THE RANDALL HOUSE BIBLE COMMENTARY

THE RANDALL HOUSE BIBLE COMMENTARY

THE BOOK OF MATTHEW

by
Jeffrey A. Crabtree

FIRST EDITION

randall house

RANDALL HOUSE
NASHVILLE, TENNESSEE 37217

RANDALL HOUSE BIBLE COMMENTARY, MATTHEW

RANDALL HOUSE
NASHVILLE, TN 37217
ISBN: 9780892657377

General Editor:
ROBERT E. PICIRILLI
Professor Emeritus, Welch College
Nashville, Tennessee

Associate Editor:
Harrold D. Harrison
Nashville, Tennessee

Dedication

To Donna,
whose labor alongside me in ministry
and sacrifice as I worked
made this book possible.

PREFACE

This volume on the Gospel of Matthew ·ings us one step nearer to the end of a ng road that began in 1986.

As we announced in the beginning, ɹr purpose was neither to be "highly chnical" nor "merely devotional," but "steer a course between these two vels of commentaries." We desire to ·ovide help in understanding both what e Scripture text says and what it eans.

The writers of these commentaries ıare certain things in common. They ·e committed Christians and firmly elieve in the plenary, verbal inspiration the canonical Scriptures as the iner- nt Word of God. Their interpretation of e written Word is grounded in the his- rical context in which the various parts the Bible were written and in the ammatical sense of the original lan- ıages. They consider the implications of ırious types of literature contained in e Bible. They are concerned to discern oth the original human author's inten- on and what the divine author intended the words. They are especially inter- sted in learning how that divine author eant the words to be applied in the lives those who desire to live in submission His revealed will.

As this indicates, the writers share a ommitment to the cardinal doctrines of e Christian faith and are therefore in ıity with all others in the tradition of storic Christianity. Even so, the writers present a particular denominational xpression of that faith known as Free 'ill Baptist. This tradition holds to a onservative theology and to a doctrine salvation that is very much like that hich was held by Jacobus Arminius in e immediate aftermath of the Protestant eformation. This "Reformation Armin-ianism" espouses: (1) a total human depravity that is mitigated by an enabling grace accompanying the intelligent hearing of the gospel and making saving faith possible; (2) a penal, substitutionary atonement, by the death and resurrection of Jesus Christ, that was designed to provide for the salvation of all and to save those who believe in Him as their Lord and Savior; (3) the electing decision of God (which has implications both for eternity and in time) to save those who thus believe; (4) and the possibility, warned against in Scripture, that those who have experienced saving grace may finally turn away from God and be forever lost. An important part of this is that human beings have, by their constitution as God's image bearers, moral freedom and accountability. This includes the freedom of choice, when enabled by grace, to receive or reject Christ.

Dr. Jeff Crabtree has written this volume on Matthew. His academic credentials speak clearly of his ability to grapple with the text of Matthew and interpret it carefully, and his writing shows this. He has considered the contributions of many other interpreters and often cites their opinions, but he thinks for himself in submission to the Spirit of God. He has extensive pastoral experience and writes with pastoral concern for all believers. What I detected as I read and edited his manuscript was the heart of a pastor. Preachers, especially, will appreciate this commentary. But so will all believers who want to know what Matthew's Gospel means for them. Crabtree speaks clearly, and when he speaks the listening soul will be enabled to hear the voice of the Lord more clearly.

Robert E. Picirilli

CONTENTS

COMMENTARY ON THE BOOK OF MATTHEW

INTRODUCTION

Author

The Gospel "According to Matthew" is, like the other Gospels, Acts, and the book of Hebrews, anonymous. However, Eusebius states that according to Papias (*Eccl. Hist.* III.XXXIX.16) Matthew originally wrote "sayings of Jesus" in the Hebrew language. Papias was the bishop of Hierapolis in Phrygia during the first half of the second century and has been thought to have been a disciple of the apostle John (ISBE I:211). Origen (ca. 185-254 A.D.; *Eccl. Hist.* VI.XXV.4) and Irenaeus (mid-late second century; *Eccl. Hist.* V.VIII.2) agreed with Papias. Irenaeus also stated that Matthew wrote his Gospel among Jewish believers "while Paul and Peter were preaching in Rome and founding the church." Eusebius (*Eccl. Hist.* III. XXIV.5, 6) evidently accepted these testimonies as accurate. He further states that there was a tradition in India that Bartholomew, one of the Twelve, had left them a copy of Matthew in Hebrew letters (*Eccl. Hist.* V.X.3). However, there is no extant Hebrew manuscript of Matthew from before the 14th century.

Scholarship today is divided over Papias' statement. It seems certain from manuscript evidence that Matthew wrote his canonical Gospel in Greek not Hebrew as Papias seems to suggest. Some recent scholarship suggests that Papias meant only that Matthew recorded some of Jesus' sayings in Hebrew, not the whole Gospel as we have it today (McDonald and Porter 298; Hagner 33A:xlvi). Other scholars accept this early church tradition as referring to the canonical Gospel and for this and other reasons believe that the Apostle Matthew wrote the Gospel record that bears his name (Blomberg 1, Evans, *Matthew* 22). According to Carson (*Matthew* 17), "the universal testimony of the early church is that the apostle Matthew wrote it." In addition, there is no surviving tradition that assigns the Gospel to anyone else (Wilkins 22; Hagner 33A:lxxvi). When one adds to these facts the truth that the Gospel of Matthew was the most widely read of the four Gospels in the early church and the most quoted by the church fathers (ISBE III:280), the testimony of those closest in time to the apostle Matthew must be given its due weight. Until evidence surfaces that more solidly argues otherwise, there appears to be no reason to disagree with unanimous, early church tradition.

Matthew is first named in 9:9. He was a tax collector by profession. At Jesus' call, Matthew left his tax booth and followed Jesus full time. One of the first things he did after his conversion was host a dinner for Jesus and invited his tax collector friends, apparently for evangelistic reasons. Matthew's conversion probably took place a few months into Jesus' Galilean ministry. In 10:3, he identified himself as Matthew the tax collector and included himself as one of the original Twelve. Mark (2:14; 3:18) and Luke (5:27-29; 6:15) know him as Matthew and Levi. They both record Matthew's conversion and Jesus' choosing him as an apostle. Mark adds that Levi was the son of Alphaeus. Matthew was present in the Upper Room in Acts 1:13 but is named in the Scriptures nowhere else after that.

Date

There are no specific statements that reveal the date of this Gospel's composition. Matthew's "to this day" references (27:8; 28:15) are general and vague and suggest that some time had passed between Jesus' death and resurrection and the writing of this Gospel record (E. Harrison 175). If one assumes Markan priority and that Matthew copied from him—these assumptions still have their detractors (see Hagner 33A:xlvii, for a summary discussion)—Matthew's date for writing would follow Mark's. If Luke used Mark and Matthew both, then Matthew would predate the Gospel of Luke. Jesus' promise in 24:2 that the temple would be destroyed and the invitation for the reader to understand in 24:15 suggest that the destruction of Jerusalem had not yet taken place at the time of this Gospel's writing and that the author believed Mark's warning still to be beneficial. Despite the claims of some writers that references to the destruction of Jerusalem were written after the fact, there is nothing in the text to suggest that Jesus could not have foretold these events (Evans and Porter 277, 278) or that the author did not record these events before they happened. In fact, as Carson (*Matthew* 20) points out, if a reference to the destruction of the temple indicates a post-70 date, then the multiple references to the temple as still standing (5:23-24; 12:5-7; 23:16-22; and 26:60-61) indicate a pre-70 date.

The *Didachē* (A.D. 70-90; McDonald and Porter 75) alludes to and quotes sayings of Christ that are part of Matthew's Gospel. These are 1:3 (Mt. 5:44-46), 1:4 (Mt. 5:39-41), 1:5 (Mt. 5:43), 8:2 (Mt. 6:9-13), and 16:8 (Mt. 24:30). The unknown author may have shared the source material with Matthew or more probably copied from Matthew's Gospel, which would mean that this Gospel was in circulation very early.

Here, then, are five reasons that one might consider a pre-A.D. 70 circulation of Matthew's Gospel: (1) the Gospel's use in the *Didachē*; (2) the statement from Irenaeus mentioned earlier about Paul and Peter still living at the time Matthew wrote his oracles; (3) the absence of any historical description of Jerusalem's destruction; and (4) the invitation to the reader to understand (24:15). If one understands this to be a warning, one could argue that Matthew was in circulation a few years prior to the A.D. 70 destruction of Jerusalem. (5) The material common to Matthew and Luke that may result from Luke copying from Matthew rather than that they shared a common source ("Q") besides Mark's Gospel. Several scholars believe Matthew wrote his account before A.D. 70. Tenny (151) thinks

Matthew may have written his Gospel as early as A.D. 50.

Methodology

My hermeneutical approach for this commentary is historical-grammatical-theological. Historical-grammatical means that the interpreter exegetes each text for its original meaning in its original contexts. My goal has been to be aware of each text's historical setting as well as its literary contexts in Matthew. For an example of interpretive conclusions based on syntactical relationships of words, see 16:18, "Upon this rock I will build my church," and the English imperatives in 28:19-20. For an example of how the historical setting influenced my conclusions, see comments on 24:15 and the A.D. 70 destruction of Jerusalem.

I have included "theological" in my methodology because theology influences exegesis. I have not tried to hide or neutralize my personal beliefs in my comments. Where I deemed it appropriate and space permitted, I have included comments to help the reader understand how my exegetical conclusions inform my theological position and vice versa. For example, in my comments on 1:18, I summarized the doctrine of the incarnation as part of my explanation of the virginal conception. In my explanation of 1:23, I include comments on who I believe Isaiah's "virgin" was and why. In my comments on 3:6, I explain why I believe immersion is the proper mode of baptism and in my comments on 28:19 the importance of Christian baptism. In 13:1-23, my belief in human responsibility and free will is clear. In 26:28, I include my thoughts on the meaning and implications of the cross for lost mankind's salvation.

Even though contemporary scholarship remains convinced that the author of the first Gospel used both oral and written sources, I have not engaged in that discussion (source criticism). Whether Matthew used Mark, "Q" (in common with Luke) and/or another source or sources ("M") available only to Matthew is not part of this discussion. Rarely have I interacted with this. I am inclined to believe that even though Matthew used sources that are discernible, he contributed from his own memory and perhaps personal notes more than some critics want to allow. For materials that were outside of his personal experience as an eyewitness, Matthew of necessity did some information gathering much like Luke (Lk. 1:1-4). These include records of events and teachings that predate Matthew's conversion such as materials contained in the first four chapters, including those portions of the genealogy not found in the O.T. See comments on 1:2 and 1:13.

I have also abstained from speculating on Matthew's editorializing (redaction criticism). This is to say that I refrained from suggesting why Matthew (apparently) modified and expanded on Mark's wording. I have not tried to identify a theological backdrop or practical need in the Christian community to which he wrote. I have consulted commentaries by Gundry and Osborne, both redaction critics, and have benefited from their studies but I have not made redaction criticism a part of this study. However, I compared the synoptics throughout and noted differences and similarities when helpful for the purposes of this commentary. One example mentioned already is 24:15 and Luke 21:20.

Finally, throughout the commentary I have included an application section, as required by the editors of this series. I have therefore included in application sections teaching and preaching points that speakers, teachers, or group leaders might emphasize. At times, I have ordered my suggestions in a list fashion. At other times, I have provided an outline. Some are exegetically organized while others are topical.

Organization

Matthew told his story in narrative fashion. There are eight major narrative sections, the last of which is Matthew's conclusion. Each section focuses on a major segment of Jesus' life and ministry. See the outline. The final section, Matthew's conclusion and the great commission, bridges the post-resurrection, pre-Pentecost days with the church era. There are also five major blocks of teaching materials interspersed throughout the narrative: (1) the Sermon on the Mount (5-7); (2) instructions to the Twelve before their first missionary effort (10:1-42); (3) the kingdom parables (13:1-52); (4) instructions for living in the kingdom community now (18:1-35); (5) and the Olivet Discourse (24-25).

Setting and Purpose

There is nothing in the book that specifically reveals the historical context in which the author wrote or the first readers lived. Unlike the authors of most N.T. epistles, Matthew addresses no named Christian community. Scholars speculate that a community of Greek-speaking Jews and Gentiles were the target audience and suggest mainly Palestine or Antioch of Syria (Elwell and Yarbrough 79; Nolland 18). Wilkins (24) thinks the "field of blood to this day" phrase (27:8) and the continued telling of the story "to this day" that the disciples stole Jesus' body (28:15) suggest that Matthew was still at least in contact with Palestine at the time he wrote. Gundry (5-6) believes Matthew wrote to a mixed church, i.e., a church with converts from all nations, and a church that was having difficulty enduring its persecution. Matthew's heavy use of the Old Testament points to a predominantly Jewish-Christian audience but their location is unknown.

Matthew's purpose for writing was first and foremost to provide a record of the life of Jesus Christ (Elwell and Yarbrough 80). Second, Matthew wrote to prove that Jesus is the King of the Jews, the royal Messiah. Third, Matthew wrote to prove that Jesus is the God-man, the Son of God and Son of Man. He is Immanuel and Messiah (Carson, *Matthew* 25). Fourth, he seems to have written with non-Christian Jews in mind for his opening lines as well as the fulfillment passages scattered throughout seem apologetic. Jews knew that the Messiah had to descend from King David and fulfill some very specific prophecies (Mic. 5:2). Matthew addressed these questions directly. Fifth, with Jesus' death, burial, resurrection, and Great Commission in mind (28:18-20), Matthew wrote evangelistically (Hendriksen 97). Jesus came as God's Savior of the world. Matthew sought to introduce Him to the world. Sixth, it seems clear that for discipleship reasons he intended his work to be didactic. He was teaching all things Jesus commanded (28:20). Seventh, Matthew wrote to confirm for Jewish Christians, his apparent primary target audience, that their centuries old faith and Scriptures are true and are fulfilled in Jesus, their Messiah. Christianity is the fulfillment of God's promises to Israel (Hagner 33A:lxx). The kingdom had arrived. Thus, this Gospel was designed to record, reach, teach, and defend.

The early church accepted Matthew's Gospel as Scripture. It was held in such high regard that (1) it was the most widely read of the four Gospels in the first and second centuries (Wilkins 19) and (2) when the four Gospels began circulating as a single corpus, Matthew was most often first in both the Greek manuscripts and versions (Aland and Aland 79).

Special Doctrines and Emphases

Christology. At first, it may seem that Matthew's Gospel is not as forthright about Jesus' deity as the Gospel of John, which begins with a clear statement of Jesus' deity. However, Matthew has a high Christology. In the birth narrative, Jesus is "God with us" (1:23). At His baptism (3:17) and at His transfiguration (17:5), a voice from heaven declared, "This is My beloved Son." He is twice addressed as the "Son of God": at His temptation by the evil one (4:3, 5) and again by the demons of Gergesa (8:29). He possesses a unique, close relationship to the Father (11:27). His disciples confessed Him to be the Son of God after He walked to them on water (14:33) and again at Caesarea Philippi when Peter confessed, "You are the Christ, the Son of the living God" (16:16). At His trial, He did not deny it when asked if He is God's Son (26:63). His accusers knew His claim (27:40, 43). Jesus is King David's Lord who sits at the right hand of God Almighty (22:44) and the Son of Man the prophet Daniel spoke of in Daniel 7:13-14. So powerful and unusual were the events in nature that accompanied and immediately followed His death that the Roman soldiers who oversaw the crucifixion confessed this man truly was "Son of God" (27:54). To corroborate His claim to be the Son of God, Jesus healed all diseases (4:23-24), cast out demons (8:28-34), raised the dead (9:25), created (14:19-20), walked on water (14:25-26), was transfigured (17:2), foretold events that have now happened (24:15; 26:34, 69-75) and arose from the dead (27:50; 28:9).

The Gentile mission of the church. Though Jesus at first limited His ministry and the offer of the kingdom to Jews (10:5, 23; 15:24, 26), from the inclusion of Gentiles in the genealogy (1:3, 5; Ruth, Rahab) to the final command of Jesus to take the gospel to the nations (28:19), Matthew consistently shows that Jesus' intent was and is that the whole world receive an invitation to join His kingdom. Jesus is the Savior of all nations. God gave a heavenly sign to the Magi who then came to worship the King (2:1-12). The centurion who had such great faith will not be the only Gentile present at the Messianic feast (8:5-13). Jesus is the chosen servant in whom the Gentles will hope (12:21). There are sons of the kingdom throughout the whole world (13:38). Gentiles share in the new people of God who received the kingdom (21:43). Jesus spent several months of His final year ministering in predominately Gentile territories (Mt. 15:21-31, etc.; Mk. 7:31), and until the Lord returns Gentiles will receive an invitation to join the kingdom (22:1-14; 24:14; 28:19).

The King and His kingdom. Matthew began His Gospel with evidence that Jesus is a royal descendant of King David and thus a legal heir to David's throne (1:1-17). He followed the genealogy with the birth narrative in which he identified Joseph, Jesus' stepfather, as a descendant of David also (1:20). Some months after Jesus' birth, the Magi came looking for the one who was born "king of the Jews" (2:2) and worshiped Jesus as that king. The two blind men in Capernaum called Jesus "the Son of David" (9:27) and after He healed a demon-possessed, blind and mute man the crowd wondered if Jesus might be "the Son of David" (12:23). The Gentile woman who begged for her daughter's healing called on Jesus as "Son of David" (15:22), as did the two blind men in Jericho (20:30-31). During His ride into Jerusalem on the colt, the crowds praised Him as "Son of David" (21:9) and the next day the children did the same (21:15).

John the Baptist preached the nearness of the kingdom (3:2) and Jesus began His ministry preaching the kingdom's nearness as well (4:17). See comments on 3:2. Soon He preached not that the kingdom was near but that it had arrived. The good news of the kingdom was its arrival and its accessibility (7:13; Lk. 16:16). In proof that it had arrived were the miracles and the freeing from bondages (11:2-5). In 12:28 Jesus said plainly that the kingdom had arrived. It had arrived in His Person and work.

The juxtaposition of "church" and "kingdom" in 16:18-19 supports the understanding that these two have some type of relationship but the text is a seedbed of questions (see ISBE I:693). It seems clear enough that Jesus was preaching the kingdom of heaven, not the church, which means that the terms are not synonymous. It is also clear from Acts that the early preachers proclaimed the kingdom (Acts 8:12; 19:8; 20:25; 28:23) to both Jews and non-Jews and the Lord added to the church. These same preachers also preached a future aspect of the kingdom that disciples will "enter" at a later time (Acts 14:22). All of this together suggests that kingdom preaching included past (John and his forward-focus on Jesus; Acts 19:1-7), present (the church and its present focus on Jesus; Acts 19:1, 8; 20:17, 25, 28) and future aspects of the kingdom (the return of Jesus and the consummation of the kingdom at that time). So while it is not accurate to say that the kingdom and the church are one and the same, it is accurate to say the church is part of the kingdom. Folks entered the kingdom after John the Baptist began preaching "the kingdom is at hand," prior to the cross. Folks joined the church after Pentecost and thus became part of the kingdom as well. Carson explains (*Matthew* 369, 370) that the kingdom and the church are two different concepts; one deals with ruling and reigning and the other with people. See this distinction in Matthew 13:36-43. However, Carson continues, the same people occupy both at the same time. In as much as the kingdom has been launched but its final consummation is still to come, so "Jesus' church is an outpost in history of the final eschatological community." The church is proof that the kingdom has come and when the kingdom finally reaches consummation, the church will enjoy the "richest blessings the Messiah's reign can give."

Use of the O.T. Matthew's use of the O.T. is a study in itself and has been one focus of Matthean scholarship. Matthew's use of both the Hebrew and Greek (LXX) versions of the O.T. as well as his application of O.T. texts to Jesus' life and events (e.g., 2:15; Hos. 11:1) continue to rouse the interests of contemporary writers. Matthew quoted and alluded to the O.T. more than any of the other Gospel writers. One source says there are "over sixty explicit or substantial quotations (not including far more numerous allusions) of the O.T., more than twice as many as any other Gospel" (ISBE III:284). Matthew states several times that Jesus did what He did the way He did and where He did because prophecy said He would. Matthew used these prophetic fulfillments to prove the identity of Jesus. In 21:10, the whole city of Jerusalem asked, "Who is this?" One might suggest Matthew answered this question throughout his record with many O.T. quotes and allusions that he declared Jesus fulfilled or that spoke directly or typologically to Jesus' person and ministry. In 1:23, Mary is the virgin spoken of in Isaiah 7:14, and her baby, Jesus, is Immanuel. In 2:6, Jesus was born in Bethlehem exactly as prophesied in Micah 5:2. In 2:15, Jesus is God's Son called from Egypt (Hos. 11:1). Herod's slaughter of the innocents (2:16-18) as he tried to murder baby Jesus moved Rachel to cry again over the loss of her children (Jer. 31:15). Jesus grew up in Nazareth that He might be called a Nazarene (Mt. 2:23). Jesus was the one for whom John the Baptist prepared the hearts of people (Mt. 3:3; Is. 40:3). Jesus' primary place of ministry was Galilee, as foretold by Isaiah (Mt. 4:12-16; Is. 9:1-2). He was the Suffering Servant who carried on Himself mankind's sicknesses and diseases (Mt. 8:14-17; Is. 53:4). He was the humble and meek Servant Isaiah promised would come (Mt. 12:15-21; Is. 42:1-3) and He taught with parables as the Psalmist foretold (13:34-35; Ps. 78:2). Jesus made a humble entry into Jerusalem on a donkey's colt as prophesied by Zechariah (Mt. 21:1-11; Is. 62:11; Zech. 9:9). He was the Lord children praised (Mt. 21:15-16; Ps. 8:2, LXX). He was the stone the builders rejected and the Lord chose to use anyway (Mt. 21:42; Ps. 118:22, 23). He was the son and Lord of King David who sits by the Lord of the universe (Mt. 22:41-45; Ps. 110:1). He is the subject of Daniel 7:13, 41 (Mt. 26:64) and the one who felt forsaken in Psalm 22:1 (Mt. 27:46). Jesus was sold for thirty pieces of silver (Mt. 27:9-10) as anticipated in the prophets' promise (Jer. 18:3; 19:1-13; Zech. 11:13).

The Synoptic Problem

The Gospel according to Matthew is one of the three Synoptic Gospels. Matthew, Mark, and Luke each tell the story of Jesus and there is considerable similarity between them. The problem of accounting for the similarities and differences is called "the synoptic problem" and it has held the interest of scholarship since the second century (McDonald and Porter 276-277). The synoptic problem is beyond the scope of this commentary. A harmony of the Gospels with the sayings and events of Christ in parallel columns will demonstrate the complexity of the issue. This study will focus primarily on the Gospel of Matthew in its completed form, not on critical thought that evaluates proposed processes of its compilation.

This is not to say that the other Gospel writers have not been consulted. While each writer selected materials according to his own divinely-inspired interest and purpose, what the other Gospel writers wrote can at times shed considerable light where clarity is needed. For example, in 24:15 Matthew did not explain the "abomination of desolation." Luke, however, explained that this is Jerusalem surrounded by armies (Lk. 21:20). Mark and Luke, then, have been consulted throughout this study for their perspectives when they add clarity to Matthew's record.

TEXT

One can approach the Greek text of Matthew with confidence. There are no major sections that are questioned. Most textual variants are minor and can be easily explained. See 24:48 and 25:13. Those that appear more challenging can be explained as well, so the doctrine of inspiration remains intact. For examples, see 12:47; 17:21; and 21:28-32. Because of the nature and limitations of this commentary, only obvious differences between the KJV and certain more recent translations will be noted. Rationales for preferred readings are not discussed.

MATTHEW

OUTLINE OF THE GOSPEL ACCORDING TO MATTHEW

I. The Birth Narrative: The Royal Messiah's Birth and Early Childhood, 1:1—2:23
  A. The Genealogy of Jesus, 1:1-17
    1. Introduction: Jesus as King of the Jews, 1:1
    2. Jesus' genealogy from Abraham to King David, 1:2-6a
    3. Jesus' genealogy from David to the Babylonian exile, 1:6b-11
    4. Jesus' genealogy from the Babylonian exile to Jesus, 1:12-17
  B. The Birth of Jesus, 1:18-25
  C. The Visit of the Magi, 2:1-12
  D. The Flight to Egypt, 2:13-18
  E. The Return to Nazareth in Galilee, 2:19-23
II. The Preparation Narrative: The Introduction of the Royal Messiah and His Kingdom, 3:1—4:11
  A. The Ministry of John the Baptist, 3:1-12
  B. The Baptism of Jesus in Judea, 3:13-17
  C. The Temptation of Jesus, 4:1-11
III. The Galilean Ministry Narrative: The Royal Messiah Shined a Great Light in a Dark Region, 4:12—18:35
  A. From Obscurity to Popularity: The Royal Messiah Began Growing His Kingdom, 4:12-25
    1. Jesus moved from Nazareth to Capernaum, 4:12-17
    2. Jesus called His first disciples, 4:18-22
    3. Jesus entered a period of increasing popularity, 4:23-25
  B. Discourse One: The Sermon on the Mount, 5:1—7:29
    1. The attitudes of kingdom citizens, 5:1-12
    2. The influence of kingdom citizens, 5:13-16
    3. The kingdom of heaven and the Law of Moses, 5:17-20
    4. The law of Christ, 5:21-48
      a. Murder and anger management, 5:21-26
      b. Adultery and the lustful eye, 5:27-30
      c. Divorce, remarriage, and adultery, 5:31-32
      d. Oaths and personal integrity, 5:33-37
      e. Revenge and meekness, 5:38-42
      f. Hate and love toward one's enemies, 5:43-48
    5. Life-habits of kingdom citizens, 6:1—7:12
      a. Private benevolence, 6:1-4
      b. Prayer, 6:5-15
      c. Fasting, 6:16-18
      d. Eternal investments, 6:19-24
      e. Possessions and faith, 6:25-34
      f. Honest judgment, 7:1-5
      g. Wise witnessing, 7:6
      h. Earnest petitions, 7:7-11

i. The Golden Rule, 7:12
6. Choosing the kingdom, 7:13-27
   a. Choosing the right gate and the right road, 7:13-14
   b. Choosing the right prophet leaders, 7:15-20
   c. Choosing to be the right kind of disciple, 7:21-23
   d. Building on the right foundation, 7:24-27
7. The impact of Jesus' teaching, 7:28-29

C. The Royal Messiah's Day-to-Day Miracles and Teachings, 8:1—9:38
1. Jesus healed a leper, 8:1-4
2. Jesus healed a centurion's servant, 8:5-13
3. Jesus healed many in Capernaum, 8:14-17
4. Jesus explained the cost of being His disciple, 8:18-22
5. Jesus calmed the storm on the Sea of Galilee, 8:23-27
6. Jesus healed two demon-possessed men at Gergesa, 8:28-34
7. Jesus healed a paralytic, 9:1-8
8. Jesus called Matthew to follow Him, 9:9-13
9. Jesus taught about fasting, 9:14-17
10. Jesus healed a hemorrhaging woman and restored life to a dead girl, 9:18-26
11. Jesus healed two blind men, 9:27-31
12. Jesus healed a demon-possessed mute man, 9:32-34
13. Jesus expressed the need for many more field workers, 9:35-38

D. The Royal Messiah Enlisted the Aid of His Disciples, 10:1—11:1
1. Discourse two: The mission—short term and long term, 10:1-42
   a. The appointment of the Twelve, 10:1-4
   b. The training of the Twelve for their first mission outreach, 10:5-15
   c. The training of the Twelve for church-age mission outreach, 10:16-39
   d. Rewards for all who contribute to the spread of the Gospel, 10:40-42
2. Separate ministries for Jesus and the Twelve, 11:1

E. The Royal Messiah Assesses the Ministries of John the Baptist and Himself, 11:2-24
1. Jesus discussed and evaluated John the Baptist's ministry, 11:2-15
2. Jesus assessed His generation's response to the gospel, 11:16-19
3. Jesus scolded the cities where He did most of His miracles for their rejection of Him, 11:20-24

F. The Royal Messiah Explained His Ministry: He Introduces to the Father All Who Come to Him, 11:25-30

G. The Royal Messiah Encountered Increasing Opposition, 12:1-50
1. Jesus is Lord of the Sabbath, 12:1-8
2. It is lawful to do good on the Sabbath, 12:9-14

3. Jesus avoided the Pharisees who were intent on destroying Him, 12:15-21
4. Jesus healed a demon-possessed man and warned against blaspheming the Holy Spirit, 12:22-37
5. Jesus warned His generation of their spiritual state, 12:38-45
6. Jesus' identitied His true family, 12:46-50

H. Discourse Three: Teaching Through Kingdom Parables, 13:1-52
1. Parables to the crowds, 13:1-35
   a. The audience, 13:1-2
   b. The parable of the sower, 13:3-9
   c. The purpose of parables, 13:10-17
   d. The parable of the sower and the soils explained, 13:18-23
   e. The parable of the wheat and tares, 13:24-30
   f. The parable of the mustard seed, 13:31-32
   g. The parable of the leaven, 13:33
   h. New revelation: Another reason for parables, 13:34-35
2. Parables to the disciples alone, 13:36-52
   a. The meaning of the wheat and the tares, 13:36-43
   b. The parable of the treasure, 13:44
   c. The parable of the expensive pearl, 13:45-46
   d. The parable of the net, 13:47-50
   e. The parable of the homeowner, 13:51-52

I. The Royal Messiah Continued His Itinerate Ministry, 13:53—15:20
1. Jesus left Capernaum, 13:53
2. Jesus taught in His home town of Nazareth, 13:54-58
3. The death of John the Baptist, 14:1-12
4. The feeding of over five thousand, 14:13-21
5. Jesus walked on water and enabled Peter to do the same, 14:22-33
6. Jesus healed many at Gennesaret and its surrounding regions, 14:34-36
7. Tradition, commandments, and defilement: Another confrontation with the Pharisees, 15:1-20

IV. The Syria, Decapolis, and Northern Palestine Ministry Narrative: The Royal Messiah Travels Between Israel and Gentile Territories, 15:21—18:35

A. The Faith of the Canaanite Woman, 15:21-28
B. Jesus Fed Over Four Thousand, 15:29-39
C. The Pharisees and Sadducees Asked for a Sign, 16:1-4
D. Jesus Warned the Twelve About the Teachings of the Pharisees and the Sadducees, 16:5-12
E. Peter Confessed That Jesus Is the Divine Messiah, 16:13-20
F. Jesus' First Prophecy of His Death and Resurrection, 16:21-23
G. Jesus Taught the Twelve the High Cost of Discipleship, 16:24-28
H. The Transfiguration, 17:1-9
I. Jesus Explained That John the Baptist Is Malachi's Elijah, 17:10-13

J. Jesus Healed the Demon-Possessed, Epileptic Son, 17:14-21
K. Back in Galilee, 17:22—18:35
  1. Jesus' second prophecy of His suffering and resurrection, 17:22-23
  2. Jesus paid the annual temple tax, 17:24-27
  3. Discourse Four: Life in the Present Kingdom Community, 18:1-35
    a. Importance in the kingdom, now and in eternity, 18:1-4
    b. Warning against sinning against the vulnerable, 18:5-7
    c. Warning against allowing oneself to sin, 18:8-9
    d. The loving concern of the Father and the Son for humble believers who stray into sin, 18:10-14
    e. Dealing with the brother who sins, 18:15-20
    f. Forgiving the brother who sins: A parable, 18:21-35

V. The Perean Ministry Narrative, 19:1—20:34
  A. Jesus Headed for Jerusalem by Way of the Transjordan, 19:1-2
  B. A Test Question About Divorce, 19:3-12
  C. Jesus Received Children, 19:13-15
  D. The Rich, Young Man: Temporary Riches Over Eternal Riches, 19:16-22
  E. Riches, Sacrifices, and Rewards: The Promise of Just Reward for Great Sacrifice, 19:23-30
  F. The Parable of the Laborers: A Lesson in Gracious Rewards, 20:1-16
  G. Jesus' Third Prophecy Concerning His Own Death, 20:17-19
  H. A Mother Requested Special Consideration for Her Sons, 20:20-28
  I. Jesus Healed Two Blind Men, 20:29-34

VI. The Passion Week Narrative, 21:1—27:66
  A. Sunday: The Triumphal Entry, 21:1-11
  B. Monday: Jesus Initiates a Confrontation, 21:12-22
    1. The royal Messiah cleansed the temple, 21:12-17
    2. The fig tree cursed and withered, 21:18-22
  C. Tuesday: Debates and Questions, 21:23—25:46
    1. Temple court debates, 21:23—22:46
      a. A question of authority, 21:23-27
      b. Three parables to illustrate the unbelief and disobedience of the Jewish religious leadership, 21:28—22:14
        (1) A question of obedience: The parable of the two sons, 21:28-32
        (2) A question of justice: The parable of the householder, 21:33-46
        (3) A judgment based on response and privilege: The parable of the wedding feast, 22:1-14
      c. Four questions, 22:15-46
        (1) Question one: Should God's people pay taxes to secular governments? 22:15-22

   - (2) Question two: Whose wife will she be in the resurrection? 22:23-33
   - (3) Question three: Which Bible command is the most important? 22:34-40
   - (4) Question four: Whose Son is He? 22:41-46
2. Further warnings to the religious leadership, 23:1-39
   - a. A warning about the scribes and Pharisees, 23:1-12
   - b. A warning to the scribes and Pharisees, 23:13-36
   - c. A warning to Jerusalem, 23:37-39
3. The Olivet Discourse, 24:1—25:46
   - a. The prophecy concerning the destruction of the temple, 24:1-2
   - b. General signs that indicate God's plan for this age is unfolding, 24:3-8
   - c. Signs that indicate when the end is nearing, 24:9-14
   - d. Signs that indicate the nearness of the destruction of Jerusalem and of the temple, 24:15-22
   - e. More information on the coming and work of false christs and false prophets in the days leading up to Jesus' return, 24:23-28
   - f. Signs that will immediately precede Jesus' coming, 24:29-31
   - g. The certainty of Jesus' words stressed, 24:32-35
   - h. The need for constant readiness for Jesus' return emphasized, 24:36-44
   - i. Three parables to illustrate the need for constant readiness for Jesus' return, 24:45—25:30
     - (1) The parable of the faithful and wise servant, 24:45-51
     - (2) The parable of the ten virgins, 25:1-13
     - (3) The parable of the talents, 25:14-30
   - j. A scene from the final judgment, 25:31-46

D. Thursday Through Saturday: The Royal Messiah's Death and Burial, 26:1—27:66

1. Events leading up to the royal Messiah's Crucifixion, 26:1—27:31
   - a. Jesus' fourth prophecy of His death, 26:1-5
   - b. Jesus' early anointing in preparation for His burial, 26:6-13
   - c. Judas made plans to betray Jesus, 26:14-16
   - d. Jesus observed His final Passover and instituted the Lord's Supper, 26:17-30
   - e. Jesus foretold the disciples' flight, 26:31-35
   - f. Jesus prayed in the Garden of Gethsemane, 26:36-46
   - g. Jesus' betrayal and arrest, 26:47-56
   - h. Jesus' first trial before the Sanhedrin, 26:57-68
   - i. Peter's denials of Jesus, 26:69-75
   - j. Jesus' second trial before the Sanhedrin and other leaders, 27:1-2

k. Judas' suicide, 27:3-10
l. Jesus' trial before Pilate, 27:11-26
m. Jesus' abuse and mockery at the hands of the Roman soldiers, 27:27-31

2. The royal Messiah's crucifixion, 27:32-44
3. The royal Messiah's death and the supernatural events that followed, 27:45-56
4. The royal Messiah's burial, 27:57-61
5. The royal Messiah's tomb secured, 27:62-66

VII. The Resurrection Narrative: The Royal Messiah Raised From the Dead, 28:1-15

A. The First Appearance of the Resurrected Jesus, 28:1-10
B. The Testimonies of the Guards, 28:11-15

VIII. The Great Commission: Matthew's Conclusion to His Gospel, 28:16-20

I. THE BIRTH NARRATIVE: THE ROYAL MESSIAH'S BIRTH AND EARLY CHILDHOOD (1:1—2:23)

The title "According to Matthew" denotes that this Gospel record is Matthew's testimony. See "author" in the Introduction. As one of the original twelve apostles, Matthew had a story to tell. This Gospel is his record.

A. The Genealogy of Jesus (1:1-17)

Each of the Gospel writers began his record differently. John began with Jesus' pre-existence (Jn. 1:1-3). When the beginning began, Jesus was there. Jesus is deity. John wrote to convince unbelievers that Jesus is the Christ, the Son of God (Jn. 20:31).

Luke began his account by stating his reason for writing a record of Jesus' life (Lk. 1:1-4). His goal was to convince Theophilus of the "certainty" of the events and teachings of Jesus' life and ministry. He started his story at one year and three months before Jesus was born. For Luke, Jesus is the anointed Son of God.

Mark began his testimony of Jesus' life with a record of John the Baptist's wilderness ministry. John the Baptist presumably began his public ministry just a short time before he baptized Jesus. Following His baptism and temptation, Jesus began His own public ministry. After approximately 430 years of silence, Israel now had two prophetic voices. Unlike the apostle John and the historian Luke, Mark does not specifically state his purpose for writing.

Matthew began with a genealogy. Though not specifically stated as such, his purpose for writing is hinted at in verse 1: Jesus is a descendant of Abraham and more particularly a descendant of King David. Jesus is an Israelite by birth and a legal descendant of King David. Such a genealogy was especially important if Matthew's primary audience was Jewish (Hendriksen 106).

Matthew divided this genealogy into three major sections in keeping with key events in Israel's history. He moved from Abraham, the father of the nation, to King David, the great king to whom the promise of an eternal successor was made; from King David to the Babylonian exile, Judah's punishment for breaking the Sinai covenant; and from the Babylonian exile to the birth of Jesus the Christ.

1. Introduction: Jesus as King of the Jews (1:1)

1 The book of the generation of Jesus Christ, the son of David, the son of Abraham.

Matthew began his record of Jesus' genealogy with words similar to those in Genesis 2:4 and 5:1. In these Genesis verses, the Greek version of the Old Testament (the Septuagint or LXX) has the same two words translated "generations"(Greek *biblos geneseō).* Literally, Matthew wrote, "[The] book of the genesis of": in other words, "[This is the] record of the origin of." This record covers approximately twenty-one hundred years from Abraham to Jesus. The importance of Matthew's record cannot be overemphasized since only he and Luke include birth and infancy narratives in their accounts.

This record of Jesus' ancestors supports the doctrine of His humanity. See comments on 1:21 for the meaning of the name "Jesus" and comments on 12:18 and 16:16 for a fuller discussion on the title "Christ." He is the human "son of" David and of Abraham. The word "son" (Greek *huios*) can refer to a first generation descendant or to a more distant descendant (BAGD 833; 1 Chr. 4:1). Matthew used the term both ways in these first seventeen verses.

Matthew introduced Jesus first as the "son of" David, which means He fulfills the covenant promise to David recorded in 2 Samuel 7:16: "And thine house and thy kingdom shall be established for ever before thee: Thy throne shall be established for ever." See also 1 Chronicles 17:11-14. Jesus is the Davidic son upon whose shoulder the government rests, the Wonderful Counselor, Mighty God, Everlasting Father, and Prince of Peace of Isaiah 9:6-7. Jesus as Son of David is a reoccurring theme in Matthew's Gospel (9:27; 12:23; 15:22; 20:30, 31; 21:9, 15; 22:42-45). Other N.T. writers also referred to Jesus by this title (Acts 2:29-36; Rom. 1:3; 2 Tim. 2:8; Rev. 22:16; Barclay 1:17). Scripture describes this covenant with David as irrevocable (Jer. 33:20-22, 25-26). It was important that Matthew address this. The Jews knew the Scriptures and understood that the Messiah would descend from King David. See 22:41-46 and comments.

In this way Matthew introduced Jesus as the Messianic fulfillment of the Davidic Covenant. His opening words prepare the reader for Gabriel's promise to Mary: "The Lord God shall give him the throne of his father David: And he shall reign over the house of Jacob for ever; and of his kingdom there shall be no end" (Lk. 1:32b, 33).

Matthew also introduced Jesus as the son of Abraham. As such, Jesus fulfilled the promise to Abraham in Genesis 22:18—"And in thy seed shall all nations of the earth be blessed." See also Genesis 12:3. Peter later proclaimed that Jesus is the seed of Abraham sent to bless the world with deliverance from sin (Acts 3:26). According to Paul this link between Abraham and Jesus is foundational to Christianity (Gal. 3:16; Carson, *Matthew* 62).

Verse 1, then, reveals Matthew's intentions. He sought to demonstrate that Jesus is the Messiah "in the kingly line of David, heir to the messianic promises, the one who brings divine blessings to all nations" (Carson, *Matthew* 63). As such, the genealogy focuses mainly on the royal line of David while at the same time including names of non-Jews who joined the O.T. community of faith.

2. Jesus' genealogy from Abraham to King David (1:2-6a)

2 Abraham begat Isaac; and Isaac begat Jacob; and Jacob begat Judas and his brethren;
3 And Judas begat Phares and Zara of Thamar; and Phares begat Esrom; and Esrom begat Aram;
4 And Aram begat Aminadab; and Aminadab begat Naasson; and Naasson begat Salmon;
5 And Salmon begat Booz of Rachab; and Booz begat Obed of Ruth; and Obed begat Jesse;
6a And Jesse begat David the king;

Matthew's source for names from Abraham to Zerubbabel appears to have been 1 Chronicles 1-3 and Ruth 4:12-22. His source for names from Zerubbabel to Joseph is unknown today. Carson (*Matthew* 63) says there is "good evidence that records were kept at least till the end of the first century" so there is no reason to think that Matthew's record is unreliable.

The differences between Matthew's genealogical record and Luke's (Lk. 3:23-38) are many. Eusebius reported in the fourth century that explanations (he calls them "guesses") were offered in his day (*Eccl. Hist.* VII.I.1) and commentators today continue to suggest possible solutions (see Marshall 157-161). Some suggest Luke gave Mary's genealogy and Matthew gave Joseph's. Others think one recorded Joseph's real genealogy and the other the throne succession from King David (Hill 74). This question is unanswerable given our present state of knowledge.

Regardless, this much is clear: Matthew (vv. 16, 18, 20) presented Jesus as the legal son of Joseph ("there was no other way of reckoning his descent"; Marshall 157) and the biological son of Mary. Luke is just as clear. Joseph is "of the house and lineage of David" (Lk. 2:4; also Lk. 1:27) and Gabriel seems to imply the same about Mary (Lk. 1:32—"his father David"). Zechariah corroborated this when he praised God "who raised up a horn of salvation for us in the house of his servant David" (Lk. 1:69).

Abraham, the father of natural Israel and of all people of faith, heads the genealogical list. The Messianic line went through Abraham's son Isaac (Gen. 17:19-21; 21:12), not Ishmael or the sons of Keturah (Gen. 25:5-6). Isaac fathered Jacob and Esau, but the Abrahamic promises and the messianic line are traced only through Jacob (Gen. 27:29; Mal. 1:2). Jacob, whose name was changed to Israel, fathered twelve sons. All of these sons were included in the covenant people ("and his brethren") but Judah (Judas) was designated as the clan through which the Messiah would come (Gen. 49:10).

Judah married a Canaanite woman and had three sons (Gen. 38). The Lord killed the oldest son, Er, for his wickedness. Judah instructed his second oldest son, Onan, to marry his brother's wife, Tamar (probably a Canaanite, Gundry 14), perform the duty of kinsman redeemer and raise a son to carry on his brother's name. (For a fuller discussion of levirate marriage, see 22:23-33.) Onan did not want to raise a son for his brother, possibly because he did not want to give up his brother's inheritance. His sin cost him his life as well.

Judah, not wanting to lose another son, sent Tamar back to her father's home with a promise that he would have his third son, Shelah, marry her when he was grown. After some time passed, Tamar realized that Judah had no intention of effecting her redemption so she disguised herself as a harlot and went to meet him. Judah did not recognize her. He hired her and she conceived and gave birth to twins, Pharez (Perez) and Zarah (Zerah). In effect, Judah was her redeemer. Judah and Tamar's firstborn (Judah's fourth son) became the legal heir of Er and the son through whom the Messiah came. Though born of an incestuous relationship and half Canaanite, Pharez was included in the Messianic line.

Little is known about Hezron (Gen. 46:12; Num. 26:21; 1 Chr. 2:5, 9;

4:1), Ram (Ru. 4:19; 1 Chr. 2:9-10), Amminadab (Ru. 4:19-20), Nahshon and Salmon (Ru. 4:20-21). Amminadab's daughter married Aaron (Ex. 6:23) and his son Nahshon was the leader of the tribe of Judah while Israel was in the wilderness (Ex. 6:23; Num. 1:7; 2:3; 7:12; 10:14; 1 Chr. 2:10). Ram, son of Hezron and father of Amminadab, had a nephew also named Ram (1 Chr. 2:9, 25). Since Israel spent four hundred and thirty years in Egypt (Ex. 12:40-41) there are probably some gaps in this genealogy (Wilkins 59).

Salmon's descendant Boaz (Booz) was the kinsman redeemer (Dt. 25:5-10; Lev. 25:25-34, 47-54) of Naomi and Ruth. Boaz redeemed Naomi's land by purchasing it and Mahlon's name by marrying Mahlon's widow, Ruth the Moabitess (Ru. 4:9-10). Boaz and Ruth's first son was Obed, the grandfather of King David. Because of this levirate marriage, Obed was the legal son of Mahlon and Ruth though he was the natural son of Boaz and Ruth. Obed became the father of Jesse (Ru. 4:22; 1 Chr. 2:12), the father of David.

Matthew is the only biblical writer to mention Salmon and Rahab (Rachab) together. Rahab lived at the time of the conquest, a couple hundred years before Boaz (1 Kg. 6:1). Nevertheless, N.T. writers have some knowledge of her beyond the O.T. records (Heb. 11:31; Jas. 2:25). This is one of those instances where Matthew passed over several years of descendants in order to include only select persons in his genealogy of Jesus (Hendriksen 116).

3. Jesus' genealogy from David to the Babylonian exile (1:6b-11)

6b And David the king begat Solomon of her *that had been the wife* of Urias;
7 And Solomon begat Roboam; and Roboam begat Abia; and Abia begat Asa;
8 And Asa begat Josaphat; and Josaphat begat Joram; and Joram begat Ozias;
9 And Ozias begat Joatham; and Joatham begat Achaz; and Achaz begat Ezekias;
10 And Ezekias begat Manasses; and Manasses begat Amon; and Amon begat Josias;
11 And Josias begat Jechonias and his brethren, about the time they were carried away to Babylon:

David was Israel's finest king. God's promise to David that he would have an eternal dynasty (see above) became part of prophetic literature and the hope of Israel (Ps. 89:3-4, 35-37; 132:10-12). He was recognized by O.T. prophets as a type of the Messiah to come (Jer. 23:5-6; 30:9; 33:14-26; Ezek. 34:23, 24; 37:24-28; Hos. 3:5). This is one point of Matthew's genealogy. The other is that Jesus descended from Abraham. Jesus is the promised son of David. And unlike Luke, who traced Jesus' ancestry through David's son Nathan (Lk. 3:31), Matthew traced His genealogy through King Solomon and the descendants who actually sat on David's throne. According to Matthew, Jesus is the divinely designated heir to the throne.

Solomon was David's eighth son (1 Chr. 3:1-5) and God's chosen heir to the throne (1 Chr. 22:9). His mother was

Bathsheba "of Uriah," possibly a Gentile (v. 6; Nolland 75). He was Israel's wisest (1 Kg. 4:29-34) and wealthiest king (1 Kg. 10:14-27). His was the golden age of Israel. God repeated the words of the covenant He had made with David and assured Solomon of his place in the covenant promise if he too obeyed the Lord (2 Chr. 7:17-18).

Rehoboam (Roboam) was Solomon's son and successor. Just a few days into his reign, as a judgment against Solomon's idolatry, God divided the kingdom and it has never reunited (1 Kg. 11:9-13, 31, 33; 12:1-19). Because of His promise to David (1 Kg. 11:13, 32), God did not totally destroy Israel. The rejoining of Israel and Judah into one kingdom has been prophesied to happen during the Messianic Age (Ezek. 37:15-22).

Abijah (Abia), Rehoboam's son and successor, was a wicked king. Like his father, Abijah was permitted to reign only because of the Davidic Covenant (1 Kg. 15:4). He believed that this covenant gave him, as David's descendant, a guaranteed right to rule over all Israel (2 Chr. 13:5).

Asa was Abijah's son and successor. He was a good king at first but in his later years he sinned by not relying totally on the Lord (2 Chr. 16:7). Scripture makes no reference to the Davidic Covenant in its record of Asa's reign or of his son's, Jehoshaphat's (Josaphat).

The Lord blessed Jehoshaphat with a secure kingdom because he followed the example of King David (2 Chr. 17:3). His son and successor, Jehoram (Joram), did not follow the Lord. He did great evil, following the example of his father-in-law, King Ahab, king of the Northern Kingdom. Scripture states that God would not destroy the house of David because of the covenant (2 Kg. 8:19; 2 Chr. 21:7).

Without explanation, Matthew passed over the next four rulers of Judah—Ahaziah, Athaliah, Joash, and Amaziah (2 Chr. 22—25)—reigns that covered a period of about forty-five years (Wood 294-295). All were evil rulers though Joash and Amaziah started out serving the Lord. Athaliah, the daughter of Israel's King Ahab, was the only woman to rule over Judah and the only ruler in Judah not in the Davidic royal line. She tried to eradicate the "whole royal family" (2 Kg. 11:1) but the priest Jehoiada used the Davidic Covenant as legal basis to unseat Athaliah and restore the throne to a descendant of David (2 Chr. 23:3b). This is the last specific mention of the Davidic Covenant by the writers of First and Second Kings and First and Second Chronicles.

Uzziah (Ozias or Azariah), descendent of Jehoram and son of Amaziah, was one of Judah's greatest kings. Scripture states that he did what was right in the eyes of the Lord as did his son and successor, Jotham. Jotham's son Ahaz (Achaz) was a wicked king. Scripture makes no mention of the Davidic Covenant in the accounts of these men. However, it was to Ahaz as the official representative of the "house of David" that Isaiah delivered the prophecy of Immanuel's birth (Is. 7:13-14), which shows that God's faithfulness to the Davidic Covenant was behind this sign of a son born to a virgin.

Hezekiah (Ezekias), son of Ahaz, was a righteous king. When Sennacherib, king of Assyria, came to attack Jerusalem, God promised to defend the city for His "sake and for the sake of David [his] ... servant" (2 Kg. 19:34;

20:6; Is. 37:35). Hezekiah was succeeded by his son Manasseh.

Manasseh was Judah's longest ruling (fifty-five years) and worst king (2 Kg. 21:9-11). His sins were so offensive to God that even though he repented (2 Chr. 33:12-17) and God heard his prayer, God would not spare the city of Jerusalem (2 Kg. 23:26-27; 24:3; Jer. 15:4). Jerusalem's fall to Nebuchadnezzar was in large part a judgment because of Judah's sins under the leadership of King Manasseh. Manasseh's evil legacy lived on in his son and successor, Amon. Amon was evil like his father but unlike his father he did not repent (2 Kg. 21:20-22; 2 Chr. 33:21-23).

Josiah (Josias), Amon's son, followed his father's reign but not his ways. Josiah was a good king who attempted thorough reform in Judah (2 Kg. 22:1—23:30; 2 Chr. 34:1—36:1). He was killed in battle by Pharaoh Necho. Josiah is the only king to have three sons reign.

Jehoahaz was Josiah's first son to reign. He only reigned three months. Matthew does not mention him. Pharaoh Necho took Jehoahaz to Egypt where he died and set up his brother, Jehoiakim (Eliakim), to rule instead. Jehoiakim ruled eleven years. Matthew does not include this son of Josiah in his genealogy either (Gundry 16—17). (Hagner 33A:6 thinks an early copyist confused Jehoiakim and Jehoiachin because of similar spellings, but there is no manuscript evidence to support this.)

Matthew included Jehoiakim's son, Jehoiachin (Jechonias, Jechoniah, Jeconiah, Coniah), who succeeded his father. He ruled three months. Nebuchadnezzar carried him to Babylon in 598/597 B.C. where thirty-seven years later Merodach, then king of Babylon, released him from prison and permitted him to eat regularly at the king's table (2 Kg. 25:27-30). Evidence suggests that the Babylonians and the Jewish exiles both considered him to be "the legitimate claimant to the throne of Judah" (ISBE II:976). This was in spite of Jeremiah's prophecy that Jehoiachin would have no biological successor to sit on the throne (Jer. 22:24-30), none who would reign or prosper.

However, Jeremiah 23:5—6 show that this prophecy against Jehoiachin did not cancel the Davidic Covenant. It remained in force and is still in force today. A descendant of King David—Jesus Christ—will reign over Judah and Israel. Jeremiah's prophecy to Jehoiachin did not speak of an end to the Davidic throne succession.

Jehoiachin's uncle, Zedekiah, Josiah's third son to occupy David's throne, succeeded Jehoiachin when he was taken to Babylon. Zedekiah was Judah's final king but he died before Jehoiachin. This made Jehoiachin Judah's final living king and with the cessation of his throne rights, the stage was set for the Lord to raise up a new King (Jer. 23:5-6; Feinberg 516).

As Jeremiah promised, Jehoiachin did not have offspring to sit on the throne of David. Neither his own sons, nor any descendants after them, returned from the exile to assume the throne. If Jeremiah's prophecy (22:30) was limited to Jehoiachin's own sons, as Gundry (17) argues, then there is no concern about Jesus being linked to the Davidic throne through Jehoiachin. If, however, Jeremiah's prophecy included all of Jehoiachin's future descendents, then the question arises how Jesus can be king if His lineage is traced through Jehoiachin who is cursed. The answer is this: because Jesus is only the legal son of Joseph, not his biological son, Jesus is not disqualified from the throne by this relationship (Wilkins 62). Or, it may be that Luke is saying in his genealogy that Jesus' biological heritage is from David through his son Nathan (Lk. 3:31), which would mean that Jesus is both a biological as well as legal heir to the Davidic throne (Archer, *Encyclopedia* 316).

4. Jesus' genealogy from the Babylonian exile to Jesus (1:12-17)

12 And after they were brought to Babylon, Jechonias begat Salathiel; and Salathiel begat Zorobabel;
13 And Zorobabel begat Abiud; and Abiud begat Eliakim; and Eliakim begat Azor;
14 And Azor begat Sadoc; and Sadoc begat Achim; and Achim begat Eliud;
15 And Eliud begat Eleazar; and Eleazar begat Matthan; and Matthan begat Jacob;
16 And Jacob begat Joseph the husband of Mary, of whom was born Jesus, who is called Christ.
17 So all the generations from Abraham to David *are* fourteen generations; and from David until the carrying away into Babylon are fourteen generations; and from the carrying away into Babylon unto Christ are fourteen generations.

At the end of the seventy years, Cyrus permitted the exiles to return home (2 Chr. 36:22-23). Shealtiel (Salathiel, Hag. 1:1) was Jehoiachin's son (1 Chr. 3:17) and father of Judah's first governor following the exile, Zerubbabel (Ezra 3:2; Hag. 1:1). Zerubbabel (Zorobabel), himself a former exile, was the man the Lord chose to rebuild the temple (Hag. 1:1-12; Zech. 4:9). Haggai 2:23 seems to hint that Zerubbabel was made a type of Christ, a further indication that Jehoiachin's own children, not the entire royal line after him, may have been rejected and not permitted to sit on David's throne rather than his entire lineage. See comments above on verse 11. Both Shealtiel and Pedaiah, Shealtiel's younger brother (1 Chr. 3:17-18), are said to be Zerubbabel's father (1 Chr. 3:19; Ezra 3:2, 8; 5:2; Hag. 1:1), a possibility if a levirate marriage took place. Zerubbabel could be the natural son of Pedaiah and the legal son of Shealtiel.

The remaining names in Matthew's genealogy from Abiud to Jacob, the father of Joseph, are unmentioned by other Scripture writers. One can only say that they lived during the intertestamental period and are part of the ancestral line of Jesus. As mentioned earlier, Matthew's source for these ancestors is unknown today but there is no reason to doubt his accuracy.

Matthew brought the genealogy to Joseph and then stopped. He identified Joseph as the "husband of Mary," but unlike Matthew's description of Joseph's ancestors, Matthew did not want his readers to believe that Joseph fathered Jesus (v. 16). Jesus was born of Mary, not of Joseph. See comments on verse 20. This change prepares the reader for the birth narrative to follow, which will explain how Jesus can be called the son of David through Joseph and how though He is David's son He is also David's Lord (22:41-46; Hendriksen 107). As will be seen below (v. 25),

Joseph's role was not as natural father but as legal father.

Verse 17 identifies Jesus as "Christ" even as Matthew did in verse one. No article precedes this name in the Greek text in either of these two places. Writing as a mature Christian, Matthew knows Him by this name. Later (16:16) Matthew will introduce Him as "the Christ" where "Christ," i.e., Messiah, is Jesus' title. See comments on 1:2; 12:18 and 16:16 for further discussion of the meaning of Christ.

Jesus is the culmination of the genealogy, the goal realized. God did as He promised. Many centuries had passed since the promises to Abraham and David but the promises are now fulfilled. God is faithful (Bruner 1:14).

The inclusions of only select names in the genealogy plus Matthew's division of the genealogy into three groupings of fourteen names show that our writer was intentional with his list. He was interpreting history (Hagner 33A:9). Some commentators look at Matthew's genealogy with skepticism. Three areas of concern are generally raised.

First, most wonder why each list does not have the full fourteen names (Hill 74, 76; Wilkins 64, etc.). Explanations vary. Commentators suggest that Matthew or copyists may have made a mistake with the count or confused one of the names, or Jesus may have been Matthew's intended fourteenth generation in the third part of his genealogy (Hill 76; Bruner 1:7-22; Carson, *Matthew* 68; and Wilkins 64).

However, it is possible to understand Matthew's genealogy as he divided it. If one (1) follows verse seventeen literally and counts David twice (as the end of one group and the beginning of another), (2) divides the second and third fourteen at the exile, and (3) includes Christ as part of the third fourteen, then the list makes perfect sense. Matthew's count is exact. Just as King David is the hinge pin between the first and second set of names, so the exile, not a person's name, is the hinge pin between the second and third sets. The following table demonstrates this explanation.

1. Abraham	David	Jeconiah, father of post-exilic descendants
2. Isaac	Solomon	Shealtiel
3. Jacob	Rehoboam	Zerubbabel
4. Judah	Abijah	Abiud
5. Perez	Asa	Eliakim
6. Hezron	Jehoshaphat	Azor
7. Ram	Joram	Zadok
8. Amminadab	Uzziah	Achim (Akim)
9. Nahshon	Jotham	Eliud
10. Salmon	Ahaz	Eleazar
11. Boaz	Hezekiah	Matthan
12. Obed	Manasseh	Jacob
13. Jesse	Amon	Joseph
14. David	Josiah, father of the exilic kings	Jesus, the Christ

Second, it is clear that Matthew did not include a *complete* ancestral genealogy for Jesus. He never says why he included some names and not others. Commentators suggest various possible reasons but Matthew gave no hint. All agree that Matthew was deliberate in choices of who to include and who to leave out.

Third, commentators ask why Matthew used the number fourteen. Again, explanations vary. It may be that fourteen is the sum of the numerical value of the consonants in the name David since David is the key person in this genealogy leading up to the Messiah king (Evans, *Matthew* 45; Nolland 86-87; Gundry 19). Hagner (33A:7) disagrees, noting that without some explanation Greek readers would not understand the numerical value of a Hebrew name. The suggestion that Matthew also used this equal division as a memory tool is possible (Keener, *Background* 47; Hill 74) because as an oral society schemes to help people remember were common in Israel. See Ong (34-41) for a discussion of memory tools in an oral society.

Matthew's inclusion of women in this genealogy is noteworthy. Scholars offer different suggestions for why Matthew included the women he did. Some point out that these women were Gentiles and were listed to prepare Matthew's readers to understand that Jesus is for all peoples (Keener, *Matthew* 80). Hagner (33A:10) says the women serve to remind that God sovereignly works in surprising ways and prepares the reader for God's unusual working in Mary. Though Matthew's reasons for including these women are unknown, one thing is apparent: God in His grace included men and women, Jews and Gentiles, and saints and sinners in His plan. Seeing this, Matthew also included some very unlikely persons in his Messianic genealogy to carry on the story that God's Christ is Savior of the world.

Summary
(1:1-17)

Matthew's genealogy provides evidence that Jesus is a descendant of Abraham and a legal descendant of the royal line of King David. Using three groups of fourteen, Matthew developed a genealogy that demonstrated God's will acted out by Jews and Gentiles. The first list of fourteen reaches from the birth of the nation in Abraham to the height of the kingdom under King David. The second list of fourteen includes the decline of the nation from its height under King David to the Babylonian exile. The third list of fourteen goes from Israel's low point as a nation in captivity to her restoration to the land and the birth of her new and eternal King, the Christ.

Application: Preaching and Teaching the Passage

A genealogy might not be a text of choice for a lesson or sermon. However, great spiritual riches can be discovered and applied from this text. One might develop a lesson or sermon on why Jesus is qualified to be Messiah. Matthew gave two reasons: He is a descendent of Abraham (see the commentary above for why this is important to Christianity, Gal. 3:16) and second, He is a descendant of King David and as such the rightful heir to the eternal throne of David. These two criteria had to be met before Jesus could be called Christ.

A lesson on the sovereign purposes and control of God might also be taught from this passage. Though twenty-one hundred years had passed, God's purpose still stood. Neither the passage of time, the imperfections of humanity, nor the rebellion and wickedness of man, could stop the intentions of God. In like manner, two thousand years have come and gone since Jesus walked on this earth. God's promises through Jesus still stand.

A sermon might be developed on the breadth and depths to which God's grace will go to deliver from sin. This genealogy includes those forgiven of sexual sins, idolatry, and murder. Men who committed horrible sins and crimes were permitted a place in this list. Judah hired a harlot and fathered two sons in an incestuous relationship. David committed adultery and murder. Solomon was an idolater. Manasseh was the most wicked ruler of the Southern Kingdom. Yet, these men and others with serious imperfections were included in the Messianic lineage.

Four women were also included in the genealogy and each stands out as an example of God's grace. Tamar was a Canaanite daughter-in-law who used sex to deceive her father-in-law and secure a redeemer. Rahab had been a Canaanite harlot. Ruth was a Moabite, part of a nation who had been forbidden access to Israel's worship (Dt. 23:3). Bathsheba committed adultery with one of Israel's kings. Yet, these women were included in the lineage, a mark of God's purpose and grace overpowering the corruption of sin.

Finally, by joining these verses with the remainder of this chapter, the importance of the humanity of Jesus can be discussed. Jesus became human so He would be qualified to redeem us. He joined the human race (Jn. 1:14) in order to redeem the race. There is at least one clear example of a kinsman redeemer (Boaz) and possibly another (v. 12) in this genealogy. Jesus is our near kinsman who came to redeem us.

By using Boaz as an example of a close relative who was qualified, willing and able (he had the means) to redeem, the kinsman redeemer can be shown to be a type of Christ. Jesus is our redeemer (Gal. 4:4-5) who sets the believer free from sin (Mt. 1:21; Tit. 2:13-14). He is our blood relative (Heb. 2:11-17), He wants to redeem everyone (1 Tim. 2:3-6), He had the means to affect our redemption and He was willing to pay the price of our redemption (1 Pet. 1:18).

B. The Birth of Jesus (1:18-25)

18 Now the birth of Jesus Christ was on this wise: When as his mother Mary was espoused to Joseph, before they came together, she was found with child of the Holy Ghost.
19 Then Joseph her husband, being a just *man*, and not willing to make her a publick example, was minded to put her away privily.
20 But while he thought on these things, behold, the angel of the LORD appeared unto him in a dream, saying, Joseph, thou son of David, fear not to take unto thee Mary thy wife: for that which is conceived in her is of the Holy Ghost.
21 And she shall bring forth a son, and thou shalt call his name JESUS:

for he shall save his people from their sins.
22 Now all this was done, that it might be fulfilled which was spoken of the Lord by the prophet, saying,
23 Behold, a virgin shall be with child, and shall bring forth a son, and they shall call his name Emmanuel, which being interpreted is, God with us.
24 Then Joseph being raised from sleep did as the angel of the Lord had bidden him, and took unto him his wife:
25 And knew her not till she had brought forth her firstborn son: and he called his name JESUS.

Verse 16 of this chapter prepares the reader for the birth account by identifying Joseph as the "husband" of Mary and Mary as the parent "of whom was born" Jesus. Matthew goes into great detail to explain specifically what he meant by these words. He emphasized Joseph's role at the birth of Jesus whereas Luke focused on Mary's role. Just as surely as Mary was the chosen mother, Joseph was Jesus' chosen legal father.

The birth (Greek *genesis,* v. 1) of Jesus Christ was "on this wise," i.e., "like this" or "in this manner." Matthew begins with the espousal of Mary and Joseph (see also Lk. 1:27). Unlike Luke, Matthew does not discuss Mary separate from Joseph (Nolland 93) nor does he mention that these events took place in Nazareth.

Espousal can mean "to betroth" or "to marry." Our text makes it clear that they were not married. If Joseph and Mary followed the Jewish customs of the day, their marriage would have been an arranged marriage and their betrothal would have been for no more than two years. Generally betrothals were for one year or less (Gower 64; Keener, *Matthew* 89). According to Keener *(Background* 47) Jewish betrothals required "two witnesses, mutual consent (normally) and the groom's declaration." Jewish men generally married around eighteen to twenty years of age, and Jewish women around thirteen to sixteen (Evans and Porter 684).

These verses indicate that betrothal in that culture and time was more binding than engagements today. Mary was called Joseph's "wife" (v. 20) during the time of the betrothal and Joseph was called "her husband" (v. 19). Mary and Joseph's betrothal would require a formal divorce if the marriage were called off (v. 19). According to the Mosaic Law, unfaithfulness during the betrothal period was adultery and punishable by stoning (Dt. 22:23-24). However, scholars agree that stoning was rare in N.T. times (Jn. 8:2-11; 2 Cor. 11:25; Hagner 33A:18; Wilkins 74).

During the espousal period, prior to the actual wedding ceremony, Mary's pregnancy became known. Both Mary and Joseph were convinced of her pregnancy and perhaps the word was beginning to spread, especially if she could no longer conceal her pregnancy. One might think that Mary told Joseph of Gabriel's visit and her pregnancy soon after she returned from her visit with Elisabeth (Lk. 1:39-56), but the text nowhere suggests this. "She was found" suggests that she told Joseph when she could hide it no longer. She was at least in her fourth month by this time and apparently not sharing with many people the details of Gabriel's visit to her—some think not even with Joseph

(Wilkins 74). If Luke's record is complete, Gabriel said nothing to Mary about Joseph's role in all of this except by inference that he would not be the natural father (Lk. 1:26-35).

Matthew's account agrees with Luke's. Joseph was not the natural father of Mary's child. She was with child "of the Holy Spirit." While there are differences in the genealogies of Matthew and Luke, there is no difference between their teaching on the origin of the conception (Lk. 1:35). Both state unequivocally that the conception was miraculous. It was divinely accomplished. It was "by the Holy Spirit."

Joseph at first knew only two things for sure (v. 19): Mary was pregnant and he was not the father. If Mary told Joseph Gabriel's explanation of her pregnancy, Joseph did not believe her story or he would not have considered divorcing her ("put her away"). Gundry's (22) position that Joseph did believe her story about the supernatural conception and that was his quandary seems highly improbable in light of the angel's need to explain that "that which is conceived in her is of the Holy Ghost."

Joseph was himself chaste. He was a righteous man and as such he wanted to obey the law as well as protect his reputation in the community. It is apparent that Joseph cared for Mary for he had no desire to disgrace her publicly. However, there may have been more to it than this. Keener says Joseph really had no choice, that Jewish laws of the day required that he divorce her (*Matthew* 91).

Joseph was a thoughtful man (v. 20). He did not act rashly. He wanted to obey the Law and yet at the same time he wanted to spare her public disgrace, so he thought about divorcing her secretly rather than subjecting her to public humiliation (Hagner 33A:18). As Joseph tried to decide what to do, the Lord intervened by sending an angel to him in a dream. This is the first of five dreams mentioned from here to the end of chapter two. An angel appeared to Zacharias, John's father, and to Mary in human form (Lk. 1:11, 26, 28) but according to Matthew, God communicated with Joseph only in dreams. Dreams had been a common means of communicating divine truth in the O.T., so Joseph would not have thought this strange (e.g. Jacob, Jacob's son Joseph, King Solomon, Nebuchadnezzar, Daniel, and others).

The angel identified Joseph as a "son of David," a description that connects this passage with the above genealogy. The angel calmed Joseph's fears about the marriage to Mary by answering two of Joseph's most troubling questions. The conception of Mary's child was the working of God the Holy Spirit, and God wanted Joseph to go ahead with the wedding. It was God's will for this righteous man to marry this expectant mother whose child was not his. He could be confident that Mary was innocent of any wrongdoing.

That Jesus was conceived by the Holy Spirit speaks of Jesus' humanity and deity from the moment of conception and answers the question of paternity. There was no human father. See Gabriel's comments to Mary (Lk. 1:31-35). Though Joseph did not understand, the conception that the angel spoke of was the incarnation, the point in time that Jesus, the Second Person of the Trinity, took on humanity. In this birth narrative, then, Matthew introduced the Persons of the Trinity: the Lord God had given the prophecy to Isaiah (v. 22; Is.

7:13-14), the Holy Spirit brought about the conception (vv. 18, 20), and the Son became incarnate (v. 23).

It is not within the scope of this commentary to address exhaustively the doctrine of the incarnation. However, the essential nature of this doctrine both to the text and to our salvation requires some comment and can be summarized as follows. The Son of God, the Second Person of the Trinity, possesses all of the divine attributes. He is equal with the Father in every way. He has always been (Jn. 1:1). There never was a time, even before time, when He was not. He was with the Father before the world was (Jn. 17:5).

This same Person took on humanity, both flesh and nature. He became something that He originally was not, a human. He was conceived in and born of a woman (Mt. 1:25; Lk. 2:7; Gal. 4:4). He experienced the usual human development (Lk. 2:52). He had a human body (Jn. 2:21; 1 Jn. 1:1; Heb. 10:5; Mt. 26:12), a human will (Mt. 26:39; Heb. 5:7-8). His human nature was not corrupted by the original sin or by personal sin (1 Pet. 2:22) but was sinless like Adam's prior to the fall.

He had the weaknesses of humanity, sin excluded. He became tired (Jn. 4:6). He became hungry (Mt. 4:2). He became thirsty (Jn. 19:28). He was tempted (Mt. 4:1-11; Heb. 2:18; 4:15). He suffered and died (Is. 53:8; Mt. 27:26, 35, 50). His humanity was necessary in order for Him to be qualified to make atonement for the sins of the human race (Heb. 2:17).

All the while, He experienced humanity, He was divine as well. He was conscious of His Father's will (Lk. 2:49) for He and the Father maintained perfect unity (Jn. 10:30). He claimed deity (Jn. 8:58; 10:33; 17:5) and equality with the Father (Jn. 5:18). He is the only visible manifestation of the Godhead (Jn. 1:18), the image of the invisible God (Col. 1:15; Heb. 1:3). He is the LORD of the O.T. (Jn. 12:41; Is. 6:1), the Creator (Jn. 1:1-3; Col. 1:16) and Sustainer of all creation (Col. 1:17). When He came to earth, He emptied himself of His heavenly glories but not His divine nature (Phil. 2:6-8) that He might live as a human and die on the cross. Though He died, He rose again to live forever (Mt. 28:7, 9; Rev. 1:18).

He was God (Rom. 9:5; Tit. 2:13) in the flesh (Jn. 1:1, 14), the proper object of true worship (Mt. 14:33; 28:9; Jn. 5:22-23; 20:28; Phil. 2:9-11; Heb. 1:6). He is the same yesterday, today, and forever (Heb. 13:8). Though He veiled His glory in flesh, His essential essence never changed (Mt. 17:2). For this reason, He is rightly called the God-man. Jesus possessed two natures, human and divine. While on this earth, He could act through either. See Matthew 9:6 where, as Son of Man, a human, Jesus forgave sin, something only God can do. He was one hundred percent divine. He was one hundred percent human.

Acceptance of the biblical doctrine of Jesus' incarnation is an essential doctrine for one's salvation (Jn. 6:25-51, esp. vv. 29, 36, 38-40). Christianity's worship of Jesus as the God-man is uniquely Christian and sets followers of Jesus apart from adherents of all other religions. As Bruner (1:46) rightly states, this is a "nonnegotiable" doctrine. For further study of the doctrine of Jesus' incarnation, see Forlines 167-182, Erickson 610-758, and comments on 4:1, 8:26, and 24:36 in this commentary.

The angel told Joseph the child's gender (v. 21) and that he, Joseph, would name Him Jesus. Gabriel likewise had directed Mary to name her son Jesus (Lk. 1:31). This name was given for a special reason. This son would "save his people from their sins." Jesus is the Greek equivalent of the Hebrew name Joshua. Both mean "the Lord saves" or "Yah is salvation" (BDB 221) or "Yahweh saves" (Allen 806). Twice in the N.T. the Greek name translated Jesus actually refers to the O.T. Joshua (Acts 7:45; Heb. 4:8), whose name Moses changed from Hoshea ("salvation"; BDB 448) to Joshua ("Yahweh saves"; Num. 13:16). Jesus is the name of the incarnate Son beginning at Bethlehem. It is His human name (Bruner 1:5).

There were and are many benefits connected with Jesus' coming, but, the main benefit concerns mankind's salvation. The name Jesus designates Him as God's provision for man's salvation. Who is included in "his people" and how He will accomplish this salvation will unfold as this gospel record advances (Bruner 1:32). One might think that the angel meant Jesus came only to save Israelites (Jn. 1:11) but "his people" are "Messiah's people" (Carson, *Matthew* 76), the new people of God (Mt. 21:43), Jew and Gentile alike (Mt. 28:19).

"From their sins" (v. 21) describes the work and ultimate goal of Jesus' work of salvation. Deliverance from the penalty, power, and presence of sin are all included in the salvific work of Jesus (Rom. 6:6-14). Jesus' coming was not to bring about a political deliverance from the Gentiles, something Jesus' contemporaries and Matthew's readers needed to know (Evans, *Matthew* 47). Rather, Jesus would sacrifice Himself as payment for all mankind's sins (Mt. 26:28), both racial (Rom. 5:12-14) and individual (Rom. 3:23).

The miraculous conception happened in fulfillment of Isaiah 7:14. That "all of this was done" (v. 22) is literally, "All of this has taken place" (Greek perfect tense), which may put these words in the mouth of the angel rather than of Matthew (Carson, *Matthew* 76; *contra* Nolland 99; Hagner 33A:20; Wilkins 78). If the angel was speaking, he wanted Joseph, even as the Holy Spirit wanted Matthew's readers, to recognize that the original promise was from the Lord. Whether the angel or Matthew referenced Isaiah's prophecy, the Lord had spoken through the eighth century B.C. prophet specifically stating that a virgin would give birth to a son. Mary's conception happened as it did so that the prophecy would be fulfilled exactly as promised. This was no divine afterthought. God's predictive prophecy is undeniable. There are two miracles, then, a virginal conception and birth, and fulfilled prophecy.

Isaiah's original statement was made to Ahaz, a wicked king of Judah (2 Kg. 16; 2 Chr. 28; Is. 7). (See comments on Matthew 1:9.) Rezin, king of Syria, and Pekah, king of Israel, joined forces to attack Jerusalem and overthrow King Ahaz. Ahaz and his people were terrified of this impending attack, so the Lord sent a message of hope through Isaiah that this confederacy would not stand. The Lord promised Ahaz that Syria and the Northern Kingdom would be brought to an end soon.

The Lord directed Ahaz to ask for a sign, even a difficult sign, as proof that the Lord would bring about what He promised, but the king refused. The Lord then gave His own sign, a deep-as-

Sheol/high-as-heaven sign (Is. 7:11; ESV). A virgin (Hebrew, lit. "the virgin") would give birth to a son, which would be a sign of "God with us" (Is. 7:14). How this was a sign for Ahaz has been variously understood (for a list of possible interpretations, see Grogan 62-63; Wilkins 79-80; and Hendriksen 135-140).

The precise meaning of Isaiah's word translated "virgin" (Hebrew *`almāh*) is debated among scholars. Some understand the word to designate a young woman, either a virgin or one newly married (BDB 761). Carson argues that the Hebrew word might be used of a woman who lacks sexual experience but "one cannot be certain the word necessarily means that" because of Proverbs 30:19 ("the way of a man with a *maid*"), of which he says the "focus is not on virginity" (*Matthew* 77). Macrae, however, believes that there is no instance in the O.T. where it "can be proved that *`alma* designates a young woman who is not a virgin" (TWOT II:672). In the final analysis, Matthew's record settles this question of the Lord's intended meaning in Isaiah 7:14. The woman would remain a virgin through childbirth.

The pregnancy of a woman who was at the same time a virgin was not all Isaiah's words meant. From the N.T. perspective, it seems probable that the prophecy was intended to have a double fulfillment (Blomberg 5; Wilkins 78-81). Judah would experience God's deliverance in two stages. The prophetic son was first a sign of God's presence for Ahaz and the entire "house of David" (Evans, *Matthew* 47; Is. 7:13-14; the Hebrew "you" is plural in both verses) and a sign of His intended preservation of the Davidic throne (2 Sam. 7:13, 16). A young woman who was a virgin at the time of this prophecy would have a son. In order to have a legitimate son, this virgin must marry either an unnamed man known to Ahaz, King Ahaz himself, or, Isaiah (cf. Is. 8:3; Wilkins 79). Before the child reached the age of moral awareness (Is. 7:16) the two enemy kings would no longer be a threat. If this prophecy came in ca. 735 B.C., the son needed to be born within three years because in 732 B.C. Rezin and Pekah were both killed.

The sign for Ahaz was intended to impress on him God's planned overthrow of the Northern Kingdom of Israel and Syria by Assyria. The house of David and all of Judah would experience a deliverance from this enemy coalition very soon. Ahaz and Judah needed to rely on God who is "with us," not on the king of Assyria (2 Kg. 16:7-9). Ahaz hardened his heart against God and rejected His offer. Ahaz trusted Assyria rather than the Lord and because of this the whole land suffered God's judgment (Is. 7:17-25; 8:5-8). The son (Is. 7:14) would reach the age of accountability during the time of the Assyrian oppression (Is. 7:16-17).

Isaiah 8's contextual proximity to the Isaiah 7:14-16 promises strengthens the probability that the sign was for Ahaz in his time and that Isaiah married the virgin. This means that the first promised son was Isaiah's (Blomberg 4; Keener, *Background* 48) and his second wife's (see 7:3). Isaish's first wife may have died or he may have had two wives since polygamy was common at that time.

Isaiah 8 records that Isaiah and the "prophetess" (8:3) had a son as a sign (8:18). The Lord told Isaiah to name the child Mahershalalhashbaz which means "quick to the plunder" or "swift to the spoil" (NIV margin) signifying Assyria's quick and ravenous plundering of Damascus and Samaria (8:4). He was to name the child this because, "Before the child shall have knowledge to cry, `My Father,' and `my mother,' i.e., to say his first words, the riches of Damascus and the spoil of Samaria shall be taken away before the king of Assyria" (v. 4). In other words, by putting the promises of Isaiah 7 and 8 together, Ahaz learned that in the time it would take for a virgin to marry, carry and bear a child (7:14), and that child learn its first words (8:4), the powers of the two enemies would be gone and their lands would be emptied of their people (7:16; 8:4). Also, by the time the child reached the age of accountability, the Assyrians would have removed most everything of any value from Judah as well (Is. 7:16, 20; 8:8).

All of this came to pass. The Assyrian king, Tiglath-pileser III, captured Damascus and killed Rezin, king of Syria, in 732 B.C., the same year Pekah was killed by his successor (2 Kg. 15:30; 16:9; Wood 281, 302). Assyria carried Syria into exile and a portion of Israel as well. In 722 B.C. Samaria, the capital of Israel, fell to Assyria and another group of Israelites was deported by the Assyrians. The deaths of these kings and the exiles of the Northern Kingdom of Israel and Syria fulfilled Isaiah 7:16 and 8:4. The Assyrians' later assaults into Judah (2 Chr. 28:20-21) fulfilled Isaiah 7:20, 23-25 and 8:7-8. However, even with all of this, there was still hope for Judah. See "Immanuel" and "God *is* with us" in Isaiah 8:8, 10.

This sign child was Immanuel in the sense that he symbolized God's continuing presence with Judah and the house of David. When their enemies to the north were no more, as God had promised, Judah remained, also as God had promised. Ahaz could look at the sign son and the survival of the little nation of Judah and know that God had been with them.

The second intended fulfillment of the Isaiah 7:14 prophecy was the sign of the future Messiah, the ultimate Deliverer. This was the angel's point to Joseph. Jesus' birth was a further sign from God of His immediate presence and the fullest fulfillment of His promise to Ahaz and the house of David through Isaiah. In this second fulfillment another unmarried virgin would have a legitimate pregnancy and give birth to a son, though this time while remaining a virgin. The son born in Ahaz and Isaiah's day was a type of the Son born to Mary, further signifying God's nearness and deliverance.

This explanation does not answer all of the questions about this passage but its strengths are that both Ahaz and Joseph received recognizable and indisputable signs from God in the contexts of their own historical circumstances and needs. It also means the promised signs are recorded in Scripture as proof that God did as He promised.

Young (1:289-291) disagrees. He says that in any interpretation of this passage three points must be stressed: "(1) the birth must be a sign; (2) the mother of the Child is one who is both unmarried and a good woman; ... [and] (3) the very presence of the Child brings God to His people." For these reasons, Young limits his interpretation to only "Jesus the Christ, the Son of the Virgin and the Mighty God." In Young's view, there was no contemporary sign for Ahaz in Isaiah 7:14. Hendriksen (134-140) and Delitzsch (VII:228) agree.

Regardless how the interpreter understands Isaiah 7:14 in relation to King Ahaz, this much is certain: Isaiah's words find direct fulfillment in Mary's virginal conception. That Isaiah's words are quoted as a prophecy of a virgin birth makes this clear (TWOT II:672; Carson, *Matthew* 76). The reference to Isaiah means that Mary's pregnancy was foretold and therefore believable. Joseph could more readily believe what the angel told him about Mary because Isaiah had promised this would happen. Such a miraculous birth has no precedent in Scripture. Though miraculous conceptions are recorded in the O.T. (Sarah, Rebekah, Rachel, Manoah's wife, Hannah), none claim virginal conception. Matthew's view of Scripture is also evident in this quote (Keener, *Matthew* 87). Jesus' birth happened as it did that Scripture "might be fulfilled" (v. 22).

Barclay (1:23) states concerning the virgin birth that "we are not compelled to accept it in the literal and physical sense," just that it was of the Holy Spirit. He fails, however, to explain what he believes to be the means of Mary's conception, leaving the reader to wonder if it was even a legitimate conception. The writer of our Gospel will tolerate no such error or confusion. For a summary of those who discount the historicity of the virgin birth and their arguments, see Bruner 1:37-43.

The miraculous birth would yield a son who would be known as "God with us," the meaning of Immanuel (v. 23). Jesus was His human given name. That the Child would be named Jesus was not part of O.T. prophecy. In Isaiah 7:14, "she" would name Him Immanuel; in Matthew "they" will name Him.

Immanuel was a description of Jesus' person and presence as Messiah. For Ahaz and Isaiah, "God with us" was declared in the sense that God was with them to accomplish His promise of keeping the royal Son of David on the throne. Immanuel was the message of the sign of the virgin who would bear a son (ESV Study Bible 1254). The full Christian understanding of this is that Jesus *is* God, and this emphasizes both His nearness and His deity. The virgin-born Child is both a sign from God and God Himself. God's revelation of Himself as Trinity now becomes clearer.

Nolland (102) views such an understanding of Immanuel as too strong, given Matthew's immediate concern of placing Jesus in the Davidic line. He states that such an understanding is too "overwhelming" at this early stage in Matthew's narrative since Matthew "cumulates" the understanding of who Jesus really is throughout his Gospel. In response to Nolland one might answer that Matthew has already pointed to this Child's deity by stating that the virgin Mary was with child "of the Holy Spirit" (vv. 18, 20). Matthew was not writing a suspense novel; he wrote to prove the identity of Jesus as the divine King of the Jews.

Having heard the instructions of the angel and the prophecy of Isaiah, as soon as he woke from sleep, Joseph immediately obeyed the Lord's command. Immediate, unquestioning obedience was Joseph's hallmark through these first two chapters. He took Mary as his wife, i.e., he took her home "in wedlock" (Gundry 25) but did not consummate the marriage until after the birth of Jesus (v. 25). Different translations reflect the fact that some Greek manuscripts have "first-born" while others do not. Luke 2:7 states clearly that Jesus was Mary's firstborn. Matthew's silence about a wedding leads only to speculation about whether there was the usual wedding celebration though it seems possible (Keener, *Background* 48; Hagner 33A:21; Wilkins 92). Luke 2:5, however, seems to infer that the usual wedding contract was not drawn up or put into effect until after Jesus was born.

In obedience to the angel's message, Joseph named the baby "Jesus." On the child's eighth day, Jesus was circumcised in compliance with God's instructions to Abraham (Gen. 17:10-13) and named (Lk. 2:21). Jesus was at this time declared to be Joseph's legal son and according to Matthew's genealogy in verses 1-17 part of the Davidic line (Gundry 26).

Zerwick (2) says the grammar here does not necessitate an understanding that Joseph and Mary ceased their celibacy after Jesus' birth since the author was "only concerned here to indicate virginal conception." However, if a supposed perpetual virginity of Mary is protected—or even allowed for—by this text, then the words "until she bore a son" become meaningless and in fact confusing. Also, the N.T. writers tell a story different from that which Zerwick suggests. Matthew (12:46-50; 13:55, 56), Mark (3:31-34), Luke (8:19-21; Acts 1:14) and Paul (1 Cor. 9:5; Gal. 1:19) each speak of Jesus' siblings. Matthew was not describing a lifetime of celibacy between Joseph and Mary but celibacy until Jesus' birth. Forty days after Jesus' birth (Lev. 12:2-4, 8; 15:25-30; Lk. 2:22) Joseph and Mary would have been able to consummate their marriage vows and live in accordance with God's created design and purpose for husbands and wives (Gen. 1:27-28). The angel commanded Joseph to take Mary as his wife, not as a lifetime celibate (v. 20). For summary arguments against the doctrine of the perpetual virginity of Mary, see Bruner (1:48-52).

By stating that Joseph "knew her not till she had brought forth her first-born son," Matthew did three things. First, he protected the doctrine of the virgin birth. Joseph, in literal fulfillment of Isaiah 7:14, "knew her not" to insure that there was a virgin birth as well as a virginal conception (Nolland 103). Second, by inference Matthew showed that the marriage relationship between Joseph and Mary was honorable (Heb. 13:4) and normal. Third, he explained how Jesus could have had brothers and sisters, as many would have known, and yet be divine. Jesus was miraculously conceived in a virgin by the Holy Spirit. This virgin wife, after the birth of her first son, became a wife who bore other children in a normal marriage relationship (Wilkins 82).

Luke 2:1-7 contains the only other N.T. account of Jesus' birth. Though told from different perspectives, it is clear that both Matthew and Luke tell the same story. Each corroborates and adds understanding to the other.

Summary (1:18-25)

In verses 1-17 Matthew disclosed Jesus' regal heritage. In verses 18-25 he revealed Jesus' divine and human union. Without telling any of Mary's story, Matthew told of Joseph's discovery of his espoused wife's pregnancy before they became physically intimate. Joseph was concerned, wondering what would be a lawful and yet merciful course of action. God sent a messenger, an angel, to provide details and direction for this righteous young man. The angel told Joseph that Mary's conception resulted from the Holy Spirit's work in her and that he was to go ahead with the marriage. Joseph learned that the Lord had promised just such a birth over 700 years earlier. In obedience to the messenger of God, Joseph took Mary home with him. Yet they remained celibate until the miracle was complete and Jesus was born of the virgin. Joseph named his wife's son showing that Jesus was his legal son and thus a son of King David.

Application: Teaching and Preaching the Passage

The record of Jesus' birth is easy to grasp on a surface level but there are also unfathomable depths of spiritual truth in this narrative. The text needs an interpreter. Matthew set the example by interpreting "Immanuel" (v. 23). Teachers and preachers can follow Matthew's example and interpret for their hearers unfamiliar words and doctrines.

One might focus a lesson on the supernatural events of Jesus' birth that serve to demonstrate God's power and presence among men. The miracle of the virgin conception and the virgin birth, an appearance of an angel and a seven hundred year old prophecy all speak of God's power and presence among men. They also speak of God's plan to save mankind and His power to execute that plan.

Using the entire chapter, one might present a lesson or sermon on the meanings of Jesus' names and titles used in this portion of His story. He was called Jesus, Christ, Son of David, son of Abraham, "child of the Holy Ghost," "that which is conceived in her," Immanuel, and first-born son. He is Savior, also, for He will "save his people from their sins."

The teacher or preacher might examine this passage for doctrines that can be discussed in light of this birth account. These could include the incarnation, predictive prophecy, angels as God's messengers, sin and people's need for a savior, Jesus' role as Savior, God's immanence, the revelation of the Trinity in Jesus' birth, the Person and work of the Holy Spirit, and God's foreknowledge and power over time and chance.

A study of Joseph might also be a profitable lesson or sermon. (1) Though a young man, Joseph was concerned to live a life obedient to the Mosaic Law and at the same time show mercy. (2) Joseph was a righteous man to whom God entrusted His Son. God picked the home in which Jesus would be raised and the kind of parenting Jesus would have. (3) Joseph was a thoughtful man, careful to do what was right and best for all concerned. (4) Joseph practiced instant obedience to the Lord, which points to a ready and confident faith. On the bases of the message of an angel in a dream and the Word of God in Isaiah, Joseph acted. (5) Joseph was a role model of self-control and sexual purity (Keener, *Background* 47). Keener suggests that both were teenagers, Mary 12-16 years of age and Joseph 18-20 years of age, and that they restrained themselves in order to fulfill literally Isaiah's words that "a virgin would both conceive and bear" (*Matthew* 88-90). (6) Joseph was a generous man, willing to raise a son not his own.

C. The Visit of the Magi (2:1-12)

1 Now when Jesus was born in Bethlehem of Judaea in the days of Herod the king, behold, there came wise men from the east to Jerusalem,
2 Saying, Where is he that is born King of the Jews? for we have seen his star in the east, and are come to worship him.
3 When Herod the king had heard *these things*, he was troubled, and all Jerusalem with him.
4 And when he had gathered all the chief priests and scribes of the people together, he demanded of them where Christ should be born.
5 And they said unto him, In Bethlehem of Judaea: for thus it is written by the prophet,
6 And thou Bethlehem, *in* the land of Juda, art not the least among the princes of Juda: for out of thee shall come a Governor, that shall rule my people Israel.
7 Then Herod, when he had privily called the wise men, enquired of them diligently what time the star appeared.
8 And he sent them to Bethlehem, and said, Go and search diligently for the young child; and when ye have found *him*, bring me word again, that I may come and worship him also.
9 When they had heard the king, they departed; and, lo, the star, which they saw in the east, went before them, till it came and stood over where the young child was.
10 When they saw the star, they rejoiced with exceeding great joy.
11 And when they were come into the house, they saw the young child with Mary his mother, and fell down, and worshipped him: and when they had opened their treasures, they presented unto him gifts; gold, and frankincense and myrrh.
12 And being warned of God in a dream that they should not return to Herod, they departed into their own country another way.

Following the birth narrative in chapter one, Matthew turned his attention away from Joseph and Mary. Everything is this chapter is about "the child." The child is worshiped, taken to Egypt, called out of Egypt, and taken to Nazareth.

Matthew, in agreement with Luke, located the birth of Jesus in Bethlehem. He said nothing about Joseph and Mary's hometown of Nazareth or of their trip to Bethlehem before Jesus' birth (Lk. 2:1-5). Matthew's purpose for writing did not require that he include all of Luke's details; and vice-versa. Neither Matthew nor Luke wrote so that readers could later "fit everything together into one harmonious whole" (Hagner 33A:35). The Messianic King needed to be virgin born in the city of David. These important details Matthew states.

Nevertheless, this historical record (Wilkins 112, 122; Keener, *Matthew* 98; Hagner 33A:25-26; Carson, *Matthew* 83) of the visit of the Magi, Jesus' escape to Egypt, and His return to live in Nazareth support Matthew's thesis that Jesus is the prophesied Son of David. The Magi especially point to Jesus as king. Hill (80-81, 84) and Gundry (26-41) do not view this chapter as historically accurate. They believe that Matthew's record was meant to teach theological truths, not record history. However, Scripture claims accuracy even in its record of history (2 Tim. 3:16; Jn. 10:35). So one should expect that Matthew's record is historically accurate.

Jesus was born during the reign of King Herod (Mt. 2:1; Lk. 1:5). This Herod was Herod the Great whom Rome had appointed as King of Judea in 40 B.C. He reigned until his death in 4 B.C. (ISBE II:688-693). Matthew was clear on which Herod he meant (v. 22). Jesus' birth year could have been as much as two years before Herod died, around 6-4 B.C. Luke gave more information on Jesus' birth year than Matthew but determining the exact year of His birth is difficult. See Marshal's (100-104, 133, 134, 162) comments on Lk. 2:1-2, 3:1, and 3:23 for a summary discussion of the historical references and dates that help determine the time of Jesus' life and ministry. For a summary of issues concerning dating Jesus' birth, see P. Harrison (75-80).

A few months after Jesus' birth, possibly as much as two years after but definetly not the night of His birth, Magi came to worship him. These visitors present something of a mystery. Their homeland and identities are unknown. What Matthew meant by the word "Magi" (KJV wise men) is also unclear.

Some writers suggest Persia or Mesopotamia ("from the east"; ISBE IV:1084) or Chaldea (Evans, *Matthew* 57; Hill 82) as their homeland. They were at least from another country (v. 12) where they were a safe distance from Herod's authority and reach. They had been exposed to O.T. Scriptures, possibly through Jewish exiles who remained in their area following the Babylonian captivity.

The Greek word translated *Magi* was used to designate members of a Persian priestly caste who specialized in astrology, interpretation of dreams, or magic—or who were, according to Nolland (108), oriental sages. More narrowly, and as used here, the word referred to a person who was "the 'possessor of special (secret) wisdom,' especially concerning the meaning of the course of the stars and its interconnection with world events" (TDNT 4:358; Hagner 33A:26). Luke uses this same noun and cognate verbs to describe the satanically empowered sorcery of Simon (Acts 13:8-9, 11). The Magi were not kings.

The Magi knew something of the O.T. Scriptures and they believed them. As Daniel demonstrated, it was possible to be a member of such a group and be a worshiper of God (Dan. 5:11). Scriptures consistently teach that Gentiles can be God-fearers too (Job 1:1; Gen. 14:18; Dan. 4:37; Rom. 2:13-15). These men joined the privileged group of unlikely people to be told of the Messiah's birth.

Matthew does not tell how many Magi there were. The word is plural and might require only two persons, but the passage seems to infer at least a small group (Keener, *Background* 49). By recounting this visit, Matthew shows that the circumstances of Jesus' birth, even as the birth itself (1:22), were rooted in Scripture and open to Gentiles.

Verse 2 suggests that the Magi did not go first to King Herod but rather were asking around Jerusalem about the birth of a king. Perhaps they assumed a Jewish king would be born in Jerusalem or more particularly in Herod's palace (Keener, *Background* 49; Keener, *Matthew* 98). They were badly mistaken if they thought the King of the Jews would be born in Herod's palace.

The Magi were searching for the one "born" king (Greek adjectival participle, attributive use), not the one "born to be king" (Carson, *Matthew* 86, 89). Rome gave Herod the title of king. Jesus is king because He is the Son of David (1:1-17). These men called the one for whom they searched the "King of the Jews." These words appear once more in Matthew's Gospel. They are above Jesus' head, fastened to the cross (27:37).

The Magi claimed that from their home they saw (Greek aorist tense) a star in the east (v.2, Greek "in the east" or "at [its] rising") that they believed announced the birth of the long awaited Jewish king, the Messiah. The text does not say that they came to Jerusalem "following yonder star" ("We Three Kings of Orient Are"). The star appeared and then was gone, subsequently to reappear (v. 9).

No clear O.T. prophecy speaks of a star to mark the birth of the Messiah. These men may have been referring to Balaam's prophecy recorded in Num. 24:17 ("there shall come a Star out of Jacob"). The problem is, in Balaam's prophecy the star is not a sign. It is the Messiah Himself (Nolland 111).

Different explanations have been offered to describe this star, including a documented alignment of planets in 7 B.C., a special "astral phenomenon that God used to herald Jesus' birth," or an angel (Wilkins 95-96, 99; Wilkins leans more to an angel). Though Matthew gave no description of the star, it is clear these men saw a stellar event that they accurately interpreted. The heavenly sign prompted the Magi to search for the king so that they might show Him due honor (worship) and give Him gifts. They probably came to pay homage to Him as king, not as one who was Divine (Evans, *Matthew* 57; Wilkins 100) but surely they believed that one whose birth was marked in such an extraordinary way would Himself be extraordinary. In all of this, Matthew's point must not be missed. This was no regular king. The reason these Gentiles came was to worship the Messianic King (Hendriksen 155).

Both Bruner (1:59) and Keener (*Matthew* 100) speak of the limitation of this natural revelation. The Magi gained some understanding from the star but this would only take them so far. In order to find the Christ, they needed special revelation, God's Word, something that only the Jewish people had.

All Jerusalem was disturbed by the Magi's questions (v. 3). Herod heard about their questioning and was disturbed as well, so he also sought to determine where such a king would be born. Herod called in the Jewish chief priests and scribes and they immediately told him the answer. He realized the King of the Jews and the Christ were one and the same (v. 4; Hendriksen 167). The Magi's testimony, plus the prophecy, convinced Herod, and he at once determined to destroy the child. The Magi's visit to Herod suggests that they lived a great distance away for they apparently knew nothing of his paranoia. Herod eliminated anyone he thought to be a rival to his throne, even immediate family members.

According to Nolland (112) the chief priests as a group consisted of "the upper echelon of the priestly order: the chief priest (and his predecessors), the captain of the temple, those who headed the twenty-four courses into which the priesthood was divided for service in the temple, the priest who had charge of the treasury, and other high-ranking priests." The chief priests (see comments on 16:21) were mainly wealthy Sadducees. The scribes (see comments on 13:52) were expert teachers of the law (Keener, *Background* 49). What is surprising is that these men, with all of their knowledge, appeared to be neutral about the entire exchange. None of them went to Bethlehem.

Freely quoting Micah 5:2, they stated that the village of Bethlehem, located just five miles (8 km.) from Jerusalem, was the designated birthplace of the Christ. (The Bethlehem of Joshua 19:15, a short distance from Nazareth, was not the city Micah meant.) This part of Micah's prophecy was clear and answered the Magi's question. The remainder of their quote differs somewhat from Micah 5:2 and suggests that they were clarifying and interpreting Micah. Though Bethlehem seemed small and insignificant, humanly speaking, that Israel's greatest leader would be born there gave it immediate importance.

The Jewish leaders combined Micah's prophecy with another Scripture. Combining Scriptures that referred to the same thing was a common rabbinic practice according to Hagner (33A:29). These leaders understood that the Christ would rule—literally, "shepherd" (Greek *poimainō*)—Israel (v. 6; from 2 Sam. 5:2 and 1 Chr. 11:2). Prophets Jeremiah and Ezekiel agreed. This is one of the Messiah's job titles and descriptions. The Lord would replace the bad shepherds of Israel (Jer. 23:1-6; Ezek. 34:1-31; esp. vv. 23-24) with a Shepherd of His own choosing. The Messiah and this coming Shepherd are one and the same. These men failed to mention Micah's reference to the Messiah's eternality.

One may conclude that Micah's prophecy was common knowledge. John (7:40-43) wrote: "Many of the people therefore, when they heard this saying, said, Of a truth this is the Prophet. Others said, This is the Christ. But some said, Shall Christ come out of Galilee? Hath not the Scripture said, That Christ cometh of the seed of David, and out of the town of Bethlehem, where David was? So there was division among the people because of him."

During Jesus' ministry, people considered His claims and checked Him against Scripture. Matthew was addressing questions like these. Though some people familiar with Jesus' Galilean home believed Jesus was from Nazareth and therefore had no rightful claim to David's throne, Matthew records that this question was credibly answered when Jesus was but an infant. He also shows that Jesus had to be from Galilee, something that some of the Jews of Jesus' day did not know. See 4:12-16 and the commentary on that passage.

Herod understood, at least at some level, the implications of the Magi's quest. If these men had in reality seen a heavenly sign that marked the birth of the Messiah in fulfillment of Jewish prophecy, his own throne and dynasty were threatened. He did what he could. Calling the Magi in for a private meeting, he asked specifically when the star appeared (v. 7). If the star marked the birth, he could determine the age of this Child. Second, he feigned honest interest and intent to worship (v. 8) and asked that the Magi continue their search in Bethlehem and, report back to him.

All seemed fine to the Magi. In fact, as they left Jerusalem they experienced a second miracle: the star reappeared and went before them. Hearing the prophecy and seeing the star again must have added to their sense of urgency and excitement as they realized the nearness of their goal. Seeing the star a second time confirmed that they were indeed right (v. 10). The star led them to "where the child was" (v. 9). This time the light moved as they did and stopped at their destination.

Carson states that the "Greek text does not imply that the star pointed out the house where Jesus was; it may have simply hovered over Bethlehem as the Magi approached it" (*Matthew* 88). He says they would have had to find "the exact house through discreet inquiry." Perhaps, but Carson's comment is no less speculative than suggesting that the star marked the house. In fact, "where the young child was" (v. 9) seems to be "the house" in verse 11.

Having led the Magi the last few miles (Greek progressive imperfect "was going," v. 9), the star stopped, marking the exact house. By now Joseph, Mary, and baby Jesus were residing in better living conditions than Luke described for their first days in Bethlehem (Lk. 2:7). No longer in an animal shelter (possibly a cave; see Keener, *Matthew* 103 for early sources), they were at the time of the Magi's visit in a *house*. Contrary to popular belief, the Magi did not arrive in Bethlehem the night Jesus was born and the star did not mark the place of His birth. The star announced His birth and later, several months or perhaps as much as two years later (v. 16), reappeared and led the Magi to His home in Bethlehem.

Matthew's comment about the second appearance of the star raises questions we cannot answer. It seems possible that either a light hovered over the house—which could look like a star though much closer to the earth's surface—or a light beam might have shown from heaven upon the house. God lit the night for the shepherds (Lk. 2:9). Paul had such an experience and spoke of it often (Acts 9:3; 22:6; 26:13). God did something of the same nature for these Magi. We do not have to discount this as poetic legend (like Barclay 1:36).

Practically, the star did two things: it minimized the Magi's travel time so they did not need to search for the child; and, second, it removed any need to ask questions in Bethlehem as they had done in Jerusalem and thus direct too much attention on the Christ Child. Jesus was not the only baby in Bethlehem (v. 16). In light of Herod's impending actions, both were necessary for Jesus' safety, although the Magi might not yet have sensed any danger.

Upon seeing the Child, the Magi did as they purposed. They worshiped Jesus. Though they saw the Child and Mary, they worshiped only the Child. In their worship, they bowed before Him, expressing honor and worth to this Infant. Jesus was apparently a toddler at this time, somewhere between six months and two years of age (v. 16).

What a scene this must have been for Joseph and Mary! Unexpected and unannounced, visitors, a group of foreigners from a distant land, entered their home at night to worship the baby. Following prophecies and a star, these visitors had come to the precise location of this holy family in Bethlehem, corroborating that this Jesus was the Christ whom they sought.

These men opened their treasure chests (v. 11) and presented costly gifts to the Child: gold, frankincense, and myrrh. Frankincense, meaning pure incense, is a aromatic gum extracted from certain trees that "has a strong balsamic odor when heated" (ISBE II:360). It was used in the special incense mixed exclusively for use in worship of the Lord (Ex. 30:34-38). It was also used as a personal fragrance (S. of S. 3:6).

Extracted from any of several shrubs, myrrh is also an aromatic resin mentioned several times in Scripture (ISBE III:450, 451). Scripture texts testify of its popularity and value in Bible times. The Ishmaelites who purchased and sold Joseph had camels loaded with spices, balm and myrrh (Gen. 37:25). Jacob sent myrrh as a gift (Gen. 43:11). Myrrh was an ingredient in the anointing oil (Ex. 30:23). Esther 2:12, Psalms 45:8, Proverbs 7:17 and eight references in the Song of Solomon speak of its use as a personal fragrance. In the N.T. in addition to being one of the Magi's gifts to Jesus, myrrh was used as a narcotic to dull pain for those being executed (Mk. 15:23; Keener, *Background* 181) and Nicodemus used it in his mixture of spices to anoint Jesus' dead body.

It is likely that these gifts funded the emergency trip to Egypt (vv. 13-14). With the gold and funds generated from the sale of the frankincense and myrrh, Joseph would have been able to cover the travel costs and living expenses until he could find work in Egypt and until such time when they could return to Nazareth.

God's direction of the Magi continued even after their arrival. Knowing Herod's intent, God warned the Magi against reporting to Herod and directed them to return home by another route. Thus God directed these men from start to finish (Hagner 33A:30). This is the second dream mentioned in the birth and infancy narratives recorded by Matthew. The first was to Joseph (Mt. 1:20).

Matthew gives no indication of the Magi's length of stay. Verse 13 suggests that the Lord wanted Joseph to move quickly. It seems likely, then, that the Magi came and left in the same night, perhaps after only a short rest during which time they had the dream. Wanting to put as much distance as possible between themselves and Herod (v. 16), they left Bethlehem while it was still night. They had accomplished their goal. They had seen the King.

Some commentators suggest that these Magi were fulfilling prophecies found in Psalm 72:10-11, 15 and Isaiah 60:6 (Blomberg 5). But if Psalm 72 is Messianic, then it is yet unfulfilled for Psalm 72:11 says, "All kings shall fall down before him: all nations shall serve him."

Summary (2:1-12)

Following the birth record, Matthew gave information on three events in Jesus' early childhood life: the visit of the Magi, the flight to Egypt, and the return to Nazareth. The first twelve verses of chapter two tell the story of the Magi's visit.

The Magi were God-fearing Gentiles who came to worship Jesus. These men traveled a great distance to see the Baby they believed to be the King of the Jews. They were convinced of this because of a supernaturally placed star that marked His birth, reappeared several months later and stopped over His home. The

Micah 5:2 prophecy provided support also. For Matthew, the Magi's visit further substantiated his claim made in chapter one that this child was the prophesied Son of David.

Jewish leaders knew the Scriptures but apparently were not interested in finding their newly born king. No one from Jerusalem went with the Magi, not even the Jewish leaders who were asked specifically about the prophecy. Perhaps they were afraid of Herod but Matthew gave no hint that any were even interested. "He came to his own, and his own received him not" (Jn. 1:11).

Application: Teaching and Preaching the Passage

A sermon or lesson could be developed around the idea of responses to Jesus' birth. One significant response to Jesus' birth was worship by Gentiles. Their worship was characterized by (1) great effort (traveled a long distance), (2) great personal sacrifice (travel expenses, gifts), (3) great persistence (asked around Jerusalem for information), (4) a show of great honor (bowed before Him), (5) great faith (believed the heavenly signs and Micah 5:2), and (6) great faithfulness to God (obeyed the signs and the dream).

Historically, the first series of recorded responses to Jesus' birth comes from Luke 2. According to Luke, angels sang, shepherds came to Bethlehem and worshiped the newborn Child. Simeon praised God and prophesied of His salvation for all people, Gentile and Jew. Anna thanked God and spoke of Jesus as Jerusalem's redemption.

However, Matthew shows another side of Jesus' birth story, a darker side. Like the dragon of Revelation 12, Christ's enemies were poised to destroy Him from the earliest days of His incarnation. After the quiet, "silent night" of Luke 2 came another scene—and it was violent (v. 16).

Barclay (1:35) sees in the three reactions to Jesus' birth a pattern still observable: (1) Like Herod, some hate Him and want Him dead; (2) like the Jewish leaders, some are indifferent to him; and (3) like the Magi, some want to fall before Him and worship Him with the gifts they bring.

D. The Flight to Egypt (2:13-18)

13 And when they were departed, behold, the angel of the Lord appeareth to Joseph in a dream, saying, Arise, and take the young child and his mother, and flee into Egypt, and be thou there until I bring thee word: for Herod will seek the young child to destroy him.

14 When he arose, he took the young child and his mother by night, and departed into Egypt:

15 And was there until the death of Herod: that it might be fulfilled which was spoken of the Lord by the prophet, saying, Out of Egypt have I called my son.

16 Then Herod, when he saw that he was mocked of the wise men, was exceeding wroth, and sent forth, and slew all the children that were in Bethlehem, and in all the coasts thereof, from two years old and under, according to the time which he had diligently inquired of the wise men.

17 Then was fulfilled that which was spoken by Jeremiah the prophet, saying,

18 In Rama was there a voice heard, lamentation, and weeping, and great mourning, Rachel weeping *for* her children, and would not be comforted, because they are not.

After the Magi left, following God's directions, God's angel once again spoke to Joseph in a dream. This was Joseph's second visit by an angel and the third dream mentioned in this passage. It became clear that rearing Jesus was going to be anything but easy. Herod would wait only so long before he would aggressively search for the Child. God's protection of the Child was immediate and effective, while at the same time insuring that Jesus experienced being fully human. Joseph's faith was challenged with the virgin birth and now he is directed to move the Child and His mother into another country because a paranoid, evil king will try to kill him. As a young man, Joseph was given great responsibilities but there is no hint of hesitancy or unbelief on his part. He took seriously his responsibility as protector of Jesus and Mary.

Probably the same night the Magi left, God directed Joseph to take the Child to Egypt. Matthew does not say where Joseph took the family exactly, only that they went to Egypt. The distance from Bethlehem to the nearest Egyptian border was approximately eighty miles (one hundred and thirty kilometers) and from Bethlehem to the Egyptian city of Memphis was approximately two hundred and fifty miles (four hundred kilometers). Scholars estimate that the average daily travel distance for walkers was twenty-four miles (thirty-nine kilometers) per day (ISBE I:879). Though we have no idea where in Egypt Joseph settled with his family or how quickly he could travel with a mother and toddler, it seems probable that he would have put as much distance between his family and Herod as necessary to insure their safety. They possibly traveled for several days.

The angel told Joseph to stay in Egypt until he, the angel, told him to leave. This told Joseph several things: the Child was in real danger; God was protecting the Child; Joseph needed to take his family to Egypt; he needed to go immediately; his stay in Egypt would be temporary; he, Mary, and the Child would be safe in Egypt; he would hear from God again; and he would be told when to leave Egypt and return to Israel.

As with the first angelic visit and instructions (Mt. 1:24), Joseph immediately obeyed. Joseph took "the young child and his mother" (note the primacy of the Child) to Egypt while it was still dark (v. 14), before anyone could identify them or the direction of their travel. The impression is that they conferred with no one. The word "flee" (v. 13) translates the same word used of the disciples when they "fled" from the soldiers who arrested Jesus in the Garden of Gethsemane (Mt. 26:56). Joseph, Mary, and Jesus were fleeing for their lives. The Child had to be protected. As directed, Joseph kept his family in Egypt until an angel told him of Herod's death (v. 19).

Quoting Hosea 11:1, Matthew continued his focus on the Child. He made the point that Jesus' return from Egypt paralleled the experience of the nation Israel (Blomberg 7), also called God's son. Hosea did not prophesy that Jesus would go to Egypt and then go back to the land of Judah. Rather he reminded Israel of God's great love and care for the nation in that He brought it out of Egypt's slavery (see also Num. 23:22; 24:8). He did not leave Israel there. Like God's son Israel, Matthew said that Jesus, God's Incarnate Son, was called out of Egypt as well. A new deliverance was being enacted through Jesus (Keener, *Matthew* 108). This began Matthew's comparisons between Jesus and the nation of Israel. Such a comparison is not unique to Matthew. Isaiah also compared the nation of Israel with Jesus, God's ideal Servant in Isaiah 49.

In vv. 15, 17, and 23 Matthew used the word "fulfilled" not to suggest that an event happened because it was foretold, as he did in 1:22 and 2:6. Instead, he used "fulfilled" in 2:15 to mean that a past event or Scripture passage has a connection with the event being discussed. The connection between the O.T. passage might be typological or in some sense a foreshadowing of N.T. events, but more specifically each O.T. passage mentioned points to the goal of all O.T. promises, Jesus. (Hagner 33A:liii-lvii, 36).

Matthew's use of the word "fulfilled" might also suggest that the O.T. passage under consideration can now be understood to have a fuller sense of meaning than it originally had (the hermeneutical principle called *sensus plenior*) in light of a N.T. event and knowledge. Thus Hosea did not prophecy that Jesus would follow the path of ancient Israel but there is a parallel in the two experiences indicating that there is something more than mere coincidence happening. (See Carson's caution against unrestrained use of the *sensus plenior* principle in *Matthew* 92-93.)

Herod waited for the Magi to report back, probably no more than a few days since Bethlehem was located just five miles (eight kilometers) south of Jerusalem. When they did not return, and after investigation he understood they were gone, he realized his scheme had not worked. He was furious. He had been tricked (v. 16), so he thought, by the Magi. The reader knows it was God who outwitted the king.

The Magi's evasive action perhaps suggested to Herod that there was something to hide. Acting on information he had gained from the Magi concerning the timing of the star's appearance, Herod had his soldiers kill all baby boys two years old and younger in the town of Bethlehem and in the area surrounding Bethlehem. Estimates range from twelve to twenty killed (Carson, *Matthew* 94; Keener, *Matthew* 111; Hagner 33A:37). However, God had kept Herod from accomplishing his purpose. The Christ Child was safely out of Herod's reach by this time. Even as Moses escaped from Pharaoh's efforts to kill all Hebrew baby boys (Ex. 1:15-16, 22; 2:1-10), so Jesus escaped from Herod. Matthew likely saw the parallel and intended that his readers see it.

Matthew reminded his readers that such calamity had befallen the region of Bethlehem before, the burial spot of Jacob's wife Rachel (Gen. 35:19). Ten miles (sixteen kilometers) to the north of Bethlehem and five miles (eight kilometers) north of Jerusalem was Ramah, the place where Jeremiah prophesied Rachel's weeping voice would be heard. Ramah was located inside the tribal allotment of Benjamin and thought by some to be Rachel's actual burial site (Blomberg 9; Gen. 35:19-20; 1 Sam. 10:2). From Ramah, Rachel's descendants would go into captivity (Jer. 31:15).

Rachel was Joseph and Benjamin's mother. In 722 B.C., Joseph's descendants, Manasseh and Ephraim, went into Assyrian captivity. Benjamin's descendants went into Babylonian captivity in 586 B.C. when Judah, the Southern Kingdom, was carried away. According to Jeremiah 40:1, captives after the final siege on Jerusalem were gathered at Ramah before they were taken to Babylon. The prophet announced that, figuratively speaking, this mother who had been barren so long would be weeping because she would once again be without children (Feinberg 570).

Matthew saw in Jeremiah's prophecy and initial fulfillment a parallel with what happened at the slaughter of the innocents. Surely Rachel must be weeping again over the loss of her children at the hand of King Herod. The "lamentation" intensifies the grief statement and agrees with the Greek translation (LXX) of the Hebrew O.T.

Matthew might also have recalled the context of this Jeremiah quote (Keener, *Matthew* 112). Following his warning of impending sorrow, Jeremiah conveyed God's message of hope (Jer. 31:16-17): the exiled will return. Carson (*Matthew* 95) agrees that there is a message of hope in Matthew's quote but understands that hope to be in the arrival of the new Son of David. Rachel's tears begun in Jeremiah's day are now fulfilled, i.e. "climaxed and ended by the tears of the mothers of Bethlehem." The arrival of the new Son marked the end of the exile and His soon introduction of the new covenant (Jer. 31:31).

Summary (2:13-18)

This portion of Jesus' infancy stories tells about His flight to Egypt and King Herod's attempt to kill Him. In his own paranoid way, Herod believed the Magi. He believed the King of the Jews had been born in Bethlehem, especially after the Magi slipped away without reporting back as he had instructed them. Jesus' time in Egypt and the slaughter of the infants in and around Bethlehem provided two more opportunities for Matthew to link Jesus' life with the O.T. writings and the historical past of the nation of Israel.

Application: Teaching and Preaching the Passage

This passage builds on theological truths. One might ask, What does this passage teach us about God? This passage teaches several important truths about God. (1) God's omniscience is demonstrated in His knowledge of the heart and plans of Herod. (2) God's sovereignty is seen in His orchestrating of lives so that His Son would be protected and provided for in these early, defenseless days. (3) God's immanence and self-revelation are seen in the dreams. (4) God's acceptance of Gentile worshipers is seen in His provision of the star and access to special revelation in Jewish Scriptures.

Herod's slaughter of the babies (1) illustrates that Jesus came to an unfriendly world. Enemies wanted Him dead, out of the way. The slaughter also (2) demonstrates the depths of human depravity. Herod is a picture of humanity's terrible sin nature. The slaughter of the innocents shows just how greatly this world needs a Savior.

One might develop a sermon or lesson on the opposition of Satan to Jesus at His birth. Revelation 12 alludes to this. Jesus' birth was not a harbinger of immediate, universal peace. In fact, His birth escalated the spiritual warfare between Satan and God. John's description of Satan's intention to destroy the Savior and God's constant and perfect protection depict in part Matthew's account of Herod's plan to kill this rival to his throne. King Herod was motivated by Satan. His murderous actions clearly show the depth of evil that was present in the world into which Jesus was born.

Matthew did not address the question of theodicy, i.e., why God would allow such evil as killing those babies to take place. Answers to this question will come from other Scriptures and one's theology, but at some point, teachers and preachers should include this question in their practical application of this passage.

E. The Return to Nazareth in Galilee (2:19-23)

19 But when Herod was dead, behold, an angel of the Lord appeareth in a dream to Joseph in Egypt,
20 Saying, Arise, and take the young child and his mother, and go into the land of Israel: for they are dead which sought the young child's life.
21 And he arose, and took the young child and his mother, and came into the land of Israel.
22 But when he heard that Archelaus did reign in Judaea in the room of his father Herod, he was afraid to go thither: notwithstanding, being warned of God in a dream, he turned aside into the parts of Galilee:
23 And he came and dwelt in a city called Nazareth: that it might be fulfilled which was spoken by the prophets, He shall be called a Nazarene.

As promised (v. 13), the angel appeared to Joseph again, also in a dream, the fourth so far in this narrative. The angel told Joseph to move his family back to Israel, without specific instructions as to where exactly. The angel also told him that those who had wanted Jesus dead were themselves now dead. The angel's use of the plural "those" may refer to Herod and the soldiers who carried out his order in Bethlehem. Herod's final days and death were torturous. For a description of his illness, see Maier (255) and Josephus (*Antiquities* XVII:6.5).

As before, Joseph obeyed without hesitation but upon arriving in Israel learned that Herod's son Archelaus reigned in his father's place. Archelaus was ethnarch (not king) from 4 B.C. to A.D. 6 (ISBE II:694). His rule was brutal and oppressive. For these reasons, Joseph was afraid to settle in his jurisdiction. Again the Lord warned Joseph in a dream, the fifth and final dream in this narrative. The warning apparently concerned Archelaus, so Joseph returned to his home town of Nazareth in southern Galilee (v. 23) where Jesus would spend His years from childhood into adulthood in relative obscurity.

Matthew's wording suggests that Joseph originally intended to take his family back to Judea, perhaps to

Bethlehem. Joseph may have been thinking of the angel's statement to Mary that Jesus would receive the throne of David (Lk. 1:33) and the Magi's report that told how, in light of Micah 5:2, they found the baby. Joseph and Mary knew that Bethlehem was an important town in Jesus' life. However, for the continued safety of the Child, the Lord directed them to their home town of Nazareth. Joseph and Mary had left Nazareth while Mary was pregnant with Jesus. Now, after Bethlehem and Egypt, they returned with a little boy walking beside them.

No Scripture writer mentions that Jesus ever visited Bethlehem again.

Matthew, like Mark and John, passed over the years of Jesus' life from His arrival in Nazareth to His adult baptism without any comment. Luke alone records the episode of Jesus' temple visit at age twelve (Lk. 2:41-51) and he summarized Jesus' childhood years in two short verses (Lk. 2:40, 52).

Nazareth was a small town located fifteen miles (twenty-four kilometers) west of the Sea of Galilee and twenty miles (thirty-two kilometers) east of the Mediterranean Sea. Recent studies suggest that the population was around five hundred (Nolland 128; Keener, *Matthew* 113). No prophet had ever come from Nazareth (Jn. 7:52).

Matthew's final statement, "that it might be fulfilled which was spoken by the prophet, 'He shall be called a Nazarene'" has occasioned considerable discussion. Nowhere in the O.T., or any other extant writing that claims to be Scripture for that matter (Blomberg 11), is there a verbatim prophecy that uses these words. Three possible explanations are generally offered according to Blomberg.

Matthew may be making a play on words, emphasizing the similarity between Nazarene and the Hebrew word for "branch" (*nēṣer*), an O.T. referent to the Messiah (Is. 4:2; 11:1; Wilkins 116-117; Hagner 33A:41-42; Keener, *Matthew* 114). This seems to be the one most favored by commentators.

Second, some writers suggest that Matthew is using "Nazarene" as a derogatory term referring to the insignificance of Nazareth (Bruner 1:78). Wilkins (116-117) and Carson (*Matthew* 97) say this follows a common O.T. prophetic and Matthean theme of the Messiah being despised. Hendricksen (190) agrees that Nazareth does speak of Jesus' lowly origin but argues that it "does not *necessarily* imply disdain" because Jesus even referred to Himself as "Jesus of Nazareth" (Acts 22:8). Others also challenge the notion of disdain for the city (ISBE III:500).

Third, some suggest Matthew is alluding to Judges 13:7 where the angel told Samson's mother that her child would be a Nazirite. Evans (*Matthew* 62) says Matthew is blending Isaiah 11:1 and Judges 13:7 because the N Z R consonants are in both Hebrew words.

Walvoord (25) offers a fourth possibility. He agrees that Matthew most probably is making an indirect reference to Isaiah 11:1 but then says "there is always the possibility that Matthew referred to an oral prophecy not recorded in Scripture."

Either of the first two seems possible. The last two seem less probable. Matthew knew Jesus was not a Nazirite (no haircuts, do not touch dead bodies, do not drink fruit of the vine, etc.; Num. 6:1-21) and never claimed to be. The best one can say is that Matthew was alluding to an O.T. Messianic understanding, but one cannot be too dogmatic about what or where that was.

Concerning Jesus' home in Nazareth (v. 23), according to Mark (1:9), Jesus was still living in Nazareth when He went to be baptized by John. Jesus lived in Nazareth until after John the Baptist's arrest, after which He moved to Capernaum (Mt. 4:13). Jesus returned to Nazareth (Lk. 4:16; Mt. 13:54) but they rejected Him. Nevertheless, even though Jesus moved to Capernaum and that city became the center of His ministry, He was always identified with His hometown of Nazareth. He was known as "Jesus of Nazareth" (Mt. 26:71; Mk. 1:24; 10:47; 14:67; 16:6; etc.) and as "Jesus the prophet of Nazareth" (Mt. 21:11). By Paul's day, Jesus' followers came to be known as the "sect of the Nazarenes" (Acts 24:5).

This is Matthew's final mention of Joseph. Joseph had been privileged to witness the birth and infancy miracles: the virgin birth, the angelic announcements in dreams (four times: Mt. 1:20; 2:13, 19, 22), the shepherd's announcements (Lk. 2:16), the Magi's visit, and perhaps the star (Mt. 2:9). Joseph and Mary fulfilled the requirements of the Law for a newborn son (Lk. 2:21-24) and then settled down in Bethlehem until the angel instructed Joseph to take his family to Egypt. Later he moved his family back to Nazareth and from there he took his family annually to Jerusalem to celebrate the Passover (Lk. 2:41). He was known as Jesus' father (Jn. 1:45; 6:42).

Sometime between Jesus' twelfth birthday and His crucifixion, Joseph must have died because at His crucifixion Jesus entrusted His mother's care to John (Jn. 19:26-27). From the silence of Scripture, it seems probable that Joseph passed away before Jesus began His public ministry. However, see John 6:42.

Summary (2:19-23)

Following a brief stay in Egypt, God directed Joseph to take his family back to Israel. The new ruler was evil like his father, so God directed Joseph to settle in Galilee. Joseph chose Nazareth, his and Mary's hometown. The relocation to Nazareth gave Matthew another opportunity to suggest a connection between the life of Jesus and O.T. Scripture.

Application: Teaching and Preaching the Passage

World leaders come and go. Herod died. His reign of terror ended. God was still on heaven's throne and the Baby was still alive. God's purpose stands. King Herod should have kissed the baby (Ps. 2, esp. v. 12). A study could be done on the parallels between Ps. 2 and Mt. 2.

When this section is considered along with the earlier verses in chapter two, a lesson might be developed that shows that the baby Jesus was (1) worth searching for, (2) worthy of worship, and (3) worth protecting. Or, one might teach that God rules the heavens (appearances of the star) and the earth. On earth He rules over (1) those who willingly bow (Magi) and (2) those who refuse to bow (Herod). He rules over (3) time and all events that take place in time. As an example of this last in this chapter, we see that He can foretell the exact city of a prophesied birth (Mic. 5:2).

This passage might also serve to encourage young parents. Raising any child is a challenge. Raising Jesus was no easier. He was hated, hunted, and hidden. However, God entrusted Him to godly parents, provided for Him, and protected Him.

Finally, this chapter is a call for decision. Everyone sides with Herod, the apathetic Jewish leaders, or God's anointed Ruler. Everyone wields the sword of Herod, stands in the ranks of the indifferent, or bows with the Magi. There is no neutral position. Everyone makes a choice.

II. THE PREPARATION NARRATIVE: THE INTRODUCTION OF THE ROYAL MESSIAH AND HIS KINGDOM (3:1—4:11)

The silent years were over. John, the prophesied messenger of the Lord (Mal. 3:1), had arrived. He was the first prophet since Malachi (ca. 430 B.C.). His public appearance apparently gained him instant popularity.

After living in virtual obscurity with His family in Nazareth for twenty-seven—perhaps twenty-eight—years, Jesus emerged from silence to begin public ministry also. He began by going to John for baptism. The Holy Spirit anointed Him at His baptism and then directed Him into the wilderness where He was tested and tempted. Following the temptation Jesus began His own ministry.

A. The Ministry of John the Baptist (3:1-12)

1 In those days came John the Baptist, preaching in the wilderness of Judaea,
2 And saying, Repent ye: for the kingdom of heaven is at hand.
3 For this is he that was spoken of by the prophet Esaias, saying, The voice of one crying in the wilderness, Prepare ye the way of the Lord, make his paths straight.
4 And the same John had his raiment of camel's hair, and a leathern girdle about his loins; and his meat was locusts and wild honey.
5 Then went out to him Jerusalem, and all Judaea, and all the region round about Jordan,
6 And were baptized of him in Jordan, confessing their sins.
7 But when he saw many of the Pharisees and Sadducees come to his baptism, he said unto them, O generation of vipers, who hath warned you to flee from the wrath to come?
8 Bring forth therefore fruits meet for repentance:
9 And think not to say within yourselves, We have Abraham to *our* father: for I say unto you, that God is able of these stones to raise up children unto Abraham.
10 And now also the axe is laid unto the root of the trees: therefore every tree which bringeth not forth good fruit is hewn down, and cast into the fire.
11 I indeed baptize you with water unto repentance. but he that cometh after me is mightier than I, whose shoes I am not worthy to

bear: he shall baptize you with the Holy Ghost, and *with* fire:
12 Whose fan *is* in his hand, and he will throughly purge his floor, and gather his wheat into the garner; but he will burn up the chaff with unquenchable fire.

Matthew, Mark, and Luke speak of John's ministry. Luke is the only writer who gave historical reference points that help locate the time period (Lk. 3:1-2; Evans, *Matthew* 67-68; see discussion on Mt. 2:1). Matthew only says, "In those days," a phrase that supports the account's historicity (Carson, *Matthew* 99) and loosely connects John's ministry with the historical time period Jesus lived in Nazareth (2:23; see comments on 3:13).

John was miraculously conceived. He was the Levite son of the priest Zachariah and his wife Elizabeth (Lk. 1:5-13, 24-25, 57-60). Since Elizabeth was related to Jesus' mother Mary (Lk. 1:36), John and Jesus were relatives. This is interesting in light of John's Levite heritage and Jesus' lineage from the tribe of Judah. Luke's word translated "cousin" (Greek *suggenis*) means a kinswoman. The Greek word can denote a cousin, but it is broader and more general.

John was six months older than Jesus and according to Luke 3:1-6 probably began his ministry just a few months before Jesus began His. He grew up in an unnamed city in the hills of Judea (Lk. 1:39, 65) and eventually moved to an unnamed location in the Judean desert where he lived until he began public ministry (Lk. 1:80). He began his desert ministry after being called by God. Luke states, "the word of God came to John" (3:2). This is reminiscent of the call of prophets in the O.T. ("the word of the LORD came to"; Hos. 1:1; Joel 1:1; Jon. 1:1, etc.). John was possibly a Nazirite from birth (Lk. 1:15).

Baptism so characterized John's ministry that Matthew identified John as "the Baptist." Mark at times (6:14, 24) called him "John the baptizer." John's baptism publically testified that the candidate was prepared to enter the "at hand" kingdom, had repented of his or her life of sin, and turned to righteousness. This turning from sin and believing the message satisfied the criteria for entering the kingdom (Mt. 21:31-32).

John's ministry marked a stage in God's dealing with mankind. The law and the prophets were until John (Mt. 11:13; Lk. 16:16). An old era ended with John's ministry. His message was forward-looking and required that people believe in the Messiah once He arrived (Acts 18:24-26; 19:1-7). John preached (1) repentance (v. 2), (2) the soon arrival of the long anticipated kingdom of heaven, (3) baptism as the public sign of confession of personal sin and a testimony of readiness for the kingdom, and (4) the soon arrival of one greater than he (Mt. 3:11). After John baptized Jesus and recognized Him as God's Son, (5) he preached faith in Jesus as the one who was to come (Acts 19:4).

John's baptism differed from N.T. Christian baptism in meaning, not in mode. Immersion was the mode for both. For both, baptism followed repentance and a decision of faith. However, John's baptism was forward-looking. Christian baptism is backward-looking. John's baptism looked forward in faith to the coming Messiah and His kingdom. Christian baptism looks back to the death, burial, and resurrection of Jesus (Rom. 6:4-5) and the new believer's identification and union with Christ (Forlines 192).

John came preaching (v. 1). The word (Greek *kērussō*) means to herald or announce as a herald, to publicly proclaim something (Louw and Nida I:412; Mk. 5:20; Lk. 9:60). Rather than preach in Jerusalem, the religious center of Judaism, John preached in the Judean deserts. This area encompassed the portion of land on both sides of the Jordan River north of the Dead Sea and the desert west of the Dead Sea. Judea was also the birthplace of Jesus' ministry. After John's arrest (Mk. 1:14), Jesus went back to Galilee for the greater portion of His remaining ministry. See comments on 11:7 for other locations where John ministered.

John's message was straightforward and suggestive of O.T. prophets (v. 2). By calling on his fellow countrymen to repent, John claimed that sin was present. The Greek word for repent (*metanoeō*) means to change one's mind. The word can mean to change from good to bad or from bad to good. For John and in the Christian gospel repentance means to change one's mind from bad to good, i.e., to be sorry for actions offensive to God and to turn away from them to God. Such repentance included remorse (Carson, *Matthew* 99). True N.T. repentance is a change of mind that always leads to a changed life (v. 8). For John's Jewish audience with their O.T. background, repentance meant the return of those who had broken faith to the Covenant God of Israel (Hill 89-90).

John's call for repentance was because ("for") the kingdom of heaven (same as the kingdom of God; Hagner 33A:47-48; Carson, *Matthew* 100; *contra* Walvoord 30) was near. John proclaimed the kingdom's nearness in time and opportunity (people could enter it) and that heaven, i.e., God, was the source of this kingdom ("of heaven"; Gundry 43). Daniel 2:44 is the backdrop for this announcement. Repentance and faith (Mt. 21:32) in John's message prepared hearers to enter that kingdom once it arrived, which it would do when Jesus appeared. Once Jesus arrived, faith in His gospel was required as well (Mk. 1:15). Participation in the kingdom resulted from spiritual preparation, not from alignment with a Messianic figure who came to set up a political rule.

In Scripture, both Old and New Testaments, the concept of the "kingdom of heaven" has more than one referent. God's kingdom can refer to God's rule over everything in the universe (Dan. 4:34-37). The kingdom that John (and Jesus, subsequently) proclaimed, however, was the earthly portion of this universal kingdom promised in Daniel 2:44. Jesus was its initiator and king (Dan. 7:13-14; Mt. 26:64). The kingdom was His even as it was the Father's. Once Jesus began preaching, as people submitted to His lordship and rule they became citizens of His kingdom (Picirilli, *Mark* 40). The full manifestation of the kingdom was not seen or realized in Jesus' earthly ministry though Jesus stated unequivocally that with His ministry the kingdom had come (Mt. 12:28). The fullest manifestation of the kingdom is still to come (Wilkins 132; 2 Tim. 4:18). Matthew will say more about this kingdom.

The kingdom for Matthew and each of the Gospel writers was both immediate and future. Theologians call this the "already-not yet" aspect of the kingdom (Hays, Duvall, and Pate 22). The kingdom of heaven that John the Baptist

The Kingdom of Heaven: Already — Not Yet

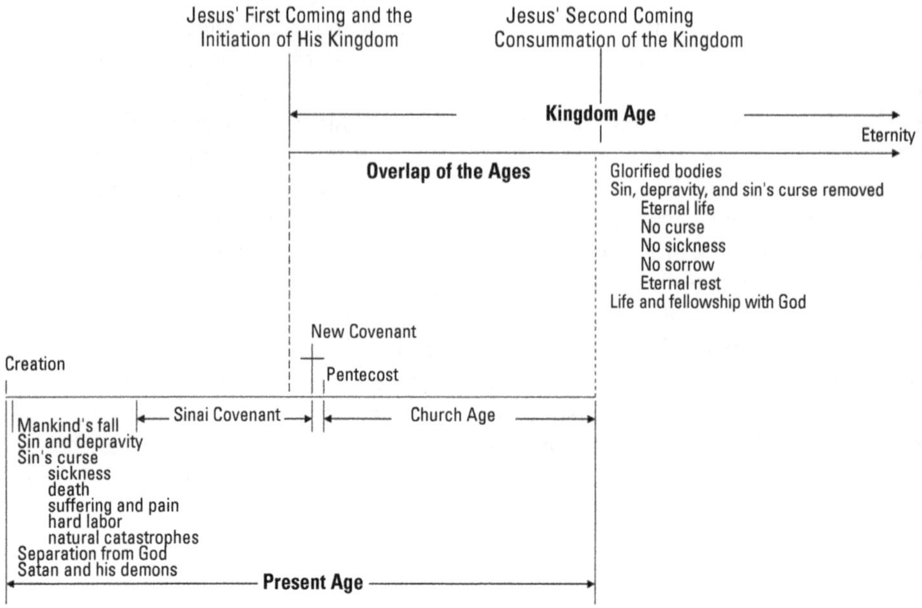

announced was the initial stage of God's rule among men and at the front end of the age to come. The Son of David introduced in chapter one was about to begin building His kingdom. This eternal kingdom and the age of sin will exist alongside each other until the Lord returns (Mt. 13:36-43). At the end of the age when Jesus returns, this age of sin will cease and the full kingdom of heaven will be revealed (Mt. 25:31-34).

Matthew turned to the O.T. for support (v. 3). According to John's own testimony (Jn. 1:23), which Jesus later corroborated (Mt. 11:10), John's ministry fulfilled Isaiah 40:3. Isaiah 40 first spoke of returning exiles to Israel (Blomberg 13; Grogan 242). The returns described in Ezra 1 would surely be included here. In this passage of hope Isaiah prophesied that one would announce the appearance of the Lord, tenderly bringing His flock back to Judah (Is. 40:1-11). All four Gospel writers declared that John was that voice. John's message and baptism were just as much founded on God's call and purpose as that of Jesus (Mt. 21:25-27; Mk. 11:27-33; Lk. 20:1-8). John, as fulfillment of prophecy, shows that Isaiah's words were about more than a return of exiles from Assyria or Babylon (Blomberg 13). These were Messianic words. If John was the forerunner, Jesus was the coming Lord. See comments on 11:10. This is especially clear with Matthew's use of "his" (v. 3) in place of "God" (Is. 40:3). Jesus is deity. In other words, if John prepared a highway for Jesus, then Jesus is the God of Isaiah 40:3.

According to the prophet, the forerunner's ministry would take place in the desert, not in cities. It seems probable, because of parallelism (Young 3:27), that in the Hebrew text of Isaiah, "in the desert" goes with "prepare the way" rather than with "a voice calls" (NIV; ESV, NASB; Hill 91). John's preparation of the highway was in the desert as the O.T. prophet foretold, not in the temple with ceremony and sacrifices. From the N.T. writers' perspectives, John was crying in the wilderness and so their statements that John was the "voice crying in the wilderness" are not in error but rather are their application of the Isaiah text to their own time (Young 3:27).

John proclaimed the coming of the Lord (v. 3). His was a literal message with a literal fulfillment. He was the voice crying in the wilderness. However, there was also symbolism. The Judean wilderness where John preached was a metaphor for the dry and barren landscape of the Judeans' hearts. John's contemporaries were in spiritual deserts. Because of their arid hearts, John called upon the people to prepare the "way of the Lord," i.e., the road by which the Lord would come to establish His rule. Righteous living was Isaiah's "way of the Lord" (Gundry 46). Evil hearts were the wilderness through which the way was to be prepared (Hendriksen 199). They were to put their lives in order by repenting and forsaking sin and by beginning to practice righteousness (vv. 2-3). Using the analogy of making a highway smooth, John called on his hearers to remove all hindrances to the Lord's coming and prepare to receive Him upon His arrival.

John's lifestyle was simple and symbolic. His wardrobe was rustic (v. 4; 11:8) and reminiscent of O.T. prophets (Zech. 13:4; ISBE: I:584), particularly Elijah (2 Kg. 1:8; Nolland 139), the one whose work he mirrored (Mal. 3:1; 4:5). His garment was made of camel's hair and his belt (girdle) was a strip of animal hide. His diet was plain also (v. 4), consisting of locusts and wild honey. Locusts (Greek *akris*, grasshoppers—not carob pods; BAGD 33) were edible and clean according to Jewish dietary laws (Lev. 11:22). Like Elijah his foreshadow, John lived "outside society" (Keener, *Background* 51-52) and by his dress and diet called on the Jews and all who would follow Jesus to stop living for this world and live for the kingdom (Keener, *Matthew* 119). But for the call of God, John probably would not have had to live like this. Being a Levite and part of the rotation of temple workers like his father, he would have been supported by the temple ministry (1 Cor. 9:13). Instead he lived a plain life in a wilderness ministry.

At first, John baptized in the Jordan, a river of great symbolism for the Jewish people (Evans, *Matthew* 66). Using the Jordan River as a setting for his ministry while quoting Isaiah 40:3 suggested that God was again bringing deliverance to His people (Keener, *Matthew* 118). Many people from cities and the surrounding country were going out (Greek descriptive imperfect; Hagner 33A:49) to hear John (v. 5; Mk. 1:5) and were being baptized. "The whole region of Jordan" includes both sides of the river from the Dead Sea up to the Sea of Galilee. The Apostle John recorded that the Baptist ministered as far north as Aenon (Jn. 3:23). Apparently all of Jesus' apostles were impacted by the ministry of John (Acts 1:22). Those who had been his disciples would have been baptized by him (Jn. 1:35-40) and possibly some of the other apostles as well.

John's ministry was fruitful (v. 6), which shows that the people saw him as a prophet and his message as a warning from God (Mt. 21:26; Wilkins 134).

People agreed that they had sinned and needed to change. They confessed the same and permitted John to baptize them. Their baptism and confession testified of repentance of personal sin and faith in John's message. As with Christian baptism, repentance and conversion preceded baptism. Although baptism was required, it did not bring about conversion (*contra* Beasley-Murray 34-35). Baptism symbolized conversion and testified that the repentant, converted, and baptized person was ready for the coming kingdom and publically identified as part of the "gathering Messianic community" (TDNT I:537).

The word baptism is almost a letter-for-letter transliteration of the Greek word from which it comes (*baptizō*). Most Bible translations transliterate the word rather than translate it. The Greek word means to dip or immerse (TDNT I:530) both here and in verse 11 where the wicked are baptized with fire. A proper translation of the Greek in these baptism passages would be "immerse." Since at least the late first century (*Didache* 7) other modes have been used in some church traditions as substitute forms of baptism. However, neither John, Jesus (Jn. 4:1-2), nor the early church in Acts spoke of baptizing anyone out of water. John picked baptismal sites because they had lots of water (Jn. 3:23), something unnecessary for modes other than immersion.

John's popularity eventually attracted the attention of the Jewish religious leaders (v. 7). Representatives from two religious sects, the Pharisees and the Sadducees, came to John's baptism. They might have come simply to observe (Gundry 46; Hagner 33A:49) or they might have come for baptism themselves (Evans, *Matthew* 70; Hendriksen 203). The latter makes sense in light of John's question in verse 7 (Nolland 142). Regardless, John was not convinced of their sincerity and he directed some very strong words at them (and to some extent to the multitudes in general, Lk. 3:7-9). These two groups later became enemies of both John and Jesus.

The Pharisees were devout, law-abiding Jews (Picirilli, *Paul* 22-24; ISBE III:823-829). They made up the largest religious sect in Judaism at that time. They meticulously sought to observe the letter of the law believing that their strict obedience would give them a righteous standing before God (Phil. 3:6). They also had oral traditions that they considered just as binding as Scripture, something that earned them a stinging rebuke from Jesus (Mt. 15:1-9). They believed in angels, a resurrection, and an afterlife (Acts 23:6, 8). As a group, they became antagonistic toward Jesus to the point of wanting to see Him dead (Jn. 18:3). Some priests were Pharisees.

The Sadducees did not believe in an afterlife, a resurrection from the dead (Mt. 22:23; Lk. 20:27), or angels and spirits (Acts 23:8; Picirilli, *Paul* 24-26). It is probable that they accepted only the first five books of the O.T. as Scripture (ISBE IV:279). They did not accept as binding the oral traditions of the Pharisees. The ruling ("chief") priests of that day possibly mainly consisted of Sadducees (2:4; Acts 5:17; Evans, *Matthew* 423).

"Offspring of vipers" (brood) is harsh name-calling (v. 7) and gives Matthew's readers a view into the messages John preached. John believed these men to be deadly. Their message poisoned people. Jesus later directed words very similar to the Pharisees and scribes (Mt. 12:34; 23:33). John had little regard for such religious leaders. They were no more righteous than anyone else who had not repented. He directed them to demonstrate repentance (v. 8), which meant to stop sinning (profession and practice must agree; Keener, *Matthew* 123) and not try to hide behind their physical descent from Abraham. Jews were not children of the kingdom just because they were Jews (v. 9). God wanted more than flesh and blood descendants of Abraham (Jn. 8:37-47; Rom. 2:17-29). Everyone, even the most religious who thought they needed no repentance, had to make a personal decision to repent and be baptized (Wilkins 136) if they were to be part of the coming kingdom. Using the images of fruit trees and wheat, John warned that judgment was imminent (KJV now; NIV already), thorough (axe laid at the root), and final (v. 10). This provided the sense of urgency to his message (Nolland 144). God would judge all the unfruitful, including all hypocrites (fruit trees that produce no fruit). The hypocrisy of these men meant that they too were not ready for the kingdom and they too were targets of God's coming judgment. These Jewish leaders just could not accept this. They did not believe John (21:25).

While John immersed people in water as a sign that they were confessing personal repentance, one who was his superior would follow (v. 11). John described Him as "mightier" and as vastly more important—John was not even worthy to be His servant (carry His sandals). As the messenger, John's might was limited. In contrast, the coming One would effect supernatural change. He would immerse in the Holy Spirit (a reference to the Spirit-birth and baptism begun at Pentecost according to Jesus; Acts 1:5; 11:16; Jn. 3:5; Rom. 8:9) those who join the kingdom and in fire (the final judgment; v. 12) those who do not. In fact, He was ready to begin: His "fan"—a winnowing fork—was in His hand. As wheat is separated from chaff (v. 12), so the coming one (assisted by angels; Mt. 13:41-43, 49-50; 24:31; Hill 95) will separate His people from those who are not His people. John described the Messiah as gathering a people, an ongoing process and the point of the winnowing fan (Beasley-Murray 33). Unlike the chaff, the wheat fare well. They will be placed in His garner or granary (Greek *apothēkē*, barn; 13:30).

The Messiah will thoroughly clean His threshing floor, meaning that those people not in His kingdom will be as chaff, discarded and burned with the unquenchable fires of judgment. These fires are a "fearful reality" (Carson, *Matthew* 105). Unfruitful trees will be discarded and burned as if on a burning brush pile. John spoke of the fires of eternal judgment, a topic that Jesus later addressed as well (13:40, 42, 50).

John's message, then, had two main thrusts. First, repent. Turn away from the practice of sin as preparation to enter the kingdom of heaven. Second, look for the one to come. He was close. By His coming everyone would either be saved or destroyed (Evans, *Matthew* 76). These are the only two possibilities.

B. The Baptism of Jesus in Judea (3:13-17)

13 Then cometh Jesus from Galilee to Jordan unto John, to be baptized of him.

14 But John forbade him, saying, I have need to be baptized of thee, and comest thou to me?
15 And Jesus answering said unto him, Suffer *it to be* so now: for thus it becometh us to fulfil all righteousness. Then he suffered him.
16 And Jesus, when he was baptized, went up straightway out of the water: and, lo, the heavens were opened unto him, and he saw the Spirit of God descending like a dove, and lighting upon him:
17 And lo a voice from heaven, saying, This is my beloved Son, in whom I am well pleased.

Jesus lived in Nazareth of Galilee (2:23; 3:1 "in those days," i.e., while still living in Nazareth; Gundry 49; Nolland 135) in the early days of John's ministry. Jesus traveled from Nazareth (Mk. 1:9) to where John was baptizing so John would baptize Him. At first, John refused. Though his recognition of Jesus' complete identity would grow (Jn. 1:33-34; Mt. 11:2), at this point John recognized only that Jesus was greater than he. Carson (*Matthew* 107) suggests that John hesitated because he knew of Jesus' miraculous birth and he knew of no sin Jesus should confess. Perhaps. However, John had already stated that by comparison his water baptism was not as powerful as the Spirit baptism the coming One would perform (v. 11). Clearly, John believed that the lesser should not baptize the greater (Evans, *Matthew* 79). He did not understand why Jesus needed his water baptism.

Jesus explained that He too should be baptized. His explanation is difficult to understand. Apparently Jesus' meant that He wanted to demonstrate His alignment with John's "way of righteousness" (Mt. 21:32; Hill 96), which meant avoiding sin and living holy. Hearing Jesus' explanation, John "suffered him": that is, he permitted Him; he consented and performed the baptism. Only Matthew mentions the exchange recorded in vv. 14 and 15. Jesus' baptism also marked His identification with, and endorsement of, John's message and ministry. He was publically identifying with the forerunner who was announcing the coming King and kingdom of heaven. From this point on John began specifically proclaiming that Jesus was the One whom he had been announcing would come (Jn. 1:29-31). The coming One had arrived.

Jesus' baptism accomplished several other things. (1) Jesus' baptism set an example for all of His followers (v. 15; 28:19). As Captain of their salvation, He led the way. He got into the water with them because He was one with them (Wilkins 140; Keener, *Matthew* 132). (2) Jesus' baptism marked the beginning of His Messianic ministry. (3) Jesus' baptism was the occasion of God's visible confirmation to Jesus of His anointing ("he saw"; v. 16; Mk. 1:10) and to John that Jesus was the One who would baptize with the Holy Spirit. John recognized and later testified that Jesus was the Son of God (Jn. 1:32-34). Jesus did not turn John's baptism into a means to receive the Spirit's baptism (*contra* Bruner 1:103-104, 110-111), a sacrament. These remained two distinct baptisms in the Gospels even as they do today; albeit since Pentecost Spirit baptism precedes water baptism.

After His baptism (v. 16), Jesus immediately ("straightway") got out of the water. Unlike the others who were baptized (v. 6), Jesus' did not confess any sin. Instead, He prayed (Lk. 3:21). According to Luke, while He was praying the Father opened heaven and the Holy Spirit anointed Jesus. This anointing set Him apart, empowered Him for public ministry and marked its inception (Carson, *Matthew* 110). The Father had anointed His Servant (Is. 11:2; 42:1; see Mt. 12:18), His Christ (16:16).

An audible voice from heaven (Ex. 20:1-19; Dt. 5:4) spoke above the sounds of the river. The unseen Speaker claimed paternity of this One in the water and expressed pleasure in Him (v. 17). This was the first of three times the Father did this (at the transfiguration, Mt. 17:5; during Passion Week; Jn. 12:28). This Anointed One was none other than God's Son (Ps. 2:2, 7; Keener, *Matthew* 135). The one "in whom I am well pleased" is surely the Servant in whom the Lord delights (Is. 42:1). This anointing was God's commission of Jesus to bring salvation to the nations (Is. 42:1, 4; Wilkins 143).

"This is" (compare Mk. 1:11 and Lk. 3:22 "you are") suggests that more than just Jesus heard the heavenly voice (*contra* Hagner 33A:54, who thinks this was a "subjective experience"). Matthew does not tell us who was present for this baptism or specifically who heard the voice. Nolland (157) suggests the voice was limited to the "heavenly court," but why would Matthew describe a dove visible to human eyes but a voice heard only in heaven? Both marked the uniqueness of the One in the water. Surely human eyes and ears witnessed these heavenly signs.

Mark states that the heavens were rent (Mk. 1:10) at Jesus' baptism. John was enabled to see into the spiritual heaven (Ezek. 1:1; Acts 7:56, 10:11) and he watched as the Holy Spirit in the form of a dove (Mt. 3:16; Lk. 3:22) descended and lit upon Jesus where He remained visible for a time (Jn. 1:32-33). This anointing highlighted an important aspect of Jesus' ministry (Lk. 4:18). The dove, not an axe, fire, or winnowing fork (Bruner 1:110), was the manifestation of the Holy Spirit sent from God to anoint His Son (12:18). The voice from heaven and the dove together were indisputable sensory proofs to John that he had found the One he had been sent to announce. "Like" (Greek *hōsei*) means "as if it were, as." This same word is translated "as" in 9:36 and "like as" in Acts 2:3. The Holy Spirit manifested Himself as a dove at Jesus' baptism and as flames of fire on Pentecost. Similes, figures of speech that compares two unlike things, are common (Mt. 28:3; Lk. 22:44; Heb. 1:12).

The witnesses to Jesus' identity are strong (Keener, *Matthew* 134). Scripture prophesied His coming. His forerunner, the prophet in the desert, declared His arrival. The audible voice affirmed His deity. The dove confirmed His anointing.

Matthew's account of Jesus' baptism contains the second reference to the Trinity in the N.T. as we have it today. Here the Father spoke, the Son was baptized and the Holy Spirit manifested Himself in the form of a dove. John was possibly the first human to be shown such a clear distinction of the Persons of the Triune Godhead. The first reference to the Trinity is in the birth account (Mt.1:18, 20, 22, 23).

Summary (3:1-17)

After four centuries of silence, a new prophet appeared in Judea: John the Baptist. Mirroring the O.T. prophet Elijah, John lived out Isaiah 40:3 and Malachi 3:1. He burst into this world with a call for spiritual renewal and a promise that the kingdom of God was near. He also spoke of One soon to appear who would immerse in the Holy Spirit and in fire. Those who received the messages of John and Jesus would receive the baptism of the Holy Spirit. Those who rejected their message would receive fiery judgment.

John's ministry consisted of helping people prepare for the coming Messiah. One day Jesus went to John for baptism. Though John's knowledge of Jesus was limited, he understood enough to hesitate, knowing that Jesus' baptismal ministry was more powerful than his own. Jesus explained that He needed John's baptism too. John baptized Jesus and supernatural signs followed which showed God's approval of Jesus' baptism and His Person and provided John proof that Jesus was Messiah. Jesus of Nazareth was God's Son on earth.

Application: Teaching and Preaching the Passage

One might develop a sermon or lesson on John the prophet: (1) the man, (vv. 1, 3-4, 7): his name, his prophetic wardrobe, his sacrificial lifestyle, and his boldness; (2) the method (vv. 1, 5): his preaching, his pulpit (wilderness), and his boldness; and (3) his message (vv. 2, 6-12): its divine source and its content (repentance, baptism, faith in the One to come).

John spoke of several items that still need to be taught and preached such as fulfilled prophecy, repentance, and its evidence (Acts 26:20), confession of sins, baptism, the Person of the Holy Spirit, baptism by the Holy Spirit, and judgment. Each of these could be used in topical lessons or sermons.

One might develop a sermon on the implications of Jesus' baptismal experience for the Christian under the heading of "gospel baptism" to set it apart from the watered-down practices of some faiths. Gospel baptism (1) is by immersion (v. 6); (2) is a testimony of a spiritual work done (v. 8); (3) is a fitting experience for the righteous (v. 15); (4) was practiced by our Savior (v. 16); (5) was endorsed by God the Father and the Holy Spirit (vv. 16-17); (6) is one of two baptisms followers of Christ receive (the other being Spirit baptism at conversion).

A lesson or sermon might also be prepared on the reasons Jesus' baptism was an important event. See comments on verse 15.

C. The Temptation of Jesus (4:1-11)

Immediately following His baptism, the Holy Spirit directed Jesus to a place of testing (Mk. 1:12-13; Lk. 4:1-13). This test would verify Jesus' determination to obey the Father. Theologians debate whether these were real temptations. Those who believe that Jesus could not sin cite James 1:13: "God cannot be tempted with evil." Explanations vary. Blomberg (17) believes that Jesus' human nature was "completely temptable" and His divine nature was "untemptable." Wilkins (165) agrees that Jesus' human nature was tempted but believes that in the final analysis He was not able to sin. Forlines (178-179) says that since deity cannot sin, the union of the divine nature with the human nature prevented Jesus from sinning.

As with many aspects of the incarnation, Jesus' openness to temptation is shrouded in mystery, well beyond our present level of knowledge (Hendriksen 224). Carson (*Matthew* 115) rightly cautions that no matter how one formulates his explanation of this question, he must make certain that he does not diminish either the deity or humanity of Jesus. From Satan's perspective the temptations were real and he approached Jesus as if Jesus could have yielded (*contra* Walvoord, 35, who says Satan knew before he began that Jesus could not sin). It appears the Gospel writers intended to communicate that these were real temptations to which Jesus could have yielded (Bruner 1:130).

Each of these temptations was external (Erickson 598). Jesus' human nature was not depraved; He did not have the corrupt human nature that all others have inherited from their parents. No temptation could arise from within (Jas. 1:14) nor did He have any desire to sin when Satan offered Him the opportunity. Regardless of how one understands Jesus' ability to sin, the temptations came at more than a merely human level (Barclay 1:76). The ability to turn stones into bread required supernatural power on Jesus' part. Satan was tempting the God-man.

1 Then was Jesus led up of the spirit into the wilderness to be tempted of the devil.

2 And when he had fasted forty days and forty nights, he was afterward an hungered.

3 And when the tempter came to him, he said, If thou be the Son of God, command that these stones be made bread.

4 But he answered and said, It is written, Man shall not live by bread alone, but by every word that proceedeth out of the mouth of God.

5 Then the devil taketh him up into the holy city, and setteth him on a pinnacle of the temple,

6 And saith unto him, If thou be the Son of God, cast thyself down: for it is written, He shall give his angels charge concerning thee: and in *their* hands they shall bear thee up, lest at any time thou dash thy foot against a stone.

7 Jesus said unto him, It is written again, Thou shalt not tempt the Lord thy God.

8 Again, the devil taketh him up into an exceeding high mountain, and sheweth him all the kingdoms of the world, and the glory of them;

9 And saith unto him, All these things will I give thee, if thou wilt fall down and worship me.

10 Then saith Jesus unto him, Get thee hence, Satan: for it is written, Thou shalt worship the Lord thy God, and him only shalt thou serve.

11 Then the devil leaveth him, and, behold, angels came and ministered unto him.

The Holy Spirit led (v. 1; Mk. 1:12 "drove") Jesus to an undisclosed wilderness location to be tested (Greek infinitive of purpose). The one who anointed Him at baptism immediately directed Him into a direct conflict with the evil one (Erickson 871). Matthew says the

Spirit led Him "up" (Greek *anagō*). The location was remote. He was with wild beasts (Mk. 1:13) and away from people.

The word translated "tempt" (Greek *peirazō)* can mean to tempt in the sense of trying to persuade someone to do something wrong and it can mean to test in the sense of trying someone to determine one's nature or character (Louw and Nida I:775, 332). The Holy Spirit did not side with Satan and try to lead Jesus to sin. Rather, the Holy Spirit placed Jesus in a situation where Satan would tempt Him, which temptations were tests of Jesus' determination always to be the obedient Son (Hill 101; Hagner 33A:65). Jesus' answers demonstrate that He understood the tests and what was at stake (Carson, *Matthew* 112).

Jesus' humanity is in full view in these tests. He limited His use of His divine attributes (Wilkins 163-164) in order to experience as a human the full force of the temptation. However, He was "full of the Holy Spirit" (Lk. 4:1) who enabled Him to withstand each temptation.

The tempter was Satan, the devil himself (Greek *diabolos,* accuser, slanderer; the Greek text has the definite article). He crafted temptations especially for Jesus. Matthew introduced Satan as a personal source of evil, the enemy of God. He is an intelligent spirit-being whose desire was and is to stop any advancement of the kingdom of God (Wilkins 154-155). See also 13:19, 39, and comments. From Adam to Jesus, Satan had never met any human he could not deceive at some point. He met his first human overcomer in Jesus.

According to Matthew, the test began at the end of a forty day fast (v. 2). The fast was part of the Spirit's directive to Jesus (Hagner 33A:64). Jesus fasted the same number of days as O.T. prophets Moses (Ex. 34:28) and Elijah (1 Kg. 19:8). The wilderness setting, the number forty, and the historical context of the Scriptures Jesus quoted remind one of Israel's forty year journey in the wilderness and the many tests Israel faced designed to teach her to rely on the Supernatural, not the natural (Dt. 8:2-3; Keener, *Background* 53; Hagner 33A:61-62). This was Jesus' test also. For forty days, He wandered in the wilderness (Lk. 4:1; Gundry 54). During this time He ate nothing (v. 2; Lk. 4:2). Scripture says nothing about fluid intake but since there was no miraculous intervention until after the temptation was over, Jesus had to keep drinking (unlike Moses, Ex. 34:28; Dt. 9:9, 18, 25; 10:10). After such a lengthy fast and being human, He was emaciated and hungry. He received no divine aid these forty days.

No Gospel writer records Jesus' activities during the forty days. Since this was a spiritual exercise, prayer was probably His main focus. It seems probable from Mark 1:12 and Luke 4:2 that Satan throughout the forty days tried to interrupt Jesus' communion with His Father (Marshall, 170). After forty days of fasting and prayer, Jesus was strong spiritually and weak physically. These three temptations began at the end of the forty days and with an appeal to the flesh's weakest point.

The tempter appealed to Jesus' hunger first. He was not challenging Jesus' sonship as the English might suggest (*contra* Bruner 1:123). "If you are God's Son" means "since" or "because you are God's Son" (Greek 1st class condition). Satan challenged Jesus' necessity to wait on the Father to meet

His physical needs and inferred that Jesus should take action Himself because of His sonship (Evans, *Matthew* 84). Had the Father not just declared Jesus' special relationship to Himself (Mt. 3:17)? Why should God's Son, of all people, be hungry (Wilkins 158)? The temptation was for Jesus to avoid the suffering the Father had planned for Him and use His own power in a self-serving manner, the power He had voluntarily laid aside (Blomberg 14; Carson, *Matthew* 113).

Jesus' answer supports this understanding (v. 4). He never sought to prove His relationship with the Father. Rather, by quoting Deuteronomy 8:3 He addressed Satan's temptation that He should take care of Himself instead of waiting on the Father. The Deuteronomy passage reveals God's explanation to Israel for why He allowed them to be hungry in the wilderness. He did this so they would learn to live by His spoken word, i.e. His commands, even if it meant going hungry. "Shall" is a future tense used here as an imperative.

The Israelites needed to trust God regardless of what was taking place in their lives. If it was God's will for them to be in the wilderness, He would feed them there even if the situation looked impossible (Wilkins 158). Jesus said the same principle applied to His situation. Jesus was in the wilderness and hungry because it was His Father's will (Hagner 33A:65). The Father would feed Him in His time. It was the Son's responsibility to obey by waiting on the Father. He learned obedience throughout His life ("in the days of his flesh"; Heb. 5:7-8), including during this great temptation.

Jesus did not teach that man does not need bread to live but that he does not need bread "alone." Jesus later taught that the need to eat is part of man's earthly existence (Mt. 6:11). God is aware of creature needs (Mt. 6:31-32). Jesus' use of Deuteronomy 8:3 also supports the doctrine of His humanity. In this conversation with Satan, He called Himself a "man" (Erickson 711).

Each time Jesus quoted Scripture in this temptation, He began by saying, "It is written" Grammatically, the stress is on the continuing result of a past event (Greek perfect tense). In other words, God's Word stands in writing. God's Word to Israel was God's Word to Jesus and it is God's Word to all generations. Scripture came from the "mouth of God" (v. 4). This anthropomorphic description emphasizes the source and character of Scripture. God's Word has His attributes. It is eternal, infallible, inerrant, holy, immutable, etc. Jesus' quotes give credibility to Deuteronomy as Scripture to the dismay, no doubt, of higher critics (Walvoord 36).

Satan next took Jesus to Jerusalem, the holy city (v. 5; Lk. 4:9). Luke has the order of the last two temptations reversed. Satan placed Jesus on an unspecified high pinnacle and encouraged Him to jump (v. 6). Gundry (56) suggests that the possible location of this temptation was the southwest corner of the outer court which drops off into the Kidron Valley. The author does not say whether this temptation is literal or visionary (like Ezekiel's visionary travel from Babylon to Jerusalem, Ezek. 8:3). Most commentators understand the last two temptations to be visionary (Barclay 1:74-75; Evans, *Matthew* 85; Hendriksen 231-232; Hagner 33A:63, 66) but it is difficult to understand how Jesus could jump *in His mind*. Some writers suggest that Satan thought such a jump might be a temptation to Jesus because God's rescue of Him would be a public display of His Messiahship and result in an immediate following, making the cross unnecessary (Wilkins 160). Others disagree. They say that the absence of spectators and Jesus' reply to Satan both argue against this (Hendriksen 230; Nolland 165).

The temptation was to put God, His Word, and Jesus' faith in that Word to the test. Jesus would create a need (Nolland 165) and test God's promise. If God would take care of Jesus as Jesus claimed in verse 4 based on Deuteronomy 8:3, then Jesus could test this very quickly by jumping (v. 6). Did Scripture not also promise that God would not permit His children even to stumble over a stone, a figure that suggests God's extreme and minute care (Ps. 91:11-12; Gundry 57)?

A literal jump would have been disastrous. The fall either would have killed Jesus or if angels had caught Him, Jesus would have demonstrated His lack of trust in the Father by having forced Him to intervene. Regardless of the physical outcome, He would have disobeyed the Father's will for Him and been disqualified as our sinless and compassionate high priest (Heb. 2:17-18; 4:15).

Satan used Psalm 91:11-12 incorrectly, thus also putting Jesus' understanding of Scripture to the test (Bruner 1:128). These verses contain a conditional promise. The promise is to those who trust the Lord (Ps. 91:9) and encounter unexpected harm (Blomberg 16). Jesus' jump would have been an act of distrust, an action designed to force God to intervene. Psalm 91 does not promise to stop attempted suicide.

Jesus answered Satan with another Scripture from Deuteronomy (v. 7; Dt. 6:16) showing that this temptation was not new. Israel had put God to the test (Ex. 17:2, 7) intending to force the Lord to miraculously provide them water. God's later Word through Moses forbade such testing (Dt. 6:16). God will not be manipulated and so Jesus would not yield. He would not jump in order to force God to prove Himself on Jesus' behalf.

For the final temptation Satan transported Jesus from the high temple pinnacle to a high mountain (v. 8; cf. Ezekiel's experience, Ezek. 40:2). Satan used his power to show Jesus all of this world's kingdoms and their glory (minus their sin; Carson, *Matthew* 114) at a glance (Lk. 4:5). Keener's suggestion (*Matthew* 141) that Satan showed Jesus a "good representative sampling of the nearer kingdoms" does not seem to fit the context. Satan gave Jesus a view of the nations around the globe. Satan knew that Jesus was a king and He was to receive a kingdom. Jesus' kingdom was to come by way of the cross. Satan's offer was for Jesus to possess all of this world's kingdoms without a cross. There would be no suffering if Jesus went Satan's way. Bluntly and plainly Satan stated his conditional offer. All Jesus needed to do to possess all of these kingdoms was fall down before Satan and worship him. Here is the heart of all such testing (Hagner 33A:68). Luke (4:6) adds that Satan claimed that he had received these kingdoms along with the right to give them to whomever he chose.

Was this a real temptation for Jesus? Did He struggle over the suffering He was sent to endure? Jesus' impending suffering and death were a struggle for Him (Lk. 12:50; Mt. 26:39; Hendriksen 234). Satan knows the role pain has in human existence and humanity's efforts to avoid it. Though Jesus struggled in prayer about His suffering, yet He never permitted Satan's offer to distract Him even slightly from His Father's will.

The kingdom offer might have sounded appealing but Satan lies (Jn. 8:44). He is god of this world (2 Cor. 4:4) but not God Almighty (Gen. 17:1; 35:11). He is powerful (Eph. 2:2) but not all-powerful. His power is a derived power, not an inherent power. He rules but not absolutely. He influences the nations (Dan. 10:13) but has neither ownership nor final control over them (Ps. 2:8). His offer to Jesus was limited at best. Only God can give kingdoms to "whomsoever he will" (Dan. 4:32).

Jesus' final answer was sharp: "Get thee hence" means "Be gone" or "Go away." Once again quoting Deuteronomy, Jesus refused to worship Satan because Scripture forbids worship of anyone or anything other than the Lord (v. 10; Dt. 6:13-14).

As commanded, Satan left (v. 11) for a time (Lk. 4:13). Jesus' refusal to follow Satan and His ability to resist Satan were firmly established. However, Satan continued working against God's purpose in Jesus throughout the remainder of His earthly life (Mt. 16:23; Lk. 22:3, 31).

At this point, angels came to care for Jesus. There is an O.T. precedent for this (1 Kg. 19:5-8). After forty days of fasting and testing, Jesus was physically exhausted and almost certainly skeletal. Unlike Moses who evidently showed no adverse signs after fasting forty days (he walked down the mountain even carrying the stone tablets; Ex. 24:18; 32:15), Jesus needed help. Interestingly, it was angels (see comments on v. 6) who ministered to Him, probably by feeding Him (v. 11; Mk. 1:13) and otherwise caring for Him until He regained enough strength to come down from the mountainous wilderness, which adds further proof of God's approval of His Son (Evans, *Matthew* 83-84).

Jesus' love for and determination to obey the Father were tested and He passed the tests. He loved the Father with His whole heart (Hagner 33A:66-67; Dt. 6:5). In contrast to Israel who had failed these same three temptations, Jesus passed each one (Osborne 26).

Summary (4:1-11)

Following His baptism, the Holy Spirit directed Jesus into a wilderness area to be tested by Satan. Satan tested Jesus' resolve to remain obedient to the Father. While Jesus was suffering from extreme deprivation after a forty-day fast, Satan tried to entice Him to eat rather than wait on the Father. Satan then encouraged Jesus to force God to demonstrate His care of His Son immediately. Finally, Satan tried to lure Jesus to himself by offering Jesus all of earth's kingdoms. These He could have, according to Satan, without His present and future sufferings. Jesus refused each temptation and remained obedient to His Heavenly Father.

Application: Teaching and Preaching the Passage

Teaching the whole Bible (Acts 20:27) includes sermons and lessons on temptations and testings. All of God's servants are tested. Jesus' temptation, response, and victory hold many valuable lessons for all who follow Him. One might develop lessons or sermons using these points.

First, Satan uses different avenues to bring temptation before us. Three of those are (1) natural needs (hunger), (2) desire to be in control (I can make God bless me), and (3) desire for power and glory (I can have everything now).

Second, the tempter uses different lures to test mankind's loyalty to God. He will attempt to lead God's children to think (1) "I deserve better than this. I am a child of God." (2) "I can manipulate God using His Word." (3) "I can have it all, the whole world, at no eternal cost to me."

Third, Jesus' temptation teaches valuable lessons about spiritual tests: (1) Some of our greatest temptations can come just after a great spiritual experience (Jesus' baptism). (2) God will design some of our greatest tests to come when we are alone. (3) Temptations will ultimately and always challenge God's will for us. (4) Satan lies. (5) Satan is powerful, but not more powerful than God or God in us. (6) Lean times are teaching times. (7) There is more to life than bread. (8) God is taking care of us even when it seems He is not. (9) The soul is worth more than the whole world. (10) The Father tests, Satan tempts. (11) Being full spiritually and being full physically are two different things (Liefeld 863). (12) Satan sometimes tempts at the place of worship. (13) Tests sometimes come when believers are weak physically. (14) Satan plays to win, not win by the rules. (15) Victory against temptation is possible. (16) Scripture answers Satan.

Jesus provided the following keys to successful resistance to temptation: (1) extended time with the Father (forty days fast); (2) patient, faithful obedience to the Father; (3) confident and accurate use of God's Word; (4) consistent resistance to temptation; and (5) renewed spiritual and physical strength received from God.

Finally, one thought from Bruner (1:126): if men do not live on bread alone, then there must be many hungry people in this world.

III. THE GALILEAN MINISTRY NARRATIVE: THE ROYAL MESSIAH SHINED A GREAT LIGHT IN A DARK REGION (4:12—18:35)

The Gospel writers sometimes compiled their materials thematically rather than according to strict historical chronology and each was selective about what material to include (Jn. 21:25). Because of this arrangement of materials, it is difficult to determine the exact order of events in Jesus' adult life. For a summary discussion of issues germane to the study of the length of Jesus' ministry, see P. Harrison (80-87).

Matthew did not record any events of Jesus' ministry immediately following His temptation. We do not know how much time Matthew passed over in his record (possibly as much as one year) but the Gospel writer John suggests that Jesus at first traveled between Galilee and Judea where John the Baptist was ministering (Jn. 1:19, 29, 35, 43; 2:1, 12; 2:13; 3:22-24). It was apparently during His first year of ministry that Jesus met Andrew, Simon Peter, Philip, and Nathaniel (Jn. 1:35-51), turned the water into wine (Jn. 2:1-11), attended His first Passover after His baptism (Jn. 2:13), cleansed the temple the first time (Jn. 2:14-17), did several miraculous signs in Jerusalem (Jn. 2:23), and met

Nicodemus (Jn. 3:1). John the writer makes special mention of Jesus' early Judean ministry (Jn. 3:22) that followed this first Passover and specifically states that this ministry took place in Judea before the Baptist was put in prison (Jn. 3:24). Following John the Baptist's imprisonment and the Lord's awareness that the Pharisees were attentive of His growing popularity (Jn. 3:26, 30; 4:1-3), Jesus went to Galilee where He spent the larger portion of His ministry time over the next two to three years (Hendriksen 240). Instead of ministering in the Jewish religious center of that day, Jerusalem, Jesus went to Galilee, an area populated by Jews and Gentiles. Matthew tells us why in verses 12-17.

A. From Obscurity to Popularity: The Royal Messiah Began Growing His Kingdom (4:12-25)

At first Jesus ministered in relative obscurity. Neither Matthew, Mark, nor Luke say anything about the earliest months. In these early months following His temptation, Jesus worked alone though He did attract some followers. After John's imprisonment, according to the three Gospel writers, Jesus' most effective ministry began (Hill 102). His popularity had begun (Jn. 3:26-30), but after John's imprisonment Jesus' popularity grew even more (Lk. 4:14-15). In these verses, Matthew set the stage for his description of that growth.

Verse 12 is transitional (Nolland 171), a literary hinge. It closes out the temptation account as well as begins the discussion of Jesus' ministry.

1. Jesus moved from Nazareth to Capernaum (4:12-17)

12 Now when Jesus had heard that John was cast into prison, he departed into Galilee;
13 And leaving Nazareth, he came and dwelt in Capernaum, which is upon the sea coast, in the borders of Zabulon and Nephthalim:
14 That it might be fulfilled which was spoken by Esaias the prophet, saying,
15 The land of Zabulon, and the land of Nephthalim, *by* the way of the sea, beyond Jordan, Galilee of the Gentiles;
16 The people which sat in darkness saw great light; and to them which sat in the region and shadow of death light is sprung up.
17 From that time Jesus began to preach, and to say, Repent: for the kingdom of heaven is at hand.

John's preaching cost him his freedom (Mt. 11:2; 14:4). Because he denounced the adulterous relationship of Herod Antipas and Herodias, Herod had him arrested. John's arrest (v. 12) was a turning point in Jesus' ministry and in Matthew's record. He might have left Judea because He wanted to avoid Herod and persecution (Gundry 59), or He might have been distancing Himself from political unrest caused by John's arrest (Maier 271-272). Hendriksen (241) thinks that Jesus was avoiding a premature crisis with the Judean religious leaders. Regardless what might appear to have motivated Jesus to return to Galilee, Matthew knew the real reason.

Up to this time, Nazareth had been Jesus' home. Following the early Judean ministry summarized above, Jesus moved from Nazareth to Capernaum (v. 13), a town located on the northwest shore of the Sea of Galilee. One can assume that Jesus had a home in Capernaum at this time (Mk. 2:1), or at least a place to stay (Keener, *Matthew* 202). However, though He had a place to stay, He evidently did not purchase a home (Mt. 8:20). See also "the house" in 9:28 and 17:25.

John's arrest was the earthly event that prompted Jesus to move His ministry focus to Galilee (v. 12), but God's plan revealed in Isaiah 9:1-2 was the prophetic reason behind the move. This prophecy was to two tribes of the pre-captivity Northern Kingdom, Naphtali (Nephthalim) and Zebulun. Naphtali was the first tribe to go into Assyrian captivity (2 Kg. 15:29), approximately ten years before the entire Northern Kingdom fell in 722 B.C. Though Scripture does not specifically say, Zebulun may have been carried away the same time as Naphtali (ISBE IV:1181).

Isaiah promised these two tribes that their ill fortune brought on by God's chastisement (Is. 10:5-6) would be reversed. They would be favored with special grace. It seems improbable that Isaiah was speaking of the glory of the exiles' physical return to the land, although their return must be assumed (*contra* Blomberg 18 who sees a double fulfillment in this prophecy).

Rather, he spoke primarily of those Jews who lived in spiritual darkness (symbolized by their Assyrian captivity) and secondly of their numerous Gentile neighbors who also lived in Galilee and in spiritual darkness (v. 15; "Galilee of the Gentiles"; Beitzel 18). These would see a great light (Grogan 73; Young 1:323-325). They would be favored with a special presence. It was to these two tribes and their Gentile neighbors that Isaiah wrote in this passage, "For unto us a child is born; unto us a son is given" (Is. 9:6). This Son was none other than the Prince of Peace who would govern from the throne of David (Is. 9:6-7). Jesus' ministry to Gentiles is a significant point in this prophecy, as is its fulfillment in Galilee.

Isaiah directed his prophecy to those who lived "by the way of the sea." This was a reference either to the land area west of Zebulun and Naphtali bordering the Mediterranean Sea (Hendriksen 243) or more probably the land areas of Zebulun and Naphtali located west of the Sea of Galilee (Nolland 173). Isaiah also wrote of those "beyond Jordan" (v. 15), but scholars disagree which side of Jordan he was referring to. Generally, Biblical usage seems to locate "beyond Jordan" to the area east of the Jordan River (Mt. 4:25; 19:1; Hagner 33A:73). Beitzel (23) identifies Isaiah's "beyond Jordan" with the district of Perea. Carson (*Matthew* 118), however, shows that "beyond the Jordan" can also refer to the west side of the river depending on the speaker's vantage point (Num. 32:19; Dt. 11:30; Josh. 5:1; 22:7). If the prophet was referring to the west side, by quoting this passage Matthew taught that the people living on the west side of the Sea of Galilee were the blessed subjects of this prophecy. They saw the greatest light as Jesus lived among them and focused a great portion of His ministry among them. Matthew also taught, by this prophetic reference, that Jesus ministered where the Lord's prophet had foretold He would.

Jesus, then, moved to Capernaum in fulfillment of Isaiah's prophecy. Zebulun was favored in that the Messiah lived in one of her cities, Nazareth, for the better part of His life. Naphtali was favored in that Jesus did a major portion of His ministry in Galilee, the O.T. land area of Naphtali. Keener's point is valid: the Messiah did not have to be only from Bethlehem (*Matthew* 147; Mt. 2:5-6), an O.T. teaching that the Jews had apparently missed (Jn. 7:42).

Isaiah 7:14 was a promise to Judah, the Southern Kingdom. See the discussion on 1:23. Jesus was born in Bethlehem of Judah. Isaiah 9:1-2 was a promise to the Northern Kingdom of Israel. This was where Jesus lived most of His life and where He practiced most of His ministry. Prophetically, the ultimate son promised in Isaiah 7:14 is born in Isaiah 9:6 and ministering in 9:1-2 and Matthew 4:12-17. Historically, the virgin-born Son born in Bethlehem ministered in Galilee where He, the light of the world (Jn. 8:12; Lk. 1:79), proclaimed the light of the gospel. Jesus was the Light the Jewish and Gentile residents in Galilean darkness would see (v. 16). Though future from Isaiah's perspective, yet he described the event as if it had already happened.

Sitting in darkness and "in the land of the shadow of death" (v. 16) suggests gloom, despair, and hopelessness (Hendriksen 245; Is. 8:22). The Hebrew word translated "shadow of death" is "the strongest word in Hebrew for darkness" (TWOT II:767) and means deep darkness. It speaks of the darkness before creation (Am. 5:8) and the deep darkness of a mining shaft (Job 28:3). Metaphorically, it can speak of spiritual darkness, as here, or even of physical death (Ps. 23:4; Job 3:5).

Zebulun and Naphtali had been lands of oppression since the Assyrian captivity. At the time of Jesus' ministry, Galilee was under the iron fist of Rome. According to Isaiah, the Messiah would be a light of hope. He would restore joy in places of despair and gloom. According to Matthew, Jesus was that Messiah.

John's imprisonment and Jesus' return to Nazareth and subsequent move to Capernaum marked a major turning point in Jesus' ministry (v. 17: "from that time forward"; Mk. 1:14-15; Lk. 4:14; Nolland 174). Matthew and Mark summarized Jesus' message as being exactly like that of John the Baptist at first (Mt. 3:1-2). Jesus preached repentance and He preached that the nearness of the kingdom was the reason for His call to repentance. The Kingdom had arrived, certain aspects of which could be experienced immediately. The change that Matthew wrote about at this point was that Jesus began taking the message where John had not been (Hendriksen 244). Everyone heard the same message, "Repent." "Turn your lives around, because here comes the kingdom of the heavens" (literal Greek; Bruner 1:138)! See comments on Mt. 3:2 for a discussion of "repentance."

Unlike the apostle John, Matthew never mentioned that Jesus and His disciples baptized converts. John says they baptized in Judea (Jn. 3:22-26; 4:1-3) at the beginning of His ministry and he leaves open the possibility in John 10:40-42 that they continued baptizing. However, there is no mention that Jesus and the Twelve baptized anyone during the Galilean portion of His ministry, nor did Jesus command the Twelve to baptize when He sent them on their preaching tour (Mt. 10:5-42).

Jesus' move to Capernaum put Him in the path of international travelers. One branch of the Great Trunk Road went through Capernaum. Beitzel (65, 171) calls this road that linked Egypt and Mesopotamia the "most important international artery of the Fertile Crescent." It is easy to see how word about Jesus could travel great distances quickly.

Summary (4:12-17)

When word of John the Baptist's arrest reached Jesus, Jesus' ministry took a decisive turn. Leaving Judea, He returned to Galilee. He went back to Nazareth, only to move to Capernaum to make that city His home base.

Jesus' ministry in Galilee fulfilled a specific prophecy in Isaiah 9:1-2, which foretold that residents of the Zebulun and Naphtali tribal allotments would receive a special favor. The light of hope would rise in their communities with the coming of the Prince of Peace, the royal Son of David.

As His forerunner John had done, Jesus preached repentance. However, unlike John who preached only the nearness of the kingdom, Jesus preached repentance because of the arrival of the early stages of the kingdom. The light had dawned.

Application: Teaching and Preaching the Passage

A sermon or lesson might be developed around the idea of profiling this portion of Jesus' ministry: (1) Jesus was no isolationist. He ministered where people lived. (2) Mankind is in spiritual darkness and Jesus is the Light lost mankind needs. (3) Jesus preached the same kingdom message to everyone.

2. Jesus called His first disciples (4:18-22)

18 And Jesus, walking by the sea of Galilee, saw two brethren, Simon called Peter, and Andrew his brother, casting a net into the sea: for they were fishers.
19 And he saith unto them, Follow me, and I will make you fishers of men.
20 And they straightway left *their* nets, and followed him.
21 And going on from thence, he saw other two brethren, James *the son* of Zebedee, and John his brother, in a ship with Zebedee their father, mending their nets; and he called them.
22 And they immediately left the ship and their father, and followed him.

As Jesus ministered around the Sea of Galilee (also called the Lake of Gennesaret, Lk. 5:1, and Sea of Tiberias, Jn. 6:1; 21:1), He encountered fishermen "casting a net." Though Matthew wrote as if this was a radical call reminiscent of Elijah's call of Elisha (1 Kg. 19:19-21; Nolland 178; Hill 106), if we follow the chronology suggested in the previous section, this was not the first time Jesus met some of these men. He had met Peter and Andrew some months earlier during His early Judean ministry. Andrew was a disciple of John the Baptist. He heard John say that Jesus was the Lamb of God and the Son of God (Jn. 1:29, 34, 34-42). He spent part of a day with Jesus and was so convinced that Jesus was who John said He was that he brought his brother Simon to meet Jesus as well. It was at this time that Jesus named Simon "Cephas" (Aramaic, *rock*), which in the Greek language is "Peter" (Greek *petros*, rock).

Matthew and Mark (1:16-20) record the same details of this call. Luke (5:1-11) seems to give a fuller account of this encounter. In Luke's account, Jesus called the four only after He demonstrated His power with the miraculous catch of fish and Peter realized Jesus' holiness (Marshall 199-200). Hendriksen (246, 248) believes that Matthew (4:18-22) and Luke (5:1-11) described two different events, Luke's record being when these men left all. He thinks these men did some occasional fishing while they were in Capernaum between these two calls. However, it seems improbable that Jesus called these men twice to follow Him to become fishers of men. Rather, it is more probable that Matthew and Luke wrote separate accounts about the same event and that Luke's account is the fuller of the two (Lk. 5:1-11).

Andrew and Peter were originally from the town of Bethsaida (Jn. 1:44) but at the time of their call to discipleship, they lived in Capernaum (Mk. 1:16-21; Lk. 4:31, 38). Though little is known of these men's background, Andrew's place as a disciple of John the Baptist and his desire to learn more about Jesus (Jn. 1:37-38) speak of his interest in spiritual matters and especially the kingdom of heaven. John did not say Peter was a disciple of the Baptist's though it is possible that he was (ISBE III:803; Acts 1:22). Peter's later claim that he strictly followed Jewish dietary laws (Acts 10:14) speaks of his devotion to the things of God as well. This, plus their earlier times with Jesus, helps us understand why these men would walk away from their family business with just a "follow me" from Jesus. Andrew and Peter already knew from John the Baptist that the kingdom was near and who Jesus was, and Jesus knew from their earlier meeting the interest of these men in spiritual matters.

Peter and Andrew were by occupation professional fishermen (ISBE II:309). Jesus called them to be "fishers of men" (Greek *anthrōpos*, used generically of persons male and female). They would now labor to encourage people to become disciples of Jesus (Gundry 62) and to enter the kingdom. Matthew gives the impression they left their nets cast but not gathered in (Nolland 179), but Luke (5:6-7, 11) states otherwise. After emptying their nets, they brought their equipment to shore. Then they followed Jesus, leaving everything behind, even the immediate gain that could have been realized from the miraculous catch. The other two men Jesus called to discipleship at this time were James and John, business partners with Peter and Andrew (Lk. 5:7). They too were brothers.

Two types of nets are mentioned in verses 18 and 20. The net in verse 18 (Greek *amphiblēstron*) was a bell-shaped net that was ten to twenty feet in diameter (ISBE III:524). The perimeter was weighted so when the net was cast it sank and trapped the fish inside. The net in verse 20 (Greek *diktuon*) usually referred to a larger seine net (Jn. 21:6, 8, 11). This vertical net had floats on the top and weights on the bottom. Boats dragged it in a circular fashion trapping fish inside. (See a Bible dictionary for more complete descriptions of these and other fishing nets used in Bible times.)

The response of all four men to Jesus' command was immediate. Peter and Andrew left their nets. James and John left their nets, their boat, and their father. (For description of a Galilean fishing vessel of the first century A.D. and discussion of boats, see comments on 8:23.) They too "followed Him" (v. 20), an intimation of their discipleship (Gundry 63). This was no small action, especially since they were married (Mt. 8:14; 1 Cor. 9:5). Keener states that fishermen of that time had above average income for that day, something that makes their discipleship appear even more radical (Keener, *Background* 55; Evans, *Matthew* 93). Jesus' call had economic, familial, and personal comfort ramifications (Keener, *Matthew* 151, 153). Peter later described what happened that day as leaving "all" (Mt. 19:27; Wilkins 177). One can only imagine the content of the discussions between these men and their wives later that day.

The next months were spent in training. Soon these men, plus another eight, would be sent out on their own to proclaim the kingdom's arrival (Mt. 10:1-11:1). Nonetheless, three of the four men became special in the work. James was the first apostle martyred (Acts 12:2) and according to church tradition John, the special friend of Jesus (Jn. 13:23; 19:26), was the only apostle to die a natural death. Peter became the spokesperson of the group. These three men became Jesus' inner circle and were privileged to see portions of Jesus' ministry that no one else, not even the other apostles, were permitted to witness (Mt. 17:1-7; Mk. 5:37-43; and Mt. 26:37).

Summary (4:18-22)

After ministering alone for several months, perhaps as long as a year, Jesus called His first full-time disciples. Without giving many details, Matthew simply states that Jesus called four men to follow Him full time, and without hesitation they did. Leaving their livelihoods, they followed this Galilean Prophet/Teacher to fish for men.

Application: Teaching and Preaching the Passage

Though everyone who follows Jesus is a disciple, Jesus calls some of His followers to a more radical discipleship. This passage illustrates the reality and cost of radical discipleship for these men. (1) The call was powerful (it was from Jesus). (2) The call was a crisis call (they were interrupted during their normal workday). (3) The call was costly (these men left all: boats, nets, and livelihood). (4) The call was disruptive (it required extended times of separation from family; Nolland 181). (5) The call was specific (devote their lives to reaching people for Jesus). (6) The call's reason was understood and accepted (they viewed the kingdom to be worth their sacrifice; their sacrifice agreed with their expectations of the kingdom). (7) Finally, the call was personal. Jesus called specific individuals to this level of service. Such is the way with those who hear Jesus' call to radical discipleship and service.

3. Jesus entered a period of increasing popularity (4:23-25)

23 And Jesus went about all Galilee, teaching in their synagogues, and preaching the gospel of the kingdom, and healing all manner of sickness and all manner of disease among the people.
24 And his fame went throughout all Syria: and they brought unto him all sick people that were taken with divers diseases and torments, and those which were possessed with devils, and those which were lunatick, and those that had the palsy; and he healed them.
25 And there followed him great multitudes of people from Galilee, and *from* Decapolis, and *from* Jerusalem, and *from* Judaea, and *from* beyond Jordan.

In summary fashion, Matthew gave a brief overview of Jesus' ministry at this time. Jesus traveled all about Galilee teaching, preaching, and healing. He fulfilled Isaiah 9:1-2. See comments on 4:15-16. Matthew repeated these words in 9:35, suggesting that he deliberately bracketed this section (4:23—9:38) to illustrate the various facets of Jesus' ministry (Bruner 1:145).

Jesus addressed both spiritual and physical needs in His travels. Unlike John whose ministry was more localized, Jesus walked about all Galilee. Jesus' ministry consisted of three actions mainly. First, He taught, i.e., He provided instruction (Greek *didaskō;* Louw and Nida I:413). He spent Saturdays teaching those who honored the Sabbath by studying Scripture in local synagogues. Synagogues during Jesus' earthly ministry were local gatherings of individuals who met to pray and study the Torah (ISBE IV:676, 681; Keener, *Matthew* 156-157). Some communities, like Capernaum, had a synagogue building, but not all. The devout who lived in communities that could not afford a building still had meetings.

Second, He preached, i.e., He "publically announced" (Greek *kērussō*) the gospel of the kingdom, the good news about the kingdom (objective genitive; Carson, *Matthew* 121), and urged acceptance of His message (Louw and Nida I:417). The kingdom was His focus. The gospel was the good news that after all of these years the kingdom had come.

Third, He healed. He healed everyone regardless of his or her illness. He healed those who were demon possessed (v. 24), those who were epileptics (KJV lunatick; Greek *selēniazomai)* and those who were paralytics (KJV palsy; *paralutikos*). These miracles proved that the kingdom had arrived (Is. 61:1-2; Lk. 4:18-21; Mt. 11:2-6; 12:28; Wilkins 182) and that Jesus was aggressively attacking the enemies of soul and body. These miracles also proved Jesus' unlimited power to heal all human troubles.

Jesus' interaction with demons verified their reality, their ability to live in people, and their subjection to the Son. His actions confirmed His warfare against Satan (Mt. 8:28-29; 9:32-34; 12:22-29) and His ability to free individuals from even the most powerful antagonist of men's souls. Jesus has ultimate power over Satan (Jn. 14:30), the one who put Him to the test in His great temptation. Jesus' actions also demonstrated that the kingdom of heaven and the kingdom of darkness are opposites (Mt. 12:25-26).

Jesus was entering the most popular time of His ministry. People from all around (v. 25) came to be with Jesus. Every area of Palestine except Samaria is mentioned (Gundry 65). Decapolis (literally "ten cities") was a "loose confederation of ten essentially independent Hellenistic cities" located southeast of the Sea of Galilee (ISBE I:906-907), all but one of them east of the Jordan.

Apparently, Jews and Gentiles were among those who came, although most would have been Jews (Nolland 183), for the areas Matthew listed had both Jewish and Gentile residents. The miracles resulted in such fame that even the people of Syria (v. 24), Galilee's neighbor to the north, were among those who brought their sick to Jesus for healing. The Roman province of Syria included all of Palestine with the exception of Galilee (Carson, *Matthew* 121). The antecedent of "they" (v. 24) should probably not be limited to Syria only but understood to include all the areas Matthew mentioned in these verses.

Matthew's point seems to be that Jesus' popular ministry spanned ethnic, geographical, and political boundaries. Nolland (183) and Hill (107) think that for Matthew "Syria" referred to the area surrounding Galilee (Mk. 1:28) rather than the entire Roman province of Syria proper. However, Mark (3:8) states that people from Tyre and Sidon followed Jesus, which suggests a larger portion of Syria than the northern border area of Galilee. Jesus' popularity was widespread and growing at this time.

Matthew's use of "all" and "every" in verses 23-24 speaks of the widespread nature of Jesus ministry and not of every person in the world or even in that area. Jesus' ministry eclipsed that of John the Baptist in its scope, attraction of crowds, and kingdom signs (Mt. 3:5).

During this time, Jesus' ministry changed. At first His ministry and message mirrored John's. However, Jesus' Galilean ministry was characterized by teaching, preaching, and healing, whereas John preached and baptized. Healings receive greater attention than baptisms, and there is no record John ever preached or taught in a synagogue. John preached more about judgment than Jesus did.

It is difficult to gauge the level of discipleship of those who "followed Him" (v. 25). Some would have been committed disciples and others would become such. But there is nothing in the text to require the understanding that everyone who was following Jesus around Galilee at this point was a faithful disciple.

Summary (4:23-25)

Without giving any specific place names or recording any sermons, Matthew summarized Jesus' Galilean ministry. Taking His new disciples with Him, He traveled throughout all of Galilee teaching, preaching, and healing. His popularity grew well outside the boundaries of Galilee and people came from all around to be with Him. Many remained with Him and followed Him as He went from preaching point to preaching point.

Application: Preaching and Teaching the Passage

Wilkins (184) reminds us that Matthew is all about Jesus. Regardless of whom else Matthew included in his account, whether Joseph, the Magi, King Herod or John the Baptist, the story was really about Jesus. In one way or another, everything pointed to Jesus. This passage can be a lesson to illustrate this point.

This passage might also serve as a pattern for how Jesus' followers should practice ministry. (1) Jesus went to the people (Bruner 1:146). He did not expect them to come to Him. (2) Jesus addressed both spiritual and physical needs in His kingdom work. (3) Understanding that Jesus had the four disciples with Him (vv. 18-22), we see that Jesus modeled ministry. He taught and showed others how to assist Him and carry on His work.

B. Discourse One: The Sermon on the Mount (5:1—7:29)

In chapter four, Matthew described Jesus' temptation and ministry following His baptism. Jesus moved from Nazareth to Capernaum and began His own public ministry separate from the ministry of John the Baptist, who was in prison at this time (4:12). He called His first full-time disciples and took on an intensive itinerate ministry throughout Galilee. The immediate result was increased popularity. He went from obscurity to area-wide fame in a very short time.

The Sermon on the Mount, as chapters 5-7 are called, is bedrock kingdom teaching. This sermon is the first of five major blocks of teaching materials in Matthew. The other blocks are chapters 10, 13:1-52, 18:1-35, and chapters 24-25. Up to this time, Matthew has recorded only brief statements of Jesus: to John (3:15), to Satan (4:4, 7, 10), to Capernaum and its surrounding territory (4:17), and to His first four disciples (4:19).

This sermon is all about the kingdom. Interpretations are many and beyond the scope of this commentary. Keener (*Matthew* 160) counts thirty-six distinct views. Wilkins (195-199) and Bruner (1:363-364) give helpful summaries of various interpretations.

It is sufficient to say that this writer understands the Sermon on the Mount to be for the present kingdom life and age. The already-not-yet tension continues (see comments on 3:2) with the emphasis in this Sermon being on living as a citizen of the kingdom now. Future aspects of the kingdom are part of this sermon (7:21) but Jesus was inaugurating His kingdom and these are the moral and ethical standards for all who become and then live as kingdom citizens in the present age. These standards are for the present life, life upon this earth now that the kingdom of heaven has arrived (Wilkins 197). Later N.T. writings as well as the *Didache* (ca. A.D. 70-90), a non-canonical Christian document, clearly demonstrate that early Christians understood the ethical demands of this Sermon to be binding on kingdom citizens now.

1. The attitudes of kingdom citizens (5:1-12)

1 And seeing the multitudes, he went up into a mountain: and when he was set, his disciples came unto him:

2 And he opened his mouth, and taught them, saying,

3 Blessed *are* the poor in spirit: for theirs is the kingdom of heaven.

4 Blessed *are* they that mourn: for they shall be comforted.

5 Blessed *are* the meek: for they shall inherit the earth.
6 Blessed *are* they which do hunger and thirst after righteousness: for they shall be filled.
7 Blessed *are* the merciful: for they shall obtain mercy.
8 Blessed *are* the pure in heart: for they shall see God.
9 Blessed *are* the peacemakers: for they shall be called the children of God.
10 Blessed *are* they which are persecuted for righteousness' sake: for theirs is the kingdom of heaven.
11 Blessed are ye, when *men* shall revile you, and persecute *you*, and shall say all manner of evil against you falsely, for my sake.
12 Rejoice, and be exceeding glad: for great *is* your reward in heaven: for so persecuted they the prophets which were before you.

Matthew did not identify the specific location of this sermon (v. 1). While Matthew spoke of a mountain (NIV mountainside), Luke said Jesus, coming down from a mountain, gave this message on the plain (Lk. 6:17; ESV level place). This suggests that if both writers were speaking of the same event (not all interpreters think they were the same), the location was perhaps a flat area in the lower parts of a mountain. Luke's record of this sermon is abbreviated but should be consulted for a fuller appreciation of Jesus' teachings (Lk. 6:17-44).

"His disciples" are at least the four chosen in 4:18-22 but the multitudes mentioned in 4:25 and the "people" of 7:28 suggest that Jesus did not limit His comments to Peter, Andrew, James, and John (Nolland 191-192; *contra* Walvoord 43). Gundry (66) believes that Matthew used "the crowds" and "his disciples" interchangeably. The switch from third person (vv. 3-10) to second person (vv. 11-16) shows that at least some of the sermon was intended only for those already in the kingdom, but Luke 7:1, a probable parallel to Matthew 7:28-29, states that He gave this sermon in the hearing of the people, suggesting that the sermon was intended for everyone present.

The term "disciple" can mean a pupil or follower. In addition to these uses, its N.T. use with regard to one's relationship to Jesus means to learn from Jesus and to "share his life and his destiny" (Newman and Stine 107). It can have special reference to the Twelve or it can be broader, referring to women (Acts 9:36) as well as men. Here the term "disciples" probably included all who had committed to Him by this time, not just the four men called in chapter four. However, awareness of what it meant to be a disciple of Jesus would increase as Jesus continued to reveal more of His identity and work as well as more of the kingdom. Not everyone in the crowd was a disciple, so one of Jesus' goals was to make disciples from the crowd (Wilkins 192). The "them" (v. 2) refers primarily to the disciples (Hagner 33A:85), but all the crowd, believers and non-believers, were able to hear His teaching (Bruner 1:153; Keener, *Matthew* 165).

Matthew is thoroughly Christocentric in verses 1 and 2. This sermon is all about Jesus (Bruner 1:152). Jesus taught (v. 2) them. He instructed them in the ways of kingdom life. People needed more than physical healing (4:24). Because the kingdom had arrived and many were pressing into it, new citizens of the kingdom needed to know how life in the kingdom would be ordered. Nine somewhat cryptic beatitudes describe this new citizen. Each is "formally declarative" as well as "implicitly" imperatival (Carson, *Matthew* 130). All refer to the same group of people, not nine different groups (Hendriksen 266).

The word *beatitude* comes from the Latin *beatus* meaning "happy" or "blessed." Each beatitude begins with "blessed" (Greek *makarios*), a word that normally means "happy, with the implication of enjoying favorable circumstances" (Louw and Nida I:302). "It will go well with the one who" captures the idea well (Keener, *Matthew* 165).

However, these blessings are more than present age happiness. They are eschatological also (Carson, *Matthew* 131). In addition, they emphasize divine approval more than human happiness (Gundry 68). They speak not only of a fact (this person is blessed) but of a gift from God (this person has received help from God; Bruner 1:158). Such sayings are common in Scripture (e.g., Ps. 1:1; 32:1-2; 41:1-2; 119:1-2; Jas. 1:12). It is true that kingdom citizens possess a happiness and joy they cannot describe (1 Pet. 1:8-9) but the blessing in this Sermon is their part in the kingdom Jesus preached (Hagner 33A:91). In each beatitude, the person described in the first part has the blessing named in the second part. The second half gives the reason for the first half. In other words, the poor in spirit (v. 3) are blessed because (Greek *hoti*) they have the kingdom of heaven (Wilkins 205).

The poor in spirit (v. 3) are those who recognize that they are spiritually destitute before God (Newman and Stine 111; Hendriksen 269). They have no pride or false righteousness. Luke's tax collector (18:9-14) may well be the classic example of "poor in spirit" (Bruner 1:161). Because they recognize their emptiness of spirit, they are rich spiritually. They are also rich spiritually because they find their help in God (Barclay 1:106). They are in the kingdom now ("is," present tense) and its blessings are theirs now (Keener, *Background* 56; Newman and Stine 112) but the full realization of the blessing awaits the consummated kingdom (Carson, *Matthew* 132).

Blomberg (20) thinks the poor are probably those who are "the materially impoverished who recognize God as their only hope" (also Gundry 67; Hill 110; Hagner 33A:91; Ps. 69:32-33). He sees Isaiah 61:1 as the Scriptural backdrop (also Evans, *Matthew* 103 who sees several of these beatitudes alluded to in Is. 61:1-11). He may be partially right since Jesus saw Himself as the fulfillment of Isaiah 61:1-2 (Lk. 4:18-21), and especially since He names the poor as targets of His gospel in 11:5 in His response to John the Baptist. However, because Jesus specifically spoke of poverty of spirit in this beatitude, one should understand this as foremost on Jesus' mind, not a gospel mainly for any particular social level (Evans, *Matthew* 103). Jesus came to address the needs of all mankind, the greatest of which is spiritual need.

Continuing the thought of the previous verse, those who mourn (v. 4; Greek *pentheō*) are persons who express sadness or grief over spiritual need (Louw and Nida I:305; Barclay 1:109; 2 Cor. 7:10; Jas. 4:9). Jesus promised that God (the unnamed agent throughout these blessings; Greek: theological/divine passive; Sauer 81) would comfort such mourners. Their salvation has begun (Hagner 33A:92). This is their comfort, their blessing. See Zechariah's prophecy as an example of hope and desire on the part of the godly in Israel who at this time grieved over the spiritual darkness of the nation (Lk. 1:67-69).

Gundry (68-69) believes Matthew wrote to a persecuted church so he interprets these beatitudes in light of this. He says these mourners were persecuted disciples mourning their horrible condition, not mourning over sin or over the dead. While Matthew may have written to persecuted believers, Jesus' immediate audience must be understood as the primary audience. At this point in time, Jesus offered them spiritual deliverance, comfort, and access to the kingdom. In addition, the text does not suggest that God's comfort will be limited only to this one area of need. Mankind needs God's comfort in many areas and God is the God of all comfort (2 Cor. 1:3; Keener, *Matthew* 170).

The meek (v. 5; Greek *praus*) are the gentle, the mild. These are the non-aggressive. Citing Psalm 37:11, Jesus promised that God will give the earth to the meek. This is an act of grace (Hendriksen 272). Instead of warmongers conquering this world, the meek who trust in the Lord will inherit the earth (Ps. 37:9, 22, 29; KJV). Jesus is the perfect role model for this attitude (Mt. 11:29; 21:5).

There is a double fulfillment to Psalm 37:9, 11. Political Israel and her regaining of the land promised to Abraham are in view for the Psalmist (Is. 60:21; 65:17-25; Evans, *Matthew* 105; Nolland 202), but there is no reason to restrict this blessing to one group (Wilkins 207) nor is there reason to restrict this to this present earth (Rev. 21-22). All of God's people will inherit the whole earth (Van Gemeren 300). This is the thrust of Jesus' promise. The meek will inherit the earth.

Those who have a strong desire (hunger and thirst; v. 6) for righteousness, for themselves and for the entire earth will be filled or satisfied. This desire is an intense, from-the-heart desire. Righteousness (Greek *dikaiosunē*) is to do right, to do what God requires (Louw and Nida I:744). God will give them this desire of their hearts. First, there is immediate satisfaction for any who turn to God in the present (Jn. 4:13-14; 6:35, 51, 53-55; 7:37-39) and since the hungering and thirsting are continuous (Greek present tense) so the satisfaction will be also. Second, there is also an end-time emphasis here (Bruner 1:171; Nolland 203) as there was in verse 5, an assurance that righteousness will come to the whole earth through justice (Hagner 33A:93) in the future aspect of the kingdom age and into eternity (2 Pet. 3:13; Jer. 23:1-8, especially verses 5-6; Mt. 19:28; Lk. 1:31-33). These first four beatitudes go together and describe the attitude changes one makes when going from the kingdom of this world to the kingdom of heaven (ISBE IV:137).

The merciful (v. 7) are those who love kindness instead of oppression, and forgiveness rather than revenge. This beatitude continues an O.T. teaching. The Psalmist wrote (Ps. 18:25): "With the merciful thou wilt show thyself merciful." The prophets Micah (6:8) and Zechariah (7:9-14) stated that God wants His people to be characterized by mercy. God will be merciful to those who show mercy. He will withhold mercy from those who refuse to show mercy (McComiskey 436).

Forgiveness, an outgrowth of mercy, was a common theme of the N.T. writers (6:14-15; Mk. 11:25; Col. 3:12-13). Merciful people are forgiving. They are not seeking vengeance or opportunity to retaliate. Merciful people are exemplifying the stated desire of Jesus, "I desire mercy" (Mt. 9:13; 12:7). Rigid, religious ritual that hardens one against the needy is not the religion Jesus preached (Bruner 1:174-175). The reward of the merciful is mercy from God. See Matthew 18:32-35 where the opposite is also true.

The pure in heart (v. 8) are those whose inner person is pure. There is no hypocrisy, no pretense (15:8-9, 18-19; 23:25-28). Righteous outward actions arise from pure motives. Given Jesus' statements that follow in this sermon, love, sexual purity, and forgiveness are included in purity of heart. The blessing for such persons is an audience with God now (Ps. 24:3-6; Mt. 6:9) and, after life on earth, eternal life in God's presence, the ultimate expectation of God's people. There they will see His face (Rev. 22:4). No one without such inner purity can ever expect to see God (Heb. 12:14). Those who expect to see God will likewise work to bring their outward actions (practical holiness, progressive sanctification; Phil. 1:6; 2:12-13; 3:12; 1 Jn. 3:3) into conformity with their promised, final, perfect holiness (1 Th. 5:23; Erickson 967-971).

The peacemakers (v. 9) are those who, like their Heavenly Father, resist envy and strife (in the home, community, church, etc.) because such is the seedbed of "every evil work" (Jas. 3:13-18). God's children possess personal peace (Gal. 5:22), they want peace among themselves (Eph. 4:3), and they want others to possess that same peace. Right relationships between people are a goal for peacemakers (Barclay 1:127). They also want everyone to be at peace with God (Is. 52:7: "who publishes peace" ESV; comp. Rom. 10:15). This desire for peace is in spite of the resistance and division that Jesus and His gospel foster (5:10-12; 10:34-37).

"Sons of God" in this verse suggests character (Greek anarthrous construction) as well as relationship. The idea of relationship is a prominent theme in Jesus' teachings, especially in this Sermon on the Mount (5:16, 45, 48; 6:1, 4, 6, 8-9, 14-15, 18, 26, 32). Here, however, it seems that the God-like quality of peacemaking was what Jesus was encouraging His hearers to possess.

The persecuted (v. 10) are righteous people pursued for purposes of oppression (Greek *diōkō;* to chase, pursue, persecute; Gundry 72, "hound"). They are the faithful, those who will not compromise or apostatize (Nolland 207). They "have suffered persecution" (Newman and Stine 117; Greek perfect passive) because of their stand for righteousness seen in their righteous living (vv. 10, 20). This includes the persecuted in both Testaments (Hill 113). Though many who live for God will experience severe attacks (2 Tim. 3:12), such attacks, Jesus promises, will not detract from their eternal kingdom blessings. Persecution will not hinder full possession of the kingdom. This the persecuted are guaranteed. Matthew's original readers might have been experiencing persecution even as he wrote (Hagner 33A:95; see Gundry's remarks above on v. 4).

Religious persecution of God's people in general is not all Jesus had in mind (v. 11). He spoke specifically of religious persecution directed at His followers (1 Pet. 4:14, 16). Those who remain true through insults (KJV "revile"), persecution, and slander for the sake of—on account of—Jesus are blessed because they will receive a great reward in heaven (v. 12). "For my sake" speaks of personal identification with Jesus in the context of the kingdom (Nolland 208). "Your reward in heaven" moves the focus of the persecuted followers of Jesus from this earth to the eternal and assures them that they will be greatly rewarded for their faithfulness. This is cause to rejoice even in the midst of intense persecution.

Jesus did not tell His disciples to rejoice *because* they were being persecuted. Rather He told them to rejoice (Lk. 6:23: "leap for joy") because God would reward them (1) for their faithfulness that attracted such persecution (v. 11) and (2) for their faithfulness in the midst of such persecution (v. 12; Acts 5:41-42; Jas. 1:2-4). In addition, those persecuted for following Jesus should not think such persecution to be strange because the O.T. prophets experienced the same type persecution (Neh. 9:26; Acts 7:52; e.g. Elijah, Jeremiah, Micaiah). Knowledge of the promised reward and association with the spiritual giants of the past are causes for real joy (v. 12; Acts 5:41; Heb. 11:24-26; 1 Pet. 4:13). To make His point, Jesus used two imperatives (v. 12), "rejoice" (Greek *chairō*) and "be exceeding glad" (Greek *agalliaō*, "be extremely joyful"—Louw and Nida I:303).

Three things bear mentioning at this point: first, Jesus changed from impersonal to personal in verse 11. No longer using the less personal third person *they*, Jesus spoke directly to His audience ("you"). Second, from the earliest days of the kingdom, Jesus spoke of persecution. Kingdom life will be opposed. Those who want to be part of the kingdom must be willing to live with opposition and they must be willing to suffer for the kingdom. Third, as mentioned in v. 10, persecution has no negative impact on one's share in the kingdom blessings. God will graciously bestow eternal life in heaven on all who faithfully endure, a gift that will be "great beyond comparison" and make one's trouble here seem but "slight momentary affliction" (1 Cor. 4:7, ESV).

Summary (5:1-12)

Jesus' popularity increased in the early months of His Galilean ministry. As the crowds followed Jesus, He taught the way of the kingdom. He spoke primarily to His disciples but He also addressed the entire crowd. In this sense, His message was both edifying and evangelistic.

These twelve verses give characteristics of kingdom citizens. Those who have the nine attitudes Jesus mentioned possess special blessings. Jesus included these blessings alongside the attitudes He praised. Some of the blessings are for the present while others are for the future. All are from God.

Application: Teaching and Preaching the Passage

Preaching and teaching the beatitudes is a challenge, partly because of the cryptic nature of Jesus' sayings. However, in addition to the notes above, popular helps are readily available. Many lesson and sermon books have been written on the Sermon on the Mount, especially the beatitudes.

A series of topical sermons or lessons could be developed on the beatitudes emphasizing one beatitude in each lesson or sermon. Other Scriptures speak of these character traits and clarify what Jesus meant by mercy, poor in spirit, mourning, meek, etc. Though there are no imperatives in these verses (Wilkins 217), it is clear that these traits characterize kingdom citizens, which means that if they are not us, then we need to change so we can become the blessed.

One must take this portion of Christ's sermon from the intellectual to the practical in order to receive full benefit from these words. Any sermon or lesson on these beatitudes must include a significant application section. These beatitudes are standards for life now as well as hope for the future. The teacher or preacher should balance the present and the future aspects of these sayings. The meek (now) will (future) inherit the earth. The pure in heart (now) will (future) see God (1 Jn. 3:3; Heb. 12:14). The church needs to hear the promises of God for her future as well as what God expects of her now.

One might also emphasize how these sayings are opposite to the world's thinking, where being "poor in spirit," for example, is not highly regarded. Jesus' words run counter to our culture, but they are required nonetheless of all who would be part of the kingdom.

2. The influence of kingdom citizens (5:13-16)

13 Ye are the salt of the earth: but if the salt have lost his savour, wherewith shall it be salted? it is thenceforth good for nothing, but to be cast out, and to be trodden under foot of men.
14 Ye are the light of the world. A city that is set on an hill cannot be hid.
15 Neither do men light a candle, and put it under a bushel, but on a candlestick; and it giveth light unto all that are in the house.
16 Let your light so shine before men, that they may see your good works, and glorify your Father which is in heaven.

Followers of Christ are kingdom citizens. Jesus taught that His kingdom would grow. Growth speaks of a process and progress. This growth will happen as followers of Jesus deliberately influence their communities and the whole world ("of the earth," Greek objective genitive) for Jesus, convincing others to join the kingdom as well. Jesus made this point using two analogies. First, using the plural "ye" in emphatic position, Jesus likened *all* of His followers to salt. In the first century world, salt was used as a preservative, for purification, for seasoning, and in limited contexts as fertilizer (Carson, *Matthew 138*). For the value of salt as a fertilizer, see http://www.ipni.net/ppiweb/agbrief.nsf/5a4b8be72a35cd46852568d9001a18da/c10feca0a9a92c0485256d3500516f5c!OpenDocument; accessed August 30, 2010. According to Wilkins (212), salt was so valuable it could be used as a medium of exchange. As preservatives and purifiers, kingdom citizens preserve biblical standards and push back the corrupting influence of the evil one. As flavorers, kingdom citizens actively influence society for God (Keener, *Background* 57; Evans, *Matthew* 109). Rather than think of only one application, perhaps all of its positive uses should be understood (Nolland 212).

On the other hand, Jesus was not naïve. Some people want a place in the kingdom but not the responsibilities that go with citizenship. To this He states that salt that does not exert its influence, i.e., kingdom citizens who do not influence their world for good, is useless. As Bruner notes (1:189), "Salt does not exist for itself [and] salt a centimeter from food is useless." Kingdom citizens must be salty.

This salt influence is the reason for the persecution in verses 10-12 (Gundry 75). The salt influence, like the light influence to follow, is in spite of the wishes of the persecutors. Persecuted or not (see vv. 10-12), kingdom citizens must permeate society openly and deliberately with their good works. Those who have no good works are warned with the fate of useless salt—i.e., to be thrown out (v. 13; 25:24-30).

Second, Jesus also compared His followers to candle light (v. 14). They are lit to shine. Like the many lights of a highly visible city that one would not think of hiding and a single lighted candle openly displayed on a candle stand, "so" (v. 16, i.e., in the same way) God positions kingdom citizens so others will see their religious and pious practices. A single candle lighting the whole house (v. 15) suggests a one-room house (Gundry 77; Wilkin 215). Openly displayed righteous acts by those living out the attitudes of the beatitudes (poor in spirit, meek, hungering and thirsting after righteousness; Evans, *Matthew* 110) will motivate others presently outside the kingdom to turn in praise to God. The Apostle Peter later made this same point (1 Pet. 2:12). It is God's intent and design that kingdom citizens dispel darkness with their light (2 Cor. 4:6). (However, compare 6:1 for a caution against public show.)

These two predicate nominatives, salt and light, name characteristics of kingdom citizens. Jesus made simple declarations: "You are." He did not exhort (you should be) or prophesy (you will be). He simply stated as factual, "You are." Also, the indicative gives energy to the imperative (Hagner 33A:98): "you are," therefore "let." "You" is emphatic in verses 13 and 14.

Kingdom citizens are salt and light. The light that dawned in Jesus' ministry (Mt. 4:16) continues in His followers. The salt influence of Jesus' ministry continues in His followers' lives and ministries as well.

Summary (5:13-16)

After listing nine characteristics of kingdom citizens, Jesus spoke of the influence of kingdom citizens in the present age. Using the analogies of salt and light, Jesus said that kingdom citizens are to influence this world for the good of the kingdom of heaven. The goal of this influence is to increase the numbers of those who glorify the Father. Kingdom citizens who do not influence this world for good are opposite the plainly stated will of Jesus. They are also guilty of keeping God from getting the full amount of praise due Him.

Application: Teaching and Preaching the Passage

Jesus pointed to two activities of all kingdom citizens. They are to (1) resist the decay of society, and (2) they are to push back the darkness of society.

This subject can be developed around "who" (you, Greek plural; all kingdom citizens); "what," (the salt; see the uses of salt in the above comments); "where," (the earth; worldwide); and "when" (are; static present tense, now and ongoing). Special emphasis might be given to ways Christians can make themselves less salty (blending with the world; cloistering only with other Christians; staying too busy to reach out) and ways Christians might make themselves more salty (resist blending, be a Christian wherever one is; build relationships with non-Christians; plan personal evangelism time). The same development can be used for light as well.

The Christian has no choice in this matter. The kingdom is no place for savorless salt or darkened lights. God communicates some truths about Himself through natural revelation. Some truths He shares in His special revelation, the written Word. The gospel He communicates through His people by their actions and words.

3. The kingdom of heaven and the Law of Moses (5:17-20)

On different occasions the Pharisees accused Jesus of breaking the Law (e.g., Sabbath controversies; Mt. 12:12-14). How far Jesus was into His ministry when these allegations began is unclear. However, He addressed the challenges directly in this sermon and laid to rest the notion that He intended to set aside the "validity and authority" of the O.T. (Hill 117). In reality, the kingdom of heaven requires obedience beyond that of the old covenant.

17 Think not that I am come to destroy the law, or the prophets: I am not come to destroy, but to fulfil.
18 For verily I say unto you, Till heaven and earth pass, one jot or one tittle shall in no wise pass from the law, till all be fulfilled.
19 Whosoever therefore shall break one of these least commandments, and shall teach men so, he shall be called the least in the kingdom of heaven: but whosoever shall do and teach *them*, the same shall be called great in the kingdom of heaven.
20 For I say unto you, That except your righteousness shall exceed *the righteousness* of the scribes and Pharisees, ye shall in no case enter into the kingdom of heaven.

"The law and the prophets" refers to the entire O.T. (7:12, 11:13, 22:40; Lk. 16:16; Acts 13:15, 24:14, 28:23; Rom. 3:21). Jesus was not setting aside or negating the whole or any part of the whole. Rather, He came to fulfill the O.T., something Matthew already pointed out to his readers (1:22; 2:5, 15, 17, 23; 4:14). He came (notice His preexistence, Jn. 1:1-14, and His mission; Hendriksen 290) to complete ("fulfill") God's every intent found in the O.T. (Blomberg 20) for it pointed to Him (Carson, *Matthew* 144).

With this statement Jesus introduced His absolute endorsement of the O.T. as the eternal Word of God (v. 18; Lk. 16:17). "Verily" translates a word (Greek *amēn*) that means *truly* or *of truth* and is the speaker's way of expressing "a strong affirmation of what is declared" (Louw and Nida I:673). "Verily" indicates that what Jesus is about to say is very important. Hendriksen (291) suggests a good understanding is "I solemnly declare." Though "amen" was commonly used to end prayers and "to express emphatic agreement with something just spoken," evidently to use it at the beginning of a statement like Jesus did here was not that common (Evans, *Matthew* 112; also Nolland 219).

Jesus stated that the O.T. must be fulfilled even to the smallest letter and pen stroke in the Hebrew alphabet. (See 24:35 where Jesus claims the same for His words.) "Fulfill" means that everything will be brought to pass that the O.T. says will be brought to pass (Newman and Stine 128). The new heaven and new earth will not come until all of the O.T. has been fulfilled, as indicated by both "until" clauses in v. 18 (Hagner 33A:107-108). This is an important affirmation about the O.T., but it also has tremendous eschatological implications. For more on the cosmic renewal, see Matthew 19:28; 24:35; 2 Peter 3:13; and Revelation 21:1-5.

The jot (Greek *iōta*) refers to either the iota, the smallest letter in the Greek alphabet (Gundry 80) or to the smallest letter in the Hebrew alphabet, the *yodh*—a character a bit larger than an apostrophe (Evans, *Matthew* 112). The tittle (Greek *keraia*) is generally understood to be a small horn-like projection of a Hebrew letter. It could also refer to "an accent, a diacritical mark or a breathing mark" (ISBE I:985). Both the jot and the tittle speak of smallness, suggesting triviality. "Not the smallest letter, not the least stroke of a pen" (NIV) expresses well the essence of Jesus' words. Surely, this captured the attention of the legalistic Pharisees!

By using the jot and tittle as illustrations, Jesus taught the extent of the inspiration and inerrancy of the O.T. Scriptures (Lk. 16:17) and of the O.T.'s duration. No part of the O.T., even to the smallest detail and what may appear to be trivial, can be set aside or destroyed. Jesus held a high view of Scripture. Jesus loved Scripture and obviously had immersed Himself in it (Bruner 1:198). His followers should follow His love and His example. Jesus also, by this jot and tittle imagery, showed the extent of God's planned fulfillment of the O.T. in Jesus. From the crushing of the serpent's head in Genesis 3:15 to the final "day of the Lord" (Mal. 4:1-4), nothing prophesied will be left unfulfilled. Every prophecy, even the smallest prophetic detail, will be accomplished in the one spoken of in the Law and the Prophets.

The entire O.T., even to the smallest detail, remains germane to kingdom citizens, albeit from a kingdom perspective (v. 19). O.T. moral laws remain unchanged while ceremonial (Mk. 7:19; Acts 10-11) and sacrificial laws have been fulfilled in Christ (Heb. 7-9) and are now obeyed by trusting His finished work on the cross (Col. 2:14-17; Heb. 8:6-13, 10:1-18). Those laws that governed everyday life in national Israel (civil laws) are no longer binding, for the new covenant is not only with ethnic and national Israel but with the people of God from all nations. In addition, followers of Jesus cannot practice the works of the Law as righteous acts before God (Gal. 2:15-3:5, 4:9-11, 5:1-5) because the new covenant has made the old obsolete (Heb. 8:13). See Fee and Stuart (163-180, especially 165-169) for a summary introduction to the Christian's responsibility to the O.T. Also, see 9:14-17 and 13:52 for other comments on kingdom citizen's responsibility to the law.

Verse 19 must be interpreted with Luke 16:16. Kingdom citizens are obligated both to live and to teach the O.T. but, as previously mentioned, only from a kingdom perspective. However, lest anyone think that this means the O.T. is no longer important, Jesus adds the statements recorded in verses 19 and 20. Any who fail to practice or who teach others not to obey God's will revealed in the O.T. will be called least in the kingdom (v. 19), which means excluded from the kingdom (v. 20: "will not enter"; Nolland 222-223; Keener, *Matthew* 179; *contra* Hagner 33A:109; Carson, *Matthew* 146). Compare with Deuteronomy 4:2 and 12:32. Jesus does not fully explain the implications of "least" and "greatest" but it is clear that the two groups do not enjoy the same status. It is also clear that the determining factor in status is one's attitude toward and handling of the Scripture as the revealed Word of God and as one's rule of faith and practice. See 18:1 for further comments on greatness in the kingdom of heaven.

That Jesus did not set aside the Law was an important truth for the early church. Both Stephen (Acts 6:11) and Paul (Acts 18:13) were accused of teaching against the Law. Paul's defense before Felix included the claim that he believed everything written in the Law and the prophets (Acts 24:14). His strong and positive statements about the Law in Romans 7 add further support to his claims.

Barclay (1:155) is wrong when he says, "Now, no fewer than five times (Mt. 5:21, 27, 33, 38, 43) Jesus quotes the law, only to contradict it and to substitute a teaching of his own." Barclay (1:156) goes on to say that Jesus overturned "what up to that point had been regarded as the eternal word of God." Jesus fulfilled the Scriptures. He did not contradict or overturn them. Jesus challenged misinterpretation and misapplication—"you have heard it said, ... but I say to you"—but He never changed or contradicted Scripture.

To further make His point, Jesus called for a righteousness that exceeded and was "far more comprehensive" (Newman and Stine 132) than that of even the most law-abiding members of Judaism, the scribes and Pharisees. See Luke 10:25-28 and Matthew 19:16-22 with my comments. The authority behind His statements was the Lord Himself: "For I am saying to you" (plural, v. 20). As Nolland (225-226) observed, this statement did not sound like someone who intended to set aside the Law (Nolland 225). Rather, it encouraged an intentional, enthusiastic obedience to "the will of God made known through the Law as unveiled by Jesus."

The scribes were the expert teachers of the Law (Mt. 2:4) and the Pharisees as a group carefully tried to obey the letter of the Law (see comments on 3:7 for a fuller description of a Pharisee). Jesus was not suggesting that these groups were role models. See 23:1-36. Rather He was saying that even they were not living as kingdom citizens (Mt. 23:13). Entry-level requirements for Jesus' kingdom were high. The kingdom requires that righteous actions be more than external only; they must come from a changed heart (Jn. 3:3). Character, not external regulations, are what Jesus emphasized (Keener, *Background* 57) and what the scribes and Pharisees lacked. The remainder of this teaching sermon, and especially the remainder of this chapter, illustrates the kind of righteous acts Jesus required, actions judged right by the Father (Mt. 5:45; 6:1, 6, 18).

Looking back from the post-cross and post-Pentecost perspective, one can be sure that Jesus meant more than any of His hearers understood at this time (one must allow for progressive revelation). In time, followers of God would realize that the righteousness that exceeds that of the scribes and the Pharisees begins with the righteousness God provides through faith in Jesus (Rom. 10:3; Phil. 3:9). Only faith in Jesus opens the gate into God's kingdom (21:31-32). Then, through the power of a regenerated life, the follower of Jesus can live out the visible, practical righteousness—i.e., the practical sanctification that comes from a regenerated heart, that Jesus requires as well.

Summary (5:17-20)

Early in His ministry, Jesus explained His attitude toward the O.T. He stated plainly that He had no intention of setting aside the O.T. In fact, the opposite was true. Every letter of the O.T. would be fulfilled because it all pointed to Him. He was the fulfillment of the O.T. Not only did He continue teaching the O.T., kingdom citizens would as well. Further, the righteousness He required of all who enter the kingdom of heaven was a more perfect righteousness than that practiced by even the most law-abiding Israelites of that day, the scribes and Pharisees. This was a righteousness that God Himself provides through His sacrificed Son.

Application: Teaching and Preaching the Passage

A sermon might be developed showing the value of the O.T. to Christians. The prevailing ignorance and dislike of the O.T. is out of step with these and other words of Jesus about the O.T. Scriptures. One only needs to recall that the early church had only the O.T. and the oral testimony of the Twelve and other eyewitnesses to realize the importance of the O.T. Scriptures. They preached Jesus from the O.T. Christians need to continue that practice.

A sermon or lesson might be developed around the idea of Jesus' thoughts concerning the Old Testament's importance to the Christian: It is inerrant, eternal, and germane to all generations.

4. The law of Christ (5:21-48)

In the previous verses, Jesus taught that a more perfect righteousness than that of the scribes and Pharisees is required of all who would share in the kingdom. He followed that with six specific examples of the required, more perfect righteousness, showing differences between contemporary Jewish interpretation of the O.T. and Jesus' Messianic interpretation. The messianic interpretation included intent as well as explanation (Carson, *Matthew* 148). Evans (*Matthew* 115) says there are five examples. He joins the discussions on lust and divorce into one because they both warn against adultery.

a. Murder and anger management (5:21-26)

21 Ye have heard that it was said of them of old time, Thou shalt not

kill; and whosoever shall kill shall be in danger of the judgment:
22 But I say unto you, That whosoever is angry with his brother without a cause shall be in danger of the judgment: and whosoever shall say to his brother, Raca, shall be in danger of the council: but whosoever shall say, Thou fool, shall be in danger of hell fire.
23 Therefore if thou bring thy gift to the altar, and there rememberest that thy brother hath ought against thee;
24 Leave there thy gift before the altar, and go thy way; first be reconciled to thy brother, and then come and offer thy gift.
25 Agree with thine adversary quickly, whiles thou art in the way with him; lest at any time the adversary deliver thee to the judge, and the judge deliver thee to the officer, and thou be cast into prison.
26 Verily I say unto thee, Thou shalt by no means come out thence, till thou hast paid the uttermost farthing.

The ancients ("them of old"; Greek *archaios*) may refer to the children of Israel in the wilderness or it may refer to later generations who in Jesus' day would be "ancients" as well. If the wilderness Israel is in view, Jesus was referring to the giving of the Ten Commandments (Nolland 230; Hill 120). If later generations are in view, then the commandment and its judgment were being passed on by the ancients as a part of their oral tradition (Evans, *Matthew* 115; Louw and Nida I:642). Either understanding is possible. Regardless which view one takes, one must be careful to understand that Jesus is not giving a new law set in opposition to the original Mosaic Law. Instead, Jesus is giving the deeper intent of the Law.

Jewish interpretation taught a literal application of the sixth commandment, "Thou shalt not kill" (Ex. 20:13), the commandment that forbade murder (Wilkins 242). They also understood that God called for the punishment of any who broke this law (Gen. 4:11-16, 9:6). Jesus did not disagree with this. However, murder was not the only wrong included in the sixth commandment. According to Jesus, this commandment also condemned wrong attitudes toward one's fellow man.

The words "But I say unto you" (v. 22, etc.) include a conjunction of contrast (Greek *de*) and an emphatic use of the first person pronoun, thus providing a contrast between Jesus and then contemporary interpreters. He claimed authority to interpret correctly ("I") but did not set Himself against the O.T. (Hagner 33A:112; *contra* Bruner 1:207). He had just stated emphatically that He would not set aside the Law (vv. 17-19). Rather He went beyond a restrictive meaning to a broader interpretation (Nolland 230). According to Jesus, not just actual murder but ongoing (Greek present tense participle, evidently intense) anger deserved judgment. See James 4:1-2.

"Brother" may refer to fellow citizens in the kingdom, "Christian brothers" (so Carson, *Matthew* 149). However, the text gives no such direct limitation. It is clear from the examples that follow that relationships are involved (Carson, *The Sermon* 42). Surely angry verbal attacks against those outside the kingdom are just as wrong as anger directed at fellow citizens of the kingdom.

Anger that vents in hateful insults also deserves judgment, for it reveals a hateful heart. "Raca," an Aramaic word, means "one who is totally lacking in understanding—numbskull, fool" (Louw and Nida I:388). "Fool" (Greek *mōros*) is the Greek equivalent. James later explained that such words should not come from the mouths of Jesus' followers because such disrespect also insults the Creator of all men (Jas. 3:9).

"Without a cause," is not in some Greek manuscripts and so is not in some translations. The phrase suggests that Jesus' subject was unjustifiable anger rather than all anger, which seems right. Ephesians 4:26 and Titus 1:7 speak of anger in a way that shows that all anger is not sin. God is angry at the sin of the wicked (Ps. 7:11). Jesus was angry at the Pharisees because of their hard hearts (Mk. 3:5). However, prolonged anger, anger that harms another, and anger that turns into hatred, are sins (1 Jn. 3:15). This is what Jesus warned against, and the words "without a cause" clarify His intended meaning.

From judgment to the Council to the continuing fires of the city dump ("hell fire," *Gehenna*; see below and Bruner 1:212), Jesus used contemporary images to show the penalty for unchecked anger. There is no place in kingdom life for this sinful attitude. Instead of harboring anger and hatred, which can lead to murder (Mt. 15:19), kingdom citizens are required to seek reconciliation (v. 23).

The progressive nature of the punishment suggests that judgment (v. 22) could refer to human courts, the Council could refer to the Sanhedrin (see discussion on Mt. 26:59) and city dump fires to the final place of eternal punishment (Gundry 84; Evans, *Matthew* 115). Some commentators understand the judgment and Council to be heavenly courts described in such a way as to parallel the Jewish Sanhedrin (Keener, *Background* 58). This latter understanding is possible since the courts of the land judge murderers as an expression of God's judgment (Rom. 13:4). Murder was declared a capital offense after the flood (Gen. 9:5-6), and this same rule permeated the Mosaic Law as well (Ex. 21:12; Lev. 24;17; Num. 35:12; Dt. 17:8). However, there does not seem to be any human court that passes judgment on anger (Hendriksen 298), so Jesus may well have had heaven's courts and the final judgment in mind. Regardless, Jesus' point is that anger will be judged (Hagner 33A:116).

"Hell fire" (v. 22: Greek *tēn geennan tou puros*) is literally "the Gehenna of fire" or "the fiery Gehenna" (ESV: "the hell of fire"), the place of final, fiery punishment. Here the bodies and souls of the lost spend eternity (10:28). The presence of body and soul together requires that this punishment follow the bodily resurrection of the lost. Jesus' warning shows that murderous hatred makes one culpable.

Another Greek word translated "hell" in the N.T. is *hadēs*, a word we have adopted in English. *Hades* has different meanings, depending on the word's usage in various contexts. See comments on 16:18. In contrast to Gehenna, *hades* is where the ungodly souls go until their resurrection and final judgment. Once the ungodly receive their resurrected bodies (Jn. 5:28-29; Rev. 20:5), they are cast into the lake of fire where they will be tormented forever

(Rev. 20:14-15). This latter is Gehenna (TDNT I:658).

The concept of Gehenna as a place of punishment comes from the O.T. The Valley of Hinnom is an east-west ravine immediately outside the south wall of Jerusalem (ISBE II:717-718) where child sacrifices were made to the Ammonite idol god Molech (1 Kg. 11:7; 2 Kg. 16:3, 17:17, 21:6, 23:10; Jer. 7:31). God was so offended by this practice that He declared the Valley of Hinnom a place of punishment and destruction (Jer. 7:32, 19:5-6). The prophet Isaiah foretold its destruction as well and he included details that were later used to describe that eternal place of punishment (Is. 30:33). This understanding of Gehenna carried over into the N.T. King Josiah (2 Kg. 23:10) destroyed this vile worship site, and the ravine evidently (see ISBE II:717) became the city dump where garbage was burned. This separation and constant burning served as a "particularly suitable metaphor for eternal punishment" (Hagner 33A:117; Hill 121).

Not only should the kingdom citizen control his or her own anger but offenses that cause anger in others must be set right as quickly as possible as well. In the context of worship, i.e., altars and gifts to God in Jerusalem (v. 23; notice that Jesus endorsed temple sacrifices at this time), Jesus instructed individual ("thou") hearers to reconcile with a brother or adversary they had wronged (Is. 1:10-17, 58:3-12; Am. 5:21-24). They were to make things right with their fellow man before approaching God (vv. 23-24; see also v. 9; 1 Jn. 4:20). See comments on 9:13 and 12:7. Reconciliation must be attempted "first" (Rom. 12:18); "then" the worshiper could approach God with a gift. Travel from Jerusalem to their homes to reconcile and then back to Jerusalem to finish the sacrifice required substantial sacrifice (Wilkins 243). Jesus was serious.

To illustrate further heaven's attitude toward sinful attitudes of the heart, Jesus used a court example. He presented the benefits of reconciliation from the human perspective (v. 25). Getting on good terms with ("agree with") a litigant, someone to whom an honest debt was owed (Walvoord 49), could save the possibility of merciless punishment at the hands of a human judge (v. 26). Apparently Jesus referred to a debtor's prison, something Keener (*Background* 58) says the Jews did not use but were familiar with among the Gentiles (see also Mt. 18:34). The farthing was a Roman coin worth 1/64 of a day's wages (Louw and Nida I:62-63). Without reconciliation, one would have to pay everything that was owed plus the fine imposed by the judge (Newman and Stine 140) to the last cent. It would have been impossible to pay such a debt while imprisoned, a point probably not lost on His hearers. Only family or friends could pay the debts of those in debtor's prison.

With this illustration, Jesus warned against God's punishment, for this sermon was about kingdom life. The wronged person might rise up at the final judgment and "confront his opponent" (Marshall 552). The judge represented God and the jail represented hell (Hendriksen 301; Gundry 87). Jesus' point was this: unchecked anger and insults are sin just as surely as murder is sin. All three will be judged. All three can be prevented. Reconciliation is God's will. Reconciliation is the responsibility of the offender. Both restrained anger and the desire to reconcile characterize kingdom citizens.

Summary (5:21-26)

In this section, Jesus began explaining the intended meanings and applications of various O.T. laws. He did not set aside Moses' teachings. Rather He opened them to deeper meaning and relevance. There are six examples in the remainder of this chapter.

Jesus' first example is the sixth commandment. Surely, murder is forbidden but Jesus said the commandment forbids not only murder but also wrong attitudes toward one's fellow man. Angry, verbal attacks that denigrate God's creatures are sinful and make one an object of God's eternal judgment, as do prolonged anger and hatred. Kingdom citizens must keep their own emotions in check and refrain from arousing these same sinful feelings in others. Should a kingdom citizen sin against another, he or she must seek reconciliation as quickly as possible. It is noteworthy that in this instance Jesus placed a higher priority on reconciliation than on worship.

Jesus understood the sixth commandment to have a much broader application than His contemporaries were teaching. Feelings of anger and hatred are just as sinful as murder. Jesus wants kingdom citizens to live at peace with others and show love, not hate.

Application: Teaching and Preaching the Passage

The sixth commandment can be taught using the two perspectives Jesus mentioned. First, do not murder. Human life is sacred. This commandment is based on Genesis 9:6 and is regularly reinforced in Scripture. Second, do not harbor feelings that can lead to murder. This sin surfaced first in Genesis 4:7 and is now brought into sharp focus by Jesus.

Many Christians, laity as well as leadership, show signs of unresolved anger. Family breakdowns as well as church breakups are evidence that anger is not being managed and that the church needs to hear this passage preached today. Anger can be a sin. Anger can lead to sin. Anger is never a legitimate reason for sin. A sermon or lesson on the dangers of anger could include individual responsibility to manage anger and the need to repent quickly and reconcile when trespasses have occurred.

Verbal assaults can also be addressed as wrong. Ugly, vindictive verbal assaults are sin. Jesus is our example in speaking against such venomous words. Words can harm. They can also insult the Creator. Raca and fool are only examples. Many verbal put-downs fit this class of denounced terms. Kingdom citizens have no right to use such hate-filled words. Whether from a parent to a child, a child to a parent, one teen to another, one co-worker to another, one stranger to another, a congregational member to a pastor, or a pastor to a member of the congregation, name-calling and other verbal put-downs are wrong.

b. Adultery and the lustful eye (5:27-30)

27 Ye have heard that it was said by them of old time, Thou shalt not commit adultery:

28 But I say unto you, That whosoever looketh on a woman to lust after her hath committed adultery with her already in his heart.
29 And if thy right eye offend thee, pluck it out, and cast it from thee: for it is profitable for thee that one of thy members should perish, and not *that* thy whole body should be cast into hell.
30 And if thy right hand offend thee, cut it off, and cast it from thee: for it is profitable for thee that one of thy members should perish, and not *that* thy whole body should be cast into hell.

"You have heard ... but I say" introduces Jesus' second comparison between contemporary Jewish understanding and Scripture's intent. Jesus quoted the seventh commandment verbatim (Ex. 20:14) and then proceeded to explain its fuller meaning. Scholars report that Jewish sources considered adultery a wrong use of another man's property (Newman and Stine 141), so the idea was theft more than purity (Carson, *Matthew* 151; see the tenth commandment, Ex. 20:17). Jesus corrected Jewish understanding and showed that purity was the intent of the seventh commandment.

As translated, the prohibition condemned a lustful look (Greek, "the one who is looking ... to lust for her," infinitive of purpose). Such a deliberate look feeds lust. Any woman, not just a married woman (Greek anarthrous construction), is the object (Hagner 33A:120). The man who is doing the lusting is in the wrong. The woman in this situation is innocent. Jesus called on the men to have integrity of heart and self-control. In this interpretation no culpability is placed on the woman.

It is also possible to translate the Greek "so as to get her to lust" (Carson, *Matthew* 151-152; accusative *autēn* as the subject of the infinitive). With this translation, the man is looking at the woman with the intent of getting her to lust as well. Thus, both ("with her") would be committing adultery. With either interpretation, lust is condemned.

Adultery today is defined as voluntary, extramarital, heterosexual sexual relations between a married person and someone other than his or her spouse. In the O.T. adultery was voluntary sex between a man, married or unmarried, and the wife or betrothed wife of another man (Wilkins 244; Newman and Stine 141). According to this later definition, the term "adultery" was not used to denote voluntary sex between an unmarried man and an unmarried or unbetrothed woman.

Both of these definitions are too limited according to Jesus. He defined adultery, not simply as having intimate relations with someone other than one's spouse (whether that person is married or not), but as desiring to have intimate relations with someone other than one's spouse. In Jesus' application, marriage is not the issue. All people, whether single or married, can violate the seventh commandment in their hearts and be guilty of breaking this commandment. As with the previous teaching about murder and anger, adultery is first an issue of the heart (Mt. 15:19). The righteousness that exceeds that of the scribes and Pharisees (5:20) begins with a heart makeover. Sexual sins arise from a corrupt heart.

Using hyperbole (vv. 29-30) Jesus instructed kingdom citizens to remove whatever leads one to sin, even to the point of severing body parts. He does this twice for emphasis. (See 18:8-9 also.) The actions are dramatic, radical, and manifesting extreme self-discipline: pluck (NIV gouge; ESV tear), cut, and cast. He taught that it is better to go through this life maimed physically and have a place in the eternal kingdom than to miss the kingdom because of sin. The instruction to excise body parts and the warning about hell (Greek *Gehenna;* see v. 22) show the seriousness of lust and how important sexual purity and self-discipline are. The hyperbolic excising of body parts shows that Jesus recognized how difficult, and perhaps expensive, sacrifice for sexual purity could be (Bruner 1:223). His words show that each person is individually responsible for purity and that victory is possible. However, because lust is a sin of the heart, the mere excising of body parts will not remove lust (Col. 2:23). The heart must be cleansed and made new (2 Cor. 5:17), and the kingdom citizen must commit to a pure life (Eph. 4:17-24; Mt. 5:8).

One final comment is in order: Original sin corrupted mankind's sexuality (Gen. 3:7) even as it did every other part of his being. However, sexual desire is not sin. God created men to desire women and women to desire men (Gen. 1:27-28), but He intended that their desires be directed toward a single spouse. The creator gave Adam one wife and Eve one husband. Holy men have long recognized that monogamy and marital fidelity are God's plan (Job. 31:1, 9-12; Mal. 2:14-16). The N.T. echoes the O.T. in this area. Sexual needs are created needs and as such are legitimate and are to be addressed in marriage (1 Cor. 7:2-9). Sexual desire is normal and to be expected unless a person has the gift of celibacy (1 Cor. 7:7) or lacks the capacity to have sex (Mt. 19:12). Each spouse is to satisfy the other's needs (1 Cor. 7:3-5). In this way, both can more easily avoid unholy, sexual temptation (1 Cor. 7:2, 9).

Summary (5:27-30)

Quoting the seventh commandment, Jesus condemned adultery. He too taught that consensual sex between persons who are not married to each other is sin. However, He went beyond this basic understanding and stated that married persons commit adultery at the point desire is directed at a person who is not one's own spouse. Adultery is a sin of the heart as much as a sin of the body. Integrity to one's marriage vows is the issue and integrity is first a matter of the heart. Kingdom citizens are responsible to prevent adultery of the heart as well as physical adultery. Jesus used strong and extreme language to make His point. Though the sacrifice necessary to master desire may be great, purity of heart and body is a must for all who hope to share in the kingdom of heaven. Such purity is possible.

Application: Teaching and Preaching the Passage

At first glance, few of Jesus' words seem any more countercultural than these instructions. While they strike fear in the heart of those desiring a high degree of holiness, few in today's society—even in the church—appear interested in hearing them, let alone obeying them. However, purity of heart is a requirement and according to Jesus a responsibility of each individual. The difficulty for many to obey these words led Bruner (1:221) to say, "This had *better* be a Word of Jesus—that is, a divine Word with power in it to do what it says—or the case is hopeless."

The prohibition against a lustful look condemns as adultery a large portion of approved activities in contemporary society and entertainment. Jesus' words condemn sexual fantasies and all forms of media that show the human body immodestly and for titillating purposes. Persons who look to lust are sinning, as are persons who dress or act provocatively. These include male and female, young and old. Paul later wrote (Rom. 1:32) that all who partake of such are also condemned. As with the previous discussion against murder and hatred, there is an abundance of Bible material on this subject. The number of marriage breakups shows that the church needs to keep this command before her people. The seventh commandment is still in force.

When preaching or teaching this passage, the interpreter should communicate (1) that while Jesus' words are literally directed to men, they can be applied evenly to men and women, both young and old; (2) that if lust is wrong, encouraging the desire of a person not one's spouse is wrong also (whether by actions, words, or dress); and (3) that in addition to a personal commitment to holiness and self-control, according to 1 Corinthians 7, a healthy marriage or the spiritual gift of celibacy will also help one avoid these sins.

One might develop a message around (1) the prohibited action: lust; (2) the prescribed attitude; life without lust; (3) the preventable punishment: hell; and (4) the profitable achievement: holiness in one's thought life and experience.

Finally, the Bible teacher must tell his or her hearers that those who practice immorality, regardless of their profession of faith, are not going to heaven (1 Cor. 6:9). Only the washed, sanctified, and justified (1 Cor. 6:11) inherit that kingdom. As with all matters of this nature, the speaker must be careful to protect the church by using only terms that will not offend sanctified ears or grieve the Holy Spirit. The church is no place for cheap or vulgar terminology. This is one area where plain talk is not always best.

c. Divorce, remarriage, and adultery (5:31-32)

Marriage and family are important to Jesus. In the previous verses, Jesus spoke of the necessity for purity of thought in areas God wants reserved for marriage. He next turned to lifelong marriage. With the divorce rates being so high today, Jesus' words are a challenge. However, they must have been hard for the first hearers, too, as the Twelve demonstrated by their concerns on another occasion (19:10).

31 It hath been said, Whosoever shall put away his wife, let him give her a writing of divorcement:
32 But I say unto you, That whosoever shall put away his wife, saving for the cause of fornication, causeth her to commit adultery: and whosoever shall marry her that is divorced committeth adultery.

This is Jesus' third comparison. Deuteronomy 24:1-4 is the backdrop for these words. Three persons are in view: the husband, the wife, and the second husband. To control a practice already in the community (separation), Moses introduced divorce certificates. The practice of separation did not legally end a marriage so a wife sent away could not marry again since she was still the wife of her first husband. Polygamy was culturally approved for men but not women. Divorce freed the wife to marry again and the document proved her divorce. Once remarried, the wife could never return to her first husband. There were two benefits to these stipulations: women could legally remarry and both the divorce certificate and the prohibition against returning to the first husband cautioned against hasty divorces (Carson, *Matthew* 152).

The Pharisees of Jesus' day were divided on the question of what constituted just grounds for divorce. Some believed that Deuteronomy freed men to divorce at will, with very little reason or justification. According to Jesus, this made divorce little more than "a form of publicly sanctioned adultery" (Nolland 243). Others believed that marital infidelity was the only grounds for divorce (Blomberg 23).

Jesus' words not only offered further protection to the wife but defined more closely proper grounds for divorce and remarriage. Deuteronomy 24:1 accepted "uncleanness" (ESV "indecency"; Zerwick 13). At the least adultery was meant, and it is possible that it included something other than adultery since both pre-marital sex and adultery were capital offenses (Dt. 22:13-21; Lev. 20:10; Blomberg 23). For the first time, though, the people heard in Jesus' teaching that the first husband was guilty of multiple sins should he divorce his wife for improper reasons. They also heard that divorce is also unfaithfulness to one's spouse (Keener, *Matthew* 189) and does not keep one from committing adultery. Rather, divorce leads to adultery.

As in the previous "but I say to you" passages, Jesus now gives a clearer meaning of God's intent. God hates divorce (Mal. 2:16), so while there may be one innocent party in a divorce, there are never two. There is no "no fault divorce" in Scripture. While from a human standpoint divorce legally provides the option to remarry, from God's perspective divorce by itself does not free one to remarry. Only some form of "fornication" (Greek *pornia*, a broad word for sexual immorality) preceding the divorce does this. Such infidelity is a "rebellion against the very essence of the marriage bond" (Hendriksen 305), a destruction of "the unity between man and wife" (Hill 125). Unfaithfulness prior to marriage was probably included in this exception as well (Dt. 22:13-29). Joseph, Jesus' stepfather, grappled with this (1:18-19) when he first learned that Mary was with child.

Matthew's exception clause is unique to him. Neither Mark (10:11-12) nor Luke (16:18) include this in their records. For the supposed additional Pauline exception, see 1 Corinthians 7:15 and commentaries on that passage (e.g., Picirilli, *Corinthians*, 97-98)

Understood literally, though the instructions would be binding as well for a wife who sent her husband away (see Mk. 10:11-12), Jesus said that a husband can divorce his wife without sin if she has been sexually unfaithful to him. One assumes from Jesus' words that the innocent husband can remarry without fault since remarriage is always stated or assumed in passages dealing with divorce. There is no N.T. example of divorce and remarriage among the Jews. However, the Samaritan woman who had five husbands, as well as Herod and Herodias' divorces and marriage to each other (14:3-4), illustrate the need for Jesus' words (Jn. 4:18).

Jesus' comparison was between the hard hearts that forced Moses to permit divorce in the first place (Mt. 19:8) and those who loosened the restrictions of Moses even more. Hagner (*33A*:123-124) argues that the contrast is between Moses who permitted divorce and Jesus who did not (Mk. 10:9). However, it is the permanence of the marriage bond that lies behind verse 32 and Jesus' declaration that divorced people who remarry commit adultery (Rom. 7:2-3). According to Deuteronomy 24:4, remarriage after divorce is not a sinless action. Remarriage after divorce defiles (see Lev. 18:20 and Num. 5:13-14, 20 where this defilement is in the context of adultery). According to Jesus, remarriage after divorce is adultery. Jesus and Moses are together on this.

If the divorced wife was not guilty of sexual sin (the uncleanness of Dt. 24:1), then the divorce was groundless from God's perspective and her remarriage an act of adultery (Keener, *Background* 59). She and her new husband both were guilty of adultery. In other words, just giving a spouse a legal document that states a divorce has taken place does not negate a marriage in God's eyes. Interestingly, according to Jesus, the first husband has culpability as well because he has forced her into a situation where she had to remarry, perhaps for economic reasons (Gundry 90), loneliness (Gen. 2:18), or the sex drive (Bruner 1:229). (See 1 Timothy 5:11 where the sex drive can be an incentive to remarry.) Jesus, then, has mentioned four wrongs: the divorce, the creation of circumstances by the first husband that cause the divorcee to remarry, the remarriage of the divorcee, and the marriage of the second husband to the divorcee. See 19:8-9 where Jesus said the man who divorces his faithful wife is also guilty of hard-heartedness (Bruner 2:258) and of adultery when he remarries.

This plus other passages reveal Jesus' attitude toward marriage. First, Jesus approved of marriage. He taught that marriage is an act of God, for God joins couples in marriage (Mt. 19:6) and has since creation (Mt. 19:4-5). Also, Jesus showed His approval of marriage when He attended the wedding in Cana and provided necessary refreshments (Jn. 2:1-11). Second, Jesus protected marriage and the family. In this passage, He was especially interested in protecting the innocent spouse (Keener, *Matthew* 192). Third, Jesus did not view a couple who lived together without being married to be husband and wife (Jn. 4:18). In other words, marriage is more than sharing a domicile and having physical union. Fourth, an individual whose spouse has been unfaithful is free to divorce that person and remarry again, but only to a person who also is innocent of adultery.

What constitutes valid marriage according to human law has changed over the years (e.g., the form of the ceremony, the introduction of marriage licenses, and the redefining of legal relationships) and is still a matter of opinion—as the redefining of "marriage" by civil lawmakers shows. This writer understands that the following essentials constitute a valid marriage in God's eyes: (1) there must be one male and one female; (2) they separate themselves from all others for an exclusive husband and wife covenant relationship until death separates them (Gen. 2:24; Mal. 2:14-16; Rom. 7:2); (3) they have the approval of society for their marriage (today in North America this is given in the form of a Marriage License and a witnessed exchange of vows); (4) they consummate the marriage (the two shall be one flesh; Gen. 2:24; Mt. 19:4-5; Eph. 5:31); and (5) they have God's approval and pronouncement ("What God has joined together," Mt. 19:4-6). All five must be present before a man and woman are considered married in God's eyes. The divorce that allows for remarriage, according to Jesus, requires that the exclusive intimacy has been violated and that society grant a divorce.

The discussion on adultery in Matthew 5:27-30 has bearing on the present discussion on divorce and remarriage. The prohibition against adultery forbids divorce and remarriage by the party already guilty of adultery. The discussion on anger and reconciliation in verses 21-26 also speaks to this situation (Bruner 1:227). Sexual sins in marriage do not have to end in divorce. Forgiveness and reconciliation are possibilities for some couples.

Jesus addresses this matter more extensively in 19:1-12. See comment there. When one considers both passages together, it is hard to agree with Keener (*Background* 59) that this is another instance of hyperbole as in verses 29 and 30. The facts are clear enough from this short passage: Jesus wants His disciples to have lifelong marriages; Jesus wants His disciples to avoid sexual sins; and Jesus gives His disciples permission to remarry without sin but only when a spouse has been sexually unfaithful. While John's preaching is not in this context, Jesus' teaching on divorce and remarriage shows that John the Baptist was right to condemn Herod's marriage to Herodias (Mt. 4:12; 14:3-4).

Summary (5:31-32)

Jesus sided with the conservatives in this section. Divorce does not cancel marriage vows or automatically give one liberty to remarry. He stated that God honors divorce only when there has been unfaithfulness to the oneness principle. When unfaithfulness is present, the innocent party can divorce and remarry without sin. When unfaithfulness is not the grounds of divorce, remarriage is adultery. Both parties in the second marriage commit sin unless there was adultery in the first marriage. No one has a Scriptural right to walk away from a marriage without just cause. Marriage vows are until death (Rom. 7:2).

Application: Teaching and Preaching the Passage

Many people look to this passage for answers. The preacher and teacher must be careful to teach the truth with compassion toward those who are scarred and courage toward those who are not faithful to their vows. God hates divorce but not the divorced. This must be made clear. Adultery is pardonable. Both Testaments testify to this (2 Sam. 12:13; Jn. 8:11). While Jesus' strong position in favor of lifelong marriages must be taught, His forgiveness and healing grace to those whose lives are wrecked by sin must also be offered (Jn. 4:18, 29, 39; 8:11). Sexual immorality is condemned (1 Cor. 6:9; Gal. 5:19; 1 Tim. 1:10; Rev. 21:8) and the church cannot condone it (1 Cor. 5:6). However, forgiveness and restoration should be offered in a spirit of gentleness and spiritual alertness (Gal. 6:1-2).

Teaching and preaching this text will require the inclusion of other Scripture passages. One might include this passage in a message or series of messages that describes (1) the origin and original design of marriage (Gen. 2:21-25; Eph. 5:31); (2) the corruption that led to the legalization of divorce (Dt. 24:1-4); and (3) the permanence that is Christ's ideal for marriage in kingdom life (Mt. 5:31-32; Mt. 19:1-12).

d. Oaths and personal integrity (5:33-37)

33 Again, ye have heard that it hath been said by them of old time, Thou shalt not forswear thyself, but shalt perform unto the Lord thine oaths:
34 But I say unto you, Swear not at all; neither by heaven; for it is God's throne:
35 Nor by the earth; for it is his footstool: neither by Jerusalem; for it is the city of the great King.
36 Neither shalt thou swear by thy head, because thou canst not make one hair white or black.
37 But let your communication be, Yea, yea; Nay, nay: for whatsoever is more than these cometh of evil.

Honesty must characterize God's people (Eph. 4:25). This is Jesus' fourth comparison between common Jewish teaching (see v. 21 for comments on "them of old time") and His own interpretation of O.T. law. In this instance the Jews correctly understood O.T. teaching to forbid swearing falsely (Lev. 19:12; Num. 30:2; Dt. 23:21, 23; Zech. 8:16-17). Jesus was not quoting any specific O.T. passage. Rather, He was summarizing several passages that required that oaths be honored (Archer and Chirichigno 31). God did not command Israel to make oaths (Dt. 23:22) yet He permitted His people to use His name when they did (Dt. 6:13). He expected them to honor their promises just as He did when He swore to bless Abraham (Heb. 6:13-18).

Jesus said swearing should not be necessary for kingdom citizens. In fact, it seems He absolutely forbade it ("at all" v. 34). Straightforward, consistent honestly is enough (v. 37), a thought James (5:12) presented, possibly even quoting the very words of Jesus. To "swear by" is to promise solemnly, to bring in as a witness to the promise someone or something thought to be sacred or "an avenging deity" (Keener, *Matthew* 195). Some Jews thought that some oaths were more binding than others, depending on whom or what was included as a witness to the oath (Keener, *Background* 59; Wilkins 247). Jesus mentioned several possibilities. In reality, all things in heaven and on earth are God's (vv. 34-35), so no matter what one swears by, God is witness to the oath. The Great King (v. 35) is either God the Father or Jesus (Mt. 25:34; Carson, *Matthew* 154). He is the LORD according to Psalm 48:1-2 and the Anointed One according to Isaiah (Is. 9:6-7; 11:2, 9). Jesus denounced the idea of graduated witnesses to one's oaths when He later denounced the flawed thinking of the scribes and Pharisees (23:16-22). "Dismantling ... [this] whole lying structure" seemed to be the main goal of

Jesus (Bruner 1:239). Honesty makes such witnesses unnecessary.

Persons were not to swear by their own head either (v. 36). Hendriksen (308) understands this to mean, "May I lose my head—hence, may I lose my life—if what I am telling you is not the truth, or if I do not fulfill my promise." God controls length of life and even one's permanent hair color. Such a vow is no less binding than swearing by heaven, God's throne. He alone is in control, even of small things.

The latter part of verse 37 says that oaths suggest dishonesty and Satanic influence (Greek *ho ponēros,* "the evil one"). Satan is the father of all lies (Jn. 8:44). An honest person does not need to take an oath. Those who lack credibility do. Jesus, then, did not contradict the O.T. with these instructions (Dt. 6:13). He corrected an abuse. God never intended that His name be used to support a lie.

Was Jesus condemning all oaths? At first glance, it would seem so. However, the Apostle Paul under inspiration of the Holy Spirit called on God as his witness (Rom. 1:9; 2 Cor. 1:23, 11:10-11; Gal. 1:20; Phil. 1:8), so all oaths are not condemned. On the other hand, one cannot simply set aside Jesus' words. They are applicable and binding on today's church. If these words mean anything they surely mean that kingdom citizens must put away lying and speak only truth (Eph. 4:25) and so establish themselves as truthful so that oaths are unnecessary. Kingdom citizens do not hide lies in the skin of an oath. "Yes" must mean "Yes" and "No" must mean "No" (Jas. 5:12).

What about oath taking in courts, the military, and other political and government situations? Some who read these words of Jesus say even these types of oaths are forbidden and choose to "affirm" rather than "swear." Again, truth is the issue. Whether one affirms or swears an oath, kingdom citizens honor their word and do not search for an "out" based on a legal technicality. For a historical overview of interpretations, see Bruner 1:233-246.

Summary (5:33-37)

Once again, Jesus set Himself against an abuse of the day. The Jews had developed a system that allowed for some oaths to be broken depending on who or what was brought into the oath as witness or guarantor of the oath's intent. Jesus denounced this and called for straightforward honesty all the time. He did not condemn all oaths but He did condemn a lack of integrity that required oaths before one would be believed. Citizens of His kingdom are expected to be so honest that an oath would add nothing to support their intent.

Application: Teaching and Preaching the Passage

One can only speculate about how much attorney time and court time are spent over matters of honesty. Contracts that were signed in good faith and supposed honesty are later not honored. Sadly, the church is not exempt. For example, dishonesty has appeared in the church's financial matters, in ministerial ethics, and even with dealings between the church and the business community. Plagiarisms could be considered here as well.

The church needs to be regularly reminded that God's people are to put away every form of dishonesty (Eph. 4:25, 28). A sermon or lesson on integrity as taught in this passage is necessary in all ages of the church. One might develop a sermon or lesson as (1) the need for an oath: potential dishonesty; (2) the Witness to all oaths: God; and (3) the kingdom way: honesty that does not require an oath.

e. Revenge and meekness (5:38-42)

38 Ye have heard that it hath been said, An eye for an eye, and a tooth for a tooth:
39 But I say unto you, That ye resist not evil: but whosoever shall smite thee on thy right cheek, turn to him the other also.
40 And if any man will sue thee at the law, and take away thy coat, let him have *thy* cloak also.
41 And whosoever shall compel thee to go a mile, go with him twain.
42 Give to him that asketh thee, and from him that would borrow of thee turn not thou away.

This is Jesus' fifth comparison. These verses are quoted in the *Didache* (1:4-5), a Christian document that dates ca. A.D. 70-90. Their presence in this document demonstrates the early use of these teachings in the Christian community.

The law of retaliation (v. 38; Latin *lex talionis* "law of kind") is part of the Mosaic Law (Ex. 21:23-24; Lev. 24:17-22; Dt. 19:15-21). This law insured that the punishment fit the crime. The punishment must equal the crime in seriousness but not be excessive (an eye for an eye, not a life for an eye, etc.). The law was for community law and courts, not individual retribution (Dt. 19:15-21). Everyone was to be treated equally and fairly under this law (Lev. 24:22).

Jesus did not contradict this O.T. law (*contra* Carson, *Matthew* 155; Kalland 126). Rather, He restated its proper sphere of usage. Courts could use it to set judgment but individuals could not use it to justify personal revenge. He taught His followers not to be retaliatory or vengeful. This was not new, for Leviticus 19:17-18 also prohibited revenge.

"Evil" (v. 39) is probably the evil person who is motivated by the evil one himself (*contra* Hagner 33A:131, who understands "the evil deed," not an evil person). Jesus refers to Satan in this same way in v. 37 and again in the model prayer (6:13).

Jesus gave four areas of application: physical abuse, lawsuits, forced service, and loans. Jesus wants His followers to be passive in these instances. Was Jesus again using hyperbole? Surely. Keener (*Background* 60) says that Jesus' was emphasizing the value of relationships over material things. He might also have been emphasizing "the disciple's obligation to serve" (Wilkins 251). He might have been illustrating meekness as well (v. 5). A slap on the right cheek, i.e., a backhanded slap by a right-handed person (Gundry 94; v. 39) was a serious insult in Jesus' day and culture (Hagner 33A:131). Jesus forbade retaliation.

Was Jesus advocating passivism? Is it wrong for a Christian to protect his own life, home, or family members? Is it wrong for a nation to defend itself? Is it wrong for a Christian to bear arms as a peace officer or a soldier? No. Jesus' ethical demands in this sermon are for individuals in their day-to-day living, not for national defense, peace officers, or personal self-defense against criminals. See Romans 13:1-7. Sadly, peacekeeping is necessary in this world of "wars and rumors of wars" (Mt. 24:6-7). However, Jesus' words, "All they that take the sword shall perish with the sword" (Mt. 26:52) remind the kingdom citizen that the sword cuts both ways.

What of persecution? Should the disciple stay or place himself where he or she is most vulnerable to persecution? No (*contra* Hagner 33A:131). Unless specifically directed otherwise, believers should avoid persecution if possible (Mt. 10:23). See Paul's example in Acts 9:23-25; 17:10; 22:25 and Peter's example in Acts 12:17.

Nor did Jesus advocate submission to those who would exploit or abuse. If this instruction were taken literally, some disciples would be left stark naked (v. 40; Keener, *Matthew* 195; Mk. 14:51, 52) or at least embarrassingly clad with only a loincloth (Carson, *Matthew* 157). See John 18:23 and Acts 23:1-5 where Jesus and Paul's responses were not, "Hit me on the other cheek too." Jesus also taught, "If your brother sins against you, go and tell him his fault" (Greek *elegchō*, rebuke him, Mt. 18:15).

What, then, did Jesus mean? One must be careful not to set aside Jesus' words or make them fit one's own desired interpretation or situation (5:19). Kingdom citizens adjust their lives in obedience to the King's commands not the other way around. When Jesus required His followers to turn the other cheek, He called on them to work hard to live in peace and allow God to enact any necessary or appropriate vengeance (Dt. 32:35). Jesus did not set a limit for tolerating abuse nor establish a point where believers could begin hitting back (Keener, *Matthew* 197). In the face of insults, kingdom citizens do not retaliate (Barclay 1:191-192). Quoting Deuteronomy 32:35, Paul (Rom. 12:17-21) offered a running commentary on this portion of Jesus' instructions: do not take revenge, God will do that; as much as possible, live peaceably with everyone; treat your enemy with kindness: "Be not overcome of evil, but overcome evil with good," which is exactly what Jesus did (Mt. 26:67-68; 1 Pet. 2:23).

It is possible that this turning-the-other-cheek illustration is to be understood in a court context also. The application would mean that kingdom citizens are not to seek retaliation in a court. See Carson, *Matthew* 155-156, for a fuller discussion of this interpretation. See 1 Corinthians 6:1-8 for a N.T. application of this principle.

If someone sued for the inner garment (the coat or tunic, v. 40), Jesus said to give him the outer garment (cloak) as well. Mosaic Law forbade keeping the cloak of the poor, the outer garment, overnight (Ex. 22:25-27; Dt. 24:12-13), but no mention is made of suing for clothing. Most people in Palestine at this time wore two pieces of clothing, the inner garment, a long tunic worn next to the skin, and the outer garment, a robe or cloak (ISBE II:402). To be sued and lose one's clothing was extreme humiliation and to tolerate such without trying to get even was extreme passivity. See comments above on 5:25 for further statements about the kingdom citizen and courts.

Jesus next spoke of forced service by the military (v. 41). To be forced to carry a load against one's will and without remuneration was demeaning as well. The Roman military could force citizens to help carry military equipment for soldiers (Blomberg 26) as Simon was later compelled to carry Jesus' cross (Mt. 27:32; Mk. 15:21). Jesus told His followers to do twice what was originally demanded of them. The first they did because of the law. The second they did because of Christ (Bruner 1:255, 256).

Kingdom citizens are also to be helpful and open-handed to the needy (v. 42). God gives (v. 45) and so should His people (Wilkins 249). This teaching was not new. The O.T. writers emphasized this same attitude toward the needy (Dt. 15:7-11; Ps. 112:5; Prov. 14:21, 31; 19:17; 21:13; 28:27). Jesus and the Twelve practiced giving as well (Mt. 26:9-11; Jn. 13:29). This includes loans. Jesus' disciples also should loan to those who ask to borrow (v. 42). According to Luke (6:35) God will reward the generosity of those who give. Luke also records that Jesus stated that such liberality is a sure sign that one is a true son of God (Lk. 6:35).

As mentioned already, there is hyperbole in these instructions. However, Jesus made His point. Kingdom citizens must live differently. They must desire to live in peace. They must refuse to become vengeful (Rom. 12:19-21). They are givers. Jesus' instructions do not give lazy or undisciplined Christians the right to expect the church to give them support just because they have a need. Christians should help needy Christians (Gal. 6:10; Jas. 2:15, 1 Tim. 5:3-16), but the church should not encourage laziness by facilitating it (1 Thes. 4:11-12; 2 Thes. 3:6-15).

Summary (5:38-42)

Rather than being a people of revenge, kingdom people are peaceful, forgiving and generous. Using hyperbole, Jesus shocked His hearers with extreme examples. He was not assembling resistance fighters. He expected His followers to submit to inescapable persecution by turning the other cheek. He expected His followers to be forgiving, non-retaliatory, and generous even toward evil people. This becomes clearer in verses 43-48. See further comments there.

Application: Teaching and Preaching the Passage

Even the unchurched know about "turn the other cheek"; but perhaps few—even in the church—know its true meaning. A sermon or lesson on the true meaning of this principle could be developed around the intent of the law of retaliation (just and equal retribution) and Jesus' applications of this law (forgiveness and generosity in place of vengeance).

Kingdom citizens need to be reminded of Jesus' teaching forbidding revenge. "I don't get mad, I get even" and "I don't get even, I get ahead" are opposite the words of Jesus. The desire to get revenge expresses distrust in God's promise, "Vengeance is mine" (Dt. 32:35; Heb. 10:30), and gives opportunity for bitterness (Heb. 12:15). Jesus was not building a resistance movement. He was teaching forgiveness and not hostility.

"Turn the other cheek" is a principle that applies to more than a literal slap in the face. It applies to the whole of life. Jesus illustrated this with examples from everyday life. Kingdom citizens refrain from a vengeful response, whether physical, verbal, or legal. The ideas that the Christian has the right to hit back, that he can respond in kind to whatever is said to him, or that if he is sued he can automatically counter sue, are unChrist-like ideas. Kingdom citizens are for peaceful solutions. This does not mean that followers of Jesus are expected to volunteer for ill treatment or martyrdom or refuse to protect their families against criminals. It does mean that we are to search for peaceful solutions always.

Kingdom citizens are also to be givers. Though mistreated by evil people, they give good in return. Whether someone can legally force Christians to do something is not the issue with Jesus. Being generous is.

Kingdom citizens also give to the less fortunate. That this is part of kingdom life is clear from Matthew 6:2-4 and 25:31-46. Meeting the physical needs of the less fortunate is a habit Jesus wanted to instill in His followers. Linking this teaching with other Scriptures will make this a profitable lesson for God's people (e.g. Rom. 15:26; 1 Cor. 16:1-2; 2 Cor. 8-9; Gal. 2:10; Jas. 1:27).

f. Hate and love toward one's enemies (5:43-48)

43 Ye have heard that it hath been said, Thou shalt love thy neighbour, and hate thine enemy.
44 But I say unto you, Love your enemies, bless them that curse you, do good to them that hate you, and pray for them which despitefully use you, and persecute you;
45 That ye may be the children of your Father which is in heaven: for he maketh his sun to rise on the evil and on the good, and sendeth rain on the just and on the unjust.
46 For if ye love them which love you, what reward have ye? do not even the publicans the same?
47 And if ye salute your brethren only, what do ye more *than others*? do not even the publicans so?
48 Be ye therefore perfect, even as your Father which is in heaven is perfect.

This is Jesus' sixth and final comparison and is closely linked to the previous discussion about retaliation. The first part of the command comes from Leviticus 19:18 and is the second greatest commandment of the Law (Mt. 22:39). The words "hate thine enemy" as a command are not in the O.T. and might have been added by the rabbis; or, as some suggest, Jesus might have been referring to an oral interpretive tradition of some O.T. passages (Dt. 23:3-6, 25:17-19; Ps. 139:21; Blomberg 27; Archer and Chirichigno 31). "Hate thine enemy" appears to contradict Scripture that teaches kindness towards one's enemies (Ex. 23:4-5; Pr. 25:21-22) but seems in agreement with the Imprecatory Psalms (e.g., Ps. 58, 69, 109, 137:7-9, 139:19-22).

Jesus commanded His followers to love everyone, including their enemies. Love was foundational to the Mosaic Law and it is also foundational to the kingdom ethic (Mt. 22:34-40; Eph. 5:1-2). The enemies might be persecutors or anyone who is hostile (Nolland 264). His followers are to do better than those who act against them. They will not return hate for hate. They will respond to hatred with love and to cursing with blessing. They will do good (the meaning of love here, not the emotion; Hagner 33A:136) to those who hate them.

One way kingdom citizens will do good and show love for their enemies is by praying for them. These would be positive, not imprecatory, prayers for those who treat them wrongly. Such love and prayers identify individuals as God's children (v. 45). Jesus' example stands as the epitome of application of this principle: "Father, forgive them for they know not what they do" (Lk. 23:34), an attitude Stephen adopted as his own (Acts 7:60) and Peter passed on in his first letter (1 Pet. 2:19-24). Jesus' words are for all (plural "ye") of His followers.

Some early Matthew manuscripts do not include the words "bless them that curse you, do good to them that hate you." However, their presence in Luke's record (6:27-28) is undisputed and shows that these are indeed words of Jesus.

The role model for such love in action is God Himself (v. 45). God blesses everyone, even those who do not love Him in return. Everyone gets sunshine and rain. More specifically, God sends sunshine and rain. He is the named cause of weather (Hendriksen 314). This demonstrates God's innate goodness and His perfect love for all men, even the unrighteous. This is what theologians call natural revelation, and it testifies of God's existence and kindness (Acts 14:17; Rom. 1:20). God intends that His general blessings to everyone lead everyone to repentance (Rom. 2:4).

Jesus divides the world into two groups (v. 45): the good and just and the evil and unjust (a chiasm; Newman and Stine 158). Even though God blesses each evenly with the same weather, there is a clear distinction between the standing of each with God. God's children are to follow the example of their heavenly Father and bless everyone, whether evil or good.

Publicans were tax collectors. They worked for the Roman government and evidently had opportunity to charge more than necessary (Lk. 19:8; ISBE IV:742, 743). The Gospel writers linked them with "sinners" (Mt. 11:19; Mk. 2:15; Lk. 15:1), harlots (Mt. 21:31), and Gentiles (Mt. 18:17), which always cast them in a bad light. Jesus' reference to them here is derogatory as well, an interesting note in light of this Gospel writer's pre-conversion occupation (Mt. 9:9). By referring to the publicans as He did, Jesus placed them among the extremely unloved in society and by inference suggested that His hearers were no better than publicans if they showed love only to others in their own group. In contrast, kingdom citizens were to be like their heavenly Father, showing perfect love, love that Jesus explained was undeserved yet real and impartial.

Some old Greek manuscripts and versions have "Gentiles" (Greek *ethnikos;* pagans) instead of "publicans" in verse 47. These Gentiles are not simply foreigners in this instance but people who do not worship the true God (Grimm's 168; Mt. 6:7, 18:17; 3 Jn. 7). Jesus' point is the same either way. For a Jew to be likened to publicans or Gentiles was highly offensive.

In the Bible times, to salute or greet (Greek *aspazomai*, v. 47) was "more than a simple 'hello'" (Gundry 99). A greeting included the use of set phrases (Louw and Nida I:392; ISBE II:574) that spoke of the other person's well-being: "Peace be to this house!" (Mt. 10:12; Lk. 10:5); "Peace be unto you!" (Jn. 20:19, 21, 26). Jesus' followers are to greet even their persecutors with kindness. Otherwise, what difference has God made in their lives? True sons have their Father's traits (vv. 45, 48).

To be perfect as our heavenly Father is perfect is the goal Jesus placed before His followers (v. 48). The word "perfect" (Greek *teleios*) can mean mature and complete (Louw and Nida I:754; Blomberg 28). However, Louw and Nida (I:746) are more inclined to think that since the comparison is with God, it seems more likely that Jesus called for perfection "in the sense of not lacking any moral quality." He is perfect in all His ways. This is a strong and necessary theological statement. God is perfect. God wants His children to be perfect also.

Verse 48 is an appropriate conclusion to Jesus' final comparison. God does not hate the lost (Jn. 3:16). Neither should His children. This verse is also an appropriate conclusion to all six comparisons (Wilkins 254). To pursue God's perfection is the goal presented in both Testaments. These six examples (vv. 21-48) illustrate the perfect way of the Father. They show the righteousness that exceeds that of the scribes and Pharisees (v. 20; Blomberg 20). The true intent of the Law is in the words of Jesus.

Summary (5:43-48)

The last of Jesus' six comparisons between His teachings and the O.T. Law continued the subject discussed in verses 38-42, love for one's enemies. Kingdom citizens are not permitted to hate even their enemies. Their example is God. He treats His enemies with gracious gifts and He wants His people to follow His example. This undeserved grace from kingdom citizens sets them apart from those yet outside the kingdom. Such actions are a mark of real God-likeness.

Application: Teaching and Preaching the Passage

Rather than take revenge on one's enemies, in addition to trusting God to take care of any necessary revenge (vv. 38-42), Jesus wants His followers to act toward their enemies as God does toward those who hate and oppose Him. A message or lesson might be developed that explains these proper actions toward one's enemies: (1) Kingdom citizens are to show love in their action of kindness toward their enemies (v. 44); (2) Kingdom citizens are to pray for their enemies. (v. 44); (3) Kingdom citizens are to show in their actions that their love is real, God-like love. This love is: (a) a love that is impartial (v. 45); and (b) a love that has no boundary (vv. 46-48).

5. Life-habits of kingdom citizens (6:1—7:12)

In the previous sections, Jesus gave six comparisons between contemporary Jewish understanding of certain O.T. laws and His own (see the discussion on 5:21-48). In the next verses, Jesus gave examples of kingdom living in this world. Kingdom living begins in this world, a world that is by nature out of the kingdom.

a. Private benevolence (6:1-4)

1 Take heed that ye do not your alms before men, to be seen of

them: otherwise ye have no reward of your Father which is in heaven.
2 Therefore when thou doest *thine* alms, do not sound a trumpet before thee, as the hypocrites do in the synagogues and in the streets, that they may have glory of men. Verily I say unto you, They have their reward.
3 But when thou doest alms, let not thy left hand know what thy right hand doeth:
4 That thine alms may be in secret: and thy Father which seeth in secret himself shall reward thee openly.

Some modern translations follow some very old manuscripts that have "righteousness" instead of "alms" in verse one. This would make verse one a heading for the three acts of righteousness discussed in the following verses: almsgiving, prayer, and fasting. Also, in verse four, these same manuscripts do not have the words translated "himself" and "openly." "Himself" intensifies the idea of God personally rewarding the giver and "openly" places God's reward in antithetical contrast to the secret place (Metzger 14-15).

At any rate, kingdom citizens must guard against hypocritical attitudes in these actions: benevolent giving (vv. 1-4), prayer (5-15), and fasting (16-18). The key to each is to make sure God is the audience and not people. However, if one follows the KJV and later manuscripts, then verse one begins the discussion of almsgiving. Further, if one follows the manuscripts that do not have the word "openly," Metzger (14-15) is probably right that verse four should be understood to mean that God's reward is better than man's, rather than that a secret gift will be rewarded openly. This same contrast is repeated twice (vv. 6, 18).

The Mosaic Law included a command to give to the poor (Dt. 15:7-8, 11). Other O.T. passages assured givers that God would reward their generosity to the poor (Prov. 19:17; 22:9; 28:27). Jesus did not challenge these O.T. teachings but He did condemn giving alms for human credit or self-glory. Almsgiving is not to be for showy, public display ("in the synagogues or in the streets"). When almsgiving is done for the glory of the donor, God allows that to stand as the final reward. God will not reward charitable giving done for show or self-glory. For synagogue, see comments on 4:23.

On the other hand, God will reward (v. 4) almsgiving done secretly and for the proper reason. Jesus did not say how or when God rewards but He promises such rewards. Perhaps the judgment described in Matthew 25:31-45 or the one in 1 Corinthians 4:5 is in view.

"Blowing a trumpet" is "sarcastic hyperbole" (Gundry 102). According to Keener (*Background* 61) people did not literally blow trumpets when giving alms. However, some did let others know of their pious acts so they might as well have blown a trumpet. This Jesus condemned. Pious acts are to direct glory to God (Mt. 5:16). Instead, these hypocrites wanted the glory for themselves (Nolland 27).

A "hypocrite" (Greek *hupokritēs*) was a theatre actor, a pretender, a person who wore different masks for different roles (Wilkins 272). According to Jesus, all hypocrites were not professional actors. He used the word negatively to label and condemn the pretense of any who practiced pious actions in order to be seen of men rather than God (vv. 2, 5, 16). The pretense was that they were helping the needy when in reality they were trying to get attention for themselves (Gundry 102). Their hypocritical actions masked their selfish hearts.

Jesus taught that kingdom citizens would be givers (v. 2; "thou" is emphatic), something He taught His disciples by example (Jn. 13:29). Their giving would be private, absent of any trumpets. Their giving would be so private that the right hand would not know what the left hand was doing, a figure of speech that suggests that even the closest confidant would not know about these righteous acts of mercy (v. 3). Those who receive might not even know the donor's identity. Those who give might not know who will receive (Hill 133). Only God would be privy to this information, so the donor will receive God's reward, not man's. Later writers also commented on charitable giving (Heb. 13:16; Jas. 2:15).

Summary (6:1-4)

Jesus continued His teaching about how kingdom citizens would live. Even though they are citizens of the heavenly kingdom, they will still help address the needs of fallen man in the here and now. Benevolent giving will continue to characterize God's people. Such giving will be done as privately as possible as a service to God. No one needs to know about it except God who will then reward these actions in eternity (Hagner 33A:141; Keener, *Matthew* 209).

Application: Teaching and Preaching the Passage

A sermon or lesson might be developed simply on the "do's and don'ts" of almsgiving.

Do not announce your giving, i.e., do not put your giving on public display. Do give. Give privately. Give early, before being asked. Give without thought of human reward or glory. Give to please God and then wait for God to reward (Mt. 25:31-40).

One might also tie this instruction in with early church practice. Almsgiving was part of the early church setting (Acts 3:2-3, 10). God acknowledged almsgiving even by the unregenerate (Acts 10:2, 4, 31). Paul taught the churches to whom he ministered to give (1 Cor. 16:1-4; 2 Cor. 8-9; Rom. 15:25-28, 31; Acts 24:17). James taught that such giving can be an expression of real faith (Jas. 2:14-17). God always sees almsgiving (Mt. 6:4, 6, 18; Nolland 276).

b. Prayer (6:5-15)

5 And when thou prayest, thou shalt not be as the hypocrites *are*: for they love to pray standing in the synagogues and in the corners of the streets, that they may be seen of men. Verily I say unto you, They have their reward.
6 But thou, when thou prayest, enter into thy closet, and when thou hast shut thy door, pray to thy Father which is in secret; and thy Father which seeth in secret shall reward thee openly.
7 But when ye pray, use not vain repetitions, as the heathen *do*: for they think that they shall be heard for their much speaking.

8 Be not ye therefore like unto them: for your Father knoweth what things ye have need of, before ye ask him.
9 After this manner therefore pray ye: Our Father which art in heaven, Hallowed be thy name.
10 Thy kingdom come, Thy will be done in earth, as *it is* in heaven.
11 Give us this day our daily bread.
12 And forgive us our debts, as we forgive our debtors.
13 And lead us not into temptation, but deliver us from evil: For thine is the kingdom, and the power, and the glory, for ever. Amen.
14 For if ye forgive men their trespasses, your heavenly Father will also forgive you:
15 But if ye forgive not men their trespasses, neither will your Father forgive your trespasses.

In verse 5, Jesus turned His attention to the second of three acts of righteousness: namely, prayer and the proper attitude that must be present in prayer. Like those who gave for show (v. 2), these who prayed in a manner intended to attract men's praise would also receive no heavenly reward (v. 5). Place, not position, was the problem. Standing to pray was a normal position for prayer in N.T. Judaism (Gundry 103; Evans, *Matthew* 122; Mk. 11:25; Lk. 18:11). The synagogues and streets stood for highly visible and public places. Heavenly rewards go to those who follow Jesus' guidelines for prayer. First, as with giving (vv. 3-4), sincerity (Hendriksen 323) is necessary for personal prayers. Whether in public or private, the petitioner must approach God in sincerity.

The "closet" (Greek *tameion*) was a storeroom (Lk. 12:24) or a secret room (Grimm's 614). It was "a room in the interior of the house, normally without windows opening to the outside" (Louw and Nida I:85). In Luke 12:3, Jesus used this word to communicate the idea of complete privacy. Most people did not have individual, private quarters so this may have been the only room in the house with a door (Keener, *Background* 62; Wilkins 273). In such a place, there would be no reason for showiness. Secrecy facilitates sincerity. The door would be shut or perhaps even locked. The Greek (*kleiō*) can mean either (BAGD 434).

Jesus spoke of God's omnipresence when He stated that God is not limited to the synagogues or street corners. God is in the secret place and He is fully aware of what is said in that place (v. 6).

Jesus did not forbid praying so that others could hear (14:19; 15:36). He forbade public prayers for show and the hypocrisy masked by them. The early church practiced public prayers and the apostles commanded them (Acts 4:31, 16:25; 1 Tim. 2:1, 8). However, Jesus was clear about the place of private prayers in the lives of kingdom citizens. They must maintain a private prayer life if they want God's rewards.

See the discussion on 6:4 for the word "openly" (KJV).

Second, Jesus forbade mechanical, wordy prayers ("vain repetitions"; ESV, "empty phrases"), prayers that repeat the same words and phrases without thought. Jesus did not forbid intense praying that repeatedly asks God until He answers. He encouraged and practiced such prayers Himself (26:39-44; Lk. 18:1-8). Instead, Jesus denounced mechanical, rote praying that is mindless. The reason Jesus condemned such praying was that it is unnecessary and insulting. God is omniscient and He hears the prayer the first time (v. 8). Prayers do not inform God. Prayers request God's direct involvement and express reliance on Him (Wilkins 274). In contrast, *earnest* prayers, when repeated, show continual trust in God's awareness, ability, and desire to intervene. Praying with mind engaged pleases God. Such prayer honors God. By contrast, the heathen practiced such vain prayers (v. 7). These were Gentiles (Greek *ethnikos)* not just ethnically but in lifestyle (Carson, *Matthew* 166). They do not serve the God of Israel (see 5:45 and comments).

Third, Jesus gave a model prayer. Pray in this *manner*, He said, not this is *what* you pray for. He was not actually praying (cf. Jn. 17 for one of His prayers). This was an example of how kingdom citizens should pray in a manner pleasing to the Father. To avoid the hypocrisy seen in long prayers, Jesus gave this pattern (Hill 136).

Luke's account (11:1-4) differs from Matthew's somewhat. Luke's is the shorter of the two and the setting is different as well. Carson (*Matthew* 168) is probably right that Jesus taught this prayer on more than one occasion and Matthew and Luke are writing about two different occasions. There is evidence that this model prayer became a liturgical prayer in the last half of the first century (*Didache* 8:3; A.D. 70-90; McDonald and Porter 75), but this was not Jesus' intent. Gundry (104-106), however, believes that the "our" in "Our Father" makes this communal and Luke's, "When you pray, say," (Lk. 11:2) makes this recitative. Matthew's "manner" (v. 9) argues against Gundry's interpretation.

As a model prayer, some implications are these: (1) Kingdom people can pray this prayer. (2) Kingdom people are not commanded to say these words every time they pray. Indeed, even the "Lord's Prayer" can become "vain repetitions." (3) There is no special favor promised to those who pray this prayer. (4) As a model, it serves as a pattern and as such is a good guide for prayer and the items one should include in his or her prayers. It is short, simple, specific, and inclusive of both physical and spiritual needs. (5) Since this is a model Jesus recommended, one ignores it to his or her own detriment.

With "Our Father," Jesus began the model prayer with an assumption of familiarity and great privilege (Bruner 1:294). This speaks of at least four truths about God: God is personal and caring (as a father) as well as close and relational (our; Carson, *Matthew* 169). This "Father" is further qualified by contrast (Hagner 33A:147). He is (literally) "in the heavens." The petitioner recognizes God's place and position. He is above us, transcendent, not our equal in position or place. Prayer begins with the recognition that He is God and not any of us. This is why we pray to Him.

The model prayer includes seven specific requests (Evans, *Matthew* 124). The first three requests are presented in terms concerning God's glory: "your ... your ... your" (Carson, *Matthew* 168). The last four deal with man's need: "us ... us ... us ... us."

(1) Hallowed be your name (v. 9). This request refers to the respect all creatures should show the Lord's name. Christ's followers, especially, are to have an attitude of respect toward God

and they are to live in such a way as to show this. They must not rebel against His name or cause Him shame (2 Sam. 12:14; Rom. 2:23-24). They are to give Him reverence (sanctify, set apart as holy; Mal. 1:6). They need God's help to do this, which is the reason for this request.

(2) Let Your kingdom come (v. 10). "Let ... come" makes an urgent request (Greek imperative). Other examples of this use of the imperative are found in Matthew 14:30 ("Lord, save me!") and Matthew 17:15 ("Lord, have mercy on my son!"); and "give" (v. 11), "forgive" (v. 12), and "deliver" (v. 13). The idea is that Christ's followers are to pray urgently for the coming of the kingdom.

The kingdom Jesus spoke of is the Father's kingdom, referred to also in the Gospels as the kingdom of God and the kingdom of heaven. It is both now and future (see "kingdom" in the Introduction and comments on 3:2). Both aspects are included in this prayer. This prayer asks for more to join the kingdom now, in the present age, and for the consummation of the kingdom (Rev. 22:17, 20). The prayer is answered as people join the kingdom now and it will be answered in full at the consummation of the ages. Kingdom citizens, then, urgently pray for others to join them in the kingdom and they pray for the kingdom to come in its final, fullest, eternal sense.

(3) May your will be done on earth as [it is done] in heaven (v. 10). Exactly what is God's will? For the present order, it is at the least this Sermon on the Mount (Bruner 1:303; cf. 7:24-27). In the broadest sense, God's will is for everyone and everything in the universe to act in harmony with His purposes. This portion of the prayer assumes that God's will is not presently being done on this earth and is proof that the kingdom of heaven has not arrived in its fullest sense. However, as a legitimate prayer, Jesus taught at least six great truths with this request. First, our prayers to heaven (circumlocution for "God") change life on this earth. Second, God's goal for this earth is perfect obedience to His will ("on earth" stands for individuals and governments). Third, those who offer this petition should be living in submission to God's immediate and eternal will for themselves. If they are not, this prayer asks for God's help to bring them into conformity to His perfect will. Fourth, God's will will be done on earth as it is in heaven when His kingdom has fully come (Keener, *Background* 62; Evans, *Matthew* 124). Fifth, there is activity in heaven, in the spiritual world of God (Bruner 1:304). Sixth, God's will is being accomplished perfectly in heaven. Seventh, heaven is a place, not merely a state of existence.

(4) Give us today our daily bread (v. 11). The word translated "daily" (Greek *epiousios*) can mean either "daily" (Louw and Nida I:652), "sufficient," as in sufficient food (Grimm's 241; TDNT II:597-599); or "for the coming day." The latter would refer "in the morning to the same day and at night to the next" (Carson, *Matthew* 171). Commentators are divided. Some argue that "daily" is the intended understanding (Evans, *Matthew* 125; Nolland 290). Carson is convinced "for the coming day" is right. Hagner (33A:149-150) also argues that the word is best understood as "for the coming day," but he says "for the coming day" speaks of the coming messianic banquet. He admits, however, that Luke (11:3) does not understand this request to refer to the end times banquet.

The daily provision of manna (Ex. 16) and Deuteronomy 8:1-18 provide the background for this prayer. In the wilderness, Israel literally lived day to day and hand to mouth. Gone were the days of Egypt's excesses and variety of foods. God's daily provisions were to be a lesson to them of God's faithful, loving, and sufficient care. With this request, Jesus taught that His followers should depend on this same care.

Several conclusions can be drawn from Jesus' inclusion of this request. First, this Sermon on the Mount is for now, not a future kingdom dispensation (Nolland 289). Second, we need provisions. Third, we need provisions every day. Fourth, God knows that we have daily needs and He knows that they are ongoing and real because He created them. Fifth, God is the source of our provisions. Mankind is not self-sufficient. Sixth, we have the right to ask God our Creator to meet our created needs. Seventh, we can expect that normally, i.e., unless there are reasons for Him to do otherwise, God will supply our needs. Eighth, faith in God to meet our needs, both immediate and future, is at the heart of this prayer. Ninth, in terms of prioritizing, honoring God, kingdom matters, and obedience to God's will all take precedence over daily bread (see comments on Mt. 4:4). Some of these points Jesus made more plainly in verses 25-34 of this chapter.

(5) The fifth request asks for forgiveness: forgive us our debts as we forgive our debtors (v. 12). (Some manuscripts have "as we have forgiven our debtors.") Debts are sins as verses 14-15; 18:21, and Luke 11:4 show. The word "as" means that there is a direct correlation between our forgiveness of others and God's forgiveness of us. To forgive is to give up resentment or any desire or claim to exact punishment. Forgiveness begins with God. However, forgiveness from God requires a forgiving heart on our part (Mt. 5:24). A heart that is unwilling to forgive others will not receive forgiveness from God (vv. 14-15, 12:32, 18:21-35, Mk. 11:25; Lk. 6:37). Paul repeated this teaching but in reverse order (Walvoord 53). He instructed believers to forgive each other as God in Christ forgave them (Eph. 4:32; Col. 3:13).

The fact that Jesus spoke these words to kingdom citizens (see notes on 5:1; also comments concerning our Father, 6:9) means that confession and requests for forgiveness are part of the ongoing, normal prayers of believers (1 Jn. 1:9; 2:1). "Forgive us ... as we forgive" is not the prayer of sinners seeking salvation. It is the prayer of those already in the kingdom. This prayer also shows that believers do not attain sinless perfection in this life (1 Jn. 1:8) and so must regularly confess and forsake (1 Jn. 3:6, 9) sin in order to maintain fellowship with God (1 Jn. 1:6). Jesus' blood cleanses at conversion and throughout the believer's life as faithful confession is made.

(6) Lead us not into temptation, etc. (v. 13). The word "temptation" (Greek *peirasmos*) can mean to test, as in "put to the test," or to tempt as in to "tempt someone to sin" (BAGD 640). Clearly Jesus spoke of the first meaning, for God will never tempt believers to sin (Jas. 1:13; *contra* Walvoord 53). He will lead and allow His people to be tested (Gen. 3:1-7, 22:1; Job 1:12, 2:6; Mt. 4:1; Mk. 1:12; 1 Pet. 1:6-7; 4:12), but He will not Himself try to get His people to commit sin. See the comments on 4:1 where even Jesus was led into a rigorous test.

Though it may seem a possibility, this prayer does not contradict God's past actions of leading His people into testing (Gen. 22:1; Dt. 13:3). Keener (*Matthew* 225) recognizes the difficulty and suggests that the prayer is for protection and safe deliverance through temptation rather than avoidance of temptation. However, there is no reason to reject the apparent meaning of the text. In this request, Jesus taught that God has given His children the privilege of requesting that He not lead them into testing (Prov. 3:5-7). Jesus did not teach that all testing would be removed from our lives but rather that God would answer prayers that request an easier and safer route and, when necessary, deliverance from the test (1 Cor. 10:13).

The prayer, then, is, "Lead us not into testing," for we know that such tests are difficult and can result in sin. Evans (*Matthew* 125) and Hagner (33A:151) think that Jesus may even have had present age apostasy in mind (Mt. 24:9-10). Testings can have benefits (Jas. 1:2-3), but believers find in Jesus' words the wisdom of avoiding tests if possible (Mt. 26:41; Lk. 22:40, 46; 2 Pet. 2:9; Rev. 3:10).

(7) Deliver us from evil. "Evil" (v. 13) can be evil in general as in ethical wickedness, or the evil one, referring either to another human (5:39) or to Satan, depending on whether one understands the original adjective (Greek *ponēros*) to be neuter (evil) or masculine (the evil one; BAGD 690-691). This is probably masculine, speaking of a person rather than evil in general, and the person is most likely Satan (13:19; Hagner 33A:151-152; Carson, *Matthew* 174). He is the one who wants most to destroy God's kingdom citizens. One needs only to remember Adam and Eve's sin, Job's trials, and Jesus' temptations to realize the power and desire of this evil being. Kingdom citizens should include in their prayers a request that God deliver them from any Satanic presence, influence, design, or destruction (2 Cor. 2:11; 1 Thes. 2:18). Only God can give victory in our spiritual battles (Wilkins 280).

The concluding words "for thine is the kingdom," etc. are not included in many translations because they are not in many older manuscripts. However, the ancient *Didache* (8:2) contains a portion of the ending, "for thine is the power and the glory for ever and ever," which shows that this portion of the ending was early in church history. The words found in the KJV reflect 1 Chronicles 29:11-13: the Lord is worthy of all praise because the kingdom and all glory and power belong to Him. He can answer this prayer because with Him all power resides (Hendriksen 339).

For comments on verses 14 and 15, see above on verse 12 and later in this commentary on 18:21-35. Notice instead of "debts" (v. 12), Jesus used "trespasses" (Greek *paraptôma*), referring to sins, deviation from truth (Grimm's 485). The forgiving person has satisfied one of the conditions for receiving forgiveness from the Father (Nolland 294).

Summary (6:5-15)

God wants honest expression, not meaningless length or repetition in prayer. He especially rewards private prayer. There are no eternal rewards for prayers designed to be seen and heard by others. In order to illustrate what God wants, Jesus offered a model prayer. He gave seven examples of requests that kingdom citizens should pray. Jesus' model prayer addressed the sin of hypocrites (vv. 7-8) by demonstrating that effective prayers can be brief and nonrepetitious.

Application: Teaching and Preaching the Passage

Teachers and preachers who expound this passage might focus on improper and proper attitudes (showiness vss. private humility) in prayer. Matters that have divine approval for prayer might be considered (see the seven requests discussed above) as well. For example, one should not hesitate to pray regularly that God would meet his or her daily needs. One might deal with the essential nature of human forgiveness and its relationship to divine forgiveness (vv. 12, 14-15; 18:21-35).

Some lists are included in the commentary on these verses, above, that could serve as good bases for sermonic or lesson material. For example, the comments include lessons one might learn from the request in verse 11, "Give us today our daily bread." Finally, one might focus on the rightness of praying this prayer. Though it is a model, not a literal prayer, it is a perfect model from the lips of our Lord and one that can be prayed with great satisfaction and benefit.

c. Fasting (6:16-18)

16 Moreover when ye fast, be not, as the hypocrites, of a sad countenance: for they disfigure their faces, that they may appear unto men to fast. Verily I say unto you, They have their reward.

17 But thou, when thou fastest, anoint thine head, and wash thy face;

18 That thou appear not unto men to fast, but unto thy Father which is in secret: and thy Father, which seeth in secret, shall reward thee openly.

Private fasting is the third righteous action that Jesus used to illustrate kingdom piety. He discussed benevolent giving and prayer in the earlier verses of this chapter. Once again, Jesus focused on the need for sincerity and privacy. He rebuked the abuses of fasting but not the practice itself (Carson, *The Sermon* 72). According to Jesus, fasting is a private matter, a matter of the heart and a matter between the worshiper and God.

Biblical examples show that fasting could represent several things. For example, fasting could show mourning (Dan. 10:1, 2), seriousness in prayer (2 Chron. 20:1-4), humility (Is. 58:3), or deep concern (Neh. 1:4-11). It could also promote sensitivity to and intensify focus upon the spiritual work at hand (Acts 13:2-3; 14:23). In this Matthean passage, fasting speaks of a regular submission of physical needs and desires to those of the sanctified spirit. It is a form of self-discipline (1 Cor. 9:27) practiced to master the body and strengthen the spirit.

Fasting is one form of self-denial. In Bible times, it generally meant going without food "for a set time as a religious duty" (Louw and Nida I:541). On special fasts, some went without food and water (Moses, Ex. 34:28; Dt. 9:9, 18, 25; 10:10; Esther and Mordecai, Est. 4:16; Paul, Acts 9:9). Keener (*Matthew* 228) says that fasts typically included avoidance of water. Self-denial for religious reasons can be practiced in other ways as well. For example, in First Corinthians 7:5 Paul mentioned temporary, willful abstinence from the conjugal relations as a form of self-denial.

Unlike the O.T. law and evidently John the Baptist (Mt. 9:14; Mk. 2:18; Lk. 5:33), Jesus did not command fasting. After His temptation (4:1-11) and during His ministry (Mt. 9:14) neither He nor His disciples fasted. This was in obvious contrast to the practice of the day where the most religious fasted on Monday and Thursday of each week (Lk. 18:12; *Didache* 8:1). He did, however, say that they would fast after His departure (Mt. 9:15). It is clear, then, that Jesus expected that fasting would be part of kingdom life during the church age. This is why He said, "When you fast" (v. 16).

When fasting, kingdom citizens are to be upbeat, not sad (v. 16; Neh. 1:4; 2:22), and take care to look like they are not fasting. The word translated "sad countenance" (Greek *skuthrōpos*) is used only here and in Luke 24:17 in the N.T. and denotes having "a sad, gloomy or sullen look" (BAGD 758). According to Gundry (111), "Ancient Jews did not wash their faces and put oil on their heads daily for hygienic and cosmetic reasons. They reserved these practices for joyous occasions." He suggests that those fasting should mask their fast by looking like they are going to a "joyous occasion." Bruner (1:318) says the exact opposite, i.e., that the Jews washed their faces and anointed their heads for joyful occasions and for personal hygiene. Nolland (295) sides with Bruner. He writes, "Jews practiced washing both for ritual and hygienic reasons." Second Samuel 12:20 seems to support that there was hygienic washing and Daniel 10:3 that there was hygienic anointing, but neither passage says anything about it being a daily habit.

This much is certain: Jesus meant that the person must hide any sign of fasting so only God would know. He probably meant for His followers to look normal (Newman and Stine 181; Hill 141) and take care to make sure no one sees signs of a fast in progress (Hagner 33A:154). Intentional disfigurement (dirty faces or unkempt hair) or sad looks to attract attention are not indicators of piety and they remove any reward a person might otherwise receive from God (Nolland 295; see comments on 6:2, 5).

True fasting is more than going without food. God wants the private fast to translate into a humble attitude and positive actions (Is. 58:3-12). The hypocrites of Jesus' day had not taken on the true meaning of a fast and its sign of serious devotion to spiritual matters. As with benevolent giving (vv. 1-4) and prayer (vv. 5-13), sincerity and privacy are Jesus' emphases in this matter of fasting.

See the discussion on 6:4 for "reward" and the word "openly."

Summary
(6:16-18)

In these verses, Jesus taught kingdom citizens the correct way to fast. Attitude and action are both important. Fasting is to be done in secret as part of one's private worship of God. Those who fast are to guard against any outward signs of fasting.

Application: Teaching and Preaching the Passage

Many Jews in N.T. times were legalists. Their spiritual disciplines became their preferred means of obtaining favor with God (Lk. 18:9-14). The N.T. book of Galatians (3:1-14) sets the believer in Jesus free from such legalistic thought by showing that God's favor is not earned. It is a gift from God to all who trust in His Son for salvation. Also, Colossians 2:16-23 shows that the Jewish fasts are not carried over into the church.

Jesus' warnings, however, were not about legalism but sham. Christians are just as prone to charades as hypocritical Jews were. As Carson (*The Sermon* 73) cautioned, we must be careful that our righteous deeds are not done "to be seen by men" for their glory, but for God. Our righteous acts should express our worship to God, not be ways to get others to worship us.

This does not mean that spiritual disciplines are unimportant for the kingdom citizen. Spiritual disciplines, i.e., practices that enhance and strengthen one's spiritual nature, such as almsgiving (6:2-4), prayer (6:5-15), and fasting (6:16-18), are still worthy practices for God's children. Indeed one must wonder why Jesus taught about these virtues if He did not intend that all of His followers, not just the spiritually elite (Wilkins 287), practice them. The church needs to revive these activities, howbeit not because of a rule but because of a heart that desires closer fellowship with the Lord.

The Scriptures are filled with examples of men and women who set aside personal needs and desires in order to have the blessings of God. Sermons and lessons can be developed that examine the spiritual disciplines of our spiritual ancestors. Answering who, what, why, and when is a simple, yet rich way to consider occasions of prayer, fasting, and other spiritual disciplines practiced in Bible times. One might also consider the results of such spiritual practices and wonder if their absence might be one reason the contemporary church is anemic.

d. Eternal investments (6:19-24)

19 Lay not up for yourselves treasures upon earth, where moth and rust doth corrupt, and where thieves break through and steal:
20 But lay up for yourselves treasures in heaven, where neither moth nor rust doth corrupt, and where thieves do not break through nor steal:
21 For where your treasure is, there will your heart be also.
22 The light of the body is the eye: if therefore thine eye be single, thy whole body shall be full of light.
23 But if thine eye be evil, thy whole body shall be full of darkness. If therefore the light that is in thee be darkness, how great *is* that darkness!
24 No man can serve two masters: for either he will hate the one, and love the other; or else he will hold to the one, and despise the other. Ye cannot serve God and mammon.

After discussing the spiritual disciplines of almsgiving, prayer, and fasting, Jesus discussed the personal wealth of kingdom citizens. Possessions are not in and of themselves evil. The Bible repeatedly teaches that wealth comes from God (Abraham, Gen. 24:35; King David, 1 Chr. 29:12; Solomon, 2 Chr. 1:12). The Bible teaches also that the wise, those who live by God's directives, have some planned reserves (Prov. 6:6-8; 21:20). However, one can abuse wealth as easily as religious activities like almsgiving, prayer, and fasting.

Jesus began this portion of His lesson with a negative command that literally translated says, "Do not be treasuring up treasures, etc." (v. 19; Louw and Nida I:621). This is a life habit, an ongoing action. The reason one should not horde wealth is its transitory nature caused by earth's destructive forces such as moths, rust, and thieves.

Nice clothing in Bible times was considered treasure (Josh. 7:21; 2 Kg. 5:22, 23; Zech. 14:14) even as gold and silver were. Though there were linen garments, clothing was made mainly of wool, and moths would lay eggs in those garments. The larvae destroyed the garments "as they [fed] on their fabric" (ISBE III:426). In Scripture moths represented decay and destruction (Is. 51:8; Lk. 12:33; Jas. 5:2).

"Break through" (Greek *deoruss*ō) suggests digging or breaking through a wall or barrier, implying a clay or brick wall of a house (Louw and Nida I:227; Lk. 12:39). This would make sense in light of first century A.D. home construction. Thieves could dig through the outside wall of a home and enter, steal, and leave undetected. Jesus later spoke of this type of home burglary to illustrate the need to be ready for His return (24:43).

Some commentators (Evans, *Matthew* 128; Gundry 112; ESV margin) understand the word translated "rust" (Greek *brōsis*) to refer to worms. The word literally denotes the eating of solid food and it can refer to an insect (LXX Mal. 3:11; Louw and Nida I:28, 240). Clothing would probably again be the treasure in view if this were the meaning. Nolland (298) thinks "rust" is most likely what Jesus meant. Otherwise, Jesus' comments would be limited to textiles. Barclay (1:276) thinks that Jesus was probably referring to grain storage buildings and the worms, rats, and mice that can eat and pollute them. If Barclay is right, "worms" stand for vermin in general.

Regardless, Jesus' point is clear. Rather than keeping wealth so long that is becomes worthless, Jesus commanded kingdom citizens to be laying up treasures (also "treasuring up treasures") in heaven where it cannot decrease in value or be stolen (v. 20). He did not explain in this Sermon specifically how one does this, only that it can be done. He later told the rich young man (Mt. 19:21) that almsgiving is one way to lay up treasures in heaven. Paul later said the same thing (1 Tim. 6:18-19). Heaven is that eternal spirit-world where God dwells in all His glory. It is the opposite of this earth and is the destiny and hope of all kingdom citizens. Heaven is the present experience of all believers who have died (2 Cor. 5:8). Where one places his or her wealth shows whether one lives for this earth or for the heavenly home (Phil. 1:27; 3:20).

Though Jesus did not specifically state how to lay up treasures in heaven, He did explain why: loyalty and devotion follow treasure (v. 21; Lk. 12:34). Values reflect the heart, that part of the person that reveals itself in actions and attitudes (Mt. 12:34-35; 15:19; Mk. 7:21-22; Lk. 6:45). What one treasures, and where those treasures are, are true indicators of one's heart. In other words, we will give ourselves to what we consider valuable (Newman and Stine 186). Jesus' words assume everyone will have some treasure. Kingdom citizens must be sure to have a heart for heaven and to invest their treasures in heaven's kingdom.

To illustrate, Jesus next compared one's focus on treasures to natural eyesight (vv. 22-23). The eye is light for the whole body. If the eye is "single"—that is, healthy (Greek *haplous*; Louw and Nida I:268)—in the sense that "there is nothing complicated or confused" (Grimm's 57; no double image, Gundry 113), the whole body has light. If the eye is "evil" (Greek *ponēros*)—that is, bad (in a physical sense diseased or blind; in an ethical sense, evil; Grimm's 530), the whole body is in darkness. Understood metaphorically, then, to live focused on this earth's treasures is blindness. It is like walking in darkness. To live focused on heaven, i.e., on God, is like having perfect eyesight (Lk. 11:34-36). This illustration is especially poignant in Jesus' first century context where there were no eyeglasses, contact lenses, or corrective eye surgeries.

Some commentators understand verses 22 and 23 differently. Hill (142) and Carson (*The Sermon* 79-80) think "single" refers to undivided loyalty. Barclay (1:283) and Hagner (33A:158) on the other hand believe the word translated "single" should be understood to mean "generous" since the adverbial form of this word means "generously" in James 1:5 and Romans 12:8. Luke 12:33 supports this understanding. See also Matthew 20:15, where the "evil eye" might mean "greedy" (Newman and Stine 187; Hagner 33A:158).

While it is true that an evil eye might manifest itself in withholding from the poor, one should not limit Jesus' words to this one application. Giving to the poor is one way (Mt. 19:21; 1 Tim. 6:17-19) but not the only way to lay up treasures in heaven. One might, for example, give to support kingdom growth and sustain kingdom efforts after one has gone on to be with the Lord through such means as endowments, foundations, wills, and estate planning that support church planting, world evangelism, local evangelism, and many other worthy ministries.

Jesus further illustrated the decision everyone has to make about the use of personal wealth by comparing a person and his or her wealth to a servant (Greek *doulos,* a slave, not an employee) and his master (v. 24; Lk. 16:13). "Hold to" (Greek *antechomai*) means "to join with and to maintain loyalty to," Louw and Nida I:449). Just as a servant cannot give such wholehearted devotion to two masters at the same time, so no person can give wholehearted devotion to both God and money at the same time. The idiomatic use of hate and love is not to be understood absolutely (compare Lk. 14:26 and Mk. 7:9-13) but rather as emphasizing by contrast how strongly Jesus' disciples are to be committed to Him (Carson, *The Sermon* 80; Hagner 33A:159). Compare this with 10:37. If one looks at this from the slave owner's perspective (Nolland 303), God is not interested in a servant with divided loyalty (Ex. 20:3).

Mammon (v. 24) is a (transliterated) Aramaic word that means money, wealth, property, or possessions, i.e., property in general (Louw and Nida I: 562; Newman and Stine 191). Thus, it is acceptable to translate, "You cannot serve God and money." Jesus is probably personifying wealth as a false god (Hagner 33A:159).

Jesus went from the theoretical to the real in the final sentence in verse 24. He no longer speaks of "no man" in general. Instead, He directly addresses His audience: "*You* cannot serve God and [the god of] wealth." Whoever has money as his or her master does not have God as his or her god. See 19:16-22.

Summary (6:19-24)

Wealth is an important part of life but it must be properly managed. Proper management means personal wealth must be put to proper use. God condemns hoarding wealth but rewards laying up treasures in heaven. Proper management also means keeping wealth the servant. One way to lay up treasures in heaven is to share personal wealth with the needy.

Application: Teaching and Preaching the Passage

A sermon or lesson might be developed around the three contrasts in this passage: two treasures (vv. 19-20), two eyes (vv. 22-23), and two masters (v. 24; Wilkins 295).

This passage teaches that giving is an integral part of being a citizen of heaven. Many Christians understand that the N.T. teaches the giving of tithes and offerings through the local church. This passage, along with 6:1-4, 1 Timothy 6:9-10, 6:17-19, and Ephesians 5:3-5, could be used to teach a lesson on individual and local church systematic giving to the poor.

One might also organize one's thoughts on the subject of "The Stewardship of Earthly Treasures" or "The ABC's of Good Stewardship." (1) Avoid the money moths (v. 19); (2) Bank your wealth for the long-term (vv. 20-21); (3) Care for your eyesight, i.e., safeguard yourself against unhealthy desire (vv. 22-23); and (4) Do not serve but rather have dominion over your wealth (v. 24).

e. Possessions and faith (6:25-34)

25 Therefore I say unto you, Take no thought for your life, what ye shall eat, or what ye shall drink; nor yet for your body, what ye shall put on. Is not the life more than meat, and the body than raiment?

26 Behold the fowls of the air: for they sow not, neither do they reap, nor gather into barns; yet your heavenly Father feedeth them. Are ye not much better than they?

27 Which of you by taking thought can add one cubit unto his stature?

28 And why take ye thought for raiment? Consider the lilies of the field, how they grow; they toil not, neither do they spin:

29 And yet I say unto you, That even Solomon in all his glory was not arrayed like one of these.

30 Wherefore, if God so clothe the grass of the field, which to day is, and to morrow is cast into the oven, *shall he* not much more *clothe* you, O ye of little faith?

31 Therefore take no thought, saying, What shall we eat? or, What shall we drink? or, Wherewithal shall we be clothed?

32 (For after all these things do the Gentiles seek:) for your heav-

enly Father knoweth that ye have need of all these things.
33 But seek ye first the kingdom of God, and his righteousness; and all these things shall be added unto you.
34 Take therefore no thought for the morrow: for the morrow shall take thought for the things of itself. Sufficient unto the day *is* the evil thereof.

"Therefore" (v. 25) refers to the truth expressed in verses 19-24 (Hagner 33A:163). One can be devoted to only one of two masters, in this instance either God or mammon (v. 24). Being devoted to God instead of wealth (vv. 19-24) raises some practical questions. How are kingdom citizens supposed to eat? How are kingdom citizens supposed to get clothes? Heaven is future and another mode of existence. Earth is now and life on this earth requires nourishment and warmth.

Jesus' audience was concerned about these things. At least four (4:18-22) had been told to leave their only means of income and accompany Jesus in His ministry travels—and these were married men (1 Cor. 9:5). According to Keener (*Background* 63), most people of that time would have had only the "basic necessities: food, clothing, and shelter." There would have been no savings for an extended Sabbatical while they did kingdom work.

Jesus' instructions were forthright: "take no thought" means do not worry or be anxious about food, drink, or clothes (v. 25; Greek present imperative can mean "stop worrying"). In verses 19-24 Jesus insisted that His followers not seek earthly wealth and in verses 25-34 He insisted that they not "value possessions enough that they worry about them" either (Keener, *Matthew* 228). The essence of life is more than the nourishment and warmth that are essential to survival. This agrees with what Jesus told Satan during the temptation (4:4, "Man shall not live by bread alone, etc.") and closely parallels God's provision for Israel in the wilderness (Dt. 8:2-4). Jesus did not forbid working for food or wise planning (Barclay 1:295). Rather He forbade worry (Phil. 4:6; 1 Pet. 5:7).

"Life" (v. 25) translates the word that normally denotes the soul (Greek *psuchē*). It is used alongside "body" in this verse and does not refer in this instance to the "eternal part in man, but ... his entire being" (Newman and Stine 191-192). It is what we mean by being "alive" (Louw and Nida I:162).

Jesus gave such instructions because the Father looks after all of His creation. His words were both a command and a comfort (Bruner 1:329). He referred first to birds as an illustration of God's care. Perhaps pointing to some birds (v. 26), Jesus reminded His audience that birds do not sow, harvest, or store food and yet they eat because the Father feeds them. God continually (Greek present tense) and actively (Greek active voice) feeds the birds. They are part of His providential care. Speaking rhetorically, Jesus made His point: humans are more valuable than birds and if God cares for them He cares for us as well (v. 26). Human value is rooted in mankind's origin and divine image (Gen. 1:26-27, 9:6). See 10:31 and 12:12.

Worry yields no positive benefit (v. 27). The last part of verse 27 can be understood in either of two ways. First, as in the KJV, Jesus might have meant that people cannot worry themselves taller (one cubit equals approximately a foot and a half). Second, He might have metaphorically meant (as in the ESV and NIV), "And which of you by being anxious can add a single hour to his span of life?" See Psalms 39:5 for this same idea. This understanding would mean that no one lives longer because he worries about dying. Though the second option is probably the better understanding in light of the context, which deals with survival not growing taller (Evans, *Matthew* 133; Gundry 117; Hagner 33A:164), either understanding yields the same results: worry is powerless to make a positive contribution to life. Worry does not put food on the table. God does.

Jesus continued to drive home His point. Of lesser value than birds is the grass of the field that people burned for fuel in their small domestic ovens (ISBE III:622; v. 30); yet God dresses the field with beauty that exceeds even the best efforts of Israel's most wealthy king, King Solomon, to attire himself (v. 29; Newman and Stine 195; Carson, *Matthew* 181). Jesus' reference to Solomon speaks of His familiarity with Solomon and of Solomon's extravagance. The O.T. Scriptures are silent about the specifics of Solomon's clothes but one can conclude from the mention of his servants' clothing, the gifts of clothing he received, and his opulent wealth, that he dressed for beauty and glory (1 Kg. 10:5, 7, 20, 23, 27).

The lilies of the field—there were probably many visible in this outdoor setting—grow to adorn the field but not through their own effort. God beautifies the lilies (v. 29) and then places them in the field to beautify the field (v.30). This should encourage faith in God's care for His people. If God will clothe lilies and grass, He will surely clothe man, the ruler of God's earthly creatures (Ps. 8:3-8).

Jesus mentioned that the lilies do not "spin" (v. 28) their own beauty. He was referring to the time-consuming, spinning process that twisted plant fibers or animal hair into thread. The thread was then woven into cloth. It is probable that the women each had spindles with them and were spinning thread even as Jesus was teaching, for this was apparently their habit anytime their hands were free (ISBE IV:597-599). According to the source just referenced, thread for one garment could require as much as two hundred hours of spinning time. Then the thread would have to be woven and the garment made. This does not include the many hours required to shear, wash, comb, card, and dye the wool or ret, clean, comb, and dye plants for linen. The construction record of the O.T. wilderness tabernacle shows that thread making in this manner had a long history and skill levels varied (Ex. 35:25-35). For a fuller description of this spinning process, consult a Bible encyclopedia.

The heart of the matter is this: worriers are people of little faith (v. 30; 8:26; 14:31; 16:8; 17:20). Worriers are not trusting in God. God does not intend that His people worry about personal survival. He intends that people trust Him to supply their needs ("Will he not much more clothe you?").

Jesus gave some concluding comments to His instructions. (1) Do not worry about food or clothes (v. 31) for two reasons. First, the desire for things fuels the pursuits of the ungodly, the Gentiles (v. 32). These people have only this world. It is all they know. God's people, on the other hand, are different.

They are to have different pursuits (v. 33). Second, our Heavenly Father knows what we need. He knows "all" of our needs (v. 32). Hunger is a created need (Gen. 1:29) and God made the first set of real clothes (Gen. 3:21). Worry suggests that God is out of touch with His creation and does not know what we need or care about our needs. Nothing could be further from the truth.

(2) In contrast to those who worry and in contrast to the Gentiles who seek the things of this world, kingdom citizens are to continually "seek" (v. 33; Greek present imperative) the kingdom first. They are to order their lives in such a way that God's kingdom and His righteousness are their first and primary concern. This teaching was countercultural in Jesus' day and it remains so today in our consumerist society (Bruner 1:333); yet, this is what Jesus called His disciples, all of them, to do.

"His righteousness" refers to right living, as God requires it (Carson, *Matthew* 182; Nolland 315). Compare with 5:6. Examples of right living were what Jesus presented and required in this sermon (5:10, 20). Practical righteousness, righteousness that grows out of a right standing before God, is the focus of this sermon.

Jesus did not deal with apparent exceptions to the care He described here, although we know there have been many. Paul plainly stated that he was often hungry (1 Cor. 4:11; 2 Cor. 11:27; Phil. 4:12), and one can safely assume that his traveling companions experienced the same shortages. The hungry in our present world, affecting even Christians in some cases, is an apparent contradiction of Jesus' words as well. Animals too have died because of severe conditions, including drought and winter storms.

What answer can one give to these apparent contradictions? I suggest five broad statements: First, Jesus was not teaching that there would *never* be any hunger. This is clear from Matthew 25:35, 42. As a general rule, God provides the daily needs of His creatures (see comments on 6:11), but there are exceptions. Second, for reasons unknown to mankind, God sometimes permits human suffering through hunger (Gen. 41; Acts 11:28). We can only acknowledge His sovereignty at these times. Third, Jesus was not saying that some of earth's creatures live without problems. Even the sparrows fall (10:29), whether from hunger or some disease. Fourth, God's people who have food and clothes need to live by Jesus' teachings and care about and share with those who are without (Bruner 1:330). Sometimes benevolent giving is God's way to feed the hungry (Prov. 21:13; Mt. 25:35; Acts 11:29; Phil. 4:12-19). Fifth, sometimes hunger is the fault of man. Some of these faults are evil and result from selfish government officials, poor treatment of environment and natural resources in ways like clear cutting trees (Gen. 1:28-29; Dt. 20:19), laziness, poor planning, or the sins of the parents—to name a few.

Do Jesus' words, then, mean anything? Yes. They tell His followers to trust the Father's wise and providential care. Do not worry. Kingdom citizens who follow God's directives for using this world's wealth can expect that the Father will faithfully meet their needs unless He has a special plan for them. In such instances special grace will accompany the apparently unmet needs (Job 2:10; Mt. 4:1-2; 2 Cor. 12:9-10).

(3) Jesus' final comment in this section is this: take life one day at a time (v. 34). Each day has enough trouble of its own. There is no reason to worry about tomorrow. Jesus was not promoting laziness or poverty. Birds work. They just do not worry. Jesus was preaching priorities and trust. Put God's kingdom first. Trust Him to supply all needs. Jesus taught that kingdom citizens are to ask God for their daily needs (Mt. 6:11). Other Scriptures complement Jesus' teaching. They teach that God gives wealth and the strength to add to one's wealth (Dt. 8:11-18), that God's people ought to have a strong work ethic (1 Thes. 5:14; 2 Thes. 3:6-12), that the wise store food for the months when there is no harvest (Prov. 6:6-11), and that the wise save some of their earnings (Prov. 21:20). In this sermon, Jesus taught that faith in the Father's care is the essential ingredient in everyone's garden, pantry, and financial plans.

Summary (6:25-34)

God does not want His children primarily focused on the day-to-day needs of earthly life. He promises personally to care for these needs so that His children can concentrate on kingdom matters. God daily demonstrates His care of His creation by feeding the birds and growing flowers in the grass. These actions should serve as reminders and faith builders for God's children that He will meet their daily needs as well. Worry has no rightful place in the life of the Father's children. Jesus' words are a call to trust God. Do not depend on self. Work but do not worry.

Application: Teaching and Preaching the Passage

God's people constantly need to be reminded that earthly choices have eternal consequences. These verses apply this truth to matters of personal wealth. Resources can be spent on this world or laid up for the kingdom of God. Each individual must decide where to use his wealth and how he or she will prioritize this segment of his life. Do we meet our earthly financial goals first and then serve God with what time and energy we have left? Do we direct our children to make a living first or to live for Christ first?

A sermon or lesson might be developed around the following truths: (1) Life is more than earthly wealth (v. 25). (2) Our Heavenly Father cares for all of His creatures. God feeds animals, and since human life is more valuable than animal life, God will feed humans as well (v. 26). (3) With the bird and flower illustrations, Jesus called for an immediate and ongoing trust in God's care for daily needs (Wilkins 297; vv. 27-32). (4) Worry makes no positive contribution to satisfying need (v. 27). (5) Kingdom citizens seek God first (v. 33). (6) Faith knows that God is in control of tomorrow even as He is of today (v. 34).

f. Honest judgment (7:1-5)

1 Judge not, that ye be not judged.
2 For with what judgment ye judge, ye shall be judged: and with what measure ye mete, it shall be measured to you again.
3 And why beholdest thou the mote that is in thy brother's eye, but considerest not the beam that is in thine own eye?

4 Or how wilt thou say to thy brother, Let me pull out the mote out of thine eye; and, behold, a beam *is* in thine own eye?
5 Thou hypocrite, first cast out the beam out of thine own eye; and then shalt thou see clearly to cast out the mote out of thy brother's eye.

This chapter contains Jesus' final instructions in His Sermon on the Mount. The outline for Matthew shows that this section continues Jesus' teachings about various life habits of kingdom citizens. In the previous chapter, He discussed almsgiving, prayer, fasting, laying up treasures in heaven, and faith in God's providential care. In this section, He denounced hypocritical and hypercritical judgments.

An imperative begins this discussion, literally, "Do not be judging (Greek present imperative). Keener (*Background* 64) and Evans (*Matthew* 134) suggest that verse 1 was a common saying at that time. Grammatically this prohibition may infer that what is already being done must cease. Jesus did not say that kingdom citizens are forbidden to form an opinion or to condemn the sinful actions or character of others. Neither did Jesus say that His followers never have a responsibility to judge (Nolland 317-318; Carson, *The Sermon* 98-99). The whole of Scripture simply will not bear out such an interpretation. See verses 15-20 in this chapter, Paul's judgment of those preaching a false gospel (Gal. 1:8; 5:12), Paul's denunciation of Peter (Gal. 2:11), and John's call for all believers to be discerning (1 Jn. 4:1). Also, 1 Corinthians 5:12-13 and 6:1-8 call for judgment by Christians. What Jesus condemned was judgment that is hypercritical and condemnatory. This kind of judgment yields no positive outcome and is opposite the fifth beatitude (5:7) and the spirit of "forgive ... as we have been forgiven" in the Lord's Prayer (6:12; Wilkins 308; Bruner 1:337). This kind of judgment also puts one in the place of God, which Scriptures condemn (Rom. 14:10-13; Carson, *Matthew* 183).

According to Jesus, one should not be judging others because another will judge that one in return. Most commentaries assume that Jesus was speaking of God (Greek passive, unnamed agent) who will do the retributive judging (Newman and Stine 201; Keener, *Matthew* 240). Hill (146) is one of a few who thinks it could be other people returning judgment. If God is the judge, the final judgment is probably in view (Gundry 120; Hagner 33A:169) and this warning has serious implications. Gundry (121) believes such self-righteous judging proves that the profession of being a kingdom citizen is a false profession and that this is the reason for his eternal punishment. Perhaps, but not necessarily.

The second reason Jesus gave for not judging is that God will use the same measure or standard used by the one judging. In other words, God will consider our use of truth, mercy, grace, and forgiveness towards others when He judges us. See 18:21-35. "Mete" (v. 2) is the verb form of the noun "measure" and means to give a measured portion to someone. Here, as in Mark 4:24, it is used figuratively: "He will deal with you in the manner that you deal with others" (Louw and Nida I:568). See also Luke 6:37-38.

By illustration (v. 3) Jesus gave a third reason not to be quick to judge. Self-righteousness tends to ignore much larger personal sins than those of the one being judged. Comparing sins to different-sized pieces of wood, Jesus said the hypercritical person condemns the "mote" (Greek *karphos*, a speck or chip; BAGD 405) in the other person's eye while carrying a beam in his or her own. This is hyperbole, but it is clear: people must not judge others when they have such large faults of their own, because personal faults can skew honest and fair judgment. King David was a classic example of this (Hendriksen 357). He was quick to condemn the man who stole and killed the lamb but ignored his own horrendous sins (2 Sam. 12:1-9). The men who accused the woman taken in adultery were also guilty of this sin (Jn. 7:53-8:11).

Some commentators (Evans, *Matthew* 135; Keener, *Background* 64) suggest that this woodchip/beam comparison was humor on Jesus' part and that it reflected His carpentry background. Wood dust and chips in the eyes were hazards of the trade. Even today, with safety glasses and face shields, it is still common to get wood chips or dust in one's eyes when working with wood.

Not only is this critical person unworthy to judge another, this person has such problems of his own that he is unable even to help where there is a real need (vv. 4-5). He cannot see past the beam in his own eye to help remove a bit of wood from a "brother's" eye. "Brother" is not limited to fellow kingdom citizens (*contra* Gundry 119-120; Wilkins 307-308; Hagner 33A:169). James 4:11-12 forbids judging inside the Christian community but Romans 2:1 condemns judging of everyone.

According to Jesus, persons who insist on condemning the faults of others while ignoring their own are hypocrites (Nolland 320). See comments on 6:2 concerning "hypocrite." The hypocrisy in this instance is the portrayal of such perfection that this judge supposedly does not have even the smallest of faults when in reality he or she has major problems (v. 3). Jesus did not mean that one should never rebuke another's sin—the woodchip needs to be removed (Carson, *The Sermon* 101; Mt. 18:15-17; *contra* Hill 147)—or never try to help another with his or her problem (Gal. 6:1). Rather, before folks can help others they must have their own lives in order.

Summary (7:1-5)

Jesus spoke of making sure one's own life is in order before trying to help others. Using hyperbole and humor, Jesus illustrated His point by showing the absurdity of trying to help someone remove a small piece of foreign matter from his or her eye when there is a log-sized item in one's own eye. The parallels and point are obvious. Hypocrites do not make good eye doctors.

Application: Teaching and Preaching the Passage

This passage warns against having a critical attitude toward others with faults. A lesson or sermon might be developed using the following points: the command—do not be hypercritical (vv. 1, 3-4); the caution—God is watching (vv. 1-2); and the cure—correct your own faults first and then help others (v. 5).

g. Wise witnessing (7:6)

6 Give not that which is holy unto the dogs, neither cast ye your pearls before swine, lest they trample them under their feet, and turn again and rend you.

Jesus did not wish His disciples to be naïve (Wilkins 310), nor did He wish them harm (10:23). It is right to avoid certain people. Jesus warned that some people will not respect the holy and will harm the messenger if they can. Using detested and unclean animals—scavenger dogs (Greek *kuōn*) and swine—to emphasize His point, Jesus minced no words in His condemnation of such wicked people. Even as Jesus stayed away from Herod (cf. Mt. 4:12; Lk. 13:31-32), so Jesus' followers should identify and avoid those like him.

Scripture writers used the word "dog" to speak of a persecuting enemy (Ps. 22:16) and more particularly those who are the enemies of God (Rev. 22:15). Peter compared apostates to dogs (2 Pet. 2:21-22). Here dogs refer to bad people, Jews or Gentiles (cf. 15:26), who lack respect for that which is holy (Louw and Nida I:756; Phil. 3:2). That Jesus was not forbidding taking the gospel to Gentiles is clear because He later commanded His disciples to take the gospel to Gentiles (28:19).

Swine stand for the same type of people. Peter also places them alongside dogs in his discussion of apostates (2 Pet. 2:22). It may be that Jesus was saying both dogs and hogs could turn on a person. On the other hand, some commentators understand this verse to have a chiastic structure (a literary structure that resembles an "X"; see Newman and Stine 203-204; Carson, *Matthew* 185). This would mean that the dogs attack and the swine trample. Either way, Jesus' point is clear enough. In proverbial fashion, He warned that it can be a foolish and deadly mistake to offer some people the gospel pearl. The pearl and the "holy" (NIV, "sacred") both represent the gospel of the kingdom (Mt. 13:45-46).

Kingdom citizens are to be wise as serpents and harmless as doves in their interaction with such people (10:16). They are not to be judgmental (7:1-5) but then neither are they to be gullible (7:6). Jesus did not want His followers to place themselves intentionally in harm's way (10:23). There are times when the disciple will need to put some distance between the evil person and himself (Acts 9:23-25; 17:10). At the same time, since one cannot tell who will receive the gospel (Keener, *Matthew* 244; 13:3-23; Acts 9:1-19), one should take care not to prejudge and exclude any who need salvation. The disciples of Jesus must not avoid everyone who at first resists the gospel. Even an enemy will sometimes turn to Christ if given an opportunity (5:43-48; Acts 9:1-19).

Summary (7:6)

In this short verse, Jesus warned His followers that there will be people who will not be sympathetic to the gospel cause. Some will even try to destroy the messenger. Kingdom citizens need to use good judgment and avoid such people because they will destroy without conscience the followers of Jesus.

Application: Teaching and Preaching the Passage

Resistance against the gospel and kingdom advancement continues. Though violence against the gospel is not part of North America at this time, brutal aggression against the kingdom is present in other places. Organizations such as "The Voice of the Martyrs" show that active opposition continues in many parts of our world. However, even in North America there appears to be a building resistance, which is one reason this verse is still needed today.

This verse may not be, by itself, a good basis for a sermon or lesson. However, if used with passages like Matthew 10:17, 23 and Acts 9:23-25, it will give the follower of Christ direction when confronted by those who are antagonistic toward the gospel and its messengers.

h. Earnest petitions (7:7-11)

7 Ask, and it shall be given you; seek, and ye shall find; knock, and it shall be opened unto you:
8 For every one that asketh receiveth; and he that seeketh findeth; and to him that knocketh it shall be opened.
9 Or what man is there of you, whom if his son ask bread, will he give him a stone?
10 Or if he ask a fish, will he give him a serpent?
11 If ye then, being evil, know how to give good gifts unto your children, how much more shall your Father which is in heaven give good things to them that ask him?

Jesus returned to the subject of prayer (see 6:5-13) and gave additional guidelines and promises for prayer. Jesus was not telling His audience to ask to enter the kingdom. These instructions were for those already in the kingdom.

Three present imperatives carry the force of His teaching: be asking, be seeking, and be knocking. Prayer is to be regular and habitual (Greek iterative presents; Walvoord 56). Jesus wants kingdom citizens to pray regularly and He wants them to pray earnestly (seek, knock; Jas. 5:17). This is the gist of His statement. Prayer is a must. So is earnestness. Wilkins (312) is probably right that Jesus gave a "rising scale of intensity" in these instructions to ask, seek, and knock.

Following each command is a promise (Greek indicatives) that these prayers will be answered (vv. 7-8). "Every one" points to the great truth that all children are treated equally. Remarkably, simple asking (Bruner 1:343), not crazed frenzy or self-mutilation (1 Kgs. 18:28), is all the Father desires. Even as a parent answers a child's request for food, so our heavenly Father will answer our prayer requests (vv. 9-10). The rhetorical questions assume a negative answer. No good parent would be so cruel as to give a stone instead of bread or a dangerous snake instead of an edible fish. A stone would not address a child's need for food and a snake would be harmful to the child.

According to Jesus, people are by nature "evil" (v. 11), but God is not. If evil people are able to give good gifts, then surely God, who has no evil in Him, can be an even better parent (v. 11; "much more"). He will surely answer the requests of His children with the good things of heaven.

Jesus called people evil because all descendants of Adam are corrupted by sin. Mankind is inherently depraved and has been since the original sin of Adam (Ps. 51:5; Rom. 3:9-18; Eph. 2:1). This depravity is universal (it corrupts the entire human race) and total (it corrupts every aspect of an individual's being) but it does not erase all ability of man to do anything good. Jesus described His hearers as being "evil" but still able to give good gifts. This does not mean that mankind can earn God's favor by doing good but rather that man's morality, though damaged, is still intact after the fall. However, though mankind can do good, he does not always choose to do so (Rom. 3:10-18). This is why he needs God's Savior and regeneration.

Luke 11:13 has "the Holy Spirit" in place of the words "good things." Evans (*Matthew* 139) thinks that this may be Luke's interpretation of Jesus' "good things." The biblical doctrine of inspiration assures the interpreter that the gift of the Holy Spirit is at least included in the "good things" of which Jesus spoke.

Summary (7:7-11)

Ask, seek, and knock are prayer actions that move heaven. Jesus promised His followers that our heavenly Father is inherently good and because of this, He will answer His children's requests by giving them the good gifts of a loving Father.

Application: Teaching and Preaching the Passage

"Ask" makes a nice acrostic for these prayer instructions: ask, seek, and knock (Bruner 1:342). These verses might also be presented as the desire of God (that His children will ask Him to supply their needs), the promises of God (that He will answer every prayer), and the goodness of God (God's answers are always good and beneficial). One could teach on the several facets of prayer as Jesus taught them in this Sermon on the Mount.

One might consider the kind of Father God is. He is a Father who (1) hears the cry of His children; (2) who provides for His children; (3) who responds to His children with fairness and impartiality; and (4) who is a good Father, much better than any human father.

i. The Golden Rule (7:12)

12 Therefore all things whatsoever ye would that men should do to you, do ye even so to them: for this is the law and the prophets.

"Therefore" connects this verse with the previous discussion of the good heavenly Father who gives generously. Like their good heavenly Father, kingdom citizens are to lead the way in treating others the way they want others to treat them. This is one of the most familiar Bible verses in our society. Folks with little or no Christian training seem to know the Golden Rule. It is simple to understand but difficult to practice at times because it requires that God's people show careful consideration for others. Commentators (e.g., Keener, *Background* 65; Nolland 329) point out that Jesus was not the only person to teach this as a rule of life. However, the reason Jesus taught this rule makes His usage unique (Hendriksen 364-365). He taught this rule not as a great rule of society but as the will of God.

According to Jesus, this rule summarizes "the law and the prophets," which was one way the Jews referred to the O.T. (See comments on 5:17.) The value Jesus placed on this command makes it extremely important. The kingdom citizen's best example of this generous treatment is the Father Himself. He sends sunshine and rain (5:44-45) because He wants everyone, even His enemies, to reconcile to Him (Rom. 2:4). This rule also explains (Hagner 33A:176) the second great commandment, "Love your neighbor as yourself," one of the two pillars of the Law (Mt. 22:39-40; Lev. 19:18; Rom. 13:8-10; Gal. 5:14). Fair treatment of our fellow human beings is next in importance to loving God with our whole heart, soul, mind, and strength. Jesus' placement of this law in this sermon further supports His earlier statement that He did not come to abolish the Law or the Prophets (5:17).

Summary (7:12)

The Golden Rule is one aspect of kingdom life taught in this Sermon on the Mount. Using a familiar principle, Jesus showed that one's relationship with his or her fellow man is of primary interest to God. He stated that this rule summarizes the whole O.T. According to this rule, kingdom citizens are to be proactive. In ongoing obedience to God, they are preemptively to act graciously to others.

Application: Teaching and Preaching the Passage

Two truths are expressed in this verse that could serve as a basis for a lesson or sermon: first, good treatment of others is God's will for His children (the command, the result); and, second, fair treatment of our fellow human beings is the gist of the entire O.T. This verse should be considered along with Matthew 22:40. See comments there.

6. Choosing the kingdom (7:13-27)

Jesus brought this teaching session to a decision time. There are two roads, two kinds of prophets, two kinds of disciples, and two kinds of foundations (Wilkins 321). Kingdom truth calls for a response. No one is in the kingdom by virtue of natural birth (Jn. 3:3-8). Only those who turn into the right gate and on the right road are in.

a. Choosing the right gate and the right road (7:13-14)

13 Enter ye in at the strait gate: for wide *is* the gate, and broad *is* the way, that leadeth to destruction, and many there be which go in thereat:
14 Because strait *is* the gate, and narrow *is* the way, which leadeth unto life, and few there be that find it.

"Enter" (Greek ingressive aorist and an imperative) has a sense of urgency. Jesus wanted His hearers to make their decision to choose the heavenly kingdom immediately. The actions depicted in these verses are first, searching for (v. 14, find it) the gate to eternal life; second, entering through the gate; third, traveling on the road to eternity; and fourth, entering into the eternal home.

"Strait" (v. 13; not straight; Greek *stenē*) means narrow, i.e., constricted, not wide. "Narrow" (v. 14) means difficult (see below). Using the image of a heavenly traveler (cf. 5:20) Jesus told His hearers that entrance into the kingdom would be by deliberate choice to accept Jesus and His teachings, one by one (Gundry 127), i.e., individually, and without this world's desires and affections (Hendriksen 369).

There are only two possible destinations and everyone is on one of the two roads going to one of the two destinations. According to Jesus, most people will choose the wide gate and the broad way for they are roomy and inviting (Wilkins 321). Because of this choice many would not "find" the narrow gate (the antecedent of "it," v. 14) and difficult way. Luke's parallel (13:24) suggests that some would try to find the narrow gate and be unable to, underscoring the fewness of the saved (Evans, *Matthew* 142). A few will choose the restricted gate and difficult route but not many. Jesus' followers, relatively speaking, are in the minority (Hagner 33A:179) in spite of the promised growth of the kingdom (13:31-33).

The decision to break from the broad way to follow Jesus marks the entrance into the narrow gate (Jn. 14:6). His teachings and persecutions by others are part of the narrow way. The narrow way runs into the consummated kingdom in the eschatological end (Carson, *Matthew* 189). None enter the final phase of the kingdom except through Him and His type of discipleship (Wilkins 321).

"Narrow" (v. 14) translates a word (Greek *thlibō*) that means, "to cause some to suffer trouble or hardship." It is to make the road difficult to travel (Louw and Nida I:245). The word includes the idea of persecution. Jesus did not sugarcoat the truth and neither should His followers as they witness to others, though one should not be all negative and thus discourage people away. Jesus' invitation into the kingdom is restricted to those who accept Him, and His call to discipleship is demanding. Hardship caused by others awaits those who choose to follow Him.

Jesus had begun this sermon with both the positives and the negatives of kingdom life (Hendriksen 366). Those who enter the kingdom will be comforted, inherit the earth, and see God, etc. (5:3-9). They will also be persecuted for their choice (5:10-12; Acts 14:22). However, God's people must never forget that heaven's blessings far outweigh earth's troubles (2 Cor. 4:17; Rom. 8:18). By God's grace they are truly the favored (Hagner 33A:180).

These two choices are about eternity. Like Moses (Dt. 30:19), Jesus set before His audience "life and death." Though the kingdom route is difficult, it leads to eternal life. Though the broad road is easier, it leads to destruction. "Destruction" was Jesus' description of the place where the souls and bodies of the wicked will be punished (10:28). This verse shows that Jesus did not teach a universal salvation, the false doctrine that all will be saved.

Summary (7:13-14)

With these verses Jesus started bringing the Sermon on the Mount to a close. He did not permit His hearers to leave without confronting them with the implications of what they had just heard. There was a choice to be made. Jesus had been describing a life different from what they were used to living and a kingdom that was near. Entrance into that kingdom would be deliberate and restrictive, and it required a life of willing hardship. No decision to enter the kingdom is a choice to stay on the broad road. This broad road is easier to travel but in the end, it will be the most difficult, for it ends in destruction. Jesus wants everyone to enter the narrow gate.

Application: Teaching and Preaching the Passage

Both saved and unsaved need to hear these verses preached and taught. Hendriksen (367) offers an outline: "two gates and two ways, two kinds of travelers, and two destinations."

b. Choosing the right prophet leaders (7:15-20)

15 Beware of false prophets, which come to you in sheep's clothing, but inwardly they are ravening wolves.
16 Ye shall know them by their fruits. Do men gather grapes of thorns, or figs of thistles?
17 Even so every good tree bringeth forth good fruit; but a corrupt tree bringeth forth evil fruit.
18 A good tree cannot bring forth evil fruit, neither *can* a corrupt tree bring forth good fruit.
19 Every tree that bringeth not forth good fruit is hewn down, and cast into the fire.
20 Wherefore by their fruits ye shall know them.

Jesus continued contrasting opposites. He spoke of two types of prophets who would confront His disciples as they traveled through life on their way to the final manifestation of the kingdom. First, He warned of false prophets. The O.T. spoke of this kind of prophet often (e.g., Dt. 13:1-5; 18:15-22; Jer. 5:31;14:14; 23:32; 29:9). Jesus, however, spoke of false prophets who would present themselves as true kingdom citizens (Hagner 33A:183; Mt. 24:11, 24). He described them as hypocrites of the worst type, individuals who appear as sheep, meek and unthreatening, but in reality, they are wolves who have donned sheep's clothing. They act like sheep in order to get close enough for the kill (Nolland 336). Sheep are their prey. These hypocrites are predatory and rapacious. They try to turn the sheep from the difficult way to the broad way. Their influence is spiritually destructive. True followers must be on their guard against such "prophets" or they can lose their spiritual lives (Keener, *Matthew* 253).

Even though they are well disguised by their apparent kingdom ways (Bruner 1:352), Jesus assured His hearers that their true selves cannot remain hidden. They will at some point act out what they really are. In fact, this is true for everyone (Mt. 12:33). The true self shows up in *fruit* (a metaphor for deeds; Hagner 33A:181; 3:8, 10; Gal. 5:22; Jn. 15:2-8), because the kind and quality of fruit betrays the kind and quality of the tree. The tree stands for the person, either good (a true disciple of Jesus) or bad (a person with a false profession). In this instance, bad (Greek *ponēros*, diseased or rotten; Grimm's 530; Louw and Nida I:624) fruit is leading people away from the true God (Dt. 13) and encouraging the practice of sin (Lk. 6:43-45), an antinomian lifestyle that

Scripture so vehemently condemns (Rom. 6:1-2). True disciples will find that false prophets provide nothing spiritually helpful. Just as grapes cannot be picked from thorn bushes or figs from thistles (v. 16) so true followers will be unable to gain spiritual nourishment from the ministries of these prophets. True disciples must not be drawn into the lawless ways of the false prophet or into accepting their false doctrine. They must part ways with false prophets even as Jesus promises to do in the judgment (vv. 21-23; Gundry 128).

Jesus' words were fulfilled in the early years of the church, though not in a final sense (Acts 20:28-30; 2 Pet. 2:1-22; Rev. 2:20). Paul identified false apostles, contemporaries enabled by Satan himself to masquerade as servants of righteousness (2 Cor. 11:13-15). John warned that false prophets were present in his day (1 Jn. 4:1) and would continue until the end (Rev. 16:13; 19:20).

Jesus declared that false prophets would experience the same end as bad fruit trees. They will be thrown into the fire (v. 19), a reference to the eternal fires of hell (Gundry 130). Jesus' message mirrored the harshness of John the Baptist at this point (3:10).

The second type of prophet Jesus spoke of was the one who bears good fruit (v. 17). As with false prophets, fruit is proof of the true nature of good prophets. Good fruit includes leading people to God and living in obedience to God's laws. Disciples gain spiritual strength from the ministries of true prophets. With these words, Jesus taught there would be others who would carry the message of the kingdom. Discernment will enable kingdom citizens to distinguish the true prophet from the false prophet.

Summary (7:15-20)

The hardships of the narrow way (see comments on 7:13-14) include false prophets. These are individuals who will try to destroy the kingdom work from within. Though it will be difficult to identify them at first, because of their ability to look like real followers of Jesus, in time their actions will show the true condition of their hearts. Evil people are unable to live a righteous life.

Likewise, true prophets are proven by their good deeds. Because the person is a true follower of Jesus, his or her actions will consistently be like those of Jesus. Such actions will help the follower of Jesus identify true prophets.

Application: Teaching and Preaching the Passage

False prophets remain in the Christian community and the Church needs to be warned. Jesus gave this warning for the church age to help Christians guard against hypocritical leaders who call themselves Christians (Nolland 337). Carson (*The Sermon* 129) warns that our own souls are at stake.

By considering this passage along with others mentioned above, a lesson or sermon could be developed apprising the congregation of the real and present dangers of false prophets. Some points might be as follows: the dangers of false prophets, the presence of false prophets inside the kingdom community, the hypocrisy of false prophets, the lack of spiritual benefit provided by the false prophets, the works of false prophets, the inability of false prophets to deceive the perceptive kingdom citizen, and the final end of false prophets.

c. Choosing to be the right kind of disciple (7:21-23)

21 Not every one that saith unto me, Lord, Lord, shall enter into the kingdom of heaven; but he that doeth the will of my Father which is in heaven.
22 Many will say to me in that day, Lord, Lord, have we not prophesied in thy name? and in thy name have cast out devils? and in thy name done many wonderful works?
23 And then will I profess unto them, I never knew you: depart from me, ye that work iniquity.

Jesus returned to the truth mentioned in verse 14 of the restricted entrance into the kingdom. This time, however, He moved past the initial entrance into kingdom life, the restricted gate, and the hard way of discipleship, to the entrance into the final, eternal phase of the kingdom. Peter wrote of this entrance in 2 Peter 1:11. Jesus spoke here of two kinds of disciples. The first group does the will of the Father and will be given entrance into the final phase of the kingdom. The other group consists of false disciples who will want to enter the final, eternal phase of the kingdom but will be turned away.

While living on this earth, these false disciples called Him "Lord." It is difficult to know what Jesus intended by this. If He meant what the original hearers' understood, then it is safe to assume they understood Jesus to mean "master" or "teacher" (Hill 152). "Lord" Jesus as deity was not yet understood, even by His disciples (see comments on 14:33), though He assumed that position for Himself in verse 23. However, Newman and Stine (217) are confident that the exalted Jesus is meant here.

Simply calling Jesus master, or even Lord as divine, will not save. At the time of this sermon, entrance into the kingdom was granted to those who repented of personal sin (Wilkins 324), trusted Jesus at the level He had revealed His identity (Jn. 1:12; 2:23; 3:16)—the interpreter must allow for progressive revelation and the transition from law to grace—followed with a life lived in obedience to the heavenly Father's commands as found in the O.T. and as Jesus taught them (v. 21). Profession and holy practice were both requirements of Jesus' gospel. Jesus had no tolerance for an antinomian (lawless, refusing to live by established moral laws that apply to everyone) lifestyle (v. 23; Lk. 6:43-46; 13:25-27). Works do not bring about salvation but they are the proof, the fruits, that salvation is possessed (Walvoord 58; Jas. 2:18-26). In a fuller Christian sense, i.e., since Pentecost, entrance into the kingdom is granted only to those who turn from sin to follow Jesus and His teachings, and trust Him as Savior—which includes confessing Him as the divine Lord (Rom. 10:9) and submitting to Him as master.

Jesus stated that many will profess loyalty to Him even to the point that they will claim to have had wonderful ministries in His name. They will claim that they have prophesied (see v. 15 and the false prophets), which probably refers to proclamation of gospel truths rather than forecasting future events (Newman and Stine 219; Hagner 33A:187). They will claim they have done exorcisms. (See 12:27 and Acts 19:13-16 for Jewish exorcists.) They will claim to have done many wonderful (Greek *dunamis*, powerful) works, i.e., miracles, all in Jesus' name "as His representative[s]" (Keener, *Matthew* 252). All of these claims will be made by folks who make a false profession.

Do deceivers perform miracles? Some did and more will as the end approaches (Mt. 24:24). However, some supposed exorcisms will be counterfeit because Jesus never knew these false prophets and Satan will not fight against his own kingdom (12:25-26). Still, some exorcisms and miracles will take place (12:27; Acts 19:13-16). The result of such miracles is great deception. Jesus will tell the truth about them in "that day" (v. 22), the day of final judgment (Gundry 131), when entrance into the final phase of the eternal kingdom, heaven, is either granted or withheld.

This passage teaches there will be such an occasion when Jesus will grant entrance into heaven to those who have obeyed the Father's will (v. 21; 25:34), the standard for real discipleship (Hill 152). Those who make false professions will be excluded. Exclusion will be because of iniquitous works (lit. "are working lawlessness," v. 23) and because they did not know the Savior. These imposters do not forfeit their salvation. They never had it (I never knew you, v. 23). Compare this with 5:20 where entrance was denied because one's righteousness did not exceed that of the scribes and Pharisees.

Jesus made some strong claims about Himself in these verses. He decides who enters the kingdom (v. 21). Notice the first person "I" and "me" in verse 23. He is the authority behind true prophesying, exorcisms, and miracles. He equates Himself to the O.T. Lord in whose Name the O.T. prophets prophesied (Ezra 5:1; Evans, *Matthew* 145). He stated that some would even invoke His name but not really know Him (Jer. 14:14; Mk. 9:38; Acts 19:13).

These claims are notable because it is Matthew's first record of Jesus making such claims of divinity about Himself. They are also notable because of when this took place, possibly no later than early in the second year of His ministry according to Matthew's chronology. See comments above on Jesus' move from Judea to Galilee (4:12).

"I never knew you" (Mt. 10:33; 25:12; Lk. 13:25, 27) means that Jesus and these false prophets never had a Savior/saved relationship. "Depart from me, etc.," may allude to Psalms 6:8 (Blomberg 30) and according to Luke 13:27-28 means that these false prophets will be sent to a place where there will be weeping and gnashing of teeth. In addition, then, to the claims already mentioned, which Jesus made about Himself in this Sermon on the Mount, Jesus also stated that He has the authority to condemn souls to the eternal lake of fire. It is no wonder the people were astonished that He spoke with such authority (vv. 28-29). No mere human has such authority.

Summary (7:21-23)

Jesus wanted His teachings put into practice. A profession to be a follower of Jesus without a lifestyle patterned after the teachings of Jesus results in a rejection by Jesus. Entrance into the eternal heavenly existence will be given only to those who repent, believe, and obey Jesus' teachings. Though a holy lifestyle is not a condition of salvation, lifestyle obedience (practical sanctification) is an understood part of Jesus' salvation. Holy living is a guaranteed result of true repentance and sincere saving faith. It was in Jesus' day. It remains so today.

Application: Teaching and Preaching the Passage

Profession without obvious repentance characterizes many in today's visible church. A sermon or lesson might be developed around the theme of true discipleship: true disciples know Jesus, Jesus knows them, v. 23; true disciples submit to Him, He is their Lord, v. 21; true disciples live a holy lifestyle pleasing to the Father; Jesus will invite true disciples into His heavenly home (v. 21).

d. Building on the right foundation (7:24-27)

24 Therefore whosoever heareth these sayings of mine, and doeth them, I will liken him unto a wise man, which built his house upon a rock:
25 And the rain descended, and the floods came, and the winds blew, and beat upon that house; and it fell not: for it was founded upon a rock.
26 And every one that heareth these sayings of mine, and doeth them not, shall be likened unto a foolish man, which built his house upon the sand:
27 And the rain descended, and the floods came, and the winds blew, and beat upon that house; and it fell: and great was the fall of it.

Because everything hinges on submissive obedience to the Lordship of Jesus (Carson, *The Sermon* 131-132), Jesus ended His sermon with a warning. He wanted His hearers to obey His teaching. Jesus did not have a take-it-or-leave-it attitude nor was He promoting a gradual life change. This was a call to decision for a complete turnaround, a drastic life change. The Mosaic Law is no longer the standard for correct conduct (Hagner 33A:191); His words are.

Again, Jesus illustrated with contrasts and once more He drew from His background as a carpenter (Barclay 1:335; cf. v. 3). In His first parable recorded in Matthew's Gospel, Jesus spoke of two builders, two houses, two foundations, and two storms to illustrate the wisdom of ordering life upon Jesus' words. Hearing and putting into practice Jesus' teachings is like building a house on a rock, a solid, unmovable foundation. Hearing but not putting in practice Jesus' words is foolish, as foolish as building a house on sand, i.e., building without foresight as if every day will be sunny and bright (Hendriksen 380; Lk. 6:46-49). The issue is not laziness. The issues are personal judgment and obedience. The wise builder obeys. The foolish one does not. The descriptive "fool" connotes responsibility. In Jesus' parable, the information was available and the foolish builder is capable of making the wise decision; hence his accountability and judgment. The fall of his house is just.

Storms assaulted both houses but only the one built on the rock was still standing when the storm was over. The one built on sand was completely ruined. It was destroyed beyond repair, so great was its collapse. The fool made a poor judgment call and suffered the consequences of his foolish decision not to prepare for the inevitable storm.

Each person is a builder. Every builder decides which foundation he will build on. Storms will come. Storms will test everyone's house. Only those structures built on rock will survive the storm.

Jesus concluded with this single point: to order one's life on teachings other than His (v. 26) is foolish and will result in complete destruction. In the strictest sense, the words "of mine" are the words of this sermon (Hill 153). However, His sayings or words include all of His teachings (Mt. 28:20). Jesus is the necessary and exclusive way to heaven.

In v. 24 Jesus directed His comments to the end time judgment (Nolland 345). "Whosoever"—that is, everyone—gives these words universal application and puts them beyond the normal, everyday troubles (storms) of this life. The final judgment is the storm that will test everyone's house (Keener, *Matthew* 256).

This parable reinforces Jesus' earlier statements: rejection of Jesus and His teaching assures that one is traveling the broad way that leads to destruction (7:13, 21-23); and rejection of Jesus and His teaching is bad fruit that will cause the tree to be thrown into the fire (7:19). In fact, Jesus final four teaching points speak of hell. The broad way leads to destruction (v. 13). Those who bear bad fruit are burned (v. 19). Those who practice lawlessness and do not have a personal acquaintance with Jesus will hear the words "depart from me" (v. 23). Everyone who refuses Jesus' teachings will be destroyed (v. 27).

For this crowd of mainly Jews, Jesus set His teachings in sharp contrast to those of the religious establishment of that time. He had already denounced the scribes and the Pharisees (5:20) and in this instance He required His hearers to decide between His teachings and theirs. His were rock solid. Theirs were shifting sands (Wilkins 327). His provided stability and security. Theirs offered neither.

This ends the first of the five major blocks of Jesus' teachings recorded by Matthew. As mentioned in the discussion of verses 21-23, this sermon probably took place early in Jesus' Galilean ministry and serves as an example of the type of teaching Jesus did. It also is part of the discipleship lessons Jesus wants all converts taught (28:20; Wilkins 328).

Summary (7:24-27)

This is the fourth and final comparison Jesus used to call His audience to decision. Beginning in verse 13 Jesus spoke of two roads, two kinds of prophets, and two kinds of disciples. Now He speaks of two kinds of foundations, which illustrate the two options everyone has in life. All who choose to order their lives on the teachings of Jesus will endure forever. All who reject the teachings of Christ will be destroyed.

Application: Teaching and Preaching the Passage

Jesus' teachings in this Sermon on the Mount rebut those who teach a cheap grace (Hagner 33A:192). Works righteousness is not the gospel Jesus preached; righteous works are inextricably woven into the gospel fabric. A lesson or sermon might be developed on the subject of the wisdom of living for Jesus and the foolishness of rejecting Jesus. Using verses 13-27, a lesson or sermon might also be developed that contrasts those who follow Jesus with those who do not.

7. The impact of Jesus' teaching (7:28-29)

28 And it came to pass, when Jesus had ended these sayings, the people were astonished at his doctrine:
29 For he taught them as *one* having authority, and not as the scribes.

With these verses, Matthew brought his record of the Sermon on the Mount to a close and bridged the Sermon with the narrative of chapter 8 (Gundry 136). This was Matthew's signature transition that he used to end each of the five major blocks of teaching material (11:1; 13:53; 19:1; 26:1).

According to Evans (*Matthew* 149) and Gundry (137) the trained scribes, who were expert teachers of the law, appealed to other authorities when speaking. Jesus did not do this. He spoke as one who had authority Himself, as when He said, "You have heard ..., but I say to you" (5:21-22; etc.)

However, Nolland (346) may be right as well. The crowds' thoughts toward the scribes (see comments on 5:1) might not have been about their habits of quoting each other as much as their inadequacies. In contrast to the scribes, Jesus gave clear direction for how to please the Father and how to get to heaven. He spoke with authority. He spoke as if He had this authority within Himself. He spoke as one who has life's answers. He spoke in the first person with the authority to judge, send away to eternal punishment, and grant entrance into the kingdom (Carson, *Matthew* 195).

Matthew does not suggest that anyone was upset by Jesus' authoritative posture. They were just amazed and surprised by both His message and His delivery. As the temple guards later testified, "No one ever spoke like this man!" (Jn. 7:46); but the prophet had said He would speak with skill (Is. 50:4). See also 13:54 and Luke 4:22. Still, amazement is not saving faith (Wilkins 328). These crowds realized they had heard powerful teaching, but at this point Matthew recorded no evidence that any became followers of Jesus.

This was the first time Matthew mentioned Jesus' authority (Greek *exousia;* Nolland 346) but this was only the beginning. Matthew had more to say about Jesus' authority. See the fuller discussion on authority in 28:18.

Summary (7:28-29)

Jesus astonished the crowds with His teaching and His authoritative posture. This Sermon sufficiently surprised the people to the point that they compared Him to their trained scribes and found Him to be much more confident and competent. This carpenter, this untrained itinerate preacher, was on the threshold of the year of His greatest popularity.

Application: Teaching and Preaching the Passage

Intellectual interest in the Sermon on the Mount is good but should not be one's final goal. This sermon is about doing (Bruner 1:368-369). As mentioned in the introduction to chapter 5, this Sermon is about kingdom citizen actions, i.e., living as a citizen of the kingdom now. Any sermon or lesson that does justice to these teachings of Jesus must present them as commands to be obeyed now.

One might develop a lesson or sermon on the character of Jesus' teachings: it is astonishing (v. 28), authoritative (v. 29), and activating (the goal of the entire sermon, but especially 7:19, 24-27), emphasizing the words "do" and "does" in this last point.

C. The Royal Messiah's Day-to-Day Miracles and Teachings (8:1—9:38)

Following the Sermon on the Mount, Jesus traveled about Galilee and into Decapolis. Though Capernaum was His ministry base, He did not stay there. He took His gospel to the people, where He met their physical and spiritual needs. Chapters eight and nine are Matthew's record of ten specific miracles along with a general reference to many other miracles (8:16). These two chapters also describe various facets of true discipleship.

Matthew gave proof of Jesus' authority over nature and the spirit world. He organized this material thematically rather than chronologically (Carson, *Matthew* 197). This is clear in the four specific healing miracles in this chapter. Jesus healed an Israelite leper, a Gentile's servant, a Jewish woman, and two demon-possessed Gentile men. None of these enjoyed the social and religious standing of the ceremonially clean, Jewish male in Israel at that time.

1. Jesus healed a leper (8:1-4)

1 When he was come down from the mountain, great multitudes followed him.

2 And, behold, there came a leper and worshipped him, saying, Lord, if thou wilt, thou canst make me clean.

3 And Jesus put forth *his* hand, and touched him, saying, I will; be thou clean. And immediately his leprosy was cleansed.

4 And Jesus saith unto him, See thou tell no man; but go thy way, shew thyself to the priest, and offer the gift that Moses commanded, for a testimony unto them.

Matthew wrote of Jesus' growing popularity in 4:23-25. The healings attracted crowds and these crowds followed Him as He traveled (8:1). Their desire to be with Him was out of curiosity more than true discipleship (Hagner 33A:198). Apparently, as Jesus descended from the Sermon location, a man suffering from leprosy approached Him for healing. This was bold on his part and against the Mosaic Law (Lev. 13:45, 46; Blomberg 30). Furthermore, there is no indication that he cried out, "Unclean, unclean," as required. This leper had heard about Jesus' ability to heal and though Matthew did not mention any specific healings of lepers up to this point, it is possible that Jesus had done so (4:24). Regardless, this leper believed Jesus could heal him and he was right. The man knelt before Jesus. He did not know Jesus' true identify but he did respect Him. His posture showed honor (Newman and Stine 228).

"If you will" (v. 2) indicates confident faith and a recognition of "the supreme significance of" Jesus' will in this matter (Nolland 349). The words "if you will" show that the leper feared Jesus might not include him in His healing ministry (Carson, *Matthew* 198). "Lord" probably meant "sir" rather than deity in this request (Evans, *Matthew* 165), since Jesus' deity was recognized by so few at this time, but "Lord" is still respectful submission. See comments below on the centurion's use of "Lord" in verse 6 and the Greeks' address to Philip in John 12:21 where the same Greek word (*kurios*) is translated "sir."

With a simple statement and a heart of compassion (Mk. 1:41), Jesus touched the leper (v. 3). This might have been the first touch the leper had felt in a long time. It was surely the most powerful and yet the most compassionate touch he had ever felt. The man was full of leprosy (Lk. 5:12), yet he was made well immediately. Such was the will and power of Jesus.

Touching a leper would normally render a clean person unclean (Lev. 5:3; 22:4-6; *contra* Nolland 350). However, Jesus heals and sanctifies what He touches. His power to cleanse is greater than any sin or sickness that renders one unclean.

Both Testaments speak of leprosy. According to modern scholarship, the Hebrew term translated "leprosy" refers to a variety of skin conditions and diseases including, but not limited to, clinical leprosy (Hansen's disease) as we understand it today (Lev. 13-14; ISBE III:103-106; Newman and Stine 227-228). Some forms were more serious than others. Leviticus 13 and 14 list laws concerning this disease and the sacrifices required of the person when cured. Lepers were required to live alone outside of the camp (Lev. 13:45-46). They had to wear torn clothes, cover their mouths, and cry "Unclean, unclean." Numbers 12:12 may suggest that lepers were viewed "as good as dead" (Hagner 33A:198). Some forms of leprosy were highly contagious.

Leprosy also rendered the person religiously unclean (Lev. 13:46; Num. 5:2-4), which is why the man requested to be made clean. This was his way of asking that he be healed of his leprosy and its many restrictions, including its ceremonial uncleanness. Lepers had no access to the altar and were not permitted to participate in group worship.

This healing was an astounding miracle. Leprosy was a dreaded disease at that time. Unlike today, there was no known human cure. Divine healings occurred (Num. 12:10-15; 2 Kg. 5:1-14), but they were rare.

For some unstated reason, Jesus did not want this man to publicize this miracle (v. 4). Wilkins (341) suggests it was because Jesus did not want people "clamoring for the miracles alone." He is probably right given Mark's comment that the man did not keep quiet about this miracle and that Jesus' movement was consequently restricted (Nolland 351; Mk. 1:45; Lk. 5:15). One reason Jesus came was to deliver from illness and disease (8:16-17). He came to remove sin and its effects, one of which is human affliction.

There were witnesses to this miracle, yet Jesus instructed the healed leper to keep the healing to himself and do as the Mosaic Law commanded for anyone who recovered from leprosy. This man needed to go see the priest to get an examination and clean diagnosis and to offer the required sacrifices. Sacrificial requirements differed, depending on several factors. Read Leviticus 13 and 14 for specifics. That the man had to go to the priest shows that a priest had already declared him a leper and unclean.

Jesus' instructions indicate that He acted in accord with the priestly system at the time. Though the kingdom was being preached, the cross was still in the future. The priests were still required to assess the man's condition (Lev. 13-14) and declare him clean. Also, animal sacrifices were still necessary. Sending the healed leper back to the priest, then, accomplished five things. First, this authenticated Jesus' miracle. A third party objectively declared the former leper now clean. Second, this healing was a testimony to the priests of Jesus' miraculous powers ("them" in v. 4). Surely they must have been surprised since this was probably the first instance of healed leprosy they had ever seen (Walvoord 64), but they would see more (Lk. 17:14). Third, the priests' ruling would restore the healed man back to his home and community and permit him once again to participate in temple activities. Fourth, the man would be able to offer the prescribed sacrifices and enjoy renewed regular fellowship with God. Fifth, the priests would know that Jesus kept the law and taught others to do the same (Newman and Stine 230).

2. Jesus healed a centurion's servant (8:5-13)

5 And when Jesus was entered into Capernaum, there came unto him a centurion, beseeching him,
6 And saying, Lord, my servant lieth at home sick of the palsy, grievously tormented.
7 And Jesus saith unto him, I will come and heal him.
8 The centurion answered and said, Lord, I am not worthy that thou shouldest come under my roof: but speak the word only, and my servant shall be healed.
9 For I am a man under authority, having soldiers under me: and I say to this *man*, Go, and he goeth; and to another, Come, and he cometh; and to my servant, Do this, and he doeth *it*.
10 When Jesus heard *it*, he marvelled, and said to them that followed, Verily I say unto you, I have not found so great faith, no, not in Israel.
11 And I say unto you, That many shall come from the east and west, and shall sit down with Abraham, and Isaac, and Jacob, in the kingdom of heaven.
12 But the children of the kingdom shall be cast out into outer darkness: there shall be weeping and gnashing of teeth.
13 And Jesus said unto the centurion, Go thy way; and as thou hast believed, *so* be it done unto thee. And his servant was healed in the selfsame hour.

Luke (7:1) placed this miracle immediately after the Sermon on the Mount in time and stated that it took place in Capernaum. The centurion was at his residence, presumably also in Capernaum (Lk. 7:3, 10). While Matthew recorded that the centurion came directly to Jesus, Luke (7:3-5) reported that the request came indirectly, through Jewish elders who approached Jesus on his behalf. Either way, the question was the centurion's.

A centurion was the leader of a century (one hundred) of soldiers, though in reality they commanded about sixty to eighty (Keener, *Background* 66; *ISBE* I:629). This centurion might have been a Roman soldier (Evans, *Matthew* 167; Hill 158) or one of Herod's soldiers (Hendriksen 394). In any case, this soldier was not a Jew, which was probably why Matthew included his story. This Gentile soldier requested that Jesus heal his servant who was, according to Luke 7:2, near death. Matthew reported that the servant was suffering terribly ("grievously tormented," v. 6). He had "palsy," which means that he was paralyzed (9:2). On "Lord," see 8:2. One cannot know for certain what the centurion meant by "Lord" but Hagner (33A:204) suggests that he at least regarded Jesus as a "person uniquely endowed by God with authority, if not sovereignty, over the physical realm." His statement of faith (vv. 8-9) testifies at least to this much. Without hesitation Jesus agreed to go heal the servant (v. 7). Though most translations understand Jesus' words to be a statement, the Greek may be understood as either a question or a statement (Keener, *Matthew* 266).

Pious Jews would normally have hesitated to go to the home of a Gentile (Acts 11:3; Keener, *Background* 67) but Jesus offered to go to the centurion's home. As with the leper, Jesus' did not avoid the need. The centurion surprised Jesus (v. 8). First, he had such respect for Jesus that he felt unworthy to have Jesus in his home. Perhaps he was thinking of Jewish ceremonial separation from Gentiles (Jn. 18:28; Acts 10-11; Hendriksen 395), or more probably he might have realized his own authority paled in comparison to that of Jesus (Carson, *Matthew* 201). Second, he believed Jesus' power was not limited to His physical presence (v. 9). He believed Jesus' power could be compared to his own in that he gave orders and they were obeyed even from a distance. He believed that if Jesus gave the order, the servant would be healed. Disease had no choice but to obey Jesus (Gundry 144) regardless of its geographical proximity to Jesus. Undoubtedly, this centurion had heard of Jesus' previous healings (4:24; Wilkins 342).

This Gentile's faith so surprised Jesus that He "marveled," one of two times Jesus marveled according to the Gospel writers. Here He marveled because of the centurion's faith and in Mark 6:6 Jesus marveled because of the lack of faith in His hometown. Jesus stated that the centurion's faith was the greatest He had found so far in all of Israel (v. 10). Furthermore, Jesus assured His hearers that this Gentile's faith placed him within the kingdom (Hagner 33A:205) with the great patriarchs. He would not be the only non-Jew in the eternal kingdom. "East and west" suggests that multiple nationalities will be present. Many Gentiles will "sit down"—literally, "recline at table"—to enjoy banquet fellowship with (Keener, *Background* 67), the great patriarchs Abraham, Isaac, and Jacob (v. 11) in the Messianic kingdom. The Messianic feast represents the joys of the Messianic kingdom (Hill, 159; Mt. 22:1-14; 25:10) and alludes to the marriage supper of the Lamb (26:29; Rev. 19:6-9) that celebrates the eternal marriage of the Lord and His Bride, the church.

While believing Gentiles are enjoying the joys of the kingdom, natural born children of Abraham will be cast into eternal punishment (v. 12). Unbelief keeps natural born Jews out of the kingdom (Hill 159). The harshness of Jesus' words should not escape the Christian reader. The original audience heard it (Wilkins 343).

Jesus described the place of punishment as "outer darkness." See also Matthew 22:13 and 25:30. Louw and Nida (I:7) define this outer darkness as "a place or region that is both dark and removed (presumably from the abode of the righteous) and serving as the abode of evil spirits and devils." Only Matthew includes this way of representing hell.

Jesus further described hell as a place of weeping and gnashing of teeth (Mt. 8:12; 13:42; 13:50; 22:13; 24:51; 25:30). Other than Matthew, only Luke mentions this (Lk. 13:28), and only once. "Gnashing" in the O.T. is used of enemies who rage (Ps. 112:10; Lam. 2:16). Here the meaning is different. Gnashing (Greek *brugmos*) suggests pain-filled "desperate hopelessness" for those who reject Jesus' kingdom offer (*ISBE* II:483). It "denotes the despairing remorse which shakes the whole body and is linked with [weeping]" (*TDNT* I:642). Jesus spoke of a place of punishment, not just a condition (Bruner 1:383). He warned about it, and the wise take His warning seriously.

Jesus assured the centurion that because he believed (v. 13: "as" being used causally; Wilkins 343; Hill 159), his servant would be healed. It is possible Jesus meant that the healing would be done to the degree that the centurion believed (understanding "as" comparatively). See 9:29. Either way, the faith of another occasioned the healing of the servant (Bruner 1:384). The servant was healed immediately, which proved the genuineness of the centurion's faith and the reality of its object. The incarnate Jesus had power over sickness. He had power to heal from a distance, and He had authority to command healing and it be done.

3. Jesus healed many in Capernaum (8:14-17)

14 And when Jesus was come into Peter's house, he saw his wife's mother laid, and sick of a fever.
15 And he touched her hand, and the fever left her: and she arose, and ministered unto them.
16 When the even was come, they brought unto him many that were possessed with devils: and he cast out the spirits with *his* word, and healed all that were sick:
17 That it might be fulfilled which was spoken by Esaias the prophet, saying, Himself took *our* infirmities, and bare our sicknesses.

Following the healing of the centurion's servant, Jesus went to Peter and Andrew's home (Mt. 4:13, 18; Mk. 1:29). He was still in Capernaum. According to Luke 4:38, some asked Jesus to heal Peter's mother-in-law and He did. (On Peter's home in Capernaum, see comments on 4:18.) His power was such that with a word (Lk. 4:39) and a touch on her hand (Greek *haptō* can mean grasp, hold, or touch; Grimm's 70; Newman and Stine 241), Jesus healed her (v. 15). Men normally would not touch a woman for fear of becoming unclean (Lev. 15:19). Mark (1:31) says that He took hold of (Greek *krateō*) her hand and raised her up. Peter's mother-in-law was immediately and so completely healed (Keener, *Background* 67) that she rose from her sick bed and began ministering (Greek inceptive imperfect) to Jesus and His disciples, i.e., she worked to prepare a meal for them. Her actions surely expressed gratitude to Jesus (Wilkins 345).

According to Paul, Peter's wife later became his traveling associate (1 Cor. 9:5). At this time, they were possibly caring for his wife's aged mother (Keener, *Background* 67). Peter had family responsibilities but Jesus' call to full-time discipleship took precedence over some family matters. However, the call did not mean for him to leave his spouse. A call to follow Jesus fulltime was a shared sacrifice. One can only imagine the excitement as Peter and the others shared with their families the stories of Jesus' miracles and teachings.

That evening more people brought their sick to Jesus (Mt. 4:23-24). Matthew is not clear on this but people waited until evening because that day was the Sabbath (Mk. 1:21; Lk. 13:14) and the evening marked a new day. Jesus had healed Peter's mother-in-law on the Sabbath. He later stated that healing on the Sabbath was not wrong (12:12; Lk. 14:1-6).

Some were in need of spiritual healing while others needed physical healing. Some needed both. As the centurion observed (8:9), persons with real authority need only say the word and it will be done. With only a word (v. 16), Jesus discharged evil spirits and freed those who were possessed (4:24). Just as easily, He healed physical ailments. These (and others) were the miracles that made this community so culpable for rejecting Jesus' claims (11:23).

Jesus ministered in this manner because this was the plan of God. Citing the Hebrew text, Matthew said Isaiah 53:4 promised that the Servant of the LORD, the Messiah, would deliver from life's infirmities and sorrows (Blomberg 32; Archer and Chirichigno 121). Jesus "took ... and carried away" (v. 17). This means that He removed the diseases from the sick (Hill 161) but not that He became sick himself (Gundry 150). He would address the needs caused by the fall even during His earthly ministry (Carson, *John* 246; Carson, *Matthew* 204-207). See the discussion on 4:23-25. Jesus was saying, by these miracles, "Look at my miraculous signs. Who do they witness that I am?" For the answer, see Matthew 11:2-6 and 12:28, John 5:36 and 10:38.

One must approach this passage in an exegetically balanced manner (Blomberg 30). Matthew's distinction between the two healings shows that Satan does not cause all sicknesses (*ESV Study Bible* 1836) and that not all sicknesses are physical. That physical healing is a benefit of the atonement is certain from Isaiah and the reason Matthew included Isaiah's promise in the context of these multiple physical healings. The Lord continues to heal today—sometimes even miraculously. However, it is wrong to say that based on this passage everyone who has certain faith will receive healing. This passage does not teach "healing on demand" (Carson, *Matthew* 206-207). The Scripture simply will not support such an understanding.

On the other hand, the Bible teaches that God heals His people. The church has both a biblical basis (v. 17) and a mandate (Jas. 5:14-16) for a healing ministry. For a discussion that argues that Jesus' atonement does not provide a basis for physical healing, see Erickson (836-841).

4. Jesus explained the cost of being His disciple (8:18-22)

18 Now when Jesus saw great multitudes about him, he gave

commandment to depart unto the other side.

19 And a certain scribe came, and said unto him, Master, I will follow thee whithersoever thou goest.

20 And Jesus saith unto him, The foxes have holes, and the birds of the air *have* nests; but the Son of man hath not where to lay *his* head.

21 And another of his disciples said unto him, Lord, suffer me first to go and bury my father.

22 But Jesus said unto him, Follow me; and let the dead bury their dead.

Jesus' healings attracted crowds. Perhaps because He wanted to make disciples, not simply attract crowds, Jesus directed His disciples to go to the other side of the Sea of Galilee. Jesus might simply have needed to rest (Nolland 364).

As He was preparing to leave Capernaum, a scribe, an expert teacher of the Mosaic Law, expressed his desire to follow Jesus in His itinerate ministry. The word "another" in verse 21 suggests that the scribe was already a disciple though not one of the Twelve. If so, he wanted a closer relationship with Jesus. The scribe addressed Jesus as Master (Greek *didaskalos*, teacher), an indication that he wanted a master/disciple relationship like the one he had already experienced to become a professional scribe (Wilkins 347; Hagner 33A:216). He might have been the first official scribe to express such an interest (Bruner 1:394). For further description of a scribe, see comments on 13:52.

Jesus stated that to follow Him would be difficult and costly (v. 20). Following Jesus as a disciple was primarily about doing, not about being a professional student (Hill 162). Jesus' discipleship was task oriented, for He was an itinerate teacher. He did not have nice lodging in His travels nor did He use a nice teaching facility (Acts 19:9). Though the Gospel writers did not specifically say so, Jesus surely spent many nights outside (Lk. 22:39; Jn. 18:2). Palestine's moderate climate permitted this (Wilkins 351). Unlike animals that even have a place to rest, Jesus ministered in hardship. Jesus did not try to stop the man from following Him but He did want the scribe to count the cost (Barclay 1:361; Lk. 14:25-33). He told him up front what would be required. It would not be an easy association. Following Jesus then and now requires determined commitment and self-denial (Hagner 33A:216).

If the scribe's commitment was authentic, that very night he and some other disciples got what rest they could in a boat. Even then, their rest was interrupted by a fierce storm, which they fought with great difficulty (vv. 23-25). The scribe did not have to wait long to see the truth of Jesus' words about the difficulties of being His disciple.

Jesus' statement in verse 20 did not mean that He did not have a home in Capernaum (*contra* Barclay 1:455). Compare 4:13 and 9:1 comments and Mark 2:1. It meant that He did not have comfortable accommodations or even acceptance (v. 34) everywhere His travels took Him (Gundry 152; Nolland 366-367). It also meant that all who follow Him can expect the same sacrifice and rejections. Unlike poverty, sacrifice is voluntary and in kingdom work, required (Keener, *Background* 68). For "Son of Man," see Matthew 26:64.

In contrast to the scribe, a second man who was already a follower of Jesus but also not one of the Twelve, asked to be relieved of his discipleship responsibilities so he could bury his father. He was not asking if he could attend to an immediate burial need (v. 21; *contra* Hendriksen 408). Since Jews did not embalm, burials took place within hours after a death. Rather, this disciple asked if he could stay home, i.e., not travel with Jesus, until his father passed away (Barclay 1:364). One might wonder if he wanted to care for his parents or if an inheritance was in view. We are not told. However, Jesus' reply was short: continue following. There is no place to step away from kingdom responsibilities—"even for a time, to bury one's father" (Evans, *Matthew* 176). Let the dead, i.e., the spiritually dead, the unsaved (Jn. 5:24; Eph. 2:1), stay with the parents until they pass away (v. 22). With these words Jesus not only called this man to total commitment to Jesus but He also stated the spiritual condition of all who do not follow Him (Bruner 1:396): they are dead.

Jesus did not tell His followers to ignore family responsibilities and disassociate from their parents, nor did He absolve adult children of responsibility to care for their parents financially (see Mt. 15:1-9; 1 Tim. 5:4-8). In His dying moments He saw to it that His mother's care was provided (Jn. 19:26-27). Rather, He taught that one's devotion to Jesus and whatever demands He places on His followers must surpass all other allegiances (Wilkins 350; Nolland 368).

Others understand Jesus' words differently. Keener (*Background* 68) says the man was asking to be permitted to attend to the second burial of his father. This was after the flesh was rotted from the bones and the bones were placed in a box called an ossuary. This second burial would happen as much as a year after the first burial. This would have meant the man was asking Jesus for a year off. If this was the case, Jesus' response required that the disciple put Him before one of the greatest responsibilities a son has toward his father.

Regardless which interpretation one accepts, this much is clear: Jesus wanted this disciple to follow Him. Jesus wanted him to get into the boat (v. 18; Keener, *Matthew* 274). Apparently he did.

Newman and Stine (248, 202) believe the statement "let the dead bury their dead" is like the "log in your eye" (7:3, ESV) and the "camel through the eye of a needle" (19:24) statements. All are intentionally ridiculous and not meant to be applied literally. However, as one writer states, the call to discipleship is radical, urgent, and uncompromising, and this fundamental principle must be "heard with every invitation to, or volunteering of, discipleship to Jesus and the cause of the kingdom" (Hagner 33A:218).

This disciple would soon learn that Jesus was not calling him to a higher level of commitment than He was the other disciples. Subjecting family love and obligations to the Lordship of Jesus was the new norm for all who would be Jesus' disciples (10:35-39; Lk. 14:25-33). Subjecting family love and obligation to the Lordship of Jesus was one aspect of carrying a cross (16:24-28).

5. Jesus calmed the storm on the Sea of Galilee (8:23-27)

23 And when he was entered into a ship, his disciples followed him.

24 And, behold, there arose a great tempest in the sea, insomuch that the ship was covered with the waves: but he was asleep.
25 And his disciples came to *him*, and awoke him, saying, Lord, save us: we perish.
26 And he saith unto them, Why are ye fearful, O ye of little faith? Then he arose, and rebuked the winds and the sea; and there was a great calm.
27 But the men marvelled, saying, What manner of man is this, that even the winds and the sea obey him!

Jesus and His disciples got into a ship or boat (Greek *ploion*). Other disciples and probably the scribe from verses 19-22 went along. Mark (4:36) says there were other boats. So, more than the Twelve witnessed the next miracle.

Though one cannot be certain of the exact type of boat Jesus used, in January 1986, a boat from that time period was discovered on the bottom of the Sea of Galilee (http://jesusboatmuseum.com/themiracle/therecovery/; accessed 3-19-2012). An illustration is available at http://www.esvstudybible.org/sb/objects/illustration-galilean-fishing-boat.html; accessed 12-27-2010). According to this latter source, this boat measures 26.5 feet long, 7.5 feet wide, and 4.5 feet high (8.1 X 2.3 X 1.4m). It is obvious from these dimensions how waves could easily cover this boat (v. 24).

The Sea of Galilee measures approximately thirteen miles north to south, eight miles east to west. Its greatest depth is 165 feet deep (50 meters; Beitzel 39). It is small enough that travelers were able to go by boat from side to side in short periods of time. Sudden storms are common on the Sea of Galilee (ISBE II:392).

Tired from the day of ministry, Jesus went to sleep in the boat (v. 24). His humanity is in view. While He was sleeping, a storm suddenly arose. The disciples, being experienced fishermen, knew that this was no small storm and unless Jesus did something miraculous they could all die. They woke Him with their cries for help. One can almost hear their panic: "Lord, save us!" "Save" has a sense of urgency to it (Greek *sōzō*, aorist imperative).

The leper, the centurion and his servant, Peter's mother-in-law, and many others in Capernaum had needed Jesus (vv. 1-17). Now it was the disciples' turn (Bruner 1:397). They too needed the Master. In truth, they had followed Jesus into the storm, which was about discipleship as well (v. 23; Hill 166).

Did the disciples believe Jesus' life was in danger as well as their own? The "we" (v. 25) can include Jesus or only the disciples (Newman and Stine 250). Given the level of their understanding at this time (v. 27), they probably feared that all of them, including Jesus, were about to die. They addressed Him as Lord but they were not inferring His deity at this time. Compare verse 27 and 14:33.

The word "tempest" (Greek *seismos*) can mean storm or earthquake. The Sea of Galilee is located in the Jordan Rift Valley, which is "part of one of the longest, deepest and widest fissures in the earth's surface" where sizable earthquakes have occurred (Beitzel 37-38). However, Matthew included wind (v. 26), which suggests that this was a surface storm rather than an earthquake (*contra* Bruner 1:398). Mark (4:37) and Luke (8:23) made no reference to an earthquake. They used a different word (Greek *lailaps*), which means whirlwind or tempestuous wind (Grimm's 368).

Aroused from sleep, Jesus' first words were to His disciples (v. 26) and included an element of rebuke. According to Matthew, before He got up and with the winds still blowing and the waves still swamping the boat, Jesus spoke to His disciples (Hendriksen 411). These men were "men of little faith" (6:30). Their faith in Him was growing but it was still immature, as their fear demonstrated. Fear evidences weak faith (14:29-32). With Jesus in the boat with them, there was no reason to fear the storm.

Jesus rose (v. 26: stood up? Newman and Stine 251) in that storm-tossed boat and proved by rebuking the winds and rough waters that there was no reason to fear. His rebuke and nature's immediate obedience showed that Jesus' authority extended even over nature. Mark (4:39) included Jesus' words in his record: "Peace, be still." There was a "great calm" (v. 26). The wind and waves did not just lessen; they quieted completely.

The "men" in the boat with Him, and possibly in the other boats as well if they were close enough to see and hear, were amazed at what they had just witnessed. With just a word, He demonstrated absolute rule over the winds and the waves. Asleep one moment, the God-man checked nature the next. The disciples had asked for help, and help they graciously received though their faith was weak (Bruner 1:401), but they were surprised at the level of help Jesus provided. This one *who* taught with authority and healed with authority also possessed absolute authority over the forces of nature (Newman and Stine 248).

Christologically, this event portrays the two natures of Jesus. In His human nature He was tired, so He slept. However, He was able to wake from sleep and in His divine nature with only a word, calm the sea. As Grudem (559) states, "here Jesus' weak human nature completely hid His omnipotence until that omnipotence broke forth in a sovereign word from the Lord of heaven and earth." For further comments on the doctrine of the incarnation, see this commentary on 1:20, 4:1, and 24:36.

If the scribe in verse 19 who had just started traveling with Jesus and the man who had wanted some time away from discipleship responsibilities (v. 21) were with Jesus on this boat ride, they witnessed something that only those in the storm with Jesus ever see. They, the Twelve (assuming all twelve had been called by this time; but see 9:9) and those in the other boats (Mk. 4:36) saw such a display of power that they began to wonder who Jesus really was. They would eventually come to realize that power such as this can only mean one thing (Mt. 14:33).

6. Jesus healed two demon-possessed men at Gergesa (8:28-34)

28 And when he was come to the other side into the country of the Gergesenes, there met him two possessed with devils, coming out of the tombs, exceeding fierce, so that no man might pass by that way.

29 And, behold, they cried out, saying, What have we to do with thee, Jesus, thou Son of God? art thou come hither to torment us before the time?

30 And there was a good way off from them an herd of many swine feeding.
31 So the devils besought him, saying, If thou cast us out, suffer us to go away into the herd of swine.
32 And he said unto them, Go. And when they were come out, they went into the herd of swine: and, behold, the whole herd of swine ran violently down a steep place into the sea, and perished in the waters.
33 And they that kept them fled, and went their ways into the city, and told every thing, and what was befallen to the possessed of the devils.
34 And, behold, the whole city came out to meet Jesus: and when they saw him, they besought *him* that he would depart out of their coasts.

Somewhere on the "other side" of the lake, Jesus got out of the boat where two demon-possessed men confronted Him. Two questions immediately confront the reader. First, where exactly did this meeting take place? Translations vary because Greek manuscript evidence is divided. Some older Greek manuscripts place Jesus in the country of the Gadarenes. Gadara was a town located about five miles (eight kilometers) southeast and inland of the Sea of Galilee. Other manuscripts say Gergasenes. Gergasa was a town located on the east side of the Sea of Galilee at water's edge. Still other manuscripts identify the area as of the Gerasenes, but Gerasa's location makes this the least likely. The parallel records of Mark (5:1) and Luke (8:26) have the same possibilities. With our present state of knowledge, we cannot know for certain which is original. Gergesa seems to fit the physical requirements (v. 33-34), but a five mile walk to Gadara would not have been unrealistic. It is also possible that the areas around the towns bore the towns' names (v. 34 "their region"; Mk. 5:1; Lk. 8:37; ISBE II:375, 447), and one may suppose that where the areas met could accurately be called by either name. Gerasa and Gadara were cities of the Decapolis.

Second, how many demon-possessed men were there? Matthew mentions two. Mark and Luke mention one. One can only speculate why the records are different. Certainly there were two but Mark and Luke mention only one perhaps because he was the spokesperson for the two or because he became a solo missionary for Jesus in the Decapolis (Mk. 5:20; Lk. 8:39).

Matthew described these men as demon-possessed (v. 28). Mark wrote that the man had an unclean spirit (Mk. 5:2). Demon possession is the state where an individual is indwelt by and so under the controlling influence of one or more demons. At no time did Jesus suggest that demons were anything other than real, personal, spirit beings (*contra*; Barclay 1:370-373 who says demons are not real and that Jesus simply accommodated current belief). Demons are fallen angels, spirit beings, who are servants of Satan. Some fallen angels are permitted to oppose the work of God on earth (Dan. 10:13) while others are bound until their judgment (2 Pet. 2:4). This passage demonstrates their power, ungodliness, multitude, ability to indwell humans, ability to speak, spirit nature, and subordination to Jesus. Jesus was regularly confronted by these Satanic minions as was the early church (Mt. 4:24; 9:32-34; 12:22-29; Acts 5:16; 8:7; 13:8, 10; 19:12; 1 Cor. 12:10; 1 Jn. 4:1). Scripture shows that demonic power always impacts humans negatively. They always leave a person in a state of debilitation (Nolland 463).

These men were possessed by many demons (Mk. 5:9; Lk. 8:30). The demons had so ruined the lives of these men that they lived separate from society. They lived among the tombs, which meant that they found shelter in the burial caves (Newman and Stine 254, 255; Hill 168). Living among the tombs was also a symbol of their own spiritual condition. They were so dangerous that no one could even travel through that area.

However, their response to Jesus was different (v. 29). Rather than physically attack Him they asked, "What have we to do with thee?" (Greek, literally, What to us and to you?). Some of the older Greek manuscripts include "Jesus" (v. 29) while others do not. English translations reflect this difference. Regardless, they wondered why Jesus was coming to them in Gentile territory (Hill 168). Was He planning to torture and torment them now? They knew their judgment day was set (2 Pet. 2:4; Jude 6). Judgment day was "the time" to which they referred. Indeed judgment had begun for these demons. Jesus' exorcism of demons not only proved that the kingdom had come (Mt. 12:28), but the coming of the Messianic kingdom also meant the beginning of their demise, the end of Satan's kingdom.

"Hither" means "to here": the question is, where is "here"? Did the demons mean the particular locale east of Galilee (Hill 168), or were they speaking of earth in general, "where they had some freedom to trouble men" (Carson, *Matthew* 218)? Carson sees an implicit reference to the preexistence of Jesus in their question. If Carson is right, one may also see in this the demons' ignorance of the plan of God. They knew of their own impending doom at the hand of Jesus but they did not expect to see Him so soon.

Speaking through the men, the demons addressed Jesus as "Son of God" thus publically affirming His deity (Nolland 375). They knew who He was and they knew that they were outranked. They had to get permission before they could even enter pigs. One who was in control had stepped into their territory. He could easily overpower them though they numbered many (12:29; Mk. 5:9). He could banish them to immediate punishment should He choose.

The demons had to leave the men as Jesus commanded (Mk. 5:8; Lk. 8:29), so they requested permission to move to the pigs (v. 31). Literally, they were begging and entreating (Greek imperfect *parakaleō*). "Suffer us" means "permit us." With authority (see comments on 8:8-9) Jesus commanded them, "Go," and they went. As soon as they entered the pigs, the pigs ran into the water and drowned (Greek *apothnēskō*, to die). The pigs died, not the demons (*contra* Gundry 160; Bruner 1:405; Newman and Stine 257). If the demons died and went to hell, then Jesus would have been tormenting them "before the time" (Carson, *Matthew* 218-219).

Matthew did not say that the demons killed the pigs but it seems that they did because this apparent destruction by the demons turned some folks against Jesus. The loss of two thousand pigs (Mk.

5:13) was a severe economic blow to the community. The presence of pigs suggests that the population was mainly Gentile (ISBE I:908). Pigs were unclean by Mosaic legal standards and while it is possible that Jews were raising pigs, there is no reason to conclude that from this passage. The demoniacs could have been Jews or Gentiles. It is probable, since this was a Gentile area, these men were Gentiles; but that is not certain.

Matthew summarized the exorcism and conversion with a simple "Go ... and they came out" (Bruner 1:405). Mark (5:15) and Luke (8:35-36) gave more extensive details of the change in the demoniacs that resulted from this encounter with Jesus. Not only could Jesus calm the winds and seas (vv. 23-27), He could deliver, heal, and calm those whose lives Satan controlled and destroyed.

Such a miracle did not go unnoticed. The herdsmen were suddenly without work. They ran into the city and told everything (v. 33). They were especially careful to tell what had happened to the two men. Everyone knew about the men who lived in the tombs, for many of them had often tried, unsuccessfully, to subdue him (Mk. 5:3-4).

The events were surprising and the whole city went out to meet Jesus (v. 34). The eyewitness testimonies, along with the change in the former demoniacs, were so dramatic that the residents became afraid (Lk. 8:37). Their fear was so strong that instead of asking Jesus, the Son of God, to stay that they might learn from Him and live under His power, they begged (also *parakaleō*, cf. v. 31) Him to leave (Evans, *Matthew* 185). What a tragedy! They did not marvel at the miraculous healing of these two men. In contrast to those on the other side of the lake (8:16; 9:1-8; Nolland 377), they brought no sick to be healed (Hendriksen 415). They asked Jesus to leave and He did. It is as if they chose the demonic over the Deliverer. It is for sure that they preferred the pigs. "The eastern shore need[ed] Jesus badly" (Bruner 1:404). The darkness was extremely dark (4:16) but they wanted nothing to do with the Light. Money was their god and yet they did not realize that with Jesus' leaving they were economically and spiritually poorer (Bruner 1:406).

Jesus, however, did not leave them without a witness (Mk. 5:18-20; Lk. 8:38-39; Hendriksen 416). What grace! If these men were Gentiles, they were the first Gentiles commissioned directly by Jesus to carry the gospel of the kingdom. Jesus sent them to their home area, a largely Gentile region.

Summary (8:1-34)

Following the Sermon on the Mount (chapters 5-7) Matthew grouped together ten miracles. Chapter eight contains Matthew's record of five specific miracles and a short discussion of the cost of discipleship. Three miracles were performed in Capernaum, one on the Sea of Galilee, and one on the east side of the lake. It is apparent from Matthew's choice of miracles that he was making the point that Jesus is for everyone, Jew and Gentile, male and female, bound and free. It is also clear that Jesus had unlimited power during His earthly ministry. There was no sickness or form of demon-possession that He was unable to heal.

Application: Teaching and Preaching the Passage

Lessons and sermons can be developed from the individual pericopes or from the chapter as a whole. The healing of the leper might be presented as (1) his need, (2) his faith, and (3) his cleansing. The centurion's faith (1) gave rise to a request (from an unlikely source, a Gentile; and was for someone else), (2) came clothed in humility (his understanding of himself, in 5:3, and his understanding of Jesus), (3) was mature (its quality, its rarity), and (4) resulted in rewards (his place in the kingdom, his prayer answered).

The discipleship commitment Jesus requires (vv. 18-22) (1) must begin with self-sacrifice; (2) must supersede normal familial desires; and (3) ultimately means getting into the boat with Jesus.

The calming of the storm teaches several lessons about discipleship. (1) Disciples follow Jesus (v. 23). (2) Following Jesus sometimes means going into great storms (v. 24). (3) Storms come even when Jesus is in the boat (v. 24). (4) Storms do not worry the Savior (v. 24). (5) Prayer for deliverance does not offend the Savior (v. 25). (6) Fear is evidence of "little faith" and little faith offends the Savior (v. 26). (7) With a word, Jesus can instantly and completely calm even the greatest storms (v. 26). (8) It is right to marvel at the one who calms the storms.

One might deal topically with the subject of little faith people, using this and other passages in Matthew's record. Jesus talked on various occasions about this. Worry and faith cannot coexist in the same heart. The following qualities describe people of little faith. They are (1) worriers (6:30): people who do not trust God for their food and clothes; (2) fearful (8:26): followers who are afraid even though Jesus is with them; (3) doubters (14:31): followers who lack faith to finish; (4) immature in spiritual understanding (16:8): followers who are too natural in their thinking; and (5) spiritually anemic (17:20): followers who are too weak spiritually to battle with the forces of evil.

The healing of the Gergasean demoniacs teaches that Jesus (1) frees those under satanic control; (2) outranks evil beings; and (3) will torment evil beings on judgment day.

The story of the Gergasean demoniacs also shows that the gospel (1) confronts (vv. 28-31), (2) delivers (v. 32), and (3) offends (vv. 33-34).

One might also consider the prayers in this chapter. There was bold prayer (v. 2), intercessory prayer (v. 6), urgent prayer (v. 25), and a prayer of rejection (v. 34).

7. Jesus healed a paralytic (9:1-8)

This chapter continues Matthew's grouping of ten specific miracles to prove Jesus' authority over nature, sickness, sin, and evil spirits. See the introduction to chapter eight for further discussion. The healing of the paralytic is miracle number six and the forgiveness of sins dominates the discussion surrounding this miracle (Hagner 33A:230).

1 And he entered into a ship, and passed over, and came into his own city.

2 And, behold, they brought to him a man sick of the palsy, lying on a bed: and Jesus seeing their faith said unto the sick of the

palsy; Son, be of good cheer; thy sins be forgiven thee.
3 And, behold, certain of the scribes said within themselves, This *man* blasphemeth.
4 And Jesus knowing their thoughts said, Wherefore think ye evil in your hearts?
5 For whether is easier, to say, *Thy* sins be forgiven thee; or to say, Arise, and walk?
6 But that ye may know that the Son of man hath power on earth to forgive sins, (then saith he to the sick of the palsy,) Arise, take up thy bed, and go unto thine house.
7 And he arose, and departed to his house.
8 But when the multitudes saw *it*, they marvelled, and glorified God, which had given such power unto men.

After being asked to leave the area where He had delivered the demoniacs, Jesus returned by boat (see comments on 8:23) to Capernaum. Matthew did not identify the house where Jesus stayed. It might have been Jesus' own private home, Peter's home (Mt. 8:14), or the home of Jesus' family—if John 2:12 means that He, His mother, and His brothers relocated to Capernaum as a family (Picirilli, *Mark* 45, 63). Matthew omits some rather interesting details. Unlike Mark and Luke, he did not mention how the man with palsy—that is, a paralytic (8:6)—arrived at the house or how he came to be in front of Jesus.

Mark (2:2) wrote that the house was packed, even the doorway. Apparently folks were standing at the door listening. Luke (5:17) says that there were several Pharisees and scribes in the home as well. Matthew mentions only the scribes.

Four men wanted to bring their paralytic friend to Jesus but the crowd was a barrier (Mk. 2:3). Confident that Jesus could heal this man (perhaps they had heard of previous healings of paralytics, 4:24), they were determined. Though Matthew did not tell his readers, Mark (2:4) and Luke (5:19) both recorded that these men removed a portion of the roof and lowered him, still on his couch, down to Jesus. No one seemed to mind. Being a carpenter Himself, Jesus understood that someone would need to repair the hole but nothing is ever said about that.

Scholars have determined that roofs in biblical times were flat and usually not over six feet (1.8 meters) above the floor (ISBE II:771). A center beam with supporting posts set in stone sockets helped span larger areas. Smaller timbers were spaced out and placed across the area between the outer walls and the center beam. This was covered with brushwood and then a final covering of a mixture of mud and chopped straw was beaten and rolled into the brush. The roof could then be accessed by stairs or a ladder. Grass grew on such rooftops and became illustrative material for prophets showing the weakness of people (Ps. 129:6; 2 Kg. 19:26; Is. 37:27). When the four men removed part of the roof to make a way to get their friend to Jesus, dirt and debris would have fallen on those in the room.

Jesus recognized the faith of these men in their determination and their actions (Mt. 9:2; Jas. 2:18) and spoke encouragingly to the paralytic. "Be of good cheer" or "Take heart" means to be encouraged. Jesus later said the same thing to calm the fears of the woman who touched His garment (v. 22), to calm the fears of His disciples the night

He came walking on the water (14:27), to blind Bartimaeus (Mk. 10:49), to the Twelve in the Upper Room (Jn. 16:33), and to Paul after his arrest in Jerusalem (Acts 23:11). In light of the paralytic's condition, Jesus' calming words were needed and welcomed.

Jesus next went beyond anything He had previously done. Rather than heal the paralytic of his paralysis, and without any specific request from the paralytic or the men who brought him (Hendriksen 418), Jesus declared the man's sins forgiven (v. 2). To forgive is to pardon or to free someone from a debt. When God forgives, the sin and the penalty for sin are forever gone, never to be remembered against that person again (Mic. 7:18-19; Ps. 32:1-2; Heb. 10:17-18).

Scripture teaches that one must not assume every sickness results from specific, personal sin (Jn. 9:2-3; Job 2:3, 7). To say, however, that this is *never* true would also be an error (Jn. 5:14; 1 Cor. 11:30). Why Jesus declared the paralytic's sins forgiven rather than his body healed is open to conjecture. Some commentators believe that it was because the paralytic believed sin to be his problem (Barclay 1:379; Bruner 1:412). Carson (*Matthew* 221) thinks Jesus may have implied that there was a direct link in this instance. It may have been that Jesus was challenging any there who were judging the paralytic a sinner (Jn. 9:34).

Regardless, though each Gospel writer mentions the faith of the four friends, it seems a given that the paralytic had faith also (Keener, *Matthew* 288), for this is the means of appropriating God's forgiving grace (Eph. 2:8-9). For that matter, "their faith" might have included the paralytic. At any rate, the faith of the four friends was remarkable in that it moved them to unusual action (Jas. 2:18-26). Putting grace on display, Jesus rewarded faith with a clear declaration of forgiveness.

Some of the scribes (expert teachers of the law; 2:4) immediately judged Jesus a blasphemer (v. 3). They thought this, thinking His statement had insulted (Newman and Stine 262) and disgraced God by claiming that He was able to do something that only God can do. They believed no one could forgive sins but God (Mk. 2:7) and that Jesus claimed a divine prerogative (Wilkins 355). This was Matthew's first recorded event where the religious leaders of the day denounced Jesus. More were on the horizon (vv. 11, 34).

Jesus knew their views and accused them of evil thoughts (v. 4). Which is easier to say, i.e., claim to be doing, forgive sins or heal the paralytic? Jesus' question assumes that both actions require the power and approval of God but some writers believe Jesus was saying that healing is the harder because it is so easily verifiable (Evans, *Matthew* 188; Bruner 1:415). To demonstrate His ability to forgive (v. 6; Greek purpose clause: *hina* + subjunctive) and thus show that He had God's approval as well (Jn. 5:34-37; Acts 2:22; Heb. 2:4), He commanded the man to get up, pick up his bed (Greek *klinē,* stretcher, pallet) and go home. The man obeyed. In full sight of everyone, even Jesus' detractors, the healed man stood up, picked up his bed and went home (Mk. 2:12). Jesus demonstrated the unseen with the seen (Hagner 33A:233).The only things the healed man left were a hole in the roof, dirt and debris on the floor, stunned eyewitnesses, his guilt, and his sickness. For Son of Man, see 26:64.

The miracle was nothing short of amazing. It took four men, a stretcher, and considerable work to get this man to Jesus. With only a word from Jesus he went home on his own power (v. 7), whole physically and guiltless before God. The lay people who witnessed the miracle reacted strongly—"marveled" in some manuscripts, "feared" in others—and with praise (v. 8). They and the paralytic recognized that this man could heal and forgive sins (Evans, *Matthew* 189; Carson, *Matthew* 222). Jesus' power to forgive impressed them more than the healing (Nolland 383).

The people's observation that God had given men the authority to forgive sins (v. 8) does not mean the church has the authority to forgive sins (*contra* Newman and Stine 260, 265 and Hagner 33A:231). These folks did not know that Jesus was God. To them He was just a man. Matthew's words (v. 8) are descriptive only of the people's conclusion and were intended to communicate that Jesus had authority to forgive, not that such authority is shared by the church. Jesus' ability to forgive fulfills the promise of the angel to Joseph (1:21, 23; Carson, *Matthew* 223) and supports Matthew's claims that Jesus is the Messiah and God with us. See 16:19 and 18:18 for further discussion about the authority of the church to forgive sin.

This healing miracle is also noteworthy for the reason that it was done mainly because of the faith of persons other than the one needing the healing. All three Gospel writers indicate this. These men believed the kingdom message of Jesus (Mk. 2:2) and that Jesus could heal their friend. This points to the value of intercessory prayer and faith, a point Matthew made earlier with the account of the centurion's faith (8:8-10).

From a post-cross vantage point, it is clear that this miracle demonstrated the deity of Jesus. His ability to know their thoughts pointed to His omniscience; His ability to heal with a word pointed to His omnipotence; and His ability to forgive sins pointed to His deity and divine desire to reconcile with sinful mankind. The crowd recognized that Jesus was human but they also recognized the power of God. Such a miracle required that they believe He could forgive sin even as He claimed.

8. Jesus called Matthew to follow Him (9:9-13)

9 And as Jesus passed forth from thence, he saw a man, named Matthew, sitting at the receipt of custom: and he saith unto him, Follow me. And he arose, and followed him.

10 And it came to pass, as Jesus sat at meat in the house, behold, many publicans and sinners came and sat down with him and his disciples.

11 And when the Pharisees saw *it*, they said unto his disciples, Why eateth your Master with publicans and sinners?

12 But when Jesus heard *that*, he said unto them, They that be whole need not a physician, but they that are sick.

13 But go ye and learn what *that* meaneth, I will have mercy, and not sacrifice: for I am not come to call the righteous, but sinners to repentance.

Sometime after the healing of the paralytic, Jesus walked by Matthew's "receipt of custom: that is, his tax booth (Greek *telōnion*). Matthew would have been collecting a tax on goods brought into the area to be sold, a kind of sales tax charged to vendors before they were permitted to sell their goods (Louw and Nida I:578). Evidently this occurred in or around Capernaum, Jesus' home base (4:13).

Seeing Matthew, Jesus said to him, "Follow me." These were simple instructions with profound implications. Jesus called Matthew, a tax collector, to follow Him as a disciple as He had done Peter, Andrew, James, and John (4:18-22). For tax collectors ("publicans"), see comments on 5:46. Matthew was probably at least able to speak Aramaic, the language of Galilee, and Greek. Being a tax collector, he also needed record-keeping skills. These skills later enabled him to write this Gospel record (Barclay 1:383).

Matthew's response (he rose and followed) suggests that this was not his first encounter with Jesus (Wilkins 365) and that he fully understood what Jesus intended. Without embellishment, Matthew gave a simple testimony. This was one of his few autobiographical entries. Luke (5:28) wrote that Matthew (Levi) left everything at once. This meant he left a lucrative and secure job (Keener, *Background* 70). Jesus' call to Matthew was simultaneously a call to salvation (v. 13) and to full-time service.

Shortly after his decision, Matthew invited Jesus and His disciples to his home for a meal (v. 10), a gesture that pointed to some wealth. To "sit at meat" is literally to "recline for eating"; see 26:7. Luke 5:29 specifically identified the dinner as being at Matthew's home and called the meal a feast. Matthew invited his tax collector friends to this dinner as well. It seems clear that Matthew's first actions as a new follower of Jesus were to make public his decision to follow Jesus (Hendriksen 423) and to evangelize his friends. He chose to host a meal as his means of accomplishing these things.

Matthew's guest list is telling. In addition to Jesus and His disciples, Matthew invited tax collectors and sinners. These were the despised of society and these were Matthew's friends. Prior to meeting Jesus, Matthew's friends were not part of the religious community.

The Pharisees (see comments on 3:7) condemned Jesus for associating with Matthew and his dinner guests (v. 11). Jewish tax collectors were disliked for several reasons (Gundry 167): they were considered traitors for collecting taxes for the enslaving power (Rome or Herod), and they were considered to be at least potentially unclean because of their association with Gentiles (Keener, *Background* 70). Honesty was also an issue (Lk. 19:8). The Pharisees thought that Jesus ran the risk of becoming at least ritually unclean (Evans, *Matthew* 191), or perhaps by association He gave the impression that He agreed with their lifestyle (Newman and Stine 269). Rather than question Jesus directly, they questioned His disciples. Jesus addressed their concern. He was not with the sinners because He agreed with their lifestyles. Rather, He had what they needed. Jesus was exactly where He needed to be. Like a physician, Jesus treated the sick, not the strong and healthy (v. 12). Matthew and his friends were sick. They needed Jesus.

Further, the Pharisees were wrong in their understanding of God's requirements revealed in the Law. Quoting Hosea 6:6, Jesus showed that the eighth century B.C. prophet's message was still relevant. God wants more than a shell of religion (Carson, *Matthew* 225). He wants religion built on a lasting relationship (Hos. 3:1; 6:4), one that comes from the heart and reflects a true knowledge of God. Such knowledge shows itself in proper worship (sacrifices) and in proper actions toward one's fellowman. Loyal love for God—the Hebrew word means covenant love, mercy—and right treatment of one's fellowman are required before sacrifices are accepted: "I will have [= desire] mercy, and not sacrifice."

This same message is found in other eighth century B.C. prophets as well (Is. 1:11-17, 58:1-12; Am. 5:21-24; and Mic. 6:6-8). It surfaces again in Matthew 12:7. Further, it is in keeping with Jesus' explanation of the first and second greatest commandments: right and faithful relationships with God *and* man are required before sacrifices are acceptable (22:39; Mk. 12:28-34).

Hosea 6:6 supported Jesus' practice of extending the mercy and knowledge of God to those who needed Him. By eating with these sinners, Jesus did not become unclean. Rather, He was celebrating Matthew's "newly found purity" (Blomberg 35) and offering the same to Matthew's friends. Hosea 6:6 also condemned the Pharisees for their extreme separation even to the point of not trying to reach these sinners for God. Reaching out to sinners is exactly what God does (Hos. 6:1), and Jesus was only doing the Father's work.

As a parting explanation, Jesus gave a clear purpose statement for His mission: He came for sinners not for the righteous (v. 13). The "righteous" might be those who think they are righteous because they practice the external requirements of the law. Legalistic Pharisees would fit in this group. The "righteous" might also be individuals like Joseph (1:19), Zechariah, Elisabeth (Lk. 1:5-6), and Simeon (Lk. 2:25), people who were already right with God and needed no "special call" (Nolland 388). The "sinners" are those who have no righteous standing before God and recognize that lack. Everyone understood that Matthew and his friends were included in this group. One can imagine the negative thoughts of the Pharisees when they realized that Jesus did more than eat with Matthew, He made him a permanent member of His select disciples.

Jesus came to call sinners (v. 13) and to forgive sinners (v. 6). This "call" is the gospel call, the invitation to become followers of Jesus and be part of His kingdom (Carson, *Matthew* 225). In mercy, Jesus offers salvation to the Matthew types.

The words "unto repentance" at the end of verse 13 do not appear in all the old Greek manuscripts. Luke 5:32 makes clear that, in fact, Jesus calls sinners to repentance. It is therefore rightfully understood here.

9. Jesus taught about fasting (9:14-17)

14 Then came to him the disciples of John, saying, Why do we and the Pharisees fast oft, but thy disciples fast not?
15 And Jesus said unto them, Can the children of the bridechamber mourn, as long as the bridegroom is with them? but the days will come, when the bridegroom shall

be taken from them, and then shall they fast.
16 No man putteth a piece of new cloth unto an old garment, for that which is put in to fill it up taketh from the garment, and the rent is made worse.
17 Neither do men put new wine into old bottles: else the bottles break, and the wine runneth out, and the bottles perish: but they put new wine into new bottles, and both are preserved.

By this time John the Baptist had been in prison (cf. 4:12; 11:2) and out of active ministry for several months, yet his disciples remained loyal to him. They continued practicing his teaching (Lk. 5:33; 11:1) and his austere living (fasting). John had taught his disciples about Jesus and they expected His and John's ministries to agree. With this in mind, they approached Jesus with a "why" question. Why was Jesus not teaching His disciples to fast as John had taught them and as the Pharisees practiced? As divergent as these two groups were, even they agreed on this (Nolland 390). For fasting, see comments on 6:16-18.

It seems from Matthew, Mark 2:13-22, and Luke 5:27-39 that John's disciples raised their question in the context of the celebration feast at Matthew's home (v. 10; Walvoord 69; Newman and Stine 271). Unlike the Pharisees, their concern was not over separation issues (v. 11) but over Jesus' feasting rather than fasting. Apparently they and the Pharisees were fasting on that very day (Mk. 2:18), and their hunger pains may have brought this difference into sharp focus. Jesus would later allude to this same difference (11:18-19), which may provide the key to understanding His comments here.

In short, Jesus said that the reason His disciples were not fasting was because He was still with them (v. 15). They would eventually fast also (e.g., Acts 13:2-3; 14:23), but as the following illustrations show, such fasting would be different from the fasting of contemporary Judaism, which fasted ritualistically, i.e., on set days and occasions. Fasting in the kingdom age is not done in this manner but rather is done in the context of prayer for the purpose of concentration and seriousness (Hagner 33A:245). (The reader is encouraged to review comments on 6:16-18 where Jesus taught His disciples to fast but said nothing about set times.)

In order to explain His answer, Jesus gave three illustrations from their everyday lives. (1) Comparing Himself to a groom at a Jewish wedding party (which lasted several days; Gower 69), and His disciples to wedding guests (Greek, sons of the bridechamber, i.e., the house where the wedding is being celebrated; Zerwick 26), He says that no one fasts during the wedding feast. In other words, there are times when it is appropriate to fast and times when it is not (Keener, *Background* 70). It was inappropriate for Jesus' disciples to fast while He was still with them. Jesus' ministry was a celebration of the arrival of the kingdom (Hagner 33A:243), seen here in the context of sinners turning to God through Jesus' ministry (Keener, *Matthew* 299; vv. 10, 13). Jesus' presence was just cause for celebration (Evans, *Matthew* 193), not an occasion for mourning.

Jesus included in this illustration a subtle reference to His ascension. The groom will be taken away (v. 15). The church age is the time the groom is away and when His followers will fast (Gundry 169).

(2) Comparing His ministry and the O.T. system to a patch made of new—that is, unshrunk (Greek *agnaphos;* Louw and Nida I:525)—material placed on an old garment, Jesus meant that His gospel of grace is not a patch for the old legal system (Walvoord 70). His gospel is its own system. Using unshrunk cloth to patch old clothing results in a worse tear when the new cloth shrinks. Jesus' gospel was not to revamp the Law. It was to replace it.

Continuing the same comparison of His ministry to the O.T. system, but now using fresh and aging grape juice, (3) He showed that His gospel could not be restricted by the old system any more than new wine could be contained by old "bottles" or skin containers (Greek *askos*). "Wine" translates the same Greek word (*oinos*) all three times, which, as this passage shows, can denote either fermented or unfermented juice. The natural aging and fermentation of wine requires flexible skins (Job 32:19). Storing freshly squeezed grape juice in already stretched or hardened skin containers would be foolish because as fermentation gases form, the old container would rupture. This would result in the loss of both the wine and the wineskin. Jesus did not mean by this that the old system would be preserved alongside the new (*contra* Hill 177) but that the new wine, i.e., the new system of kingdom grace and the new skins, i.e., the new stipulations of kingdom law as taught by Jesus (e.g., the Sermon on the Mount), would both be preserved (Hagner 33A:244). Each requires the other.

Later Judaizers misunderstood this great gospel truth and caused considerable trouble in the first century church (Acts 15; Gal. 1:1—5:12). Judaizers believed that adherence to certain aspects of the Mosaic Laws (circumcision) remained a requirement of those who would be followers of Christ. See comments on 5:17-20 and 13:52.

Animal skins, especially of goats, were used for storage and transportation of liquids (ISBE IV:536). Scriptural examples include wine (Josh. 9:4), milk (Jgs. 4:19), and water (Gen. 21:14-15). The skin bottles would be made from the whole skin. The skin would be sewed together, fur side out, with only one opening, usually the neck, left unsewed (Newman and Stine 273; Carson, *Matthew* 227).

In summary, it was right for John's disciples to fast but it was wrong for them to think their fast days should be observed by every God-fearer. Unlike the O.T. legal system, kingdom life is not about rigid observance of ritual. Kingdom life is about righteousness and peace and joy in the Holy Spirit (Rom. 14:17). One may suspect that the spirit of John's disciples is still in the church today.

10. Jesus healed a hemorrhaging woman and restored life to a dead girl (9:18-26)

18 While he spake these things unto them, behold, there came a certain ruler, and worshipped him, saying, My daughter is even now dead: but come and lay thy hand upon her, and she shall live.
19 And Jesus arose, and followed him, and *so did* his disciples.

20 And, behold, a woman, which was diseased with an issue of blood twelve years, came behind *him*, and touched the hem of his garment:
21 For she said within herself, If I may but touch his garment, I shall be whole.
22 But Jesus turned him about, and when he saw her, he said, Daughter, be of good comfort; thy faith hath made thee whole. And the woman was made whole from that hour.
23 And when Jesus came into the ruler's house, and saw the minstrels and the people making a noise,
24 He said unto them, Give place: for the maid is not dead, but sleepeth. And they laughed him to scorn.
25 But when the people were put forth, he went in, and took her by the hand, and the maid arose.
26 And the fame hereof went abroad into all that land.

See the introductory comments to chapter eight for contextual matters. These verses describe miracles seven and eight in Matthew's list of ten miracles. This story stands out because two healings are intertwined, both persons are called "daughter," and the number twelve is common. The girl is twelve years old according to Luke (8:42), and the woman had suffered for twelve years (Mt. 9:20).

As Jesus explained to John's disciples why He was not teaching His disciples to fast, a synagogue leader, presumably from Capernaum (v. 5; Jairus, Mk. 5:22; Lk. 8:41) approached Him on behalf of his daughter. He knelt before Jesus, a gesture of respect. Matthew condensed his account of this miracle and his chronology is a little different from that of Mark and Luke. The result is the same: (1) Jairus showed great respect for Jesus (Hendriksen 430); (2) he prayed urgently for Jesus' assistance; and (3) he believed Jesus could do as he requested. So confident was he that he said, "Lay your hand on her and she will live" (v. 18). Without a word, Jesus got up (from the meal? v. 10; so Hill 178) to follow him and His disciples and several others (Mk. 5:31) accompanied Him. He would not run—even from death, the greatest of our enemies (Bruner 1:428).

Along the way to the ruler's house, a woman who had been hemorrhaging for twelve years came up behind Jesus and secretly touched the hem, the fringe, of His cloak. (Many others later in Jesus' ministry did the same thing; Mt. 14:36). She believed so much in Jesus' ability to heal that she reasoned that only a touch of His garment would cure—literally, "save" (Greek *sōzō*)—her. He would not have to say anything. She was right. According to Mark (5:29) and Luke (8:44) she was immediately healed.

The word translated hem (Greek *kraspedon*) can also denote the corner tassel (BAGD 448). See also 14:36 and 23:5. Both Old and New Testament Israelites wore tassels on the four corners of their garments and each tassel contained a blue thread. These tassels were to remind Israel of God's commandments so they would do them (Num. 15:37-41; Dt. 22:12; Mt. 23:5; ISBE II:363, IV:737). Such tassels implied that Jesus lived in strict obedience to the law (5:17-20; Hagner 33A:249). The woman might have touched one of these.

Her secretiveness was probably for a couple reasons. First, for privacy reasons she did not want to speak of her need publicly. Second, according to the law, she was ceremonially unclean the whole time she was hemorrhaging plus seven days after it stopped (Lev. 15:19-33). This negatively impacted her home life. Everything she sat on or laid on was ceremonially unclean as was anyone who touched her or anything she sat or laid on. Intimate relations were forbidden during this time (Lev. 20:18; 15:24). Her public life was limited, as well as was her public worship, because as long as she was ceremonially unclean she could not worship at the temple. By healing her Jesus changed her whole life.

Jesus assured her that because of her faith she was permanently healed (v. 22; Greek perfect tense of *sōzō*, lit. "has saved you"; cf. Lk. 17:19). Her faith was her belief that Jesus had the ability to heal her. She was a ready recipient of His kingdom powers (Nolland 397). She should be encouraged; there was no need for timidity or fear. He addressed her as "daughter," probably a reference to her Jewish lineage but more so to her position as a true daughter of Abraham (Evans, *Matthew* 199).

When Jesus arrived at Jairus' house, the professional mourners were in place (v. 23). Mourners were mainly women "skilled in lamentation" (Jer. 9:17-18; Am. 5:16; ISBE I:557). They included people paid to make a noise in wailing and minstrels who were flute players. Jesus commanded them to leave (v. 24) and had them put outside (v. 25; Greek aorist passive of *ekballō*). Only the inner circle of disciples (Peter, James, and John; Mk. 5:37; Lk. 8:51) and the parents were permitted to witness the miracle.

Jesus stated that the little girl was not dead but only sleeping. The mourners laughed, evidence that she indeed was dead (Bruner 1:432). Jesus knew death when He saw it. She was dead (see Jn. 11:11-14). There was no hope, humanly, of her getting up from that bed. However, Jesus is the resurrection and the life (Jn. 11:25). With Jesus in the house, there was no need for mourners (Nolland 398).

Jairus had requested that Jesus lay His hand on her but Jesus did better than that (Hendriksen 434). In Matthew's abbreviated version, Jesus took hold of her hand—touching a corpse would normally render a person unclean for seven days (Num. 19:11)—and she arose. Mark 5:41 and Luke 8:54 report that He told her to rise and Mark 5:42 says she immediately got up and walked. Mark apparently recorded the exact Aramaic words Jesus spoke.

Barclay (1:398-399) believes she probably was asleep rather than dead. He says that she might have been in a "cataleptic coma" and that Jesus really saved her from being buried alive. However, Luke 8:55 said her spirit returned to her body, which is not a suitable description for sleep or a coma.

Jesus had entered the dwelling where a person had just died and He had touched the corpse. Either would normally make one ceremonially unclean (Num. 19:11-22). By raising the dead, Jesus sanctified what would normally have been unclean and cancelled its corrupting influence. This meant that He, His disciples, Jairus, and his wife did not need to go through the law's cleaning rituals for these circumstances.

Jesus wanted this kept quiet (Mk. 5:43; Lk. 8:56), but it was too strong for that. Matthew (v. 26) reported that the whole district heard about this miracle.

11. Jesus healed two blind men (9:27-31)

This is miracle number nine in Matthew's grouping of ten miracles. These miracles show Jesus' authority over nature, sickness, and evil spirits. See the introduction to chapter eight for further discussion.

27 And when Jesus departed thence, two blind men followed him, crying, and saying, *Thou* son of David, have mercy on us.

28 And when he was come into the house, the blind men came to him: and Jesus saith unto them, Believe ye that I am able to do this? They said unto him, Yea, Lord.

29 Then touched he their eyes, saying, According to your faith be it unto you.

30 And their eyes were opened; and Jesus straitly charged them, saying, See *that* no man know it.

31 But they, when they were departed, spread abroad his fame in all that country.

In non-specific terms, Matthew wrote that Jesus left "from there," presumably Jairus's house. As He walked, two blind men began shouting after Him. They were determined. Perhaps they had learned of the resurrection that had just occurred. A person who could raise the dead would have no trouble opening blind eyes. The blind men addressed Jesus with a Messianic title (2 Sam. 7:12-16)—Son of David (see comments on 1:1)—and asked that He have mercy on them. The Jews expected the Messiah to be a descendant of King David (22:41-45; Mk. 12:35), which is what Son of David meant primarily (1:1, 20). This particular Son of David, according to 2 Samuel 7:16, would rule forever. See 22:41-45 for further discussion on Jesus as the Son of David.

By their request, these blind men showed that they believed the Messiah would heal the blind (Is. 35:5-6; Hagner 33A:253). These men knew Scriptures that gave hope to the blind and they believed Jesus to be the Messiah, the one who could heal the blind. Jesus later used healings like these to prove that the kingdom had arrived (11:2-6).

Jesus evidently did not respond until He arrived home. Compare with 15:23. They followed him—we are not told how—into His house and Jesus asked if they believed He could do what they wanted. They both answered in the affirmative so He touched them and told them they would be healed in accordance with (Greek *kata* with the accusative) their faith, i.e., in accordance with the fact that they had faith. Because they had faith they would be healed (v. 29; 8:13; Carson, *Matthew* 233). Their healings were dependent upon Jesus' power but contingent upon their faith. Immediately they received perfect eyesight. Jesus is the only person in the Bible to heal blindness (Jn. 9:32).

Once again, Jesus commanded that the newly healed persons keep their healing a secret (v. 30; 8:4). In fact, He spoke "sternly" (Greek *embrimaomai*) to them, i.e. He emphatically ordered them not to tell what He had done. Again, the thing was too amazing to keep quiet. They told their story through the whole district (vv. 31; 26).

Matthew did not explain why Jesus wanted this miracle untold. However, Evans (*Matthew* 198) is probably right that Jesus did not want His miracles to "overshadow His proclamation of the kingdom of God and His call to national repentance and renewal." See also 8:4, 12:16-21, and 17:9. Also, His claim to be the Messiah, the king of the Jews, was used against Him at His trial (26:63; 27:11). Neither Herod the Great (2:2) nor Pilate (Jn. 19:12-16) ignored this claim.

12. Jesus healed a demon-possessed mute man (9:32-34)

32 As they went out, behold, they brought to him a dumb man possessed with a devil.
33 And when the devil was cast out, the dumb spake: and the multitudes marvelled, saying, It was never so seen in Israel.
34 But the Pharisees said, He casteth out devils through the prince of the devils.

Apparently, even as the healed men left a demon-possessed mute was brought to Jesus to be healed. This is the tenth and final specific miracle gathered in these two chapters. See comments at the beginning of chapter eight.

The word translated dumb (Greek *kōphos*) means to be blunted or dull and can refer to people who are deaf, mute, or both (Grimm's 367). The context determines which is meant (Newman and Stine 285). The man in this verse was mute. The same word in Matthew 11:5 refers to deaf individuals.

Jesus exorcised the demon and healed the mute. He performed two miracles. One might assume the demon caused the muteness but the text does not state this. "When the devil (Greek *daimonion*, demon) was cast out" speaks of an immediate healing. Crowds were still around His house. People were amazed and marveled, the same reaction Jesus had earlier in 8:10. Israel had never seen such power. No prophet had ever done such miracles.

However, all were not positively impressed. The Pharisees were by this time against Jesus. They did not deny His power. They denied it was from God. They believed that God does not work the way Jesus was working (Wilkins 374). In fact, they plainly stated they believed that Jesus' power was from the prince of demons, Satan himself. The hostility of this statement is advanced from verse 11 (Nolland 404) and prepares the reader for 10:25 (Evans, *Matthew* 21) and 12:22-32. Matthew recorded Jesus' answer to this allegation in chapter twelve. For discussion of Pharisees, Satan, and demon possession, see comments on 3:7, 4:1, and 8:28 respectively.

With these ten miracles, Matthew showed that Jesus was able to heal mankind's most difficult diseases from near or far, heal lifelong handicaps, raise the dead, control nature, and overpower Satan. All of these He did at will. The kingdom of heaven had surely arrived (12:28).

13. Jesus expressed the need for many more field workers (9:35-38)

35 And Jesus went about all the cities and villages, teaching in their synagogues, and preaching the gospel of the kingdom, and healing

every sickness and every disease among the people.
36 But when he saw the multitudes, he was moved with compassion on them, because they fainted, and were scattered abroad, as sheep having no shepherd.
37 Then saith he unto his disciples, The harvest truly *is* plenteous, but the labourers *are* few;
38 Pray ye therefore the Lord of the harvest, that he will send forth labourers into his harvest.

Matthew summarized the early part of Jesus' Galilean ministry with these verses and told his readers that the miracles recorded in chapters 8 and 9 are only examples of many miracles (Keener, *Matthew* 308; Jn. 20:30). Reminiscent of 4:23 (see comments there), Matthew in these verses gave an overview of this portion of Jesus' ministry. He was "going about (Greek progressive imperfect) ... teaching ... preaching ... and healing" (Greek adverbial, modal participles; Sauer 124).

Jesus wanted people to know the truth (proper doctrine), have membership in His kingdom, and enjoy healthy living. Jesus ministered to the total person. These three activities characterized His ministry. Still, as hard as He worked and as much as He accomplished, these were not enough. In the flesh, He was localized. It was time to enlist the help of others to multiply His efforts.

The crowds continued following Him and their spiritual needs were great (v. 36). He felt deep compassion (Greek *splagchnizomai*; Louw and Nida I:295) for them. One reason was that they were faint; but the majority of manuscripts say they were harassed (Greek *skullō*, perfect passive participle; BAGD 758). Another was that they were scattered or helpless (Greek *hriptō*; here a figurative meaning of "thrown down or lying helpless from fatigue," Grimm's 563; Newman and Stine 288). Jesus saw them as sheep with no shepherd. Their shepherds, their religious leaders, were not doing their jobs. They had abandoned their sheep (Hendriksen 440). The sheep's physical needs were great and needed to be addressed, but it was their spiritual emptiness, their aimless existence and their lostness that moved Jesus' heart most (Hagner 33A:260-261). Israel's spiritual leadership had failed God and His people.

Using a second image, as a farmer, Jesus saw great needs but few workers (v. 37; cf. Lk. 10:2), so He commanded His disciples to pray that the Lord of the harvest would send out workers into His harvest (v. 38). In this way, He awakened them (1) to the great harvest that He wants gathered, (2) to their own responsibility toward the harvest, and (3) to personal prayer as the way to address the need for workers to bring lost souls to salvation. Even while Jesus was with them, He expected His disciples to pray. With this command He also awakened the Twelve to the fact that (4) they alone could not and were not expected to bring in all of the harvest by themselves.

The word translated "pray" (Greek *deomai*) means to beseech and ask. The purpose for praying (Greek *hopōs* plus the subjunctive) is that the Lord of the harvest ("his harvest") may send out (Greek *ekballō*) laborers or workers—presumably before the harvest spoils or is lost (Nolland 408). This is the reason for the urgency. Jesus' point is not so much that the harvest is wanting to be harvested—i.e., that multitudes are ready to accept the gospel message and waiting for someone to tell them how to be saved (*contra* Newman and Stine 289)—but rather that the harvest needs to be harvested. There is plenty of harvest. There are few workers. Jesus' instructions to His disciples that they should pray show that His plan calls for more than just Jesus and the Twelve to be in the field. It also shows that some folks are lost, in part, because no one goes to the field to bring them in.

Though it does not always have this connotation, the word translated "send forth" (Greek *ekballō*) can and probably does in this instance include driving out with force (BAGD 237). Grimm's (193) says it means, "to compel one to depart, in stern though not violent language." See verse 25 where the same word describes the crowd being removed from Jairus' house. This prayer asks God to thrust people into the field, implying that they will not go without His impulse. Chapter ten tells about the first wave of laborers sent, the Twelve, whom Jesus had been training by example (Keener, *Matthew* 308) and instruction.

Being one of the "workers" has little appeal to many church people. People like to be planners, organizers, or administrators. However, Jesus said the need is for workers. These are those He called "missionaries, evangelists, and disciplers" (Bruner 1:450). To this end, all who follow Christ need to pray today as well: "Lord, send workers to the fields before the harvest is lost."

Summary (9:1-38)

Chapter nine contains the last five miracles Matthew grouped together to demonstrate Jesus' authority. He had authority over death, demons, and difficult illnesses. Nothing was too hard for Him. Included in this portion of Matthew's record are discussions on fasting in the kingdom and the need for more workers to bring more people out of the lost world and into the kingdom of God.

Application: Teaching and Preaching the Passage

The miracles and instructions of Jesus teach many great spiritual truths. Some of these instructions are evident in more than one miracle. One might develop lessons or sermons on the healing of the paralytic (vv. 1-8). There is the reward of intercessory prayer (the request, the faith, the reward). There is the authority of Jesus (to forgive sins, to cause the sick to rise, to silence the unbelievers).

The call of Matthew (vv. 9-13) can be presented as Matthew's response to Jesus' call: it was (1) immediate, (2) complete, and (3) overflowing. Lessons from Matthew's conversion include: (1) great sinners can turn to Jesus, (2) those who turn to Jesus are open about their Savior, and (3) those who turn to Jesus want their friends to turn to Him too. Also, a lesson might be taught using (1) the two invitations (Jesus to Matthew, "Follow me," and Matthew to Jesus, feast with me and meet my friends), and (2) the two insinuations: the Pharisees about Jesus (v. 11: Is Jesus one of them? with "them" understood as derogatory) and Jesus about the Pharisees (v. 13: You need to learn what the Scripture really means).

For sermonic and teaching application of 9:14-17 and fasting, see the application section on 6:16-18. Jesus' ministry to Jairus and the woman who touched His garment teach truths about

Jesus' ministry and methods: (1) He responded quickly to those in need (v. 19), (2) He integrated interruptions into His ministry day (vv. 20-22), and (3) He finished what He came to do (v. 25). Both the ruler and the woman found Jesus to be (1) available, (2) compassionate, and (3) able to meet their needs. The blind men found Jesus to be the (1) Messiah, (2) merciful, and (3) a worthy object of their faith (vv. 27-31).

By considering verses 35-37 together with the first five verses of chapter ten (9:35—10:5a), one might develop a sermon or lesson on Jesus' responses to spiritual need. Jesus is committed to addressing human need (9:35: He went about all of the cities); Jesus has compassion for the needy (9:36); and Jesus commissions others to help Him address spiritual needs (9:37—10:5).

One might consider "The world through the eyes of its Savior": the world needs (1) the gospel (v. 35), (2) both physical and spiritual healings (v. 35), and (3) spiritual leadership (vv. 36-37; compare Moses' concern in Num. 27:17 with Jesus' concern in v. 36). One might also consider the attitude and action of godly shepherds: (1) they feel compassion for their sheep, and (2) they provide for their sheep (they provide comfort for the harassed, strength for the helpless, and spiritual guidance for the lost).

The entire chapter could be considered as an example of Jesus' ministry: (1) He responded to need (vv. 19, 29), (2) He rewarded faith (vv. 2, 22, 29), and (3) He regularly did the seemingly impossible (vv. 7-8, 25-26, 30-31, 33). One might follow Matthew's emphasis and use the miracles in this chapter to show that Jesus has authority over all sickness, sin, and Satan.

Finally, one might develop a message around the idea "who have you left in the field?" Jesus' words in verse 37 suggest that some lost souls would receive the gospel if they were only told. Following Jesus means following Jesus into the field.

D. The Royal Messiah Enlisted the Aid of His Disciples (10:1—11:1)

At the end of the previous chapter (9:35-38) Matthew spoke of Jesus' physical limitations. The incarnate Christ was localized. Though He traveled steadily, He was not reaching the lost as quickly as needed. He drew attention to this need and directed the disciples—these were more than the Twelve—to pray that the Lord of the harvest would push workers into the fields lest the ripe harvest spoil (see discussion on 9:38). In order to address the need for more workers He appointed the Twelve and sent them on a short-term mission trip.

1. Discourse two: The mission—short term and long term (10:1-42)

This mission trip is the historical context of Matthew's second major teaching section (vv. 5-42). The Sermon on the Mount (chapters 5-7) was the first major teaching section. (For a summary of source critical issues and possible answers from a conservative perspective, see Carson, *Matthew* 240-243.)

Though the text does not say, one may surmise that there was another reason for this short missionary trip. The Twelve needed to prepare for their ministries after Pentecost. Jesus was training these men to carry on His ministry after His ascension.

a. The appointment of the Twelve (10:1-4)

1 And when he had called unto *him* his twelve disciples, he gave them power *against* unclean spirits, to cast them out, and to heal all manner of sickness and all manner of disease.
2 Now the names of the twelve apostles are these; The first, Simon, who is called Peter, and Andrew his brother; James *the son* of Zebedee, and John his brother;
3 Philip, and Bartholomew; Thomas, and Matthew the publican; James *the son* of Alphaeus, and Lebbaeus, whose surname was Thaddaeus;
4 Simon the Canaanite, and Judas Iscariot, who also betrayed him.

Jesus at this point set aside the Twelve for a special ministry. For disciples, see comments on 5:1. This is the first time Matthew listed all twelve, but Mark (3:13-19; 6:7-13) and Luke (6:12-16; 9:1-6) indicate that they had been set aside as apostles earlier in Jesus' ministry.

An apostle (Greek *apostolos*) was a sent one, a person commissioned as a messenger (Grimm's 68; Keener, *Background* 72). This messenger shared the authority of the one he represented (Hagner 33A:265). Its N.T. usage includes the Twelve as special disciples of Jesus and men such as Barnabas (Acts 14:14) and others who were apostles in a more general sense. See 2 Corinthians 8:23 and Philippians 2:25, where "messenger" translates the same Greek word.

In its narrow sense, as here, an apostle was appointed by Jesus. This apostleship became a recognized spiritual gift (Eph. 4:11) and foundational to the N.T. church (Eph. 2:20; 3:5). Paul was an apostle in the narrower sense and testified that he too had seen Jesus (1 Cor. 9:1), had been appointed by God to be an apostle (Gal. 1:1, 15-17; 1 Cor. 1:1), and had performed apostolic miracles to substantiate his claim (2 Cor. 12:12). Commentators are in agreement that the number twelve is significant and was intended to suggest a link between the twelve sons of Jacob (Israel) and the Christian community.

This occasion is also the first time Jesus empowered the Twelve for ministry. These men would help Him gather the ripe harvest (9:37). They would do for the first time by themselves what they had been called to do—fish for men (4:19; Nolland 670). He gave them authority over (Greek *exousia*, the right to control; Louw and Nida I:476) unclean spirits (see v. 8, 4:24, 12:43) so that they could do as He had been doing and cast them out. He also gave the Twelve authority to heal all sicknesses as He did (4:23; 9:35). Bearing the name of Jesus, they were able to command every demon and every disease to leave. This was not a permanent and unconditional ability for these men or the community of disciples at large (17:16). Later they would receive the permanent anointing of the Holy Spirit and the gifts He imparted (Acts 1:8; 5:12-16; Heb. 2:3-4), but even then such gifts were not equally shared or permanent (Acts 19:11-12).

Simon, whom Jesus named Peter (Jn. 1:42; see discussion on 16:18), and his brother Andrew were sons of a man named John. Peter and Andrew were two of the first disciples Jesus called to fulltime service (4:18). They were fishermen by trade and business partners with James and John (Lk. 5:7). Jesus called all four men to follow Him at the same time. Andrew had introduced Peter to the Lord (Jn. 1:41-42).

Peter's prominence and leadership among the Twelve is seen in the word "first" (v. 2; Hagner 33A:266). He was one of the three closest to Jesus and one who saw the transfigured Lord (17:1-7; 2 Pet. 1:16-18). He became the leader and spokesperson for the post-resurrection group (Acts 2:14, 3:12, 4:8, 5:3). He also authored two N.T. letters, 1 and 2 Peter.

James and John were brothers and sons of Zebedee. Their mother at times traveled with Jesus' ministry group and was present at the crucifixion (27:55-56). James was the first of the Twelve to be martyred (Acts 12:2). John was the "beloved" disciple. He authored the Gospel that bears his name today as well as 1, 2, 3 John and the Revelation.

Jesus called Philip to follow Him and Philip then brought Nathaniel to Jesus (Jn. 1:43-51). Jesus tested Philip's faith at the feeding of the five thousand (Jn. 6:5-7). During the Passion Week, some God-fearing Gentiles approached Philip and expressed their desire to meet Jesus (Jn. 12:20). In the Upper Room Discourse, Philip requested to see the Father (Jn. 14:8). All of these references to Philip are in John's Gospel. The Synoptics do not mention any dialogue with Philip.

Scripture is fairly quiet about the rest of the Twelve. Nothing specific is said about Bartholomew in Scripture unless he is Nathaniel, a possibility raised by some commentators (Picirilli, *Mark* 98; Wilkins 405; Hendriksen 450, 453) in light of Nathaniel's presence in John 21:8. Bartholomew's name is really a reference to his paternity, *bar* (Aramaic for "son of") Tolmai (Grimm's 95). Nathaniel's hometown was Cana of Galilee and where Jesus did His first miraculous sign (Jn. 21:2).

Thomas (from Aramaic), called Didymus (Greek), was possibly a twin (both names mean twin; ISBE IV:841). He voiced his willingness to die with Jesus (Jn. 11:16). He was absent the first time Jesus appeared to the apostles as a group (Jn. 20:24) and doubted Jesus' resurrection (Jn. 20:25).

Matthew identified himself as a tax collector (9:9-13). He was the son of Alphaeus (Mk. 2:14) even as was the other James, thought to be James "the less"—perhaps equaling "younger" (Grimm's 414; Mt. 10:3; Mk. 15:40), making it appear that Matthew and James could have been brothers. Hendriksen (95, 453) believes they were not brothers. Evans (*Matthew* 205) believes that James the son of Alphaeus is not to be idenfied with "James the Smaller."

Thaddaeus is called Judas, not Iscariot (Jn. 14:22), and Judas "of James" (lit. Greek) in Luke 6:16 and Acts 1:13. The precise family relationship between Judas and this James is unknown. Greek grammar allowed for some ellipses, which is why there is ambiguity. The King James translators supplied "brother" and the New International Version and the English Standard Version translators supplied "son." Either is possible from the Greek.

Matthew 10:4 and Mark 3:18 called Simon a Canaanite: that is, a Cananaen. Luke twice (Lk. 6:15; Acts 1:13) called him a Zealot (Greek *zēlōtēs*). "Cananaean" is Aramaic for zealot (ISBE I:591; BAGD 402). Writers disagree about whether an anti-Roman Zealot party existed in Jesus' time (ISBE IV:515, 1179). Those who say that no such party existed argue that Simon was known for his zeal and devotion to God (ISBE IV:1179; Bruner 1:456; Nolland 412). That Simon was marked zealous seems certain, for no other disciple had this title (Keener, *Matthew* 311).

Judas Iscariot, son of Simon Iscariot (Jn. 6:71), was the traitor. He was the treasurer of the group (Jn. 12:6; 13:29) and empowered along with the others to command demons and heal diseases. However, he stole money from the group during their ministry years, which indicates that he had spiritual problems even before the betrayal. At what point he turned against Jesus is unknown but his hypocrisy was established by the last week (Jn. 12:6; Mt. 26:14-16, 25).

There are some differences in the N. T. listings of the Twelve, which suggests that Peter was not the only member of the group with two names (Simon-Peter; Matthew-Levi; Lebbaeus-Thaddaeus-Judas (KJV) or Thaddaeus-Judas (ESV, NIV). This was necessary since there were two apostles named Simon, two named James, and two named Judas.

The following chart shows that all lists agree for the most part and where there are differences, they can be explained easily enough. The numbers in each column represent the order of names in that writer's list. The chart thus shows that a slight reordering of the names answers most questions.

Mt. 10:2-3	Mk. 3:13-19	Lk. 6:12-16	Acts 1:13
1. Simon Peter	1. Simon Peter	1. Simon Peter	1. Peter
2. Andrew	4. Andrew	2. Andrew	4. Andrew
3. James	2. James	3. James	3. James
4. John	3. John	4. John	2. John
5. Philip	5. Philip	5. Philip	5. Philip
6. Bartholomew	6. Bartholomew	6. Bartholomew	7. Bartholomew
7. Thomas	8. Thomas	8. Thomas	6. Thomas
8. Matthew	7. Matthew = Levi, son of Alphaeus (Mk. 2:14; Mt. 9:9)	7. Matthew	8. Matthew
9. James [son] of Alphaeus	9. James [son] of Alphaeus	9. James [son] of Alphaeus	9. James [son] of Alphaeus
10. Labbaeus (KJV) Thaddesus	10. Thaddeus	11. Judas, (son NIV, ESV; brother; KJV) of James	11. Judas, (son NIV, ESV; brother; KJV) of James
11. Simon the Cananaean	11. Simon the Cananaean	10. Simon the Zealot	10. Simon the Zealot
12. Judas Iscariot	12. Judas Iscariot	12. Judas Iscariot	

The four records seem clearly to list the same twelve (eleven in Acts), although in different order. In all of them Simon Peter, Andrew, James, and John are the first four; Philip is next; Bartholomew, Thomas, and Matthew/Levi are the next three; James of Alphaeus is next; Lebbaeus/Thadeus/Judas of James and Simon the Cananaean/Zealot are the next two; and Judas Iscariot is last.

Evans (*Matthew* 207) thinks that the number of apostles fluctuated and that based on the information in the Gospels, it is impossible to reduce the number to twelve. He understands the number twelve to be symbolic in both Testaments (twelve sons of Jacob, etc.). This view does not seem probable in light of the above comparison and in light of the final reference to the Twelve in Revelation 21:14 where their names are inscribed on the twelve foundations of the new Jerusalem.

Jesus had been teaching these men kingdom truths since they began following Him. It was time for them to begin ministering apart from His physical presence, so He gave them instructions specific to their new ministry. Matthew recorded no time frame, so perhaps the trip took a few weeks. Mark (6:7) said they went out "two by two," which may be why Matthew listed them in pairs.

b. The training of the Twelve for their first mission outreach (10:5-15)

5 These twelve Jesus sent forth, and commanded them, saying, Go not into the way of the Gentiles, and into *any* city of the Samaritans enter ye not:

6 But go rather to the lost sheep of the house of Israel.

7 And as ye go, preach, saying, The kingdom of heaven is at hand.

8 Heal the sick, cleanse the lepers, raise the dead, cast out devils: freely ye have received, freely give.

9 Provide neither gold, nor silver, nor brass in your purses,

10 Nor scrip for *your* journey, neither two coats, neither shoes, nor yet staves: for the workman is worthy of his meat.

11 And into whatsoever city or town ye shall enter, enquire who in it is worthy; and there abide till ye go thence.

12 And when ye come into an house, salute it.

13 And if the house be worthy, let your peace come upon it: but if it be not worthy, let your peace return to you.

14 And whosoever shall not receive you, nor hear your words, when ye depart out of that house or city, shake off the dust of your feet.

15 Verily I say unto you, It shall be more tolerable for the land of Sodom and Gomorrha in the day of judgment, than for that city.

Some of the instructions in this chapter are limited to the Twelve and their first trip (Bruner 1:459). Some were repeated for the seventy (or seventy-two in some manuscripts here and in Luke 10:1, 17). Some of the instructions are for the church age. This makes these verses difficult to follow but this was Matthew's way. He condensed and organized Jesus' teachings thematically rather than in a general chronological fashion. See the introductory comments to chapter eight.

Before sending these men out, Jesus empowered them for ministry (v. 1). This is consistent with His post-resurrection instructions (Lk. 24:49). Attempts to have a harvesting ministry without God's power are fruitless (Lk. 24:44-49; Acts 1:8).

Second, He told them exactly to whom they were to carry the gospel of the kingdom. They were to go to the lost sheep of the house of Israel (v. 6), which refers to all Israel as lost, not to the lost *within* Israel. (This takes the Greek genitive to be epexegetical, not partitive; Gundry 185; Newman and Stine 297; *contra* Nolland 416-417.) The sheep image goes back to Matthew 9:36 (Evans, *Matthew* 209) and provides the link with 9:36-38. Jesus sent the Twelve because souls needed to be harvested and Jesus could not humanly accomplish by Himself all that needed to be done.

The limitation Jesus imposed on the Twelve was both geographical and ethnic (Barclay 1:420; Hill 185). Though Galilee was home to many Gentiles, no Gentile or Samaritan community or city was to be entered at this time (though see comments on 4:15, "Galilee of the Gentiles"). Nor were the Twelve to go beyond the borders of Galilee to the Gentiles (v. 5). Those areas would be evangelized later. Like their Master, the Twelve would focus primarily on Israel. See comments on 15:24.

This is the only time Matthew mentioned Samaritans. See ISBE IV:303-308 for a discussion of the origins, history, beliefs, and practices of Samaritans. According to some recent scholarship, 2 Kings 17 and Ezra 4 reveal nothing about Samaritan origins (Evans and Porter, *Dictionary* 1058).

The Jews had no dealings with Samaritans (Jn. 4:9). They sometimes used the term "Samaritan" as a derogatory name (Jn. 8:48). Jesus' inclusion of Samaritans in some of His parables was surprising and unexpected (Lk. 10:33; 17:16).

The exclusion of non-Jews from this mission is noteworthy because it sounds like these folks were being deliberately bypassed by Jesus' gospel and God's grace. However, Jesus taught that God loved the world (Jn. 3:16) and offered His Savior to Gentiles and Samaritans (Jn. 4:42) as well as Jews. See the earlier discussion about Gentiles in Matthew 4:12-17, 8:5-13, and 8:28-34. The Gentiles and Samaritans were not being eternally excluded. Jesus' instructions were consistent with O.T. teaching and later apostolic teaching and practice that God's salvation would go through Israel to the world (Gen. 12:2-3, 22:18; Is. 54:1-3; Jn. 4:22; Gal. 4:26-27; Acts 3:25; Rom. 1:16, 9-11; Wilkins 389; Hendriksen 456). The Gentiles would be evangelized at a later time (v. 18; 28:19; Acts 17:30).

Jesus' instructions included a job description (v. 7). These men were to preach (Greek *kērussō*; on this word, see 3:1) and heal as they traveled (Greek present tense, temporal participle, lit. "as you go, preach saying"; Keener, *Matthew* 316; for contrast see 28:19). Their message would be the same as His (4:17), "The kingdom of heaven is at hand," i.e., near and available to enter. The kingdom had been initiated and hearers were invited to enter it. For a discussion on the meaning of these words as a summary of Jesus' and John's message, see comments on 3:2.

It is clear from Mark's summary statement (6:12) that Matthew summarized the instructions as well. Though Matthew did not record it here, repentance was part of the message of the Twelve, even as it had been part of Jesus' and John's messages (3:2; 4:17; Bruner 1:462). Baptism, however, does not seem to have been part of the message and practice at this time, although it had been earlier (Jn. 3:22-23; 4:1-2) and would be again after the ascension (Mt. 28:19).

The Twelve would address physical needs, as Jesus did (vv. 1, 8), as proof of the kingdom's arrival (see comments on 4:23; 11:2-6; 12:28). They would heal the sick without limitation, even as they followed their Lord's practice (4:23; 8:16; 9:35) and instructions. The word translated sick (Greek *astheneō*) is used only here and in 25:36 in Matthew, though the other Gospel writers used it also. It means to be feeble or sick (Grimm's 80).

The Twelve would cleanse lepers. This meant they would heal leprosy, a disease that rendered the sick ceremonially unclean. Such a healing would enable the person to be restored to ceremonial cleanness and once again permitted to live and move about in society as well as worship in the temple. See this commentary on 8:3.

Jesus empowered the Twelve to raise the dead. There is no record in the Gospel accounts of anyone but Jesus raising the dead. Luke, however, records one instance following Pentecost when the Lord answered Peter's prayer and restored life to a woman (Acts 9:40).

The apostles would also cast out demons with the authority of Christ. For comments on demons, see this commentary on 4:24. There is only one recorded instance in the Gospels of the apostles' attempting an exorcism, and it was a failure (17:16). However, Mark 6:13 reported that the apostles cast out many demons, and according to Luke 10:17 the seventy did also.

The gospel and its benefits were not to be peddled (v. 8). His apostles were to give deliverance as freely as they had received authority. They were to give the kingdom blessings freely (Greek *dōrea,* adverbial accusative), i.e., as a gift, without charge. See Acts 8:20 for an example of apostolic defense of this principle and Romans 3:24, which states that God grants a right standing with Him as a free gift (Greek *dōrea*).

They were to travel light. They would carry no "scrip": that is, no traveler's bag (Greek *pēra*; Louw and Nida I:71). They would "provide"—that is, acquire (Greek *ktaomai*, Louw and Nida I:565) no money (v. 9) or extra clothes (v. 10). The "coat" is better understood as a long undershirt, a tunic, worn under the cloak next to the skin (Louw and Nida I:74). They could take no sandals or a walking-stick. Mark records that they were forbidden to take anything but the clothes on their backs, sandals, and a walking stick (Mk. 6:8), which could suggest that Matthew meant they must not take any *extra* sandals, etc. These differences are difficult to reconcile but Luke (9:3, 5; 22:35) substantiates Matthew's record, which suggests that we are missing a piece of this puzzle. Regardless, they were to travel unencumbered, as free from care as possible (Archer, *Encyclopedia* 326). In short, they would leave immediately without preparation (Wilkins 390) or provisions. They would be dependent on those who heard their message for food and lodging. The need for laborers (9:37) was urgent and they were to go immediately. The harvest was ripe.

Their appearance (barefoot travelers) and poverty might have been intended as a sign to the hearers, but obedience to these stringent instructions called for complete reliance on God's provision. This was at least one lesson Jesus wanted these men to learn (Lk. 22:35). This might have been the first time in a long time that some of them went without. Some of them might never have lived with such bare essentials before. See comments on 9:9.

Several conclusions can be drawn from these instructions. (1) The missionary and evangelistic labors of the Twelve partially addressed the need for more laborers (v. 10). Link this verse with 9:37-38 (Gundry 187). (2) Jesus required that His missionaries not be burdened down with things (extras). (3) Jesus wanted His missionaries to trust God for everything. (4) Jesus legitimized ministry as a livelihood worthy of support (Lk. 10:7). "Meat" (Greek *trophē*) is food in general. (5) Jesus sent them to live as He lived. He himself depended on this type of faith ministry support (Lk. 8:1-3). (6) Those who believed the message were immediately obligated for the material support of the messenger. The message was not for sale, but the messenger could expect that his needs be met. (7) Later writers understood this principle to be Jesus' will for all preachers and hearers of the gospel (1 Cor. 9:3-14; Lk. 10:7; 1 Tim. 5:18). Gospel preachers are to rely on their hearers for provisions, and hearers are to take care of the material needs of the gospel preacher.

The Twelve were to pick carefully their lodging. They were to stay only with those "worthy" and they were to stay there as long as they were in the area ministering. They were not to move from house to house, which might give an appearance of "freeloading" (Evans, *Matthew* 208) or that the apostles were trying to find better lodging (Newman and Stine 300). Appearance and reputation were important.

The "worthy" (Greek *axios*) might have been those who had already accepted the gospel as a result of Jesus' ministry (Gundry 188). However, it seems more probable that Jesus' call for more laborers (9:37-38) meant He wanted help reaching the unevangelized, not those who had already heard and believed. The "worthy," then, would have been those who received or were at least open to the apostles' message of the kingdom (Wilkins 391) and opened their homes to these men. Verse 14 shows that not every home would welcome the gospel. Barclay (1:426) is also probably right that the worthy are those who have a good reputation. Jesus did not want His disciples staying with those of low or questionable morals.

The apostles would offer the common greeting, "Peace to this house," (v. 12; Lk 10:5; Carson, *Matthew* 246) and if the homeowner responded positively and permitted them to stay, the home would be blessed with their presence and the hosts would be rewarded (10:40-42). If the homeowner rejected the men and would not allow them to stay, the apostles would leave (v. 14). When they were rejected by a homeowner or a city they were to kick the dust off their feet as they left as a testimony that the feet of those who preached the gospel had been in their home and city (Rom. 10:15). They had been offered the kingdom but had rejected it (v. 14; Mk. 6:11; Lk. 9:5; 10:10-12). Paul later did the same thing as he left cities that had rejected the gospel

(Acts 13:51; 18:6). By kicking the dust off their feet, the evangelists separated themselves from the city or house upon whom judgment was sure to come (Gundry 190). Both here and in Acts, Jewish hearers were the ones who rejected and the ones whose dust was left behind.

This was the first mention of possible rejection (Hagner 33A:272) in this discourse. As Hagner observes, rejection "will loom larger as the discourse proceeds." This rejection shows that the folks had a real decision to make. Their wills were functional and what made them culpable for their rejection. Rejection of the King, or of His preachers and gospel, was and is serious, more serious in fact than the sordid sins of Gentile Sodom and Gomorrah and their rejection of the angelic messengers (v. 15; Bruner 1:470; Gen. 18:20—19:29). Rejection of Jesus is the most serious forgivable sin. Compare with 12:31-32 and comments.

The Jews needed to hear this (Keener, *Matthew* 316, 320). Jesus' comparison of these cities with Sodom and Gomorrah was hyperbole, but it showed how seriously Jesus took rejection of His gospel. Jesus' reference also showed the accuracy of the historical account of Sodom and Gomorrah as recorded in Genesis. Those who reject the gospel will be severely punished on the Day of Judgment. See comments on 11:23, 24.

The Twelve did as instructed and they saw great results (Mk. 6:13; Lk. 9:6). More laborers meant more harvested souls. It still does. Mark's ordering (6:30) suggests that the Twelve might not have returned until after the death of John the Baptist.

c. The training of the Twelve for church-age mission outreach (10:16-39)

16 Behold, I send you forth as sheep in the midst of wolves: be ye therefore wise as serpents, and harmless as doves.

17 But beware of men: for they will deliver you up to the councils, and they will scourge you in their synagogues;

18 And ye shall be brought before governors and kings for my sake, for a testimony against them and the Gentiles.

19 But when they deliver you up, take no thought how or what ye shall speak: for it shall be given you in that same hour what ye shall speak.

20 For it is not ye that speak, but the Spirit of your Father which speaketh in you.

21 And the brother shall deliver up the brother to death, and the father the child: and the children shall rise up against *their* parents, and cause them to be put to death.

22 And ye shall be hated of all *men* for my name's sake: but he that endureth to the end shall be saved.

23 But when they persecute you in this city, flee ye into another: for verily I say unto you, Ye shall not have gone over the cities of Israel, till the Son of man be come.

24 The disciple is not above *his* master, nor the servant above his lord.

25 It is enough for the disciple that he be as his master, and the servant as his lord. If they have called the master of the house

Beelzebub, how much more *shall they call* them of his household?
26 Fear them not therefore: for there is nothing covered, that shall not be revealed; and hid, that shall not be known.
27 What I tell you in darkness, *that* speak ye in light: and what ye hear in the ear, *that* preach ye upon the housetops.
28 And fear not them which kill the body, but are not able to kill the soul: but rather fear him which is able to destroy both soul and body in hell.
29 Are not two sparrows sold for a farthing? and one of them shall not fall on the ground without your Father.
30 But the very hairs of your head are all numbered.
31 Fear ye not therefore, ye are of more value than many sparrows.
32 Whosoever therefore shall confess me before men, him will I confess also before my Father which is in heaven.
33 But whosoever shall deny me before men, him will I also deny before my Father which is in heaven.
34 Think not that I am come to send peace on earth: I came not to send peace, but a sword.
35 For I am come to set a man at variance against his father, and the daughter against her mother, and the daughter in law against her mother in law.
36 And a man's foes *shall be* they of his own household.
37 He that loveth father or mother more than me is not worthy of me: and he that loveth son or daughter more than me is not worthy of me.
38 And he that taketh not his cross, and followeth after me, is not worthy of me.
39 He that findeth his life shall lose it: and he that loseth his life for my sake shall find it.

As mentioned in the comments introducing the previous section, some of the instructions in this discourse were for the immediate mission of the Twelve (v. 5), while other parts of these instructions are for the church era. Some instructions are for both time periods. Because of the overlap in contexts, commentators outline these verses differently.

Verse 16 carries further the thought of opposition introduced in verse 14. Opposition to the message will not be passive or impotent. It will be deliberate and dangerous. In the previous verses, Jesus spoke of the troubles of those who reject the gospel message. In these verses, He turns attention to how this rejection will affect the messengers (Hagner 33A:275).

Jesus sent the Twelve into danger. This is a startling but unmistakable statement. He knew full well the impending dangers. His warning assured them of His knowledge and His care for them. They were going as sheep among wolves. "As" (Greek *hōs*) introduces the characteristic quality of sheep among wolves (BAGD 898): i.e., they would be defenseless against apparently superior power (Bruner 1:472). Christ's followers would not spread the gospel with human force (5:38-48). However, effective, Christ-like ministry would require the wisdom (Greek *phronimos*) of serpents, probably in the sense of shrewdness (Carson, *Matthew* 246) and the harmlessness or innocence (Greek *akeraios*, free from a mixture of evil, pure; Louw and Nida I:746) of doves. Keener (*Matthew* 322) suggests shrewdness was needed in order not to provoke unnecessarily their opponents.

In Scripture, serpents have a dark shadow over them because of their potential harm physically and, in a figurative sense, spiritually. The first mention of a snake is in Genesis 3:1 where the serpent deceived Eve (1 Tim. 2:14) by his cunning (LXX Greek *panourgia*, trickery involving evil cunning: craftiness, treachery, Louw and Nida I:771). This is the same word Paul used to describe the serpent in 2 Corinthians 11:3 and the word Jesus used here. Jesus instructed the Twelve to be cunning (wise) for good ends. Such wisdom will help them avoid certain men (v. 17) and know when to run (v. 23; Acts 14:6).

Doves, on the other hand, are harmless and gentle. They pose no danger or threat to anyone. Instead of "deceitful cunning and treacherous guile," the Twelve were to possess "harmless cunning and gentle innocence" (ISBE I:988).

Verses 17-22 parallel Mark 13:9-13. In the Gospel of Mark, Jesus clearly spoke of persecution during the church age. This helps the reader of Matthew understand that Jesus was speaking of the church age here as well.

Jesus' "sent ones" will need innocent cunning in order to avoid evil men: that is, people, including men and women (Greek masculine *anthrōpos,* used generically; Newman and Stine 305). These are wolves who will try to hurt them (v. 17). These evil men will have them arrested and scourged (flogged; Lk. 18:33; Jn. 19:1; Acts 22:25; 2 Cor. 11:24). Such scourgings were painful beatings inflicted by using a leather whip or sometimes a whip made of leather straps knotted with pieces of bone or metal (ISBE IV:358-359). Keener (*Background* 73) says the "Jewish flogging consisted of thirteen harsh strokes to the breast and twenty-six to the back."

The Councils (v. 17) are not the Great Sanhedrin but local councils from local synagogues (Newman and Stine 306; *ISBE* I:786-787). "In their synagogues" identifies some of their enemies as Jews. The book of Acts records the truthfulness of this prophecy (4:1-22; 5:17-41; 6:8—8:3; etc.). For synagogue, see comments on 4:23.

Though the apostles went with only the basics (vv. 9-10), they would give testimony before great men (v. 18), both Jews and Gentiles. With this promise, Jesus showed that the restrictions He gave in verses 5 and 6 were temporary. The gospel of the kingdom would be proclaimed to the Gentiles too, another indication that this portion of Jesus' comments was intended for the church age.

Jesus' messengers do not need to "take thought"—worry—about their testimonies when they are brought before human leaders (v. 19). They should not even *start* to worry (interpreting the Greek aorist negative command as ingressive). What they should say will be given when they need it, for (Greek explicative *gar*) they are God's mouthpieces to those in power (v. 20). "The Spirit of your Father" is the Holy Spirit; thus, Jesus promised that God the Holy Spirit will speak through the persecuted so they will give testimony (v. 18) concerning Christ (Acts 6:10, 7:55-56; 24:24-25; 26:27-29). This promise was specific and limited and has no application to pulpit ministry (Carson, *Matthew* 248).

Not everyone will receive the gospel message and messengers. Even close family members will divide over this (v. 21) and some divisions will result in death. Hatred will be directed at Jesus' followers because of their identification with Him ("for my name's sake" v. 22; 24:9). "Hated by all" is hyperbole (Hagner 33A:278) and teaches that opposition will be hate-driven and common.

Verse 21 alludes to Micah 7:6. See verses 35-36 also. Micah described a time when evil was so rampant that even the closest family and friends were untrustworthy (Keener, *Background* 75; Blomberg 36). Jesus paralleled the experiences (not the evil) of Micah's subjects with those of His followers. His gospel will be so divisive that even the closest family ties will be set aside as people polarize over Christ (Blomberg 36) and work to destroy those who choose to follow Jesus. "Shall deliver up" (v. 21 KJV) translates the same verb (Greek *paradidōmi*) that refers to John the Baptist's arrest in 4:12. It is also used several times of Judas' betrayal of Jesus (26:2, 15-16, 21, etc.)

Even though Jesus promised persecution, He also promised deliverance—i.e., salvation, not from persecution but from hell—to those who do not allow the opposition to stop them (v. 22). All who remain faithful during persecution (Evans, *Matthew* 213), i.e., all who remain faithful even in death, to the end of their persecution or to the Lord's return (Hagner 33A:278), will receive salvation. This is not a works salvation (Eph. 2:9) but a faith that shows itself in faithfulness (Jas. 2:24). Compare with Matthew 24:10-13 and Hebrews 3:14.

Still speaking of the church age, Jesus gave another straightforward guideline for dealing with persecution: run from it if possible (v. 23; Jn. 7:1). Both, persevering and fleeing help spread the gospel (Gundry 194; Acts 8:1-4, 25; 17:10, 14-15). The reason disciples were told to run is there were more cities to cover than there was time; so the disciples were being told to avoid non-receptive areas. Jesus told them not to spend time with those who did not want to hear their message. He would come before they evangelized all of Israel's cities.

The phrase "before the Son of man comes" seems at the same time both definite and vague. Commentators are divided over its meaning. Wilkins (394) calls this "one of the most problematic verses in the Bible." Barclay (1:442) goes so far as to say that Matthew read into Jesus' words something He did not intend. This verse suggests on the surface that Jesus assured the ones He sent that He would be close behind them in His own ministry (compare Lk. 10:1). A brief ministry appears to be in view. Hill (190-191) is right to understand that Jesus would return before His disciples completely fulfilled this command to evangelize but wrong to understand this promise to mean that Jesus expected an end within perhaps 40-50 years. Carson (*Matthew* 252) believes this refers to Jesus' coming in judgment against the Jews, specifically in the destruction of Jerusalem in 70 A.D. Gundry (194-195) says it is eschatological and was intended by Matthew (as redactor) to show that evangelism was to include the Jews until Christ returns (also Hagner 33A:280).

However, this portion of the discourse (beginning in v. 16) is about evangelism during the entire church age, not a limited mission in the first century. Verse 23, then, is about evangelizing until the Lord returns in His glory and kingdom (24:30; 25:31; 26:64; Keener, *Matthew* 324-325). Evangelism will not be completed even in Israel before the Lord Jesus returns to gather His workers, for there will always be those who need to be saved. See comments on 16:28, "until they see the Son of Man coming in his kingdom."

Using three illustrations from everyday life (vv. 24-25), Jesus explained why His followers would be persecuted. (1) Disciples are not greater than their master or teacher (Greek *didaskalos*). (2) Nor are servants greater than their masters (Greek *kurios*, "lord"; v. 24; Jn. 13:16). (3) Disciples work to be like their teacher (Greek *didaskalos*). This is their goal. "It is enough," means the student is satisfied to be like his or her teacher (Newman and Stine 313).

The disciples' Master, the master of the house (Greek *oikodespotēs*), was maligned and called Beelzebul or Beelzebub (9:34; 12:24), which also means "master of the house" but is a reference to Satan (ISBE I:447). The disciples should not be surprised, then, when they, as part of His household (Evans 214), are identified with Him and called the same name. Jesus suffered and so will His followers. Suffering is, in fact, one way for disciples to identify with Jesus (Acts 5:41; Phil. 3:10; 1 Pet. 4:13).

With this knowledge, the disciples were better prepared to withstand persecution. Three times in this discourse, Jesus commanded His disciples not to fear (vv. 26, 28, 31). Here (v. 26), they should not fear people's allegations. In judgment, God will reveal everything. Jesus was probably inferring that God's final judgment will reveal who is on the Lord's side. "Fear not," then, means do not be afraid of these false allegations that one is associated with Beelzebul. The truth will be told in the judgment.

Using a parallelism, Jesus described the coming work of His disciples (v. 27). He intended that they proclaim openly, loudly, and boldly what He had been quietly telling them. This is what He meant by "in the light ..., on the housetop ... [and] ... without fear." According to Hill (192), the flat housetops were used for public announcements. Keener (*Matthew* 326) suggests that "shouting from the housetops" is a hyperbolic image of boldness. "Preach" (Greek *kērussō*) is to proclaim as a herald, "to announce extensively and publicly" (Louw and Nida I:412). If Jesus were instructing the Twelve today He might say something like, "Get the message on the airwaves. Put it on the internet. Use every means available to get the message out."

Jesus had privately and quietly, i.e. in the dark, been giving them kingdom truths (cf. 16:20; Wilkins 396; Newman and Stine 315). "In the ear" means secretly or whispered. Jesus' followers would soon proclaim loudly and openly all of the words Jesus had been privately teaching them.

Second, Jesus wanted His disciples to fear God more than people (Keener, *Matthew* 326) because humans are limited in their ability to take life (v.28; 1 Pet. 3:14; Rev. 2:10). People can kill only the body. They have no power over the soul, that immaterial part of mankind that lives on after its separation from the physical body. Rather, Jesus said, His followers should fear only the one who can destroy both body and soul in hell—Gehenna (see comments on

5:22). Though Jesus did not elaborate, the punishment of body and soul in this final hell is presented as fact. Destruction is not annihilation but everlasting punishment (25:46; Mk. 9:48; 2 Thess. 1:9; Hendriksen 471-472). The one who could destroy both body and soul is God, not Satan (*contra* Walvoord 77).

However, God will not forsake His own (v. 29). Two illustrations make this point, one using sparrows and one about hair. A sparrow had the extremely low market value of a "farthing" or "penny" (Greek *assarion,* a Roman copper coin worth 1/16th of a denarius, the latter being a day's wages for a common laborer; Louw and Nida I:62-63). Even a sparrow has God's careful eye and not one dies without God, i.e., without His will and knowledge. How much more a martyr (Gundry 198)? God cares so much for His own that He maintains an accurate count of the hairs on His children's heads (v. 30).

This sounds like exaggeration, but could one expect less from God? Could one imagine any part of His creation not under His direct control? So great is the Father's care and love that He is there for every sparrow and every saint (v. 29; Bruner 1:484). Jesus sent His beloved disciples where there would be trouble (v. 16), but not because He did not care. The conclusion (Greek inferential *oun)* one should understand from Jesus' teaching of God's careful watchfulness over His people is this: a disciple is worth much more than many sparrows and each should understand that he or she has no reason for fear (v. 31; Hagner 33A:286). Even during persecution, God's love for His own remains. For human worth in comparison to animal worth, see 6:26 and 12:12.

The third prohibition against fear, then, concerns the disciples' worth in God's eyes. Christ's followers have no reason to fear people because God always loves and takes care of His own. They are most valuable to Him.

Because of this great loving care (therefore: Greek inferential *oun*), Jesus' disciples must confess their love for Him before men. So closely connected are discipleship, i.e., one's relationship to Jesus, and witnessing that Jesus promised He will confess or acknowledge (Greek *homologeō*) to the Father those who acknowledge Him before men (v. 32). However, the exact opposite will also be true. Denial of a disciple-master relationship with Jesus before men will result in a denial of the same before the Father (v. 33). To deny (Greek *arneomai*) is "to say one does not know about or is in any way related to a person or event" (Louw and Nida I:420; Mt. 7:23; 25:12; 26:34-35, 70, 72, 74). This warning takes the reader back to verse 28. Alongside one of the greatest promises in Scripture (v. 32) is one of its most somber statements (v. 33). Disciples testify of their relationship. Persons who profess a relationship with Jesus but who refuse to confess that relationship to others have no relationship. In the judgment, how one has confessed Jesus will be the decisive element of evidence (Keener, *Matthew* 329; cf. 12:36-37; Jn. 12:42; Rev. 3:5; Mk. 8:38; 2 Tim. 2:12).

Love and loyalty to Christ must surpass all other ties (vv. 35-37; 19:29). See also the discussion on v. 21. Jesus' goal was not to make everyone one big happy family ("do not think"; compare with 5:17) but rather to gather an exclusive following (v. 34). As strange as it sounds, Jesus, the God of peace (1 Cor.

14:33), came to bring division, division between those who follow Him and those who do not. He is responsible for a portion of the disciples' opposition (Nolland 439). Jesus wants His followers to have a clear commitment to Him above all others (v. 38). One of the outcomes of such commitment will be a separation between followers of Jesus and non-followers. The division will be so sharp that even family members will turn against family members in persecution. There is no mention of the husband-wife relationship (Bruner 1:489-490). As Bruner observes, Jesus did not intend to break up this relationship though at times it does happen (1 Cor. 7:10-16), nor did He intend to deny His disciples the blessings of family. However, even the husband and wife love must be second to one's love for Christ (Lk. 14:26). Jesus practiced what He preached. His mother and siblings learned that He loved the Father above all else (12:46-50; Lk. 2:49; Jn. 7:3-9).

Again, for clarification, verses 35 and 36 are not a direct quote of Micah 7:6. See the discussion above on verse 21. The translations show that they are close but Jesus alluded to the general concept of Micah's words rather than actually applying them to His situation (Archer and Chirichigno 159).

One should bear in mind that the love/hate commandment uses a common Semitic idiom and should not be understood in an absolute sense (see Mal. 1:2-3; Lk. 14:26; 16:13). Rather, Jesus was emphasizing by contrast the superior devotion He requires of His disciples. See comments on 6:24.

Jesus used two forceful instruments to make His point. Both spoke of persecution and death. He used a sword to portray the surety of this division (Greek *dichazō*, to cut into two parts, Grimm's 153). "Jesus divides families just as a sword slices in half" (Gundry 199). He used a cross to portray death (v. 38).

The cross was an instrument of capital punishment and represented death and martyrdom (Gundry 200). In these literary and historical contexts, taking up the cross meant more than simply doing God's will (*contra* Wilkins 398) or even self-denial (*contra* Hill 195). Cross-bearing included these but the ultimate application is martyrdom. Just as each person who was condemned to death by crucifixion bore his own cross to the place of crucifixion (Jn. 19:17; Hendriksen 476; Newman and Stine 322), so each follower of Jesus must take up his cross, i.e., make a decision to pick up a cross and then *continue* to carry it as he follows Jesus. (The Greek verbs "take" and "follow" are present tense.) The action is intentional (Greek active voice) and represented as reality (Greek indicative). This is a factual requirement. Each disciple must continually and sacrificially follow Jesus for the long term.

There are both active and passive aspects of cross-bearing, and Jesus' disciples are required to do both (Bruner 1:491). These verses speak of the active aspects of cross-bearing. Jesus' focus was on both the crisis experience of conversion and the lifetime of service. His own road to Calvary began at Bethlehem. In the same way, the cross-bearing of a disciple is a life-long habit. In verses 35-37, death to the closest human ties is in view. Compare this with Luke 14:25-33 where cross-bearing means renunciation of everything that challenges the supreme lordship of Christ. See especially Luke 14:33.

A person who searches for and finds (Greek *heuriskō*) his or her life will in the end lose it (v. 39). The meaning is that one who finds *in this earthly life* what he or she is looking for will lose it in the next life. Likewise, one who loses his or her life here, either through "actual martyrdom or disciplined self-denial, will find it in the ages to come" (Carson, *Matthew* 257). In other words, to paraphrase Jesus, either people live for themselves now (find life in this world) or they die to themselves now and live for Jesus and find life in the world to come. Compare with 16:24-25 and John 12:25.

These are attention-getting words. Jesus told His disciples what to expect for a reception and how painful their lives would be. The fact that these men stayed with Jesus after this, speaks of their high level of commitment to Jesus. Some would need these words before the church was very old (Acts 12:1).

d. Rewards for all who contribute to the spread of the Gospel (10:40-42)

40 He that receiveth you receiveth me, and he that receiveth me receiveth him that sent me.
41 He that receiveth a prophet in the name of a prophet shall receive a prophet's reward; and he that receiveth a righteous man in the name of a righteous man shall receive a righteous man's reward.
42 And whosoever shall give to drink unto one of these little ones a cup of cold *water* only in the name of a disciple, verily I say unto you, he shall in no wise lose his reward.

Those who accept and live by Jesus' Sermon on the Mount (chapters 5-7) will be eternally blessed (7:24-25). Those who obey Jesus' teachings in this second discourse will also be rewarded. Returning to the discussion begun in verses 11-13, Jesus assured His disciples and their hearers that He would honor both His messengers and those who accepted them and their messages. To receive (accept, welcome; Newman and Stine 324) His messengers was to receive them as Jesus' agents, and to receive Jesus was to receive Him as God's agent (v. 40; Jn. 12:44; Carson, *John* 451). He was and is (Mt. 28:18) the authority and the source of the messengers' message (Wilkins 398). Rewards will be given to both the messengers and all who receive them and help them by caring for their physical needs (vv. 41-42; Jn. 13:20). Even something as common as a cup of cold water given to the least of Christ's servants because he or she is Christ's servant will not be overlooked in the judgment (25:31-46). "Cold" suggests deliberate and considerate care. The motive more than the gift caught Jesus' eye (Hendriksen 479).

Gundry (203) sees this as a hierarchical list: apostles (v. 40), prophets, righteous persons (13:17; 23:29)—whom he understands as teachers of righteousness (v. 41)—and the little ones (v. 42). These little ones are the followers of Jesus who are not in leadership or teaching roles. Whether this is hierarchical or not, Jesus' promise is that He will reward all who are instrumental in spreading the gospel. Both missionary and supporter will receive a missionary's reward.

Jesus' origin and mission should not be overlooked. He came from the Father (v. 40). He too, was an apostle, a sent one (Bruner 1:496). He was the Father's missionary.

2. Separate ministries for Jesus and the Twelve (11:1)

1 And it came to pass, when Jesus had made an end of commanding his twelve disciples, he departed thence to teach and to preach in their cities.

After commanding the Twelve, Jesus parted for a time (11:1). The apostles went on their first missionary trip and Jesus continued His ministry in the cities of Galilee (Hendriksen 483). Thus, Matthew brought to a close this second discourse. For a discussion on the meaning of teaching and preaching, see comments on 4:23.

Summary (10:1—11:1)

Chapter ten is Matthew's record of the selection and appointment of the Twelve and their pre-service training. This is Jesus' second major teaching block. It is His response to His own expressed need for more laborers (9:35-38) and His preparation of the apostles for missionary work.

The adage "some things are caught more than taught" appears to have been Jesus' mentoring practice. Not until Jesus was well into His ministry did He send out the Twelve to minister apart from His physical presence. They first needed to learn His teachings and His ministry methodology. They needed to see Him act and react in the context of full-time ministry. They needed to observe Him as He experienced both acceptance and rejection. Having witnessed Jesus in ministry over an extended period, they were ready to go out and begin their own preaching ministries.

In preparation for sending them on their first missionary trip, Jesus empowered these men to do great miracles as they shared the gospel of the kingdom. He instructed them to live from their ministries. i.e., allow those to whom they ministered to provide for their food and clothing needs. He promised that some hearers would accept their message but not all. Some would reject the kingdom message and turn on the messengers with severe persecution. Persecution, however, would not be sufficient reason to quit. Jesus required endurance to the end. He ended this discourse by promising to reward everyone who took part in spreading the gospel.

Application: Teaching and Preaching the Passage

Preaching and teaching from this chapter might seem a challenge. However, some of the discourse can be readily turned into sermonic and teaching material. One might do a study on the Twelve: their call (v. 1), their characters (vv. 2-4), and their commission (vv. 5-15). One might follow Hagner's (33A:288) suggestion and speak of the reward of confession (v. 32) and the penalty of denial (v. 33). Three reasons God's children need not fear spiritual enemies are found in verses 26-33.

Proper techniques for handling opposition are found in verses 16-28. In such times, one should be shrewd (v. 16), rely of the leadership of the Holy Spirit (v. 20), have stamina (endurance; v. 22), steer clear of persecutors where possible (avoid, flee; v. 23), and squelch personal fear (v. 28).

One might also draw attention to Jesus' timeless principles for missionary work found in these verses. Missionary work answers a timeless need and prayer (9:37—10:5). Christ's missionaries labor under a divine call and commission (vv. 1, 5). Christ's missionaries are divinely enabled (v. 1).

Missionaries are to pick a target group or community prayerfully (v. 6), preach the gospel (v. 7), minister to the whole person (v. 8), rely on God for provision (vv. 9-10), and look for good people with whom to associate when moving into a new area of ministry (vv. 11-13). Missionaries can expect some rejection (vv. 14-15), some opposition (vv. 16-17, 21-25), and some division over their message (vv. 34-37. They should expect divine aid at the same time they are being opposed (vv. 18-20).

Missionaries should not spend all of their ministry time trying to convince those who reject their message (vv. 13-15). They should fearlessly proclaim all the words of Jesus (vv. 26-33). They should be totally committed to Jesus (vv. 38-39). Missionary work brings God and man together through Jesus (v. 40). Missionaries can expect some human aid (v. 42) and a reward from God in the next life (v. 41). Missionaries can expect that those who help them with material resources will share in the heavenly reward (v. 42).

E. The Royal Messiah Assesses the Ministries of John the Baptist and Himself (11:2-24)

Not everyone welcomed the kingdom. Both John the Baptist and Jesus encountered people who were not interested in their messages. Both encountered active and direct opposition. In this section, Jesus discussed this apathy and opposition and warned those who rejected the gospel that their judgment would be severe.

1. Jesus discussed and evaluated John the Baptist's ministry (11:2-15)

2 Now when John had heard in the prison the works of Christ, he sent two of his disciples,
3 And said unto him, Art thou he that should come, or do we look for another?
4 Jesus answered and said unto them, Go and shew John again those things which ye do hear and see:
5 The blind receive their sight, and the lame walk, the lepers are cleansed, and the deaf hear, the dead are raised up, and the poor have the gospel preached to them.
6 And blessed is *he*, whosoever shall not be offended in me.
7 And as they departed, Jesus began to say unto the multitudes concerning John, What went ye out into the wilderness to see? A reed shaken with the wind?
8 But what went ye out for to see? A man clothed in soft raiment? behold, they that wear soft *clothing* are in kings' houses.
9 But what went ye out for to see? A prophet? yea, I say unto you, and more than a prophet.
10 For this is *he*, of whom it is written, Behold, I send my messenger before thy face, which shall prepare thy way before thee.

11 Verily I say unto you, Among them that are born of women there hath not risen a greater than John the Baptist: notwithstanding he that is least in the kingdom of heaven is greater than he.
12 And from the days of John the Baptist until now the kingdom of heaven suffereth violence, and the violent take it by force.
13 For all the prophets and the law prophesied until John.
14 And if ye will receive *it*, this is Elias, which was for to come.
15 He that hath ears to hear, let him hear.

At some point in Jesus' Galilean ministry (cf. Lk. 7:18-23), John sent two of his disciples to question Jesus (some manuscripts omit "two," leaving the number uncertain). That John had disciples is clear, but the Gospels do not explain what being a disciple of John meant (Nolland 450). At any rate, they intended to learn and follow his teaching. At this time, John was in prison because of his bold and prophetic-style preaching against Herod Antipas. See 4:12 and 14:1-12 and comments there.

John's disciples had earlier questioned Jesus about fasting (9:14-17), but now the question was from John himself. He wondered about Jesus' identity. John's question may actually be Matthew's key question around which he constructed this chapter (Bruner 1:501): "Who are you, Jesus?" Matthew placed this question before his reader throughout his record (8:27; 16:15; 21:10).

Matthew did not record what triggered John's question. Luke said John's question was prompted by a report from some of his disciples who had witnessed Jesus' miracles (Lk. 7:18). One can assume that John was eager to track Jesus' ministry. Perhaps his disciples regularly carried news to John about the works "of the Christ" (lit. Greek).

Matthew, from his later perspective as the writer of this Gospel, identified Jesus as the Christ in verse 2, not John (Carson, *Matthew* 261). In other words, John was not calling Jesus the Christ but asking if He was the one who was to come. Apparently, he had lost some of his earlier certitude. He had previously identified Jesus as the Lamb of God, the one who would come after him and be much greater than he, the Son of God (Jn. 1:27-34; also John 3:28-30). John did not always know that Jesus was the Christ (Carson, *John* 151). He recognized Jesus' fuller identity only after the visible manifestation of the Holy Spirit (Jn. 1:31-33). It is doubtful that John forgot those powerful revelations from God at Jesus' baptism (Mt. 3:13-17).

John was probably the first to make such a confession. Yet now, after months in prison he was beginning to wonder. Perhaps even John expected that the Christ (for Christ, see 16:16) would set up an earthly kingdom (Keener, *Background* 75) and restore Israel to her glory. Perhaps John wondered why his own prophecies that Jesus would baptize with the Holy Spirit and judge with fire were not being fulfilled (3:11-12; Is. 35:4-5; Gundry 206; Wilkins 413; Bruner 1:505). Jesus traveled from city to city proclaiming the kingdom but He was not bringing judgment. John might have wondered, if the Messiah was to set prisoners free (Is. 61:1; Evans, *Matthew* 224), why he was still in prison.

John's disciples relayed his question to Jesus (v. 3): "Are you the coming one or are we to expect another?" Verses 4-19 answer John's question. Verses 4-6 are Jesus' answer to John through his disciples. Verses 7-19 are Jesus' explanation of who John and He both were.

The "coming one" is Messianic (Hagner 33A:300). "Another" translates a word that might suggest another of a different kind (Greek *allos;* Keener, *Matthew* 335; as in Gal. 1:6-7) or simply a different person (Gundry 205). Either meaning is possible (Louw and Nida I:590). Rather than give a direct answer, Jesus invited John's disciples to listen and watch Him and then go and tell John what they now knew firsthand from Jesus' teaching and miracles and from eyewitness testimonies (v. 4; Osborne 415). Jesus' answer was His ministry. His miracles and those to whom He preached (the poor) testified for Him (Jn. 5:36; 10:37-38; 14:11). He gave sight to the blind (9:27-31) and to those paralyzed the ability to walk (9:1-8). He cleansed lepers (see comments on 8:1-4 and 10:8) and caused the deaf to hear. He restored the dead to life (9:25) and invited the poor into God's kingdom, something that seems a bit out of place next to such miracles as raising the dead (Bruner 1:508). Newman and Stine (331) observed that He did not heal all of the diseased, only those who came to Him.

All of this was in fulfillment of Isaiah's prophecies (Is. 29:18; 35:5-6; 26:19; 61:1-2) and proved that the kingdom had arrived (Mt. 4:23-24; 12:28; Lk. 4:18-21). Jesus' healing and preaching ministry was a Messianic ministry (Mt. 8:16-17; Is. 53:4) and proof that Jesus and the Messiah are the same.

Jesus' reference to Isaiah also points to another truth: a comprehensive understanding of Jesus' person and ministry is possible only when one is familiar with the O.T. and when the O.T. is read with Jesus in mind. The O.T. is essential to knowing Jesus in His fullness.

Jesus ended His message to John with a general beatitude and a gentle rebuke (v. 6): kingdom blessings belong to those who accept Jesus' ministry as prophesied. John, his disciples, the crowd, and Matthew's readership (the church) are blessed when they trust Jesus, even though He does not appear to be the kind of Messiah they were expecting (Nolland 451). For beatitude (blessed is he), see comments on 5:1. They are blessed when they accept the present realities of the kingdom, even though the realities are not what they expected either. For example, the present stage of the kingdom includes both joy and grief (Hagner 33A:302). Many followers of Jesus have been excited at the kingdom blessings (miracles) but offended by the attacks (persecutions, martyrdom; 13:20-21) of those destined for judgment (Heb. 10:32-39). All Christians need to hear verse 6 and Jesus' rebuke of John for his doubts. Though not harshly, John was rebuked for his doubts. How one responds to the Messianic Jesus has eternal ramifications (Keener, *Matthew* 335).

The word "offended" (v. 6; Greek *skandalizō*, in the active voice) means "to offend or cause someone to stumble" (Grimm's 576), to cause someone to stop believing (Louw and Nida I:376; Jn. 6:61). But sometimes (when in the passive voice, as here) it means "to fall away" (Grimm's 576; 13:21; 24:10) or "to cease believing" (Louw and Nida I:375-376). In such passages, the verb often (but not always) denotes apostasy (26:31).

The rebuke, then, is also a warning: do not stop believing just because you do not see everything happening that you want to see happen now. Rejoice in what is happening and patiently wait for the rest to come later (Lenski 429). As verses 20-24 illustrate, judgment was still part of the Messiah's role. However, judgment was not the purpose of Jesus' first coming (Jn. 3:17; 12:47; Lk. 9:54-55). He came to save. John did not understand that Jesus' present ministry was to precede His coming in judgment (16:27; Keener, *Matthew* 335).

Jesus addressed John's doubts with His teaching and His miracles. He used these to strengthen John's faith in His identity. This was Jesus' way of turning unbelievers into believers and doubters into believers with strong and confident faith (Bruner 1:509). Matthew's inclusion of this record suggests that John was not the only one Jesus wanted to contemplate His works because they are key to recognizing His true identity (Hill 198).

As John's disciples were walking away, Jesus began teaching the crowds about John (v. 7). The presence of crowds indicates that Jesus was popular with the general population at this time. Using three rhetorical questions Jesus drew attention to John's ministry. Three times, He asked them what they had gone to see. Jesus reminded them that John's ministry was a wilderness, not urban, ministry (see comments on 3:1) and the people went to him (3:5), not the other way around. John also ministered in different places. These folks had traveled from Galilee to hear John, direct distances of approximately seventeen miles (twenty-seven km.) if they traveled from Capernaum to Bethany beyond the Jordan (Jn. 1:28), thirty-three miles (fifty-four km.) if they traveled from Capernaum to Aenon near Salim (Jn. 3:23), or ninety-six miles (one hundred and fifty-four km.) if they traveled from Capernaum to the Jordan just above the Dead Sea (Mt. 3:1). A day's journey averaged between twenty-four and thirty miles (thirty-eight to fourty-eight km.; ISBE 1:879), so they had expended some effort and resources to see him.

The people sensed that John was a person of spiritual significance and vitality, more than "a reed being shaken in the wind" (Hagner 33A:304). Some thought he might even be the Messiah (Lk. 3:15; Jn. 1:20; Acts 13:25). He did not dress like the rich and powerful (v. 8; 3:4), and the people should not have expected otherwise when they went to see him. They expected to see a prophet (v. 9; 21:26); Jesus agreed that indeed John was a prophet, but he was more than the normal prophet. John was the fulfillment of Malachi 3:1 (v. 10). By quoting this O.T. passage (which quotes the first part of Ex. 23:20), Jesus pointed His audience to John's call (Jn. 1:6: "there was a man sent from God") and prophetic role as forerunner of the Lord (Jn. 3:28). John was the prophet who first announced the Messiah's soon arrival. Jesus' statement about John's role and message ultimately pointed them to Jesus Himself. It is clear from verses 19-24 that many did not connect the ministries of John and Jesus in this manner. They did not recognize John as Malachi's messenger nor Jesus as Malachi's Lord (Mal. 4:5). Neither did they recognize Jesus as the fulfillment of John's prophecy (Jn. 1:30; 5:33). However, John did have considerable success. See 17:13 and comments.

Jesus (v. 10; Lk. 7:27) hinted at His true identity when He quoted Malachi 3:1 and used "your face" and "your way" in indirect reference to Himself, rather than the original first person in reference to God. This equated Jesus to Malachi's Lord (Bruner 1:511) and showed a distinction in the Persons of the Godhead.

A prophet was one who conveyed God's message. In the O.T., prophets were also known as men of God and seers (1 Sam. 9:8-10). The three terms were synonymous (Hays, Duvall, and Pate 266, 358). A prophet or prophetess might speak of God's workings in the past, of God's present workings, or of future events. Many times, though not always, Israel's prophets spoke of God's judgment against Israel and of her salvation and of the judgment and salvation of the nations with whom Israel interacted.

Jesus' reference to John's attire was not small talk. John dressed like the prophet Elijah (3:4; 2 Kg. 1:8). His rough prophet's clothing was the clerical robe of the O.T. prophet (Zech. 13:4) and was another sign of his identity and role. John's dress and message made it easy for the people to view him as a prophet (14:5; 21:26; Mk. 11:32; Lk. 1:76).

Though Jesus was unlike John in dress and several other respects, He too was considered to be a prophet because of His message and miracles (13:57; 21:11, 46; Lk. 7:16; 13:33; 24:19; Jn. 6:14; 7:40; 9:17). Some thought He was one of the O.T. prophets resurrected (Mt. 16:14; Lk. 9:19).

"Prepare your way before you" (v. 10) means to prepare the road so you can travel on it (Newman and Stine 336). John's ministry was preparatory. He opened and built a road for the Messiah. This figuratively refers to the spiritual heart preparation (Lk. 1:17) that John encouraged his audience to make—as he spoke of the one soon to come (Is. 40:3; Mt. 3:3; Lk. 3:16)—and baptized the repentant (Lk. 3:3; Jn. 1:33). This heart preparation was essential. Otherwise the Lord would have come only in judgment (Mal. 3:1; 4:6; Keil 457-458).

Jesus gave John a place in human history second to none (v. 11). No human ("one born of women"; Keener, *Background* 76) equaled John in position and privilege. He was the greatest, i.e., the most important (Newman and Stine 337) for several reasons. (1) Although he was both a prophet and the fulfillment of prophecy (Hendriksen 488), he was also the official announcer of God's Messiah, the Lord Himself (Lk. 1:76). (2) He was the "immediate" forerunner (Carson, *Matthew* 264). (3) He did the greatest work in preparing people to receive personally the Lord. According to Luke 7:29-30 Jesus' hearers, with the exception of the Pharisees and lawyers, agreed John was God's man (Jn. 5:35) and praised God that Jesus had such a high view of John (Marshall 298-299).

In short, verse 10 is the key to verse 11. John's greatness was not merely a matter of timing but because of who was there with him and what He was doing (v. 5; Nolland 457). John prepared people for the arrival of the King and the King was at work building His kingdom. As Bruner (1:512) detects in this text, "Jesus is talking about John; Matthew is talking about Jesus; readers are to think about God. That is the point."

For Jesus to make such a claim about John's greatness suggests that He excluded Himself from this group of mortals (Blomberg 40). As Blomberg observes, He could only do this because He was no mere mortal. He was the Lord who "came" (v. 19), also in fulfillment of Malachi 3:1 and 4:5. Both forerunner and Messiah have come and their messages deserved the people's attention.

John was a great man but everyone in the kingdom of heaven is greater. As much as Jesus valued John for his place in God's prophetic plan, yet Jesus placed a higher value on all who humbled themselves as a child to enter His kingdom (v. 11; 18:1-4; Keener, *Matthew* 339; for kingdom, see 3:2). John announced the kingdom's nearness and prepared people for its coming but he did not witness or experience the full new covenant blessings (justification by faith in Jesus' finished work, regeneration and its accompanying sanctification; Rom. 5:12-8:17) that followed the cross and Pentecost. John was part of the old era, not the new (Hendriksen 488; Carson, *Matthew* 265; *contra* Marshall 628-629, Gundry 208-209, and Hagner 33A:306). He would share in the future blessings of the kingdom even as the O.T. patriarchs would (8:11), yet his understanding of Jesus' Messianic role was incomplete (v. 3; Acts 19:1-7). In this sense, even the least in the kingdom is greater than John the Baptist for even the least understand Jesus' role as Savior who died on the cross, something John would not live to see (a veiled prophecy? Wilkins 415). Walvoord (82) thinks Jesus was speaking in verse 11 of those who will live during the millennial kingdom as being greater than John. Nothing in the context suggests any of the hearers would have understood such a reference or that Jesus was speaking of the kingdom in this manner.

John's ministry was to announce an approaching kingdom, and neither he nor his message was received well by all (v. 12). Verse 12 poses several interpretive possibilities. The problem lies with whether to understand the subjects as using force or having force used against them. In addition, if the subjects are using force, then one must determine if the force is positive or negative. Osborne (421) summarizes the possibilities:

> The problem lies in the cognates "is subject to violence" (*biazetai*) and "violent people" (*biastai*). They occur side by side and can be understood positively ("forceful advance") or negatively ("suffering violence"). Thus there are four combinations here: (1) totally positive ("the kingdom forcefully advances [through God], and forceful people [the disciples] seize it"); (2) totally negative ("the kingdom suffers violence [persecution], and violent people [the leaders] plunder it"); (3) negative/positive (the kingdom suffers violence, but forceful people lay hold of it"); (4) positive/negative ("the kingdom is forcefully advancing, but violent people plunder it").

The NIV, GW, and Wuest's N.T. translation follow the first option. The KJV, NKJV, NASB, ESV, RSV, REB, and TEV follow option two. The NLT follows the fourth option. Hendriksen (488-490) and Keener (*Matthew* 340) prefer the first option (see also Luke 16:16). Hill (200-201), Gundry (210), Evans (*Matthew* 227), Wilkins (416), Hagner (33A:306-307), and Bruner

(1:513-514) prefer the second option. Nolland (457-458) and Carson (*Matthew* 265-267) prefer the fourth option.

A clear solution is difficult. Either translation is possible. John's arrest, imprisonment, and impending death as well as the rising opposition to Jesus' kingdom ministry suggest that Jesus may have been speaking of evil's violent opposition to the kingdom (option two). However, the kingdom was aggressively advancing at the same time it was under attack (option four). Each of these two possibilities fits the context, but option four seems slightly more probable, especially in light of Jesus' later promise, "I will build my church, and the gates of hell shall not prevail against it" (16:18).

John was a key figure also because of his role as the Messianic forerunner and his place in God's calendar of events. He was the end and the beginning (v. 13). His ministry marked the end of the O.T. prophetic era, the Law and the Prophets (the Scriptures), and the beginning of the Messianic era (v. 13; Lk. 16:16; Acts 1:22; 10:37). "The prophets and the law" refers to the entire O.T. (see comments on 5:17). John was a unique person in history. His place in salvation history as the one to introduce the Messiah placed him in time as the final voice of the prophetic Law and the Prophets, a voice pointing to Jesus. As Hill (201) observed, "Prediction has now given way to realization, in the presence of Jesus." Verse 13 does not declare an end to the law. Jesus was emphatic that the law would remain (Lk. 16:17). See comments on 5:17-20. However, Christ was both the goal and the end of the covenant of law (Rom. 10:4).

Fourth, not only was John's ministry a hinge-pin in time, John was also the fulfillment of Malachi 4:5, which promised a return of the O.T. prophet Elijah before the end times (v. 14). Jesus' statement was clear: John the Baptist was Malachi's Elijah. See 17:13 and comments there.

Jesus' words "if you are willing to receive it" do not give latitude in biblical interpretation (*contra* Bruner 1:516-517). Rather, He was calling on His audience to accept all He had just said about John and by inference Himself. A proper identification of John is key to an accurate understanding of Jesus' own identity. The "if" suggests the hearers had either difficulty understanding or difficulty accepting that John was Elijah because of their preconceived ideas about the coming Elijah, especially in light of John's imprisonment (Hill 201).

Three decades earlier the angel Gabriel had spoken words similar to these to John's father Zechariah. John would minister "in the spirit and power of Elijah" and prepare a people to receive the Lord (Lk. 1:17). Surely, Zechariah recounted this angelic message to John. So while John was not a literal Elijah returned to life (Jn. 1:21), and perhaps did not fully comprehend his own Elijah-type role (Mt. 11:3, 11; Carson, *Matthew* 269), he was the Elijah Malachi prophesied to come (Mt. 17:12). He was a prophet, one to whom "the word of the Lord came" (Lk. 3:2), i.e., one whom God called to the prophetic office (Marshall 134). Like Elijah, John wore the prophet's clothing (3:4; 2 Kg. 1:8), preached God's judgment with fiery passion (3:7-12; 1 Kg. 18:18-21), and stood against the sins of all levels of society (3:5; 14:4; 1 Kg. 21:17-24). He possessed the same divine anointing as Elijah (Lk. 1:17) and like Elijah sought to bring Israel back to God (1 Kg. 18:21, 24, 36-37, 39).

Both were men of prayer (1 Kg. 18:36; Jas. 5:17; Lk. 11:1) and fasting (1 Kg. 19:8; Mt. 9:14). Both were men of God (1 Kg. 17:18, 24; 2 Kg. 1:10-13; Jn. 1:6). Both were persecuted by wicked rulers and their evil spouses (14:3-12; 1 Kg. 18:10; 19:2-3). John, however, did not do any miracles (Jn. 10:41; Keener, *Matthew* 337) or leave in a fiery chariot (2 Kg. 2:11). John suffered martyrdom instead (Mt. 14:10). For further comments on John and Malachi's prophecies, see comments on Matthew 17:10-12.

Jesus called on His audience to consider well what He had just said (v. 15). This is the first of three times (13:9, 43) in Matthew's Gospel that Jesus called for His hearers to listen closely, i.e., to give due diligence to understand His words. Both John and Jesus had spoken the words of the kingdom with clarity and both called for a decision. "If you will receive it" (v. 14) speaks of a decision concerning the prophetic identity and message of John the Baptist and a decision concerning the person and message of Jesus (Wilkins 417). The power of a free will is evident. See comments on verses 24 and 28 below. Many—yes, even most—rejected the message of these two great persons. This rejection prompted the following rebuke from Jesus.

2. Jesus assessed His generation's response to the gospel (11:16-19)

16 But whereunto shall I liken this generation? It is like unto children sitting in the markets, and calling unto their fellows,
17 And saying, We have piped unto you, and ye have not danced; we have mourned unto you, and ye have not lamented.
18 For John came neither eating nor drinking, and they say, He hath a devil.
19 The Son of man came eating and drinking, and they say, Behold a man gluttonous, and a winebibber, a friend of publicans and sinners. But wisdom is justified of her children.

In these verses, Jesus scolded His contemporaries ("this generation") for not accepting the message of the kingdom (vv. 16-17). They were like children who could not be pleased, who refused to participate regardless what was suggested when asked by their friends to join them (Newman and Stine 342).

To play the flute and dance suggested a wedding and joyous celebration. To mourn (Greek *koptō*) meant to sing a dirge or a funeral tune. Verse 17 is a common Hebrew parallel construction that makes its point by contrasting statements (antithetical parallelism; Keener, *Matthew* 341). The Bible has many of these (Ps. 1:6; Prov. 10:1; 10:12; Jn. 1:3; Ryken, *Read the Bible* 104; Giese and Sandy 226; Ryken, *Words of Life* 111, 236). On flute playing at funerals, see comments on 9:23.

Jesus' illustration in verses 16 and 17 pointed to the contrasting lifestyles of John and Himself and called attention to the rejection of the kingdom by His generation. John lived one lifestyle, Jesus another. John, represented by the funeral dirge, was an ascetic and his diet was coarse (v. 18; 3:4; Lk. 1:15) when he ate at all. "Came neither eating nor drinking" means John fasted a lot (see 6:16 for fasting), was not known for attending banquet parties, and drank no non-alcoholic grape juice or alcoholic drinks (Newman and Stine 344; Lk. 1:15; 7:33). Apparently John, for the most part, lived separate from society (Wilkins 418) and as a Nazirite (ISBE III:502).

Jesus, represented by the flute and dance, attended social celebrations (Jn. 2:1-11) and large dinners (v. 19; Mt. 9:10-13: Lk. 15:2; 19:5-10), apparently rarely fasted (9:14; Lk. 5:35; but see Mt. 15:32 and Jn. 4:31-34), did drink unfermented grape juice (Lk. 7:34; see further comments below), and provided the same for others to drink (Jn. 2:9). Both John and Jesus encouraged their disciples to live as they did (Lk. 5:33), a fact that did not go unnoticed by the general population (Mk. 2:18). Jesus' point was that both messengers were rejected ("for,"v. 18). That people were already aware of these differences between Jesus and John should have made Jesus' illustration more appreciable.

Rather than accept these men as from God, the detractors accused John of being demon-possessed and Jesus of being a glutton and "winebibber": that is, a drunkard. In short, both were considered to be evil and worthy of being ignored (Nolland 463). As seen in verse 8 and earlier (3:4), John's asceticism was prophetic and in line with his calling. He was called to be a wilderness prophet (3:3; Is. 40:3). For comments on demon possession see above on 4:24, 8:28.

Jesus was friendly toward tax collectors (see 5:46) and sinners (9:11-13; Lk. 15:1-2) because they needed Him and because winning them was in agreement with His own purpose statement (Lk. 19:10). His accusers thought otherwise, charging Him with being one of them, of "standing in the way of sinners" (Ps. 1:1).

Concerning the allegation of gluttony and drunkenness, only Jesus' detractors would believe that (Mk. 3:20; 6:31; 8:2). The purpose behind these allegations may well have been a warning, for one who was "a glutton and a drunkard" was condemned by the law (Dt. 21:20; Gundry 213). It is true that He made wine by the gallons (Jn. 2:6), but there is not a hint in the Apostle John's record that Jesus facilitated drunkenness. The N.T. word translated wine (Greek *oinos*) can denote either unfermented or fermented wine (9:17). Believers can be assured that Jesus never compromised the Spirit's control in His own life (Eph. 5:18; Lk. 4:1) by consuming anything that would negate His own sobriety or contradict His own condemnation of drunkenness (24:49). Neither would He hinder the Spirit's work in others (Jn. 3:5), while He preached the kingdom, by facilitating their drunkenness. He made unfermented grape juice out of water, wine that would not turn drinkers into drunks. In truth, Jesus' enemies were upset not because He feasted too much. Some of His feasting had been with them (Lk. 7:36)! Jesus' enemies were upset because He sometimes celebrated with folks whom the religious establishment condemned (9:10-13; Lk. 15:2; Keener, *Matthew* 342).

Jesus' responded with a brief proverbial saying—"wisdom is justified by her children"—meaning that the fruit of His actions will support His methods and message (v. 19). Some manuscripts have "children" and others have "works." Either word makes the same point. Actions have fruit. The fruits of John and Jesus' ministries testified of God's plan (see vv. 25-26) as He worked in and through both of His servants, in spite of the doubts and rejections of "this generation." The fruits (works) were those who accepted the message of the kingdom and joined as citizens (Bruner 1:520). This fruit validated the ministries of both John and Jesus. It had been several hundred years since Israel had witnessed such a godly stirring as John initiated and Jesus continued (Barclay 2:12). Shame on them for rejecting it.

3. Jesus scolded the cities where He did most of His miracles for their rejection of Him (11:20-24)

20 Then began he to upbraid the cities wherein most of his mighty works were done, because they repented not:
21 Woe unto thee, Chorazin! woe unto thee, Bethsaida! for if the mighty works, which were done in you, had been done in Tyre and Sidon, they would have repented long ago in sackcloth and ashes.
22 But I say unto you, It shall be more tolerable for Tyre and Sidon at the day of judgment, than for you.
23 And thou, Capernaum, which art exalted unto heaven, shalt be brought down to hell: for if the mighty works, which have been done in thee, had been done in Sodom, it would have remained until this day.
24 But I say unto you, That it shall be more tolerable for the land of Sodom in the day of judgment, than for thee.

These verses continue Jesus' discussion about His rejection. After scolding His generation of Jews for rejecting the message of John and Himself, Jesus began "upbraiding"—rebuking (Greek *oneidizō*, "to reproach someone, with the implication of that individual being evidently to blame," Louw and Nida I:437)—specific communities for their refusal to repent, i.e., turn from their sins and follow Him (for repent, see comments on 3:2). Jesus' rebuke demonstrates a real choice before the people of these communities and a responsible rejection. For the first time Matthew reveals how great Israel's rejection of Jesus was (Hagner 33A:313).

Woe (Greek *ouai*, v. 21) denotes a "state of intense hardship or distress, disaster or horror" (Louw and Nida I:243). It signifies "a condition of deep suffering due to a calamity that has befallen or will befall a person or community" (ISBE IV:1088). God's messengers frequently pronounced woes on the rebellious (Is. 5; Mt. 23). Jesus promised these cities that God would send severe judgment upon them. See 23:13.

The area where Jesus ministered most was not one He randomly selected (see comments on 4:14-16). Isaiah had foreseen that this portion of the nation would be favored with great spiritual light (Is. 9:1-7). Jesus was that light (Is. 42:6; Jn. 8:12), but the people refused His message and the many signs that were intended to validate Him as the light.

He started with Chorazin, a city north of the Sea of Galilee about two and a half miles inland (four km.) and north of Capernaum (ISBE I:652). This occasion (v. 21; Lk. 10:13) is the only mention of this city in both Testaments. Its inclusion as one of the cities where Jesus did "most of His mighty works" suggests that Jesus performed several miracles in this city. It also reminds the reader that the Apostle John's testimony (20:30) and his hyperbolic statement (21:25) are supported by other witnesses. The four Gospel writers recorded only a small portion of the events in Jesus' life.

Bethsaida might have been the name of two cities (ISBE I:475), one on each side of the Jordan River on the north end of the Sea of Galilee. The Scriptural evidence suggests two, but that remains to be determined. The city originally was home to three of Jesus' twelve: Philip, Peter, and Andrew (Jn. 1:44; 12:21). Scripture shows that Jesus did multiple miracles in Bethsaida. He fed the five thousand (Lk. 9:10-17) and He gave sight to a blind man (Mk. 8:22-26). Luke 9:11 says that just before the feeding of the five thousand Jesus healed those who needed healing.

Chorazin and Bethsaida were cities of great gospel privilege and responsibility. Jesus compared the hardness of their hearts to that of their Gentile neighbors to the north, the two cities of Tyre and Sidon. Tyre and Sidon in the O.T. "became proverbial for pagan peoples" (Wilkins 420) and were singled out for divine judgment by the prophets Isaiah (23), Jeremiah (25:22; 27:3-7), Ezekiel (26-28), Joel (3:4-8) and Zechariah (9:2-4). According to Jesus, these Gentiles would have shown deep repentance long ago ("in sackcloth and ashes," v. 21) if they had witnessed His miracles. Consider 15:21-28. In the final judgment, all four cities will be condemned but Chorazin and Bethsaida will receive the harsher judgment (v. 22). Jesus shamed Jewish Chorazin and Bethsaida by saying that even the pagan cities of Tyre and Sidon would have repented.

Jesus' description of the judgment and the judged in these verses, teaches the following: (1) there is coming a judgment in which everyone will be judged; (2) people who have not heard the gospel will be eternally lost; (3) there are different degrees of punishment in eternity; (4) some people who have not heard would be saved if someone would share with them God's way of salvation and give them the opportunity to accept it (compare 9:37, 38); (5) people will be judged in part according to their opportunity to hear and accept the gospel; (6) people who hear and reject the gospel will be punished more severely than those who never heard; and (7) people have a real choice about the gospel. God has not predetermined who will and who will not accept the gospel.

Jesus' reference to repentance shows that His kingdom preaching included a call to repentance (Hagner 33A:313). He had not changed His message (4:17) since His earliest preaching. Sackcloth and ashes were symbols of distress, mourning, humility, or deep repentance and were common in Bible times (1 Kg. 21:27; 1 Chr. 21:16; Est. 4:1-4; Dan. 9:3; etc.). Sackcloth was made of goat or camel hair and was dark in color (ISBE IV:256). It was generally worn as an outer garment (2 Kg. 19:1) but could be worn next to the skin as an undergarment (2 Kg. 6:30). Apparently, Jacob wore sackcloth as a loincloth (Gn. 37:34) to show grief for the assumed death of his son Joseph. Ashes could be put on the head (2 Sam. 13:19), sat in (Job 2:8; Jon. 3:6), or laid in (Est. 4:3).

Jesus ended the list with His own city, Capernaum (4:13; 9:1), where He had performed many miracles (8:14-17; 9:1-8; Mk. 1:21-28; Jn. 4:46-54). This city of all cities should have been filled with believers. Instead, most rejected Jesus' claims. In this, Capernaum mirrored Nazareth (13:53-58).

Jesus compared the spiritual hardness of Capernaum to that of Sodom and by Scriptural allusion her demise to that of Babylon (Is. 14:13-15; Blomberg 38). This is telling. Sodom stands as the epitome of wickedness and as an example of God's judgment against sin (Gen. 13:13; 18:20-21; 19:5, 13, 24-25; Jude 7) and yet Capernaum is more resistant to the miraculous signs than Sodom would have been. Given the same opportunity, Sodom would have repented and would never have been destroyed (v. 23). Did Capernaum think she would be exalted to heaven? (Some Greek MSS have a negative rhetorical question; so ESV and NIV.) Jesus warned that there would be no exaltation for this city. Even as God had humbled Babylon, who was also known for her pride (Dan. 4:30) and wickedness, He will humble Capernaum.

Because Capernaum refused to believe in Jesus as Messiah, the citizens of Capernaum would suffer a worse judgment than Sodom (v. 24) and as certain a judgment as Babylon. Like Chorazin and Bethsaida, Capernaum had great gospel privilege and therefore great responsibility. See 10:15, 12:41-42, and Luke 12:47-48 for this same idea. Greater light means greater responsibility (Hagner 33A:314; Osborne 433).

Jesus' mention of Sodom's future judgment shows that Sodom's citizens are still available for more judgment (Nolland 468). Four truths are evident: (1) though the city was destroyed by fire, Sodom's citizens did not cease to exist; (2) there will be a resurrection and final judgment of the ungodly; (3) the final judgment will be analogous to their first judgment (they will be no better off); and (4) Capernaum should take heed.

Jesus promised that these who rejected the kingdom would be brought down to hell (Greek *hadēs*, v. 23). This is one of two times Matthew uses this Greek word. The other is 16:18. It can mean the place where all dead people go, a general term denoting the spirit world of the dead (Acts 2:27, 31), and it can refer to the grave. It can also denote, more narrowly, hell fire, the place of punishment where God sends the ungodly. See comments on 16:18. This last is the meaning here. See Luke 16:23. Compare with Gehenna. See comments on 5:22. Capernaum would experience the antithesis of heaven. (The Greek *Hades* usually translates the Hebrew *Sheol* in the LXX. There is considerable disagreement among the scholars concerning the exact meaning of *Sheol*; see TWOT II:892-893. That disagreement, because it is translated mainly *Hades*, affects one's understanding of *Hades* also.)

Twice in these verses (vv. 22, 24), Jesus spoke of the day of judgment. It is clear that He spoke of that day as a reality (Hays, Duvall, and Pate 257). He also inferred a resurrection (Hill 204) and taught a judgment based on choices made in this life.

Jesus' hearers may have been shocked at these harsh words, but Israel had been compared to Sodom before (Is. 1:10). For God to live among them for over two years—in the earliest months of His ministry in Judea Jesus was close to John the Baptist—and for them not to recognize Him was equally shocking. If the records are any indication, more miracles were done in and around Capernaum than any other city.

See chapters 8 and 9. The signs should have convinced Jesus' neighbors of the kingdom's arrival (see comments on 4:23 and vv. 4-5 above) and moved them to repentance and discipleship (Jn. 2:23; 10:38; 11:45; Wilkins 420). This city's rejection shows the spiritual darkness of the citizenry and the justness of their judgment.

These words teach that the greatest sin is not the idolatry and hedonism of Tyre and Sidon or the homosexuality of Sodom. The greatest sin is willful rejection of Jesus. No one can be saved without the gospel (Rom. 10:14; Acts 4:12; 1 Cor. 15:1-5). Nor was Jesus teaching that some might be saved based on what they would have done had the miracles and gospel been offered to them (*contra* Bruner 1:525-526, 534). He was teaching that all who hear a clear presentation of the kingdom's gospel and reject it will suffer more than the most sinfully wicked societies. Rejection is a sin of choice, which will result in certain condemnation to the place of punishment.

Jesus was prophetic with these words. He sounded a bit like John the Baptist (3:7) and some of the O.T. prophets who condemned their contemporaries in plain terms. Using the second person "you" rather than an impersonal third person, Jesus directed His words to hardhearted people. "Woe to you!" Jesus knew what will happen in the final judgment to all peoples (Bruner 1:521). This was in keeping with His later teaching that He will judge all the earth (25:31-32).

One might wonder where the Jesus of love was at this time. He was present. These words were gracious words of warning and they reminded the hearers that they must accept Jesus to be part of the kingdom of heaven (vv. 11, 16-19). These words were not to push away or condemn (Jn. 3:17-18), but to invite (v. 28). Here, too, Jesus placed before His hearers a choice, a call for them to exercise their wills and make the only wise choice, the only choice that can lead to eternal life.

F. The Royal Messiah Explained His Ministry: He Introduces to the Father All Who Come to Him (11:25-30)

25 At that time Jesus answered and said, I thank thee, O Father, Lord of heaven and earth, because thou hast hid these things from the wise and prudent, and hast revealed them unto babes.
26 Even so, Father: for so it seemed good in thy sight.
27 All things are delivered unto me of my Father: and no man knoweth the Son, but the Father; neither knoweth any man the Father, save the Son, and *he* to whomsoever the Son will reveal *him*.
28 Come unto me, all *ye* that labour and are heavy laden, and I will give you rest.
29 Take my yoke upon you, and learn of me; for I am meek and lowly in heart: and ye shall find rest unto your souls.
30 For my yoke *is* easy, and my burden is light.

"At that time" may be general rather than specific (Gundry 215-216). Other examples of this are 12:1 and 14:1. Luke (10:17, 21) placed the prayer sometime after the return of the seventy-two, which suggests that at least one (perhaps both) of the writers was not following a strict, historical chronology.

Regardless of the exact timing, after having given such harsh criticism of those who were slow to follow Him, Jesus paused for prayer. With His hearers watching, Jesus addressed His heavenly Father and thanked or praised (Greek *exomologeomai*) Him. Addressing God as Father demonstrated Jesus' submission. He spoke of the Father's supreme rule over the universe. He is Lord of heaven and earth. Jesus was straightforward about the Father's sovereignty. There was no religious pluralism or syncretism with Jesus. Consider Isaiah 44:6-8; 45:18, 21; and 46:9.

Jesus next thanked the Father for designing the way of salvation so that even the simplest folks can understand. A "babe" (Greek *nēpios*) denotes "a small child above the age of a helpless infant but probably not more than three or four years of age" (Louw and Nida I:110); here it represents people who approach God in simplicity. The Apostle Paul expanded on this truth in 1 Corinthians 1:18-31. The hidden and revealed things (v. 25) refer to the events and signs (the miracles) of the kingdom that require eyes of humble faith to recognize as being from God (Wilkins 421). The "wise and prudent" are the intellectually proud who refuse to accept the signs and their meanings (v. 14) and repent. Their refusal led to more blindness, a subject Jesus discussed further with His disciples on another occasion (13:10-16). The babes are those who make no claim to "sophisticated knowledge of God" but yet "are able to recognize the presence of God in Jesus Christ" (Newman and Stine 352). Jesus stated that the Father's plan is that all come into the kingdom as a child, humble and repentant (v. 26; 18:1-5; Wilkins 421).

In their historical context, Jesus' comments toward the intellectually proud may have been directed mainly at the scribes and Pharisees or perhaps even all Israelites (Rom. 2:17-24; Osborne 439). However, since Jesus did not limit His comments to any particular group, perhaps Matthew's readers should not.

Jesus was neither praising weak and lazy minds nor condemning aggressive mental training. The human intellect is part of God's creation and human rationality is part of the divine image in mankind (Col. 3:10). Scripture encourages Christians to expend mental energies in their quest to learn the deeper truths of Christ (Col. 2:2-3). Jesus taught that only those who are diligent to learn and only those who are obedient to what they learn will understand certain spiritual truths (Mk. 4:24-25; Mt. 13:10-15). Mental training was both commanded (Dt. 6:7) and blessed (Dan. 1:17) in the O.T. and is one way believers continue to please God (Rom. 12:2). Moses (Acts 7:22), Ezra (Ezra 7:10), and Paul (Acts 22:3) were highly trained and used by God. John the Baptist's upbringing as a Levite suggests that he also was.

Jesus' words, however, teach that human intellect does not discover the way to salvation (1 Cor. 1:21). Divine revelation provides the way to salvation (v. 25). This revelation and salvation both come from the Father and through the Son (Heb. 1:2). Anyone who tries to understand or know God without learning from the Son will remain without true knowledge of God and in the end join the judged (v. 24).

Following the prayer, Jesus turned His attention back to His and His Father's unique relationship. Their knowledge of each other is complete and exclusive. Such a relationship requires that the deity of the Son equal that of the Father. Hagner (33A:318) says that this "passage constitutes without question one of the highest points of Synoptic Christology." See also 22:45 and comments.

Jesus stated that His Father had handed over (Greek *paradidōmi*) to Him everything (v. 27). What the devil claimed in finite terms, in limitation (Lk. 4:6), Jesus claimed infinitely. Nolland (472) understands this in terms of an heir and an inheritance. Because of the unity that exists between the Father and the Son, the Son has received all that is the Father's. The remainder of the verse explains that this includes a full revelation of the Father. Jesus possessed in His pre-incarnate and incarnate states a complete and exclusive knowledge of the Father as well as an exclusive right to share Him (Wilkins 422). Only in Jesus can God be known, a doctrine central to Christianity (Barclay 2:17) and at odds with all non-Christian religions.

Verse 27 has caught the attention of some theologians. Calvin (II:1152-1153) understood Jesus' statement to mean that no knowledge of God has ever been available except through the Son. Calvin meant by this that God has never revealed Himself other than through His Son, even in O.T. times. Thiessen (41), on the other hand, does not go as far as Calvin but understands Jesus' statement to teach that He is the "center ... of revelation," the omniscient God (138-139) and that "true knowledge of [Jesus] is possible through divine revelation" (303).

No one knows either the Father or the Son unless one reveals the other (Jn. 1:18; 6:44; Eph. 1:17). From this statement comes the great invitation in verses 28-30, for Jesus is the one and only perfectly qualified mediator between God and mankind (1 Tim. 2:5). This statement explains why so many (vv. 20-24) failed to recognize the true identity of the Son. The Father refuses to reveal the truth of His Son to any who proudly rely on human wisdom and understanding or to any who reject the claims of the Son. The Father requires all to believe in His Son (Jn. 6:29). Jesus requires belief that the Father is working through Him (Jn. 10:38-39).

"Come to me" is Jesus' invitation to all who would come to Him. Bruner (1:537) observes that Jesus said, "Come to me" not "Come to God" thus offering Himself as the "fully authorized representative of God." Jesus tenderly offers to provide rest to all who labor and are heavy laden. This is a clear call for hearers to exercise their power of choice. This broad invitation is genuine and universal. The hearers now have to decide whether to accept or reject it.

This same idea of choice is present with the imperatives "take" and "learn" in verse 29. Jesus' commands are invitations. He does not force His will on others.

"Labor" and "heavy laden" (v. 28) describe those who are invited. The first can mean to work or to be weary as a result of work (Greek *kopiaō*, Louw and Nida I:260, 515). The second means "to cause to carry or bear a load" (Greek perfect tense of *phortizō*; Louw and Nida I:207). Together they speak of someone who has been laboring under a heavy load and is in dire need of rest. Jesus promised to provide that rest. Compare this with 9:36.

Strangely enough, Jesus will give rest to those who put on His yoke (v. 29), a metaphor for discipleship ("learn from me"; Wilkins 424). The picture is probably of two draft animals, like oxen (1 Sam. 6:10), fastened together with "a shaped wooden bar" (ISBE IV:1164) for work purposes. Keener (*Matthew* 348) suggests that Jesus might be referring to yokes used by people to carry or pull other loads. This is possible in light of Jeremiah 27:2 and 2 Corinthians 6:14. Either way, the one who responds takes the yoke on himself (Nolland 476).

The point is clear: Jesus was not suggesting that those who come to Him add His burden to what they were already carrying but rather that He will share His yoke to help them pull or carry their load. Those willing to learn revelation that comes only from Him (v. 27; Carson, *Matthew* 278) will find His yoke will be easy to wear (v. 30; Newman and Stine 357). He will share the burden of any who submit to His yoke. Rest belongs to those who are in union with Jesus.

At the same time, the hearer must recognize that Jesus did not promise absolute rest in this life. "A yoke is a work instrument" (Bruner 1:538). He did not promise that there would be no loads. There is work to be done ("my burden") but He promises to carry the greater portion of the load. He will place light burdens on those who chose to submit to His yoke. The yoke also suggests submission (Jer. 27-28; Newman and Stine 356) and obedience (Keener, *Background* 77).

The yoke of the Law was probably part of Jesus' concern in verse 28, perhaps on three levels. First, the Law itself was a yoke. Peter stated (Acts 15:10-11) that it was an unbearable yoke and its opposite is the grace of our Lord Jesus. Paul also spoke of the Law as a yoke of slavery and of Christ as the one who sets people free from it (Gal. 5:1). As Romans 7:4 states, all in Christ have died to the Law so they might belong to another. In other words, one yoke has been traded for another, only this time Christ shares the yoke with His people to help lighten and move the load.

Second, the added rules and regulations the Jewish leaders attached to the law were an extra hardship on the people (Mt. 23:4; Lk. 11:46). See 12:1 and comments there concerning Sabbath restrictions. Hagner (33A:323) says Jesus was referring only to the "tremendous burden of the minutiae of the oral law." However, Jesus did not limit His invitation to this level of concern (*contra* Newman and Stine 354). Burdens come in many shapes and sizes, and these make up the third level of Jesus' concern. He invites *all* the burdened to come to Him for permanent respite.

"Rest for your souls" was the same invitation God gave Judah through the seventh and sixth centuries B.C. prophet Jeremiah (6:16). Jesus' quotation (v. 29) of this invitation may have been a warning, for Judah's rejection of God's invitation through the prophet resulted in their Babylonian captivity (Nolland 478). On the other hand, it was clearly an act of grace that Jesus repeated the invitation.

In verse 29, Jesus spoke of a closeness that would develop with this yoking together. Those yoked with Him will learn from Him. He will be their teacher and the lead person as they labor side by side with Him. As a work partner Jesus is gentle (Greek *praüs*, mild, meek; Louw and Nida I:749) and humble (Greek *tapeinos*, lowly) in heart. Working alongside Jesus is a positive experience for this reason (Greek *hoti*, causal; Osborne 443).

The result of being yoked with Jesus is rested souls. The soul (Greek *psuchē*) here is the whole person, not just the inner self, although that is included (Louw and Nida I:322, 106). Being yoked with Jesus provides what overburdened souls need—assistance and respite. Thus, Jesus promised all His followers (v. 30). His yoke is easy. It is not a harsh entrapment. Jesus will never overload anyone who shares His yoke. This promise assures relief to the tired and overburdened mentioned in verse 28. Jesus promised rest, a real Sabbath rest, for the troubled and sin-burdened souls who come to Him.

Summary (11:2-30)

John the Baptist had been in prison for several months and was beginning to wonder why Jesus did not minister with fiery judgment, as John had understood He would. Jesus responded to John's question by showing that His ministry was exactly as prophesied. Any problem was with John's misunderstanding, not Jesus' performance.

Jesus used this occasion to teach the importance of John's person and ministry. John was number one in privilege because God had selected him to announce the arrival of the Lord and His kingdom. John was Malachi's Elijah. Jesus' discussion of John's importance naturally led into the importance of His own person and ministry and to a severe scolding of those communities that rejected both messengers. Judgment of these cities would be sure and harsh.

Matthew closed this section of Jesus' teaching with His great and universal invitation, "Come unto me and I will give you rest." Though many rejected Jesus, none needed to. The compassionate caregiver offered His deliverance to all.

Application: Teaching and Preaching the Passage

Faith comes by hearing and hearing through the word of Christ (Rom. 10:17). John's faith was clouded with uncertainty, proof that doubts can arise in the hearts of even the greatest. Jesus addressed that doubt by what He did and said (v. 4). Preachers and teachers would do well to follow this model to arouse faith in non-believers and strengthen faith in believers who are temporarily struggling by telling them the wonderful words and works of Jesus. Using this chapter, a sermon or lesson could be organized around the (1) message of Jesus, (2) the ministry of Jesus, and (3) the man Jesus. The message is the gospel of the kingdom (the good news, v. 5, repentance, vv. 20-24, and the coming judgment, vv. 22-24); the ministry is the miracle and sign work He did as well as those to whom He ministered (v. 5 and comments above); and the man Jesus is seen in His prophetic and messianic identities (vv. 10, 13-14; use Isaiah and Malachi; see comments above).

A sermon or lesson might be developed around the following seven truths about ministry found in verses 16-24. (1) God calls and equips His ministers for different types of ministries and methodologies in kingdom work; (2) even the most godly can experience ministry rejection and disappointingly little visible success; (3) God's ministers should not allow people's opinions to negatively affect their attitude about their own ministries (some folks will not be satisfied regardless what the minister does); (4) God's ministers should not take all rejection as a personal attack (some folks will not accept the message from anyone, even Jesus Himself); (5) some folks are so dead spiritually they have no awareness of the Holy Spirit in others (these folks accused John of being demon-possessed); (6) the man of God must rely on God to justify his ministry and not succumb to the temptation to try to get his validation from the world; (7) God will one day vindicate His messengers (vv. 20-24).

Using John as an example, one might also develop a message on the character of the mature man of God. (1) He is strong and stable, not a reed easily moved by the wind (v. 7). (2) He is motivated by God's call on his life, not by creature comforts (soft clothing, v. 8). (3) He is the Lord's messenger, directing the attention of his hearers to the coming Lord and not toward himself (v. 10). It is who he is announcing (the Lord) that makes his message important, not who he, the messenger, is. It is imperative that the hearers look to the one the messenger is announcing, not to the messenger. (4) He trusts the Lord to determine the value of his ministry (v. 11).

One might also develop a lesson on "Truths for the Discouraged Servant of God." (1) Even great servants of God can have doubts from time to time (v. 3). (2) The cure for doubts is focused attention on the word and works of Jesus (vv. 4-5). (3) The servant of Christ must not allow his or her lack of understanding to feed doubts (v. 6). (4) The faithful servant of Christ must believe that Christ's valuation of his or her ministry will be positive. John was in jail, discouraged and voicing doubts but Jesus ranked him as number one (v. 11).

A sermon or lesson might be entitled "The Gracious Words of Jesus." (1) Listen: the command (v. 15), the content (vv. 10-11), and the contrast (12); (2) Receive: be one who is pleased (vv. 16-19) and convincible (vv. 19b-24); (3) Come: the invitation (v. 28), the invited ones (v. 28), and the offer (vv. 29-30).

G. The Royal Messiah Encountered Increasing Opposition (12:1-50)

Opposition against Jesus was increasing. In 9:34, the Pharisees attributed His abilities to Satan. In 11:20-24 Matthew listed Galilean cities that rejected Jesus and His kingdom preaching. This chapter records the rising of more visible opposition against Jesus, beginning with two Sabbath controversies (vv. 1-14) followed with an allegation of being demon-possessed and empowered by Satan. Jesus responded to the latter with some very strong words against the Pharisees and scribes (vv. 22-37). The scribes and Pharisees then requested a special sign, which Jesus declined to perform (vv. 38-45).

Matthew ended this section with Jesus' family wanting to see Him (vv. 46-50). Mark said they were concerned about His mental health. Jesus responded by rejecting His earthly family's attempts to get Him to slow His ministry pace (Mk. 3:20-21; 3:31-35) and identified another family as His real family.

1. Jesus is Lord of the Sabbath (12:1-8)

1 At that time Jesus went on the sabbath day through the corn; and his disciples were an hungred, and began to pluck the ears of corn and to eat.
2 But when the Pharisees saw it, they said unto him, Behold, thy disciples do that which is not lawful to do upon the sabbath day.
3 But he said unto them, Have ye not read what David did, when he was an hungred, and they that were with him;
4 How he entered into the house of God, and did eat the shewbread, which was not lawful for him to eat, neither for them which were with him, but only for the priests?
5 Or have ye not read in the law, how that on the sabbath days the priests in the temple profane the sabbath, and are blameless?
6 But I say unto you, That in this place is *one* greater than the temple.
7 But if ye had known what *this* meaneth, I will have mercy, and not sacrifice, ye would not have condemned the guiltless.
8 For the Son of man is Lord even of the sabbath day.

Matthew, Mark (2:23-28), and Luke (6:1-5) all include a record of this Sabbath controversy. This is Matthew's first mention of the Sabbath. Pharisees confronted Jesus because they believed that His disciples were breaking Sabbath laws. One wonders, given the fervor of the accusation, if the disciples had asked Jesus' permission to pluck grain or if by this time they had gained an accurate understanding of Sabbath law.

The Gospels reveal that Jesus gave most of His teaching concerning the Sabbath in six settings. Five of the six settings included healings and five of the six resulted in significant controversies (Mt. 12:1-4; Mk. 3:1-6; Lk. 13:10-17; Lk. 14:1-6; Jn. 5:1-18; 7:21-24; 9:1-41).

The Jewish community of Jesus' day, especially the Pharisees, strictly followed the Sabbath laws. The Sabbath went from sundown Friday evening until sundown Saturday evening. The Sabbath regulation had its roots in the creation account in Genesis 2:3 (Ex. 20:11) and witnessed to a literal, six-day creation (Hill 209). Though the Sabbath was made for mankind (Mk. 2:27), there is no record that the fallen race practiced its observance until the Sinai Covenant. It is certain that the Israelites were not practicing any Sabbath observances while in Egypt.

God made the observance of a weekly day of rest mandatory for the Israelite community six weeks into their wilderness journey (Ex. 16:1, 23-26). One week later (Ex. 19:1; 20:8-11) they received the Ten Commandments, the fourth of which was "remember the Sabbath Day to keep it holy." The Sabbath law was part of God's special covenant with Israel (Ex. 31:12-17; Ezek. 20:12, 20). There are four main aspects to these Sabbath stipulations. The day was declared (1) holy, (2) a day of rest, (3) a perpetual reminder of God's creative work and pattern (Ex. 20:11), and (4) a reminder of Israel's deliverance from Egypt's slavery (Dt. 5:15; Evans and Porter 1031). There is no explicit condemnation of Gentile nations in the O.T. for not observing a

Sabbath rest but there are many rebukes by the O.T. prophets directed against the Israelites for violating the Sabbath (e.g., Ezek. 20:13, 24). In fact, violation of the Sabbath laws was a capital offense (Ex. 31:15; 35:2; Num. 15:32-35).

Some of the earliest Sabbath restrictions were temporary. For example, there is no indication that in N.T. times anyone stayed in his dwelling on the Sabbath as required in Exodus 16:29. As Matthew's record shows, at times Jesus, His disciples, and even the Pharisees walked outside on the Sabbath though there is no suggestion that Jesus did any significant traveling on Sabbath days. Rabbis limited Sabbath travel distances to 2000 cubits: 3000 or 3600 feet (914 or 1097 meters), depending on which cubit was followed, the Hellenistic (the shorter) or the Roman; but the scribes invented ways to double this (ISBE IV:252). The only N.T. passage that explicitly mentions a Sabbath Day's journey is Acts 1:12.

In Jesus' day, the Sabbath was one of two distinguishing marks of Judaism (circumcision was the other; ISBE IV:251). The Pharisees' additional restrictions and extreme legalism in this area are well documented. They condemned the following activities as being in violation of the Sabbath law:

> Sowing, plowing, reaping, binding, threshing, winnowing, grinding, sifting, kneading, baking, shearing wool, bleaching or dyeing wool, spinning, weaving, tying or untying a knot, sewing or tearing two stitches, hunting, writing or erasing two letters, building demolishing, kindling or extinguishing a fire, hammering and carrying objects from one place to another, etc. (ISBE IV:251)

A full discussion of the Sabbath and the Christian is not within the scope of this commentary. However, two observations are in order: first, Sabbath regulations were not included in the Acts 15 decision, which means that the Jerusalem church and its leaders did not believe Sabbath laws to be part of the gospel teaching and binding on Gentile Christians; second, Colossians 2:16-17 states that Christians are not under Sabbath rules. Though the Sabbath was part of the first century debate between Judaizers and Paul, both passages show that Christians are free from the Sabbath regulations contained in the Mosaic Law. Romans 14:5-6 also speaks to this.

Rather than worship on the Saturday Sabbath, Christians worship on the Lord's Day, the first day of the week. This is to honor the Lord's resurrection day (28:1) and the day on which the church was born, the Day of Pentecost (Acts 2:1). Pentecost was the day after the Sabbath of Passover Week (Lev. 23:15-16), hence, the first day of the week. This means the church was born on Sunday.

Sunday worship is in obedience to apostolic command and example (1 Cor. 16:1-2; Acts 20:7; Rev. 1:10). Extra-biblical writings also testify that first century Christians worshiped on Sunday (*Didache* 14:1). For these reasons, Christians honor the first day of the week for worship, rest, and spiritual and physical renewal. Christians are not under the Sabbath stipulations of the O.T., but they are expected to honor the N.T. Lord's Day principles established and practiced by the apostles. (For a different approach and other reasons for

Christians to honor the Lord's Day as a day of worship and rest, see Picirilli, *Mark* 84-86.)

On the Sabbath in question (v. 1), because they were hungry Jesus' disciples began picking and eating "corn" (Greek *stachus*), which in the N.T. refers to grains like wheat and barley, not to the large ears we call corn. In other words, the disciples were not picking and eating ears of corn (maize). They were picking heads of grain and by rubbing them between their hands (Lk. 6:1) were able to separate the kernels from the husks so they might eat the kernels. This was technically, "threshing grain," forbidden on the Sabbath.

The law permitted travelers to eat as they went through fields (Lev. 19:9-10; 23:22; Dt. 23:24-25; 24:19-22; Ruth 2:3, 7). At issue here was whether on the Sabbath day a hungry person could pluck grain to eat immediately or if Sabbath law prohibited such an action (Nolland 483). The disciples' actions on any other day would not have been offensive. The Pharisees (v. 2) considered the disciples' actions work and thus in violation of the Sabbath law (Ex. 34:21).

Pharisees were probably walking with Jesus (Newman and Stine, 362, assume they were standing at the edge of the field watching) and held Jesus responsible for His disciples' misdoings. Rather than rebuke His disciples as the Pharisees might have expected (Hagner 33A:329), Jesus defended the Twelve and rebuked the Pharisees instead. Jesus' disciples were not Pharisees and Jesus did not teach them to follow the extreme and erroneous manmade teachings of the Pharisees (15:1-9). However, see 5:20; 23:2-3, 13.

Jesus' response shows that some circumstances took precedence over Sabbath rules. Jesus gave two illustrations of this truth, familiar to His questioners. "Have you not read" (vv. 3, 5; rhetorical questions that assume a "yes" answer; Newman and Stine, 362) and "if you had known" (v. 7) drew His accusers back to Scripture and suggested that with all of their knowledge these authorities still did not grasp the full meaning of certain key texts.

First, when David fled from King Saul he entered the tabernacle (something the 1 Samuel record does not mention) and took the showbread, the bread of the Presence (Ex. 25:30), for himself and those traveling with him (v. 4). They ate the showbread (1 Sam. 21:1-6), something normally only priests could do (Lev. 24:5-9), and priests could eat it only in a holy place. Thus David, entering the tabernacle, eating the showbread, and eating it outside the holy place violated three points of the law.

However, neither Ahimelech the priest nor Scripture condemned David's actions as sinful, but both showed mercy in the face of need (Wilkins 441). This showed that need could override normal ceremonial restrictions. David's emergency (Keener, *Matthew* 355) took precedence over the law and David was thus uncondemned by the law for his actions (Nolland 483). Ahimelech was right to allow David to take the showbread. David was right to eat and to give to his men to eat. Scripture corroborates this. By appealing to Scripture in this manner, Jesus showed that God, who gave Scripture, approved David's actions.

Jesus' followed David's understanding and rebuked the Pharisees for not doing the same (Carson, *Matthew* 281).

The Pharisees' legalistic interpretation of Scripture would not have approved David's actions or the eating of sacred bread by his men. This appears to be the main reason Jesus appealed to this O.T. incident.

It is possible the events of 1 Samuel 21:1-6 took place on a Sabbath (Youngblood 728; TDNT 7:22) and that David ate bread that was removed from the table that day (Ex. 25:30; Lev. 24:8). This could suggest why 1 Samuel 21:6, especially the last half of the verse, was included in the inspired record and why Jesus picked this event to illustrate His point. However, the text does not specifically state that David's actions occurred on a Sabbath. Rather, David's entrance into the tabernacle suggests that He actually took the bread from the table and fresh bread was not there to replace what David took.

Second (v. 5), and this was by directive, priests also regularly violated (ESV profaned; Greek *bebēloō*) Sabbath rules by working on the Sabbath and were not guilty of wrongdoing (Num. 28:9-10). David, by the Spirit's direction, added more Sabbath responsibilities to the priests to begin after the temple's construction by Solomon (1 Chr. 9:22-32; 28:11-19). These priestly activities on the Sabbath were possible because temple work took precedence over Sabbath rules. In other words, temple work had to be done even on the Lord's Day of rest. Priests worked on the day of rest but were not condemned for it because the law told them to. Jesus used the same kind of argument in John 7:21-23.

These two illustrations demonstrate that the prohibition against working on the Sabbath was not absolute (Nolland 484). Jesus referred to David's actions as a historical precedent for an exception to the law in general, and to the common actions of the priests as an exception to the Sabbath law provided by the law itself (Newman and Stine 365).

Jesus, then, tacitly agreed that His disciples, like David and the priests, had done what the Sabbath laws forbade (Ex. 20:9-10). However, the disciples were not guilty of wrongdoing for two reasons. First, they did what they did to satisfy hunger. They were not harvesting grain on the Sabbath Day in lieu of another day. They needed to eat that day, which need took precedence over Sabbath law.

The second reason the disciples were innocent of wrongdoing was that Jesus' authority took precedence over the authority of Sabbath law. Jesus inferred that His own authority took precedence over even the temple's authority (v. 6, something greater). If the temple laws took precedence over Sabbath laws and thus "shielded the priests from guilt" then He being more authoritative than the temple is also able to "shield His disciples from guilt" (Carson, *Matthew* 282). In other words, Jesus supported the actions of the disciples as they picked grain to eat on the Sabbath Day.

The Pharisees with all of their legalistic obedience failed to understand the intent and spirit of the law. In verse 7, "If ye had known" assumes they had *not* known (a Greek contrary-to-fact condition; Osborne 453). God was not interested in increased demands for more and greater sacrifice. "Sacrifice" stands for "the observance of religious prescriptions in general" (Hill 211). He desired obedience in day-to-day life. He desired merciful actions and attitudes toward the needy. He wanted and still wants His people to live out His love and mercy daily as they live out His commandments.

Jesus' teaching was not new. He quoted Hosea 6:6, one of the eighth century B.C. writing prophets, to support His point. O.T. Israel and Judah at that time (Hos. 6:4) were religious but away from God. They offered sacrifices to God (Am. 4:4-5; Is. 1:11-15), but their religious practices did not carry over into their everyday lives. The absence of a godly lifestyle showed that their love for the Lord was superficial at best. God called on them to repent and to treat their fellow men fairly and promised if they did that He would then accept their worship (Is. 1:16-20; Mic. 6:6-8). Rigid, legalistic acts of worship are no substitute for living out all of God's laws every day.

According to Jesus, these first century A.D. Pharisees were just like their eighth century B.C. forefathers. They were religious but they did not know God (Hos. 6:6). With all of their Bible knowledge, they lacked personal knowledge of God and real understanding and obedience of His laws and principles. "Have you not read" (vv. 3, 5) and "if you had known" (v. 7) point to their ignorance. They were more interested in ritual (sacrifice and Sabbath Day observances) than day-to-day godly living (mercy). This showed in their condemnation of the "guiltless" (v. 7)—here, Jesus' disciples. The disciples were not breaking the Sabbath by plucking grain to satisfy their hunger and Jesus was not wrong for not rebuking them. The Pharisees were wrong in their understanding of the Sabbath law's intent and application and in their condemnation of the disciples and Jesus. Instead of requiring more sacrifice of people by increasing their burdens (11:28), they should have offered mercy (Wilkins 441), like being sympathetic toward the disciples and their hunger, or even offering the disciples something to eat so they would not need to "work" on the Sabbath to satisfy their hunger.

See 9:13 for another application of Hosea 6:6 by Jesus. There Jesus also rebuked His critics for "overly scrupulous legislation" (Blomberg 14). Jesus repeated this reference because this was a characteristic problem of the Pharisees.

Jesus' use of Hosea 6:6 was not to teach freedom from the law's demands but rather to direct His accusers' focus to the heart of the law—life-style adherence from the heart. As the Pharisees proved, for some folks, legalistic conformity is all external and their preferred way to live. Jesus, however, taught that legalism merits no favor with God. Favor from God comes to those who love Him and their fellow men from the heart (Mt. 22:36-39).

Jesus ended His remarks by claiming authority over the Sabbath and its various regulations (v. 8). The only way He could be greater than the Sabbath is if He is the Lawgiver which He is. He is God (Bruner 1:550). Jesus had every right to interpret—or for that matter redefine—the Sabbath, "for [Greek corroborative *gar*] He is Lord of the Sabbath." But not everyone agreed.

2. It is lawful to do good on the Sabbath (12:9-14)

9 And when he was departed thence, he went into their synagogue:
10 And, behold, there was a man which had *his* hand withered. And they asked him, saying, Is it lawful

to heal on the sabbath days? that they might accuse him.

11 And he said unto them, What man shall there be among you, that shall have one sheep, and if it fall into a pit on the sabbath day, will he not lay hold on it, and lift *it* out?

12 How much then is a man better than a sheep? Wherefore it is lawful to do well on the sabbath days.

13 Then saith he to the man, Stretch forth thine hand. And he stretched *it* forth; and it was restored whole, like as the other.

14 Then the Pharisees went out, and held a council against him, how they might destroy him.

From outside to inside, from a grain field into a synagogue, Jesus' accusers followed Him. For synagogue, see 4:23. Luke 6:6 said this was on another Sabbath. Matthew is not so specific.

This synagogue visit by Jesus was probably the normal Saturday morning worship meeting (TDNT 7:16). The devoted met every Sabbath Day for prayer and to hear portions of the O.T. read and expounded (Acts 13:15-44; 15:21; TDNT 7:821-822; Evans and Porter 1032). Jesus normally attended the synagogue worship services (Lk. 4:16) and on some occasions read from Scripture and offered comments (Lk. 4:17-27).

His antagonists followed Him and began making preparations to destroy Him. Conveniently a man with a withered (Greek *xēros*, withered, paralyzed; Louw and Nida I:273) right hand was present. Jesus' enemies began with a seemingly innocent question (v. 10), but He knew their motive ("that" v. 10; Greek purpose clause; Newman and Stine 369). They wanted Him to break the Sabbath (Gundry 223). According to Wilkins (442), Rabbinic law permitted medical help on the Sabbath only when life was endangered. This is probably behind a synagogue leader's statement on another occasion that healing should be sought on days other than the Sabbath (Lk. 13:14). Mark's record (1:21, 32-34) suggests that this restriction was honored by the general population (Evans and Porter 1032). The man's withered hand was not life threatening and so could wait.

Rather than answer them directly, Jesus instructed the man with the withered hand to come forward and stand (Lk. 6:8). Jesus then asked a question in order to expose the hypocrisy of His accusers: Is it wrong to free an entrapped animal on the Sabbath? Would any in that room leave the animal to suffer when they could set it free? Silence answered Jesus (Mk. 3:4), and according to Mark's account Jesus became angry with them because they were so hard-hearted. Yet He felt sorry for them as well (Greek *sullupeomai*; Mk. 3:5). They believed and practiced exactly that for which they wanted to fault Him. Jesus inferred that everyone present would lift a sheep out of a pit or ditch (Greek *bothunos*; Grimm's 104) even on a Sabbath day (v. 11). People are more valuable than animals (6:26; 10:31). Therefore, Jesus concludes, it is also biblically right (Bruner 1:554) to help people in need on a Sabbath (v. 12). This principle is in keeping with verse 7 discussed earlier.

With this statement and His actions on behalf of the man who needed healing, Jesus again declared human worth to be greater than animal worth. Animals have worth—they deserve to be pulled from the pit—but not more worth than human life. Human worth is based on the fact that God made mankind in His unique image (Gen. 1:26-27; Carson, *Matthew* 284).

Jesus directed the man to stretch out his hand (v. 13), an impossibility for a withered hand, yet the man stretched out his hand as if it were a perfect hand—for suddenly it was! Jesus healed the hand without touching it or praying over it or doing anything that smacked of showmanship (v. 13). He had simply willed the healing (Hendriksen 518). Had His accusers witnessed Him work on the Sabbath? What did they see? No law forbade stretching out one's hand.

With this miracle, Jesus substantiated His interpretation of the law (Wilkins 443) and demonstrated again that He had the approval of God. This agrees with the explanation He gave on another occasion of a Sabbath healing: the Father works on the Sabbath doing good and so does the Son (Jn. 5:16-18; Evans and Porter 1034). The Pharisees, however, rejected this. They could not accept that Jesus could have God's approval and be in violation of Sabbath laws, as they understood them.

Matthew said nothing about anyone's response to this miracle except the Pharisees. He wanted his readers to understand the rising opposition against Jesus. The Pharisees were so upset He had broken Sabbath rules (as they interpreted them) that they blindly rejected the presence of God's grace in that room. They could not accept that Jesus could break the Sabbath and still be used by God. The Pharisees left the synagogue and, along with the Herodians, began planning Jesus' destruction (Mk. 3:6). Because of this increased hostility, Jesus began avoiding the Pharisees (v. 15).

3. Jesus avoided the Pharisees who were intent on destroying Him (12:15-21)

15 But when Jesus knew *it*, he withdrew himself from thence: and great multitudes followed him, and he healed them all;
16 And charged them that they should not make him known:
17 That it might be fulfilled which was spoken by Esaias the prophet, saying,
18 Behold my servant, whom I have chosen; my beloved, in whom my soul is well pleased: I will put my spirit upon him, and he shall shew judgment to the Gentiles.
19 He shall not strive, nor cry; neither shall any man hear his voice in the streets.
20 A bruised reed shall he not break, and smoking flax shall he not quench, till he send forth judgment unto victory.
21 And in his name shall the Gentiles trust.

Realizing the intent and determination of the Pharisees, Jesus left the synagogue (v. 15) with many new followers (Keener, *Background* 79). He might have healed more people that day (Walvoord 88) but Matthew's words appear to be more a summary of events over several days. "All" (v. 15) means all who needed healing or all who came to Him for healing (Osborne 464).

These events took place during the months of Jesus' greatest popularity. See Mark 3:7-12. He was attracting a lot of people. According to Mark's record, people came from as far north as Tyre and Sidon and from as far south as Idumea. They came from across the Jordan and from Jerusalem. This is perhaps why Matthew included verse 21 in his quote. See below.

The Pharisees' disapproval did not deter Him from continuing His healing ministry (v. 15). However, He did not want the crowds broadcasting His healings (v. 16) so He commanded that they keep this to themselves. Some have speculated, because of this and other passages (8:4; 16:20; 17:9), that Jesus wanted to be a "secret Messiah" (Osborne 465). However, Matthew indicates otherwise. As Jesus had clarified to John the Baptist the type of ministry He as Messiah had (11:2-6), so now Matthew also clarifies for his readers the kind of ministry Jesus had (vv. 18-20).

Matthew stated that Jesus quietly ministered and avoided "sensationalizing" His work (Evans, *Matthew* 244) in fulfillment of Isaiah 42:1-4 (v. 17). In other words, the kind of ministry Jesus had was according to the plan of God foretold in Isaiah. There the Father declared His choice of and pleasure in His Servant (v. 18). The Father's pleasure in His Son was stated at Jesus' baptism (3:17) and transfiguration (17:5).

The Father also promised to put His Spirit upon Him, i.e., to anoint with His Spirit this one who would do His work (v. 18; Is. 11:2; 61:1). This is a clear reference to the Trinity in both Testaments. For Matthew, Jesus is the Messiah, the Anointed One *par excellence*, the Servant of the Lord (Blomberg 44; Barclay 2:38, however, says Isaiah was speaking first of the Persian King Cyrus whom Isaiah specifically mentions in 45:1).

Jesus' anointing was not the Acts 2 Pentecost anointing though His anointing did prefigure it. His anointing was the O.T. kind of anointing by God for office and service, except without the medium of oil or human hands. Jesus was anointed at His baptism (3:16) and immediately filled with the Holy Spirit (Lk. 4:1). In other words, the Father gave His incarnate Son His Spirit without measure (Jn. 3:34). This same Spirit empowered Jesus for ministry (Lk. 4:14, 18).

The word "messiah" has a rich O.T. background and means "the anointed one" (Hebrew *māshîah*). As a verb the word "involved a ceremonial application of oil" to items such as tabernacle furniture or "the ceremonial induction into leadership offices" (TWOT I:530-532). Typically, priests (Ex. 28:41), prophets, and kings (1 Sam. 16:12-13; 1 Kg. 1:39; 19:15-16) were anointed as were furniture items in the tabernacle (Ex. 30:25-28; 40:9, 11). The original anointing oil was made according to a special recipe and had an oil and aromatic mixture (Ex. 30:22-33). Anointed persons or items had the oil poured or sprinkled on them (1 Sam. 10:1; Ps. 133:2). They were thus marked by the oil and the aroma. (Whether kings and prophets were anointed with this special mixture or with plain oil is unclear, but they probably were not anointed with the special mixture; see Ex. 30:32.)

Anointing generally meant the person or item was set apart by the Lord for special service (1 Sam. 10:1). When a person was anointed, He was also then equipped by God to complete the assignment (1 Sam. 10:6-7; 16:13). Because the Lord did the anointing, "the anointed one" was to be respected and honored (1 Sam. 26:9), and he was also held to a higher level of responsibility (1 Sam. 15:17; 2 Sam. 12:7). Generally the anointing was for a lifetime (1 Sam. 24:10) but see 1 Samuel 10:6, 10 and 1 Samuel 16:14. For further study on the O.T. practice of anointing, see ISBE I:129 and III:330.

The Messiah, i.e., God's Anointed One as Israel's coming ruler is referenced in Psalm 2 and Daniel 9:25-26. The early church and N.T. Scriptures state unmistakably that Psalm 2:2 (Acts 13:32-33) and Psalm 2:7 (Heb. 1:5; 5:5) are speaking of Jesus.

The title "Messiah" is found only two times in the N.T. (Jn. 1:41; 4:25), but "Christ," the Greek equivalent of Messiah, is found over five hundred times. As a title applied to Jesus, *Christ* denotes that He is God's special Anointed One, "the Christ, the Son of the Living God" (Mt. 16:16). For further comments on the title "Christ," see comments on Matthew 16:16.

Isaiah further prophesied that Jesus would bring judgment to the nations (vv. 17-18). Translators understand the judgment aspect of the Servant's work differently. He would either pronounce *judgment* (Greek *krisis*) on the nations that choose not to serve Him (v. 18) or proclaim *justice* (ESV, NIV) to those who do trust Him, another way of understanding the same word (vv. 20-21; Bruner 1:556; Zerwick 37). Carson (*Matthew* 289) sees a bit of both. He understands the word translated judgment or justice to mean that God reveals His character for the "good of the nations (cf. Is. 51:4), while at the same time calling them into account."

The positives in these verses are victory and trust—literally, hope (vv. 20-21), and they support the idea that justice is the main emphasis. In other words, Jesus, the Servant, would successfully bring in the justice He proclaimed (v. 20; see further comments on "justice" below). At the same time, as Carson observed, the Isaiah passage is about the salvation God's Servant would bring, a salvation that includes both warning and deliverance.

Jesus' ministry would be a quiet ministry. He would not encourage disputes or cry loudly in the streets (v. 19), i.e., He would not "through rhetoric ... arouse the multitudes to move against their present rulers" (TWOT II:272), Jew or Gentile. He would neither fight nor resist but would quietly go about His ministry (Blomberg 42). This is the part of the quote that Matthew mainly wanted his readers to see. Jesus did not leave the synagogue in fear, nor did He command the crowds' silence because He was trying to keep His identity a secret. Instead, He was ministering without encouraging His own popularity. He ministered quietly and meekly (v. 19), from His Sermon on the Mount (5:5) to His triumphal entry (21:5). Unlike John the Baptist (3:7-12), He avoided altercations. Jesus' answer to His accusers was to show more "mercy" (v. 7) to the harassed and helpless (9:36).

He was compassionate and gentle to the weak (a bruised reed, v. 20) and merciful to those who had little hope, meaning perhaps those "of little faith" (a smoldering wick; Hendriksen 521-522; Wilkins 445). The bruised reed and "smoking flax"—a smoldering wick—are used figuratively and refer to those who are near their end. Jesus compassionately received them, healed them, and gave them rest (11:28-29).

The last part of verse 20 meant that He would bring deliverance and victory (justice: see above on v. 18) to the weak and the hopeless, the "bruised reed" and the "smoldering wick." As their Shepherd, He would care for them (9:36). He would provide eternal "rest" (11:28-29) for their souls (Carson, *Matthew* 287). He was and is their salvation.

Finally, the prophecy states that He would be the Savior of the Gentiles too (v. 21). Indeed He already was (v. 15; Mk. 3:8). They would place their trust or hope in His name (Acts 4:12), which means in His person (Newman and Stine 380). Jesus would quietly minister until even the Gentiles turn to Him (Gundry 230). This ministry to the Gentiles was already taking place according to Mark 3:8 referenced above. This fits Matthew's overall emphasis wherein he repeatedly tells the reader that Jesus is interested in all nations, not just the nation of Israel (see comments on 28:19). The Lord's Servant ministers to all nations (Greek *ethnē,* heathen, pagan, Gentiles; BAGD 218), to all who are afar off and without hope (Acts 2:39; Eph. 2:17). The Servant directs His labors toward the Gentiles (v. 18) and the Gentiles respond positively (v. 21).

Verses 18-21 are a summary of Jesus' ministry (Bruner 1:558). Verse 18 is about His early calling and ministry. Verses 19 and 20 cover the bulk of His ministry years. The last clause of verse 20 and verse 21 speak of His success in bringing justice to all who place their hope, i.e., their trust, in Him (Nolland 495).

The O.T. used in Matthew's day was available in both Hebrew/Aramaic and Greek (the Septuagint, LXX). It appears that Matthew, led by the Holy Spirit (Hendriksen 519), used both in this instance, carefully choosing which phrases to quote in order to make his point. For example, the LXX in Isaiah 42:1 identifies the Servant as Jacob but the Hebrew does not mention Jacob. Also, the LXX includes in Isaiah 42:4 the phrase "in His name the Gentiles will trust"—as quoted by Matthew (12:21)—but the Hebrew does not have this phrase.

Matthew apparently, then, used the Hebrew translation of Isaiah 42:1 because the Hebrew copies do not identify the Servant. This permitted him to identify Jesus as the Servant. He then used the LXX translation of Isaiah 42:4 so he could include in his extended quote the phrase "in His name the Gentiles will trust." Matthew's inclusion of this phrase is in keeping with his overall theme that the Messiah is for the Gentiles too. The reader is referred to more technical commentaries for further discussion and analysis.

4. Jesus healed a demon-possessed man and warned against blaspheming the Holy Spirit (12:22-37)

22 Then was brought unto him one possessed with a devil, blind, and dumb: and he healed him, insomuch that the blind and dumb both spake and saw.
23 And all the people were amazed, and said, Is not this the son of David?
24 But when the Pharisees heard *it*, they said, This *fellow* doth not cast out devils, but by Beelzebub the prince of the devils.
25 And Jesus knew their thoughts, and said unto them, Every kingdom divided against itself is brought to desolation; and every

city or house divided against itself shall not stand:
26 And if Satan cast out Satan, he is divided against himself; how shall then his kingdom stand?
27 And if I by Beelzebub cast out devils, by whom do your children cast *them* out? therefore they shall be your judges.
28 But if I cast out devils by the Spirit of God, then the kingdom of God is come unto you.
29 Or else how can one enter into a strong man's house, and spoil his goods, except he first bind the strong man? and then he will spoil his house.
30 He that is not with me is against me; and he that gathereth not with me scattereth abroad.
31 Wherefore I say unto you, All manner of sin and blasphemy shall be forgiven unto men: but the blasphemy *against* the *Holy* Ghost shall not be forgiven unto men.
32 And whosoever speaketh a word against the Son of man, it shall be forgiven him: but whosoever speaketh against the Holy Ghost, it shall not be forgiven him, neither in this *world*, neither in the world to come.
33 Either make the tree good, and his fruit good; or else make the tree corrupt, and his fruit corrupt: for the tree is known by *his* fruit.
34 O generation of vipers, how can ye, being evil, speak good things? for out of the abundance of the heart the mouth speaketh.
35 A good man out of the good treasure of the heart bringeth forth good things: and an evil man out of the evil treasure bringeth forth evil things.
36 But I say unto you, That every idle word that men shall speak, they shall give account thereof in the day of judgment.
37 For by thy words thou shalt be justified, and by thy words thou shalt be condemned.

The intensity of the disagreement between Jesus and the Pharisees escalated in this exchange. Set in the context of another healing, Jesus' source of power is challenged. See also Mark 3:22-30 and Luke 11:14-15.

At a time when Jesus was healing many people (v. 15), someone brought a man with multiple problems (v. 22). He was possessed by a demon (Greek *daimonizomai*, present tense, showing the man's condition as ongoing). The demon possession manifested itself in blindness and the inability to speak. Jesus healed all three problems, which meant that Jesus set him free of the demonic possession and control and gave him eyesight and the ability to speak. He demonstrated authority over the demon and reversed his negative effects on this man.

Barclay's (II:40-41) insistence that demon possession is a delusion is surely wrong. See comments on 8:28. If there is no such thing as demon possession, then Jesus' discussion about Satan casting out Satan is nonsense (v. 25-29), as is His parable about the evil spirit in verses 43-45.

As with the healing of the withered hand (vv. 9-13), Matthew recorded no response on the part of the healed man. The crowd, though, reacted strongly. They were astonished (Greek *existēmi*; lit. "beside oneself," Grimm's 224; see also Mk. 3:21; 2 Cor. 5:13). Compare with 9:32-34. This crowd had just witnessed something that made them wonder if they had underestimated Jesus, and they began entertaining Messianic notions. They wondered if He was the "Son of David," the Messiah (v. 23; see comments on 1:1 and 9:27).

One must be careful not to read back into this context an understanding that came only with later revelation. Many of Jesus' contemporaries were expecting a Messiah different from the one that actually came (Hendriksen 524). See comments on 11:2-6. It was not until after the cross, the resurrection, further specific teaching from Jesus on this subject (Acts 1:3), and Pentecost that Jesus' followers had a more accurate and complete understanding of His role as Messiah. See comments on 22:41-46.

Hearing the people discuss the possibility that Jesus was the Messiah brought an immediate negative response from the Pharisees and scribes (v. 24). These men had traveled from Jerusalem evidently just to hear Jesus (Mk. 3:22). They refused to entertain even as a possibility that Jesus might be the Messiah. They did not deny the healings. They denied the power working through Jesus. The crowd and the religious leaders witnessed the same event but reached opposite conclusions (Hagner 33A:342).

These leaders said Jesus was empowered by Beelzebub or Beelzebul (v. 24, with different spellings in different manuscripts), a name for Satan. Scholars suggest different meanings, among them "lord/master of the dwelling" for Beelzebul and "lord of the flies" for Beelzebub (ISBE 1:447). See 10:25 also. The charge meant that Jesus was a magician, a sorcerer, and that He had Satan working on His behalf. They alleged that Jesus was Himself possessed by a demon (Mk. 3:30).

This was not a new charge. On another occasion, some people, who had some level of faith in Him for a time (Jn. 8:31), accused Him of being demon possessed (Jn. 8:48, 52). The Pharisees had also said this of Jesus (Mt. 9:34).

Jesus knew the thoughts of His accusers (v. 25). His response showed the nonsense of the allegations (vv. 25-26). Jesus described Satan's domain as a kingdom and a unified one at that. Satan is the author of strife and division but he does not tolerate either in his own ranks. If Jesus were using Satan to cast out demons, Satan's kingdom would quickly fall. It would soon disintegrate, something even the Pharisees should have realized was not happening. On the other hand, if Jesus and Satan were allies, Jesus would work to advance Satan's kingdom, not try to destroy it (Evans, *Matthew* 247).

This world is the theater where God's kingdom and Satan's kingdom join in conflict (Hill 216). Jesus spoke of Satan as a person who is powerful and the real enemy of God. See this commentary on 4:1 for additional remarks on Satan.

Grammatically, "if Satan cast out Satan" (v. 26) and "if I cast out demons by Beelzebub" (v. 27) are both conditional statements assumed true for the sake of the argument (Greek first class condition; Carson, *Fallacies* 81).

The city referenced was possibly a city-state (v. 25). The house was possibly a domestic home. Jesus' point was that division (civil war? Newman and Stine 384) will destroy any organization.

Jesus was not the only exorcist in Israel (v. 27). There were also other Jewish exorcists (your sons; cf. 7:22; Acts 19:13-16), and the Pharisees would not accuse them of using Satan's power to cast out demons. Then why accuse Jesus? Jesus told the Pharisees they should think through the implications of what they were saying (Keener, *Background* 80). The Jewish exorcists' methodology will be evidence to condemn the Pharisees in the final judgment for their allegations against Jesus (Bruner 1:562; see comments on verses 41 and 42).

Since, however, Jesus was working under (by means of) the power of God's Spirit (v. 18), i.e., by the "finger of God" (Lk. 11:20; Ex. 8:19; 31:18; Dt. 9:10; Ps. 8:3), then the Pharisees were looking at kingdom realities (v. 28). Here "if" implies "since" (another first class condition in Greek). This time, Jesus assumes it true because it is. Pharaoh's magicians had been more perceptive than these Pharisees (Ex. 8:19) in that they at least recognized God's power at work.

Verse 28 is an important verse. Jesus clearly states that the kingdom had already arrived (Greek *phthanō*, ingressive aorist). It had come in the person and work of Jesus, the Messiah King (1:1, 16-17; 2:2). Compare with 3:2 where John preached only the *nearness* of the kingdom. The visible manifestations of the Messiah's power over Satan proved the arrival and presence of the kingdom of God (Is. 61:1-2a; Lk. 4:17-21). (Matthew's interchange between "kingdom of heaven" and "kingdom of God" shows they are the same. See 19:23-24.)

Jesus healed the man (v. 22) and placed him in God's kingdom and he began living under the rule of God (Nolland 501). Jesus rebuked these Pharisees and told them to judge correctly (see vv. 33-35). They should have recognized the healing and exorcisms as "tangible confirmation" of the kingdom's arrival (Wilkins 447) and proof of Beelzebul's demise. This does not mean the kingdom *in its fullness* had arrived but that the early aspects of the kingdom had arrived (Hagner 33A:343). See the discussion on 3:2 of the already-not yet aspects of the kingdom.

Jesus' ability to cast out demons demonstrated that He has to be stronger than the evil one. One does not take possessions from a strong man's home (v. 29; fully armored soldier, Lk. 11:21) without first tying up the strong man. The only way Jesus could have forced the demon out of the man (v. 22) was first to exercise authority and power over him. The strong man represented Satan and the goods were those individuals he possessed. Every time Jesus sets a captive soul free He exercises control over Satan (He binds the strong man) and plunders his house.

Some commentators (e.g., Keener, *Matthew* 365) point out that Jesus defeated Satan at His temptation and suggest that this was when Jesus bound Satan. They argue that the earlier victory over Satan gave Jesus power over him, also allowing Jesus then to be able to delegate His authority to those who follow Him (10:8). "Except he first bind" (v. 29) is an exceptive clause that can refer to one event of binding (Greek aorist, historical momentary as Keener understands Jesus' words), or it can speak of multiple events as a single fact (Greek aorist, historical collective, as this writer understands Jesus' words). Either interpretation is grammatically possible. The main point is the same with both understandings: Jesus has absolute authority over Satan and his house. Jesus can enter Satan's home and free anyone from Satan's bondage at will and Satan cannot stop Him. That Satan lives under some constant restraint now is factual. However, Jesus further exercises that authority every time a soul turns to Him for deliverance. Such power can come only from God. Lay people had testified to this earlier (Mt. 8:27, 9:33). Jesus' accusers should have as well.

Gundry (236) interprets verse 29 differently. He says that for Matthew Jesus is the strong man and the disciples are His goods. The spoiling refers to persecution. Gundry is in error because Satan cannot bind Jesus and persecution will not prevail (Mt. 16:18). Most commentators see Satan as the strong man in Jesus' parable and so disagree with Gundry. It seems Jesus' point to the Pharisees was that His ability to bind Satan, the strong man, showed His power over Satan, not His association with him. No one has power to bind Satan but God.

At this point Jesus further distanced Himself from His accusers (v. 30). There are no half in, half out people when it comes to the kingdom of heaven. People are either for Jesus or against Him (Mk. 9:40). Jesus' accusers were not His friends. They were, in fact, warring with Satan against Him.

The last half of verse 30 summarizes Jesus' ministry. He is a gatherer. He is adding to His kingdom. All who follow Him gather with Him. This is evangelism and missions (Bruner 1:566). Folks who want to follow Jesus but are not involved in harvesting are in a dilemma because Jesus said that whoever does not gather with Him scatters.

"Wherefore" (Greek *dia touto*: literally "because of this") indicates that Jesus' next statement (v. 31) flows from the discussion in verses 24-29 (Newman and Stine 390). It contains two great truths: (1) with only one exception, all sin and blasphemy will be forgiven people; (2) the only sin that will never be forgiven is blasphemy against the Holy Spirit.

The first truth is a promise that should be proclaimed with confidence. From the lips of Jesus the promise is that every sin but one can be forgiven. The offer of forgiveness extends even to all who blaspheme Jesus Himself (v. 32). Peter's denial was surely a sin against the Lord, and Paul calls himself a blasphemer, but both received forgiveness (26:69-75; Lk. 24:34; Jn. 21:15-19; 1 Tim. 1:12-16; Hendriksen 528).

Forgiveness (Greek *aphiēmi*) means to have the guilt associated with sin removed (Louw and Nida I:503). The act of wrongdoing is not undone but the guilt that results from the wrong that was done is removed. God offers and provides forgiveness to the guilty who accept Jesus' substitutionary payment on their behalf. Once forgiven, even though the acts of sin remain part of sinners' pasts, they are without guilt because their sin debt has been paid and their sin forgiven.

The second truth is also a promise, but a negative one concerning unforgivable sin. The reality of unforgivable sin is not a new revelation. It first appears in Numbers 15:30-31 as a sin done "with a high hand," i.e., a sin done in willful rebellion against the Lord's commandments. This person reproaches or blasphemes the LORD. Unlike sins committed unintentionally (Num. 15:22-29), sin committed in willful defiance against the Lord received no forgiveness. For further study on this sin, see Forlines (467-487). The sins of Eli's sons could never be atoned for (1 Sam. 3:14), and the sins of Judah committed under

Manasseh's leadership were likewise unpardonable (2 Kg. 24:3-4).

The promise in Matthew 12:31-32 names the unforgivable sin as blasphemy against the Holy Spirit. Blasphemy, meaning to speak against, is to show disrespect. In this instance, it was a denial of the personal (Bruner 1:567) presence and workings of the Holy Spirit in Jesus and a crediting of those same works to the person, presence, and power of Satan instead. (There may be more than one way to commit this sin. See also Heb. 10:29 and its context.) These Pharisees said Jesus had an evil spirit (Mk. 3:30) when they should have said He had the Holy Spirit (Evans, *Matthew* 248). Calling the Holy Spirit Satan is blasphemous.

The problem was not simply what they said. Their sin was also a rejection of what they knew to be right. They knew that Jesus was working in the power of the Holy Spirit, yet they credited that power to Satan (Carson, *Matthew* 202). Such blasphemy is unforgiveable.

Many people have wondered if they have committed the unforgivable sin. However, since the Holy Spirit is the one who convicts of sin (Jn. 16:8), the person who senses conviction and desires forgiveness of personal sin has not committed this sin.

Jesus did not explain why some sins are forgivable and this one sin is not. Commentators offer various opinions. Nolland (505) says the reason blasphemy against the Holy Spirit is unforgivable is that it keeps people from receiving what God is doing through Jesus: namely, forgiving people of their sins. Bruner's (1:561-567) understanding is close to Nolland's. He says the Pharisees' sin was their effort to keep people from believing in Jesus as Savior. Nolland believes, however, that this sin is unforgivable only as long as one continues in it. Once discontinued, this sin may be repented of also. Such an understanding seems to negate the whole idea of an unpardonable sin.

Writers also disagree about whether Jesus' accusers actually committed the sin or were just getting close. It appears the sin had been committed (Gundry 238; Hagner 33A:348). However, see Picirilli (*Mark* 107) for a different understanding.

This passage reveals a distinction between the Persons of the Godhead. The kingdom is God's. Sins against the Son of Man will be forgiven. Sins against the Holy Spirit will not be forgiven. See verse 18 for another example.

"This world," here, is literally "this age" (Greek *aiōn*). The verse shows that the present church age, the age of grace, will end and another age will follow. To suggest that some sins might be forgiven in the next age is reading too much into this hyperbolic text. Jesus meant that this sin would never ever be forgiven.

Jesus continued defending Himself by demanding—using "make" two times—that His detractors judge Him fairly and consistently (v. 33). If He has good fruit, i.e., He casts out demons (v. 22), then judge Him to be good too and empowered by the Spirit of God. Compare with 11:19. Also, see comments on 7:15-20 concerning the quality of trees and fruit.

Jesus then confronted His accusers directly and illustrated their evil, using four images. Continuing the fruit and tree analogy from verse 33, He stated that the Pharisees' fruit, here their words (v. 32: speaks a word against; v.

34: how can you speak good), showed that they were evil at heart. This was why they spoke against the Son and the Spirit.

Second, using words reminiscent of John the Baptist, Jesus called them "offspring of serpents" (v. 34). See also 3:7 and 23:33. Serpents (Greek *echidna*) were poisonous snakes (Louw and Nida I:47). The Pharisees' words were venomous.

Third, Jesus compared the heart to a full container (v. 34; Newman and Stine 394) that overflows with words. Words reveal what the heart holds. Their words revealed an evil heart.

Fourth, Jesus spoke of the heart as also being a storage place for good or evil (v. 35, the treasure of the heart; Lk. 6:45). A man can take out only what he has stored (15:11). These men had evil hearts (15:19).

Jesus ended His defense with another solemn warning: spoken words will matter in the final judgment (vv. 36-37), even careless words. In verse 37 (in contrast to v. 34), Jesus used singular pronouns, pointedly addressing the individual.

Jesus taught that in the judgment people will give an accounting (cf. Lk. 16:2; Heb. 13:17; 1 Pet. 4:5) before God. The verb (Greek *apodidōmi*) can have a sense of obligation in it. Payment is made "in response to an incurred obligation" as in the payment of wages (Mt. 20:8; Louw and Nida I:575, 804; Grimm's 61). People owe God an accounting.

The account (Greek *logos*) is a "record of assets and liabilities" (Louw and Nida I:583). People will have a personal audit done by their Creator. The audit will be thorough, even to idle words, because words reflect the heart. The judgment will be good for some and bad for others (v. 37).

Jesus' audience probably already believed that everyone would answer directly to God. What they might not have realized was the attention to detail that will be part of that judgment. For more comments on the final judgment, see 11:23-24.

"Idle" (Greek *argos*) refers to words spoken without careful consideration (Louw and Nida I:355). Words spoken when one thinks they matter little will be part of the judgment. In this context, then, Jesus' warning means that if even small talk will be judged, then words such as these men spoke against the Savior will have serious ramifications (Hendriksen 531). These men's words against Jesus and the Holy Spirit will condemn them.

Though Jesus did not mention conversion here, the remedy for evil words is a regenerated heart. This is made possible by trusting in His name and in His finished work on the cross (v. 21; Acts 4:12).

5. Jesus warned His generation of their spiritual state (12:38-45)

38 Then certain of the scribes and of the Pharisees answered, saying, Master, we would see a sign from thee.
39 But he answered and said unto them, An evil and adulterous generation seeketh after a sign; and there shall no sign be given to it, but the sign of the prophet Jonas:
40 For as Jonas was three days and three nights in the whale's belly; so shall the Son of man be three days and three nights in the heart of the earth.

41 The men of Nineveh shall rise in judgment with this generation, and shall condemn it: because they repented at the preaching of Jonas; and, behold, a greater than Jonas *is* here.
42 The queen of the south shall rise up in the judgment with this generation, and shall condemn it: for she came from the uttermost parts of the earth to hear the wisdom of Solomon; and, behold, a greater than Solomon *is* here.
43 When the unclean spirit is gone out of a man, he walketh through dry places, seeking rest, and findeth none.
44 Then he saith, I will return into my house from whence I came out; and when he is come, he findeth *it* empty, swept, and garnished.
45 Then goeth he, and taketh with himself seven other spirits more wicked than himself, and they enter in and dwell there: and the last *state* of that man is worse than the first. Even so shall it be also unto this wicked generation.

Some Pharisees (see comments on 3:7) and scribes (see comments on 13:52) together asked for a sign (v. 38; Lk. 11:16; 1 Cor. 1:22), perhaps to validate Jesus' authority to call them into judgment (Evans, *Matthew* 251) or to provide evidence for His identity claims (Blomberg 44). If this is a continuation in the same historical context as verse 37, then it is hard to imagine such a request. They had just witnessed an exorcism and the healing of a blind and mute man (v. 22). What would it take to convince these unbelievers?

Apparently, they wanted a special sign, a "super miracle" (Newman and Stine 398). They wanted a sign that would confirm all of Jesus' miracles were of God (Hagner 33A:353; Carson, *Matthew* 294). Requests for signs were fairly common. See 16:1 where some Pharisees asked for a "sign from heaven" and John 6:30 where a crowd also asked for such a sign. Paul later referred to this tendency of the Jews (1 Cor. 1:22). See also 4:1-6 where Satan also tried to convince Jesus to put on a fantastic display of His power.

These leaders addressed Jesus as master or teacher (Greek *didaskalos*) but the reader need not be fooled. They did not fool Jesus. Their request was not an honest appeal. They probably did not believe He could give them a sign anyway (Hendriksen 533).

Jesus did not immediately oblige them with any additional miraculous signs (vv. 39-40). Their request showed their evil and spiritually adulterous or unfaithful (Hos. 1:2; 2:2; 3:1) hearts. However, He offered them one sign; but it was nothing like they imagined. The O.T. prophet Jonah was the sign (Greek appositional genitive; Lk. 11:30). As Jonah was three days and three nights in the whale (Jon. 1:17), so Jesus would be three days and nights in the grave. The great sign would be His defined grave time and His resurrection. Jonah's deliverance from death validated his message as being from God even as Jesus' deliverance from death and the grave would validate His preaching and miracles as being from God (Carson, *Matthew* 296; Rom. 1:4). See 16:1-4 for another time when Jesus spoke of Jonah as a sign.

Commentators agree that with this reference to Jonah Jesus did not say He would be in the grave seventy-two hours. He used common Jewish time reckoning, where a part of a day was counted as a whole day (Gundry 244; Gen. 42:17, 18; 1 Sam. 30:1, 12-13; Est. 4:16-5:1). See 16:21, 17:23 and 20:19 where Jesus plainly stated He would rise "on the third day."

Jesus' reference to Jonah verified the historicity of the prophet, the whale (Greek *kētos*, sea monster, whale, great fish; Grimm's 346), that Jonah lived inside the whale three days, the expulsion from the whale, the preaching of Jonah, the repentance of the Ninevites, and the fact that Jonah lived to tell about his experience. With this prophecy, Jesus also suggested that Jonah's experience was a type of His own death and deliverance from the grave.

Referring to Jonah's ministry success, Jesus again denounced His contemporaries (v. 41; 11:20-24). He contrasted their response to Him with the responses of the Ninevites and the Queen of Sheba to Jonah and Solomon (v. 42). He assured them that there is a final judgment (see 11:22, 24 and 12:36) and that they, Jesus' audience and their O.T. counterparts, will be present. The Assyrian Ninevites will fare better in that final judgment than the Israelite unbelievers of Jesus' day because the citizens of Nineveh repented when Jonah warned them but Jesus' contemporaries did not repent when He warned them. In addition, Jesus was greater than Jonah and He should have had greater success than Jonah but He did not. Jonah did not want his audience to repent but they did (Nolland 512). Jesus wanted His audience to repent but they did not.

Jesus' reference to the Assyrians is noteworthy because they carried the Northern Kingdom of Israel into captivity in 722 B.C. As in the reference to Tyre, Sidon, and Sodom in the previous chapter (11:20-24), Jesus' audience heard that they were in a more precarious position before God than the Gentiles they despised so much. Like the centurion in 8:5-13, many Gentiles will be guests in the kingdom (8:11), while many of the Jews will be shut out (8:12; Osborne 486).

Likewise, the Queen of Sheba (v. 42; 1 Kg. 10:1-10; 2 Chr. 9:1-9) will fare better than Jesus' contemporaries in the final judgment because she traveled a long distance (Greek, "from the boundaries of the earth") and made great effort to hear the wisdom of Solomon; but one greater than Solomon stood in the midst of their homeland and yet they rejected Him. As Hendriksen (539) aptly observed, "She came, but they refused."

The wisdom Solomon shared with the Queen included his worship of the Lord. No O.T. text infers that the Queen became a worshiper of Israel's Lord, but Jesus suggests that she listened with great interest (Greek infinitive of purpose: came to listen) and openness to Solomon's wisdom, something the Israelites of Jesus' day did not do. No generation is as culpable as the Israelite generation that heard Jesus teach, saw His miracles, looked Him in the eye, and yet rejected Him. These men requested a sign (v. 38), received a sign, and rejected the sign (Mt. 27:63; 28:11-15). Their Judge faced them. He was greater than the temple (v. 6), Jonah (v. 41), and Solomon (v. 42)—but they would not accept it.

Both the men of Nineveh and the Queen of the South "will rise" to condemn these unbelieving Jews. Bruner (1:576) understands "will rise" to mean that the Ninevites and the Queen will be "summoned to testify" against these men. At the least, they will stand as examples of people who had much less by way of signs and revelation than these first century leaders had but who believed anyway (Hagner 33A:354).

The words "will rise" are also a reference to the final resurrection. All parties will be alive. They will rise bodily, they will stand in judgment, they will stand in judgment together, and they will each be judged according to their own historical circumstances and opportunities. It seems certain that the Ninevites who repented were "saved," to use N.T. terminology, from immediate and eternal judgment.

Jesus ended His answer with a parable about His contemporaries (vv. 43-45). Comparing contemporary Judea with a man delivered from demon possession, Jesus said that an exorcized demon looks for another place to rest and when he finds none, returns to reoccupy his former home. He finds it clean and empty. Because there is no new occupant and the conditions are so inviting, the demon takes seven other and more evil spirits with him and they all move into the demon's former home corrupting it to a much worse state than it was before.

In the same way, Judea had benefited from Jesus' ministry. Jesus' ministry was good for Judea. There was good fruit from His ministry, with many physically and spiritually healed (vv. 13, 15, 22, 33, 35). Satan had been bound and his goods spoiled (vv. 22-29). Jesus was exorcizing that generation (Keener, *Matthew* 369). However, the positive effects of Jesus' earthly ministry among the Jews would be short-lived because they did not receive Him in place of Satan. After Jesus leaves, the consequences of national rejection will be terrible ("seven" may signify completeness or in this instance terribleness; Keener, *Background* 81). Because they did not receive Him, i.e., "embrace what Jesus brings" (Nolland 515), their latter end will be worse than before He came, much worse. Once again Jesus stressed that with increased opportunity and rejection there will be increased judgment (11:20-24). Hagner (33A:357) thinks that Jesus may have been speaking of the destruction of Jerusalem.

If this interpretation of the return of the unclean spirit is right, the modern interpreter will have little trouble seeing a parallel between Jesus' gracious effects on Judea during His incarnation and the effects of His church on society today. Society benefits in many ways from the church's presence, but as the church's presence and influence changes, so will her blessings on her society. Satan longs for an absent church.

6. Jesus identified His true family (12:46-50)

46 While he yet talked to the people, behold, *his* mother and his brethren stood without, desiring to speak with him.
47 Then one said unto him, Behold, thy mother and thy brethren stand without, desiring to speak with thee.
48 But he answered and said unto him that told him, Who is my mother? and who are my brethren?
49 And he stretched forth his hand toward his disciples, and said, Behold my mother and my brethren!
50 For whosoever shall do the will of my Father which is in heaven,

the same is my brother, and sister, and mother.

Jesus' biological family (13:55-58; Mk. 6:3) was not supportive of His ministry (Jn. 7:5). They were concerned on this occasion because He did not appear to be taking care of Himself (Mk. 3:20, 21). This might have been because of time constraints, or, as Evans (*Matthew* 245) suggests, there was standing room only in the home leaving no room to recline for a meal. Also, He was in confrontation with the religious leaders. This must have been a shock and concern for His mother and brothers. This was not the Jesus they knew. In fact, some were saying that Jesus had lost His mind (Mk. 3:21), and so His family went to intervene.

The absence of any reference to Joseph, Jesus' earthly father (1:18-25), suggests that he might have been dead by this time (Wilkins 454), but one cannot be certain (Nolland 517). See John 6:42. Matthew's mention of Mary's other children is in line with 1:25 (see comments there) and the idea that Joseph and Mary had their own children after the miraculous conception and birth of Jesus. This reference to Jesus' brothers—one assumes they were adults—is one proof that the doctrine of the perpetual virginity of Mary is false.

Matthew did not include all of these bits of information but he did state that Jesus' family came to see Him and requested to speak with Him (v. 46; Mk. 3:31-35; Lk. 8:19-21). This shows they were not part of His immediate followers.

Verse 47 is in some Greek manuscripts and absent from others, as evidenced in various translations. Mark 3:32 reflects an early tradition that suggests its inclusion in early sources. The meaning of the passage is not affected either way. However, the story does seem to read more smoothly with verse 47 included (Carson, *Matthew* 299; Metzger 32).

His family was unable to reach Him because of the crowd (Lk. 8:19). When someone told Jesus that they were there and wanted to speak with Him, He responded with a surprising answer (vv. 48-49). First, He distanced Himself from His earthly family. Second, He stated He now had another family, a family closer to Him than even His natural family. His disciples are His family. All who obey Jesus' Heavenly Father are His family (v. 50). This includes men and women (Bruner 1:583) for Jesus specifically stated that anyone who does the will of His Heavenly Father is His "brother and sister and mother." Obeying His Heavenly Father means believing on the Son (Jn. 6:40) and doing what is good and right, i.e., bearing the fruit of righteous living (7:21; 12:33).

Though the answer was to one person, these words were for the crowd, His family, and later generations of believers. He did not deny His biological connection to Mary and her other children, but rather He stated that natural ties were second to kingdom ties (4:22; 8:21-22; 10:37-38; Lk. 14:26). Jesus was part of another family, the family of God (v. 50; Lk. 8:21; Jn. 1:13). If His natural family would do the will of the Heavenly Father, i.e., believe in the Him as God's Messiah, they would be part of His kingdom family too. If they did not accept Jesus and His message, they too would find themselves eternally estranged from Him. Mary and Jesus' siblings were probably surprised to hear

Him speak like this, but His words were gracious and inviting. Jesus was calling them to Himself. They could be closer to Jesus than they had ever been, even when He had lived with them under the same roof. Jesus was evangelizing His earthly family and everyone else within hearing.

Though Jesus honored His mother (15:4-6; Jn. 19:26-27), He was not about to permit her and His brothers to take Him home. He was not beside Himself. He was about His Heavenly Father's business. However, see 13:54 where Jesus returned to Nazareth, perhaps to visit His family.

"My Father which is in heaven" might have reminded Mary of a truth Jesus' half brothers and sisters did not know. Perhaps only Jesus and Mary knew, at that time, the truth of His claim that His Father was in heaven.

One should also notice that Jesus did not give Mary special place over other humans (Walvoord 91). Quite to the contrary, she had to accept Him as Messiah and enter His kingdom just the same as everyone else. Jesus' siblings had to learn Jesus' teaching and believe in Him too. Those years He lived at home, He was God but His deity was veiled in human flesh. Once He began His public ministry, however, He called on His family to repent and believe in Him the same as He did everyone else. He directed His universal invitation, "Whosoever" (v. 50), to everyone, including His family. His family eventually believed in Him but probably not until after His resurrection (Mt. 13:55; 1 Cor. 15:7; Acts 1:14; 12:17; Gal. 1:19; 2:9).

Summary (12:1-50)

Matthew compiled events in this chapter that depicted the escalating opposition against Jesus. The first two were on Sabbath days, the only Sabbath controversies Matthew included in his Gospel. The Pharisees did not appreciate that Jesus permitted His disciples to pluck grain and eat it on the Sabbath. He responded to their challenge with two anecdotes from O.T. Scriptures. First, when David was fleeing for his life from King Saul, he entered the tabernacle and took the showbread for his men and himself. Neither Scripture nor Ahimelech the priest cited David with any wrongdoing. Jesus' reference to Scripture like this meant that God, who authored Scripture, did not condemn David. David's need took precedence over the Sabbath law on that occasion.

The second part of Jesus' defense was the normal Sabbath priestly activities. Priests were commanded by the law to do certain work every Sabbath. This meant that certain temple laws took precedence over Sabbath law. David and Jesus' disciples were not the only Sabbath breakers.

Jesus' concluding comments (vv. 6, 8) concerned His own authority over Sabbath law. He was greater than the temple (v. 6) and He is Lord of the Sabbath (v. 8). His words take precedence over Sabbath law as well.

The next confrontation also took place on a Sabbath. Jesus went to a synagogue meeting where a man with a withered hand was also in attendance. Jesus healed the man and again the Pharisees were offended. They believed that medical treatment should not be given on the Sabbath unless life was threatened. Jesus pointed out their hypocrisy. They would help a trapped animal on the Sabbath. Humans are worth more than animals. The law does not prohibit doing good on the Sabbath. The Pharisees sought ways to kill Him for this.

In order to avoid the Pharisees, Jesus left the area but continued ministering. He ministered with God's special anointing, quietly, and effectively, exactly as Scripture prophesied He would.

Another healing further intensified the tension between Jesus and the Pharisees. This time He healed a demon-possessed, blind, and mute man. The Pharisees accused Jesus of working under the power and authority of Satan. Jesus warned them about blaspheming the Holy Spirit, the unforgiveable sin. He pointed out that the healing benefited the man, a sure sign God, not Satan, was at work. If Jesus was doing good, that meant He was a good person.

The Pharisees followed up with a request for a super-miracle that would authenticate Jesus' claims. He gave them nothing immediate but promised a super miracle—one in the pattern of Jonah—in the future. As Jonah was three days in the whale, so Jesus would be three days in the earth. Jesus would rise from the grave even as Jonah came from the whale.

Jesus' generation had already received more in the way of preaching and miracles than the Ninevites received. Yet, while the Ninevites believed Jonah, the Pharisees rejected Jesus. Likewise, they had heard greater wisdom than the Queen of Sheba heard, yet their response was rejection and hers was acceptance. Because the Pharisees rejected Jesus, the Gentile Ninevites and the Queen of Sheba would witness against the Pharisees in the final judgment. Jesus had already given them more than enough reason to believe Him.

Rejection of Jesus was not without consequences. Once He was gone, the benefits of His ministry in Judea for those who rejected Him would be short-lived. Like a man who had been freed from demon possession but who at his deliverance had not invited the Savior to occupy the emptied space, so Judea, once Jesus was gone, would be repossessed by the evil one.

Matthew closed this section with Jesus' invitation to all who would like to be part of His family. Anyone who does the Father's will is close family with the Savior.

Application: Teaching and Preaching the Passage

The Sabbath controversies might seem poor instruction material for Christians. However, there are parallels between the Sabbath Day and the Lord's Day. See comments above. The following outline will help one organize thoughts found in these two stories: (1) The Lord's Day does not deny human need; (2) The Lord rules His Day; and (3) The Lord's Day is a day for doing good (gathering, prayer, worship, Scripture study, and meeting others' physical needs).

Verses 15-21 describe Jesus' ministry. All who minister in Jesus' name would do well to study Jesus' ministry habits and make them their own. One might entitle the message or lesson, "Ministering as One of the Father's Servants." The servant of God is (1) divinely chosen/called (v. 18); (2) loved by God (v. 18); (3) Spirit anointed and filled (v. 18); (4) a proclaimer of God's justice and judgment to everyone (the nations, KJV; v. 18); (5) not one given to arguing (v. 19; 1 Tim. 3:3); (6) a quiet, gentle person (v. 19; Tit. 1:7; 1 Tim. 3:3); (7) compassionate toward the weak (v. 20); (8) on the side of justice (v. 20); and (9) one who encourages all people to trust in the name of Jesus (v. 21).

The section warning against blasphemy has the gospel at its core (vv. 22-32): (1) Jesus first binds the one who captures souls; (2) Jesus frees captive souls; and (3) Jesus forgives the captured souls.

There are five characteristics of Jesus' ministry work: (1) His is a freeing work (v. 22), (2) a healing work (v. 22), (3) a kingdom work (vv. 25-28), (4) a binding work (v. 29), (5) a gathering work (v. 30), and (6) a forgiving work (vv. 31-32).

Verses 34-37 give warnings concerning the tongue: (1) the tongue tells all: the heart's character and content, whether good or evil (vv. 34-35); (2) the tongue should be controlled (v. 36; James 1:19; 3:1-12); and (3) the tongue condemns or justifies (vv. 36, 37).

One might develop "A Lesson in Contrasts" from verses 38-42 (adapted from Nolland 513): (1) a prophet and a queen; (2) a prophet who went to tell (Jonah) and an audience that traveled to hear (the Queen); (3) a negative message (Jonah's) and two positive messages (Solomon's wisdom and Jesus' gospel) (4) an audience that repented (Nineveh) and an audience that did not (N.T. Palestine); and (5) an audience that accepted wisdom from above (the Queen) and one that did not (Jesus' audience).

One might also consider "lessons from some outsiders": (1) The Ninevites learned that Israel's God is a forgiving God; (2) the Queen of Sheba learned that Israel's God is a loving and wise God; (3) the Magi (from chapter 2) learned that Israel's God is the faithful and Sovereign God (prophecy, the star, the King).

Finally, in these verses we find "the Israelites' witnesses to the nations" (adapted from Keener, *Matthew* 369): (1) Jonah to Nineveh (v. 41); (2) Solomon to the Queen of Sheba (v. 42) (3) Jesus to the Gentiles (vv. 15, 18, 21).

H. Discourse Three: Teaching Through Kingdom Parables (13:1-52)

Chapter 13 includes a collection of eight parables that Jesus told on a single day, seven if one does not consider verse 52 a parable. On this day, Jesus taught the crowds using only parables (v. 3).

A parable, as Matthew used the term, was a teaching tool. Jesus utilized them to convey truths about the kingdom of heaven. More particularly, Jesus used parables to urge His audience to respond to His teaching by accepting His call to discipleship (Fee and Stuart 152). There were different types of parables: stories, metaphors, similes, and occasional allegories (Fee and Stuart 151; ISBE III:655-656). Parables were given in such a way that insiders understood their meaning but outsiders did not (Evans, *Matthew* 261). See comments on verses 11-13. Parables were such an important part of Jesus' teaching that the Bible student is encouraged to read works on N.T. hermeneutics, especially ones written to help readers understand the Gospels and Jesus' parables. Fee and Stuart's *How to Read the Bible for All It is*

Worth, or some such work, is a good place to start.

As with all of Jesus' teachings, one will want to be aware of audiences and contexts for these parables. Who were the original hearers, unbelievers or believers? Were the unbelievers friendly or His enemies? What was the main point or points of each parable in its original context? Parables generally have one or two main points or reasons for Jesus telling them, although they can occasionally have more (Carson, *Matthew* 301). The point (or points) of each kingdom parable is some aspect of the kingdom (Hill 225).

Bible readers want to know what these parables mean today (hermeneutics), i.e., how they should be applied to the believer's life and circumstances. This must always be controlled by Jesus' original intent and the parable's original setting, since original meaning controls contemporary application. The reader should never attempt to make the Scripture mean what it never meant.

The parables in Matthew 13 are called kingdom parables. The importance of these parables is seen in the enormous amount of materials written about them, far too much for this work to interact with or summarize. This chapter is Matthew's third major block of teaching materials.

Jesus taught how to live as citizens of the kingdom (chapters 5-7), how to proclaim the kingdom (chapter 10), and now in this chapter how God grows His kingdom. In addition, chapter thirteen is to some degree Jesus' response to the rejections of His ministry recorded in chapter twelve (Hagner 33A:366-367).

1. Parables to the crowds (13:1-35)

Jesus began by teaching all who would listen. Those who accepted His teachings grew in understanding. Later that same day He met privately with His disciples and explained to them His parables.

a. The audience (13:1-2)

1 The same day went Jesus out of the house, and sat by the sea side.
2 And great multitudes were gathered together unto him, so that he went into a ship, and sat; and the whole multitude stood on the shore.

"That same day" tells the reader that the chapter division is not a real break. The house where Jesus was speaking in 12:46 is the same one mentioned in 13:1. Leaving the house, Jesus went to the Sea of Galilee where He sat for a time (Greek imperfect, was sitting) as the crowds gathered. Matthew said it was a great crowd. Luke said the people were from many towns (Lk.8:4), which suggests that the crowds were growing. Sitting was the normal posture for teaching (5:1; Nolland 523).

Because the crowd was so large, He got into a boat. Evans (*Matthew* 257) suggests that Jesus was concerned about His own safety since the circumstances seem to be identical to that described in Mark 3:9. Also, water acoustics are much better than land acoustics, so while in the boat His voice would carry better to the crowds. For a description of a first century A.D. Galilean fishing boat, see comments on 8:23. Jesus had used Peter's boat for this same reason on an earlier occasion (Lk. 5:1-3).

Jesus taught these lessons at a time when His popularity was high and growing. The placement of these parables in Mark and Luke suggests that Matthew may have gathered them into this single unit of kingdom parables much as He did the miracles in chapters eight and nine. However, it is also possible that Jesus repeatedly taught some of these parables as He traveled about preaching and teaching but on this day taught them back to back.

b. The parable of the sower (13:3-9)

3 And he spake many things unto them in parables, saying, Behold, a sower went forth to sow;
4 And when he sowed, some *seeds* fell by the way side, and the fowls came and devoured them up:
5 Some fell upon stony places, where they had not much earth: and forthwith they sprung up, because they had no deepness of earth:
6 And when the sun was up, they were scorched; and because they had no root, they withered away.
7 And some fell among thorns; and the thorns sprung up, and choked them:
8 But other fell into good ground, and brought forth fruit, some an hundredfold, some sixtyfold, some thirtyfold.
9 Who hath ears to hear, let him hear.

The first parable was the parable of the sower, so named by our Lord Himself (v. 18; Bruner 2:16), even though the focus was on the soils (Carson, *Matthew* 304). What Jesus said about the soils and seed is always true of sowing (Fee and Stuart 152). This parable is a similitude and an allegory (Evans, *Matthew* 259). The application is clear because Jesus explained it (vv. 18-23). There are similarities between peoples' responses to the kingdom invitation and the earth's responses to the farmer's sowing seed. Just as some earth receives seed more readily than others, some human hearts more readily receive Jesus' teaching than others.

Some writers understand this parable to have a different emphasis. They understand this parable to be about the overall kingdom growth. Hill (225) says that just like the farmer experienced many frustrations, so the kingdom of God "will be established in fullness only after much apparent loss. But there will be a sure and glorious harvest; the kingdom does come at last." Lane (*Mark* 154) agrees. He understands the soils to reflect diversity of responses to kingdom preaching, but he believes this was not Jesus' primary emphasis. This parable was primarily about "the coming of the kingdom of God." He says (163) that Mark shows this by his placement of Jesus' specific mention of the kingdom in 4:11-12 before giving the meaning of the parable (4:13-20). These writers interpret the parable of the sower generally to mean the same as the parables of the mustard seed (vv. 31-32) and the leaven (v. 33): although it starts small, the kingdom will grow and prevail.

What Hill and Lane say about the kingdom of God is true: it begins small and grows. However, as Carson (305) observed, this interpretation has the sower sowing "serially, [and] ... in all of the bad places first" rather than upon all soils at one time. Also, Jesus' interpretation (Mt. 13:18-23) focused on the responses of hearts to the seed. Therefore, the reader should understand this to be Jesus' intended emphasis.

First century Galilee was an agricultural community, so Jesus' illustration immediately connected with His audience. The picture was of a man broadcasting seed, probably wheat or barley (Newman and Stine 414). As he spread the seed in a side-to-side, half-circular motion while he walked, seed fell on different portions of the field. Whether he plowed the field prior to sowing, after sowing, or both (Keener, *Matthew* 376) is a matter of scholarly debate and has no effect on the final meaning of the parable. As the sower tried to get good coverage, some seed fell by (Greek "alongside"; see 20:30; Gundry 253) the footpath. Because the ground was hard, i.e., packed down from frequent traffic, the seed did not go into the ground. Lying exposed on the surface, birds came and devoured (Greek *katesthiō*, to devour completely; Louw and Nida I:250) the seed. Luke adds some seeds were trodden under foot (Lk. 8:5), suggesting that what seeds were not eaten were kept from growing.

Other seed landed on ground with rock just below the surface. The thin layer of soil on top of warm rock (Newman and Stine 415) meant the seed would sprout quickly, but because there was no depth to the soil, there was no place for root growth and development. The absence of root structure and any ability to get nutrients and moisture (Lk. 8:6) for the plant meant the plant could not survive the sun's heat. This resulted in an early death for the newly sprouted seed (v. 6). There was life but it was short lived (v. 6; when the sun rose).

The third soil group would soon be full of thorns. As with the rock, the farmer was unaware that thorns were present (Keener, *Background* 82). The seed sprouted and grew for a time, but the thorns growing alongside the good seed (Newman and Stine 416) soon took all of the ground's nutrients and moisture and choked out the grain. There was life but the plant was unhealthy and underdeveloped. Mark 4:7 said this seed, choked as it was, produced no "fruit" or grain. There was nothing to harvest.

The fourth soil type was the goal and hope of the sower. This ground was good because it was broken up, unlike the footpath. It had deep enough dirt to support a healthy root structure, unlike the rocky soil. It was free of anything that would also vie for the soil's water and nutrients, unlike the thorny soil. In short, it was productive, unlike the first three soils. Of the four soils, this soil was the only soil that was producing grain for harvest. "Brought forth" (Greek imperfect tense) suggests "continual, regular and normal action" (Bruner 2:7). It was productive because it allowed the seed in and because it provided nourishment and room for the seed to grow. Some portions of the good soil produced a harvest thirty times more than what was sown. Some produced sixty times over the amount sown. Some produced one hundred times the amount of seed put in the ground.

Jesus ended His explanation with "He who has ears to hear, let him hear." See comments on 11:15. Everyone listening heard Jesus urge for immediate acceptance, to be good soil. This is the second of three times (11:15; 13:43)

Jesus called on those who heard Him teach to give due diligence to accepting His words. "Hear" means to listen for understanding (vv. 18-19) and to obey (Louw and Nida I:467; Mt. 17:5).

Some of the older Greek manuscripts of Matthew simply say "He who has ears, let him hear." However, both Mark (4:9) and Luke (8:8) included the words "to hear" without question.

See verses 18-23 for Jesus' explanation of this parable.

c. The purpose of parables (13:10-17)

10 And the disciples came, and said unto him, Why speakest thou unto them in parables?
11 He answered and said unto them, Because it is given unto you to know the mysteries of the kingdom of heaven, but to them it is not given.
12 For whosoever hath, to him shall be given, and he shall have more abundance: but whosoever hath not, from him shall be taken away even that he hath.
13 Therefore speak I to them in parables: because they seeing see not; and hearing they hear not, neither do they understand.
14 And in them is fulfilled the prophecy of Esaias, which saith, By hearing ye shall hear, and shall not understand; and seeing ye shall see, and shall not perceive:
15 For this people's heart is waxed gross, and *their* ears are dull of hearing, and their eyes they have closed; lest at any time they should see with *their* eyes and hear with *their* ears, and should understand with *their* heart, and should be converted, and I should heal them.
16 But blessed *are* your eyes, for they see: and your ears, for they hear.
17 For verily I say unto you, That many prophets and righteous *men* have desired to see *those things* which ye see, and have not seen *them*; and to hear *those things* which ye hear, and have not heard *them*.

Some disciples, along with the Twelve (Mk. 4:10), realized Jesus had changed His method of teaching and they asked Him why (v. 10). Normally Jesus spoke plainly, as in the Sermon on the Mount. (But see 7:24-27, 9:15-17, and 11:16-19 for earlier parables; Hagner 33A:372).

Matthew did not record the timing of this question. According to Mark (4:10) the disciples asked when He was alone, which means they might have asked Him later that day (v. 36). Newman and Stine (418) suggest the disciples approached Him in the boat (v. 10, came), which seems improbable given Mark's record.

The word "because" (v. 11; Greek *hoti*) can introduce a direct quotation (as in ESV, NIV), or it can mean "because" (as in the KJV). Either is possible and in this instance the point is the same regardless which translation is followed (Newman and Stine 419).

Jesus had reason for teaching with parables. He intended that only select people understand· certain kingdom truths. The disciples—all those who believed in Jesus, not just the Twelve—had been given (v. 11) the ability to understand, but others had not. This ability came from God (interpreting "is given" as a "divine passive"), and Jesus added to the ability the truths He wanted understood.

The mysteries of the kingdom (v. 11) are previously unrevealed truths (v. 35) about the kingdom of heaven: namely, that the kingdom had arrived in Jesus and was in a different form than expected (Wilkins 477). As verse 35 states, the parables teach many previously unknown truths. The main truth is that the kingdom is here now and fully operative but also hidden. These parables speak mainly about the kingdom from Jesus' earthly ministry until the final judgment. For the kingdom of heaven, see comments on 3:2.

Some who understand Scripture to teach that saving faith is God's gracious gift find verse 11 a challenge: "to them it is not given." Bruner (2:10) says, "This is hard," and wonders why more people are not given this gift. He writes, "The sentence cannot be explained away. And we will accept it as it stands only if we are prepared to let God be God." However, see further the discussion of verses 14-15. This passage is about human responsibility in the face of the divine offer, not about double predestination. God gives to those willing to receive (Hagner 33A:372-373). Here He gave to those willing to believe in Jesus.

Verse 12 further explains (Greek explicative *gar*, for). To those who received initial understanding from God and are receptive to His offer, He will give even greater understanding so that they will have no shortage. Those who do not understand because they rejected God's offer will lose even the most basic understanding that comes with the offer to join the kingdom. The next verses explain why this is. See also verse 35 and the deliberate use of parables and Mark 4:24-25 for human responsibility for understanding Jesus' sayings. This same kingdom principle is repeated in 25:29.

The reason, then, for these parables was to provide a way for Jesus to get His message out openly and publicly while at the same time insuring that unbelievers would not understand all that was being said (v. 13). The same words taught believers and hardened unbelievers. In this way Jesus' ministry paralleled Isaiah's. Both spoke the Word of God. Both preached to unbelieving, spiritually blind people (Wilkins 478; Is. 6:9-10). Both witnessed the hardening effects of the gospel when rejected. Kingdom truths are "understood only from the inside" (Barclay 2:77).

Because (v. 13; Greek *hoti*) they refused to believe Jesus' claims, i.e., because they refused to really look at or consider what they saw and they refused to pay attention to what they heard, the people heard the words but did not understand the meaning. As an act of judgment, God withheld understanding from those who refused to believe (Gundry 256). They saw—probably a reference to Jesus' miraculous signs (Jn. 12:37-40)—but did not recognize God at work.

The Pharisees who blasphemed (12:24) are among those who did not understand. They saw Jesus' works and they heard His teaching, but they did not receive His message and so did not fully comprehend His word. The residents of Nazareth also did not understand, again because of their unbelief (13:54, 58). See comments there.

In this manner, Jesus' ministry also fulfilled (v. 14) Isaiah's words. Isaiah was not speaking prophetically of a future hardening that would be realized in Jesus' ministry. Rather, Jesus saw Isaiah's ministry as being typical of His own. Isaiah's audience paralleled the audience of Jesus' day. Even though many gathered to hear Jesus, most were not believers. They were curious but not committed. They saw Jesus and His works but did not see the complete Jesus (v. 13). They did not see the Father at work in Jesus. They heard but did not recognize God's voice in Jesus. See John 5:36-40 and its context for further comments by Jesus on this matter.

The Hebrew text behind verse 14 (Is. 6:9) is literally, "See and see, hear and hear." The construction intensifies the basic meaning (Williams 38). The result is that the people really see and they really hear. Matthew's wording agrees grammatically, indicating that the audience will surely hear and surely see, but will not understand because understanding comes from God and God does not give understanding to those who reject Him. In this sense, Isaiah's prophecy, which saw its primary fulfillment in his own day, continued to be fulfilled in Jesus' day (Blomberg 48). In keeping with the timelessness of the truth in verse 12, Jesus' application of Isaiah 6:9 remains applicable.

Continual rejection resulted in gross or calloused hearts. The word (Greek *pachunō*) literally means "to become thick" and figuratively means "to become unable to understand or comprehend as the result of being mentally dull or spiritually insensitive" (Louw and Nida I:386). "Ears are dull of hearing" is an idiom that means they were slow to understand the message from God because they turned a deaf ear to Him. They also closed (Greek active voice) their eyes against God's revelation.

They turned deaf ears and shut their eyes, willfully resisting understanding, because they knew if they listened to God they would turn to Him for healing and renewal (Newman and Stine 424). God's word through Isaiah was emphatic: "lest" (Greek *mēpote* + subjunctive) indicates negative purpose, i.e., "so that [they would] not see ... and hear ... and understand ... turn again, and be healed" (v. 15). Such an attitude toward God meant they would by no means ever (Greek emphatic negative; Osborne 511) understand or see (v. 14).

God did not initiate the people's blindness to His Word. God said that the people themselves shut their eyes. Because people rejected God's invitations, they became increasingly insensitive to His offers of grace. According to John 12:37, people could have believed but did not. See John 12:40 and Acts 28:25-27 and their contexts for further references to this same quotation from Isaiah. Israel chose not to believe God's message to them (Is. 53:1; Jn. 12:38), thus hardening their hearts. God then further judged the unbelievers by not giving them any additional understanding and finally removing what little understanding they originally received from Him (Mt. 13:12). This resulted in an even greater hardening of hearts by God.

Matthew recorded Jesus' answer to His disciples in verse 15 from the LXX of Isaiah 6:10 rather than from the Hebrew text. The Hebrew text implies that *Isaiah*, by his preaching, would harden the hearts of the people. However, the LXX wording focuses the responsibility for their lack of understanding on the *people* themselves. By quoting the LXX, Jesus placed the blame on the Jews for their rejection of Him and His kingdom. They, not God, shut their eyes to His offer of salvation through Jesus. Their rejection of the gospel resulted in calloused hearts.

Jesus' reference to His pre-incarnate words to Isaiah (vv. 14-15; Is. 6:9-10; Jn. 12:37-41) explained the reason for the people's dullness. The people's unbelief and rejection in Jesus' day mirrored that of late seventh century B.C. Judah. First century Israel was just as resistant to Jesus' word as she had been seven hundred years earlier in Isaiah's lifetime. For O.T. Judah, their continued rejection of and increasing hardness toward God's word to them meant they would be exiled and only a remnant would remain of the people of God (Is. 6:11-13). For Jesus' audience, their rejection of God's word through Jesus meant they would miss the kingdom of heaven and be exiled for eternity in the fire of God's judgment.

There is a theological camp that teaches that people are lost because God in eternity past decreed they would be lost. God's explanation recorded in this Isaiah passage and its N.T. quotations show the error of this doctrine. Unsaved people do not want to hear and understand God's word because they do not want to turn from their sin and be converted (v. 15). The unsaved that shut out God's message of salvation are responsible for their own lost condition. In other words, rejection begins in the heart of sinful man, not with God. The reader is directed to verses 54-58 for an example of a community's rejection of God's Word to them. Nazareth rejected Jesus and refused to believe in Him. They were responsible for their decision not to believe Jesus. Jesus marveled at their rejection of Him, not God's rejection of them (Mk. 6:6).

Barclay (2:83) says Jesus was teaching His disciples a common Jewish belief that "it was as much God's will when people did not listen as when they did." Such an understanding of God is wrong. Jesus wanted and still wants everyone to hear, i.e., understand and obey (v. 9). Evans (*Matthew* 263) agrees that Matthew teaches human responsibility but believes that Mark teaches divine judgment. Understanding Mark 4:12 to begin with a purpose clause (that seeing they might see, etc.), Evans says, "God does not want his people to repent, not until judgment has run its course" and gives Isaiah 6:11-13 as support. This makes God responsible for people's rejection and ultimately their lost condition. However, grammatically, Mark's "that" can be understood to introduce *result* rather than purpose. This would mean the people's unbelief resulted in their inability to perceive and understand Jesus' teachings, making Matthew and Mark agree. People who do not understand are under divine judgment but it is because they have already rejected the message of the kingdom and its invitation. See Picirilli (*Mark* 117-118) for further comments on Mark's intent.

The importance of Isaiah 6:9-10 is seen in the fact that each of the Gospel writers and Luke in his Acts of the Apostles include this passage in their records. John 12:37 and Acts 28:24 state plainly that the people's unbelief and rejection kept them from turning to God for spiritual healing. God did not shut out the people. The people shut out God. Isaiah 6:9-10 is simply God's confirmation of Israel's "repeated, freely chosen decisions to reject him"

(Blomberg 46). Jesus quoted Isaiah to state that the prophet's experience foreshadowed His own (Hagner 33A:374).

Jesus told His disciples that believers who lived at the time of the incarnation were especially blessed (v. 16). They received and understood Jesus' signs and teachings. They understood beyond the basics because they believed and God then gave them increased understanding and perception (v. 12).

The blessings to Jesus' immediate disciples (v. 16) were rare and precious. Many of God's faithful in times past had greatly desired (v. 17; Greek *epithumeō*) to see and hear what these disciples were seeing and hearing. Peter also later referred to this truth (1 Pet. 1:10-12). God blessed the O.T. saints with prophetic insights into the Lord's earthly ministry and they looked forward with great faith and anticipation. However, they were not blessed to actually experience the Lord's incarnate ministry, the initiation of God's kingdom on earth (Hill 228).

d. The parable of the sower and soils explained (13:18-23)

18 Hear ye therefore the parable of the sower.
19 When any one heareth the word of the kingdom, and understandeth *it* not, then cometh the wicked *one*, and catcheth away that which was sown in his heart. This is he which received seed by the way side.
20 But he that received the seed into stony places, the same is he that heareth the word, and anon with joy receiveth it;
21 Yet hath he not root in himself, but dureth for a while: for when tribulation or persecution ariseth because of the word, by and by he is offended.
22 He also that received seed among the thorns is he that heareth the word; and the care of this world, and the deceitfulness of riches, choke the word, and he becometh unfruitful.
23 But he that received seed into the good ground is he that heareth the word, and understandeth *it*; which also beareth fruit, and bringeth forth, some an hundredfold, some sixty, some thirty.

Later that day, a smaller group of disciples, along with the Twelve, asked Jesus about the parables in general and specifically about the meaning of this parable (v. 10; Mk. 4:10, 13). For a summary of various views, see Bruner (2:3). After His explanation about His use of parables recorded in verses 10-17, Jesus interpreted the parable of the sower. This parable was not limited in its application to Jesus' day. It speaks of the preaching of the gospel throughout the church age and its truths should be spoken of in the present tense. Not only did the sower sow, the sower and those who follow Him continue sowing.

According to Mark 4:14, Jesus began His explanation with, "The sower sows the word." The seed is the word of the kingdom (Mt. 13:19), the word of God (Lk. 8:11). This is the message of the kingdom of God, which Jesus and His followers communicate to all people with the hope that it will take root and grow. All four soils hear the same word. For the kingdom of God, see comments on 3:2.

Seed sown along the footpath represents the kingdom message proclaimed to hardened hearts. The hard ground is the heart, i.e., the inner being, of the person who hears the kingdom word but does not understand it (v. 19). Compare this with verses 15-17 and comments about why this hearer does not understand. Because this person refuses to receive the word, i.e., to allow the seed entrance into the heart, he or she is farthest removed from personal salvation. The hard ground represents people like the Pharisees in 12:24-32.

Hendriksen says the hard ground represents those who do nothing about the seed sown to them (560). However, as seen from verses 14 and 15, a hard heart is a heart that rejects God's Word. Hardened hearts, then, act with rejection. They refuse it entrance into their hearts.

The birds stand for Satan who steals the seed before it can grow. He removes the word before hearers can understand it (v. 19) and decide to believe and be saved (Lk. 8:12). Seed that is received grows and results in salvation—to use Luke's post-Easter term (Evans, *Matthew* 266).

With these words, Jesus described some of the works of the evil one. Satan works to keep the gospel out of people's lives, to keep people from receiving the word in order to keep them from being saved. He works through demons (Mt. 8:28-29), the ungodly philosophies of the age (Rom. 12:2), the ungodly people who assist him in opposing the work of God (Acts 13:8; Eph. 2:2), and all that is against (anti-) Christ (1 Jn. 2:18).

The rocky soil represents the person who receives the message of the kingdom immediately upon hearing it (v. 20). This person is excited about the gospel message and receives it "with joy." This decision, however, is superficial in the sense that it is "for a while": that is, short-lived (Greek *proskairos*; Louw and Nida I:643), represented by the thin soil over rock and the absence of deep, stabilizing roots. The acceptance is real but temporary. Luke (8:13) says these believe (Greek *pisteuō*) for a while. "He has no root in himself"—that is, in the human heart (cf. v. 19; Nolland 540). This suggests he did not give serious thought to the kingdom message and its sure opposition by enemies of Christ (Lk. 14:28).

With the same speed this hearer accepted the gospel message he falls away ("is offended," v. 21; Greek *skandalizō*, to cease believing; Louw and Nida I:276; Grimm's 576; for this same meaning, see 24:10; 26:31, 33; Mk. 4:17; 14:27, 29; Jn. 16:1). He endures for a while, but when trouble comes in response to his acceptance of the kingdom message, he is unable to survive spiritually. Shallow commitments are short-lived and unable to withstand the certain attacks by the evil one. See comments on 11:6. "By and by" (Greek *euthus*) means "immediately" rather than "at some time." (See Luke 17:7 and 21:9 for other examples where this understanding applies.)

The thorn-infested ground (v. 22) is the heart that is too crowded with matters of this life for healthy seed growth and development. Verse 7 suggests the ground was never totally clear of thorns and that when the seed was sown the thorns grew with the seeds' sprouts and overpowered the plants, keeping them from bearing fruit.

The thorns represent the day-to-day cares of life and the deceitfulness of riches. The word "cares" (Greek *marima*) can also be translated worries and refers to those concerns easily encouraged by the needs of living in this world (e.g., food and clothes, 6:25). Jesus warned against both anxiety and riches in His Sermon on the Mount (6:19-34; Hagner 33A:380). The cares of life are not in and of themselves sin. God knows we have need of these things (6:32). The problem here is of importance and priorities. Earthly matters are allowed to dominate kingdom matters when kingdom matters should be given priority over earthly matters (6:33).

The deceitfulness of riches means deception that comes from riches (Greek subjective genitive). Jesus did not explain how riches deceive and mislead. However, other Scripture texts reveal that riches teach erroneously that they are essential to life and will satisfy human cravings. The more wealth one has, the more satisfaction; enough wealth, enough satisfaction. All of this is a lie (Eccl. 5:10). Wealth also erroneously teaches that it can permanently provide this world's pleasures and security (Eccl. 2:1-11). Worldly wealth is not a guaranteed, permanent asset (6:20). It can be stolen, devalued or destroyed. Scripture on the other hand teaches that only God provides (Mt. 6:26, 30, 33), and that wealth should be used for life's necessities and eternal matters, not hoarded (6:19-21; Lk. 16:9). In the end, how one uses wealth will be judged (Jas. 5:3).

When permitted to grow alongside the gospel seed, earth's cares and the desire for riches will keep the seed from ever reaching maturity. It becomes "unfruitful," which means that the seed will never make a harvestable head of grain. This means the seed never accomplishes in the hearer what the sower wants it to accomplish. The sower wants the seed to change the life of the hearer from living for this world to living for the kingdom of heaven. This hearer joins the first two in their failure. Neither of the first three soil types produced a harvestable crop for the sower.

The fourth soil type is good ground (v. 23). Good ground is cultivated and loose, ground that has sufficient depth to grow a strong root and provide nourishment needed to withstand the sun's heat (persecution and troubles). It is ground that has been cleared of everything that would compete for nourishment (thorns). Jesus identified this soil-type as the person who hears. The messenger shares the gospel with him and he listens and receives. He also understands. In light of Jesus' previous discussion (vv. 12-15), this good heart understands because he believes and wants to hear more. His ears and eyes are open; he has received Jesus' message and has thus been awarded greater understanding (Hagner 33A:380). See the discussion above on verses 10-17.

Jesus says this kind of soil "also" or surely (Greek *dē*; indeed, really, doubtless; "denotes that a statement is definitely established," BAGD 178) bears fruit. There is no doubt that the seed had matured and produced a harvestable crop. The sower is pleased. The seed is so productive that it multiplies in some instances one hundred times over what was sowed, in some instances sixty times over what was sowed, and in some instances thirty times over what was sowed.

To summarize, the hard ground is the person who wants nothing to do with the gospel. He shuts it out and Satan easily removes it from his life. The rocky ground is the person who wants to be part of the kingdom but is superficial about the whole thing. This person "believes," but that is all. Below the surface is strong resistance against the demands of the gospel for kingdom life. Such a person would be saved if he or she would allow God to change the heart of stone into a heart of flesh (Ez. 11:19; 36:26). He has faith but not saving faith (Jas. 2:19).

The thorny ground is the person who wants salvation but no discipleship. This person accepts a gospel that requires neither sacrifice of goods nor separation from worldly concerns. This person tries to hold on to both worlds, never realizing that a true disciple cannot love this world and the next (1 Jn. 2:15-17). This person would be saved if he or she would stop relying on personal wealth, stop loving this world, and start trusting Jesus as Lord and loving Him supremely (19:16-30). Jesus later warned that a saved person can fall into this lifestyle and miss out on the blessings of the return of Christ (Lk. 21:34). Thorns are dangerous. Nolland (541-542) argues that both the rocky ground and the thorny ground are addressed to the Christian church as well as the crowds. If so, these persons' salvation is short-lived because the rocky ground person "falls away" (v. 21, as above; Lk. 8:13) and the thorny-ground person never bears fruit. However, see additional comments below. Whether one believes the persons represented by the second and third soil types were never saved or were saved and then backslid into apostasy, the end state is the same: such persons are lost. For further observations about whether the second and third soil types speak of apostasy, the reader is referred to Picirilli's comments (*Mark* 119-124).

The good ground welcomes the seed and provides for it the ideal growing conditions. By receiving the seed, the good ground keeps or holds fast the seed (Lk. 8:15) and thus prevents Satan from stealing it. The seed in good ground grows deep roots and is able to withstand troubles and persecution. By clearing itself of other affections, the good ground is able to devote all its resources to the growing seed, which results in an abundant harvest. The good ground perseveres and according to Luke brings forth fruit with patient endurance (Lk. 8:15; Evans, *Matthew* 267).

The good ground is the only ground that received Jesus' approval because it alone bore fruit. This was the reason for His appeal (v. 9) and the point He was making. The parable is not about barely getting into the kingdom or even about gaining and losing citizenship; it is about the one way to enter. The end goal of the seed is not growth; it is a harvest. The one way into the kingdom is to be good ground and permit the seed to grow to fruition.

The Sower was sowing the word. The message of the kingdom was being preached at that time. The crowd needed to apply the message to themselves immediately because the kingdom was already being initiated in Jesus (Fee and Stuart 158) and judgment loomed (vv. 24-30). Jesus called on the crowd to receive His message rather than harden their hearts against it or try to receive it half-heartedly. He called on them to give no place for anything else to grow alongside their devotion to His kingdom, no desire for wealth and no place for this world's concerns. They were not to try to bring into the kingdom a life crowded with affections for this world. Each person was and is to receive the word of the kingdom without resistance or hindrance. As mentioned already, this parable is about "human responsibility" (Evans, *Matthew* 270) when confronted with divine opportunity.

It is clear that Jesus preached for decisions. The crowds gathered to listen and watch, many out of curiosity, but Jesus called for a change of hearts. He was not a show. He was their Savior—if they would have Him. He was the Sower. Jesus preached to each soil-type but only one type became citizens of the kingdom. His disciples now knew this. They would encounter the same four types of soils.

e. The parable of the wheat and tares (13:24-30)

24 Another parable put he forth unto them, saying, The kingdom of heaven is likened unto a man which sowed good seed in his field:
25 But while men slept, his enemy came and sowed tares among the wheat, and went his way.
26 But when the blade was sprung up, and brought forth fruit, then appeared the tares also.
27 So the servants of the householder came and said unto him, Sir, didst not thou sow good seed in thy field? from whence then hath it tares?
28 He said unto them, An enemy hath done this. The servants said unto him, Wilt thou then that we go and gather them up?
29 But he said, Nay; lest while ye gather up the tares, ye root up also the wheat with them.
30 Let both grow together until the harvest: and in the time of harvest I will say to the reapers, Gather ye together first the tares, and bind them in bundles to burn them: but gather the wheat into my barn.

The second kingdom parable also uses farming as a teaching tool and appears only in Matthew. By using something common to first century Galilean life, Jesus' parable immediately connected with His audience. For parables, see the introductory comments to this chapter. "The kingdom of heaven is likened unto" includes the entire parable, not just the sower (Keener, *Background* 83), and means that there are similarities between what will happen in the kingdom and what will happen when a man sows (Hill 231).

Good seed was seed that was pure. It had only the seed of the desired crop in it. The farmer was careful to protect his field from unwanted growth. Corrupted crops were harder to harvest, so if the value of the crop was to be protected the seed had to be kept pure. The first parable was about different soil types but assumed good seed. This parable is about different seeds but assumes a single type of soil. The seed in the first parable represents the word of God. The seed in this parable represents people.

This farmer carefully sowed (Greek *speirō*) good seed, but during the night an enemy came in while everyone else was asleep and resowed (Greek *epispeirō*) the same field. The enemy used seed that produced a harmful plant (Greek *zizanio*) but that resembled the good seed's plant in its early stages. Most commentators identify the enemy's seed as darnel, a grass that resembles wheat or rye and if infected with a particular mold can produce "vomiting, malaise or even death. Thus the tares have to be separated very carefully from the wheat, but usually only as harvest approaches" (ISBE IV:1045).

Only as the wheat matured and heads of grain began to appear (Newman and Stine 434) did the tares become identifiable (v. 26). Darnel grain heads are black and light, allowing the plant to remain upright whereas wheat grain heads are brown and heavy resulting in the plant bending over (http://en.wikipedia.org/wiki/Lolium_temulentum; accessed 06-21-12). The farmer quickly concluded that some enemy—literally, "an enemy, a man"—had deliberately corrupted his pure crop (v. 28) and that pulling the darnel out before the harvest would destroy the wheat as well. This was because the roots would be intertwined and pulling one would uproot the other also. This destruction of good plants would result in no harvest at all or a severely reduced harvest.

The servants wanted to pull out the weeds immediately, but the farmer forbade this action in order to spare the wheat. Bruner (2:29) thinks this ethical dilemma is the point of the parable: "How should we fight this evil?" However, Jesus' silence in His later explanation concerning this question argues against Bruner. The parable is not about how the church is to fight evil. Instead, it teaches us that the church exists alongside evil and God perfectly judges all people in the last day. See below on verses 36-43 for additional comments.

The farmer decided to allow the darnel to remain in the field until the harvest. At harvest time, he will command his servants to separate the tares from the wheat, bind and burn the tares, and store the wheat. (For barn, see 3:12.)

According to Gundry (265), in such situations harvesters would usually cut the grain heads off the good stalks and leave the shorter tares in the field. Then they would burn both the tares and the stalks of the grain plants in the field. He suggests that Jesus described an unusual way of dealing with the problem to emphasize the final judgment of false disciples.

See verses 36-43 for Jesus' explanation of this parable.

f. The parable of the mustard seed (13:31-32)

31 Another parable put he forth unto them, saying, The kingdom of heaven is like to a grain of mustard seed, which a man took, and sowed in his field:
32 Which indeed is the least of all seeds: but when it is grown, it is the greatest among herbs, and becometh a tree, so that the birds of the air come and lodge in the branches thereof.

This parable is recorded in all three Synoptics (Mk. 4:30-32; Lk. 13:18-19). "The kingdom of heaven is like" means that certain aspects of the kingdom can be compared to aspects of a mustard seed when planted. The growth of the mustard seed means the kingdom is present and growing (Wilkins 483). The extent of the mustard seed's growth seen in its height and size at maturity points to the unexpected growth of the kingdom. Though small, the mustard seed grows to become the largest of the garden plants (Greek, *lachanon*; Louw and Nida I:32).

Likewise with the kingdom of heaven: what appeared small and insignificant in the early days of Jesus' ministry (the preaching and any visible manifestation of the kingdom) would one day be surprisingly large and well able to support all who would place their trust in it. Its humble beginnings were no indication of its final glory. The kingdom's hidden potential paralleled that of the mustard seed (Hill 233).

While the mustard seed is not the very smallest seed known today (Newman and Stine 439), it was apparently used by the rabbis to "characterize something very minute" and was the smallest seed of its kind in that part of the world at that time; some species could grow as tall as fifteen feet (4.6 meters; ISBE III:449).

"Lodge" (Greek *kataskēnoō*) normally means to settle or dwell (Grimm's 337). Here it seems to mean to nest (Louw and Nida I:71). The nesting of the birds may suggest that the seed will mature quickly since birds nest in the springtime, the same time seeds are normally planted (Gundry 267). Gundry points out that there are multiple hyperboles in this parable, one of which is the seed's speedy growth.

Some commentators find meanings in this parable that Jesus did not specifically mention. Some (Evans, *Matthew* 273; Bruner 2:36; Barclay 2:89) understand the birds to represent Gentiles who will be saved. This is consistent with O.T. imagery (Ezek. 31:6; Dan. 4:21). The kingdom, then, will include people from all nations. Evans (*Matthew* 272), commenting on a description of the mustard plant by the Roman writer, Pliny the Elder (A.D. 23-79), also suggests that there may be more to this parable than kingdom growth. He suggests that because the mustard plant, once rooted, is extremely difficult to get rid of, perhaps this was partly Jesus' point.

g. The parable of the leaven (13:33)

33 Another parable spake he unto them; The kingdom of heaven is like unto leaven, which a woman took, and hid in three measures of meal, till the whole was leavened.

Another similitude (Fee and Stuart 152), this parable is found also in Luke 13:20-21. Jesus spoke of the custom of mixing yeast or "a piece of fermented dough reserved from a previous baking" (ISBE III:97) with new dough. Women normally did this work; though see Genesis 40:2. The hidden yet pervasive action of leaven in flour (Greek *aleuron*, wheat flour; Grimm's 26) illustrates the unseen and gradual—yet thorough—spreading of the kingdom of heaven (of God, Lk. 13:20) in society. As with the parable of the mustard seed, Jesus set up a contrast between the small beginnings of the kingdom and its much larger consummation. Hidden potential is the point (Hill 234).

Barclay (2:93) understands Jesus Himself to be the transforming power of leaven. However, the words "hid" and "whole" suggest pervasive power more than transformation, though transformation is surely included in the yeast's pervasive influence. All of the world will be touched by the gospel, but not all will be transformed by it. The kingdom will grow to be present throughout the entire world (26:13; 28:19). Like leaven placed in dough, the gospel will completely accomplish its purpose (Nolland 554).

Walvoord (103-104), on the other hand, understands the leaven to represent evil in the church, even as he understands the tares (v. 25) and the discarded fish (v. 48). This way, the point of the parable would be that evil will completely permeate the church, not that kingdom influence will permeate the world. This does not seem to fit the overall theme of the chapter: namely, the growth of the kingdom. Leaven in the Bible does not always have to represent evil (Lev. 7:13; 23:15-18; Carson 319).

A measure (Greek *saton*) was about a peck and a half (Louw and Nida I:709). Three measures would be about nine gallons. This was a large amount of flour to be preparing at one time and has been estimated to provide enough bread to feed over a hundred persons (Newman and Stine 440). Again, Jesus exaggerated to make His point clear. A little leaven influences a large amount of flour. In the same way, the kingdom, though small initially, will thoroughly permeate this world (24:14).

h. New revelation: another reason for parables (13:34-35)

34 All these things spake Jesus unto the multitude in parables; and without a parable spake he not unto them:
35 That it might be fulfilled which was spoken by the prophet, saying, I will open my mouth in parables; I will utter things which have been kept secret from the foundation of the world.

Matthew explained that on this occasion Jesus chose to teach only in parables. See comments above on verses 10-17 for Jesus' reasons for doing this. Verses 34 and 35 take earlier comments about hearers a step further: hearers represented by the good soil are given fresh opportunities to receive and understand new revelation.

The O.T. quotation is Psalm 78:2. The Psalmist (possibly Asaph; 1 Chr. 25:2 and 2 Chr. 29:30; Hagner 33A:390) taught the people using conventional methods of the day—wisdom sayings, dark sayings, and parables. This verse is an instance of structurally synonymous parallelism, where the second line restates the meaning of the first (Gundry 270). The Hebrew word translated "parable" has a wide range of meanings: proverb, parable, allegory, byword, taunt, and discourse (TWOT I:533). The purpose of Psalm 78 was to communicate God's revelation in law and life (His past works) so each successive generation would learn to trust God also and not forget God as their fathers had done (Ps. 78:7-8). According to Matthew, Jesus was doing the same with His parables. Like the prophet Psalmist, Jesus imparted previously unknown truths (Blomberg 49). "Secret" (Greek *kruptō*) means hidden. As in the wilderness, God was still in the events of their lives and they needed to recognize Him and turn to Him. Indeed God was teaching them at that very moment from a boat.

In addition to parables concealing truth from non-responsive hearts (people who rejected Jesus' gospel, vv. 10-17), parables also required hearers to focus their attention in order to understand. Accurate discernment belonged only to those who were willing to devote the mental energy to understand them (v. 9; Mk. 4:24-25). Mark 4:33-34 adds that once they were in private, Jesus explained each of His parables to His disciples. This prevented misunderstanding and doctrinal disagreements as the disciples passed Jesus' teachings on to others.

With this quote, Matthew showed that Jesus claimed to be a teacher (Evans, *Matthew* 275). He was a revealer of God's hidden truths. A greater than Solomon was present (12:42), one who explained the secrets of the kingdom (v. 11).

"Of the world" is not in some Greek manuscripts. Carson (*Matthew* 323-324) argues that its absence in the original suggests the writer meant only that the truths were hidden "from of old," from old times. If "of the world" is original—which is certainly possible given our present knowledge—Jesus' reference to the foundation of the world assumes a literal understanding of Genesis 1. The world has not always been. God brought the world into existence. All Scripture writers, Old and New Testaments both, speak of the creation account of Genesis 1 and 2 as if it is to be understood literally. See comments on 19:4.

2. Parables to the disciples alone (13:36-52)

After giving the parables, Jesus returned to the house (v. 36). This was presumably His own house in Capernaum (4:13; 9:28; 12:46; 13:1), not that of one of His disciples, since they "came to him" (v. 36). However, most commentaries seem to prefer that Jesus stayed with Peter or Andrew when He was in Capernaum rather than in a house of His own.

The disciples approached, wanting Him to "declare"—to explain in detail (Greek *diasapheō*; BAGD 188)—the parable of the wheat and the tares (darnel) as He had done the sower (vv. 18-23). This explanation and the remaining parables were given to the disciples alone (Newman and Stine 411).

a. The meaning of the wheat and the tares (13:36-43)

36 Then Jesus sent the multitude away, and went into the house: and his disciples came unto him, saying, Declare unto us the parable of the tares of the field.
37 He answered and said unto them, He that soweth the good seed is the Son of man;
38 The field is the world; the good seed are the children of the kingdom; but the tares are the children of the wicked *one*;
39 The enemy that sowed them is the devil; the harvest is the end of the world; and the reapers are the angels.
40 As therefore the tares are gathered and burned in the fire; so shall it be in the end of this world.
41 The Son of man shall send forth his angels, and they shall gather out of his kingdom all things that offend, and them which do iniquity;
42 And shall cast them into a furnace of fire: there shall be wailing and gnashing of teeth.
43 Then shall the righteous shine forth as the sun in the kingdom of their Father. Who hath ears to hear, let him hear.

Jesus briefly identified each important point of reference in this parable about the final division between the righteous and the unrighteous, and especially about the delay of judgment by God (Hagner 33A:382, 392). Jesus is the sower of the good seed, the field is the whole world (Nolland 559), and the good seed are His followers, those who have joined the kingdom. Unlike 8:12, where the children—literally, sons—of the kingdom are unbelieving Jews, in this passage sons of the kingdom are believers in general, people who are part of the kingdom of God (Newman and Stine 444). The seed in this parable does not represent the gospel (as in the parable of the sower, v. 18) but rather those who accept the gospel message and are part of the kingdom. The Hebraistic expression "children/ sons of" is descriptive of the persons' character and identifies their close association with someone or something (Hagner 33A:393), here with the characteristics of the kingdom.

The good seed are sons of the kingdom (Carson 326). It is the incarnate Jesus' business to sow His children in this world. His sowing is ongoing. It continues today and will continue (Greek present participle) until the end (Bruner 2:41).

The bad seed are those who are outside the kingdom. The devil is the enemy who sows bad seed. The bad seed follow Satan, i.e., they have the characteristics of the evil one (Jn. 8:44; Acts 13:10; 1 Jn. 3:10; Eph. 2:2-3). They have no part in God's kingdom. For Satan, see comments on 4:1. Jesus described the devil as the evil one and the enemy of God (vv. 38-39). For a time, there is no perceptible difference between those who are in the kingdom and those who are not. Both live in the same world. Why evil is permitted to exist Jesus did not explain. He only says that He will deal with evil on Judgment Day (Bruner 2:41).

Gundry (272) and Bruner (2:27) understand the tares to be false disciples, persons who have professed discipleship but in reality are not. Gundry (279) understands false disciples to be represented by the bad fish (v. 48) as well. However, Jesus said the field is the world. He said nothing to suggest that the field stood for the church, visible or invisible. While it is true enough that hypocrites are not children of the kingdom, this parable is about the co-existence of the righteous and wicked in this world until the judgment, not about unsaved people who try to be part of the visible church without being regenerated. Because this parable is not about the makeup of the visible church, it has nothing to say about church discipline. Church discipline concerns actions regarding those who profess to be saved but whose lives are obviously opposite godliness (e.g., 1 Cor. 5:9-13). See 18:15-20 for church discipline.

"Therefore" identifies the point of the parable: the harvest is the judgment at the end of the age (vv. 39-40; "world" is Greek *aiōn*), when Jesus will send His angels, the reapers, to gather the weeds and burn them (Hagner 33A:392). "Harvest" appears in other Scripture texts representing judgment (v. 30; Jl. 3:13; Rev. 14:14-16; Evans, *Matthew* 277). The angels will gather and burn the darnel (v. 40): namely, those who are not numbered with the righteous. See 25:46 for the duration of their punishment. "This" (v. 40) is not in all Greek manuscripts so some translations do not include it.

Matthew mentions angels and their work several times in His Gospel. Angels are personal beings who sometimes communicate God's messages to mankind (1:20, 24; 2:13, 19) and care for God's children while they live in this world (4:6; cf. Heb. 1:14). They ministered to Jesus after His temptation (4:11) and announced His resurrection to those who first visited the empty tomb (28:2, 5). They minister before God for the benefit of God's children (18:10). They are not a race and do not reproduce (22:30), nor do they know everything God knows (24:36). They will accompany Jesus when He returns to earth (16:27; 25:31). They will be God's agents to separate the righteous from the unrighteous and carry out His judgment at the end times (13:39, 41, 49; 24:31). At Jesus' command they will gather the sinners and cast them into the fiery furnace (13:42), the place of eternal punishment of the wicked (25:41). The fiery furnace imagery may be from Daniel 3:6 (Newman and Stine 447; Archer and Chirichigno 139).

The tares or darnel represent all causes of sin ("all things that offend") as well as all who practice iniquity (v. 41: Greek *anomia*, lawlessness). Because Jesus has all authority in heaven and earth (28:18), He can eradicate sin and all its sources in each realm as well (Carson, *Matthew* 326). The fire will be their painful end (v. 42). They will be gathered like weeds and burned. "Weeping and gnashing of teeth," indicates the hopelessness and pain of this punishment. (See comments on 8:12 for this phrase.) Verses 41 and 42 serve as a warning to those who are not children of Jesus' kingdom. The sons of the wicked one (v. 38) face a painful eternity.

Jesus' (His) kingdom (v. 41) has its broadest sense here and means the world. Even though all have not submitted to His rule, He is still the rightful ruler of this earth. It is from the world that His angels will gather all that causes and all who practice sin.

The wheat, then, are children of the heavenly kingdom. Whereas the children of the devil are gathered for punishment, the righteous will be gathered to share in the glory of the Father's kingdom (vv. 30, 43). The promise that they will shine is reminiscent of Daniel 12:3 and looks forward to the full glory of the resurrected body (1 Cor. 15:43). The glorious body will be like that of Jesus' (17:2; 1 Jn. 3:2; Hagner 33A:394). The believers' glory is part of the "not yet" aspects of the kingdom. See comments on 3:2 for the already-not yet aspects of the kingdom.

Jesus ends His explanation by repeating to His disciples what He had earlier told the crowds (vv. 9, 43): Pay attention. Listen well. Understand. Obey. This is true wisdom (7:24-27). (See the discussion on verse 9 for why some translations say, "He who has ears, let him hear.")

The kingdom has arrived. It will not totally crush the enemy at this time. Considerable time will pass before the enemy will be finally judged in that final judgment (Wilkins 482). In the meantime, the righteous and unrighteous will exist alongside each other in this world. Because of that, to some extent, the professed, visible church will also contain both.

b. The parable of the treasure (13:44)

44 Again, the kingdom of heaven is like unto treasure hid in a field; the which when a man hath found,

he hideth, and for joy thereof goeth and selleth all that he hath, and buyeth that field.

In this parable, Jesus compared the response of one who finds the kingdom to the response of one who unexpectedly finds buried treasure. According to Newman and Stine (448) burying wealth was common in that day (25:25), so Jesus' reference to buried treasure was readily understood by His audience. He may have been speaking only to His disciples at this point (v. 36).

The finder recognized the supreme worth of the treasure and immediately reburied it. He was so filled with joy that he willfully sacrificed everything he had to purchase the field. The finder may well have been a peasant farmer plowing the field (Keener, *Background* 84).

The parable stresses the supreme worth of the kingdom and its hiddenness from the eyes of most. It also teaches urgency, sacrifice (Newman and Stine 448), and wise choices. The parable shows the good fortune of those who discover the message of the kingdom (the hidden message of the parables, v. 35) and the kingdom itself. Mostly this parable teaches the sheer joy of finding something so valuable (Fee and Stuart 160; Bruner 2:47). The supreme value of the treasure justifies the total sacrifice of everything to possess a place in the kingdom (Wilkins 488; Phil. 3:8).

c. The parable of the expensive pearl (13:45-46)

45 Again, the kingdom of heaven is like unto a merchant man, seeking goodly pearls:

46 Who, when he had found one pearl of great price, went and sold all that he had, and bought it.

Like the previous parable this one speaks of the joy of finding the kingdom and its supreme value. Jesus likened the kingdom to a very valuable pearl that a businessman found while searching for good pearls for investment or resale. Most commentators think Jesus was speaking of a wholesaler. Unlike the previous parable, where the farmer (or laborer) happened upon a treasure, this businessman was deliberate in his search.

However, this businessman evidently found more than he expected. He found one pearl that was extremely valuable (Greek *polutimos;* of great value, Louw and Nida I:620; Jn. 12:3). As soon as he found that pearl, the one of highest quality, he, like the man who unexpectedly found the treasure (v. 44), sold everything he had to get it because he realized that the pearl was worth all he possessed (Wilkins 488).

This parable teaches there are people who are actively searching for the right relationship with God (6:33; Acts 8:27-28; 10:1-2). When they find the kingdom, they gladly give all because they recognize its extreme worth. "Selling all" was the condition for possessing, not finding, the treasure (Bruner 2:48). Jesus was not advocating a vow of poverty as the condition of entering the kingdom. He taught that all who find the kingdom willingly and joyfully lay aside everything to possess what they deemed so valuable. See comments on 7:6 where Jesus used pearls to speak of the value of the gospel message of the kingdom.

d. The parable of the net (13:47-50)

47 Again, the kingdom of heaven is like unto a net, that was cast into the sea, and gathered of every kind:
48 Which, when it was full, they drew to shore, and sat down, and gathered the good into vessels, but cast the bad away.
49 So shall it be at the end of the world: the angels shall come forth, and sever the wicked from among the just,
50 And shall cast them into the furnace of fire: there shall be wailing and gnashing of teeth.

Jesus continued privately teaching His disciples (v. 36). As in verse 41, the kingdom in this instance refers to all under Jesus' reign, not just the church (Carson, *Matthew* 330). This is the seventh and final kingdom parable in this chapter.

The previous two parables spoke of the value of the kingdom. This parable of the net speaks of another aspect of the kingdom of heaven: the final judgment and separation of the good from the bad. In this respect, this parable teaches a truth also taught in the parable of the wheat and the tares. At some future date, at the end of the "world" (Greek *aiōn*, "age"), the kingdom will be fully realized. At that time, as fishermen cull out the bad fish from good fish, so angels will divide the wicked from the just and cast the wicked into the fiery furnace. For the fiery furnace, see comments on verse 42. See comments on 8:12 for "wailing and gnashing of teeth."

The disciples understood the imagery since Capernaum was a fishing community (4:18-22) and some of the disciples had been fishermen. Good fish were kept. "Rough" fish, not good for food, were discarded. Devout Jews in obedience to the Mosaic Law culled out fish without fins or scales (Lev. 11:9-12).

The net (Greek *sagēnē*) was a large seine net (Louw and Nida I:55). This type of net hung on floats and was weighted at the bottom. The disciples, especially the fishermen of the group, were familiar with these nets and readily understood the imagery. This net caught all varieties of fish. Once the net was full, men working in boats or on shore dragged the net in and sorted the fish. God's net, here God's call to judgment, will gather every person and the angels will divide them into two groups (Wilkins 489), those who followed Jesus and those did not.

Not all interpreters agree with this understanding. Hendriksen (578) views the net as the gospel that catches men (Lk. 5:10), some of whom are not saved even though they have made a profession. Hagner (*33A*:399) says the bad fish are false disciples which means this parable is about good and evil in the kingdom. Barclay (2:104) believes the net is the visible church. According to Carson (*Matthew* 331; v. 49), this parable is a picture of the state of the kingdom at the time of the judgment. These interpreters have an understanding of the wicked in this parable that is too narrow (v. 49). The wicked are not only those who make false professions of faith in Christ but all who are not true believers, regardless of their professed association with the visible church. When it comes to eternal salvation, Scripture knows only two groups of people: the saved and the lost. The parable of the wheat and the tares teaches the same truth as this one. The final consummation of the kingdom will include a judgment where there will be a final separation of the wicked from the just. For angels, see comments on verses 39 and 41.

Jesus' point is evangelistic. With this parable, He urged His hearers to tell others to follow Him into His kingdom. Otherwise, they will experience eternal, hopeless, and horrible punishment. For verse 50, see comments on verse 42 and 8:12.

e. The parable of the homeowner (13:51-52)

51 Jesus saith unto them, Have ye understood all these things? They say unto him, Yea, Lord.
52 Then said he unto them, Therefore every scribe *which is* instructed unto the kingdom of heaven is like unto a man *that is* an householder, which bringeth forth out of his treasure *things* new and old.

With these words and the final parable in this section, Matthew brought the kingdom discourse to a close. These two verses are unique to Matthew. The words translated "Jesus saith to them" are not in all Greek manuscripts. For this reason, some translations do not include them. The meaning of the text is unaffected either way.

"Them" is possibly only the Twelve (though see comments on v. 18), since they went into the house (v. 36). Jesus wanted the Twelve to understand fully the parables (vv. 14, 19, 23). They assured Him they did. Their understanding demonstrated that the disciples were good soil (v. 23) and were not part of the group who would be judged as prophesied by Isaiah (vv. 14-15; Evans, *Matthew* 283). Because they understood ("therefore," v. 52; Greek *dia touto*), Jesus gave the following conclusion to the previous parables. Jesus compared His followers to a discipled scribe. This scribe was not a listener only. He listened, accepted, and understood Jesus' kingdom teachings and joined His ranks. Because he has been instructed or discipled, he is now ready to share what he knows with others. Some knowledge will be from previous learning. Some knowledge will be from more recent kingdom instruction. In the phrase "being instructed unto the kingdom" (v. 52), the "unto" probably has the idea of "for."

Scribes were skilled writers. In O.T. times, because of this skill, scribes could rise to powerful political positions (1 Kg. 4:3; 2 Kg. 18:18; 25:19; Evans and Porter 1086). They could be professional secretaries (2 Kg. 12:10; Jer. 36:4, 18, 32) and in some instances become scholars (Ezra 7:6). Because all copies were done by hand, a scribe filled an essential role in the pre-printing press community.

In N.T. times, scribes studied the Scriptures in order to understand and teach them. Here Jesus commends those who labor to understand Scripture and then pass that understanding on to others (Bruner 2:54). Not all scribes were bad (23:1, 13, 15, 23, 25, 27, 29). At least one approached Jesus to join His ranks (8:19) and perhaps others did as well (Mk. 12:28-34). Jesus later promised that He would use scribes in His kingdom work as well (23:34).

Like a householder, the scribe who is in the kingdom now has a treasure chest from which he takes out old and new treasures. Householder (Greek *oikodespotēs*) can refer to either the owner or the manager of the house. In the parable of the wheat and the tares, it referred to Jesus, the owner (vv. 27, 37; BAGD 558). Treasure (Greek *thēsauros*) can refer to the place where treasures are kept or to the treasure itself. Apparently, Jesus had the first in mind (treasure box, storeroom, storehouse; BAGD 361) since the scribe brought out multiple items.

The kingdom scribe possessed some truths of the kingdom of heaven from the O.T. and after hearing and believing the message of Jesus, he possessed more. All knowledge from his pre-kingdom past was not discarded. Rather, it remained useful and necessary information. See 5:17-48. With this, Jesus taught there is linkage between the Old and New Testaments. The trained kingdom scribe is able to understand the mysteries of the kingdom (v. 11) and "is able to maintain a balance between the continuity and the discontinuity existing between the era inaugurated by Jesus and that of the past" (Hagner 33A:402).

Jesus spoke of His disciples as being now "knowledgeable scribe[s]" (Gundry 280). His disciples were enlightened to new truth by the parables. They were now kingdom savvy and they were responsible to bring out for others the kingdom truths Jesus had taught them (Wilkins 490). Peter's sermon on Pentecost (Acts 2) illustrates how Jesus' disciples were able to bring out both old and new treasures. They had been discipled by the Master Teacher and they were equipped to pass that knowledge on to others.

"Instructed" (Greek *mathēteuō*) is the same word translated "teach" or "make disciples" in 28:19. Jesus spoke of the scribe as having been trained by another, assuming another who was already in the kingdom. What Jesus after His resurrection told His disciples to do—make disciples—He and His disciples were doing at this time also. They were making disciples of the kingdom. Joseph of Arimathea (27:57) and Apollos (Acts 18:24-26) are examples of devout Jews who had been taught to believe in Christ. Apollos is an example of one who brought out of his treasure box things old and new. See further discussion of this concept in 27:57 and in 28:19.

Summary (13:1-52)

Following Jesus' confrontation with the Pharisees (12:24) and His statement that He had closer affiliation with His followers than His own earthly family (12:46-51), Jesus went outside Capernaum to a spot next to the Sea of Galilee (13:1). There, using only parables, He taught great truths about His kingdom. Matthew recorded seven of those kingdom parables. The eighth parable (vv. 51-52) is not a kingdom parable *per se* but an application of Jesus' teaching specifically for the disciples, first for the Twelve and then for all who would follow.

Jesus explained that He used parables to both reveal and conceal truth. For all who want to understand and accept His teachings, the parables reveal truths hidden since creation (vv. 10-17, 34-35). For all who reject His teachings, He removes any previous understanding they had.

Application: Teaching and Preaching the Passage

These kingdom parables are a primary resource for sermonic and lesson materials. One might give a lesson or sermon as an overview of all seven kingdom parables in a single setting (as Jesus originally gave them) emphasizing the main point or points of each. (1) Entrance into the kingdom requires acceptance of the gospel and is a personal choice (vv. 1-9; 18-23). (2) The present stage of the kingdom will coexist alongside the kingdom of the evil one (vv. 24-30). (3) Kingdom growth in the present age will be phenomenal (vv. 31-32). (4) The kingdom will almost imperceptibly spread into the entire world (v. 33). (5) The kingdom is worth more than all of this world's goods one might possess (two parables; vv. 44-46). (6) The Lord will punish the wicked in the end (vv. 47-50).

The parable of the sower (vv. 1-9, 18-23) might be considered under the heading "Four Types of Hearers." (1) Those who turn a deaf ear, i.e., totally reject the gospel message. (2) Those who are shallow, i.e., they outwardly receive the message but permit no real penetration of the word into the depths of their inner beings. (3) Those who receive the message initially but do not subject the cares of this world and its wealth to the demands of the gospel. (4) Those who totally receive the gospel message and permit it to complete its work in their lives. Essentially, the same thought could be developed as responses to any gospel message: (1) rejection; (2) shallow reception; (3) acceptance without denial; and (4) full acceptance.

One might consider the purpose of parables: (1) to reveal (vv. 10-12, 34-35); and (2) to conceal (vv. 12-15).

The parable of the wheat and the tares (vv. 24-30; 36-43) might be treated under the heading "The Existence of Good and Evil." (1) The present coexistence of saint and sinner; (2) the future separation of saint and sinner; and (3) the future reward of saint and sinner.

The growth of the kingdom might be developed topically as the kingdom's growth in size (vv. 31-32) and the kingdom's growth in influence (v. 33).

The parables of the hidden treasure and the pearl of great price (vv. 44-45) could be considered as "The Kingdom Search": (1) some find the kingdom accidently; (2) some find the kingdom after extensive searching; and (3) all who find the kingdom and recognize its supreme worth readily give all they have to possess it.

There are four timeless truths in the parable of the fishing net (vv. 47-50): (1) God's judgment will include everyone (vv. 47-48); (2) God's judgment will mean separation (vv. 48-49); (3) God's judgment will mean punishment for the wicked (v. 49), and (4) the wicked will be discarded and detained where there will be extreme pain (v. 50).

The two roles of kingdom scribes are presented in verses 51 and 52. (1) The kingdom scribe was himself a student and (2) is now responsible to disciple others. This might be a good devotional passage for a teachers' meeting: (1) having been trained for the kingdom, (2) now be a trainer of others.

This chapter also contains several topics of interest to the believer that can be treated individually. For example, the final judgment as Jesus taught it in these seven kingdom parables is sure (vv. 40,

49), is about separation (vv. 30, 41, 49), ends in one of only two possible destinies for everyone (punishment with fire for the wicked, vv. 30, 41-42, 50; reward for the righteous, vv. 30, 43), and will take place at the end of this age (v. 40).

One might present a lesson or sermon on the kingdom and each individual as Jesus emphasized them in these parables. (1) This world is part of the larger kingdom over which the Lord Jesus reigns (vv. 24, 27, 37-38). (2) Satan, Jesus' enemy, is working subtly yet aggressively to prevent a good harvest of souls (vv. 25, 38-39). (3) At the end of the age, Jesus will destroy Satan, his work, and all who follow him (vv. 40-42). (4) The sons of the kingdom will experience the fullest glory of the heavenly kingdom at the end of the age (v. 43). (5) With the gospel message, Jesus gives each person the opportunity to choose which kingdom to join (v. 43).

Finally, one might compare the Jews who heard and rejected the gospel (Mt. 13:14-15; Acts 28:25-27) with the Gentiles who heard and accepted it (Rom. 15:21; Is. 52:15).

I. The Royal Messiah Continued His Itinerate Ministry (13:53—15:20)

Following the day of kingdom parables, Jesus left Capernaum and began traveling through Galilee again. This portion of His itinerary took Him back to the area of His childhood and early adulthood. Perhaps He returned home to visit His family, a possibility in light of 12:46-50 (Wilkins 509).

1. Jesus left Capernaum (13:53)

53 And it came to pass, *that* when Jesus had finished these parables, he departed thence.

Verse 53 brings the kingdom parables to an end and marks the end of Matthew's third major block of teaching materials (cf. 7:28; 11:1). This verse also introduces the next section. The following verses document Jesus' continuing ministry in the midst of increasing resistance against Himself and His message.

2. Jesus taught in His home town of Nazareth (13:54-58)

54 And when he was come into his own country, he taught them in their synagogue, insomuch that they were astonished, and said, Whence hath this *man* this wisdom, and *these* mighty works?
55 Is not this the carpenter's son? is not his mother called Mary? and his brethren, James, and Joses, and Simon, and Judas?
56 And his sisters, are they not all with us? Whence then hath this *man* all these things?
57 And they were offended in him. But Jesus said unto them, A prophet is not without honour, save in his own country, and in his own house.
58 And he did not many mighty works there because of their unbelief.

One assumes Nazareth (2:23) was Jesus' home, but neither Gospel gives the name. Country (v. 54; Greek *patris*) can mean hometown (ESV) or homeland (BAGD 637). On a Sabbath day (Mk. 6:2) He was teaching (Greek imperfect) them and did some miracles (Greek *dunamis*) in their synagogue (Mt. 13:54). Their reaction at first was surprise. They knew him. He had lived there most of His life. His teaching ability, and probably the subject matter as well (Evans, *Matthew* 284), caught them by surprise (cf. 7:28; Lk. 4:24; Is. 50:4). They knew Jesus had not formally studied under recognized rabbis. How did He know so much about the kingdom? What right did He have to preach the arrival of the kingdom of heaven or call them to repentance?

His healing miracles also surprised them (Mk. 6:5). They wondered how He was able to perform miracles. Compare this with the Pharisees' doubts and comments in 12:24. They too questioned the source of His power (Osborne 550).

If Luke 4:16-30 is Luke's record of the same visit to Nazareth, then we know that Isaiah 61:1-2 was His text. Perhaps Jesus visited Nazareth multiple times, the first being the one recorded in Luke 4:16-30 and this one—recorded by Matthew and Mark (6:1-6)—a later visit (Wilkins 508-509). In all three accounts the residents apparently first appreciated Him and His message but then turned on Him—in part when He refused to do major miracles (Lk. 4:22-27). Jesus' visit in Matthew and Mark ended in rejection because they did not believe in Him. The visit in Luke ended with their trying to kill Him (Lk. 4:28-29) because He stated that God does not always send His favors to Israelites. Sometimes Gentiles receive greater blessings than Israelites.

The question in verse 54 (Mt. 13) supports the understanding that Jesus did no miracles while He lived in Nazareth. All they had ever seen Him do was carpentry work. Mark (6:3) speaks of Jesus as a carpenter. Matthew (v. 55) speaks of Jesus as the carpenter's son.

Joseph, Jesus' legal father (1:25), was a carpenter. Assuming Jesus learned His father's trade, He worked in that trade until His baptism. If Joseph was dead by the time Jesus began His ministry, Jesus may have carried on the family business for a while, which is why they knew Him as "the carpenter."

It is possible that carpenters in Nazareth were primarily stonemasons, since wood was scarce in that area (Newman and Stine 458). Campbell (510-519) argues that evidence from that time period strongly favors understanding that Joseph and Jesus worked with stone more than wood in their construction work. Evans (*Matthew* 284) understands "carpenter" (Greek *tektōn*) to denote a woodworker.

The men in attendance also knew Jesus' mother, Mary, and they knew His biological brothers and sisters (vv. 55-56). Joses is the Galilean pronunciation of the Hebrew Joseph (Metzger (34). Mary and Joseph had named one of their sons after his father.

Jesus was part of a large family, at least four brothers and possibly as many sisters—or more, as "all" of His sisters may suggest. This reference to Jesus' biological siblings teaches against the doctrine of Mary's perpetual virginity. See comments on 1:25 and 12:46. Clearly, Joseph and Mary had children of their own after Jesus was born.

Nazareth knew Jesus well, or so they thought, and He had given no indication while He lived in Nazareth that He was someone special. In fact, His humanity was so dominant that the people of Nazareth were unable to see His glory.

They were offended by Him, apparently because they knew too much about Him. They had seen no evidence of divine power the years He lived among them. Though the text does not say, they might have reached the same conclusion as the Pharisees; His powers were Satanic (Osborne 551). They asked where he obtained the power to do mighty works.

Jesus responded to their rejection with a proverbial saying that means much the same as "over familiarity breeds contempt" (v. 57). This saying is repeated in John 4:44, but there it evidently refers to His rejection by the whole of Galilee (Carson, *John* 236). Even though those who knew Him best as brother, neighbor, friend, or business acquaintance in Nazareth rejected Him, still Jesus claimed to be a prophet. As such, He deserved their honor (Hendriksen 582).

Not only did the general population of Nazareth reject Him so did His siblings ("in his own house"). They did not believe in Him until after His resurrection. Luke mentioned that His mother and brothers were in the upper room as part of the one hundred and twenty (Acts 1:14). Jesus appeared to James (1 Cor. 15:7), who eventually became a key leader in the Jerusalem church (Acts 15:13; 21:18; Gal. 1:19; 2:9, 12) and authored the N.T. book that bears his name (Jas. 1:1). Jude (Judas), who identified himself as James' brother (Jude 1), also later wrote a short letter that bears his name. Nothing specific is known of the other brothers or sisters. One might suspect that given their stage in life as young adults, the sisters might have had family responsibilities that kept them from being in Jerusalem with the others on Pentecost.

Unbelief was the problem (v. 58) in Nazareth and this unbelief was their own choosing (Mk. 6:6). According to Mark, Jesus marveled at the unbelief of His family and acquaintances even as He had marveled at the faith of the centurion (Mt. 8:10). The result of such unbelief was few healings and no recorded kingdom conversions. Unbelief kept Him from helping the needy. Unbelief also kept His family and acquaintances from gaining understanding of His message and joining His kingdom (vv. 13-15). What sad days! Those who had the greatest light will receive the harshest judgment (11:20-24).

Summary (13:54-58)

Matthew wrote of various people and groups who rejected God's message to them. Isaiah saw it in his day (Isaiah 6:9-10; Mt. 13:14-15) and Jesus saw it in His. The Pharisees rejected Jesus' teaching (12:22-42), as did some in the crowds who listened to Jesus preach (13:11-15). Even Jesus' family and friends in His own hometown of Nazareth would not accept Him as a legitimate messenger of God. Like the Pharisees, the Nazarenes wondered where Jesus' power originated and what gave Him the right to speak so authoritatively about the kingdom. In short, they did not believe Him, which led to further misunderstanding and rejection.

Application: Teaching and Preaching the Passage

This passage illustrates the tragedy of unbelief. The teacher or preacher might explain that unbelief blinds the unbeliever to Jesus' person and power (vv.

53-57) and stops the work of God (v. 58).

3. The death of John the Baptist (14:1-12)

1 At that time Herod the tetrarch heard of the fame of Jesus,
2 And said unto his servants, This is John the Baptist; he is risen from the dead; and therefore mighty works do shew forth themselves in him.
3 For Herod had laid hold on John, and bound him, and put *him* in prison for Herodias' sake, his brother Philip's wife.
4 For John said unto him, It is not lawful for thee to have her.
5 And when he would have put him to death, he feared the multitude, because they counted him as a prophet.
6 But when Herod's birthday was kept, the daughter of Herodias danced before them, and pleased Herod.
7 Whereupon he promised with an oath to give her whatsoever she would ask.
8 And she, being before instructed of her mother, said, Give me here John Baptist's head in a charger.
9 And the king was sorry: nevertheless for the oath's sake, and them which sat with him at meat, he commanded *it* to be given *her*.
10 And he sent, and beheaded John in the prison.
11 And his head was brought in a charger, and given to the damsel: and she brought *it* to her mother.
12 And his disciples came, and took up the body, and buried it, and went and told Jesus.

"At that time" is indefinite, as is the time lapse between verses 2 and 3. In verse 3, Matthew went back in time to tell the story of John's death. He inserted the record here to provide the reader with needed information about John's death while at the same time keeping his story about Jesus intact. This is a literary practice called flashback (Newman and Stine 462).

Herod heard about Jesus' and the Twelve's (Mk. 6:12-14) ministries and miracles and Jesus' growing fame. These reports disturbed Herod because he had already had some contact with another holy man, John the Baptist, and though John was dead, Herod could still hear his voice. How Herod heard about Jesus is uncertain, though it may have been through his household manager Chuza (Lk. 8:3; Carson, *Matthew* 337). Jesus had healed Joanna, Chuza's wife, and she along with other women followed Jesus and supported Him financially. She would have had firsthand knowledge of Jesus' miracles.

This Herod was Herod Antipas, a son of King Herod the Great (2:1). Among his siblings were a full brother Archelaus and three half-brothers, Aristobulus and two named Philip (2:22; ISBE II:693-694). Herodias, the daughter of Aristobulus, married one Philip (Mt. 14:3) and their daughter, Salome, married the other Philip, Philip the Tetrarch (Lk. 3:1). Herod Antipas divorced his first wife and Herodias divorced Philip in order to marry each other (A.D. 27). Thus, both husbands of Herodias were her uncles. John the Baptist publicly denounced this marriage and made these two his enemies.

Antipas is identified as a tetrarch in verse 1, which originally meant "ruler of a fourth part" (ISBE IV:798). In N.T. times, however, the term was "used more loosely of rulers with status less than that of a king." Matthew referred to Herod as "king" in verse 9, a loose description since he was never officially given that title by Rome.

Jesus had very little respect for Herod Antipas and no fear. He would not run from Herod because He still had ministry to complete (Lk. 13:31-32). Jesus called Herod a "fox" and refused to be intimidated by his sly, nocturnal ways. At His own trial Jesus refused even to speak to Herod when Herod questioned Him. Herod and his soldiers shamefully treated Jesus (Lk. 23:11). Antipas and Herodias were the N.T. counterparts of the O.T. Ahab and Jezebel (1 Kg. 18:17—19:1).

Jesus' ministry reminded Herod of John the Baptist's (v. 2), although there is no evidence that John ever performed miracles (Jn. 10:41). John's had been a powerful ministry, and because of that Herod and others were convinced (16:14) that Jesus was John resurrected and come back more powerful than before. He wanted to see Jesus (Lk. 9:9) to learn more about Him and to get Him to perform some miracle for him (Lk. 23:8-9). Herod was, of course, wrong on both conclusions. John had not arisen and Jesus was not John.

John had preached against many evils Herod had committed (Lk. 3:19-20). That Matthew used the word "said" (v. 4) may mean that John said this on more than one occasion (taking the Greek imperfect to be iterative) that Herod and Herodias' relationship was sin (Ex. 20:14, 17; Lev. 18:16; 20:21). By Mosaic Law standards, they were guilty of adultery and incest because Herodias was Antipas' sister-in-law—and there were no Levirate marriage provisions in this instance (Keener, *Matthew* 401). According to Newman and Stine (465; also Hill 244), Herod Antipas claimed to be a loyal Jew. This gave John the right to appeal to the Mosaic Law to condemn Herod's sinful lifestyle. Jesus also taught that such relationships were sin.

Herod and Herodias had agreed to divorce their spouses to marry each other. John dared to defend the sanctity of marriage (Bruner 2:63) and denounced this relationship as sin. The only way their marriage might have been approved was if Herodias' first husband had died without a male heir (Dt. 25:5-6; see Mt. 22:24 and comments).

Neither Herod nor Herodias accepted John's condemnation of their sinful lifestyle. Herod added to his sins the arrest and imprisonment of John (Lk. 3:20) for Herodias' sake, but he seems to have had mixed feelings about John himself. He wanted to silence John permanently (v. 5), and yet he wanted to hear him as well. He gave John opportunity to speak even while he had John in prison (Mk. 6:20).

Matthew records that Herod was afraid to kill John because of the people. They had great respect for John (3:5-6). The general population considered John a prophet, even as they did Jesus (16:14). Herod had enough political savvy to know that killing John could have enormous political fallout if the people turned against him. Josephus reports that Herod was motivated by political fears when he arrested John, afraid John had such influence that he could turn the people against him (Maier, 271-272). With John preaching to large crowds and publically denouncing Herod's sins, Herod may have been losing favor with the people. This could have been another reason Antipas decided to stop John. He also feared John because he knew John was "a righteous and holy man" (Mk. 6:19-20). Because of this fear and knowledge of John's holiness, not only would Herod not kill John, he would not permit Herodias to kill him either. John apparently languished in prison for some time, perhaps as much as a year or more (4:12; 9:14; 11:2; Wilkins 510).

During Herod's birthday celebrations (v. 6; perhaps not exactly on his birthday), his step-daughter danced for him, his officials, and his politically influential guests (Mk. 6:22; Newman and Stine 466). Herod so enjoyed her dance that he swore to give her whatever she asked (v. 7), up to half his kingdom (Mk. 6:23). Matthew does not describe the dance. "Pleased" (Greek *areskō*) means only that Herod enjoyed her dance. Though her dance may have been sexually provocative, the word does not necessarily infer that (*contra* MacArthur 421).

Hill (244; also Newman and Stine 469) suggests that Herodias' daughter was probably at least in her upper teens at this time, but Hagner (33B:412) thinks she was no more than twelve. So angry and filled with hate for John was Herodias that when presented with such an opportunity she coached her daughter to request John's head on a charger or platter (v. 8). She chose her sin over repentance and forgiveness.

Her request evidently caught Herod by surprise. No doubt, he thought she would ask for something for herself. Herodias has outfoxed the fox. In spite of his distress and grief (v. 9), because he had taken an oath and because of the witnesses present, Herod ordered that John be killed and his head given on a platter to the girl. It was done, and this adolescent girl carried John's head to her mother (v. 11). Such proofs of death were not unheard of (2 Kg. 10:6-9; 1 Sam. 17:54; Keener, *Matthew* 402). Such was this family: adulterers, murderers, and cold-blooded killers.

Herod ended John's earthly life but not before John accomplished his God-given assignment (11:10-11; Lk. 1:16-17). Born a miracle baby (Lk. 1:13), he died a martyr. What Herod and Herodias viewed as antagonistic was more properly a merciful warning from God. John's message should have brought conviction and repentance. Rather it brought rejection, a hardened heart, and revenge on the messenger.

John's disciples cared for his body by giving it a proper burial, probably without the head (Evans, *Matthew,* 296). Then they told Jesus of John's death. John's arrest months earlier triggered Jesus' relocation from Judea to Capernaum in Galilee (4:12-17). John's death was another marker pointing to Jesus' own impending death (Keener, *Matthew* 401). "They did to him whatever they pleased" (17:12), and they would do the same to the Son of Man.

4. The feeding of over five thousand (14:13-21)

Mark (6:30-31) wrote that the Twelve returned from their preaching trip (cf. 10:1-15; Mk. 6:7-13) at this time and because of the busyness of ministry Jesus decided to take the Twelve somewhere private where they could rest.

Instead, the crowds followed them and Jesus and the Twelve spent another busy day in ministry.

13 When Jesus heard *of it*, he departed thence by ship into a desert place apart: and when the people had heard *thereof*, they followed him on foot out of the cities.
14 And Jesus went forth, and saw a great multitude, and was moved with compassion toward them, and he healed their sick.
15 And when it was evening, his disciples came to him, saying, This is a desert place, and the time is now past; send the multitude away, that they may go into the villages, and buy themselves victuals.
16 But Jesus said unto them, They need not depart; give ye them to eat.
17 And they say unto him, We have here but five loaves, and two fishes.
18 He said, Bring them hither to me.
19 And he commanded the multitude to sit down on the grass, and took the five loaves, and the two fishes, and looking up to heaven, he blessed, and brake, and gave the loaves to *his* disciples, and the disciples to the multitude.
20 And they did all eat, and were filled: and they took up of the fragments that remained twelve baskets full.
21 And they that had eaten were about five thousand men, beside women and children.

Verses 3-12 were parenthetical. Verse 13 resumes where verse 2 left off (Carson, *Matthew* 340). When Jesus heard that His and His disciples' ministries and miracles had roused the attention of Antipas, He left the area.

Taking a boat (v. 13; see comments on 8:23), Jesus tried to escape the crowds, but the people sought Him out. His popularity was at its peak at this time (v. 1) and the people—guessing His destination—traveled ahead of Him on foot (Mk. 6:33, ran) to be with Him. A normal day's journey for someone traveling light would have been somewhere around twenty-five or thirty miles (40 – 48 km.; ISBE I:897). If one assumes Jesus left Capernaum and traveled by boat directly to Bethsaida (Lk. 9:10), some folks would have been walking (or running) for only an hour or two—depending on their starting point and how far from the city of Bethsaida He landed. Others might have traveled a half day or more. See verse 15, which suggests that this wilderness (Greek *erēmos*, desolate; BAGD 309) place was a considerable distance from the people's homes. Traveling difficulties would have been compounded by the need to transport the sick.

Jesus' desire to be alone took Him to a desolate area. Luke 9:10 says He went to the city of Bethsaida. Luke and Matthew mean that Jesus went to a desolate area in the vicinity of Bethsaida, a city on the northeastern shore of the Sea of Galilee. However, the people went on foot ahead of Him and were waiting for Him when He stepped from the boat. That He "went forth" means he disembarked from the boat; he went ashore. Gundry (291) says He was coming out of His place of privacy.

When He stepped out of the boat, He saw a great crowd, numbering in the thousands (v. 21). Their needs touched

Jesus' heart and He had compassion on them (v. 14). He healed their sick and spoke to them of the kingdom of God (Lk. 9:11). As the day neared its end (literally, the hour [to eat?] had already passed), the disciples strongly implored Jesus to send the people away so they could go into the nearby villages and buy "victuals": that is, food (v. 15).

Jesus healed the sick and the multitudes heard the gospel (Lk. 9:11). It had been a good day of ministry, but the people still needed to eat. Jesus told the disciples to feed the crowds (v. 16). They responded that the cost for such an undertaking would be prohibitive (Mk. 6:37; Jn. 6:7). The only food they knew about in that lonely place (Lk. 9:12) were five loaves and two fish (Mt. 14:17), one lad's meal (Jn. 6:9). (Some mother is to be commended for her foresight.) Andrew told Jesus about the boy's lunch and asked, "What are they among so many?" (Jn. 6:8-9). The disciples' response shows they had no means of feeding the crowd. Apparently, they had no food for themselves either (Wilkins 514), and there was no cash or food reserve in their group to cover this. Besides, the logistics of purchasing, transporting, and serving such a crowd would have been enormous.

The loaf (Greek *artos*) was a small, generally round loaf of bread. Louw and Nida (I:50) suggest in size the loaf was more like present day rolls or buns. Fish was normally preserved in salt for the market (ISBE II:309). These fish, however, were probably smoked or pickled (Newman and Stine 475).

Jesus told the disciples to bring Him the loaves and fish (v. 18) and to make the crowds sit down (Greek *anaklinō*, recline to eat) in groups of fifty (Lk. 9:14; Jn. 6:10) on the grass. Mark 6:39 adds that the grass was green: it was spring (Jn. 6:4). Jesus blessed the food and began breaking the bread and the fish (Lk. 9:16) and gave the pieces to His disciples to give to the people. In this manner, they were able to do as Jesus had initially instructed them (vv. 16, 19; Nolland 594). They distributed bread and fish (Mk. 6:41) until all had eaten as much as they wanted (Jn. 6:11).

Jesus did not make a large batch of food to feed the crowd. He just kept distributing pieces of bread and fish until no one wanted any more. The miracle was open and undeniable. The Twelve and the multitude witnessed this miracle as it was happening over the extended time it took to break enough bread and fish to feed and serve these thousands of people. In other words, it was not an instantaneous miracle but one that kept happening, like the oil in 2 Kings 4:5-6. It must have made a deep impression on the Twelve. It is the only miracle recorded in all four Gospels (Mk. 6:30-44; Lk. 9:10-17; Jn. 6:1-14). Compare this miracle with the one recorded in 2 Kings 4:42-44.

Some commentators (Gundry 292; Nolland 592) point to the words common to this miracle and the Lord's Supper: He took the bread, blessed it, broke it, and gave it to His disciples. Matthew (26:26) describes the initiation of the Lord's Supper with the same words and sequence. However, the same sequence was part of ordinary Jewish meals (Acts 27:35; Hagner 33B:418). In the final analysis, Jesus' own comments in John 6:27-59 tell what this miracle was about. It was to encourage faith in Him as the one and only one who gives eternal life. He is the Bread that gives and sustains life.

Following the meal, Jesus instructed His disciples to gather the fragments (v. 20; Jn. 6:12), and they gathered twelve baskets full of leftover broken pieces. Every piece was broken. Every piece had been miraculously provided.

The exact size and construction of the baskets (Greek *kophinos*) are unknown (Louw and Nida I:71), as is the significance of the number of baskets. Perhaps each of the Twelve apostles stood before Jesus with a full basket in hand as a lesson of Jesus' ability to provide for more than mere needs. In response, they should recognize their responsibility to rely on Jesus for life's needs (6:11, 25-34; 16:8-11). They should also recognize that Jesus' abundant provisions are no license to waste (Keener, *Matthew* 405). Neither writer tells what happened to the extra food.

Jesus miraculously fed about five thousand men, plus perhaps a few thousand more women and children (v. 21). He blessed and multiplied a boy's personal provisions to the degree that all were fed and satisfied. He made more than enough food to feed this crowd. Neither His power nor His provision was limited. He created at will. He fed both genders. He provided for all ages.

Barclay (2:120-121) suggests that perhaps Jesus did not multiply the loaves and fish. He suggests rather that the people had food but did not want to tell anyone lest they have to share it. They were selfish. He further suggests that when Jesus began sharing with His disciples the loaves and fish, the people seeing His example did the same and there was more than enough food for everyone. Hagner (33B:416) rightly calls explanations such as this "implausible naturalistic explanations," that "are far from the intention of the evangelists and out of line with the Gospel narratives."

John (6:14-15) recorded that the crowd understood what had just happened to be a miracle and quickly recognized some implications of this sign. They identified Jesus as the Prophet who was to come (Dt. 18:15-18) and began discussing making Him king. Jesus did not allow them to make Him king but rather sent them away. The day following this miracle, these same people came looking for Jesus again, only to realize He had left the area. When they found Him in Capernaum and began to question how He got there (Jn. 6:25), He told them that they were not seeking Him because of the signs—and by inference the implications of the signs—but because He provided them with a free meal. This led into the bread of life discourse (Jn. 6:27-59). This miracle was more about Jesus, the Bread of Life, than about feeding hungry men, women, and children. Jesus was not going to feed them with the miracle bread every day, as their ancestors had experienced in the wilderness for forty years. Instead, He wanted to give them bread that would give and sustain life forever. Matthew did not record any of John's observations about this miracle.

5. Jesus walked on water and enabled Peter to do the same (14:22-33)

22 And straightway Jesus constrained his disciples to get into a ship, and to go before him unto the other side, while he sent the multitudes away.
23 And when he had sent the multitudes away, he went up into a

mountain apart to pray: and when the evening was come, he was there alone.
24 But the ship was now in the midst of the sea, tossed with waves: for the wind was contrary.
25 And in the fourth watch of the night Jesus went unto them, walking on the sea.
26 And when the disciples saw him walking on the sea, they were troubled, saying, It is a spirit; and they cried out for fear.
27 But straightway Jesus spake unto them, saying, Be of good cheer; it is I; be not afraid.
28 And Peter answered him and said, Lord, if it be thou, bid me come unto thee on the water.
29 And he said, Come. And when Peter was come down out of the ship, he walked on the water, to go to Jesus.
30 But when he saw the wind boisterous, he was afraid; and beginning to sink, he cried, saying, Lord, save me.
31 And immediately Jesus stretched forth *his* hand, and caught him, and said unto him, O thou of little faith, wherefore didst thou doubt?
32 And when they were come into the ship, the wind ceased.
33 Then they that were in the ship came and worshipped him, saying, Of a truth thou art the Son of God.

After the feeding of the five thousand, Jesus directed His disciples to proceed by boat to the western side of the lake toward Gennesaret (v. 22) while He sent the crowds away. According to Matthew, Jesus wanted His disciples to go before Him to the other side of the lake. His walk across the lake that night was no spur-of-the-moment decision. He then went up into the mountain to pray (v. 23).

Jesus taught about prayer in the Sermon on the Mount (6:5-13) and had instructed His disciples to pray for additional laborers (9:38). However, this is the first time Matthew recorded a prayer of Jesus Himself. The only other such prayer was in the Garden of Gethsemane (26:39, 42, 44). Mark (1:35) and Luke (6:12; 9:28-29; 22:32, 44-45), however, spoke of other occasions when Jesus prayed, which suggests that the disciples would not have viewed Jesus' desire for private prayer as unusual.

While Jesus prayed, the disciples rowed. "But ... now" (v. 24) is literally "but ... already." By the time Jesus sent the crowds away and went up into the mountain to pray, these experienced fishermen had already traveled a considerable distance.

Instead of "in the midst of the sea" (v. 24), some manuscripts read "many *stadia*," with each *stadion* being more than 600 feet. The meaning is the same, regardless: they were a considerable distance from land. John 6:19 is even more specific, saying they had rowed "twenty-five or thirty furlongs," which is three or four miles (five or six and a half km.). They were just over halfway to Gennesaret. (See the discussion about boats on 8:23.)

Sometime in the night a strong wind arose (Jn. 6:18). The boat was tossed about by the waves. "Tossed" (Greek *basanizō*) is the same word used to describe the distress of the centurion's servant in 8:6. The disciples were in rough water and were rowing (Jn. 6:19) with great difficulty (Mk. 6:48) as they struggled against a headwind.

Jesus was able to see them and their difficulty from His vantage point up on the mountain (Mk. 6:48). Sometime between three and six a.m. (v. 25: the fourth watch of the night; Keener, *Background* 86), He walked to them on the rough water against the headwind. Mark 6:48 says Jesus intended to walk on by the boat.

Apparently the disciples saw Jesus walking *across* (v. 25, Greek *epi* with the accusative) and *on* (v. 26, Greek *epi* with the genitive) the water but did not recognize Him. They thought He was a ghost (v. 26) and cried out in fear. Jesus immediately spoke both to calm their fears by identifying Himself (v. 27: literally, "I am," = "It is I") and to end their fears. To the Christian reader, the "I AM" (Ex. 3:14) overtones are clear (Hagner 33B:423).

Peter responded with a surprising answer: literally, "If you are" = "If it is you," a condition assumed true (Greek first class condition). He believed Jesus was walking on the water and he believed Jesus could enable him to do the same. For these reasons, he asked that Jesus "bid" (v. 28; Greek *keleuō*, command, order; Grimm's 343) him to get out of the boat and join Him on the water's surface. In other words, Peter made his request because he believed, based on Jesus' self-identification that he was looking at Jesus walking on the water's surface.

Only Matthew recorded this part of the miracle with Peter. In answer to Peter's request, Jesus obliged and commanded him, "Come." Peter stepped out of the boat that was still in the deep, dark waters of the lake and walked upon the water's turbulent surface to Jesus. Only the other disciples were privy to this miracle and the reader can be sure they were in awe at what they were witnessing.

All of this happened while the strong winds continued. Peter was so focused on Jesus that he apparently temporarily forgot about the wind and waves. When Peter once again became aware of his surroundings, that he was standing on the water's surface in the middle of a storm (v. 30), he began to doubt Jesus' ability to keep him on the surface (Carson, *Matthew* 344), and he began to sink. He cried out (Greek *krazō*), "Lord, save me." Compare 8:25 and comments. One may imagine that the other disciples felt fear as they witnessed Peter's sudden drop. Peter was a strong swimmer (Jn. 21:7), but he was having difficulty keeping his head above water. In fact, Matthew's word for sink (Greek *katapontizō*) can mean to sink, be submerged, or to drown (18:6; Louw and Nida I:197; Grimm's 335). Peter was powerless against such winds and waves, and he knew that body of water well. The Sea of Galilee is one hundred sixty-five feet (50 meters) deep at its greatest depth (Beitzel 39).

Limited natural strength was not the cause of Peter's new danger. Doubt (v. 31) was his problem. For a moment, he believed the winds and waves were stronger than Jesus. Responding immediately to Peter's cry for help, Jesus "reached out His hand" and took hold of Peter, lifting him back to the water's surface.

Once again (cf. 8:26) Jesus described Peter as one of "little faith" (Greek *oligopistos*). See 6:30 for comments on this word. The question pointed to the reason for Peter's failure. He did not stop believing completely. He stopped believing in the complete adequacy of Jesus (Osborne 576). Why did he doubt?

He had walked on water, but had he become afraid of the waves? He should know that the one who enabled him to walk on water could keep him safe from the winds or waves.

Peter called Jesus *Lord* in the prayer he cried out. Newman and Stine (484) suggest that Peter probably did not yet use the title "Lord" in the full Christian sense, since verse 33 records the disciples' first strong confession of Jesus' deity. Compare 8:25 and comments there. Experience and emergencies can cause one's theology to develop quickly. Peter had seen Jesus multiply the loaves and fish, walk on water, and enable him to do the same. The one who could empower another human to live above the forces of nature is surely more than a man. To such a one Peter cried, "Lord!" and was saved. Together Jesus and Peter walked to the boat.

"Boisterous" (v. 30, Greek *ischuros*) is not in many of the Greek manuscripts. However, the context requires its presence—at least in understanding. The meaning is obvious, whether the word was part of the original or not.

Peter had weakened while on the water, yet he did something that even the greatest servants of the Lord had never done (Keener, *Background* 86). God *parted* the waters for Moses, Joshua, Elijah, and Elisha but none of them *walked* on it!

Matthew recorded the final miracle of that night. The winds calmed as soon as Jesus and Peter stepped into the boat. Matthew's record shows that this was not lost on the disciples. Though Jesus did not audibly rebuke the winds, as in 8:26, He was the reason for the calm. Those in the boat immediately worshiped Him confessing, "Of a truth thou art the Son of God."

The word translated "worship"(Greek *proskuneō*) means "to prostrate oneself before someone as an act of reverence, fear or supplication" (Louw and Nida I:218) or to "express by attitude and possibly position one's allegiance to or regard for deity" (Louw and Nida I:540). The Magi (2:11), a leper coming to be healed (8:2), and Jairus (9:18) had prostrated themselves before Him. Now with the fullest understanding so far, the Twelve—at least in attitude and possibly even in position—bowed before Him in the boat, and worshiped Him as one worships God. This is the first time Matthew records that the Twelve worshiped Jesus.

Hagner (33B:424-425) is probably right to suggest that their understanding was short of the church's later and fuller understanding of Jesus as the incarnate Deity, but the Twelve were growing in their understanding and perception. See Mark 6:51-52. This was their strongest confession yet. In 8:27, they had been amazed and wondered aloud about His identity. This day they were convinced that they were looking at Deity.

Up to this time, the Father had called Jesus His Son only at Jesus' baptism (3:17). Presumably, none of the Twelve were present to hear that. Satan, twice at Jesus' temptation (4:3, 6), spoke of Him as God's Son. The only other time Matthew records that anyone called Jesus "Son of God" was when the demon-possessed men prior to their healing addressed Jesus with this title (8:29).

On this day, the Twelve worshiped Jesus as God and vocalized that understanding. Jesus did not object or correct them. As with Peter's great confession (16:16) and Thomas's post-resurrection confession (Jn. 20:28), Jesus did nothing to stop these men from believing that He was God. This is an important truth since, though Jesus never called Himself God, yet He never corrected anyone else who did. See 16:16 and comments about the "Son of God" title and its use in the disciples' confession.

The day had been busy and long. Jesus showed the Twelve more and more of His glory (Jn. 1:14; 1 Jn. 1:1, 2). Many were healed, over five thousand were miraculously fed, Jesus walked on water across a large portion of the lake, Jesus enabled Peter also to walk on water to meet Him, and Jesus calmed the sea. The Twelve had served the miracle food to the five thousand, gathered up the uneaten food, and had rowed against a headwind across a significant portion of the lake. Evidently, no one had slept. Jesus had prayed on the mountainside and the Twelve had wrestled against the waves, perhaps most of the night. So much for a getaway for rest (Mk. 6:30-31); yet this was a day etched forever in their memories. This day they recognized that Jesus was no mere human. He was God's Son. Perhaps this was why Jesus chose to disclose such power at this time.

To Mary (Lk. 1:35), Jesus was God's Son because He had no human father. He was her miracle baby. The Twelve probably knew nothing of Jesus' birth circumstances at this time. To the Twelve He was the Son of God (v. 33) because He possessed and displayed divine qualities. He clearly was not subject to human limitations. Though He rode in a boat most of the time, that was not the only way He could cross water!

Because of the night circumstances, only the Twelve witnessed Jesus and Peter walking on the water. Some miracles were for the crowds. Others were only for the Twelve.

All this did not mean that the disciples from this point on had perfect understanding or faith (Mk. 6:52). They failed to perceive the fullest implications of the miracle of the feeding of the five thousand, even as they would later do the miracle of the feeding of the four thousand (15:32-16:10). They still had much to learn. However, they were making progress.

6. Jesus healed many at Gennesaret and its surrounding regions (14:34-36)

34 And when they were gone over, they came into the land of Gennesaret.
35 And when the men of that place had knowledge of him, they sent out into all that country round about, and brought unto him all that were diseased;
36 And besought him that they might only touch the hem of his garment: and as many as touched were made perfectly whole.

Jesus and the Twelve went to Gennesaret, a heavily populated, fertile plain located on the northwest side of the Sea of Galilee. The plain of Gennesaret is about three miles (5 km.) long and one mile (1.6 km.) wide. It extends northward along the coast from Magdala almost to Capernaum (ISBE II:443).

After landing in Gennesaret, Jesus and His disciples apparently first went up to Capernaum (Jn. 6:22, 59) where Jesus gave the Bread of Life discourse. Though no Gospel writer ever suggests this, one can assume that those disciples with families (all of them? 1 Cor. 9:5) visited them as often as they could (8:14). Several of the Apostles lived in or near Capernaum, so this would have been a home visit for them. One can imagine the excitement as the Twelve recounted for their families the events of the previous twenty-four hours. Following this Capernaum visit, Jesus and the Twelve returned to Gennesaret where He ministered for some time. John 7:1 seems to allow for the extended Galilean ministry Matthew summarized in these verses (14:34-36).

When the local people learned that Jesus was in their community, they advertised His presence. They even went to neighboring communities and brought their sick to Him. These sick folk asked that He permit them to touch only the hem of His garment. All who touched Him were healed. Touching the hem of His garment showed their respect for Him. As He would walk by, the people would bow down in homage and humbly reach out to touch Him. Touching His hem also demonstrated their faith in Him. They believed His powers were such that this would be enough to bring healing (Wilkins 519). See 9:20 for another example of this kind of miracle and a discussion of the garment hem.

Matthew says all were "made perfectly whole." This verb (Greek *diasōzō*) literally means to preserve through danger, to bring safely through. For examples of this in a literal sense see Acts 23:24; 27:43-44; 28:1, 4; and 1 Peter 3:20. Here, as in Luke 7:3, it apparently means to cure (Grimm's 142). (It is possible that the *dia* on the front of the Greek *sōzō* intensifies the meaning as "to cure completely," as Carson, *Matthew* 347 notes, *contra* Hagner 33A:427; but neither BAGD, Grimm's, TDNT, Louw and Nida, nor Liddell and Scott mention this meaning.)

Matthew's description shows that his and Mark's portrayals (Mk. 6:56) of this time of ministry were summaries of an extended ministry. See 4:24-25; 8:16-17; and 9:35 for other summaries. As Jesus traveled to various communities, people would place their sick where they knew He would pass. Though Jesus healed the sick, this was not His primary ministry (11:4-5; 12:28; Hagner 33B:427). His primary ministry was providing access into the kingdom. Healings indicated that the kingdom Jesus was preaching had arrived (Mt. 11:2-6; Lk. 4:18-21; Is. 61:1-2). Matthew's point in these verses is not so much the faith of the people as it was the power of Jesus (Hendriksen 604). He who had fed the five thousand and walked on water now healed every disease brought to Him. Bruner (2:79-81) points out that Matthew used "five excited absolutes" in his description: "all that country, ... all that were diseased, ... only touch, ... as many as touched, ... [and] perfectly whole."

Summary (14:1-36)

Following the kingdom parables, Jesus left Capernaum and traveled to Nazareth where He had been raised (13:53-58). He taught His former neighbors kingdom truths, but they were offended that He would think that they should listen to Him. They rejected Him. Around the same time, John the Baptist was killed. Herod Antipas had John beheaded because he denounced the ruler's adulterous and incestuous marriage to his sister-in-law (14:1-12). When

Jesus learned that Herod had an interest in Him, He left the area, apparently Capernaum or at least on the western side of the Sea of Galilee, and took a boat to a remote area near Bethsaida. In addition to getting away from Herod, Jesus wanted some time alone to provide rest for His disciples and for personal devotion. Not everyone was like Jesus' acquaintances in Nazareth. Thousands of people wanted to be with Him, so when they determined Jesus' destination they hurried ahead of Him and were waiting when He arrived.

Can God prepare a table in the desert (Ps. 78:19)? He did for the O.T. wilderness sojourners and He did again for the five thousand. With only five small barley loaves and two fish, Jesus fed the multitudes their evening meal. This was a miracle of creation.

Following the miraculous meal, Jesus sent His disciples toward Gennesaret by boat while He sent the crowds away. He apparently spent several hours in prayer. While Jesus prayed, the disciples struggled with the boat. They found themselves in the midst of another storm and labored most of the night. Sometime between 3:00 and 6:00 a.m. Jesus came to them walking on the water. This was a first. Peter asked to join Him and Jesus enabled Peter to walk on the water also. When they returned to the boat, the winds ceased. These miracles demonstrated Jesus' power over nature.

They arrived on the western shores of the Sea of Galilee, just south of Capernaum. He ministered in this area for a time, healing everyone who came. These miracles further proved that the kingdom Jesus preached had arrived.

Application: Teaching and Preaching the Passage

The feeding of the five thousand and Jesus' walking on water are two of the most familiar stories found in the N.T., probably because the reader can easily apply their lessons to life's struggles and victories. However, the story of John's martyrdom holds valuable lessons for God's people as well.

John's demise teaches these three lessons: (1) God's law convicts transgressors (vv. 1-2); (2) transgressors reject God's standard for living (vv. 3-4); and (3) some transgressors do all they can to silence the messenger (vv. 5-12).

One might also develop a lesson or sermon from the records of John the Baptist's murder in the following manner: (1) Unholy matrimony is a violation of the moral laws of God; (2) marriage does not make an unholy relationship holy; (3) murder is a violation of the moral laws of God; and (4) the death of the messenger does not silence the voice of the guilty conscience.

John's death was (1) preceded by his biblical stand on moral issues, (2) precipitated by a dance and a foolish promise, (3) prompted by a vindictive and evil woman, and (4) empowered, rather than cancelled, his influence on the one who killed him.

What Herod learned from John was: (1) his own high political position was still under God's sovereign rule; (2) right will not go away; and (3) murder does not silence the voice of God's messenger.

Some lessons ministers of the gospel can learn from John's experience with Herod are: (1) even earth's most powerful, political figures are not above God's law; (2) God's call can place His servant to bear witness of God's truth before even the most powerful people; (3) evil can be a powerful presence; (4) faithful messengers can be the target of vicious attacks; (5) standing for truth can be costly; and (6) a godly minister's influence for God and right can continue even after he has gone on to be with the Lord.

One might consider that even the wicked get a witness. God's three witnesses to Antipas were (1) John the Baptist, whose "you are sinning" was convicting (14:4); (2) Joanna (Lk. 8:3; 9:7; Mt. 14:1-2), whose testimony that Jesus healed her (cleansed her if she had been possessed) was a reminder of another holy person, and (3) Jesus Himself, whose words (Lk. 13:32) and later silence (Lk. 23:6-12) testified, "I am not answerable to you."

The miracle of the loaves and fish shows that (1) physical needs can be one reason people come to Jesus (vv. 13-14), (2) disciples need to believe beyond apparent limitations (vv. 15-18), and (3) Jesus can more than meet every need of every person (vv. 19-21). This last point can be expanded to include (a) the truth of the statement (vv. 18-20) and (b) the extent, i.e., unlimited numbers, each gender and all ages (v. 21). A fourth point might be added from John 6 (see comments above): people need the provider, Jesus, not just His day-to-day provisions for this life (both miraculous, Jn. 6:22-59, and providential, Mt. 6:25-33).

The feeding of the multitudes shows that (1) human need stirs the compassion of Jesus; (2) human limitation does not limit Jesus; (3) Jesus' blessing turns scarcity into bounty; and (4) there is more to Jesus' miracles than first meets the natural eye (Jn. 6:22-59).

Some lessons disciples learn about storms and Jesus from the miracles of Jesus and Peter walking on the water are: (1) Jesus sometimes sends His disciples into the path of a storm; (2) storms come; (3) strong and boisterous waves are no hindrance to Him who walks on water; (4) Jesus comes to His own in their storms; He does not remain aloof from their struggles; (5) Jesus enables the faithful to walk with Him in the storm; (6) Jesus is Savior, the one who raises His followers from the depths and calms their storms; (7) Jesus deserves worship for His care during the storm and His ability to control the storm; and (8) calm times are good times to worship.

These miracles teach that (1) Jesus can heal all diseases; (2) Jesus can create at will; (3) Jesus rules nature; and (4) Jesus is God.

One might observe that Jesus did three things of great spiritual significance immediately following the feeding of the five thousand: (1) He prayed; (2) He administered a faith test to His disciples by sending them into a storm; and (3) He delivered His disciples from deep and dark dangers.

7. Tradition, commandments, and defilement: another confrontation with the Pharisees (15:1-20)

1 Then came to Jesus scribes and Pharisees, which were of Jerusalem, saying,
2 Why do thy disciples transgress the tradition of the elders? for they wash not their hands when they eat bread.
3 But he answered and said unto them, Why do ye also transgress

the commandment of God by your tradition?

4 For God commanded, saying, Honour thy father and mother: and, He that curseth father or mother, let him die the death.

5 But ye say, Whosoever shall say to *his* father or *his* mother, *It is* a gift, by whatsoever thou mightest be profited by me;

6 And honour not his father or his mother, *he shall be free*. Thus have ye made the commandment of God of none effect by your tradition.

7 *Ye* hypocrites, well did Esaias prophesy of you, saying,

8 This people draweth nigh unto me with their mouth, and honoureth me with *their* lips; but their heart is far from me.

9 But in vain they do worship me, teaching *for* doctrines the commandments of men.

10 And he called the multitude, and said unto them, Hear, and understand:

11 Not that which goeth into the mouth defileth a man; but that which cometh out of the mouth, this defileth a man.

12 Then came his disciples, and said unto him, Knowest thou that the Pharisees were offended, after they heard this saying?

13 But he answered and said, Every plant, which my heavenly Father hath not planted, shall be rooted up.

14 Let them alone: they be blind leaders of the blind. And if the blind lead the blind, both shall fall into the ditch.

15 Then answered Peter and said unto him, Declare unto us this parable.

16 And Jesus said, Are ye also yet without understanding?

17 Do not ye yet understand, that whatsoever entereth in at the mouth goeth into the belly, and is cast out into the draught?

18 But those things which proceed out of the mouth come forth from the heart; and they defile the man.

19 For out of the heart proceed evil thoughts, murders, adulteries, fornications, thefts, false witness, blasphemies:

20 These are *the things* which defile a man: but to eat with unwashen hands defileth not a man.

What appears to be an official delegation of Jewish leaders from Jerusalem came to Jesus in Galilee to question Him about His teaching and practice. The question concerned the Twelve, but because they were Jesus' disciples, the inference was that He was responsible for their alleged sins. (For Pharisees, see 3:7 and for scribes, see 13:52.) The Pharisees asked Jesus why His disciples were transgressing the tradition passed down from the elders. To transgress (Greek *parabainō*) means to disobey or break an established custom or law (Louw and Nida I:469). Their complaint was the disciples' failure to observe ceremonial hand-washing before eating. The apparent assumption behind the question was that unclean hands would defile (make unclean) the food, which would then defile the person (Nolland 612, 615), thus breaking fellowship with the Lord. See comments on verse 11 for further explanation of defilement.

The "tradition of the elders" was a body of oral interpretations of the written law. In some instances, they were viewed as equally authoritative to written Scripture (ISBE IV:884). The Sadducees did not accept these oral interpretations as binding (Maier, 266) whereas the Pharisees did.

The allegation against the disciples was that it was their habit to eat (transgress is Greek present tense, signifying ongoing action), without first ceremonially washing their hands. The elders required ceremonial washing in case contact had been made with some type of uncleanness. This washing was not about sanitation or hygiene but about ceremonial cleanliness. God required priests to wash their hands and feet prior to entering the tabernacle and prior to approaching the altar (Ex. 30:17-21). City elders were required to wash as part of the atonement offering for unsolved murders (Dt. 21:6). Rinsing of hands was required of laity in certain situations threatening uncleanness as well (Lev. 15:11).

According to scholars, the elders had extended these priestly washings and the commandments concerning personal purity for individual Israelites to include ritualistic washings prior to the blessing given before eating meals (Hagner 33B:430). Jeremias (265) writes, "Whereas the Torah laid down the rules of purity and rules on food for the officiating priests alone, the Pharisaic group made these rules a general practice in the everyday life of the priests and in the life of the whole people." Mark (7:3-4) writes that all Jews, not just the Pharisees, would not eat unless they purified themselves. This cleansing was done by pouring water over the hands or immersing the hands up to the wrist (Keener, *Background* 153). The Jews did this each time they came from the market. They also ceremonially washed cups and pots as well as cookware. This could require considerable amounts of water, especially for large gatherings. Compare John 2:6 and the capacities of the stone water pots.

The problem with these requirements was that the elders had added them to Scripture (Dt. 4:2; 12:32). In their efforts to honor God's Word, they went too far and broke it. They broke it by making extra rules that God did not give and by making rules that contradicted rules God had given. The men confronting Jesus thought the elders' traditions had authority over the disciples. They also acted as if their traditions had more authority than God's law. To "eat bread" was Semitic for eating a meal (Zerwick 48).

Jesus did not deny the allegations but countered with a charge of His own: "Why do you transgress (Greek present tense; ongoing action) the commandment of God for the sake of your tradition?" The elders questioned Jesus' disciples' violation of their tradition, inferring that the disciples had broken fellowship with God. Jesus questioned their violation of God's law, inferring that they were out of fellowship with God. His allegation was much more serious than theirs. They had the bigger transgression. Jesus' primary point was "God commanded." The Pharisees and scribes quoted tradition. Jesus quoted God.

Jesus' second point to His accusers was that they were in violation of these two commandments in God's law. First, their tradition set aside God's law requiring honor to parents, the fifth commandment (Ex. 20:12; Dt. 5:16); and, second, their tradition set aside God's punishment for violators (Lev. 20:9). God had declared dishonor toward parents a capital offense (Ex. 21:17).

To honor (Greek *timaō*) means to "show high status to someone by honoring" (Louw and Nida I:735). It can also mean to "provide aid or financial assistance, with the implication that this is an appropriate means of showing respect" (1 Tim. 5:3; Louw and Nida I:571). These two meanings are closely connected, as Paul demonstrated in his instructions about parental support (1 Tim. 5:3-8). Adult children and grandchildren are responsible to honor their parents and grandparents by caring for their material needs. This was Jesus' point as well.

To curse or revile (v. 4) means "to insult in a particularly strong and unjustifiable manner" (Greek *kakologeō*; Louw and Nida I:434; Grimm's 320). The Hebrew word (Ex. 21:17) means to treat with contempt or dishonor (BDB 886). This Hebrew word and form were used in Genesis 12:3 ("that curseth thee") in God's covenant blessing to Abram. See also Leviticus 24:14, 23, Proverbs 20:20, and Jeremiah 15:10 for other examples.

Some writers think this "curse" refers to speaking a curse formula intended to bring harm, "as by sympathetic magic" (TWOT II:800). One may speculate that Israel's background in Egypt, where sympathetic magic was practiced (ISBE I:838), might have encouraged such practices in Israel. However, the N.T. context does not suggest this. Jesus did not accuse the Jewish leadership of encouraging people to speak curse formulas against their parents. Rather, He condemned their failure to honor their parents by properly caring for their material needs.

The grammatical structures of the punishment commands (v. 4) are emphatic in both Testaments. The violator was to die a violent death, i.e., violators would not be permitted to die a natural death (Ex. 21:17). The grammatical construction (Hebrew infinitive absolute for emphasis, Gesenius' 342; literally, put to a violent death, BDB 559) intensifies the verb, which the translators represent with "surely." The LXX, which Jesus quoted, likewise uses an intensive construction.

Jesus accused these men of not obeying the fifth commandment. Jews of that day, according to Jewish sources quoted by Blomberg (50-52), saw this commandment as second only to honoring God. As Blomberg explains, Jesus accused these men of providing a legal way out for people to avoid responsibility that the law clearly assigned to them. One practical outworking of this tradition was the teaching that if a man devoted his goods to God he was no longer obligated to support his parents financially (vv. 5-6). What the parents might have gained or benefited from such a gift, the adult child claimed to have set apart as God's. The child thus violated both the spirit and the letter of this commandment (Hagner 33B:431). For further discussion, see Picirilli's comments on Mark 7:11 and *Corban* (*Mark* 196-197).

The elders' teaching, Jesus said, was based on tradition and made of no effect (Greek *akuroō*; to refuse to recognize the power or force of something; Louw and Nida I:683) God's written instructions. The way the elders had interpreted and applied Scripture was not according to God's original intent.

"Or his mother" in verse 6 is not in some older Greek manuscripts so some translations do not include it. However, the words are part of Mark 7:10 and are understood in Matthew from verses 4 and 5, so their meaning belongs.

Jesus called His accusers hypocrites (v. 7; see comments on 6:2). They presented themselves as loyal worshipers of God, but He declared that their hearts were not true to God (v. 8). They claimed to be loyal teachers of the law, but in reality, they were teaching only man's thoughts (v. 9).

Quoting Isaiah 29:13 (vv. 8-9), Jesus made His point: these men had an external religion but no internal reality with God. They could talk a good claim, but neither their hearts nor their day-to-day actions supported their claims. Isaiah's and Jesus' generations were more loyal to human applications of Scripture than they were to God's original intent. God condemned this through Isaiah and Jesus. Jesus' accusers prided themselves that they were loyal to ancient traditions (Carson, *Matthew* 349). Jesus and Isaiah both condemned traditions that usurped the position reserved for God's commandments alone. The spirit of the religious leaders in Isaiah's day lived on in the leadership confronting Jesus (Carson, *Matthew* 349).

As the Isaiah quote shows, this lax attitude and practice—an interesting condemnation since few would have denounced the Pharisees for being lax about the law—was disobedience. When tradition, whether oral or written, old or recent, contradicts God's Word, that tradition is wrong. Further, Isaiah taught that God rejects hearts that are far from Him, i.e., hearts that do not love Him and are not loyal to Him. Love and loyalty are heart matters. A heart not right with God cannot produce a life right with God.

Some Christian groups today also rely heavily on tradition at the expense of Scriptural authority. The Roman Catholic Church, for example, teaches three sources of authority: (1) Scripture, (2) the infallibility of the pope when speaking *ex-cathedra,* i.e., "as the head of the Church on earth concerning faith and morals" (Cairns 427), and (3) church tradition. Roman Catholic doctrine has long taught that Scripture alone is not enough for salvation and holy living and that church tradition "as it was expressed in the decrees of popes and councils, [is] the only permissible, legitimate and infallible interpreter of the Bible" (Dowley 366). In 1545, the Council of Trent affirmed that the Bible and tradition are equally authoritative. This remains the official position of the Roman Catholic Church.

Protestants strongly disagree with this Catholic valuation of tradition and the authority of the pope and believe that Scripture alone contains all that is necessary for salvation and holy living (2 Tim. 3:15-16). There is a place for gifted pastors and teachers (Eph. 4:11), for commentaries (such as this one!), and for teachings that have been passed on from one generation to the next—even from the earliest centuries of Christianity to now. But none of these is equal to Scripture in authority. God's Word is the final authority because it is His word. No human tradition, regardless of its age or historical circumstances, equals the authority of God. Each generation of Christians must be careful to keep their valuations of their own traditions in check. Tradition, whether individual, local church, denominational, or that of the entire visible church, can serve well only as long as it agrees with and remains subservient to Scripture.

Jesus' condemnation of these men (v. 9) is also a clarion call for careful and honest hermeneutics. Man has no right to interpret and apply Scripture any way other than what God intended when He gave it. Scripture can never mean what it never meant. Religious integrity requires loyalty to the original text and meaning. The elders had replaced God's truth with tradition, and for that, God judged them. Part of this judgment was an increased inability to understand and properly interpret God's written Word (Is. 29:9-14). Perhaps this judgment was one reason Jesus chose to quote this Isaiah passage (Blomberg 53). To understand and then reject that understanding, results in a loss of understanding. They were now blind (Mt. 15:14). See comments on Matthew 13:15.

These men's sins were multiple. They rejected God's original intent. They gave Scripture their own interpretation and application (Grogan 188). They taught their interpretation, "the commandments of men" (v. 9), as if it was more authoritative and binding than God's Word (Mk. 7:8-9). They did not show godly honor to their parents. For that matter, they broke many laws in the same manner, i.e., through their traditions (Mk. 7:13; Evans, *Matthew* 306). The result was worthless worship actions. Jesus declared them "in vain." No good comes from such worship, only rejection. See Isaiah 1:10-15, Malachi 1:6-14, and John 4:22 for other examples of worthless worship. How sad that men gave their entire lives to religious observances and yet gained nothing positive in return either in this life or in the life to come. As Walvoord (117) observed, these men did not need more religious traditions. They needed a changed heart.

After rebuking His accusers, Jesus turned His attention to the crowd (vv. 10-11) and denounced the tradition of ceremonially washing before eating. He stated unequivocally that "what enters the mouth," such as food the elders considered ceremonially unclean (see comments on v. 2), does not defile a person before God. Rather, it is what comes "out of the mouth" that defiles. What defiles are evil intents and actions that originate from inside persons, i.e., in the heart.

To become defiled (Greek *koinoō*) means "to become unclean ... or ritually unacceptable" (Louw and Nida (I:536). Defilement destroys "the capacity for fellowship with God" and makes one unable to approach God in worship (Newman and Stine 500). Personal sin destroys fellowship with God, not ceremonially unclean food or hands (TDNT III:809). These scribes and Pharisees were wrong.

Defilement originates inside each person as evil desire, not in or on objects outside the person. James (1:13-15) explained that desire that lies dormant is not sin. Dormant desire has the potential to sin but it is not itself sin. However, when desire is nurtured, it can give birth to sinful actions. James teaches that sin comes from within, from the depraved nature. God cannot sin because God cannot be tempted with evil. He has no capacity to sin. His nature is absolutely holy. Mankind can sin because the human heart is by its depraved nature evil, and the heart's desires can be enticed and tempted to follow evil.

The clean/unclean precepts began with Noah and the ark (Gen. 7:2) and were for worship distinctions (Gen. 8:20). Only animals were at first divided into these two categories, and this was apparently for worship matters only. For food purposes, the only unclean or separated meats were those that had not been bled properly (Gen. 9:3-4). Years later, at the giving of the Law to Moses, the Lord gave more instructions defining what would be labeled clean and unclean. These laws included food laws plus much more. These restrictions applied only to Israel, not to other nations or people groups.

There were several ways Israelites could defile themselves or become defiled. Certain bodily emissions (Lev. 15:2, 16, 25), having leprosy (Lev. 13:14, 46), touching a carcass of an animal (Lev. 11:8, 24; 17:15) or a human (Num. 19:11), touching certain "creeping things" (Lev. 22:5), and touching (Lev. 11:26) or eating animals declared unclean (Lev. 11:8; Dt. 14:3-21) are some ways. By the N.T. times rabbis had expanded "the scope of defilement in its various degrees" into an elaborate and burdensome system (ISBE I:912). They further defined various degrees of uncleanness (multiple degrees of separation) and applied their own rules of ceremonial cleanness. One example is the washing of one's hands before eating in case one had unknowingly come in contact with some form of uncleanness and become defiled before God. The O.T. law contains no such stipulation. For a fuller treatment of the biblical concept of cleanness, uncleanness, and defilement, see a Bible encyclopedia (e.g., ISBE I:718-723, 912).

During His earthly life, Jesus and His disciples obeyed the food laws of the O.T. Peter was still able to say in Acts 10:14 that he had never eaten unclean food. It is therefore an error to understand Jesus' words here to set aside immediately the O.T. food laws. Jesus' teaching (v. 11), however, showed the error of the elders' tradition in this matter of ceremonial cleansing. His comments also became the foundation for the post-cross end to fourteen hundred years of certain separation laws (Bruner 2:93), some that dated back even to Noah's day. Writing several decades after the cross, Mark (7:19) in his Gospel account inserted a parenthetical remark that Jesus' comments about food not defiling meant that all foods are now clean. After Pentecost, Peter received further instruction from the Lord about this in preparation for his visit to Cornelius (Acts 10:9-16). The Christian's freedom from the O.T. ceremonial laws became a major doctrine in the early church (Acts 11:1-18; Gal. 2:11-14; Col. 2:16-23). It was a point of division, or perhaps one should say growth, for several years in the first century church.

Romans 14, especially verse 14, builds on this portion of Jesus' teaching and restates with apostolic authority that no food is unclean. Galatians 2:11-21 condemned Peter, Barnabas, and other Christian Jews in Antioch who sought to maintain the Jewish-Gentile distinction by observing food laws. Colossians 2:16-17, 21-23 specifically warns that observing food laws provides no spiritual benefit to those who are in Christ and states that these food laws were part of the legal system that pointed to life in Christ (cf. Heb. 8:5; 10:1). First Timothy 4:1-5 warns that observing food laws is a departure from the faith and contrary to God's declaration at creation that all creation was good.

Whatever the original intent of the clean/unclean distinction under Moses—and one cannot be sure what that was except that it was one of the ways Israel lived "holy to the Lord" (Dt. 14:21) and thus different from other nations—in Christ that distinction is removed (Eph. 2:14-15). The Law specifically stated that unclean food was unclean to Israel ("to you"; Lev. 11:4, 5, 6, etc.), not to other nations (Dt. 14:21), but now the law expressed in ordinances has been abolished that Christ might create in Himself one new man, the Church.

What Jesus' words taught this immediate crowd was that the elders' traditions were never God's Word and so could not affect one's holiness before God either positively or negatively. God's holiness is not offended by hands that have not had ceremonial water poured over them. Such hands are not, nor have they ever been, sinful hands.

Jesus' disciples observed that the Pharisees were "offended" (Greek *skandalizomai*; be offended, displeased, indignant; Grimm's 577) and reacted negatively to His words, and they told Jesus (v. 12). They apparently were concerned that Jesus would directly confront these powerful leaders (Keener, *Matthew* 413). It was no wonder the Pharisees were offended. Jesus appeared to have set aside a significant portion of the law, had publically disagreed with the Pharisees and scribes, had struck down the tradition of the elders—and that openly, and had thus publicly challenged the authority of these men, their elders, and their traditions.

Jesus responded to His disciples with two parables about the Pharisees (vv. 13-14). They would be uprooted, i.e., removed from their places of influence, because the Father had not planted them. They were not part of true Israel. "Rooted up" signifies direct judgment (Dt. 29:28; Zeph. 2:4; Gundry 307). If Isaiah 60:21 and 61:3 are behind verse 13, then Jesus was condemning the Pharisees as glory seekers (Mt. 23:5-7) instead of being righteous oaks planted by the Lord for His own glory (Is. 61:3; Grogan 334).

Second, "they were blind and failed to comprehend" spiritual truth in "the Scriptures they claimed to follow" (Carson, *Matthew* 350), as were those who followed their directions. These who taught that observance of human tradition was the proper way to worship God were blind to truth and unable to give directions that would help other blind people know where to go (Newman and Stine 502). See also 23:13-22. They were blind leaders of the blind, but this was not the opinion they had of themselves (Rom. 2:19).

Jesus left the crowds and His accusers and entered "the house" (Mk. 7:17). Peter, probably on behalf of the Twelve (Mk. 7:17; Wilkins 537), asked for clarification of the parable about what really defiles a person (vv. 11, 15). He was not speaking of verses 13 and 14 as Jesus' answer in verses 17-20 shows. Jesus had implied that the entire tradition of the elders was flawed. Peter and the others recognized the implications of Jesus' statement and so wanted further explanation.

Jesus obliged, but first He rebuked Peter and the others for not understanding (v. 16). He inferred that they, of all people, should have understood the separation between ritualistic washing and defilement of the inner person. He then gave a straightforward explanation (v. 17). What a person eats goes into the stomach, through the digestive system, and into the latrine (Greek *aphedrōna*, latrine, toilet; Louw and Nida I:92). Food does not enter the human *spirit*.

However, what comes out of the mouth (v. 18), i.e., words, doctrines, worship practices and all sorts of actions, originate in the heart, the volitional seat of man. It is probable that Jesus used "mouth" here to stand for the whole person and actions of the whole person. All that a person says and does comes from the heart. If the heart is evil, and everyone's is by nature (7:11; Wilkins 538), it produces evil thoughts and actions (Mt. 15:19; 12:34). See also James 3:6-12, especially verses 11-12, and the various ways the writer depicts the source of evil actions. Actions motivated by evil defile the person (vv. 18, 20). The elders' understanding was backward. Causes of defilement originate from within, not from without.

Matthew listed seven examples of activities that defile a person before God. Mark's list (7:21) has thirteen. Matthew included one not in Mark's list, false witness, which shows that neither list is meant to be exhaustive, only representative. Both lists teach that people who live in sin are not right with God. Evil thoughts are evil meditations, sins without bodily action. Murders, adulteries, fornications (Greek plural *porneia*), and thefts are actions of the body that are motivated by an evil heart. These all defile. The body does not act independently of the human spirit. The spirit wills and moves the body.

Perjuries (false witnesses) and blasphemies (Greek pl. *blasphēmia*) also defile. The latter probably refers to slandering others rather than God (Newman and Stine 506; Louw and Nida I:434). These complete the list and are sins of the heart and mouth. Jesus identified these actions as defiling. Lies and blasphemous words defile. Any action of the body that violates God's holy law defiles that person before God.

Jesus ended with the plainest statement possible: literally, "To eat with unwashed hands does not defile man." Jesus was not about to require His disciples to practice ceremonial washings. See Matthew 23:25-26 and Luke 11:37-41 for further teaching by Jesus on ceremonial washing.

The cure for defilement was not ceremonial washing. The cure for human defilement is a cleansed heart (Wilkins 538), made new by the new birth (Ezek. 36:25-26; Jn. 3:3-8; Tit. 3:4-7). This new birth belongs to all whose heart of faith moves them to repent of their sins (Acts 2:38; 3:19; 17:30; 26:20) and to confess with their mouth Jesus as Lord (Rom. 10:9-10).

This exchange between the Jewish leadership and Jesus contributed to the growing divide between them. In 9:3, some of the scribes accused Jesus of blaspheming because He claimed to be able to forgive sin. In 9:11, the Pharisees questioned the propriety of Jesus' willingness to eat with sinners. In 12:1-8, some Pharisees challenged Jesus for allowing His disciples to break the Sabbath law. In 12:24, they accused Jesus of being empowered by Satan rather than God's Spirit and He warned them that such statements are blasphemous and unforgivable. Later some scribes and Pharisees approached Jesus asking for a super sign (12:38). He rebuked them and promised them a great sign to come. Now representatives from the same two groups challenge Jesus again, this time on His failure to teach His disciples to obey the tradition of the elders. Jesus called them hypocrites and told everyone within earshot that these men were wrong. They were unhappy. The dislike would soon be hatred.

IV. THE SYRIA, DECAPOLIS, AND NORTHERN PALESTINE MINISTRY NARRATIVE: THE ROYAL MESSIAH TRAVELS BETWEEN ISRAEL AND GENTILE TERRITORIES (15:21—18:35)

Jesus' did not usually travel into Gentile areas. Earlier in His ministry, He visited the east side of Galilee where He healed the Gergasean demoniacs (8:28-34). Most of His time, especially the early years of His ministry, was devoted primarily to reaching lost Israelites (10:6; 15:24; Jn. 1:11). He did, however, preach the gospel to Gentiles as well. See the discussions on 4:15, 24; 8:5; 12:15, 21.

It seems, at this point in His ministry, that Jesus began spending more time in areas mainly populated by Gentiles. Perhaps what is often called His Galilean ministry was over (Wilkins 538; Hendriksen 621), but not all agree with this. Hagner (33B:444) thinks the Decapolis miracle summary in 15:29-31 is the climax of Jesus' Galilean ministry. Regardless, Jesus left Galilee for a few months and traveled first north into the areas of Tyre and Sidon (v. 21; Mk. 7:24). Whether He actually visited either city is unclear (Newman and Stine 508). Jesus visited Galilee again but the larger portion of His ministry in Galilee was behind Him.

A. The Faith of the Canaanite Woman (15:21-28)

21 Then Jesus went thence, and departed into the coasts of Tyre and Sidon.
22 And, behold, a woman of Canaan came out of the same coasts, and cried unto him, saying, Have mercy on me, O Lord, *thou* son of David; my daughter is grievously vexed with a devil.
23 But he answered her not a word. And his disciples came and besought him, saying, Send her away; for she crieth after us.
24 But he answered and said, I am not sent but unto the lost sheep of the house of Israel.
25 Then came she and worshipped him, saying, Lord, help me.
26 But he answered and said, It is not meet to take the children's bread, and to cast *it* to dogs.
27 And she said, Truth, Lord: yet the dogs eat of the crumbs which fall from their masters' table.
28 Then Jesus answered and said unto her, O woman, great *is* thy faith: be it unto thee even as thou wilt. And her daughter was made whole from that very hour.

News of Jesus' miracles had previously reached Tyre and Sidon (Mk. 3:8), and many from there had brought their sick to Galilee for healing. Jesus had earlier shamed the Galilean cities of Chorazin and Bethsaida by stating that the Gentile citizens of Tyre and Sidon would have accepted His message and ministry whereas these Jewish cities had rejected Him (Mt. 11:21, 22). He even stated that these Gentile cities would receive an easier judgment than

Chorazin and Bethsaida because these Jewish communities had refused His message.

When He arrived in the area of Tyre and Sidon, it was not to extend His ministry. He wished to remain unnoticed (Mk. 7:24), but people recognized Him. As Jesus walked along, a woman came out (Hill, 253, suggests out from her house) and began calling after Him for help for her daughter, following Him.

Matthew called her "a woman of Canaan." Mark says she was a Gentile, a Syrophoenician by birth. Both make the same point: she was not a descendent of Abraham. Blomberg (54) thinks Matthew was deliberately introducing offensive memories of these two pagan cities from O.T. times. It is noteworthy that the account of this Canaanite woman's faith follows Jesus' discussion of clean and unclean, since by Jewish standards this Gentile was unclean. The Jews believed she was unqualified to approach God in worship (Newman and Stine 507).

Approaching Jesus, she began calling out (Greek inceptive imperfect) to Him as He walked along (v. 23, after us; Newman and Stine 511). She addressed Him as Lord, probably showing honor in the same way we say, "Sir" (Greek *kurios* three times, vv. 22, 25, 27). Matthew, writing later (his Christian readers also), understood more (Newman and Stine 512). She also used the Messianic title, Son of David, showing she had some knowledge of Jewish history and promise as well as some information about Jesus. (See comments on 1:1, 9:27, and 22:41-45 for "Son of David.") Rather than addressing Him as Jesus, a name she undoubtedly knew, she used this title of respect and prophetic meaning.

She begged for mercy and did not presume on His favor. She asked on behalf of her daughter, whom she described as being "grievously vexed with a devil." For demon possession, see 8:28 and comments.

At first Jesus appeared to ignore the woman (cf. 9:27-28) but she persisted. She was so vocal and insistent that the Twelve asked Jesus to tell her to leave (v. 23), but He did not (Hendriksen 622). Jesus finally answered, but it was not the answer she (or probably we) expected. He stated that He was sent to lost Israelites, not to anyone else (v. 24; see 10:6, which contextually is connected to 9:36-38). That He was sent by God is assumed (10:40). As in 10:6, all of Israel is in view, as lost (Wilkins 539). God's blessings to the world came through the seed of Abraham, the nation of Israel and the Messiah (Jn. 4:22). The Messiah came to His own first (Jn. 1:11).

Interpreters debate whom Jesus was speaking to in verse 24 since He did not specifically address His comments to either the woman or His disciples. Gundry (312-313; also Walvoord 118) says Jesus was talking to His disciples and the woman overheard him. He says that Jesus' restricted calling and His disciples' antagonism were obstacles that highlighted this Gentile's faith. Bruner (2:99) suggests He may have been talking to Himself.

Whether speaking directly to her or not, He was clearly talking about her and intended that she hear. She seized the opportunity to beg and came closer. Apparently, she had been crying out from a distance (Gundry 312) as they approached the house. Hers was the cry of a hurting, loving mother, a cry that others uttered as well: "Lord, help me"

(v. 25). Peter had cried out, "Lord, save me" (14:30). A father would soon cry out and say, "Help my unbelief!" (Mk. 9:24). These pleas were short, intense, to the point, and effective prayers.

The woman "worshipped" Him: that is, she knelt before Him (v. 25: Greek *proskuneō*; to prostrate one's self in worship; Louw and Nida I:218, 540). The woman was convinced Jesus was Israel's Messiah and He could help her (Hagner 33B:442). Her position reflected her submission, and her persistence showed her faith.

Jesus' next response seemed an insult (v. 26), that He called her a dog. According to Keener (*Background* 154; also Nolland 634), Jews did not normally call Gentiles dogs, but Guthrie (160; also, Hill 254) says they did. Opinions about how this applies to the woman vary. Some writers note that Jesus used a different word for dog this time than in 7:6 (Nolland 634). There the scavenger dogs (Greek *kuōn*; Lk. 16:21; Phil. 3:2) were the enemies of the gospel, both Jew and Gentile. Here He probably spoke of smaller house pets (Greek *kunarion*, Louw and Nida I:44), but Hendriksen (623) notes that house pets, regardless of how they are loved by their owners, "are not children and have no right to be treated like children." Evans (*Matthew* 308; also Newman and Stine 512) believes that Jesus was simply using common eating habits of the day—that children were fed before house pets—and meant only that His focus was at that time on lost Israelites. They were at the table to be fed first. The Gentiles would be fed later.

These scholars are surely correct but there may be more to this. Jesus might have used the term "dog" as a metaphor to speak of those who were not normally part of Israel's covenant community (Wilkins 539), and thus it was not a term denoting dignity. In fact, it was very uncomplimentary. Jesus used this term to put her off (Keener, *Matthew* 417) and to make sure she understood that the Son of David was first for the Jews (Carson, *Matthew* 355). This does not mean that Jesus was opposed to Gentiles. He wanted Gentiles as well as Jews in His kingdom (8:11).

Also, Jesus was out of country. He was a godly Jew in a Gentile land. Surely, ungodliness (idolatry, etc.) prevailed and was open. Jesus was not in Tyre to share God's blessings with the decidedly wicked and ungodly (7:6; 10:14). As Nolland (635) observes, had this woman not been a woman of faith, this story would have turned out much differently.

The woman did not take offense at Jesus but instead quickly identified with the "dogs" metaphor and asked that like a pet she be permitted to pick up the crumbs that fell from the masters' table during the meal (v. 27). She asked that Jesus not make her wait (Evans, *Matthew* 308). She wanted to be "fed" now.

The woman's self-identification with dogs shows that she understood what Jesus meant and accepted her place as one outside the covenant community. She had no right to ask this favor. She understood that Jesus was speaking of "order of priority" (Newman and Stine 512-513). He was the Jews' Messiah first. She believed, though, that her needs could be met immediately.

Her answer pleased Jesus (Mk. 7:29; Guthrie 160). Answering her directly, Jesus acknowledged her great faith and answered her prayer (v. 28). Without seeing the daughter or speaking directly to the evil spirit, Jesus immediately healed the girl. As with the centurion who wanted Jesus to heal his servant (8:8-9), authority, not proximity, was the issue. Jesus assured this mother that the demon was already gone and when she went home she found the child healed and resting (Mk. 7:30). Jesus had ministered to both mother and daughter (Bruner 2:103). Matthew's comments about the daughter's immediate healing and Mark's (7:30) about the child found lying in bed suggest that this was not the last they heard from this woman (Walvoord 118). The age of the daughter is unknown but Mark's description of her resting in bed suggests that she might have been young.

This is the second time Jesus acknowledged great faith (8:10). Both times, it was a Gentile's faith He commended. Both times the faith was great because it was unlikely (Wilkins 540). In this instance, this Gentile woman, outside of God's Israel-based, salvation program, believed in Jesus as God's fulfillment of His O.T. promises. Against her Gentile background, the desire of the Twelve that she be gone, and Jesus' delay in answering her request, she persisted. Such persistence, born of faith, Jesus honored. She proved the truth of Jesus' words in 11:21. Those of Tyre and Sidon accept Jesus' gospel when they hear it.

Neither Matthew nor Mark explained why Jesus did not answer this woman's request immediately—He did the same with the two blind men (9:27)—or how this story fits into the development of their overall Gospel accounts. Romans 9 and 10 are helpful. God desired to show mercy to those who previously had received no mercy (Rom. 9:24-25). Gentiles, who did not pursue God's righteousness, received it by faith, whereas the Jews tried to obtain God's righteousness by works (v. 2) and were rejected (Rom. 9:30—10:4). This Gentile woman's faith was in sharp contrast to the unbelief and works of the Jewish authorities (vv. 1-9; Hendriksen 622), and upon her profession of faith in Jesus, she became part of the believing community and a recipient of the Master's care and blessings.

B. Jesus Fed Over Four Thousand (15:29-39)

29 And Jesus departed from thence, and came nigh unto the sea of Galilee; and went up into a mountain, and sat down there.
30 And great multitudes came unto him, having with them *those that were* lame, blind, dumb, maimed, and many others, and cast them down at Jesus' feet; and he healed them:
31 Insomuch that the multitude wondered, when they saw the dumb to speak, the maimed to be whole, the lame to walk, and the blind to see: and they glorified the God of Israel.
32 Then Jesus called his disciples *unto him*, and said, I have compassion on the multitude, because they continue with me now three days, and have nothing to eat: and I will not send them away fasting, lest they faint in the way.
33 And his disciples say unto him, Whence should we have so much bread in the wilderness, as to fill so great a multitude?
34 And Jesus saith unto them, How many loaves have ye? And

they said, Seven, and a few little fishes.
35 And he commanded the multitude to sit down on the ground.
36 And he took the seven loaves and the fishes, and gave thanks, and brake *them*, and gave to his disciples, and the disciples to the multitude.
37 And they did all eat, and were filled: and they took up of the broken *meat* that was left seven baskets full.
38 And they that did eat were four thousand men, beside women and children.
39 And he sent away the multitude, and took ship, and came into the coasts of Magdala.

Jesus left the vicinity of Tyre and continued north to the area of Sidon (Mk. 7:31). From there He went back to an area close to the Sea of Galilee where crowds again gathered to Him. He was avoiding Judea because the leaders were trying to kill Him. The travel from Galilee to Tyre, on to Sidon, and then back down into the Decapolis, would have taken a few weeks, perhaps as much as six months (Barclay 2:147). The feeding of the five thousand was in the spring (Jn. 6:4) and by the fall Jesus was back in Galilee with His family (Jn. 7:2-3)—and six months from the cross! The Decapolis ministry and miracles, then, took place in mid to late summer of the final year of Jesus' ministry and was in an area populated mainly by Gentiles.

When Jesus arrived in the Decapolis, He did as He had done in the Jewish communities. In summary fashion, Matthew records that Jesus healed the lame, the blind, the maimed (Greek *kullos*; a disability in one or more limbs, ... often the result of some deformity; crippled; Louw and Nida I:273), and many others with various diseases. Placing their loved ones and friends at Jesus' feet, the people hoped for a miracle. None were disappointed. As Jesus made clear to John the Baptist, healing was part of the Messiah's ministry (Newman and Stine 515). Healing proved that the Messiah had come and that Jesus was the Messiah (see comments on 11:3-5). See 4:23-25; 8:16-17; 9:35; and 14:35-36 for other summaries.

Unlike the feeding of the five thousand, when Jesus fed the crowd at the end of the first day, this time people did not eat for three days while they watched Him perform miracle after miracle. It must have been a marvelous experience, watching healing after healing, hearing mutes talk for the first time, watching people take their first steps, watching as people who had been crippled were made whole, and seeing the reaction on the faces of those who saw or heard for the first time or at least in a long time.

As a result of these miracles the people, surely both those who were healed and the onlookers, responded with wonder and praised the God of Israel (v. 31). They were amazed at the signs and gave God credit, so amazed that they would not leave even to get food.

"The God of Israel" is a common O.T. designation that appears in the N.T. only here and in Luke 1:68. (Acts 13:17 has "the God of the people of Israel.") In Matthew, it draws attention to the Gentile crowd's recognition that the "God whom the people of Israel worship" (Newman and Stine 517) was at work in Jesus. This God was not their

God but the God of another people (Hendriksen 627). Perhaps after these miracles they trusted Jesus and the God of Israel.

Hagner (33B:446) says to limit these miracles to Gentiles makes verse 24 and the story of the Canaanite woman absurd. As mentioned above, he sees this Decapolis ministry as the climax of Jesus' Galilean ministry. This is, of course, possible and the easiest answer. However, because the Decapolis was mainly Gentile, most scholars disagree with Hagner. The crowd was probably mainly Gentile, although Jews would also have been present.

This begs the question why Jesus was so willing to help these Gentiles and so hesitant to help the Canaanite woman in the previous pericope? If He was sent only to the lost sheep of Israel, why is He now ministering to thousands of Gentiles? It is difficult to be certain. Carson (*Matthew* 357) suggests that based on the priority interpretation of feeding the children before the dogs (v. 26), the "blessing for the Gentiles is about to dawn." The fact is, the only thing that changed when Jesus went into the region of Tyre and Sidon was His location. He had been ministering to Gentiles throughout His ministry (4:25; 8:5-13; 28-34). However, His ministry to Gentiles was not the specific, targeted ministry that characterized His approach to lost Israelites (10:6), and even when in the region of Tyre He was not there on a campaign. He was there to rest and to avoid those who wanted Him dead. That avoidance took Him to the Decapolis as well.

After three days of ministry and no food, Jesus decided to send the crowds away but He wanted to feed them first. He felt pity (Greek *splagchnizō*; have pity, feel sympathy; BAGD 762; Mt. 9:36; 14:14; 18:27; 20:34) for them and did not want them to faint (Greek *ekluō*, become weary or slack, give out; BAGD 243) on their way home (v. 32). Some had traveled a great distance to be with Jesus (Mk. 8:3).

When Jesus mentioned this to the Twelve, they did not suggest another miracle. In fact, it seems they had already forgotten about the miraculous feeding of the five thousand (14:19-21). They wondered how they could get enough loaves in the wilderness (Greek *erēmia*, a largely uninhabited region; Louw and Nida I:17) to satisfy (Greek *chortazō*; 14:20) so large a crowd. There were only seven loaves and a few fish (v. 34; see comments on 14:17). Jesus commanded the crowd to sit—to recline for eating (v. 35; cf. 14:19). He took the bread and fish, then broke them and gave the broken pieces to His disciples. They, in turn, gave to the crowd. As with the feeding of the five thousand, this miracle was ongoing (Greek imperfect, He "was giving").

Everyone ate and everyone had enough to eat (v. 37). Again, Jesus provided more than was necessary. The disciples collected seven baskets full of bread and fish fragments. The basket (Greek *spuris*) was a large basket, perhaps larger than the basket in 14:20 (Greek *kophinos*; Louw and Nida I:71, 72)—but the difference in size is not certain. The total number of people who ate was four thousand plus women and children.

After feeding the crowd, Jesus sent them away. Matthew wrote as if Jesus then got into a boat by Himself (15:39) and His disciples later joined Him (16:5). Newman and Stine (522) understand the text to mean this. However, Mark plainly states that Jesus got into a boat with His disciples (Mk. 8:10).

They traveled to the region of Magadan or Magdala. Some Greek manuscripts have one name, some the other. Scholars are not sure where Magadan is located or even from which side of the sea Jesus sailed after this miracle. Mark (8:10) is little help for he reports that Jesus went to the area of Dalmanutha. Variant readings in Mark include those in Matthew's Gospel also.

Some commentators think that the two feeding miracles are separate traditions of a single event (Evans, *Matthew* 312; Hill 255-256; Hagner 33B:449-450). Hagner goes so far as to say that Matthew and Mark both believed that the two feedings were separate events, although they were not. Such a position requires that the Gospel writers erred. The doctrine of Scriptural inerrancy (e.g. 5:18) will not tolerate this. It is important to note that Matthew and Mark record Jesus' later reference to both feedings as separate events (16:9-10; Mk. 8:19-20).

Summary (15:1-39)

This chapter teaches the need for obedience to God's Word, regeneration, and faith. On one occasion when Pharisees and scribes accused Jesus of not teaching His disciples the traditions of the elders, Jesus responded with an accusation of His own: the elders were teaching traditions rather than God's commandments. Jesus also made the following points: the elders' traditions are non-binding, ceremonial washings are of no advantage before God, ceremonial washings have no effect on the heart, God's Word is supreme, and unclean hearts cause uncleanness before God, not hands that have not been ceremonially rinsed with water. The only way to have a clean heart is to have the heart regenerated. Though Jesus did not specifically mention regeneration at this time, He did condemn the people's distance from God and the vanity of their worship habits. He warned of God's sure judgment.

Jesus left Galilee after this and traveled north to the regions of Tyre and Sidon. Upon His arrival at Tyre, a Canaanite woman approached Him asking that He heal her daughter of demon possession. The account of the Canaanite woman's request illustrates that what pleases Jesus is faith. The nationality of the believer does not make one unacceptable before God. The woman had no bloodline connection to Abraham, yet she approached Jesus in faith, asking for His help. She believed He was the Messianic Son of David and could and would help her. She was right.

Jesus left the region of Tyre and Sidon and traveled south to the predominantly Gentile Decapolis where He ministered as He had been doing in Galilee. He healed all the sick that were brought to Him and He miraculously fed over four thousand at one time. The same miracles He had been performing for Jews, He now performed for Gentiles. These Gentiles recognized God in Him and worshiped the God of the Israelites. Though the text does not say, it seems probable that many of them accepted Jesus' gospel and joined His kingdom community.

Application: Teaching and Preaching the Passage

Teaching and preaching verses 1-20 requires some familiarity with appropriate sections in Leviticus and Deuteronomy. See comments above for those references. These verses are important because they teach two essential truths: God's Word takes precedence over tradition, and personal defilement comes from within, not from without. With these in mind, one might talk about (1) the supremacy of God's Word over man's tradition and (2) the source of personal defilement (which will show the need for inner cleansing and regeneration; Jn. 3:3; 2 Cor. 5:17; Eph. 5:26; Tit. 3:4-7). A third point might be added from 2 Timothy 3:16-17 concerning the sufficiency of the Word ("profitable for ... training ... that the man of God may be competent," ESV).

One might consider the weaknesses and limitations of human tradition: (1) human tradition originates with mankind so it has all of his limitations; (2) human tradition does nothing to gain God's acceptance or approval; (3) human tradition cannot take the place of God's directives and commands; and (4) human tradition does not sanctify the human spirit.

The Canaanite woman illustrates effective, intercessory prayer. When she prayed, she was (1) persistent, (2) made a profession of faith, and (3) was rewarded with a positive answer. From her we learn that when we pray we should (1) make our requests known, (2) be specific, (3) be persistent, (4) have faith in Jesus' person and power, and (5) have faith in our privilege (to come to Him in prayer).

For application ideas for verses 32-39, see the application section for 14:14-21. Further, one might consider that (1) Jesus is compassionate toward all, regardless of nationality (assuming these were mainly Gentiles in these verses; v. 32); (2) Jesus extends His abundant care to all (v. 33-36); and (3) Jesus more than addresses the needs of all (vv. 37-38).

C. The Pharisees and Sadducees Asked for a Sign (16:1-4)

1 The Pharisees also with the Sadducees came, and tempting desired him that he would shew them a sign from heaven.
2 He answered and said unto them, When it is evening, ye say, *It will be* fair weather: for the sky is red.
3 And in the morning, *It will be* foul weather to day: for the sky is red and lowering. O *ye* hypocrites, ye can discern the face of the sky; but can ye not *discern* the signs of the times?
4 A wicked and adulterous generation seeketh after a sign; and there shall no sign be given unto it, but the sign of the prophet Jonas. And he left them, and departed.

Jesus' enemies continued pushing Him. Whereas the Pharisees and scribes came (in 15:1) to question Jesus, on this occasion the Pharisees and Sadducees came specifically to "tempt" or test Jesus by requesting a miraculous sign. Paul later wrote that this was a Jewish characteristic (1 Cor. 1:22). Clearly, the motive of these men was evil. They did not believe Jesus could give them such a sign, which for them was proof that He was not of God. Their question was a trap (Newman and Stine 524).

For Pharisees and Sadducees, see comments on 3:7 where these same two groups approached John the Baptist and received a scathing rebuke from him. This is the first time Matthew mentioned specifically that these two groups approached Jesus together. Mark 8:11 says they were arguing (Greek *suzēteō*) with Jesus. Both Matthew and Mark record that they came to tempt or test Him, the same word used in 4:1. There Satan tried to entice Jesus to sin. Here Jesus' enemies tried to get Him to demonstrate special powers by showing them a heavenly sign, a special and spectacular miracle that only God could do. See comments on 12:38.

"Heaven" stands for God's realm, thus God Himself, not the sky. Hendriksen (635), however, interprets the request to mean for Jesus to do something like bring manna or fire down from heaven, or make the sun and moon stand still. Either way, these men asked Jesus to perform a sign that would be indisputably of God.

Jesus directed their attention to the sky and started talking about the weather and these men's ability to forecast weather. In the evening when the sky was red and clear they knew no rain was coming. In the early morning when the sky was red and gloomy (Greek *stugnazō*, to be dark and gloomy, lowering, threatening; Louw and Nida I:176), they knew a storm was coming their way. See Luke 12:54-56 for additional elements. However, Jesus was not teaching weather forecasting. Instead, He condemned these men—calling them hypocrites (in many but not all Greek manuscripts)—because they had learned the weather signs in the sky but not the signs of the times. They should have recognized the signs of the times all about them. The signs were Jesus' miracles (12:28). Jesus was not operating in a vacuum. There were many evidences if these men had just been open to them (see comments on 13:13-15). On hypocrites, see comments on 6:2.

The words "a wicked and adulterous generation" connect these critics with the O.T. Israelites who tested the Lord in the wilderness (12:39; Ex. 17:1-7; Ps. 78:41, 56; Blomberg 54-55) and with Jesus' earlier rebuke to some scribes and Pharisees who had also asked for a sign. "Wicked" describes the evil hearts of these men. "Adulterous" speaks of their spiritual unfaithfulness and the absence of exclusive love and loyalty to the Lord (Hos. 1:2; 2:2; 3:1). Jesus was not fooled by their outward religiosity. He knew their hearts.

Jesus' answer was the same as it had been to the earlier group: the only sign they would receive was Jonah. See comments on 12:39-40. Of course, for the Sadducees, the promise of a resurrection meant nothing to them, but then neither did the actual event (28:11-15). Jesus did not stay for debate (v. 4). His answer was final.

D. Jesus Warned the Twelve About the Teachings of the Pharisees and the Sadducees (16:5-12)

5 And when his disciples were come to the other side, they had forgotten to take bread.
6 Then Jesus said unto them, Take heed and beware of the leaven of the Pharisees and of the Sadducees.

7 And they reasoned among themselves, saying, *It is* because we have taken no bread.
8 *Which* when Jesus perceived, he said unto them, O ye of little faith, why reason ye among yourselves, because ye have brought no bread?
9 Do ye not yet understand, neither remember the five loaves of the five thousand, and how many baskets ye took up?
10 Neither the seven loaves of the four thousand, and how many baskets ye took up?
11 How is it that ye do not understand that I spake it not to you concerning bread, that ye should beware of the leaven of the Pharisees and of the Sadducees?
12 Then understood they how that he bade *them* not beware of the leaven of bread, but of the doctrine of the Pharisees and of the Sadducees.

Matthew identified their last location as Magadan. See above on 15:39. Reaching the other side of the Sea of Galilee, they realized they had forgotten to bring food. Mark 8:14 says they had only one loaf, surely not enough for all thirteen men. Some interpreters think Matthew writes as if the disciples caught up with Jesus after He had left ahead of them (cf. 15:39; Gundry 322; Hagner 33B:458), but Mark (8:10, 13-14) says plainly that Jesus got into the boat with His disciples.

Matthew's description reveals a little about the day-to-day life, travel, and itinerate ministry of Jesus and the Twelve. Traveling as much as they did required significant and ongoing planning just to meet daily needs, for there were none of today's conveniences of travel.

Jesus used this shortage of food to teach the Twelve a valuable lesson. He cautioned them to be on guard against the teachings of the Pharisees and Sadducees. Mark has, in place of Sadducees, "Herod" (8:15), which Gundry (325-326) suggests may be because the Sadducees supported the Herodian family. The high priest was a Sadducee and appointed by Herod (ISBE III:962; VI:279). It may also be that Jesus originally included all three groups in His warning and Matthew and Mark recorded only two each. There was probably a common thread tying all three together: namely, "believe only if signs which compel faith are produced" (Lane, 281; also Carson, *Matthew* 362).

"Take heed" and "beware" mean to be on one's guard against. The teachings of these groups might appear to be true but Jesus warned against them. Jesus spoke of the teachings (doctrine, v. 12) of the Pharisees and Sadducees as leaven. Leaven is used throughout the Scripture in both positive (13:33) and negative contexts (Lk. 12:1; 1 Cor. 5:6-8; Gal. 5:9). Here it is negative. He had earlier stated that the Pharisees were evil (12:34-35). They claimed righteous standing before God, but the claim was hypocritical (15:7). They were blind leaders and all who followed them would end up in the ditch (15:14).

At first, the Twelve did not understand Jesus and thought He must be speaking of food (v. 7). Perhaps they thought He was telling then not to buy food from the Pharisees or Sadducees. They "reasoned"—talked among themselves—trying to figure out what He meant. Jesus perceived their discussion and rebuked their small faith (v. 8; see comments on 6:30; 8:26; 14:31; and 17:20). After what they had just witnessed (vv. 9-10), they should have known that Jesus was not concerned about where they would get food for the day. Had they needed food, with none available through normal channels, Jesus could provide it supernaturally—with more leftovers than the original amount (vv. 9-10; 14:13-21; 15:32-38). The rhetorical questions were designed to rebuke the disciples for their lack of mature thinking (vv. 9-10; Newman and Stine 531). They remembered the specifics of the miracles. However, they had not given thought to what those miracles should mean to them. If He could feed thousands, He could feed thirteen. In addition to learning that He could meet all their needs, they should also have learned that the miracles He worked were sufficient to validate His Messianic claims. Mark (8:17-18) records a much harsher rebuke. With this Jesus showed that He expected His disciples to be more perceptive and different from the crowds who saw only food.

Jesus' warning about the Pharisees' and Sadducees' leaven had nothing to do with food (v. 11). Rather, it had everything to do with their doctrine, or—more specifically—their opinion of Him. Like leaven, false doctrine can permeate and corrupt what is at first pure and wholesome (Wilkins 556). The doctrine of these two groups was actively corrupting all who allowed it to enter their hearts. The Twelve must not allow the Pharisees' and Sadducees' critical attitude toward Jesus and their call for a spectacular sign (v. 1) to corrupt and destroy their own faith.

Luke (12:1) wrote of another occasion when Jesus gave this same warning to His disciples, only that time it was the leaven of the Pharisees alone in view. On that occasion, Jesus explained the leaven as the Pharisees' hypocrisy. Those Pharisees claimed to love God but in truth they lived for people's praise (Lk. 11:43). With people literally walking over each other to get to Jesus, He warned the Twelve that popularity is not what following Him is about (Bock 221).

E. Peter Confessed That Jesus Is the Divine Messiah (16:13-20)

13 When Jesus came into the coasts of Caesarea Philippi, he asked his disciples, saying, Whom do men say that I the Son of man am?
14 And they said, Some *say that thou art* John the Baptist: some, Elias; and others, Jeremias, or one of the prophets.
15 He saith unto them, But whom say ye that I am?
16 And Simon Peter answered and said, Thou art the Christ, the Son of the living God.
17 And Jesus answered and said unto him, Blessed art thou, Simon Barjona: for flesh and blood hath not revealed *it* unto thee, but my Father which is in heaven.
18 And I say also unto thee, That thou art Peter, and upon this rock I will build my church; and the gates of hell shall not prevail against it.
19 And I will give unto thee the keys of the kingdom of heaven: and whatsoever thou shalt bind on earth shall be bound in heaven: and whatsoever thou shalt loose on earth shall be loosed in heaven.

20 Then charged he his disciples that they should tell no man that he was Jesus the Christ.

Jesus led the Twelve to the region of Caesarea Philippi, located twenty-five miles (forty km.) north of the Sea of Galilee. This area was part of N.T. Palestine and was ruled by one of the sons of Herod the Great, Philip the Tetrarch (4 B.C.—A.D. 34; ISBE II:694-696; Lk. 3:1). Philip married Salome, the daughter of Herodias. It was this Salome who danced before Herod Antipas and asked for the execution of John the Baptist (14:6-11).

At the foot of Mt. Hermon in Caesarea Philippi was a cave that had been a Canaanite shrine to Baal (Jos: 11:17; Jg. 3:3; 1 Chr. 5:23; ISBE I:569). The Greeks dedicated the cave shrine to Pan, a Greek god of nature, and named the cave Paneion. After Caesar Augustus gave Herod the Great control of this area in 20 B.C., Herod erected a marble temple there in honor of Caesar Augustus (Evans and Porter 178). The presence of the shrine and temple may have influenced Peter's answer enough that he included the modifier "living" when he confessed Jesus as the Son of the living God. See below.

Jesus stayed in this area for at least a week (17:1). His reputation had reached this mainly Gentile area (Carson, *Matthew* 364), as evidenced by the crowd that assembled after the transfiguration (17:14). It was here that He healed the demon-possessed boy (17:18).

Upon His arrival at Caesarea, according to Luke 9:18, Jesus spent time, away from the crowds, in prayer with only His disciples. Jesus' prayer habits were an example to the Twelve and should be to all of Jesus' followers. Regular, private prayer times are a must (Mt. 6:6; Lk. 18:1; 1 Th. 5:17).

This prayer time might have focused on the question Jesus was about to ask His disciples. He first asked them what they were hearing about Him. What were people saying about Jesus? Exactly who did the crowds believe Him to be (v. 13)? For "Son of Man" see comments on 26:64.

The Twelve told Him what they were hearing (v. 14; Mk. 6:14-15; Lk. 9:7-9). There were several suggestions as to Jesus' identity: John the Baptist (cf. 14:2), Elijah (Mal. 3:1; 4:5-6), Jeremiah, or one of the other O.T. prophets. Though people knew Jesus was no ordinary man, no one got it right (Carson, *Matthew* 365). They equated Him with the great prophets of old. This was quite a compliment. It also required a miracle. He had to be a resurrected person to be either of them. However, as great as either of these would have been, such an identification was inadequate. He was neither, yet He was much more.

He asked the group directly: "Whom do *you* say that I am?" The "you" is in emphatic position (in the Greek order), signaling a contrast between the people's opinions and that of the Twelve (Osborne 625). Apparently, this was the first time He asked them so directly about what they had already come to know (14:33). Hagner (33B:468) suggests that this was something they had discussed many times.

Simon Peter, one of Jesus' first full-time disciples (4:18), and the group's leader and spokesperson (10:2) answered (v. 16), "You (Greek emphatic pronoun) are the Christ, the Son of the Living God." Peter's answer was first and foremost his own confession, but the others probably had the same understanding. Mark 8:29 and Luke 9:20 also record this, but neither is as full as Matthew's record. There is no parallel account in John's Gospel, but he did record another confession (Jn. 6:67-69).

"Christ" (Greek *Christos*) is the translation of the Hebrew "Messiah." It is a title, not a personal name. It means "anointed (one)." In the O.T., the word could apply to the Aaronic priests (Lev. 8:12; Num. 3:3), the king of Israel (1 Sam. 10:1; 16:13; 2 Sam. 19:10; 1 Kg. 1:39), anointed prophets (1 Kg. 19:15-16), the nation of Israel as a whole (Ps. 28:8; 105:15), or even to a heathen king who had been specially chosen to assist Israel in God's redemption plan (Is. 45:1). The most frequent use was of a king of Israel (TWOT 1:530). The Anointed One *par excellence* is the *Messiah* (Is. 61:1; Ps. 2:2; Acts 4:26-27; 10:38; Ps. 45:7; Heb. 1:9). The Authorized Version translates the Hebrew word as "Messiah" only twice (Dan. 9:25-26). The Greek transliteration of it (*Messias*) is likewise found only two times in the N.T. (Jn. 1:41; 4:25). John 1:41 says clearly, "We have found the Messias, which is, being interpreted [translated] the Christ."

Peter probably meant that Jesus was Israel's prophesied and anointed kingly Son of David (Evans, *Matthew* 317-318), the heir of David who would lead Israel into their promised age of renewed glory (Acts 1:6; Nolland 665). He viewed Jesus to be the fulfillment of the O.T. Messianic prophecies. This does not mean he had perfect understanding of Jesus' Messianic mission (vv. 22-23), but at least he understood some basics. For further comments on the meaning of "Christ," see comments on 12:18. For further discussion of the Christ as the promised descendant of King David (2 Sam. 7:16), see comments on Matthew 1:1.

"Son of the living God" further identified "the Christ" and was a faith statement. The transfiguration had not happened yet and neither had the resurrection, yet Peter and the others knew. In fact, they had known for some time that He was the "Holy One of God." See Peter's confession recorded in John 6:69 and the confession of the Twelve in Matthew 14:33 (Wilkins 560). The Father had revealed Jesus' true identity through His signs and teachings, and Peter had received understanding (13:10-17). Jesus was God's Son (1:20; Lk. 1:32, 35). He was deity. Peter and some of the others had even heard demons confessing His identity (8:29; Mk. 3:11).

The Jews for the most part rejected as blasphemous the idea that a man could also be God (26:63-65; Jn. 10:33) and killed Jesus for making this claim about Himself (Jn. 19:7). See also comments on Mt. 22:41-45. For Peter to call a man God demonstrated just how far he had grown in his own personal understanding of the true identity of Jesus.

However, there were some Jews at that time who believed, based on 2 Samuel 7:14 and Psalms 2:7, that the Messiah would be the Son of God. Nathanael (see comments on 10:3) believed Jesus was God's Son from the first (Jn. 1:49). The writer of Hebrews 1:5 later brought together these two O.T. passages and joined them with the idea of the special designation "My Son" (Lane, 1-8, 25), thus reminding his

Jewish readers that the promised Messiah is incarnate deity.

The "living God" is a common (thirty times) Scriptural description of God. Scripture writers in both testaments used this to contrast the God who lives with lifeless idols (1 Sam. 17:26; 2 Kg. 19:16-19; 2 Cor. 6:16). In Peter's confession, the contrast with lifeless idols may be inferred (see comments on v. 13), but in the fuller biblical sense "Son of the living God" means that Jesus shares in the unique, eternal life of God and has power to share that life as well (Jn. 1:4; Newman and Stine 536).

Peter's answer was exactly what Jesus wanted and was categorically different from the suggestions of the general population (Hagner 33B:468). Jesus responded by declaring Peter blessed (v. 17).

Calling Peter by his given name (v. 17), Simon son of Jonah (*bar,* is Aramaic for son; see also Jn. 1:42; 21:15-17, Simon son of John), Jesus focused on this one disciple. Peter did not discern Jesus' identity on his own nor did another human tell him. According to Jesus, Peter knew that He was the Son of the living God because God the Father had made this known to him. Unlike the Pharisees and Sadducees, who required signs (vv. 1-4), Peter accepted the Father's revelation (Carson, *Matthew* 362). Because he believed the Father's revelation about Jesus, Peter also now knew the Father. See comments on 11:27. Jesus was clear about who He meant by "Father": it was His Father in heaven not His earthly, adoptive father. Peter was indeed blessed. See comments on 5:3 for the word blessed (Greek *makarios*).

The Father's choice of Peter to receive this revelation made him the Son's choice as well, and just as Peter confessed Jesus (v. 16) so Jesus also confessed Peter (v. 18): I say also to you, you are a rock. "Also" links verse 18 with verse 16 (Nolland 667). Jesus would use Peter in a special way in the construction of the church.

This conversation between Jesus and Peter was probably in Aramaic, the Galilean tongue, rather than in Greek (Wilkins 562). Indeed most of Jesus' teachings were originally in Aramaic, the common tongue in His home area of Galilee and so Jesus' own mother tongue. This means that Matthew as well as the other Gospel writers translated Jesus' original Aramaic words into Greek (e.g., Mk. 5:41). When the N.T. authors felt it would be helpful, such translations were specifically noted for the sake of non-Aramaic readers (1:23; 27:33, 46; Mk. 5:41; 7:11; 15:22, 34; Jn. 1:38, 41, 42; 9:7; 19:17; 20:16; Acts 1:19; 4:36).

If Jesus originally spoke verse 18 in Aramaic, He would have used the one Aramaic word for rock, a masculine word (probably vocalized *kēphā*, as Matthew McAffee indicated in personal correspondence on 10-02-2012), both times. Jesus' statement, then, would have been something like this: "You are *Cephas*, and upon this *cephas* I will build My church." Verse 18, then, in the Greek N.T., is Matthew's translation of Jesus' words in Aramaic to Peter.

Matthew recorded that Jesus continued His comments to Peter (v. 18, using the singular pronoun) and addressed Peter with the name He had given him when they first met (Jn. 1:42). "Peter" (Greek *petros*) is the Greek equivalent of the Aramaic name *Cephas*. *Petros,* Peter, can denote a stone, rock (as in bedrock), cliff or a ledge (Grimm's 507), but because *petros* here translates the Aramaic word that denotes rock, in this instance *petros* must also mean rock, not a small stone.

Jesus next made a statement playing on the word *Petros*, Peter's name, and its meaning: "and upon this rock I will build my church" (Carson, *Matthew* 367-368). "And" connects the promise with the preceding "you are a rock" (Greek *petros*) and thus limits the possible antecedents to "this rock" to the first clause. In this clause "rock" translates a word (Greek *petra*) that normally means rock, as in bedrock (BAGD 654). The identity of "this rock" has consumed considerable mental energy throughout church history. Bible scholars and theologians have tried to determine the identity and the antecedent of "this rock" but have arrived at no clear consensus. Would Jesus build His church on a human foundation, especially one as unstable as Peter (Mt. 26:69-75; Gal. 2:11-14)?

In the original, "Peter" (Greek *Petros*) is a masculine word and "rock" (Greek *petra*) is feminine. Normally a word and its antecedent must agree in gender, leading some interpreters to suggest that "this rock" does not refer to Peter because rock is feminine and Peter is masculine. However, if both uses in verse 18 (*petros* and *petra*) accurately translate the masculine Aramaic word for rock (*cephas*), then Matthew simply continued Jesus' play on words (rock and rock). He used the masculine word because it would have been incorrect grammar to use a feminine word to refer to Simon, and he used the feminine word to preserve Jesus' play on words and because it usually denoted rock. Thus Matthew's use of the Greek masculine and feminine forms are not intended to distinguish between Peter as a small and loose stone and Jesus as the bedrock foundation of the church. In other words, Jesus did not contrast Peter with Himself but promised Peter that he would be foundational in the construction of Jesus' church. This means, then, that in verse 18 Jesus spoke of Peter's upcoming role in the startup of the church. Thus Peter was a rock, one on which Christ would build His church.

There are other explanations of Jesus' promise, the identity of "this rock," and possible implications of both for the church and her leadership. In fact, this verse has been a seedbed of spirited discussions. There are at least four views, each of which has truth to it: (1) Peter is "this rock" (Wilkins 563-564; Hendriksen 645, 647-648); (2) Peter's confession is "this rock," i.e. the truth in his confession; (3) Jesus is "this rock" (Walvoord 123); and (4) the law of Christ is "this rock" (Mt. 7:24-27; Gundry 334).

If Jesus meant that the church would be built on Peter as leader—as some interpreters believe (Hagner 33B:471-472)—then Peter is the designated representative of the Twelve, for all of the apostles are later called the foundation of the church and Jesus is the chief cornerstone (Eph. 2:20; Rev. 21:14; cf. 1 Cor. 3:11 also). In this view, Peter is "this rock." Even if one adopts this understanding, this verse says nothing about Peter being Jesus' designated leader of the universal church, only that Peter would be foundational in the beginning of the church.

If the second interpretation is right, i.e., that the truth of Peter's confession (or the confession itself) is the foundation upon which the church is built, then Jesus the Christ, the Son of the living

God, is the embodiment (Is. 28:15-18) of that confession. He is the chief cornerstone, the foundation of the church that is sure and the confidence of all who believe (Rom. 9:33; 1 Pet. 2:6). This is the bedrock doctrine of the church (Rom. 10:9, 11), and all who become part of the church make this confession (2 Jn. 9). In this view, "this rock" does not refer to Peter. Jesus spoke of Peter as a rock (*Petros*) to set up His point about the real rock (*petra*), the truth of the confession.

If one adopts the third interpretation, i.e., that Jesus spoke of Himself as "this rock" in contrast to Peter, then He is the foundation upon which the church is built and there can be no other (1 Cor. 3:11). N.T. writers sometimes spoke of Jesus as a stone though they at times used a different word (Greek *lithos*; Mt. 21:42, 44; Mk. 12:10; Lk. 20:17-18; Acts 4:11; 1 Pet. 2:6-7). When they spoke of Jesus as a rock and used a Matthew 16:18 word, they used the feminine word each time (Greek *petra*; Rom. 9:33; 1 Cor. 10:4; 1 Pet. 2:8).

In the fourth interpretation, the teachings of Christ are "this rock" and Jesus will build His church "only on the bedrock of His law (cf. 5:19, 20; 28:19), not on the loose stone of Peter" (Gundry 334). Gundry believes "these words of mine" (7:24, 26) are "this rock." While Gundry's argument is appealing, to expect the disciples to associate Jesus' earlier remarks (at the end of His Sermon on the Mount) with "this rock" (spoken at least a year later) seems unrealistic. Still, even though Gundry's interpretation of "this rock" is unlikely, there may be a link between "this rock" and the rock in 7:24 (also Greek *petra*) upon which wise men build (Nolland 672).

A combination of the first two views is probably what Jesus meant by "this rock" (Nolland 669; Keener, *Matthew* 427). Peter, by confessing Jesus as the Christ, the Son of the Living God, is the rock upon which the church is built. Even as Jesus blessed Peter for making this confession, He called Peter to a higher role in the Christian community. By confessing Jesus as incarnate Deity and by leading in proclaiming this confession after Pentecost, Peter became "the foundation stone for the church" (Nolland 669). In other words, Peter is not the rock because of any personal characteristics or special place among the apostles (as leader; *contra* Hagner 33B:471), but because he first confessed Jesus as the Christ and would therefore be the first to proclaim Him as the resurrected Savior of the world—in Acts 2:14-41. Peter's confessing these great truths of Jesus' identity and resurrection and his calling to be "this rock" placed him at ground level of Christ's great edifice, the church.

Regardless which understanding one adopts, the reader can be certain that the foundation of the church is sure. This was Jesus' point as much as anything else. The church is built on solid rock. Also, if the reader adopts the interpretation preferred here, one can be sure that Peter and the others understood that Jesus was calling Peter to a role of extreme importance. Peter had a designated role to play in the soon-to-be-begun church. The church would initially be built on his proclamations of Jesus' identity (Acts 2:14).

As important as the designation of the foundation are the words "I will build My church." Speaking as a carpenter, Jesus used the image of a building under construction (v. 18; cf. 1 Cor. 3:9).

Jesus is the person responsible for the birth and growth of the church. Though He will commission His followers to carry His message to the ends of the earth (28:18-20), He and He alone can and will begin and add to the church (Acts 2:47). He said "I" when He spoke of the church being brought into existence and built.

His determination and purpose are seen in His "I will." The church is the result of divine purpose (Eph. 1:4), not of men's plan or religious tendencies. One of Jesus' eternal purposes will be accomplished in the building of the church. Furthermore, the church is a project that will progress over time until its final completion. Jesus will build His church. It will not be done quickly (13:24-33, 36-43), but it will be finished.

The church belongs to Jesus. He called it "my" church. The church is Christ's building, bride, and body. It belongs to Him. He loves her, died for her, redeemed her, sanctified her, and will come again for her (Eph. 5:25-27).

"Church" (Greek *ekklēsia*) suggests by its etymology a calling out. It has both secular and biblical uses and in both spheres of usage can denote "the assembling of men and the men thus assembled" (TDNT III:503). In the N.T. the word can refer to a local assembly of citizens (Acts 19:32, 39, 41), to the O.T. "congregation" assembled before the Lord (Acts 7:38), to a local congregation of N.T. believers (the house church; Mt. 18:17; Acts 14:23; 1 Cor. 1:2; Philem. 2), or to the universal church, i.e., all believers, dead and alive (Eph. 1:22; 5:23-24; Heb. 12:23). Here in Matthew 16:18, Jesus was speaking of His new people (Evans, *Matthew* 319), the universal church which encompasses all believers of all time. The only other time the Gospel writers record Jesus speaking directly of the church is in Matthew 18:17 where the local congregation is in view. Mark, Luke, and John do not mention the "church."

The gates of hell speak of something other than the entry point into the place of punishment. Hell (Greek *hadēs*) has three main meanings in the N.T. In some contexts, it is the place where all dead people go, righteous and unrighteous, and is equivalent to the Hebrew *sheol* (translated grave, Ps. 6:5; hell, Ps. 16:10; Is. 5:14). Acts 2:31 and Revelation 1:18, 6:8, 20:13-14 fit here. It can denote the earthly grave (1 Cor. 15:55; not in all manuscripts). In other contexts the word means the place of eternal torments for the wicked (Mt. 11:23; Lk. 16:23). See comments on Matthew 11:23.

In O.T. usage, the city gates were sometimes where city leaders gathered to conduct business (Gen. 19:1, 9; Dt. 22:15; Ruth 4:1-2, 11; Prov. 31:23; Am. 5:15). If this was what Jesus meant, He pictured Satan and His powerful demons gathered in collusion at the entrance of the underworld and joining forces to overcome the church. "Prevail" can denote some form of aggression, meaning that Jesus pictured these gates as attacking the church. One may see Revelation 6:8, 9:1-11, and 20:7-8 as depicting such a struggle with hades and Satan as the aggressors (Bruner 2:131). Multiple scholars understand it this way (TDNT VI:927; Hendriksen 649).

Hill (262) finds this interpretation forced and unnatural. Using Isaiah 38:10 as a background, he and other interpreters understand the gates of hell to mean the powers of death (ISBE II:408; TDNT VI:924-927; Gundry 332) or the entrance into the world of the dead (Newman and Stine 539). See also Job 38:17, Psalms 9:13, and Psalm 107:18. In Isaiah 38:10, Hezekiah complained he was so sick that he was near death. He feared that the remainder of his days on this earth would be at death's door.

Understood this way, Jesus' promise meant that even death (martyrdom, Gundry 335; natural death, Newman and Stine 539; death in general, Hagner 33B:472) would not stop the church (Wilkins 565). If church tradition is right, all of the apostles but John died a martyr's death. Add all of the believers who have given their lives for their faith or have simply died in faith and it is clear that death cannot stop the church. The church lives on today and those members of the church of Jesus Christ who have died will arise in final victory over her last enemy, death (1 Cor. 15:26, 54-57).

Carson believes Jesus meant that because the church is Jesus' assembly, the church itself cannot die (*Matthew* 370). Nolland (674-675) understands the gates of hell to represent the entrance to the place of the dead and prevail (Greek *katischuō*) to mean something like "be stronger than" or "make themselves strong against." He sees the church as the aggressor. The church can "batter down the gates of Hades" and through the preaching of Peter, who has the keys of the kingdom, rescue "people from the grip of Hades" and open "for them a future in the kingdom of heaven."

The question, then, becomes, did Jesus mean the church will successfully stand against the aggressions of hell, or, did He mean that the church will overcome the gates of hell? Is the church the aggressor or the target of aggression? Jesus' earlier words in Matthew 11:12 help here. The church is aggressively moving forward even while she is under attack by the forces of the evil one. There is aggression both ways. Thus, the first interpretation is probably the correct one. The gates of hell represent the forces of evil gathering to plan their attack against the church.

Regardless how one identifies these gates or decides which of the two parties mentioned is the aggressor, Jesus promised victory for His church (the antecedent of "it"). The church will win. Jesus guarantees this. While "this rock" is the foundation of the church—and, as such, part of the reason for the church's strength—it is the builder, owner, and protector who is the reason the church is immoveable and triumphant.

Still focusing on Peter (the singular pronoun in v. 19), Jesus also promised him the authority to loose and bind on earth. Keys speak of authority and access (Is. 22:21-22; Rev. 3:7-8). Here they speak of authority to bind or set free. Without giving specifics, Jesus gave Peter certain authority.

Some commentators (Nolland 677, 682) separate keys and the authority to loose and bind, understanding that two types of authority are in view. Nolland sees the keys as representing Peter's new ability to open the gates of the kingdom of heaven. Peter's ability to loose and bind is about his ability to apply Jesus' teachings to people's lives.

That Jesus delegated to Peter authority seems clear enough. Protestants are confident that Catholic theologians are mistaken to use this verse to teach that an order of priestly successors who have the Apostle Peter as their head is necessary for the church to offer sacrifices to God (sacerdotalism). Neither does this verse teach that these same priests have the authority to absolve sin.

The words "shall be bound" and "shall be loosed" can also be translated "shall have been bound" and "shall have been loosed" (Greek future perfect passive). This could mean that Peter's binding and loosing would simply be an extension of what had already happened in heaven—but not necessarily. Again, opinions vary. Carson (*Matthew* 372) argues that Matthew did not have to use the perfect tense for these two words, so he must have done so for a reason. Using Luke 11:52 to illustrate (Luke's version of Matthew 23:13), Carson compares with Peter the scribes who misrepresented Scripture to the extent they kept people from entering the kingdom. They had the key of knowledge, i.e., they knew about God and they knew how to get to God (Marshall 507), but they took the key away from the people. For this Jesus pronounced on them a solemn woe.

In contrast to what the scribes failed to do, i.e., to lead the people into the kingdom, Peter would do. Jesus gave him the key of knowledge as well. He was the new scribe (13:52).

Matthew, then, used the perfect form of loose and bind because Peter would bind and loose "by proclaiming a gospel that has already been given and by making personal application on that basis" (Carson, *Matthew* 373). Peter would proclaim the gospel message that Jesus gave to him and all who accepted it would enter the kingdom (Acts 2:41) and all who rejected the gospel Peter preached would be excluded (Acts 4:11-12). Thus, Peter was empowered to declare folks outside the kingdom bound in their sin because they rejected his message (as in Acts 8:10, 20-23), and to declare folks inside the kingdom loosed from their sins because they accepted his message (Acts 10:47).

Other passages help explain more about Peter's new authority. He was not the only person to receive it. In Matthew 18:18, Jesus gave this same apostolic authority to all of the Twelve, to the universal church, and to each local church in matters of church discipline (1 Cor. 5:1-13; 2 Cor. 10:8; 13:10; 1 Tim. 5:20; Tit. 2:15; 3 Jn. 9). In 18:18 the "you" is plural in the Greek, whereas here (16:19) "you" is singular and refers only to Peter. See comments on 18:18 and its context.

In 28:19, Jesus sent His followers all over the world with His authority to proclaim the gospel as His plan of salvation. In John 20:23, Jesus gave His followers the authority to preach His message of forgiveness. The book of Acts illustrates that Peter did indeed minister with great authority as he directed lost souls to the door of the kingdom (Acts 2:37-41) and disciplined sinful members (Acts 5:1-11). He also argued before the Jerusalem church for Gentile believers' freedom from the demands of the Mosaic Law (Acts 15:7-11). Through changed lives and visible signs of the Holy Spirit (Acts 8:17; 10:44-46), heaven supported Peter and the others as they proclaimed the gospel of the kingdom.

Peter's privilege is in his place and role as first proclaimer. The Jews, the Samaritans, and the Gentiles all first received confirmation of their place in the kingdom through the baptism of the Holy Spirit at the preaching and invitation of Peter (Acts 2:14-41; 8:14-17; 10:44-45), something Peter and the

Jerusalem church both acknowledged (Acts 15:7-9).

To summarize, then, the keys that Jesus spoke of were (1) the possession of the gospel message, (2) the right to proclaim the gospel and offer access into the kingdom, and (3) the exercising of discipline within the Christian community (Hendriksen 651). The "whatsoever" referred to people (18:15-18). Everyone in the Christian community is under the authority of the church in matters of church discipline, though not for personal salvation, and is required to live under Jesus' teachings for life as recorded and taught by the Apostles. "In heaven" teaches "God stands behind" the gospel the church preaches (Bruner 2:132-133), accepting those who accept the gospel and rejecting those who reject the gospel.

Now that the Twelve knew Jesus' true identity, He insisted they keep it to themselves (v. 20). The disciples' excitement must have surged with Peter's confession and Jesus' admission, yet Jesus quickly set boundaries. At this time, they would preach the kingdom but not the king, i.e., they would not travel around Galilee openly proclaiming Jesus the Messianic king. Such preaching would have caused major trouble for Jesus. The Apostles would openly proclaim Jesus as their king after His ascension (Acts 17:7). Now was a time when sign miracles (11:4-6) and divine revelation (11:25-27; 16:17) would give birth to faith in Jesus as the Christ, the Son of the Living God (Carson, *Matthew* 374).

As the next verses show, the Twelve did not understand what Jesus as Messiah fully meant (Barclay 2:171-172). Had they begun proclaiming Jesus as the kind of kingly Messiah expected by many in Judaism at that time, they would have been preaching a false gospel. Jesus needed more time to help them understand the full meaning of His Messiahship. Only then could they be permitted to publically identify Jesus as the Christ, the King.

F. Jesus' First Prophecy of His Death and Resurrection (16:21-23)

The Twelve now knew Jesus was the Messiah, the Christ. After Peter's clear statement of faith in verse 16, and Jesus' promises in verses 18-19, Jesus began to explain to the Twelve more fully what His Messianic mission meant. Being Messiah meant that He must go to Jerusalem where He would suffer at the hands of the Jewish leadership, be killed, and rise from the dead.

21 From that time forth began Jesus to shew unto his disciples, how that he must go unto Jerusalem, and suffer many things of the elders and chief priests and scribes, and be killed, and be raised again the third day.
22 Then Peter took him, and began to rebuke him, saying, Be it far from thee, Lord: this shall not be unto thee.
23 But he turned, and said unto Peter, Get thee behind me, Satan: thou art an offence unto me: for thou savourest not the things that be of God, but those that be of men.

"From that time forth" marks this as a transition time in Jesus' ministry (4:17) and the second major section of Matthew's Gospel (Hagner 33B:478-

479). Matthew recalled how from this point on Jesus began speaking clearly about His upcoming death and resurrection in Jerusalem (17:22-23; 20:17-19; 26:2).

Jesus showed His disciples that He must die. "Show" (Greek *epideiknumi*) means "to demonstrate that something is true, ... to prove" (Louw and Nida I:673). Mark (8:31) says He began to teach (Greek *didaskō*) them, but Matthew suggests by his choice of words that Jesus did more. He was proving to them, perhaps with references to O.T. passages, that He as the Messiah must suffer and die.

"Must" is key to Jesus' teachings and grammatically connected with the verbs go, suffer, be killed, and be raised. It was God's plan for Jesus to die at the hands of the religious establishment in Jerusalem and be raised again. Though Jesus did not want to suffer, He was willing to submit in obedience to His Father's will (Mt. 26:39, 42). Consider 17:10, 24:6, 26:54, Mark 13:10, Luke 9:22, 17:25, and 24:7 for other uses of "must" in this sense.

Jesus gave several specifics in His prophecy. He would die in Jerusalem. The Jewish elders, chief priests, and scribes would make Him suffer many things and then kill Him. However, He would rise from the dead on the third day. The specifics could be easily checked. Either they would come true or they would not.

Matthew uses the word "elders" more frequently than any other Gospel writer (twelve times). Apparently the title could refer to leaders of local synagogues (Lk. 7:3), chief priests, scribes (Lk. 22:66), Pharisees (Mk. 7:3, 5), or to lay members of the Sanhedrin (26:3, 57, 59; 27:1; TDNT VI:659-661). The latter seems to be meant here. Jeremias (222-232) identifies them as lay aristocrats of lesser importance than the priestly nobility but whose influential place in society afforded some of them a place on the Sanhedrin. He believes Joseph of Arimathea was one such elder since the N.T. writers never call him a priest or scribe, the other two groups who made up the Sanhedrin.

Chief priests were the leading, influential priests. They were members of the Sanhedrin and instrumental in Jesus' death (26:59; 27:1). Apparently most were Sadducees (Acts 5:17), but Evans (*Matthew* 423) cautions against such an assumption because Josephus never makes that claim. For scribes see comments on 13:52.

Jesus spoke plainly (Mk. 8:32) and the disciples understood. In fact, Peter rebuked the Lord for talking like this. Having just had the conversation about Jesus' true identity, Peter could not understand why Jesus would now speak of dying. This was not the destiny of the Messiah he had understood Jesus to be. There was still much to be learned (Lk. 9:45).

Peter so strongly opposed this talk of Jesus' death that he took Jesus aside privately (Greek *proslambanō*) and began to rebuke Him. Literally translated, Peter said, "Mercy to you, Lord. This will never happen to you!" Peter rejected any thought of a dying Messiah. Peter could not fathom how one who was Son of the Living God could experience what Jesus foretold.

Jesus quickly stopped Peter and rebuked him instead. Peter was to return to his "position of discipleship" (Keener, *Matthew* 433). The one who just moments before was declared "blessed" and a rock now was called Satan. Jesus' answer was harsh because Peter's words did not agree with God's will for Jesus. Peter's words were an offense or hindrance (Greek *skandalon)* and came from his human way of thinking. The one who moments before was commended for receiving special revelation from the Father (v. 17) was now carnal in his thinking. Jesus would allow no one, not even Peter, to keep Him from the cross. Satan had earlier also offered Jesus a kingdom without a cross (4:8-9), but Jesus remained committed to the Father's will for Him.

The name "Satan" means opponent or adversary. Because of this, some writers wonder if Jesus was calling Peter an opponent rather than the devil (Evans, *Matthew* 323). Grimm's (572) also understands "Satan" here as descriptive. He believes Jesus called Peter a "Satan-like man." Either way, the rebuke was stern, for Peter's word had a satanic overtone.

G. Jesus Taught the Twelve the High Cost of Discipleship (16:24-28)

24 Then said Jesus unto his disciples, If any *man* will come after me, let him deny himself, and take up his cross, and follow me.
25 For whosoever will save his life shall lose it: and whosoever will lose his life for my sake shall find it.
26 For what is a man profited, if he shall gain the whole world, and lose his own soul? or what shall a man give in exchange for his soul?
27 For the Son of man shall come in the glory of his Father with his angels; and then he shall reward every man according to his works.
28 Verily I say unto you, There be some standing here, which shall not taste of death, till they see the Son of man coming in his kingdom.

Not only did Jesus speak of His own death (v. 21), He also required all His followers to die as well. Compare with 10:38, 39 and other parallel accounts (Mk. 8:34—9:1; Lk. 9:23-27; 14:27). Peter did not want Jesus to die but Jesus said that death was also a reality for all who follow Him. "Any" means there are no exceptions. Mark says that there was a multitude present for this portion of Jesus' instructions. Surely Jesus surprised the Twelve with these words about what they should expect as they followed Him (19:27-30; 20:20-28; Hagner 33B:487). This was not what they thought following the Messiah would mean.

Jesus spoke of voluntary association with Him. "If any will" focuses on the universal invitation of Jesus' gospel and the free will of man (Nolland 691). Following Jesus means first surrendering one's life to Him (Keener, *Matthew* 434). This is a decision point (Greek aorist) that precedes taking up one's cross (Hagner 33B:483) and is a non-negotiable mandate (imperative). Following Jesus means leaving one's own way of life with its goals and ambitions and adopting Jesus as sovereign Lord (Jn. 8:12; 12:26; 21:19). Adopting Jesus as Lord means submitting to His rule. Self's pleasures, goals, desires, and ambitions must all be renounced in favor of following Jesus (Rom. 14:7-9; Carson, *Matthew* 379).

Second, following Jesus means dying to self, which includes crucifying the flesh with its passions and desires (Gal. 5:24). As Jesus completely subjugated

His will to the Father's—and the cross showed this pointedly—so anyone, i.e., everyone, who follows Jesus must bear his or her own cross (v. 24) for the same reason (Wilkins 572; Rom. 15:2-3). Cross bearing is proof that the disciple's will is subject to the will of his Lord (Gal. 2:20; 1 Pet. 2:21). Carrying the cross does not mean one could die (martyrdom) or that one is going to die. It means that the cross-bearer is dead. He has already died. In 10:35-39, death on the disciple's personal cross meant subjecting the closest family ties to the supreme Lordship of Christ. See comments on 8:22 also. Here in 16:24-26 death on one's cross means death to personal goals, ambitions, passions, and desires. In Luke 14:25-33, death on one's cross means death to anything that competes with the Lordship of Christ.

Third, having denied self and having picked up the personal cross, followers must then continually (Greek present imperative) follow Jesus, carrying their crosses. This is no single decision event, nor does it mean to start, stop, and start again. Following Jesus continues on from the initial decision and means wherever He leads the disciple will follow. Following Jesus is full time and for a lifetime.

Hill (264) says these three actions "describe, not conditions for discipleship, but the attitudes in which the *whole* life of the disciple must consist." True enough. Salvation is by grace through faith and not of works (Eph. 2:8-9). However, the sincere decision to follow Christ begins with self-denial, cross-bearing, and acknowledging and submitting to Jesus as Lord (Rom. 10:9)—both of the world and of oneself. These attitudes and actions coincide with conversion. They are not part of a post-conversion, more committed discipleship, a deeper life experience, or a separate or second definite work of grace.

Notwithstanding what was said in reference to the second point, above, following Jesus and carrying a cross can result in persecution and even martyrdom. Anyone who rejects Christian discipleship because of the fear of persecution will miss eternal life (v. 25; Gundry 340). Anyone who loses life because of persecution on account of allegiance to Christ will find eternal life. Even so, martyrdom is not the only way a person can "lose" his life.

The first century cross was a symbol of death and thus for Jesus expressed total commitment. It held no attraction in itself. Verse 25 explains why the cross is necessary for the disciple. This is the first of three successive uses of "for" (vv. 25, 26, 27; Greek explicative *gar*) to explain the reasons for the preceding statement of verse 24 (Hagner 33B:484). Verse 25 explains why all followers must pick up a cross: life is found by losing it. By giving up earthly desires and ambitions for Jesus' sake now, one will find life in the eschatological consummation, i.e., eternal life at the judgment (Bruner 2:154). The person who tries to save life for himself, so he can live it to the fullest now, will ultimately lose it in that eschatological end (Carson, *Matthew* 379). Noah's generation and Sodom's citizens illustrate how one can lose life by trying to save it for the here and now (Lk. 17:26-37). Paul's testimony illustrates how one can find life by losing it (Phil. 3:7-11; Wilkins 573).

In these verses "life" and "soul" translate the same word (Greek *psuchē*), which can refer to physical life, i.e., the breath of life, "the vital force which animates the body" (Grimm's 677); or to the soul, the psychological faculties of "thinking, willing and feeling" (Louw and Nida I:261, 321-322). Luke (9:25) uses "himself" instead of this word. At the least, physical life is meant in verse 25, but it is probable Jesus had the whole person in mind (Newman and Stine 546), the deeper self that does not die (Hagner 33B:484). The eternal soul is clearly meant in verse 26.

Verse 26, with its "for," explains why verse 25 is true: when one stands before God in judgment, all of this world's goods will not be enough to purchase salvation of the soul. Verse 27 explains the reason for the truth in verse 26: Jesus will return to judge according to works, not possessions.

Verses 25 and 26 both speak hyperbolically and both use profit and loss images (Nolland 693). Psalm 49:7-8 is a probable backdrop for these verses. The Psalm teaches that the rich and the poor, the wise and the fool, will alike die empty-handed. The rich will be unable to purchase his way out of the grave or have someone die for him so he can continue living (Ps. 49:7-12, 17; VanGemeren 369).

Jesus explained what He meant in verse 25 with two rhetorical questions in verse 26. Both require the answer, "Nothing" (Newman and Stine 547). A person who lives only for this world and dies lost has realized no real benefit in the end. The individual who loses his soul, though he dies wealthy, has gained nothing. "Lose" (Greek *zēmioō*) means to lose or forfeit something that one previously possessed (Louw and Nida I:566). The person who loses his soul has forever forfeited the only thing he could have saved.

Jesus' second question in verse 26 focused on the value of the soul over anything in this world. Nothing in this world is valuable enough to purchase a soul. Once lost, the soul is forever gone. All of man's accumulated wealth will not redeem the soul.

These are important concerns because Jesus is coming again (v. 27). His incarnation visit to the earth was not His last. The next coming will be different, for He will come in the splendor and glory of Almighty God (Mt. 16:27; 24:30; 25:31; 26:64). He will not be shrouded in humanity or Galilean dust and sandals. His entourage will not be Galilean fishermen but His own angels. His first visit to earth marked the inauguration of the kingdom. His return will mark the consummation of the kingdom (Carson, *Matthew* 379). For Son of Man, see discussion on 26:64.

At the time of Jesus' return, He will judge everyone and will give sentence according to what each person has done. This is not a works-based salvation. However, everyone's deeds will be judged, for works demonstrate the love of the heart. For those carrying their cross, this will be a great experience (5:12). The Bible mentions a judgment of works several times (e.g., Rom. 2:6-10; Rev. 20:12-13).

Jesus' final recorded words on this occasion are somewhat surprising (v. 28). Having just spoken of His own death (v. 21) and the deaths of all who follow Him (v. 24), He now promises that some of those standing there would not physically die until they see Him coming in His kingdom. Some of the Twelve will remain alive until this promise comes to pass.

If verse 28 continues the thought begun in verse 27—that Jesus' coming promised in verse 27 is the coming kingdom also assured in verse 28—it seems that Jesus promised something that has not happened yet. Keener (*Matthew* 435) says the prediction did not happen. If, however, Jesus spoke of two separate events, His return in glory (v. 27) and a revelatory preview of Himself in His kingdom glory, then the interpretive problem lessens. Many writers see this promise as referring to the transfiguration. See below.

Carson (*Matthew* 380-382) argues that Jesus promised His kingdom would be seen and this had nothing to do with the transfiguration. He understands verse 28 to find fulfillment in the rapid expansion of the kingdom after Jesus' resurrection and the mission to the Gentiles. He believes only this allows enough time for the phrase "some standing here will not taste death" and demonstrates that the kingdom has come in power. One weakness with Carson's view is that *all* of the Twelve, not just some (except for Judas, who is not specifically being discussed) saw the kingdom as he explains it.

Luke says that some will see the kingdom of God (9:27). Mark (9:1) writes that some will see the kingdom of God in its "power." According to Matthew, some will see the "Son of Man coming in His kingdom" (16:28). Mark indicates that Jesus spoke of the coming transfiguration as powerful proof that the kingdom had come (Evans, *Matthew* 326). Matthew's abbreviated account omits the words that speak of Jesus' coming with power (Mk. 9:1) and so might be understood to refer to Jesus' second coming (so Gundry 341 and Nolland 695). However, Mark's fuller account shows that Jesus was not speaking of His second coming but of His transfiguration. Three disciples would witness that, and it so overwhelmed them that they were overcome with fear (Mk. 9:6; cf. Mt. 17:6).

Jesus temporarily disclosed His majesty (2 Pet. 1:16) and the glorious power of His kingdom in the transfiguration. Peter, James, and John (the "some") saw Jesus in the glory that will be His in His eternal kingdom (16:27: "the glory of his Father"; 17:2: "His face shone, etc."). The transfiguration was, then, a preview of Jesus' kingdom glory to be revealed at His second coming and a glimpse of what is rightfully and eternally His (Jn. 17:5; 2 Pet. 1:16-18; see comments on 17:1-9).

Matthew recorded several definitive proofs that the King and His kingdom have come. The most obvious to the Twelve were (1) the presence of the forerunner (3:2-3; 11:10), (2) Jesus' spectacular physical healings (11:4-5; compare with Jn. 9:32), (3) and Jesus' ability to cast out demons (12:28). There would be more, the most obvious being Jesus' transfiguration (16:28-17:8) and His resurrection (28:6-10).

Summary (16:1-28)

This section began with the enemies of Jesus gathering to test Him. He condemned their hypocrisy and cut them short. They asked for a super sign as proof of His claims. Jesus refused, saying their request was itself a sign, a sign of an evil and spiritually unfaithful heart. The only sign He offered was Jonah. Jonah's resurrection from his grave, the whale, validated his message. The same would be true for Jesus.

Jesus left with His disciples and used the request of the Pharisees and

Sadducees to warn the Twelve not to be like them. The Twelve needed to guard against having a critical spirit against Jesus and against any temptation to build their faith on the spectacular. Though they witnessed many great miracles, such as the feeding of the multitudes, yet they needed to be careful lest they join Jesus' detractors and lose their faith.

Traveling twenty-five miles north of the Sea of Galilee to Caesarea Philippi, Jesus called on the Twelve to confess their faith. He asked them to state plainly who they believed Him to be. Peter spoke on behalf of the Twelve and gave a clear confession of Jesus' person as Messiah and Son of God. This is a bedrock doctrine of the church, the essential confession of Christianity (Hagner 33B:474). Without it Christianity would not exist.

Because Peter expressed this confession, Jesus designated him to be the person who would first proclaim it to the world. Peter and his confession together were the foundation rock upon which Jesus would build His church. All who accepted the confession as Peter proclaimed it would gain entrance into the kingdom. All who rejected Peter's confession would be turned away.

Once the disciples articulated a clear understanding of Jesus' Person, He began explaining to them the purpose of His coming as the God-man. He had to suffer, die, and be raised again. Peter, who had just confessed so eloquently, began to rebuke Jesus. Jesus rejected Peter's rebuke and rebuked him for what would hinder His way to the cross. Jesus concluded His rebuke by speaking to all of His disciples. Death was not just for Him. Death was for all who would follow Him. Every person who would follow Jesus must deny self, take up his cross, and follow Jesus bearing that cross. Death to self is a non-negotiable. It is a prerequisite for receiving eternal life.

Eternal life is worth more than the sum total of everything this world has. When life on earth is over—and it will be over—every person will stand before Jesus with nothing but how he lived. If he followed Jesus, he will receive eternal life. If he tried to gain everything this world could give him, he will lose his only opportunity for eternal life. This judgment will take place when Jesus returns in glory. At that time, He will judge everyone according to his or her life's works.

Perhaps to calm their fears and to prove that His death would not change anything about Him as Messiah, Jesus promised to reveal His kingdom glory to some of His disciples before they die. Such a promise anticipated the transfiguration. It also looked forward to the consummation of the kingdom.

Application: Teaching and Preaching the Passage

This chapter is a treasure. Pastors and teachers must from time to time revisit this chapter because it contains the biblical basis for the church's existence as well as Jesus' requirements for discipleship. Both need to be kept before God's people even though both are thought by some to be optional for Christians. Nothing could be further from the truth—whether one is speaking of the visible (local) or invisible (universal) church or discipleship.

The idea that one can be saved and then decide whether to serve the Lord through a local church is foreign to

Scripture. The same is true for discipleship. The Bible does not describe a two-tiered Christianity. Discipleship is not limited to the committed in the sense that uncommitted Christians need not concern themselves about it. Jesus' discipleship requirements are inclusive of all Christians. Any who refuse to shoulder a cross are not following Jesus.

With these thoughts in mind, perhaps the following ideas will be helpful for lesson or sermon preparation: Verses 1-12 suggest three very practical and timeless lessons for Jesus' disciples: (1) do not worry about the little things; (2) Jesus is our provider; and (3) do not allow critics to destroy your faith in Jesus. Several doctrines of Christ are taught in this chapter: (1) He is the creator (16:9-10); (2) He is divine (16:16); (3) He rules angels (16:27); (4) He was destined for the cross (16:21, 23); (5) He will judge everyone (16:27). Using verse 18 as a lesson text, one might explain (1) the greatness of the church, (2) the greatness of her founder and owner, (3) the greatness of her opposition, and (4) the greatness of her security (Bruner 2:514).

Verses 13-19 suggest several possible outlines for lessons and sermons on the church. One might develop a lesson or sermon using (1) a personal confession, (2) a promised construction, and (3) a permanent creation. Verse 18 speaks of (1) the foundation, (2) the founder, and (3) the founding of the church. The same verse speaks of (1) the greatest assembly, (2) the greatest leader, (3) the greatest purpose, (4) the greatest conflict, and (5) the greatest stability.

The five words of Jesus' statement, "I will build My church" can be expressed in five confessions: (1) "I": Jesus possesses the authority needed to build the church; (2) "will": Jesus' own resolve and purpose are evident in His desire to build the church; (3) "build": Jesus will build the church over time; (4) "my": Jesus alone possesses ownership of the church; and (5) "church": what Jesus perceived as the completed project is in the name itself.

Jesus was headed for the cross. It was the Father's plan. Verses 21-23 speak of (1) the Messianic must, (2) the Messianic reprimand, and (3) the Messianic mindset.

Jesus' call to discipleship can be expressed in various outlines. Following Jesus requires (1) a decision, (2) a death, and (3) a lifelong determination (v. 24). See explanation above. There is (1) a call to discipleship, (2) a cost of discipleship, and (3) a revealed consequence of discipleship. Discipleship is (1) offered to all, (2) carries the same requirements for all, and (3) brings rewards to all. Verses 24-27 speak of (1) each soul's potential (live or die), (2) each soul's price (value), and (3) each soul's payday (judgment).

H. The Transfiguration (17:1-9)

Following Peter's confession, Jesus acted to strengthen the faith of His inner circle more than anything He had done up to that point. Aside from the resurrection, this is the greatest sign Jesus did, for in this one act He revealed His normally hidden but true glory. The human Jesus was divine. This was His eternal nature and essence and on this occasion He chose to reveal a portion of His divine glory to Peter, James, and John.

Jesus had called for undivided commitment (16:24) to Him. Nothing is more important (16:25-26), for He will one day come to judge every fallen being. This transfiguration was proof of His coming in glory and power.

The transfiguration was also Jesus making good on a promise (16:28). Here some of the Twelve saw heavenly glory with a human eye. This scene was indelibly impressed in their memories (Jn. 1:14; 2 Pet. 1:16-17).

1 And after six days Jesus taketh Peter, James, and John his brother, and bringeth them up into an high mountain apart,
2 And was transfigured before them: and his face did shine as the sun, and his raiment was white as the light.
3 And, behold, there appeared unto them Moses and Elias talking with him.
4 Then answered Peter, and said unto Jesus, Lord, it is good for us to be here: if thou wilt, let us make here three tabernacles; one for thee, and one for Moses, and one for Elias.
5 While he yet spake, behold, a bright cloud overshadowed them: and behold a voice out of the cloud, which said, This is my beloved Son, in whom I am well pleased; hear ye him.
6 And when the disciples heard *it*, they fell on their face, and were sore afraid.
7 And Jesus came and touched them, and said, Arise, and be not afraid.
8 And when they had lifted up their eyes, they saw no man, save Jesus only.
9 And as they came down from the mountain, Jesus charged them, saying, Tell the vision to no man, until the Son of man be risen again from the dead.

Matthew, Mark (9:2-10), and Luke (9:28-36) each record the account of the transfiguration. About a week after Peter's confession (16:13-20), apparently while Jesus and the Twelve were still in Caesarea Philippi, Jesus took Peter, James, and John "up into a high mountain" to pray (Lk. 9:28). The mountain is not named. Mounts Tabor and Hermon are generally suggested although Hendriksen (665) thinks Jebel Jermak is more likely and Carson (*Matthew* 384) prefers Mount Miron. All of these but Mount Hermon are located in Galilee. The presence of a crowd (17:14) and scribes (Mk. 9:14) suggests a mountain in Galilee as a probable site but Matthew's note in verse 22 (see the discussion there) may indicate they gathered back in Galilee afterward, making Mount Hermon seem the most likely (Wilkins 590).

Luke says the transfiguration happened about eight days after Peter's confession and Matthew says it was after six days. One should understand that neither was trying to be exact. About a week later is probably the correct understanding. (See John 20:26 for another example of eight days that probably means a week.) Luke also mentions that Jesus and His three disciples were on the mountain two days (Lk. 9:37) and that the disciples were asleep (Lk. 9:32) at the beginning of the transfiguration. The transfiguration took place at night.

Jesus went up the mountain to pray, and as He prayed (Lk. 9:28) He was changed so that His face began to shine as brightly as the sun (cf. 13:43). His clothing began to shine and became "white as the light." His entire being was glorified. This fulfilled the promise (16:28) that some of His disciples would see Him coming in His glory and in the power of His kingdom before they died. See comments above.

"Transfigured" (Greek *metamorphoō*) means to be changed in form. Jesus' physical being was altered by the Father to reveal His preincarnate glory (Jn. 17:5) and the glory that will be His in His kingdom. Peter wrote (2 Pet. 1:16-17) that the Father honored and glorified Jesus on this occasion. Luke 9:32 said they saw His glory. John later wrote that he had beheld Jesus' glory, glory as of the only begotten of the Father (Jn. 1:14). Matthew's three uses of the word behold "stresses the marvel of the experience" (vv. 3, 5; Carson, *Matthew 385*).

Jesus' transfiguration paralleled Moses' experience (Ex. 34:29-33) but went much further. Moses' face shone, whereas Jesus' entire being shone. Moses covered his face and hid his glowing skin. Jesus' clothing did not hide His glory.

While Jesus prayed, Moses and Elijah appeared in glorified form. They talked with Jesus about His upcoming death in Jerusalem (Lk. 9:31). The three disciples recognized Moses and Elijah and heard their conversation with Jesus.

Peter and the others were very afraid (Mk. 9:6). As Moses and Elijah were about to leave (Lk. 9:33), Peter stated that it was a good place for all six of them to be. He offered to set up shelters (Greek *skēnas*, shelter, tent) or brush booths for Jesus, Moses, and Elijah (v. 4). "If thou wilt" = "If you will/desire" and is a condition assumed true (Greek first class condition). Perhaps Peter assumed that to stay on the mountain and prolong this event was Jesus' will, but Mark 9:6 and Luke 9:33 both add that Peter did not know what to say. Peter's offer suggested the three were equal (Gundry 344) and he might have thought this was the beginning of the fulfillment of 16:28 (Nolland 703).

While Peter was still speaking (v. 5), a bright cloud—reminiscent of God's cloud of Presence in the O.T., the Shekinah glory (Ex. 24:15-18)—overshadowed or enveloped them all, and God the Father spoke. The Father answered (rebuked?; Evans, *Matthew* 329) Peter's offer. There was no need for three booths. Moses and Elijah were important figures of the past but Jesus is God's voice today (Heb. 1:2).

The words "This is my beloved Son in whom I am well pleased" are the same as the Father said at Jesus' baptism (3:17). In the transfiguration context, the Son has greater standing than the servants Moses and Elijah (Heb. 3:5-6). The Father's command, "Listen to him," also pointed to the same superiority. It seems probable that Moses represented the Law and Elijah represented the Prophets. These great men and their messages pointed to Christ, but the reality in Christ is greater than the types and promises of these O.T. men (Heb. 3:3). He was the Prophet to whom Moses said that his hearers should listen (Dt. 18:15; Blomberg 56; Acts 3:22-23; 7:37; Gundry 343). When there was a question of who or what to follow—whether Jesus' teachings or the O.T.—the transfiguration answered that question: hear Jesus (Bruner 2:168).

The three disciples reacted to God's voice with reverence. "They fell on their faces" (v. 6) means they prostrated themselves and put their faces to the ground in weakness, worship, and fear (Ezek. 1:28; Dan. 8:18; 10:9). Jesus came to them and calmed their fears. When the disciples looked up, Moses and Elijah were gone and they and Jesus were alone on the mountain. Jesus' glory was again hidden.

As they descended (v. 9), Jesus instructed the disciples not to tell anyone about the experience until after His resurrection. This included the other disciples. The vision was privileged. No one else had seen such a revelation of Jesus' true identity. No one else would know about it until after His resurrection. The Twelve knew that Jesus was the Christ (16:20), and Peter, James, and John saw Him glorified; but none were permitted to tell anyone what they now knew from personal experience.

Jesus probably required secrecy because publicity of this event would have negatively impacted His ministry. See comments on 9:30 and 12:16-21. Mark 9:10 said they did as Jesus instructed and kept this to themselves, but they did not understand Jesus' resurrection comment. According to Matthew's record, this was only the second time Jesus had spoken of His resurrection to them (16:21). For Son of Man, see comments on 26:64. This was one of Jesus' ways of referring to Himself, a circumlocution for "I" (Hagner 33B:498).

Matthew offered no explanation for the transfiguration other than the promise in 16:28. See comments on that verse. For these three it was undoubted proof, as their question in verse 10 assumes, that He was the Messiah (Carson, *Matthew* 387).

Peter later wrote briefly about this event (2 Pet. 1:16-18), saying that it was a foretaste of His second coming (Picirilli, *2 Thessalonians* 113). This means that Jesus had come in His kingdom (Mt. 16:28) and with power (Mk. 9:1) in the transfiguration. The transfiguration was a preview of Jesus' kingdom glory and a glimpse of what is rightfully and eternally His (Jn. 17:5). See comments on 16:28.

There are other implications of this event. Moses and Elijah demonstrate some precious truths for God's people about the intermediate state. (1) Dead saints are very much alive. Indeed the soul is immortal. (2) Dead saints are already experiencing a level of glory. (3) Dead saints are conscious. (4) Dead saints are able to communicate and otherwise socialize. They continue to function as full persons. (5) Dead saints have some form even in their intermediate state—even though they have yet to receive the resurrected and glorified body (2 Cor. 5:1-4; 1 Cor. 15:42-57).

I. Jesus Explained That John the Baptist is Malachi's Elijah (17:10-13)

10 And his disciples asked him, saying, Why then say the scribes that Elias must first come?
11 And Jesus answered and said unto them, Elias truly shall first come, and restore all things.
12 But I say unto you, That Elias is come already, and they knew him not, but have done unto him whatsoever they listed. Likewise shall also the Son of man suffer of them.
13 Then the disciples understood that he spake unto them of John the Baptist.

Only Matthew and Mark (9:11-13) recorded the follow-up question of the three disciples. The transfiguration greatly impacted them. They realized they had just previewed some aspect of the eschatological kingdom (Nolland 708; 16:28), and they had just seen Elijah. This caused them to ask a question (Hagner 33B:496, 498). Jewish teachers understood from Malachi 3:1 and 4:5 that Elijah the prophet would precede the visitation by the Lord. Some scholars suggest this might have been an objection the scribes raised against Jesus' claims about Himself (Evans, *Matthew* 331). To their understanding, Jesus could not have been the Messiah because Elijah had not come yet. Were the scribes wrong? This was the three disciples' question. The transfiguration convinced them that they were on the verge of the kingdom's appearance, but what they had witnessed did not line up with the scribes' teachings.

Jesus stated that the scribes were right. Elijah would come and turn people back to God, the meaning of "restore all things." See Luke 1:16 (Hagner 33B:499). Furthermore, Elijah had indeed come, but the scribes had misunderstood Malachi 3:1 and 4:5. Elijah had come in the person of John the Baptist. The Jews expected the O.T. Elijah to reappear, but this was not Malachi's intent. John was like Elijah (v. 12), but John was not Elijah reincarnate (Jn. 1:21, 25) or returned.

The Jewish teachers did not recognize John's Elijah-like ministry (Mt. 21:23-27). John, though, was like Elijah in many respects. See comments on 11:14. Like his O.T. counterpart, John sought to turn Israel back to God even to the point of preaching directly against the sins of her leaders (3:7; 14:4). He was successful at turning many back to God (3:5-6, 11-12) by pointing them to Jesus (Bruner 2:183), so those who repented and received John's baptism were ready to receive Jesus when He came (Jn. 1:29-31, 35-40; 3:26, 30). John's success was seen in that the Lord was able to come in grace instead of judgment (Mal. 4:6).

John the Baptist was not recognized and neither would Jesus be (v. 12; Bruner 2:183; Jn. 1:10). Even as John suffered, so would Jesus. Here again Jesus told His disciples of His upcoming death. For "shall," see comments on verse 22 "shall be."

"They" had caused John to suffer, an allusion to his death by Herod. "They" may be a reference to all of John's detractors, since the scribes were not directly responsible for his death (Gundry 348). "List" is archaic and means to wish or choose. Rather than listen to John and prepare to receive the Messiah, they chose to kill him.

Some interpreters see John as the first of two fulfillments of Malachi 4:5, in part because they understand that all things have not yet been restored (v. 11; Wilkins 594; Nolland 708). See comments on 11:14. See also commentaries on Malachi. Though Jesus did not use John's name, He spoke of Elijah's coming and martyrdom. The disciples understood enough from this to know that Jesus was referring to the Baptist.

J. Jesus Healed the Demon-Possessed, Epileptic Son (17:14-21)

14 And when they were come to the multitude, there came to him a *certain* man, kneeling down to him, and saying,
15 Lord, have mercy on my son: for he is lunatick, and sore vexed:

for ofttimes he falleth into the fire, and oft into the water.
16 And I brought him to thy disciples, and they could not cure him.
17 Then Jesus answered and said, O faithless and perverse generation, how long shall I be with you? how long shall I suffer you? bring him hither to me.
18 And Jesus rebuked the devil; and he departed out of him: and the child was cured from that very hour.
19 Then came the disciples to Jesus apart, and said, Why could not we cast him out?
20 And Jesus said unto them, Because of your unbelief: for verily I say unto you, If ye have faith as a grain of mustard seed, ye shall say unto this mountain, Remove hence to yonder place; and it shall remove; and nothing shall be impossible unto you.
21 Howbeit this kind goeth not out but by prayer and fasting.

Jesus and the three disciples came down from the mountain and rejoined the nine at the bottom. The mountain scene and the valley scene were worlds apart (Hendriksen 673). From the heights of glory to "the shame and confusion" in the valley Jesus went.

According to Mark, the scribes were arguing with the nine. See Mark 9:14-29 and Luke 9:37-43 for parallel accounts. Mark includes many details Matthew does not mention.

As Jesus approached them, He asked what they were discussing with His disciples. The father of an epileptic son spoke up and asked Jesus for help with his son. For "Lord," see comments on 8:2. Matthew says the son was a "lunatick," a severe epileptic (v. 15), while Mark and Luke both focus on the root cause, demon possession. Each writer notes that the boy's life was at risk (Hagner 33B:503). For demon possession, see comments on 8:28. Jesus had healed epileptics before (4:24).

The father explained that he had asked Jesus' disciples for help but they could not heal him. This is surprising in light of the fact that Jesus had given the Twelve power to heal sickness and cast out demons (10:1, 8). It was also a surprise to the nine. Apparently the disciples and the scribes were arguing about this failure on their part.

In one of the harshest rebukes ever of His disciples (v. 17), Jesus scolded the nine and linked them with their unbelieving contemporaries (Nolland 712; Keener, *Matthew* 441). Some writers think Jesus addressed unbelieving Israel (Gundry 350; Evans, *Matthew* 334; Wilkins 596), while others think He was mainly addressing the crowds (Hagner 33B:504). One difficulty with understanding that Jesus directed His rebuke toward the disciples is the word "generation." In contexts like this, "generation" normally had a negative connotation and referred to those characterized by wickedness and unbelief. See for example 11:16; 12:39, 41-42, 45; 16:4; and 23:36. On the other hand, one wonders why Jesus would rebuke people in general (the crowds or that generation of Israelites) who were not empowered to cast out demons.

It seems better to understand that Jesus rebuked His disciples. The nine should have been able to cast out this demon. They were impotent when they should have been victorious. They had two problems. (1) They were not strong enough in their faith, i.e., they lacked confidence in God to accomplish the healing. (2) They were "perverse" (Greek *diastrephō*), which means "to depart from correct behavior" (Louw and Nida I:770), to be perverse, corrupt, or wicked (Grimm's 142). This probably does not mean that there was some hidden sin among them but that, as Jesus later told them, they were lax in their prayer lives (Mk. 9:29).

"How long shall I be with you?" supports the understanding that Jesus was speaking to the nine rather than to the crowd or to unbelieving Israel. The reference to His ultimate departure is clear to post-ascension readers. For the disciples it meant they should be able to heal and cast out demons even in His physical absence.

Jesus asked, rhetorically, how long He must "suffer" or put up with them. One can feel the sting in His words. Matthew, one of the nine, surely felt it then and remembered it. These men should have been carrying on Jesus' ministry while He was up on the mountain. Instead, they were shamed in front of the father and the crowds when they tried unsuccessfully to heal the boy. Jesus told them to bring the boy to Him. The failure of the nine might have stirred doubt in the father. By the time he spoke to Jesus, according to Mark (9:22), he wondered out loud if Jesus could do anything. He also admitted his own lack of faith (Mk. 9:24).

Matthew summarized the exorcism (v. 18). Jesus rebuked the demon and he came out. The child was healed immediately. See Mark for more details. Jesus regularly cast out demons (Mt. 4:24; 8:16, 28-34; 12:22; 15:22), each time without delay.

Later, when they were alone, the nine asked Jesus why they had been unable to cast out the demon. They were obviously surprised and disturbed by their inability to heal (Nolland 715) and by Jesus' rebuke. Jesus' response is debated. Some Greek manuscripts name "unbelief" (Greek *apistia*) the problem. Others have "little faith" (Greek *oligopistia*). As an ongoing problem among the Twelve (8:26; 14:31; 16:8), "unbelief" might suggest the nine had no faith at all, whereas "little faith" suggests that they had some faith, just not have enough to gain the victory over this demon. More likely, either word can mean the latter.

Speaking hyperbolically, Jesus said faith as little as a mustard seed could accomplish even the most difficult challenges. With faith these men could even move the mountain He had just descended, "this mountain." See comments on 21:21. In fact, "nothing will be impossible" for them if they have faith.

This is the point of Jesus' comments. With faith these men could cast out powerful and contrary demons (Nolland 717) and much more. With the omnipotent power of God they would find nothing impossible. This promise is, of course, qualified by the overall biblical teaching that God only acts according to His will and by the contextual parameters of kingdom work (Hagner 33B:505). In other words, no obstacle could successfully withstand their faith as they labored for the advancement of the kingdom of heaven. Faith is so effectual that even a little will enable believers to accomplish great things. The failure of these nine disciples showed they had very little at this time.

(Some translations have verse 21 in their margins because of its absence in some Greek manuscripts of Matthew. The Greek text of Mark 9:29 unquestionably includes the verse, with some variations, including that some manuscripts there do not include "and fasting.")

Verse 21 (as well as Mark 9:29) adds two other reasons the nine were unable to overpower the demon: no prayer and no fasting. The nine disciples had commanded the demon to come out thinking their command was sufficient (Bruner 2:192). Perhaps before their simple command had always made demons flee. However, this demon refused to leave at their command and they were confused and defeated. Rather than ask God for help, they tried to overpower this demon on their own, perhaps repeatedly commanding him to leave. Jesus' words that this kind requires prayer suggests that these men should have prayed as soon as they realized their commands were not obeyed. Even little faith (like their own?), if coupled with prayer, would have resulted in victory. In other words, little faith was not their only problem. In addition to having limited faith, the faith they had was not expressed in prayer.

Jesus' rebuke also concerned the disciples' lack of habitual spiritual preparation for ministry. Jesus' going up on the mountain to pray should have been an example for the nine to follow, not viewed as an opportunity for rest and relaxation. For more on prayer and fasting, see comments on 6:6-18. For Jesus' expectation of the Twelve to practice fasting, see comments on 9:14-17.

Concerning confrontation with evil spirits, this passage teaches that (1) such encounters happen; (2) some demons are more powerful than other demons and the exorcist requires more power with God to drive such demons away; (3) serious and habitual spiritual habits are essential for any who desire victory over evil spirits, and (4) people who are possessed cannot deliver themselves. Deliverance requires the aid of believers who have power from God. See comments on 12:28.

K. Back in Galilee (17:22—18:35)

Jesus and the Twelve left Caesarea Philippi and returned to Galilee. He wanted private time to teach the Twelve more about His upcoming suffering. See Mark 9:30-32 and Luke 9:43-45.

1. Jesus' second prophecy of His suffering and resurrection (17:22-23)

22 And while they abode in Galilee, Jesus said unto them, The Son of man shall be betrayed into the hands of men:
23 And they shall kill him, and the third day he shall be raised again. And they were exceeding sorry.

Some Greek manuscripts say they abode (Greek *anastrephō*) and some say they gathered (Greek *sustrephō*). Either way, Jesus was back in Galilee when He gave this second of four notices of His upcoming death (but see 17:12). The first announcement had been in Caesarea Philippi (16:21). Others would follow (20:18-19; 26:2). Mark 9:30-31 says that Jesus and His disciples were alone because Jesus was teaching them.

Jesus added a new fact to His prediction: He would be betrayed (Wilkins 598). See also 20:18-19; 26:2; etc.). "Shall be" (Greek *mellō*) has the sense of "must" in this instance. (See verse 12 for this same construction in the context of Jesus' coming suffering.) In 16:21 "must," though a different word in the original (Greek *dei*), conveys the same meaning: "it is inevitable." Jesus came to die. It was the unalterable plan of God that Jesus be betrayed and die (1 Pet. 1:20). However, speaking in the third person, Jesus told the Twelve again that though men would kill Him, He would not remain dead. He would be raised (a divine passive, implying that the agent is God) on the third day.

The specificity of the prophecy is undeniable. His enemies understood it and planned accordingly (27:64). However, God's plans took priority over theirs.

The disciples reacted with much sadness (cf. 26:22). They were *very* sad (Greek *lupeō sphodra*). (See this same expression in 26:22.) Though they had many questions they were afraid to ask for an explanation (Mk. 9:32; Lk. 9:45).

2. Jesus paid the annual temple tax (17:24-27)

24 And when they were come to Capernaum, they that received tribute *money* came to Peter, and said, Doth not your master pay tribute?
25 He saith, Yes. And when he was come into the house, Jesus prevented him, saying, What thinkest thou, Simon? of whom do the kings of the earth take custom or tribute? of their own children, or of strangers?
26 Peter saith unto him, Of strangers. Jesus saith unto him, Then are the children free.
27 Notwithstanding, lest we should offend them, go thou to the sea, and cast an hook, and take up the fish that first cometh up; and when thou hast opened his mouth, thou shalt find a piece of money: that take, and give unto them for me and thee.

Only Matthew records this exchange. Jesus had returned to Capernaum. Persons responsible for collecting the annual temple tax for Jerusalem approached Peter wanting the tax payment (Greek *didrachmon*; a two drachma coin; Grimm's 145) from Jesus. The drachma was a Greek silver coin approximately equal to the Roman denarius (Louw and Nida I:62-63), the standard day's wage for a common laborer. The two drachma coin, then, was worth two day's wages.

There is some question about this tax, but apparently it was a half-shekel tax that began as an annual, one-third shekel temple tax under Nehemiah (Neh. 10:32-33). It might also have had connections with the annual taxes instituted under Moses (Ex. 30:11-16; 2 Chr. 24:6-10; Evans and Porter 1166). If so, it was required of all males, twenty and older, and was for the maintenance of the Jerusalem temple (ISBE IV:742).

Those collecting the temple tax asked if Jesus paid this tax. Peter answered in the affirmative and headed for the house either to get some money to pay the tax for Jesus or perhaps to talk to Jesus about this. Why the tax collectors targeted Jesus is not stated. Before Peter could say anything, Jesus "spoke first" ("prevented" is an archaic usage that means going ahead of), demonstrating that He already knew what Peter had been asked and said (Hendriksen 678). He asked a question that inferred that He and Peter really did not owe this tax. Kings exempted their own children from taxation. Because He was the child of the King, the Lord of the temple (Mal. 1:14; Mt. 12:6; Lk. 2:49; Jn. 2:16), Jesus was exempt from the temple tax (Keener, *Background* 92) and He was not alone. All who are children—literally, sons (v. 26)—are exempt from the temple tax (12:47-50; 13:38; Wilkins 600).

Others understand that "sons" stands for citizens of the king's own country (Newman and Stine 571). Jesus' point, then, would have been that kings of that day normally taxed those they conquered, not their own citizens. He and Peter should not be taxed because they are citizens of the heavenly kingdom. Jesus probably used "sons" in a familial sense rather than as a descriptive for citizens.

Jesus did not want to offend the Jews, i.e, place an unnecessary stumbling block (Keener, *Matthew* 445) between them and the kingdom. He did not want the Jews to misunderstand what He was doing and unfavorably judge Him (Grimm's 577), so He agreed to pay the tax. Paul later used this same principle in the context of Christian liberty in pagan circumstances and when around weak believers (Rom. 14:13-23; 1 Cor. 8:13; 9:1, 12, 22; Wilkins 600).

Jesus instructed Peter to go fishing. The first fish he caught would have a coin in its mouth sufficient to pay the tax for both. The piece of money (Greek *statēr*) was "a silver coin worth two didrachma" (Louw and Nida I:63).

This account teaches several truths about Jesus. (1) It illustrates an aspect of Jesus' submission and His love for His nation (Evans and Porter 1166). In order not to offend unnecessarily those He was trying to reach, He paid taxes that He really did not owe. (2) The miracle demonstrates the absolute control of Jesus over all creation. He commanded a fish to pick up a coin from the bottom of the Sea of Galilee and then bite a specific fishhook (one may assume that Peter's hook was not the only one in the water). All of this was to place that coin in the hand of a particular individual. (3) The miracle further shows Jesus' ability to meet need, even financial ones, and to do so in miraculous ways. As Scripture repeatedly states, the earth and everything in it belong to the Lord (Ex. 9:29; Ps. 24:1; 1 Cor. 10:26).

One might infer from this that since Jesus only provided enough money for Peter and Himself the other disciples were not present. Since they were in Capernaum the other disciples may have been with their families. See comments on 14:34. One might also infer that Jesus was not carrying any money (10:9).

Barclay (2:199-201) denies the miraculous in this story. He says Jesus was telling Peter to catch enough fish to sell and make the necessary money to pay the tax. Barclay believes Jesus would not have commanded Peter to pay his bills by finding money in a fish's mouth because (1) God does not do for us what we can do for ourselves; (2) this would mean that Jesus transgressed His decision not to use His powers to meet His own need; and (3) God did not order life so that people could meet their needs in such "lazy and effortless" ways.

Barclay's reasons are without Scriptural basis. First, when Jesus miraculously fed the five thousand (14:13-21), which Barclay also denies happened (II:121), there was no serious hunger as there had been when He fed the four thousand (15:32-39), so these people could have gone home to eat. Second, surely Jesus and His disciples also ate of the multiplied loaves and fish, so Jesus would have benefited from His powers at that time also. Third, there is nothing in the text to suggest that God was ordering life so people can make a living from the money they find in fishes' mouths. Barclay's unbelief is by decision not reason.

Summary (17:1-27)

About a week after Peter's confession in Caesarea Philippi, Jesus took three of His disciples high up on a mountain to pray. The other nine disciples remained at the foot of the mountain. While Jesus prayed and Peter, James, and John slept, Jesus' countenance changed and He began to shine. He was so transfigured that even His clothing was bright beyond imagination.

Moses and Elijah appeared on the mountain with Him and as the three of them talked the disciples woke to a glory as bright as the sun. Peter suggested they make preparations to stay, but God spoke audibly and commanded that they listen to Jesus, not the trio of glorified persons. The three were not equals. As the four came off the mountain, Jesus instructed them to keep this event to themselves until after His resurrection.

The three disciples had seen undisputable proof that Jesus is God's anointed one and they had just seen a preview of the eschatological kingdom. They had also seen Elijah. These facts caused the three disciples to ask about Elijah's promised return. Jesus identified John the Baptist as the fulfillment of that promise.

When Jesus and the three disciples arrived at the foot of the mountain, a man with a demon-possessed son met them. He had brought his son to the nine but they had been unable to exorcise the demon. The demon manifested his presence in life-threatening, epileptic-type seizures. Jesus scolded His disciples for their inability to cure the boy and then rebuked the demon and healed the lad. When they were alone, the nine asked why they had been unable to cure the boy. It was because of their weak faith and their failure to pray.

Following these events, Jesus and the Twelve went back to Galilee. There Jesus told them that His future was determined. He would die but He would remain dead only until the third day.

When they arrived at their home in Capernaum, tax officials approached Peter and asked if Jesus paid the temple tax. Peter answered in the affirmative and prepared to pursue the matter with Jesus. However, even though Jesus did not owe the tax, He sent Peter to fish with instructions to find money in the fish's mouth and to pay the temple tax with that. Jesus wanted to win the Jews to the kingdom, not distance them from Himself, so He was careful not to give them any unnecessary reason to reject Him or His gospel.

Application: Teaching and Preaching the Passage

The transfiguration is a magnificent story that can bolster the faith of God's children. One might develop ministry outlines on this passage as follows: There were at least four ways God strengthened the faith of the three disciples in this divine event: (1) by glorifying the Son; (2) by sending two prominent O.T. witnesses; (3) by manifesting a visible Presence in the Shekinah cloud;

and (4) by audibly declaring the Son's preeminence. The transfiguration was all about Jesus: (1) Jesus' glory; (2) Jesus' O.T. company; (3) Jesus' heavenly endorsement; and (4) Jesus' priority. One might discuss Jesus' transfiguration as (1) Jesus' transfiguration; (2) Jesus, Moses, and Elijah's conversation; (3) the Father's declaration; and (4) Jesus' consolation.

A lesson or sermon might be developed around the topic of Elijah and the Christ: (1) Elijah's place in prophecy: first (vv. 10-11); (2) Elijah's role in God's plan: restore in preparation for the Lord's coming (v. 11b); and (3) Elijah's misunderstood ministry: rejected (vv. 12-13).

Concerning the father with the demon-possessed son, one might follow a teaching outline: (1) A father's request, vv. 14-16; (2) the Savior's rebuke, vv. 17-18; and (3) the disciples' reaction, vv. 19-21. Or: (1) the father's desire; (2) the Savior's disappointment; and (3) the son's deliverance. One might consider the topic, "A real power failure": (1) the need for power; (2) the absence of power; (3) the display of power; and (4) the promise of the availability of power. It is time to pray (1) when there are folks who need deliverance; (2) when the evil enemy refuses to flee; (3) when failure will hurt our testimony; (4) when failure will bring divine rebuke; (5) when we are faced with seemingly insurmountable obstacles; and (6) when only God's power will do.

Verses 14-21 suggest five truths about faith failures and spiritual power: (1) this world needs followers of Jesus who possess God's power in their lives (vv. 14-16); (2) faith failures disappoint Jesus (v. 17); (3) faith failures reveal the absence of suitable faith (v. 17); (4) faith failures should be cause for concern (v. 19); and (5) faith failures can be prevented (v. 21; Mk. 9:29).

Using verses 22 and 23 along with 16:21 and 17:9, one might discuss the foreknowledge of Jesus. He foreknew that (1) He would suffer, (2) He would be betrayed, (3) He would be killed, (4) He would be in the grave an exact predetermined length of time, and (5) the Father would raise Him from the dead. One notes that the events in the prediction passages are at the heart of the gospel (1 Cor. 15:1-4).

The story of the temple tax highlights three truths about the incarnate Jesus: (1) He knew the thoughts of those around Him, vv. 24-27; (2) He determined not to place a stumbling block in front of those He wanted to win, v. 27; and (3) He controlled with precision earth's resources, v. 27.

On the lighter side, one might prepare a devotion entitled "Taxes and Fishing" using the following thoughts—while at the same time honestly and accurately teaching the text. (1) Sometimes one may be charged a tax he does not owe. (2) Sometimes it is wisest just to pay the tax, even if one does not owe it, to keep from "offending" the tax people. (3) Sometimes it just pays to go fishing, especially at tax time. (4) Sometimes it is God's will for His servants to go fishing. (5) Sometimes God will miraculously put a fish on the hook. (6) Sometimes fishing is a good deal all the way around. (7) Not all fish stories are fabrications.

3. Discourse Four: Life in the Present Kingdom Community (18:1-35)

Chapter 18 contains Jesus' fourth major teaching block. The first three are the Sermon on the Mount (chapters 5-7), the instructions to the Twelve (chapter 10) and the kingdom parables (chapter 13). This teaching block covers various matters about life in the kingdom community, namely present kingdom life and humility, sin, and forgiveness. The fifth major block of teaching material is the Olivet Discourse (chapters 24 and 25). Jesus delivered this fourth discourse in Capernaum after He and the Twelve returned from Caesarea Philippi.

a. Importance in the kingdom, now and in eternity (18:1-4)

1 At the same time came the disciples unto Jesus, saying, Who is the greatest in the kingdom of heaven?
2 And Jesus called a little child unto him, and set him in the midst of them,
3 And said, Verily I say unto you, Except ye be converted, and become as little children, ye shall not enter into the kingdom of heaven.
4 Whosoever therefore shall humble himself as this little child, the same is greatest in the kingdom of heaven.

"At that time" is a non-specific time marker placing these teachings during the same time in Capernaum mentioned in 17:24. Parallel accounts are in Mark 9:33-37 and Luke 9:46-48. According to Mark 9:34, as the group traveled toward Capernaum, the disciples, here probably the Twelve, argued about who was and would be the "most important" (Newman and Stine 574) in the kingdom. For kingdom, see comments on 3:2. These men were convinced they were on the verge of the kingdom's fuller revelation.

Hendriksen (684-685) suggests that Peter's apparent increasing prominence—Matthew names him more than any other disciple from 14:28 to 17:25—among the Twelve may have occasioned this. It is clear from 20:20-28 that there were ongoing struggles inside the group. The mother of James and John even tried to get special places of honor for her two sons. It is also clear from 19:27-28 that these men expected places of privilege in the final stages of the kingdom and were to some extent right in doing so. However, these men allowed their prospects of privileged positions to degenerate into sinful rivalry. Records of less than flattering discussions among the Twelve support the integrity of the text. One could argue that records of such negative tensions inside the group would serve no good purpose other than that they reflect truth.

After they arrived in Capernaum and entered "the house" (Mk. 9:33; see comments on Mt. 4:13; 9:28; 13:1, 36; 17:25), the Twelve brought the question to Jesus. The fact that all three Synoptics mention this issue shows that this was no little matter. Six items are apparent from this question and its multiple contexts in Matthew, Mark, and Luke: (1) the Twelve were convinced that Jesus was the Messiah; (2) they were convinced they were already seeing the kingdom unfold; (3) they were looking for a fuller revelation of the kingdom soon; (4) they expected to share in the governing of the kingdom (see also 19:28; 20:20-28; and Lk. 22:24-30); (5) they expected that some of the Twelve would enjoy greater privilege than others; and (6) the apostles were not perfect.

Jesus answered the question with an illustration. He called to a nearby child and sat him by His side (Lk. 9:47). For "child" see comments on 19:13. Jesus called on these men to change immediately. He insisted that they turn from their pride and assume the humility of a child. "Be converted" (v. 3) does not refer to salvation conversion in this instance. These men were already disciples of Jesus. The word means "to turn oneself, namely, from one's course of conduct, i.e., to change one's mind" (Grimm's 591). Here, rather than to conversion (as in Jn. 12:40), the word refer to the disciples' need for a deep-seated attitude change. They needed to become as humble as the child.

According to Mark, at some point He took the child in His arms (Mk. 9:36). Referring to the basic humility of children, Jesus taught two things. First, decisive and characteristic humility in this life is foundational to any greatness in the eschatological kingdom. The disciples' desire to have the highest positions stemmed from pride and was opposite Jesus' teaching (5:3). According to Jesus, such attitudes do not bring greatness in the kingdom. In fact, pride will keep people, even the Twelve, from participating in future aspects of the kingdom (v. 3). "Ye shall not enter" is emphatic in the original: literally, "You will never or by no means enter" the eschatological kingdom (Hagner 33B:519). These disciples who had entered the narrow gate (7:13) would find themselves outside the kingdom if they did not turn from their sinful pride.

Jesus mentioned entrance standards and requirements on various occasions. See 5:20; 7:13; 7:21; 18:8-9; 19:17, 23-24. The other Gospel writers also included statements Jesus made about entering the kingdom (e.g., Jn. 3:5).

Second, children do not aspire to greatness. They do not focus on personal position, power, or influence (Walvoord 135). The disciples' desire to rule over others was carnal and opposite Jesus' teaching. "Blessed are the meek, for they will inherit the earth," Jesus had said (5:5). Rather than striving in this life to position oneself for the most prestigious and powerful positions in Christ's kingdom, Christ's followers are to serve in humility in this life and then Christ will reward with greatness in the next life. Mature Christ-likeness includes childlike humility.

Jesus wanted to be clearly understood. This is not a gray area. "Verily" or "truly" (v. 3, Greek *amēn*) shows the absolute nature of His statement. Pride such as caused these men to argue among themselves (Mk. 9:34) concerning top positions was not an approved kingdom attitude. The humility Jesus wanted of His disciples He modeled (11:29: lowly in heart; Phil. 2:8) and later rebuked the proud for not having (23:12).

Greatness in the future manifestation of the kingdom, however, is a real and worthy goal and one that is attainable. The way to greatness, however, even in the future aspect of the kingdom, is through humble service in the present stage of the kingdom (v. 4). Who is the greatest (v. 1)? The one who serves in humility now is the greatest now and will be the greatest in the future (v. 4).

Jesus places high value on those who lay aside aggression and pride for humility. Their decision to follow Him in humility results in His identification with them (v. 5). See further comments on the humble believer in the next section.

b. Warning against sinning against the vulnerable (18:5-7)

5 And whoso shall receive one such little child in my name receiveth me.
6 But whoso shall offend one of these little ones which believe in me, it were better for him that a millstone were hanged about his neck, and *that* he were drowned in the depth of the sea.
7 Woe unto the world because of offences! for it must needs be that offences come; but woe to that man by whom the offence cometh!

Mark 9:42 and Luke 17:1-2 also record this portion of Jesus' teaching. Jesus wants all of His humble followers to be received by others already in the kingdom community (v. 5). Receive (Greek *dechomai*) has several connotations, depending on context. It can mean "to receive to friendship" (Lk. 9:11; Jn. 4:45), "to receive to hospitality" (Mt. 10:14, 40), and "to receive into one's family in order to bring up and educate" (Grimm's 130). Grimm's places verse 5 with the latter and if he is right, this saying shows Jesus' awareness and heart for orphan children. Following Grimm's understanding, Jesus spoke of children in the most humble circumstances—children with no adult guardians or home—to illustrate the humility necessary for kingdom citizens.

Children, though, were the illustration, not the point. The words "one such ... child" and "receives me" (v. 5) indicate that Jesus was speaking of the kind of disciple who will enter the kingdom (vv. 3-4) and as such the kind of disciple who should be welcomed into the church community (Gundry 361). In other words, "receive" speaks of church life in general and may even be the main emphasis (Osborne 674).

Jesus' previous reference to His disciples as "little ones" (10:42) further identifies the humble, little ones in 18:5-6 as His disciples of all ages, including children. In 10:42, Jesus spoke of believers who because of their association with and work for Jesus are to be welcomed and assisted in their labors (10:40-42; Hagner 33B:521). Here in 18:5, He spoke of welcoming humble believers into the Christian community. Jesus was talking about believers who have certain child-like attitudes.

Jesus identified Himself closely with His followers. Folks who welcome into the kingdom community Christ's little ones in His name will be welcoming Christ Himself. Compare 10:42 and 25:40, 45 and comments. "In My name" has been variously interpreted. It might mean "because of your dedication to Me" (Bruner 2:211) or, more likely, "as though he or she was I" (Nolland 733).

Jesus warned of severe punishment for any who would offend His humble followers. Offend (v. 6, Greek *skandalizō*) here means to "cause to stumble in faith or entice to sin" (Grimm's 576). Jesus, then, in this discussion was not speaking of personal offenses as in 17:27 but of occasions to sin (Hagner

33B:522). To offend or cause to sin in verse 6 is the verb form of the word translated offences in verse 7.

Jesus placed a strong emphasis on the "one" in these verses (Bruner 2:213; vv. 5-6, 10, 12, 14). Every believer is important. Jesus condemned causing even one of these little ones, whether a child or an adult believer, to lose faith in Him (Newman and Stine 578) or sin (see comments on v. 7 below) and be lost (v. 14). See 13:21 and 24:10 for other examples of offend in the sense of fall away.

Jesus' severe warning can be understood in at least one of two ways. First, the person who would cause one of Christ's little ones to sin would be better off dead before he had opportunity to do such a thing in order to avoid judgment. Or, second, as Keener (*Matthew* 449) prefers, God's judgment against the offender will be so severe that inescapable drowning would be preferred. Either way, the outlook is grim for the one who influences God's children to sin. It is God's will that all of His children know and serve Him without enticement, influence, or occasion to sin.

Both the word "depth" (Evans, *Matthew* 341; Ex. 15:5; Neh. 9:11; Ps. 63:9) and the size of the millstone intensify through hyperbole (Wilkins 614) the image of judgment. "Depth" (Greek, *pelagos*) speaks of the open sea (Acts 27:5), that deep part of the sea where ships travel (Grimm's 499). The millstone was the size and kind turned by a donkey, not the hand mills women normally used (ISBE III:356). Donkeys pulled this wheel-shaped stone around a center pole over a flat bottom stone to crush grain. The millstone was so heavy and the water so deep that a person could not possibly free himself. Jesus' point was God's judgment against those who lead others to sin should be feared more than inescapable death by drowning.

Jesus gave a second warning (v. 7): the world, which is responsible for providing all temptations to sin, will face severe judgment. Here, "offences" are enticements and occasions to sin (Louw and Nida I:774). The word implies providing "special circumstances which contribute" to sinful behavior.

"Woe" points to the harsh and sure judgment the tempters will receive. See comments on 11:21. Jesus taught that occasions to sin will of necessity (Greek *anagkē*) confront God's people (v. 7; Lk. 17:1-2) but individuals who provide such occasions are condemned and will face severe judgment. This necessity of "offences" comes from the nature of sin and its presence in this world. Temptations confront everyone. Even Jesus was confronted by temptation. However, through God's grace sin has been and will continue to be overcome (Rom. 5:20-6:4). False teachers are one group Jesus identified and condemned for leading others to sin (7:15-23; 24:4-5; Gundry 362; 2 Tim. 3:2, 6).

c. Warning against allowing oneself to sin (18:8-9)

8 Wherefore if thy hand or thy foot offend thee, cut them off, and cast *them* from thee: it is better for thee to enter into life halt or maimed, rather than having two hands or two feet to be cast into everlasting fire.

9 And if thine eye offend thee, pluck it out, and cast *it* from thee: it is better for thee to enter into life

with one eye, rather than having two eyes to be cast into hell fire.

Only Matthew and Mark (9:43-48) record this portion of Jesus' teaching. Even though persons can be led into sin, still each person (singular pronoun) must discipline himself against temptations to sin (vv. 8-9). In these verses Jesus switched from the impersonal third person (v. 6) to the second person, showing that even though occasions for sin come, still individuals are responsible for their own sins (Nolland 737-738). Using hyperbole, Jesus said that it is better to excise a portion of the body or tear out an eye and spend the rest of one's time on this earth crippled, lame, or blind than to allow a member of the body to lead one into sin and ultimately to hell. Because sinners go to hell, individuals should do whatever is necessary to avoid temptation and sin. "Cast them off" depicts complete separation from whatever encourages sin.

These are words for individual believers. Professed repentance sometimes appears to be less sin-killing than it ought to be. Bruner (2:215) writes, "Jesus' approach to such problems is not to humor them; it is to cut them out immediately and to throw them as far away as possible." People do not need to wean themselves from temptation or sin. People need a firm decision that purposes from the heart to eradicate sinful practices from one's life (Rom. 6:1; Col. 3:5-6). Compare these verses with 5:29-30 where instead of speaking of resisting sin in general as here, Jesus spoke of resisting lust.

Verses 8 and 9 are about individual believers, not the corporate body (*contra* Osborne 675-676). Jesus' use of the singular personal and possessive pronouns (vv. 8-9) argue for this understanding. See verse 18 where the church is represented by a plural "you." Here in verses 8 and 9 Jesus spoke of practical sanctification on an individual level. The sinning individual, not the church, is warned of judgment because of sin.

"Life" (vv. 8-9, twice) is eternal life and the hope of the pure (7:14; 19:16-17, 29; 25:46). It is the opposite of everlasting fire (25:46). "Life" stands for the eternal and final experience in the kingdom of God (see Mk. 9:47). Eternal fire (v. 8) on the other hand, is the destination and despair of sinners (25:41). Verse 9 calls this place of punishment, literally, "the gehenna of fire." For gehenna, see comments on 5:22. Mark (9:43, 48) called this place hell (Greek *gehenna*), the fire that will never be quenched. Jesus warned that the sinner's punishment is eternal, fiery, bodily, and to be avoided at all costs.

d. The loving concern of the Father and the Son for humble believers who stray into sin (18:10-14)

10 Take heed that ye despise not one of these little ones; for I say unto you, That in heaven their angels do always behold the face of my Father which is in heaven.
11 For the Son of man is come to save that which was lost.
12 How think ye? if a man have an hundred sheep, and one of them be gone astray, doth he not leave the ninety and nine, and goeth into the mountains, and seeketh that which is gone astray?
13 And if so be that he find it, verily I say unto you, he rejoiceth more of that *sheep*, than of the

ninety and nine which went not astray.
14 Even so it is not the will of your Father which is in heaven, that one of these little ones should perish.

Having warned about sinning against humble believers (v. 6), Jesus next warned against looking down on His little ones, the humble, as if they have no value in God's economy. "Take heed" suggests warning and responsibility. "Despise" (Greek *kataphroneō*) means "to feel contempt for someone or something because it is thought to be bad or without value" (Louw and Nida I:763). The more powerful (prideful?) believers must respect Christ's humble servants. Little ones are of great value to God, so valuable that they have angels assigned to watch over them. Keener (*Matthew* 451) believes these are guardian angels. Though possible, one should be cautious since there is so little about this in Scripture; however, see Daniel 10:21 (Michael, your prince).

These angels reside in a place of great privilege (see also Lk. 1:19). They have constant access to the Father (Newman and Stine 582). Exactly what Jesus intended to indicate about the role of these angels in caring for humble followers is unclear. Regardless, the role is positive for these little ones and negative for those who would cause them harm! One may suspect that at God's direction these powerful beings give particular protection to His little ones even as they do for all God's people in a general way (Gen. 32:1; Ps. 34:7; 91:11-12; Mt. 4:6; Acts 12:7; Heb. 1:14; Grudem 399-400). Apparently they can also inflict some kind of earthly judgment against those who seek to harm God's humble servants (Gen. 19:11, 13; 2 Kg. 6:17). Consequently, what is clear is that if God and His angels have such concern for His little ones, all believers should have that same concern for each other (Hagner 33B:527). Also, one does not want the Father and His angels to become one's enemies.

Jesus' instructions are to be understood on two levels. One, God cares for all children (this is what makes the illustration work) and will punish those who despise and abuse them. Second, God cares for all who are His kingdom children (Jn. 1:12) and He will take vengeance on all who harm them as well (2 Th. 1:6).

Verse 11 is in many of the older Greek manuscripts of Matthew's Gospel but not all. It is also in Luke 19:10, so one can be certain these are Jesus' words. In this context, the verse substantiates what Jesus has said about honoring humble believers and links verse 10 with verses 12-14 (Newman and Stine 582). Jesus' whole purpose for coming was to save the lost. Those who cause or bring occasion to sin to these little ones are working against Jesus.

With a question (v. 12) Jesus called for His audience to think about what He was saying. This question also joined a shepherd's care for wandering sheep with the Father's concern for the wandering believers. Neither wants those cared for to perish. So intent is the Father on locating the one wandering sheep that for a time—and this is the first point of this parable—the one sheep receives more attention and effort than the ninety-nine (Nolland 742). Jesus exaggerated to emphasize His point (Newman and Stine 583): the Father wants lost sheep found.

This sheep had gone astray—that is, wandered away (Greek *planaō*) from the rest of the flock. As this applies to believers, this means they can wander off into sin or false belief (cf. offense in v. 6) and be lost (v. 11). See 24:4-5, 11, 24, and 1 John 2:26 for the metaphorical use of going astray as meaning being seduced or led astray into false doctrine (Grimm's 514). See also Revelation 2:20 for its metaphorical use of being led astray into immorality.

The shepherd's excitement when he finds the lost sheep shows the high value the shepherd places on each sheep. Jesus again emphasized this with "verily." See comments on verses 3 and 18. Verses 12 and 13 are also found in Luke 15:4-5.

The second and overarching point of this parable in Matthew is stated in verse 14: God the Father does not want—literally, it is not the will of the Father—to lose even one child. The concern is for sheep who yield to sin's temptation and head for apostasy. The possibility of a sheep becoming lost and perishing teaches that believers can be lost and apostatize (Gundry 365). The possibility of finding the sheep before it perishes teaches that straying little ones can be rescued before they commit apostasy (Jas. 5:19-20). The possibility of apostasy (perish, v. 14) is what motivated the shepherd to search "persistently" (Hill 274) for the sheep and then to rejoice greatly when the sheep was found.

Though this passage is not specifically about infant salvation, it and 19:14 teach that all children are in the kingdom and should they die before reaching the age of accountability and personal choice they will go to heaven (Walvoord 136). Compare with 2 Samuel 12:23. Forlines (208) says Jesus' statement about children's angels being in God's presence implies that children are in a "favorable relationship with God."

This passage also teaches that children can be encouraged to follow kingdom teachings or be led astray. This places a great responsibility on parents, guardians, and others in positions of influence to lead children to Jesus and not into the ways of the world. When children mature to the point of understanding God's existence and characteristics and their own personal guilt (Dt. 1:39; Rom. 1:19-20), and they reach the level of maturity where they are able to trust Jesus as personal Savior, they become personally responsible and accountable for their own sins (Forlines 211) and to find forgiveness and salvation in Jesus.

There is a difference between the sheep in Luke 15:3-7 and the sheep here in Matthew (Gundry 366). In Luke the sheep who has gone astray is the sinner, the person who has never been saved (Lk. 15:1-2; Is. 53:6: "All we like sheep have gone astray; 1 Pet. 2:25). There Jesus used the parable to rebuke His antagonists (Newman and Stine 581) because they condemned Him for receiving and eating with sinners. In Matthew 18, the sheep is a believer, a little one (v. 14), who has gone astray (v. 12). He has fallen into sin or stumbled in faith and must be rescued before he apostatizes. The Father seeks the sheep who has never been saved, in Luke 15:1-7, and He seeks the wandering sheep, in Matthew 18:12-14.

e. Dealing with the brother who sins (18:15-20)

15 Moreover if thy brother shall trespass against thee, go and tell him his fault between thee and him

alone: if he shall hear thee, thou hast gained thy brother.
16 But if he will not hear *thee, then* take with thee one or two more, that in the mouth of two or three witnesses every word may be established.
17 And if he shall neglect to hear them, tell *it* unto the church: but if he neglect to hear the church, let him be unto thee as an heathen man and a publican.
18 Verily I say unto you, Whatsoever ye shall bind on earth shall be bound in heaven: and whatsoever ye shall loose on earth shall be loosed in heaven.
19 Again I say unto you, That if two of you shall agree on earth as touching any thing that they shall ask, it shall be done for them of my Father which is in heaven.
20 For where two or three are gathered together in my name, there am I in the midst of them.

Still teaching about sin, Jesus turned His discussion from sins against children and other vulnerable believers to dealing with other types of sin within the church. Consider Luke 17:3 along with this passage. "Brother" (v. 15) and "church" (v. 17) show that Jesus was speaking of the Christian community.

These verses provide instructions for finding one type of lost sheep described in verses 12-14. Here a brother who has fallen into sin (Newman and Stine 585) needs to be restored. The contextual connection with verse 14 shows that the sin potentially could result in apostasy (Gundry 368).

The words "against thee" are absent from some of the oldest Greek manuscripts. If they are original, the sin is directed against another Christian. Otherwise, that might still be the case, or the offense may simply be a sin that one believer is aware of in another.

"If" introduces a condition not assumed true or untrue but a reasonable possibility (Greek third class condition, as in vv. 16-17, 19). Jesus was making provision for sins that may occur within the Christian community. There is proper procedure for dealing with sin in the Christian community even as there is for the individual disciple who must deal with personal sin.

"Trespass" is the usual word for "sin" (Greek *hamartanō*) that means to violate God's law (Grimm's 30). If the sin is against another believer then it is not merely a personal offense, hurting another's feelings, but an offense that is also a violation of God's law. One may think of something like stealing, a violation of the eighth commandment (Ex. 20:15; Eph. 4:28), or dishonesty (Eph. 4:25), or some other type of unsanctified behavior (1 Th. 4:3-8) that violates God's code of conduct. Ephesians 4:26-27 teaches that reconciliation should be pursued quickly (Picirilli, *Ephesians* 211).

This is only the second occasion Matthew mentions the word church (once in 16:18; twice here). None of the other Gospel writers mention the church at all. Jesus' reference to the church prior to the cross shows that the church was part of God's plan and not an afterthought.

Walvoord (137) understands this in terms of a Jewish assembly rather than the N.T. church since the church had not been established yet. Walvoord's understanding is improbable since the promises Jesus later made about being in their midst and having heaven's authority would then have been for Jewish assemblies before the cross rather than church assemblies. Jesus was speaking prophetically of the church.

Jesus gave a four-step process for dealing with a sinning brother (Wilkins 618) who has not repented (Nolland 745). Here the offense appears to have targeted another believer but the process Jesus presented could also be followed when any sin is discovered in the church. See 1 Corinthians 5.

First, the offended party (or the one who is aware of the sin) is to approach the offender in private ("between you and him alone") with the goal of bringing the offender to repentance and the two parties to reconciliation. The offended person is to speak the truth in love (Lev. 19:17; Lk. 17:3-4). If the brother who sinned listens—i.e., if repentance happens—reconciliation can take place and fellowship restored. Nothing more needs to happen. One may consider King David and Nathan's discussion of David's sin as an O.T. example of how repentance should follow rebuke (2 Sam. 12:13; Ps. 32, 51).

However, if the offender does not respond positively (v. 16), then the offended party can proceed to step two and take one or two others along and try again to get the offender to repent and reconcile. The others are along as witnesses, as prescribed in Deuteronomy 19:15. See also 2 Corinthians 13:1 and 1 Timothy 5:19. The witnesses go so that every "word" may be established.

The "word" can be the allegation from the aggrieved brother or the conversations of the two persons (Newman and Stine 587). In Deuteronomy 19:15 the witnesses were witnesses of the wrongdoing. Here, however, that does not seem to be required. The text assumes the guilt of the offender so the witnesses are not present to determine guilt or innocence but to witness the offended party's attempt to gain repentance and reconciliation (Hagner 33B:532; Carson, *Matthew* 403). They add credibility to the offended, affirm that sin has been done (Osborne 686), and can testify of the offender's defiance if he refuses to repent and the offended party goes to step three and takes his grievance to the church.

Some commentators understand the role of the witnesses differently. Nolland (746) thinks the witnesses are of necessity witnesses to the sin. Gundry (368) says the witnesses strengthen the rebuke and help encourage the brother to repent and be restored.

If the second attempt also fails, the offended party takes the third step and goes to the church, the assembly of believers. How this is done in practice, e.g., whether before a committee or board or the entire congregation, will depend on church size and form of government. Congregations will want to have this properly defined in their governing documents (church Constitution and By-Laws) and then will need to follow these written directives in order to obey Jesus' instructions and protect the church from possible conflicts with the law of the land. Congregational authority is the highest authority in this grievance process (Bruner 2:228). The congregation may delegate this to a representative group (special committee, deacons, etc.), but according to Jesus' words the final authority to loose or bind rests with the congregation.

Fourth, if the offender refuses to repent, "even" (v. 17, Greek ascensive *kai*; Osborne 686) to the church, both the offended party (v. 17, "thee") and the church (v. 18, "ye") are to withdraw fellowship and treat the offender as an unsaved person with no rights and privileges normally associated with congregational life. For example, while under disciplinary action the church might restrict the offender from holding office, participating in worship leadership, teaching classes, or leading small groups. In more serious offenses, the offender should be removed from the membership roll. Blomberg (56) rightly sees a link between this withdrawal and the law's requirement to cut off offenders from Israel (Gen. 17:14; Ex. 12:15, 19; 30:33, 38; Lev. 17:10; Num. 19:13). Godly communities in both testaments were instructed to keep the community clean by disciplining antinomian and errant members.

In each step the goals are repentance and restoration to holy living and full fellowship within the Christian community (Gal. 6:1; 2 Th. 3:14-15; Jas. 5:19-20). If the brother who sinned refuses to repent, the final actions of the church are to withdraw fellowship (see 1 Cor. 5:2, 13) and to continue praying for his repentance (1 Jn. 5:16). "Heathen" is Gentile (v. 17, Greek, *ethnikos*). The point is not ethnicity but the Gentiles' characteristic failure to worship the only true God and their practice of a lifestyle that is opposite God's holy law. See comments on 5:47. For "publican" (tax collector), see comments on 5:46.

The point of this separation is that the sinning brother is to be denied fellowship privileges in the local church until he admits and renounces his sin. He is to be treated as an unsaved individual. However, Jesus' called on His followers to love their enemies (5:43-48; Nolland 748). God's children must love and pray for the "heathen" and "publican," even if they are under church discipline. Nonetheless, believers must not associate with them as long as they continue in their sin (1 Cor. 5:9-12).

The Gentile and publican pejoratives point to a Jewish audience. This was clearly the original historical context, for Jesus spoke these words to the Twelve. Some commentators point to this verse to support their understanding that Matthew wrote mainly to a Jewish Christian audience (Osborne 687).

This is the only mention of church discipline in the Gospels. The Apostle Paul later spoke of it in his writings. See 1 Corinthians 5; 2 Corinthians 13:1-4; Galatians 6:1; 2 Thessalonians 3:14-15; and 1 Timothy 5:19-22. Taken together, these passages teach that local congregations as well as the apostles have been assigned the responsibility of disciplining sin within the Christian community.

The entire church (v. 18, with plural pronouns), not just the leadership, is to be characterized by confrontation of sin and compassion toward the repentant. Each local congregation has authority from heaven and the responsibility to act against sin (1 Cor. 5:4-5, 12-13). See comments on 16:19 where Peter is the subject. There Peter was given authority to lead people into the church (Acts 10:34-43, 46-47) or declare them outside it (Acts 8:21). What Jesus earlier gave Peter, in this discussion He gave to the whole church. Only here, He focused on the church's authority to excommunicate sinning members rather than on bringing people into the church.

The authority of the church is so strong in this matter that Jesus emphatically (verily, truly; see comments on vv. 3, 13) committed heaven to the church's decision. This is startling, to say the least, but the wording supports this understanding. "Will be bound" and "will be loosed"—as in 16:19 (see for comment)—could be rendered "will have been bound" and "will have been loosed" (Greek perfect tense). The emphasis is on the completed actions. Jesus guaranteed that heaven will honor the decision of the collective body of believers who act to purify the body. The church cannot declare or withhold God's forgiveness, but if the church agrees to excommunicate members who refuse to repent, heaven will support those decisions. See also John 20:23. Divine discipline will accompany church discipline as well (1 Cor. 5:5), with the goal to correct and save the wayward brother. Christ has given His church great authority and responsibility for the sake of saving the errant brother or sister.

The church should not only be characterized by confrontation of sin and compassion toward repentant brothers but also consensus in its disciplinary action (Wilkins 620). This entire disciplinary procedure is to be bathed in unity and prayer (v. 19). The church that agrees to carefully contemplate God's will in disciplinary matters will find that God will reveal His will to them and support their disciplinary actions against the wayward brothers or sisters. The word "two" links this promise with the offended believer and the one or two witnesses in verse 16 (Blomberg 57) and assures the Father's involvement in each step of the disciplinary process.

Verse 19 has become a favorite text for prayer in general. However, the asking here is for the wayward member's repentance and restoration (1 Jn. 5:16), for the Father's direction (Hendriksen 702), and for support of the church's disciplinary actions. The attention-getting portions of this promise are that heaven will move in response to earth and only a small number of believers is required to meet the conditions of this promise. Jesus promised that God would answer the prayers of a group as small as two or three, which shows that Jesus was speaking of a local church, not the universal church. (See also 7:7-11 and 21:22 for other prayer promises equally amazing.) Jesus could guarantee heaven's involvement because He would be present for the meetings also (v. 20).

Verse 20 is sometimes understood in popular settings to teach that only a few believers meeting together can constitute a church meeting, which is a truth. This context, however, is about church discipline. Jesus promised He would be present even at the meeting between the offended party, witnesses, and the sinning brother. Christian disciplinary authority is not dependent on a quorum of participants but on Jesus being present. See 1 Corinthians 5:4.

Gathering in Jesus' name in this context is when people who are called by His name assemble with His authority. However, gathering in Jesus' name applies to more than gathering for church discipline. Church discipline is only one function of the assembled church. Gathering for worship is also gathering in Jesus' name. Gathering in Jesus' name generally means gathering as followers of Jesus who believe His message, adopt His teachings, and rely on His word (Nolland 750). In this sense, the church gathering at its most basic level is not about numbers but about Jesus' followers meeting with Jesus. Yet the church is an assembly, so more than one person must be present for there to be church. No one person can be a church nor can one person alone have a church worship experience. Private worship is possible (6:6), and even desirable as a daily practice, but private worship is not a church worship service.

To say this another way, the church is more than individual people who call themselves believers but who never meet together in Jesus' name as a group. The church Jesus described in Matthew's Gospel has several characteristics. It is both (1) universal (16:18) and (2) local (18:20). It is the (3) assembling (gathering; 18:20) of (4) baptized (28:19) (5) believers (18:6) who (6) meet in Jesus' name (18:20) and so (7) have His unique presence with them (18:17). Jesus' unique presence is what sets a church assembly apart from every other gathering of people.

Other N.T. passages expand on this limited definition of church. For example, later writers described the local assembly as where believers practice the gospel ordinances, exercise spiritual gifts, discipline wayward believers, and cooperatively work to bring the world to Jesus Christ for salvation. See comments on 16:18 for further observations on the meaning and use of the word church.

Jesus' presence is an important gospel teaching. Jesus came as the incarnate God to be with people (Immanuel, 1:23). In 18:20, He promised to join with believers when they meet as His assembly, His church. He also promised to be with His people throughout the ages as they share His gospel around the world (28:20).

Carson (*Matthew* 403-404) cautiously follows the lead of others and suggests that verses 19 and 20 are about the two parties reaching an agreement and reconciling instead of being about prayer. He suggests the promises are that God will ratify their agreement (v. 19: it will be done, etc.) and that Jesus will be with the judges (v. 20) who are brought together by the church to render a decision. This commentator, however, as mentioned above, understands verse 19 to promise heaven's direction and support in disciplinary matters if the church agrees prayerfully to seek God's direction. Verse 20 is about the offended brother, the witnesses, and the sinning brother, rather than believers set aside to judge this matter. Either way, Jesus is present with authority when the local church or its representatives meet to confront and correct sin among its membership.

f. Forgiving the brother who sins: A parable (18:21-35)

21 Then came Peter to him, and said, Lord, how oft shall my brother sin against me, and I forgive him? till seven times?

22 Jesus saith unto him, I say not unto thee, Until seven times: but, Until seventy times seven.

23 Therefore is the kingdom of heaven likened unto a certain king, which would take account of his servants.

24 And when he had begun to reckon, one was brought unto him, which owed him ten thousand talents.

25 But forasmuch as he had not to pay, his lord commanded him to be sold, and his wife, and children, and all that he had, and payment to be made.

26 The servant therefore fell down, and worshipped him, say-

ing, Lord, have patience with me, and I will pay thee all.
27 Then the lord of that servant was moved with compassion, and loosed him, and forgave him the debt.
28 But the same servant went out, and found one of his fellowservants, which owed him an hundred pence: and he laid hands on him, and took *him* by the throat, saying, Pay me that thou owest.
29 And his fellowservant fell down at his feet, and besought him, saying, Have patience with me, and I will pay thee all.
30 And he would not: but went and cast him into prison, till he should pay the debt.
31 So when his fellowservants saw what was done, they were very sorry, and came and told unto their lord all that was done.
32 Then his lord, after that he had called him, said unto him, O thou wicked servant, I forgave thee all that debt, because thou desiredst me:
33 Shouldest not thou also have had compassion on thy fellowservant, even as I had pity on thee?
34 And his lord was wroth, and delivered him to the tormentors, till he should pay all that was due unto him.
35 So likewise shall my heavenly Father do also unto you, if ye from your hearts forgive not every one his brother their trespasses.

Jesus had just taught the Twelve how to properly deal with sin in the church community. He spoke of confrontation, repentance, reconciliation, and restoration. He had not specifically mentioned forgiveness, but reconciliation requires repentance and forgiveness. Being willing to forgive was also part of Jesus' message. See Luke 17:4 for a summary statement of these verses in Matthew.

Peter understood the necessity of forgiveness and raised the question about how many times he should be expected to forgive someone who had sinned against him. Brother, as in verse 15, is another believer. For forgive, see comments on 6:12.

Peter suggested seven times, the number of completion in Scripture (Gen. 2:2; TWOT II:898). He must have considered this sufficient. Jesus, however, expected more of His disciples and used hyperbole to make His point. One should forgive not just seven times but an unlimited number of times. He should not keep a record of the number of times he has forgiven (Newman and Stine 594).

The Greek can be translated seventy times seven or seventy-seven times (Grimm's 163). See Genesis 4:24 where the Hebrew is, literally, seventy times seven (TWOT II:899; BDB 988) and the LXX translation of the Hebrew is identical to Jesus' words here. If Jesus alluded to Genesis 4:24, seventy times seven may have been His intent. Regardless, offended believers must be ready and willing to forgive offenders every time they repent, no matter how many times (even in a single day, Lk. 17:4) they have repeated the offense (Nolland 754). If Jesus was alluding to Lamech's words, then perhaps He was indicating that unlimited forgiveness rather than unlimited revenge must characterize His followers (Hill 277).

This call for forgiveness did not nullify the previous instructions concerning personal offense or sin in the church (vv.

15-20; Carson, *Matthew* 405). Instead, Jesus cautioned that forgiveness must be part of the restoration process and cannot be limited. He then told a parable to show why He has such high expectations of His disciples. This is a kingdom parable. (See introductory remarks for chapter 13 for comments on kingdom parables.) In this parable, the king represents God and the first servant represents each person who has experienced God's forgiveness but who then refuses to show forgiveness to others. Debts, as in 6:12 and Luke 11:4, are sins.

In order to demonstrate what He requires of those to whom He extends forgiveness, Jesus compared the kingdom of heaven to certain court practices of a Gentile king (Keener, *Matthew* 457) who wished to review the financial records of his servants (v. 23). One of the first servants audited, perhaps the first (v. 24), showed an enormous shortage. He owed the king ten thousand talents. According to Keener (*Background* 95) one talent was worth approximately six hundred days' wages, so the servant owed the equivalent of six million days' wages, a debt so large no average worker could ever repay the debt. The debt seems unimaginably high (Newman and Stine 595), but see Esther 3:9 and 1 Chronicles 29:4, 7. The reader can consult Bible encyclopedias for further information on talents, weights, and measures.

When it was determined the servant could not repay the debt, the king ordered that he, his family, and all his possessions be sold to go against the debt. The king was well within his rights to do this (Dt. 15:12; 2 Kg. 4:1; Neh. 5:4-5). The servant immediately fell before his king, i.e., he fell to his knees and put his face to the ground to pay homage. He asked that the king be patient and he would repay the debt, which was an impossibility (Hagner 33B:538). The king felt compassion and instead of selling the servant, his family, and his possessions, he cancelled the debt and released the servant.

This is one of the amazing turns in this story. The servant received much more than he asked (Bruner 2:238). He had asked only for time to repay, but the king completely forgave him (v. 27). He did not sell the servant or send him to prison even for limited punishment. Evidently, the servant remained in the king's service.

Following his own forgiveness, that same servant met a fellow servant who owed him one hundred denarii. A denarius was a day's pay for a common laborer and a Roman soldier (ISBE III:406). The first servant grabbed his fellow servant around his neck, choked him, and demanded that he pay the debt. The second servant fell down, begged for mercy, and promised to repay, even as the first servant had done before the king, but the first servant refused to show mercy. Literally, the text says, he "did not want to" (v. 30). He had the second servant thrown into prison until he could repay the debt. (For debt and prison, see comments on 5:25-26.)

Other servants witnessed the first servant's actions and were deeply grieved (cf. 17:23; 26:22). They explained everything in detail (Greek *diasapheō*; BAGD 188; see introductory remarks to 13:36) to their king. The king called the first servant back before him and rebuked him for his unwillingness to forgive his fellow servant after he had been forgiven so much himself. The king described the servant as evil and confronted him with his evil actions. Verse 33 is the point of the parable and the answer to Peter's question: "Should not you have had mercy on your fellow servant, as I had mercy on you?" The king was angry at the servant and delivered him to tormenters or torturers (Greek *basanistēs*, prison guard, torturer; Louw and Nida I:487) until he paid off his debt—which would be never. The servant was not to be sold as the king first considered. This time he was imprisoned (Nolland 760). Because the servant would never be able to repay his debt, "his situation was helpless and his punishment endless" (Newman and Stine 601).

Jesus had made His point: "Forgiveness received [must] be forgiveness given" (Bruner 2:240). All whom God has forgiven owed Him such an enormous sin debt that they could not possibly repay it, even in many lifetimes, yet God forgave them. Furthermore, no matter how much others sin against us, they will never owe us as much as we owed God and we will never have to forgive them for as much as God has forgiven us. Therefore, God expects that all who receive His unlimited forgiveness give the same to others (6:12, 14-15).

To further answer Peter's question, Jesus taught that God will treat kingdom citizens the same way the king treated this unforgiving servant. If they do not forgive from their hearts, i.e., for real, every time others sin against them, not only will God not forgive, He will place those who refuse to forgive in a place of eternal torture.

Persons who were once forgiven "can fall away and lose forgiveness" (Bruner 2:245). Bruner, of the Reformed tradition, wrestles with this text yet acknowledges its warning. Walvoord (140) believes this parable has only partial application to Jesus' disciples and warns of chastisement on earth (1 Cor. 11:27-32; Heb. 12:5-11) rather than of a possible loss of justification and eternal punishment. However, see verses 12, 14; John 15:2; Galatians 5:4; Hebrews 3:12-19; 6:4-8; 10:26-31; and 2 Peter 2:20-22, which teach that personal salvation can be forfeited. Verse 35 is a clear warning: "So likewise," Jesus said, "will My Father do to you." As the king revoked the earlier cancellation of the debt, so the Father "will revoke His forgiveness of a disciple's sins if that disciple, like the servant in the parable, refuses to forgive the sins of another disciple" (Hagner 33B:540). Each individual believer is required to practice forgiveness.

The king's condemnation of the unforgiving servant was just. The king had shown him undeserved and extensive grace, forgiven an enormous debt, and responded to a mere plea (Gundry 375). Kingdom citizens must do the same.

This lesson is consistent with Jesus' teaching in His Sermon on the Mount. See 6:12, 14-15. A forgiving heart is an ongoing requirement God has for all who receive His ongoing forgiveness. The heart is that inner consciousness that is the real self. It is from there that forgiveness must flow (Nolland 762). Forgiveness is at the heart of God (Ps. 86:5) and is part of His long-term plan for the salvation of lost people (Jer. 31:34). He promised to remember their sin no more.

The O.T. character Joseph is a classic example of the type of forgiveness Jesus requires of all of His followers (Gen. 50:17-21). See also Stephen's prayer in

Acts 7:60. However, none can compare to the Savior who prayed while dying on the cross, "Father, forgive them; for they know not what they do" (Lk. 23:34).

Summary (18:1-35)

In this fourth teaching section, Jesus explained to the Twelve several aspects about life in the Christian community. Jesus first addressed pride and position. Using a little child to illustrate, He explained that kingdom life requires humility. There is not now nor will there ever be any place for prideful rivalry among His disciples. The characteristic humility of little children illustrates the humility required of all members of the kingdom.

Jesus wants those already in the kingdom to welcome all of God's children into the kingdom community. He warned that a terrible judgment awaits any who provide opportunity or encouragement to such little ones to sin. He also warned that those who commit sin are culpable and therefore His followers must do everything possible to avoid sin.

All humble believers are precious to God. Angels in heaven watch over God's children and He searches for wandering sheep in order to save them from apostasy. God does not want any of His children to perish.

Jesus gave a four-step process for handling sin inside the church community in order to encourage repentance, forgiveness, and reconciliation. Persons who refuse to repent are to be excommunicated from the community of believers until they do. Handling personal offenses naturally led to the question of how many times an offended party should be expected to forgive. Jesus taught that forgiveness is to be unlimited in both quality and quantity and He gave the parable of the unforgiving servant to illustrate His expectations.

Application: Teaching and Preaching the Passage

This entire chapter is a good text for a series of lessons or sermons on the subject of "How to live in the Christian community." One might also develop a single overview lesson or sermon using the following: (1) serve each other in humility (vv. 1-4); (2) welcome all who enter the church (v. 5); (3) refuse to harm another spiritually (v. 6); (4) expect temptation and opportunities to sin (v. 7); (5) avoid temptation and sin (v. 8, 9); (6) love all of God's children (v. 10); (7) seek the wayward (v. 11-14); (8) confront sin Christ's way (v. 15-20); and (9) forgive without limit (vv. 21-35).

This chapter also teaches the importance of each believer to Jesus and the Father. The church is to (1) receive each one (v. 5); (2) present no stumbling blocks before anyone (vv. 6-7); (3) refuse to look down on anyone (v. 10); (4) proclaim Jesus' desire to restore each lost one (v. 11; Lk. 19:10); and (5) search for each one who strays (vv. 12-14).

One might develop a sermon on saving the sinning brother. (1) Do not treat brothers or sisters who fall into sin as unimportant (v. 10). (2) Follow the example of the Good Shepherd. Search for and go after lost sheep, sheep who have gone astray, in order to bring them back into the fold (vv. 11-12). (3) Recognize the real and present danger of sheep lost in the wilderness. They can perish spiritually (v. 14). (4) Accept God's will in this matter of reaching out in order to retain all sheep in the fold (v. 14). (5) Celebrate the return of lost sheep to the fold (v. 13).

Three times this Gospel promised Jesus' presence: (1) when He came as the incarnate God (Immanuel, 1:23); (2) when He joins with believers while they meet as His assembly, His church (18:20); and (3) when He is with His people throughout the ages as they continually share His gospel around the world (28:20). To put this another way, Jesus lived where we (all humans) live (1:23), meets where we (His followers) meet (18:20), and goes where we (His witnesses) go (28:20).

Another way to present the truths of Jesus' presence might be: in 1:23 He is Immanuel, the incarnate God with us; in 18:20 He is the immanently present God (as opposed to being transcendent only): "I am with you"; and in 28:20 He is the eternal God, one who is with us always: "I am with you always."

A sermon or lesson might be developed around Jesus' four steps for dealing with personal offenses (vv. 15-20). See comments above. A lesson on forgiveness might be presented as the extent of forgiveness questioned, illustrated, and required (vv. 21-35).

V. THE PEREAN MINISTRY NARRATIVE (19:1—20:34)

The most extended portion of Jesus' ministry in one area, His Galilean ministry, ended in 15:21. At that time, He traveled north into Syria. From Syria He traveled down around the eastern side of Galilee into the Decapolis (15:29), back up the coastline (which side is unclear; see comments on 15:39) and then on to Caesarea Philippi (16:13). From Caesarea Philippi He returned to Galilee (17:22) and back to Capernaum (17:24), perhaps for a final visit before His crucifixion. Afterwards, Jesus headed south into the region just across the Jordan River (and so called "Transjordan") from Judea in Perea. The cross was on the horizon. Interpreters believe Jesus left Galilee about six months before His crucifixion (Wilkins 642).

A. Jesus Headed for Jerusalem by Way of the Transjordan (19:1-2)

1 And it came to pass, *that* when Jesus had finished these sayings, he departed from Galilee, and came into the coasts of Judaea beyond Jordan;
2 And great multitudes followed him; and he healed them there.

As Jesus slowly made His way to Jerusalem, His popularity continued. Large crowds still followed Him. Some writers suggest (e.g., Grogan 285) that toward the close of Jesus' ministry the great crowds were no longer thronging Him. Matthew (19:2) and Mark (10:1) say otherwise.

Jesus did not change His ministry practices. He continued healing (v. 2; Greek historical, collective aorist) people and teaching (Mk. 10:1). One wonders how many thousands Jesus healed during His short ministry.

B. A Test Question About Divorce (19:3-12)

3 The Pharisees also came unto him, tempting him, and saying unto him, Is it lawful for a man to put away his wife for every cause?

4 And he answered and said unto them, Have ye not read, that he which made *them* at the beginning made them male and female,
5 And said, For this cause shall a man leave father and mother, and shall cleave to his wife: and they twain shall be one flesh?
6 Wherefore they are no more twain, but one flesh. What therefore God hath joined together, let not man put asunder.
7 They say unto him, Why did Moses then command to give a writing of divorcement, and to put her away?
8 He saith unto them, Moses because of the hardness of your hearts suffered you to put away your wives: but from the beginning it was not so.
9 And I say unto you, Whosoever shall put away his wife, except *it be* for fornication, and shall marry another, committeth adultery: and whoso marrieth her which is put away doth commit adultery.
10 His disciples say unto him, If the case of the man be so with *his* wife, it is not good to marry.
11 But he said unto them, All *men* cannot receive this saying, save *they* to whom it is given.
12 For there are some eunuchs, which were so born from *their* mother's womb: and there are some eunuchs, which were made eunuchs of men: and there be eunuchs, which have made themselves eunuchs for the kingdom of heaven's sake. He that is able to receive it, let him receive *it*.

It was apparently during His Transjordan, southward travels (see comments in section V) that the Pharisees asked Jesus about divorce. The Scriptural backdrop for their question is Deuteronomy 24:1-4. The Pharisees' goal was to entangle Jesus in their ongoing debate about approved grounds for divorce. Tempt here means to test. See 4:1; 16:1; 22:18, 35 and accompanying comments. See also Mark 10:2-12 and Luke 16:18.

The Pharisees believed in divorce (v. 7), but they disagreed among themselves about what constituted proper grounds for divorce. Deuteronomy 24:1 says "if she finds no favor in his eyes" and speaks of "some uncleanness" or indecency in her. The Pharisees debated the meaning of these two descriptors. Some Pharisees believed that "gross indecency" (adultery or other forms of sexual misconduct) was the only God-approved basis for divorce (Carson, *Matthew* 411, 413). Others believed divorce could be granted for just about any reason (ISBE I:976). These differences were the reason Pharisees included the phrase "for every cause" in their question to Jesus.

Josephus, the first century Jewish historian, was a Pharisee and he illustrates the problem of the day. He was married four times (ISBE II:1132) and wrote this about divorce (*Antiquities* IV.VII.23):

> He that desires to be divorced from his wife for any cause whatsoever, (and many such causes happen among men,) let him in writing give assurance that he will never use her as his wife any more; for by this means she may be at liberty to marry another husband, although before this bill of

divorce be given, she is not to be permitted so to do.

In order to answer their question, and rather than take sides in the debate, Jesus referred His questioners to day six of creation. There God made the first two humans. His opening words assume the Pharisees' familiarity with this passage. Primary guidelines for marriage and divorce come from Genesis 1 and 2, not Deuteronomy 24.

Alluding to Genesis 1:1 (Nolland 771) and quoting a portion of Genesis 1:27, Jesus pointed out that in the beginning God made two people, one a male and the other a female. Some manuscripts say He "made" and some He "created." The meaning is the same. This was how God started the human race. The creation of the two sexes was foundational to God's order. God's creation of Adam as male and Eve as female shows God planned for their physical union from the beginning (Hendriksen 715). Their potential for union is one basis for the permanency of marriage.

Second, according to Jesus, God the Creator spoke (v. 5) on the day He created Adam and Eve and brought them together as husband and wife (Gen. 2:24). Gundry (378) thinks the subject of "and [He] said" is Jesus, not the Father. However, the most natural understanding of Jesus' quotations is to link "he which made them" (v. 4) with "and said" (v. 5). This means the Creator is the source of Genesis 2:24.

The Creator said, "For this cause": that is, because they are male and female. In the Genesis 2:23-24 context, "for this cause" links verse 24 with verse 23. Jesus' use of this connector suggests He was not just quoting these words to make verse 24 complete. Rather, He was also linking Genesis 2:24 (Mt. 19:5) with Genesis 1:27 (Mt. 19:4; Nolland 771).

At least six timeless, life principles are established in these Genesis verses. (1) When a man is ready to establish his own home, he will separate from his parents. (2) He will then marry a woman. (3) These two as husband and wife will establish a union and family unit that will take precedence over every other human tie and relationship, including that which each has with his or her own parents (ISBE I:975). (4) The marriage will include sexual union ("the two will be one flesh"). (5) Those two will no longer be two single people (ESV 1860). They will be one married couple. "They are no longer two but one flesh" (v. 6). This implies that the oneness is more than sexual or temporary; it is a "persistent state" of oneness in purpose and living (Nolland 772). (6) They will be exclusively for each other (Gundry 379).

Jesus' statement about the Creator speaking is important also for it teaches that though Moses wrote the words in Genesis 1 and 2, they originated with God. Moses did not write millennia later about something (marriage) that had become society's idea over a period of time as an outgrowth of the male and female differences. Rather, Moses recorded what God revealed to him as His divine intention when He created Adam and Eve as male and female. God's commands to be fruitful and multiply (Gen. 1:28), immediately after He stated that He made them male and female, show they "belong together" (Bruner 2:251). Hence, the bases of marriage are the created ability of the male and female for physical union (Hendriksen 715) and the divine prescriptions in both Genesis 1:28 and 2:24.

Jesus prescribed monogamy when He quoted the words "his wife" and "two" (v. 5). God made Adam one wife. God created Eve for one husband. The "two," not three or more, become one.

Jesus also taught marriage as a prerequisite to intimate relationships. Sexual intimacy without holy commitment is not marriage, is not approved by God, and is not an acceptable "alternative lifestyle." Two who unite physically are to do so only in the context of the highest level of commitment to each other and in holiness before God (1 Cor. 6:13-20; 7:1-5). God joins couples in holy matrimony who meet His criteria. See comments on 5:32.

"Cleave to" (v. 5, *kollaō*) can mean to glue or colloquially "to stick to" (Zerwick 61). Joined together in a God-intended sense requires a level of commitment that will last a lifetime (Mal. 2:10-16). God intended that marriage last as long as both live (Rom. 7:2; 1 Cor. 7:39). The Hebrew words translated "cleave" and "shall be one flesh" in Genesis 2:24 both signify the purpose of leaving parents (Hebrew perfect tense, Gesenius 315-316, 332) and the ongoing state of oneness. Permanency of marriage is also seen in that God "joined" (v. 6; Greek *suzeugnumi*) the man and woman as husband and wife. "Joined" (Greek *suzeugnumi*, v. 6) is different from "cleave to" (v. 5) and can mean "to yoke," including the idea of two permanently joined in effort and purpose. (See Mt. 11:29-30 for the cognate Greek noun *zugos*.) Because God joined the man and women in marriage, neither has the right to destroy that union. "Man" is probably generic and although Jesus almost certainly was speaking mostly to husbands, since they were normally the instigators of divorce (Nolland 773), His comments are equally applicable to wives (Mk. 10:12; Carson, *Matthew* 418). The words of the original question—"to divorce one's wife"—also show that husbands were primarily in view. Josephus (*Antiquities* XV.VII.10) states that according to Jewish laws wives could not divorce their husbands. A woman who left her husband could not be married to another man unless her husband divorced her.

The short answer to the Pharisees' question, then, was "No." God hates divorce (Mal. 2:16; Evans, *Matthew* 346-347). As Evans states, "Divorce is tantamount to undoing the created order." Jesus might have meant more: the syntax in verse 6 may mean "stop divorcing" (Greek *mē* plus the present imperative; Bruner 2:254). See comments below on verses 8 and 9.

In addition to the principles mentioned above, one can also conclude the following: (1) marriage is first and foremost an institution of God. He planned marriage, prepared mankind for marriage, and ultimately performs the marriage. (2) God made the rules for marriage. (3) God joins a man and a woman in marriage for a lifetime. (4) Since God puts the man and woman together as husband and wife, no human has the right to break it up. (5) In the beginning God made provision for marriage but not for divorce.

It is worth noting that Jesus taught the literal creation accounts of Adam and Eve. He accepted as completely accurate Scripture's record of mankind's origin. God created both the man and his wife. God created Adam first, and Scripture describes Adam as fully functional physically, intellectually, morally, and volitionally from his first breath (Gen. 2:7-8, 15-17). Later that day God created Eve (Gen. 2:22). She was His final created being. God's presentation of Eve to Adam and her later conversations with the serpent and God demonstrated that like Adam she was fully functional physically, intellectually, morally, and volitionally. Together they shared the responsibility of ruling the earth (Gen. 1:29). The Genesis description of Adam as being fully functional, as well as the separate and later creation of Eve, argues strongly against any evolutionary development of the human race. Adam and Eve were the first and only human beings on the earth at the end of creation week.

The Pharisees (v. 3) were not satisfied with Jesus' answer and asked why, if divorce was wrong, did Moses command that a certificate of divorce be given and to divorce her (v. 7). Jesus answered that Moses did not command divorce but rather permitted it (v. 8). Pharisees saw Deuteronomy 24:1-4 as a command; Jesus said it was a concession. Moses permitted divorce because the people were hard-hearted; their minds were closed to the truth (Newman and Stine 609; 13:15, 19). Their homes were breaking up because they were not living according to the divine pattern of Genesis 2:24. Even though Moses permitted divorce, Jesus said, "from the beginning it was not so" that marriage would end in divorce. Divorce is not a true reflection of creation or of God's perfect will. Divorce comes from man's spiritual hardness, i.e., his rebellion against and resistance toward God's revealed truth.

Adam and Eve's marriage was God's perfect will. The world of Genesis 1 and 2 was the world before sin. Deuteronomy 24:1-4 is God's permissive will for a broken home after the fall (Bruner 2:260-261). The home suffered greatly in the fall (Gen. 3:16) and divorce is one, sad evidence of that. However, God's gospel of grace is also for those who have been divorced and remarried (Rom. 5:20-21; Jn. 4:18, 29).

Wilkins (643) summarizes the intended benefits of Moses' divorce document. (1) Divorce protected marriage by providing a way to keep it holy, i.e., to keep "something indecent from defiling the relationship." (2) Divorce protected a woman from a man who might send her away for no reason. (3) Divorce provided the woman with legal documentation that she was divorced, which protected her from allegations of being "a harlot or a runaway adulteress."

Jesus thus showed that He had a high view of Scripture, marriage, and women. Scripture is the record of God speaking and is binding on the human race. Marriage is God's way to provide and protect the holiness of the physical union. Declaring two to be one for a lifetime was Jesus' way to protect the sanctity of marriage and in this context to protect the woman from brute males.

The plural pronouns in verse 8 referred to the people in general (Newman and Stine 609), but it seems probable that some of those men had divorced their wives. According to Hill (280), "In certain Pharisaic circles, the frequency of divorce was often an open scandal." The question, then, was not totally hypothetical. Any of these religious leaders who had sent their faithful wives away with divorce papers were out of step with God's created pattern, spiritually insensitive to God's desires for their homes, and adulterers (v. 9).

"I say to you" is emphatic (Hagner 33B:549) and points to the authority of Jesus, the same authority He used in His Sermon on the Mount (5:22, 28, 32, 34, etc.). Jesus gave only one legitimate basis for divorce and remarriage: fornication. Fornication (Greek *porneia*) is sexual sin in general and speaks of any form of sexual infidelity including adultery. The physical relationship between husband and wife is divinely provided, protected, approved, and defended (1 Th. 4:3-8; Heb. 13:4). Spouses who violate their "oneness" with their marriage partner are guilty of sin.

The committing of adultery referenced in verse 9, even though present tense refers to the establishment of the second marriage, not their whole married lives together (Greek aoristic use of the present). The innocent spouse is free to divorce and remarry if he or she chooses (v. 9). Jesus permitted this but did not command it, thus allowing for repentance, forgiveness, and reconciliation. For a fuller discussion of different views of this exception clause, see Carson (*Matthew* 413-418). (For the clause, "and whoso marrieth her which is put away doth commit adultery" (v. 9), which is not in all the Greek manuscripts, see comments on 5:32.)

One of the great blessings of the gospel of grace is God's forgiveness. Adultery, though awful, is forgivable (1 Cor. 6:9-11). God forgives folks who divorce and remarry wrongfully if they come to Him for cleansing.

To summarize, Jesus was closest to the conservative Pharisaic interpretation of Moses' divorce laws (although He was even more conservative!) and condemned divorce for these reasons. (1) Divorce divides "one." (2) God made no provision for divorce in the original institution of marriage. (3) Man has no right to divide what God joins. (4) Divorce comes from a spiritually hard heart. (5) Divorce does not release faithful married people from their vows. (6) Folks who divorce without Biblical grounds commit adultery when they remarry and need God's cleansing and forgiveness (v. 9). And (7) folks who divorce because of their mate's unfaithfulness are free to remarry.

Later when Jesus and the disciples were in the house, perhaps where they were staying (Mk. 10:10; Mt. 10:11), the disciples brought the subject up again (v. 10). Their comments revealed their own misunderstanding and preference. For them divorce was a necessary option for more reasons than fornication. They concluded that if one can divorce and remarry only if there has been sexual unfaithfulness then it would be better never to marry. Keener (*Background* 97) reminds us that marriages were arranged by parents at that time and the prospect of marrying someone who might not be all one expected was frightening. The Twelve evidently believed that to view the marriage bond as being insoluble, except for fornication, was extreme.

Jesus responded, however, that not everyone can live unmarried (vv. 11, 12). "Receive" (Greek *choreō*) is to accept what is being said and do what is being recommended (Louw and Nida I:373). "This saying" refers to the disciples' conclusion, not to Jesus' teaching (*contra* Gundry 381-382). Jesus was not giving permission for some to disagree with Him, nor did Jesus mean, as Barclay (2:240) suggests, that His words are only for His followers.

Jesus taught that "some people will not marry because" (an ellipsis that is understood to follow "for"; Newman and Stine 612) they are born as eunuchs, meaning they were born without the ability to have sexual intercourse (Louw and Nida I:107). Others were made that way by being castrated. Others made themselves that way for the kingdom's sake by choosing to exercise the ability God gave them to live without sexual intimacy (v. 11). These people could marry but have decided that for kingdom reasons they will live celibate. Their sex drive is such that they can control it without sinful desire.

The Apostle Paul later provided additional information about celibacy and marriage. He was celibate and he attributed that to a spiritual gift (1 Cor. 7:7). He taught that remaining single was normally better for kingdom work; but like Jesus he acknowledged that most people need to be married to satisfy desire and lessen temptation (1 Cor. 7:2, 5, 8-9, 32-38).

In addition to the Apostle Paul, John the Baptist and Jesus lived celibate. Also, Anna, the prophetess (Lk. 2:36, 37), did not remarry after her husband passed away. Apparently, all the Twelve were married (1 Cor. 9:5).

Neither Jesus nor the Apostle Paul advocated castration as a means to a higher level of spirituality or approval by God. Origen, a second century A.D. church leader, reportedly applied Jesus' words literally (Eusebius: *Eccl. Hist.* VI.VIII.1)—although some wonder about the accuracy of Eusebius' record (Bruner 2:275). However, Jesus, by quoting Genesis 2:24, approved sexual intercourse, stating plainly that this was God's design from the beginning (Picirilli, *1 Corinthians* 82-83). Paul likewise, in 1 Corinthians 7:2-3, stated that physical relations in marriage were right and one of the mutual responsibilities of married couples. Paul's warning in 1 Timothy 4:3 that in the latter times some would forbid marriage shows that God's plan for persons of the opposite sex to marry will remain in effect until He ends life on this earth as we now know it.

Some religious groups and churches have emphasized celibacy more than others. For example, the Catholic Church ordains to certain leadership positions only those who are celibate. However, Jesus recommended celibacy only for those who are able to live single (v. 12). If a person can live celibate and wants to do so for the sake of the kingdom, then that person should do so. If, however, a person has desires that make a celibate life difficult, then that person should marry. He or she is not sinning by marrying. See 1 Corinthians 7:9, 36-38 for the Apostle Paul's teachings about celibacy and marriage.

Jesus, then, provided three options for His followers: (1) celibacy, (2) marriage for a lifetime, and (3) divorce and remarriage when there has been sexual unfaithfulness. Once again, Jesus demonstrated the superiority of kingdom standards to those of the Mosaic Law.

C. Jesus Received Children (19:13-15)

13 Then were there brought unto him little children, that he should put *his* hands on them, and pray: and the disciples rebuked them.
14 But Jesus said, Suffer little children, and forbid them not, to come unto me: for of such is the kingdom of heaven.
15 And he laid *his* hands on them, and departed thence.

"Then" suggests another occasion. Some parents brought their children to Jesus that He might lay hands on them and pray for them. See also Mark 10:13-16 and Luke 18:15-17. Such was the respect these parents had for Jesus. They believed that Jesus was a godly man and at His request, their children would be blessed. Would that all parents would bring their children to Jesus!

"Little children" (Greek *paidion*) is a general word that can denote infants (Lk. 2:21, 27), toddlers (Mt. 2:11), preschoolers (Mk. 9:36), or preadolescents (Lk. 7:32). The word normally denotes children below the age of puberty (Louw and Nida I:110). Luke 18:15 uses a word (Greek *brephos*) that clearly denotes infants, so it seems probable the mothers were bringing their very young children to Jesus for His blessing at this time.

The Twelve tried to keep the children away. They rebuked the parents (v. 13). It is easy to imagine, once Jesus started blessing children, that many other parents would want Him to bless theirs also. Perhaps the Twelve thought Jesus was too busy for children. Maybe there were many children. However, Jesus rebuked the Twelve and told them to allow the children to come to Him. Mark says Jesus was "much displeased" (10:14; Greek *aganakteō*, indignant). Jesus' reason was that the kingdom belongs to people who are like children (Evans, *Mark* 94). Children have characteristics that all kingdom people have. He did not say which characteristics He had in mind, but 18:3-4 require childlike humility of all kingdom people so this is at least included. Some of the beatitudes might also fit here, like being poor in spirit, meek, pure in heart (5:3, 5, 8). By inference, Jesus taught that children are kingdom people too.

Mark and Luke both include Jesus' requirement of receiving the kingdom in the same way or manner as a child does. This means to submit unquestioningly to kingdom authority (Evans, *Mark* 94). Children have no authority of their own whereas adults do. Adults must submit to the Lord's authority before they can enter the kingdom.

Two additional truths are apparent from Mark and Luke: (1) Children who allow someone to hold them (Mk. 10:16) are completely trusting. A child will not go to someone he does not trust. Jesus wants everyone to come to Him with childlike—fearless, comfortable, no-hesitation—trust. (2) Children can and must at some point receive the gospel and be born again to enter into the kingdom. Though they are in the kingdom from conception until they reach the age where they can turn away, when they come to understand their personal sin and guilt and Jesus' offer to forgive them, they are required to reach out to Him and trust Him for personal salvation and regeneration. Hence, little children in the age of innocence and children who, after they reach the age of accountability, respond to the gospel in faith, are both in the kingdom.

Jesus laid hands on the children, and one assumes that He prayed for them as requested. Mark (10:16) says He held them, blessed them, and laid hands upon them. Jesus took time for children. His actions showed everyone that children are accepted and valued in His kingdom (Evans, *Matthew* 352). Jesus was not, however, imparting saving faith to these children with this blessing (*contra* Bruner 2:281). As already mentioned, children along with all innocents (mentally challenged, etc.) are already saved until they reach the maturity level of moral responsibility. Saving faith is required only of those who are morally aware and mature enough to exercise saving faith in response to the gospel (Rom. 10:9-17). The study of child salvation is a thorny issue doctrinally. For further discussion, see comments on 18:2-4, 10-14 and Forlines (208-215).

After blessing the children, Jesus began to leave the area (v. 15).

D. The Rich, Young Man: Temporary Riches Over Eternal Riches (19:16-22)

16 And, behold, one came and said unto him, Good Master, what good thing shall I do, that I may have eternal life?
17 And he said unto him, Why callest thou me good? *there is* none good but one, *that is*, God: but if thou wilt enter into life, keep the commandments.
18 He saith unto him, Which? Jesus said, Thou shalt do no murder, Thou shalt not commit adultery, Thou shalt not steal, Thou shalt not bear false witness,
19 Honour thy father and *thy* mother: and, Thou shalt love thy neighbour as thyself.
20 The young man saith unto him, All these things have I kept from my youth up: what lack I yet?
21 Jesus said unto him, If thou wilt be perfect, go *and* sell that thou hast, and give to the poor, and thou shalt have treasure in heaven: and come *and* follow me.
22 But when the young man heard that saying, he went away sorrowful: for he had great possessions.

As Jesus was leaving (Mk. 10:17), a young man (v. 20) ran up to Him with life's most important question. He was a man of some means (v. 22). Luke (18:18) called him a ruler and said he was very rich (18:23). For these reasons, he is called "the rich, young ruler." Mark (10:17-22) records this man's story also.

"Ruler" (Greek *archōn*) in the N.T. is a "general term for someone in a prominent position in which he exercises authority" (ISBE IV:241, 241; TDNT 1:489). In the N.T. it can refer to a Jewish (Acts 23:5) or Gentile (Acts 16:19) leader, a synagogue leader (Mt. 9:18; Mk. 5:22; Jairus), a member of the Sanhedrin, or simply a prominent individual. Scripture does not identify this man's specific position.

Mark 10:17 says the young man ran to Jesus. The man did not know it but this would be his final opportunity to see Jesus like this. Jesus was headed for the cross and after His death and resurrection, He did not appear in the Transjordan area or personally evangelize again. This was a very important meeting.

The young man's desire was right and his question revealed that he understood the purpose of Jesus' message. Jesus was offering eternal life. However, the young man did not understand how to receive it. He was thinking works: "What good thing can I do?" Matthew's readers know that humble belief, not works, is required (18:6) for entrance into the kingdom (21:31-32; 13:19; Lk. 8:12; Jn. 1:12; Eph. 2:8-9).

The young man asked about eternal life (v. 16). Jesus spoke of entering life (v. 17) and entering the kingdom of heaven (v. 23). The disciples subsequently asked who could be "saved" (v.

25). It is clear that they all were speaking of the same experience (Wilkins 650). One must enter the kingdom now (7:13-14) in order to be saved from the wrath of God's judgment and enter the realm of the blessed (25:46).

The man had respect for Jesus. He addressed Him as "good Teacher"; although some manuscripts of Matthew do not include "good" with "teacher," Mark 10:17 and Luke 18:18 do. Furthermore, that the young man addressed Jesus as Good Teacher may explain why Jesus responded as He did (v. 17).

Jesus first spoke about the "good" title and stated that no one is good, i.e., totally, except God. The various translations have minor differences (involving some differences in the Greek manuscripts), but all of them mean that only God is good. Jesus did not deny His own absolute sinlessness (Carson, *Matthew* 422). Indeed the inference is that if Jesus is good, He is also God. He was not rejecting the title. To suggest that Jesus was asking this young man to consider He was God may be reading too much into the text, but for the Christian Jesus' deity is plain.

Jesus stated that to enter life the young man needed to keep the commandments. When asked which ones, he named five of the Ten Commandments and the commandment "to love your neighbor as yourself" (Lev. 19:18). This may appear at first glance to be an unusual answer for various reasons: (1) Jesus was preaching the gospel of the kingdom. Why did He answer the young man's request by referring him to the Law? (2) How would the Ten Commandments give eternal life? (3) Jesus answered with only the horizontal commands, those dealing with human relationship and interaction. He said nothing about the first four commandments or the great commandment (22:37).

One may respond to these reasons as follows: first, Jesus taught throughout His ministry that if a person lives by the law, not legalistically but from a heart that loves the Lord and his fellowman, that person will have eternal life (Lk. 10:25-28; Evans, *Matthew* 358). Such love for the Lord always includes faith (Gen. 15:6; Hab. 2:4). See also 5:17-20 and comments.

Second, Jesus may have used these particular commandments to show the young man his sin. The law promised life (Lev. 18:5; Dt. 30:11-20; Rom. 7:10; 10:5) to all who obeyed it but because no one was able to obey it fully (Rom. 8:3), the law only brought condemnation and death. As Paul later taught in Romans 7:7-8, one function of the law is to show sinners their sin and sinfulness (also 3:20). Jesus may have referred this man to the law, then, to convince him of his sin.

The first five commandments Jesus used were all from the second half of the Ten Commandments. The last commandment Jesus mentioned (v. 19) was a summary of all those commandments dealing with the proper attitude and actions toward one's fellowman and is said to be the most quoted Pentateuchal verse in the N.T. (Bloomberg 61).

For the prohibition against murder, see comments on 5:21; and against adultery, see comments on 5:27. The commandment against stealing applies to all types of thefts, including but not limited to personal property, money, and intellectual property regardless of its form or format (hard copy, digital, etc.). The commandment also teaches that it is God's will for individuals to own personal property. The law against "false witness" prohibits false testimony in court. For "honor you father and mother," see comments on 15:4.

The commandment to love one's neighbor as oneself (Lev. 19:18) Jesus later called the second greatest commandment (22:39). See comments there and on 5:43. Loving one's neighbor as oneself is described in Leviticus 19:9-18 and illustrated in Luke 10:25-37. This may have been the young man's root problem and one reason Jesus told him to give his wealth to the poor. This may have been one facet of the law he neglected.

The young man thought he was satisfying all the requirements of the law, but he knew he still did not have eternal life. Jesus knew why. The man's primary love was not the Lord. For this man, the only remedy was getting rid of his personal wealth before he could follow Jesus as a disciple (Greek *akoloutheō*; Grimm's 22; 4:20, 22; 8:22; 9:9); his wealth would always be a spiritual stumbling block (13:22). This is the only individual Jesus specifically commanded to give away all of his possessions (Blomberg 62), but see Luke 12:33. Everyone has to abandon whatever is keeping him or her from entering the kingdom. Heart and treasure must be in heaven (Mt. 6:19-21; Lk. 12:33-34).

"From my youth" (v. 20) are not in some older Greek manuscripts of Matthew. However, Mark 10:20 and Luke 18:21 both include them. The young man claimed long-term obedience already. What more could he do? Mark 10:21 says that Jesus "looking upon him loved him." Jesus was not being harsh. To the contrary, He wanted the young man to experience eternal life and He told him how.

"If you would be perfect" (v. 21; Greek *teleios*; wanting nothing necessary to completeness, perfect; Grimm's 618; 5:48) cuts to the heart. The man was trying to work his way into eternal life by perfectly obeying every requirement of the law—an impossibility. Eternal life comes to those who are committed to the Lord above all else, not to those who obey a list of rules (8:22; 10:38-39; 16:24-26; Hagner 33B:558).

Jesus was specific about how the young ruler could possess eternal life, requiring three things: (1) The young man was to dispose of his wealth. He was to liquidate everything. (2) He was to give the proceeds to the poor. This was one way he could love his neighbor as himself, and his almsgiving would be transformed into eternal riches (Lk. 12:33). See comments on 6:1-4, 19-20. Ridding himself of his possessions would also free him of his worship of mammon (6:24) and the deceitfulness (13:22) and snare (1 Tim. 6:9) of riches. Then (3) he would follow Jesus.

Jesus' words were imperatival and called for a decisive exercise of the will: "Go!" "Sell!" "Give!" "Come!" "Follow Me!" Jesus did not choose for the man. He presented the requirements and encouraged the young man to make the right choices. "Sell" and "give" are decisive and denote urgency (Greek ingressive aorist). "Go" and "follow" denote positive commands that expect continuing action (Greek present). To "follow" Jesus is not a single event as when a person receives Him as Savior but an ongoing action beginning at conversion and continuing through life in a disciple-Lord relationship.

In order to possess eternal life, this man had to separate himself from the object of his present trust and follow Jesus, even as the Twelve were doing. Eternal life is not just another possession. Eternal life belongs to those who follow Jesus into the final kingdom.

At first impression, it may seem as if Jesus expected him to walk away from his possessions immediately. However, Jesus told him to sell his properties. This would take time, depending on how much property he owned. However, he would need to do this as quickly as possible so he could follow Jesus on to Jerusalem.

Selling his property and giving the proceeds to the poor was not earning him salvation. Ridding himself of his wealth meant making room for Jesus to be his Lord. The center point around which all else turned was Jesus' command to follow Him.

The young man was sorrowful and probably surprised by Jesus' answer. He wanted eternal life *and* wealth. He had great wealth (Greek *ktēmata polla*; many possessions; possibly referring to property and lands; Grimm's 363; Acts 2:45; 5:1) and evidently placed considerable trust in that fact. To move his trust from wealth to the Lord would require a radical act on his part.

Matthew's syntax, literally "was having," may suggest that this young man had possessed this wealth for some time. He was accustomed to wealth. Hagner (33B:558) thinks the words suggest that he was preoccupied with his wealth. Apparently, wealth was so important to him that he would not do as the Lord required and he walked away. In exchange for his soul (16:26), he chose wealth. He chose his present possession over the one pearl of great value (13:46) and over the treasure in the field (13:44). He did not get past the first requirement of discipleship (16:24). The young man whom Jesus loved walked away from the one who was on His way to the cross to save his soul.

As mentioned above, this is the only person according to the Gospel records that Jesus told to sell everything. The Twelve "left all" to follow Him (v. 27), but even they had not given away their properties (Mt. 8:14). This means that complete obedience to Jesus is required of all, but the individual orders are not always the same. All who would follow Jesus are required to repent and trust Jesus as Savior and Lord. How that is lived out will be different for each person and can mean selling all, leaving family (Mt. 8:22), leaving occupations (Mt. 4:18-22; 9:9), staying home and witnessing (Mk. 5:18-20), or whatever He directs (Mt. 16:24-25; Jn. 21:22).

E. Riches, Sacrifices, and Rewards: The Promise of Just Reward for Great Sacrifice (19:23-30)

23 Then said Jesus unto his disciples, Verily I say unto you, That a rich man shall hardly enter into the kingdom of heaven.
24 And again I say unto you, It is easier for a camel to go through the eye of a needle, than for a rich man to enter into the kingdom of God.
25 When his disciples heard *it*, they were exceedingly amazed, saying, Who then can be saved?
26 But Jesus beheld *them*, and said unto them, With men this is impossible; but with God all things are possible.

27 Then answered Peter and said unto him, Behold, we have forsaken all, and followed thee; what shall we have therefore?
28 And Jesus said unto them, Verily I say unto you, That ye which have followed me, in the regeneration when the Son of man shall sit in the throne of his glory, ye also shall sit upon twelve thrones, judging the twelve tribes of Israel.
29 And every one that hath forsaken houses, or brethren, or sisters, or father, or mother, or wife, or children, or lands, for my name's sake, shall receive an hundredfold, and shall inherit everlasting life.
30 But many *that are* first shall be last; and the last *shall be* first.

As the rich, young ruler walked away without the eternal life he desired, and about which he had inquired, Jesus used the young man's disappointing decision to make a sobering observation: rich people rarely enter the kingdom of heaven. Based on Jesus' hyperbolic comparison, it may be that rich people have so much baggage that for them to enter the narrow gate of the kingdom (7:13) is like a camel trying to pass through the eye of a needle.

Jesus' saying may have been a common saying in His day (Newman and Stine 624), or it might have originated with Him. The absence of extant materials from Jesus' day using this saying other than the Gospels makes the latter seem the most probable. Also, there is no evidence that Jerusalem in Jesus' day had a small gate through which a camel could just barely squeeze. Such explanations nullify the punch Jesus intended in His surprising statement.

The Quran (7:40; Hill 284), written in the early seventh century A.D., uses this proverb. However, the primary referent is not the wealthy but those who reject the Quran: "Indeed, those who deny Our verses and are arrogant toward them - the gates of Heaven will not be opened for them, nor will they enter Paradise until a camel enters into the eye of a needle."

A few late manuscripts of Matthew, Mark, and Luke have "rope" instead of camel. The words are spelled similarly (*kamēlon*, camel; *kamilon*, rope; BAGD 410) and were pronounced the same in later Greek (Metzger 169). Clearly, "camel" is original.

The disciples were amazed. They had never heard Jesus describe entrance into the kingdom as having anything to do with personal wealth, nor had they heard Him suggest that too much personal wealth could keep some out of the kingdom. Wealth was normally viewed as a sign of God's blessing and favor to the righteous (Dt. 28:1-14; Hagner 33B:561). Here the kingdom of God and the kingdom of heaven are used interchangeably (vv. 23-24). See 3:2 and comments.

The disciples' question, "Who then can be saved?" might have concerned them also, for some of them, like Matthew (9:9), might have been well off by the standards of that day. Whether any of the Twelve qualified as wealthy is unknown, but there were wealthy individuals like Zacchaeus (Lk. 19:2) and Joseph from Arimathea (Mt. 27:57) who later became followers of Christ. This was an important question.

The disciples used the word "saved." By this they inferred this was the point of Jesus' life and gospel. It was why Jesus came (1:21; 18:11; Lk. 19:10).

Folks like the young man who asked how to receive eternal life (v. 16) needed to be saved, and they understood Jesus to mean it is impossible for the wealthy to be saved.

Jesus saw their concern and answered it. Looking straight at them (v. 26; Greek *emblepō*, beheld) He said, "With men this is impossible; but with God all things are possible" (v. 26). God can get the camel through the eye of the needle, i.e., God can save the wealthy also. His answer was about getting the wealthy through the narrow gate but the principle is all-encompassing. According to Jesus, God can do anything. No one is beyond God's saving power. Jesus' answer about God's unlimited abilities comes from Genesis 18:14 and the context of Sarah's barrenness (Evans, *Matthew* 362). However, as Jesus taught here—and other Scriptures substantiate—the principle is unlimited (Job 42:2; Jer. 32:17, 27; Mk. 14:36; Lk. 1:37).

This discussion about personal wealth prompted Peter to ask what he and the others would receive since they had given up everything for the kingdom. He was speaking of personal wealth. What "treasure in heaven" (v. 21) would they have because of their sacrifice? See 4:18-22 and 9:9 where Peter, Andrew, James, John, and Matthew gave up their businesses and livelihoods. From Peter's statement, it is clear that all twelve did the same thing. Though they had not sold everything (8:14) and given the proceeds to the poor, as Jesus had told the rich young ruler to do, still they had set aside everything to follow Jesus. They went where He went. They slept under the open sky when He did. They suffered hunger the same as He did. Would they be any better off in the long term for sacrificing at this level?

Jesus' answer was a resounding yes. There are different opinions about what Jesus meant by the details of this promise but His point is clear enough: the Twelve will receive special rewards for their calling and earthly sacrifice for the kingdom (v. 28). This world did not respect these men or the calling Jesus had placed on their lives. However, Jesus guaranteed them that their poverty and humiliation was only temporary. (For Son of Man see comments on 26:64.)

The regeneration (ESV, new world; NIV, the renewal of all things) translates a word (Greek *paliggenesia*) which is only here and in Titus 3:5 in the Greek N.T. The word can denote a new birth, reproduction, renewal, or re-creation (Grimm's 474). In Titus, the new birth, i.e., initial sanctification, is in view. Here in Matthew's Gospel it can refer to the millennium (so Walvoord 146; Hagner 33B:565) or to the eternally new or renovated earth. The word speaks of a new beginning, another "genesis," so Jesus probably spoke of the new and eternal earth (Is. 65:17; 66:22; Mt. 5:18; 24:35; Acts 3:21; Rom. 8:20-23; 2 Pet. 3:10-13; Rev. 21-22; Hendriksen 739), not the millennium (Rev. 20:4-6). Believers will reign with Christ during the millennium (Rev. 20:4), and they will also reign forever, after the new heaven and earth are (Rev. 22:5). Those who serve the Lord faithfully to death will accompany Him as He judges the ungodly (1 Cor. 6:2; Ciampa and Rosner 711), and the Lord will place in positions of oversight and service those who sacrificially and faithfully served Him on this earth (Rev. 2:26, 27; 20:4).

Jesus told the Twelve they would sit on twelve thrones judging the twelve tribes of Israel. The number twelve and the specifying of Israel suggest that both should be taken literally. Israel here does not stand for the church (*contra* Hill 284). The number of disciples corresponds to the number of tribes of Israel (Hagner 33B:565). See comments on 10:1.

That Jesus' promise is based on Daniel 7:9, 13-14 seems clear. In Daniel 7:9-10 thrones are set up, possibly referring to the thrones for the saints, for judgment. In Daniel 7:13-14 the Son of Man is given dominion, glory, and a kingdom. This is the throne He spoke of when He said, "The Son of Man will sit on His glorious throne" (Mt. 19:28). See comments on 26:64.

"Judging" can refer to adjudicating or governing. See also Luke 22:28-30 and 1 Corinthians 6:2. If the millennium is in view, at that time Jesus will sit on the glorious throne of David in Jerusalem. The Twelve will also reign and assist in governing (adjudicating?) Israel at that time. Carson (*Matthew* 426) thinks instead that the Twelve will assist in judging Israel for her rejection of their Messiah. The Twelve apparently understood these as literal thrones and Jesus never told them differently. They would reign but only under the King of Kings. Their thoughts of reigning might have been included in their question in Acts 1:6.

The Twelve will not be the only disciples rewarded for kingdom sacrifice (v. 29), although it appears they will receive unique and special places in the eternal kingdom. Everyone who left home, immediate family, or homeland because of identification with and service to Jesus will receive a rich reward: a hundred times as much as given up (Mk. 10:30; Lk. 8:8) and eternal life. Mark 10:30 says they will receive some of their reward even now in this life. All of the saved receive eternal life as a gift. All who sacrifice will receive rich rewards because of their sacrifice. Those who follow the example of the young ruler (vv. 16-22) will not receive eternal life or eternal, rich rewards.

Jesus spoke of immediate family members, i.e., brothers, sisters, parents, and children. Here "children" (Greek *teknon*) are apparently grown children (Bruner 2:313). (This Greek word is different from the one is in vv. 13-14.) Jesus did not advocate abandoning small children who are dependents. He did teach that parents might be required to serve Christ away from grown children (and grandchildren as well!). The closest natural ties, the most precious loved ones, and the most binding securities are to be brought in submission to Christ and His service. One does this by willfully deciding to put Christ first. See comments on 10:35-37.

Some Greek manuscripts of Matthew (and therefore some translations) do not include "wife" in this list. However, most textual scholars agree that Luke 18:29 included it, so apparently Jesus included "wife" in His demand.

This is a text for missionaries, traveling evangelists, the persecuted (Heb. 10:34), and all others who sacrifice in their service for Jesus. It is especially for all who are required to relocate or spend significant portions of time away from family as they serve Christ. Jesus is fully aware of the sacrifices.

Verse 30 (also Mk. 10:31) concludes this teaching with a proverb that teaches a principle of reversal. This principle means that the status of folks now will be different in the age to come (Newman and Stine 629). See comments on 20:16 for further explanation.

Throughout His earthly ministry, Jesus promised rewards (6:2, 4, 6, 16, 18; Osborne 724). However, our Lord is a gracious Lord and all rewards will come from God's grace (Mt. 20:15-16). While there will be distinctions for faithfulness, rewards will not be based on things that seem most important in earthly labor and remuneration. Peter was not wrong to ask the question, but he and the others needed to know that God's pay standard is different from the pay standards of this earth. God rewards for faithfulness and service (Mt. 25:29; Lk. 19:26; and 1 Cor. 3:8, 10-15).

Summary (19:1-30)

Jesus ended His teachings in Galilee and headed south through Perea, probably in the fall of the year before His crucifixion. He was going to Jerusalem to die. This was the final portion of His earthly ministry.

Along the way, some Pharisees came to Him with a test question about divorce. They wanted Jesus to give His opinion as to what constituted legitimate grounds for divorce. Jesus answered their question but in doing so explained that the Creator designed marriage to last a lifetime. Any marriage breakup is a sin on someone's part. There may be one innocent party in a divorce but never two. People should not look for a way out of marriage or a way to get a new marriage partner. People should remain with their present mates.

The Twelve struggled with Jesus' answer and wondered if one should get married at all. Jesus explained that marriage is God's will for most people. Some people can live single, but most by God's design cannot.

Some parents wanted Jesus to pray for and bless their children. The Twelve tried to stop them from getting to Jesus but He strongly rebuked the disciples for this and encouraged parents to bring their children to Him. Children are kingdom people, too, and they have every right to the King's favor.

As Jesus prepared to leave this unidentified community, a young man approached Him seeking the way of salvation. Jesus told him to obey the commandments, but the man claimed to be doing this already. Recognizing the man's honesty as well as his sin, Jesus told him to sell everything, give the proceeds to the poor, and then come follow Him. The young man would not do this, so he went away sad and lost.

Jesus used this occasion to teach the Twelve about the hindrance wealth can be to personal salvation. Most wealthy people will not be saved. Even though God can save anyone who comes to Him, the wealthy will rarely come for salvation.

The disciples had left everything to follow Christ. The cost was high but they willingly paid it. Would it matter? Would they be rewarded in any way for their sacrifice? Jesus taught that they and all who sacrifice for Him will be greatly rewarded.

Application: Teaching and Preaching the Passage

Jesus' teachings are timeless. Chapter 19 illustrates this perfectly. His words concerning marriage and divorce, the salvation of children, personal wealth and salvation, the way of salvation, and eternal rewards for sacrificial service to Christ all are as needful today as they were when Jesus first gave them.

Jesus' teaching on marriage and divorce might be presented as follows: (1) marriage is for a lifetime (vv. 3-6); (2) marriage breakups are always at least one person's sin (vv. 7-9); and (3) marriage is for everyone—almost (vv. 10-12). Marriage breakups (1) are against God's perfect will (vv. 6, 8); (2) are always a result of sins (vv. 7-8); and (3) can lead to further sin (v. 9).

A sermon or lesson might be developed on the subject of Jesus and children (vv. 13-15). (1) Adults do right when they bring children to Jesus (vv. 13-14a). (2) Children are symbols of the true kingdom citizen (v. 14b; 18:3-4). And (3) children find in Jesus a welcome heart, a caring hand, and a generous blessing (v. 15; Mk. 10:16).

Concerning personal wealth and the kingdom: (1) one must not permit personal wealth to keep him or her from personal salvation; (2) God can help people overcome whatever hinders them and save them (vv. 25-26); and (3) the Lord will abundantly reward those who sacrifice personal wealth for the kingdom's sake (vv. 27-30).

Jesus answered three important questions in verses 16-30: (1) what must I do to inherit eternal life? (v. 16); (2) who can be saved? (v. 25); and (3) what will we receive for our sacrifice for Jesus? (v. 27).

Verses 16-22 illustrate three common mistakes unsaved people make: (1) some assume good deeds are the way to heaven; (2) some assume they have the ability to do whatever is required to get to heaven, not recognizing the sinful wretchedness of everyone but God; and (3) some assume what they have (wealth) is worth more than what they need (God's forgiveness and eternal life).

F. The Parable of the Laborers: A Lesson in Gracious Rewards (20:1-16)

1 For the kingdom of heaven is like unto a man *that is* an householder, which went out early in the morning to hire labourers into his vineyard.

2 And when he had agreed with the labourers for a penny a day, he sent them into his vineyard.

3 And he went out about the third hour, and saw others standing idle in the marketplace,

4 And said unto them; Go ye also into the vineyard, and whatsoever is right I will give you. And they went their way.

5 Again he went out about the sixth and ninth hour, and did likewise.

6 And about the eleventh hour he went out, and found others standing idle, and saith unto them, Why stand ye here all the day idle?

7 They say unto him, Because no man hath hired us. He saith unto them, Go ye also into the vineyard; and whatsoever is right, *that* shall ye receive.

8 So when even was come, the lord of the vineyard saith unto his steward, Call the labourers, and give them *their* hire, beginning from the last unto the first.

9 And when they came that *were hired* about the eleventh hour, they received every man a penny.

10 But when the first came, they supposed that they should have

received more; and they likewise received every man a penny.
11 And when they had received *it*, they murmured against the goodman of the house,
12 Saying, These last have wrought *but* one hour, and thou hast made them equal unto us, which have borne the burden and heat of the day.
13 But he answered one of them, and said, Friend, I do thee no wrong: didst not thou agree with me for a penny?
14 Take *that* thine *is*, and go thy way: I will give unto this last, even as unto thee.
15 Is it not lawful for me to do what I will with mine own? Is thine eye evil, because I am good?
16 So the last shall be first, and the first last: for many be called, but few chosen.

This parable continues the discussion introduced in 19:27 and appears only in Matthew. Peter had asked Jesus what he and the other disciples would receive for their great sacrifices. Jesus assured them that they would be well rewarded, they and everyone who sacrificed for His gospel (19:29). This parable illustrates that the Lord will pay everyone who serves Him and He will pay everyone fairly and graciously. It also explains the great reversal of 19:30. The rewards received, and by whom, will be different from what many would expect.

For the words, "the kingdom of heaven is like," see comments on 13:24. They mean that there are similarities between what will happen with kingdom workers on judgment day and what happens when a landowner hires laborers to work in his fields and then pays them. It also tells the reader that Jesus was giving a lesson on kingdom work in the present age (Wilkins 664).

The owner—here the master of the house—went to the marketplace, a local gathering place for day workers, to hire hands to work in his vineyard. From later details, one assumes that this was around 6:00 a.m. Jesus gave no details of the kind of labor they would be doing, whether pruning, harvesting, or working the winepresses. (See 18:6, 21:33-34 and comments as well as John 15:1-6 for further information on vineyard work.) The owner and the workers agreed to their work and pay, and he sent them into his vineyard to work the entire day. The pay was a denarius ("penny" is misleading in our day), the normal day's pay for a common laborer (ISBE III:406; 18:28).

The owner went back to the marketplace at around 9:00 a.m. (the third hour) and saw other men waiting to be hired. He told them to go work in the vineyard and promised to pay them "whatever is right." This was repeated at noon and at 3:00 p.m., and he also promised these groups that he would pay what was right. He even hired some men at the eleventh hour (5:00 p.m.). The landowner's visit to the marketplace at that late hour shows there was still work to be done (9:37-38). Again (in some but not all of the Greek manuscripts) he promised to pay what was right.

At the end of the day, the landowner instructed his steward (*epitropos*, manager, foreman; BAGD 303; not the usual *oikonomos*, steward) to pay each worker for his day's work. This was according to the law (Lev. 19:13; Dt. 24:15; Blomberg 62). Instead of beginning with those who had worked the longest, he started with those he had hired last. He paid each a denarius, the same wage he had agreed to with those he hired first.

Because those hired last received a full day's wage, those who had worked all day—even through the hottest (Greek *kausōn*; scorching heat; BAGD 425) time—thought they should have received more. They grumbled against the "goodman" (same as "householder" in v. 1), implying that they thought he was being unfair toward them for these two reasons.

The surprise is the turning point of the parable, the "reversal of expectation" (Osborne 731). The first was not only paid last, they were also paid a single denarius. They thought they deserved more than the latecomers. They did not complain that the latecomers received too much, only that they had received too little and should have been compensated proportionally. However, the landowner reminded them that he had paid them exactly what they had agreed to (v. 13). He had done them no wrong. They should take their pay and go. He also pointed out that while he owed them a denarius, he *desired* to give the last workers a denarius. His gift to the last workers was just that, a gift. He had every right to do that, for the money was his to do with as he pleased. Furthermore, the first had no right to envy his gifts to the last.

The "evil eye" (v. 15) was mentioned in 6:22-23. See comments there. Here it speaks of envy (Evans, *Matthew* 364). However, Nolland (812) thinks resentment, not envy, was visible in their eyes.

Verse 16 summarizes the parable. Whether this is Matthew's summary (Evans, *Matthew* 364) or Jesus' is hard to determine. Regardless, the saying in 19:30 is here reversed, "The last shall be first and the first last." See comments on 19:30. Primacy will be given according to the Master's gracious desire, not according to human reckoning, such as is based on type or length of service and personal sacrifice.

"For many be called, but few are chosen," at the end of verse 16, are not in the Greek manuscripts relied on by many textual scholars. These words end the parable of the wedding feast in 22:14 without question and so are genuinely words of Jesus. Some would say that they do not seem to contribute to the point of the parable of the laborers.

Commentators understand this parable differently. Hagner (33B:572) thinks this parable teaches the Twelve that the unworthy, the last in rank, will receive God's grace too. While it is true that the last in rank will receive God's grace, the unworthy in this parable are not the harlots and tax collectors as Hagner suggests (33B:571). The Twelve are never depicted in the Gospels as objecting to harlots and tax collectors coming into the kingdom, and their acceptance has nothing to do with Peter's question in 19:27. The unworthy in the minds of the first group of workers were those who did not work as long or as hard as they did. This included all four groups that were hired later in the day. Peter had asked what difference their level of sacrifice would make (19:27). Jesus assured them they would receive a very gracious reward. However, this parable cautioned them not to think of themselves too highly, for all who join in the work will receive a full and gracious reward.

Gundry (399), on the other hand, understands Jesus to mean that the early workers represented the first disciples (Jews) and the latecomers were Gentiles who had entered the church more recently (from Matthew's perspective). Gundry thinks Jesus' point was that the Jewish believers must accept Gentile believers. See Luke 13:30 where on another occasion Jesus made this very application with these words. However, such an understanding seems foreign to Matthew's context.

It seems probable that to Peter and the other Apostles Jesus was saying, in effect: "Yes, you will receive reward for your sacrificial labors for Him (19:27-30), but you will not be alone. Others who have not sacrificed at the level you have will be rewarded well also, and you apostles need to have the right attitude about this. You must not be swollen with pride (Bruner 2:321) or envy. God can be gracious to whomsoever He desires." Thank God for His grace.

This parable is not a promise to lazy Christians that they will receive the same rewards as those who work hard for the Master. Compare with 1 Corinthians 3:8. Neither is this parable for procrastinators, those folks who wait until they have one foot in the grave to turn to Jesus. This parable is about obeying the Lord's call to join His workforce and God's gracious rewards for service. "God's grace makes some who are last equal to the first." In this sense, "the first" are the Twelve and everyone who has been called to extreme sacrifice, and "the last" are all who work in the kingdom vineyard but are not called to extreme sacrifice. All will receive a gracious reward.

G. Jesus' Third Prophecy Concerning His Own Death (20:17-19)

17 And Jesus going up to Jerusalem took the twelve disciples apart in the way, and said unto them,
18 Behold, we go up to Jerusalem; and the Son of man shall be betrayed unto the chief priests and unto the scribes, and they shall condemn him to death,
19 And shall deliver him to the Gentiles to mock, and to scourge, and to crucify *him*: and the third day he shall rise again.

This third of four predictions of Jesus' death (though see 17:12 also) is recorded in all three Synoptics with slight differences (Mk. 10:32-34; Lk. 18:31-34). Neither writer records exactly where Jesus spoke these words, only that He was on His way up to Jerusalem. For Jesus' earlier predictions of His death, see 16:21; 17:22-23. One more will follow (26:2).

"Up to Jerusalem" means up in elevation from Jericho. See "down to Jericho" in Luke 10:30. Jericho is located about eighteen miles (29 kilometers) northeast of Jerusalem. Jerusalem is about 2400-2526 feet (640-770 meters) above sea level. Jericho is about 820 feet (250 meters) below sea level. The road from Jericho to Jerusalem, then, rose approximately 3350 feet (1019 meters).

Separating the Twelve from the others who were traveling with Him, Jesus took them aside and told them again of His approaching death. He knew where He would die (Jerusalem), that He would be betrayed to the Jewish leaders, and that His trial would end with Him condemned to die. For betrayed, see the discussion on 26:2. The leaders would then hand Jesus over to the Gentiles to ridicule, whip with a scourge, and crucify. However, Jesus would not stay dead. He would rise on the third day after His crucifixion. All of this happened exactly as Jesus foretold. He went to Jerusalem fully aware of the details of His imminent suffering. (For "Son of Man" see comments on 26:64; for chief priests 16:21; and for scribes 13:52.)

Matthew says no more about this. However, Luke 18:34 says the disciples did not understand what Jesus meant because the meaning was hidden from them. This means that for some reason the Father kept the disciples from understanding this plain statement about Jesus' death (Marshall 691).

H. A Mother Requested Special Consideration for Her Sons (20:20-28)

20 Then came to him the mother of Zebedee's children with her sons, worshipping *him*, and desiring a certain thing of him.
21 And he said unto her, What wilt thou? She saith unto him, Grant that these my two sons may sit, the one on thy right hand, and the other on the left, in thy kingdom.
22 But Jesus answered and said, Ye know not what ye ask. Are ye able to drink of the cup that I shall drink of, and to be baptized with the baptism that I am baptized with? They say unto him, We are able.
23 And he saith unto them, Ye shall drink indeed of my cup, and be baptized with the baptism that I am baptized with: but to sit on my right hand, and on my left, is not mine to give, but *it shall be given to them* for whom it is prepared of my Father.
24 And when the ten heard *it*, they were moved with indignation against the two brethren.
25 But Jesus called them *unto him*, and said, Ye know that the princes of the Gentiles exercise dominion over them, and they that are great exercise authority upon them.
26 But it shall not be so among you: but whosoever will be great among you, let him be your minister;
27 And whosoever will be chief among you, let him be your servant:
28 Even as the Son of man came not to be ministered unto, but to minister, and to give his life a ransom for many.

As Jesus continued toward Jerusalem (20:17), the Twelve and some others accompanied Him. Included in this larger group were certain women disciples who had ministered to Jesus' needs as He traveled about preaching and healing (Lk. 8:1-3; Mt. 27:55). The mother of James and John was one of these. She was accompanying her sons as they followed Jesus, at least on this occasion. It is possible that her name was Salome (ISBE IV:286; Wilkins 667). From the crucifixion texts in Matthew (27:56), Mark (15:40), and John (19:25-27) it also seems possible that Salome was Jesus' aunt and that James and John were His cousins on His mother's side.

Somewhere on the road to Jerusalem, this faithful woman approached Jesus and knelt before Him to make her special request. Perhaps she knelt in homage to Jesus as the Messianic King rather than as Deity (Carson, *Matthew* 431). Though her understanding was growing, the reader of Matthew has a greater understanding of Jesus' person than Zebedee's wife at the time. It is clear from Matthew's use of the first and second person plurals (we, you) that all three were involved (v. 22-23) in the request. This was a family idea.

She asked that her sons might sit in the highest places of privilege in Jesus' kingdom (v. 21). His kingdom was the same as the kingdom of heaven and God's kingdom (Bruner 2:328). To sit on the right and left meant to be the closest to Jesus in His rule. Which of the disciples would be the greatest in the kingdom had been on the disciples' minds for some time (18:1; Wilkins 669).

John, the beloved disciple, was evidently the closest of the Twelve to Jesus. He and his brother James and Peter made up the inner circle. Only these three were permitted to accompany Him into Jairus' house where Jesus raised his daughter from the dead. Only these three were permitted on the Mount of Transfiguration and were nearest to Him in the Garden of Gethsemane. Even though Peter appears to have been the leader of the Twelve by this time, perhaps James and John were attempting to eclipse Peter.

Jesus' response was kind but firm: neither the mother nor her sons understood what she was asking or the implications (v. 22). First, they did not have all of the facts of the kingdom and they surely did not fully understand the greatness of His throne. Would mere mortals be permitted to sit in such company? Further, they did not even know what was about to transpire in Jerusalem. They were looking for the visible Messianic kingdom. Jesus was not close to sitting on an earthly throne. He was close to dying. Finally, those who share the throne in the future aspects of the kingdom must share in Christ's suffering now. The "cup" in this instance stands for "suffering." The "cup" generally refers to that which God administers, whether good or evil (Ps. 16:5; Jer. 25:15). Here, as in 26:39, the cup refers to the suffering God has determined for the Son. James and John wanted to share in Jesus' glorious throne. Did they also want to share in His suffering?

The words "and to be baptized with the baptism that I am baptized with" (vv. 22-23) are not in all the Greek manuscripts. Even so, they are certainly in Mark 10:38-39 and were part of what Jesus said. Like the cup symbol, baptism is a symbol for Jesus' suffering (Lk. 12:50) and suggests immersion in or being overwhelmed by a situation, here negative (Picirilli, *Mark* 294). Wessel (720) points to Psalms 18:16 and 69:1-2 and says baptism "is a symbol of a deluge of trouble." The baptism to which Jesus looked was more than mere trouble: He referred to the cross, when the wrath of God would be poured out upon Him. See Psalm 88:7 and Jonah 2:3 where overflowing waves are a figure of God's wrath (ISBE I:411).

James and John thought they could drink from the same cup as Jesus, but when His "cup" came, they could not (26:40, 43, 56). These two men were not elevated with Him, but two thieves were (Evans, *Matthew* 372). From the

Gospels it appears that of the Twelve only John stayed near the cross of Jesus. James is not mentioned. Neither of them was as committed to Jesus as they thought (26:31, 56; Hendriksen 746).

Still, it was true that these two would share in Christ's cup; they too would suffer (v. 23). In this they were right, although they surely did not understand at the time. James died a martyr's death (ca. A.D. 44) but John did not. James was the first of the Twelve to die for the faith (Acts 12:2). John was exiled (Rev. 1:9). However, Jesus said that only the Father could answer their request. He alone decides who sits next to Jesus in the kingdom.

The limitations of the incarnate Jesus are in view, much as in 24:36, Mark 5:30-34, and 11:13. The explanation for how Jesus, as omniscient God (Jn. 1:48, 50; 2:24-25; 16:30; 21:17), could *not* know some things is wrapped up in the mystery of the incarnation and the union of His two natures. The God-man was in some way limited in His use of His omniscience. For further comments on the incarnation, see the remarks on 1:23 and 24:36.

Jesus did not correct the belief that there would be such a kingdom with such positions (Acts 1:6-7). Rather, He supported such a belief when He declared that the places of privilege belong to those for whom it was prepared (Thiessen 509). Jesus had told them they would rule along with Him in the new world (19:28). Evidently, that was not enough for these two. They also wanted to rule over the other ten apostles as well. One wonders what the others in this traveling company thought about such a strong disagreement among Jesus' disciples.

The other apostles overheard the discussion and reacted with anger (Greek, *aganakteō*; "to be indignant against what is judged to be wrong," Louw and Nida I:762). Like a festering sore, the debate about who would be the greatest resurfaced (18:1) and would surface again (Lk. 22:24). It is clear that the Twelve had not internalized the lessons of 18:1-9 (Erickson 624).

Jesus called the Twelve together and explained their wrong thinking. Unlike the political order in this world, where rule by tyrants was common (v. 25; Keener, *Background* 100), in Jesus' kingdom those who minister and serve are the greatest. Jesus did not limit His comments to preachers and deacons, but He spoke of all who willingly serve others for Him. In Christ's order, positional authority over others in the Christian community is forbidden. "It shall not be so among you" (v. 26). This future tense is imperatival (Newman and Stine 648). The Twelve were worldly in their thinking (Osborne 741) and out of line with the will of Christ.

The desire to be great must ("let him be" is also imperatival) manifest itself in service. Jesus modeled this mindset (even as, v. 28; Phil. 2:7-8). First, He came to this world to serve not to be served. His claim that He "came" to this world presupposes His preexistence (Carson, *Matthew* 433). Second, He came to give His life a ransom for the sake of many. Ransom (Greek *lutron*) means "the price of release" (BAGD 482). Jesus planned to die to set mankind free. He would die to bear mankind's iniquities (Is. 53:11-12) in order to set them free from their guilt and deserved punishment before the holy God. He voluntarily took on this guilt and punishment (Is. 53:4-6), thus providing a way for sinners to be free from sin's bondage and guilt and become righteous before God (2 Cor. 5:21). "For" (Greek *anti*) means "instead of, in the place of" (Grimm's 49). Jesus gave His life as a substitute for sinners (Is. 53:6, 8, 10-12) and as a ransom to purchase their freedom (Hagner 33B:583).

"Many" denotes many as opposed to a few (Grimm's 529). Compare with 7:13, 22; 8:11; 12:15; 24:5 (two times). Jesus did not limit the extent of His atonement. He came for the whole world (Jn. 3:16; 1 Jn. 2:2) and His death was sufficient for the whole world (1 Tim. 2:6). However, Jesus promised that though not all would receive His provision for salvation, many would.

Evans (*Matthew* 373) points out that neither one of the Twelve became the leader of the Jerusalem church. It was a family member, Jesus' half-brother James, who became the leader. Apparently, the apostles finally got the point. Greatness in the kingdom belongs to those who serve.

I. Jesus Healed Two Blind Men (20:29-34)

29 And as they departed from Jericho, a great multitude followed him.
30 And, behold, two blind men sitting by the way side, when they heard that Jesus passed by, cried out, saying, Have mercy on us, O Lord, *thou* son of David.
31 And the multitude rebuked them, because they should hold their peace: but they cried the more, saying, Have mercy on us, O Lord, *thou* son of David.
32 And Jesus stood still, and called them, and said, What will ye that I shall do unto you?
33 They say unto him, Lord, that our eyes may be opened.
34 So Jesus had compassion *on them*, and touched their eyes: and immediately their eyes received sight, and they followed him.

This healing gives rise to questions that are unanswerable at the present state of knowledge. Mark 10:46-52 and Luke 18:35-43 record this healing also but mention only one blind man. On another occasion Matthew recorded two healings where Mark and Luke mention only one (cf. 8:28; Mk. 5:2; Lk. 8:27). Also, according to Matthew and Mark, as Jesus left Jericho He healed the blind men. Luke says it happened as they approached Jericho. Since there were two Jerichos at this time located about a mile (1.6 kilometers) apart, Matthew and Mark probably referred to one and Luke to the other (Carson, *Matthew* 435; Wilkins 671). However, more information is needed before a clear harmony of these records can be established for certain.

Jesus left Jericho and headed for Jerusalem by way of Bethany, approximately sixteen miles (26 kilometers) away. A typical day's journey on foot was about twenty miles (thirty kilometers; ISBE IV:895). If this was Friday, one week before His crucifixion, He needed to arrive in Bethany by evening before the Sabbath began. At Bethany He and the Twelve would stay with friends, probably Lazarus and Mary and Martha or with Simon the Leper. These loyal followers had a banquet planned (26:6-13) to honor Jesus—and perhaps Lazarus because of his resurrection.

A great multitude followed Jesus partly because they wanted to be with Him and partly because of the upcoming Passover in Jerusalem. Travelers to the pilgrim feasts often traveled in groups. The road from Jericho to Jerusalem was notoriously dangerous (ISBE IV:203; Bock 198; Lk. 10:30).

Just outside Jericho, two blind men were seated by the roadside, desiring alms (Mk. 10:46; Lk. 18:35). When they heard Jesus was passing by they began crying out, begging for mercy from Jesus. They did not ask for money. They asked that He take time for them.

They had heard of the one who could give eyesight to the blind. Their only hope was passing within shouting distance of them. Above the noise and rebukes of the crowd, these two men shouted to get Jesus' attention. They addressed Him as Son of David, a clearly Messianic title. See comments on 1:1 and 9:27 for its meaning and implications. Restoring sight to the blind was one sign that proved the kingdom of heaven had arrived and that Jesus was the Messiah. See comments on 11:5.

In spite of the crowds' attempts to silence them (compare 15:23; 19:13), the blind men continued their attempts to get Jesus' attention and were rewarded for their efforts when He called for them to come to Him. He asked them what they desired. They wanted their eyes opened. Jesus felt compassion (cf. 9:36; 14:14; 15:32) and healed their eyes. Matthew alone records that Jesus touched their blind eyes (v. 34; cf. 8:3, 15; 9:29). The healing was instantaneous, confirming that their faith in Jesus as Messiah was right (Nolland 829; Mk. 10:52). The first person they saw was Jesus. These men responded by becoming immediate followers of Jesus, both spiritually and physically. Apparently, they became part of the crowd headed for Jerusalem. If they stayed for Passover, one week later they saw the great healer and their Savior die on a cross. They might even have witnessed His resurrection (Acts 13:31). According to Luke 18:43, the great multitude that followed Jesus (Mt. 20:29) gave praise to God when they saw the men healed.

Summary (20:1-34)

The parable of the laborers in the vineyard illustrates the proverb that many who are first will be last, and the last first (19:30). All who serve Jesus faithfully, regardless of the length of their call or service, He will reward out of His abundant grace. Believers need to leave fair and gracious compensation matters up to the Lord,

As Jesus walked on toward Jerusalem, He pulled the Twelve away from the crowds traveling with them to Passover and again told them what awaited Him in Jerusalem. With specific language, Jesus spoke of His betrayal and condemnation and the fact that He would be handed over to the Gentiles to be tortured and finally crucified. His death, however, would be temporary, for on the third day He would be arise.

The Twelve did not comprehend His words. They were not thinking about Jesus dying. They supposed that He was going to set up the kingdom while He was in Jerusalem. Because of their kingdom expectations, James and John and their mother approached Jesus with a request for James and John to sit by Him in His kingdom. Jesus could not give what they asked but promised instead that they would suffer with Him. Then He called the Twelve about Him again and told them that they would not be permitted to rule over each other. If they wanted to be great, they had to become everyone's servant. This included serving each other.

As they continued on their way toward Jerusalem, they passed through Jericho. Just outside the city, two blind men began shouting at Jesus, begging for His attention. He asked what they wanted and they requested that He open their eyes. With compassion, He healed their eyes and they became immediate disciples and followed Him on to Jerusalem.

Application: Teaching and Preaching the Passage

One might present the message of the parable of the laborers by explaining that being first in the kingdom means (1) working from the time you are called until quitting time, (2) accepting whatever wages God gives as a gift of His grace, and (3) submitting to God's sovereignty in calling and rewards.

Hendriksen (740) describes how one can avoid being among the first who become last. (1) Avoid a work-for-wages spirit for things that are spiritual. (2) Recognize God's sovereignty in His right to distribute favors as He pleases. (3) Avoid envy.

For preaching or teaching Jesus' prediction of His suffering, see the application section on 17:22-23.

Using the Twelve as an example (vv. 20-28), one could discuss disunity among Christ's followers: (1) its cause (worldly ambition), (2) its corrupting influence (infected all of the Twelve), and (3) its cure (humble service).

A sermon or lesson might be developed explaining three reasons these blind men were successful in gaining their eyesight. They received their eyesight because (1) they had faith that Jesus could heal them, (2) they were persistent against resistance, and (3) they made their request known to the Lord.

One might consider all of chapter twenty in an overview fashion as a contrast in thinking. Three examples of upside down thinking, i.e., thinking that was opposite that of Jesus: (1) some thought they should have received more (vv. 11-12); (2) some thought they should have the highest places of privilege (vv. 20-21); and (3) some thought Jesus should not be bothered with such people (v. 31). In contrast, right side up thinking is: (1) the last shall be first; (2) the Father sovereignly and graciously gives places of privilege to those who humbly serve; and (3) Jesus has compassion for the less fortunate.

VI. THE PASSION WEEK NARRATIVE (21:1—27:66)

Toward this week, all of Jesus' life and ministry were directed. He came to give His life a ransom for many (20:28). Every message preached and every miracle performed pointed to the crucifixion (Wilkins 700), the place, and time where the propitiatory sacrifice (Rom. 3:25; 1 Jn. 2:2; 4:10) for lost humanity would be offered. The culminating and climaxing events of this week, the death and burial of Jesus, along with His resurrection on the first day of the next week, together make up the foundation of the new community, the one body, the church (Eph. 2:11-22).

It appears that John recorded details in a more strictly chronological order than Matthew. The feast in honor of Jesus, and possibly Lazarus, whom He had raised from the dead (Jn. 11:43-44), was given the evening before the triumphal entry. This feast followed the ending of the Sabbath at sundown (Jn. 12:1-8). Matthew recorded the events of this dinner in 26:6-13 where he emphasized Jesus' anointing. Here in chapter 21, however, he recorded nothing about either event. He went from the healing of the two blind men in Jericho (20:29-34) to the Triumphal Entry, passing over Jesus' stop in Bethany and the celebration dinner in His honor. (See notes on 26:2, 6 for more comments on the chronology of the Passion Week.)

A. Sunday: The Triumphal Entry (21:1-11)

1 And when they drew nigh unto Jerusalem, and were come to Bethphage, unto the mount of Olives, then sent Jesus two disciples,
2 Saying unto them, Go into the village over against you, and straightway ye shall find an ass tied, and a colt with her: loose *them*, and bring *them* unto me.
3 And if any *man* say ought unto you, ye shall say, The Lord hath need of them; and straightway he will send them.
4 All this was done, that it might be fulfilled which was spoken by the prophet, saying,
5 Tell ye the daughter of Sion, Behold, thy King cometh unto thee, meek, and sitting upon an ass, and a colt the foal of an ass.
6 And the disciples went, and did as Jesus commanded them,
7 And brought the ass, and the colt, and put on them their clothes, and they set *him* thereon.
8 And a very great multitude spread their garments in the way; others cut down branches from the trees, and strewed *them* in the way.
9 And the multitudes that went before, and that followed, cried, saying, Hosanna to the son of David: Blessed *is* he that cometh in the name of the Lord; Hosanna in the highest.
10 And when he was come into Jerusalem, all the city was moved, saying, Who is this?
11 And the multitude said, This is Jesus the prophet of Nazareth of Galilee.

This is Sunday of Passion Week, the week of the crucifixion. Hill (290) suggests the triumphal entry took place six months before Passover, probably during the Feast of Tabernacles. However, compare John 12:1 ("six days before the Passover") and John 12:12 ("the next day"). The biblical evidence argues that He rode the colt the Sunday before His crucifixion. All four Gospel writers narrate this event (Mk. 11:1-11; Lk. 19:28-40; Jn. 12:12-19).

Jesus approached Jerusalem from the east. The exact location of Bethphage is unknown but it was a small village possibly located on the west side of the Mount of Olives between Bethany, where Jesus had lodged Saturday night, and Jerusalem. Newman and Stine (656) suggest Bethphage was located east of Bethany, which would place it on the east side of the Mount of Olives

(ISBE I:474). If one understands that Jesus was just arriving from Jericho and had not yet been to Bethany, then the chronology of events surrounding the feast given in Jesus' honor suggested above would need to be revised.

Once Jesus arrived at Bethphage, He stopped and sent two of His disciples into the village (Hagner 33B:593, thinks the two went into Bethany) to borrow a donkey and her colt. Mark 11:2 and Luke 19:30 both mention He wanted a colt that had never been ridden. He gave His two disciples specific instructions about where (in the village), when (immediately), and how they would find and get this donkey (v. 2). He also assured them no one would stop them (v. 3). Evans (*Matthew* 381) thinks Jesus prearranged this. The text does not say if this was prearranged or if He was exercising supernatural foreknowledge, but verse three seems to suggest arrangements had not been previously made.

Jesus acted as He did to fulfill a specific prophecy found in Zechariah 9:9. He moved deliberately, in accordance with Scripture (v. 4). Hill (290; also Carson, *Matthew* 437) calls this messianic entry an "acted parable."

The first portion of Matthew's quote (v. 5) came from Isaiah 62:11: "Say to the daughter of Zion." This was part of the prophet's message of the Lord's restoration and salvation in which He extends His invitation to the whole earth to join in Zion's renewal. Zion was originally the name of the mountain ridge upon which Jerusalem sat (1 Kg. 8:1). The phrase "daughter of Zion" became synonymous with Jerusalem and her people (ISBE I:870; IV:1198). This message is specifically for the people who live in Jerusalem. Why Matthew quotes first from Isaiah is unclear unless he wants his readers to link the one bringing salvation in Isaiah with the one riding the colt in Zechariah 9:9. Zechariah began his sentence with "Rejoice greatly" where Isaiah has "You say."

The post-exilic, fifth century B.C. prophet Zechariah told Jerusalem's inhabitants to take note because their king would come to them just or righteous and having salvation, humble and riding on a donkey's colt. God promised Jerusalem her king would be a righteous deliverer, but humble and riding a lowly beast normally used to carry men's burdens? What kind of a king is that? Humble is lowly, opposite to being haughty (TWOT II:683).

Even though Jesus instructed His disciples to bring two animals, neither Zechariah nor Matthew intended to convey that Jesus would ride two animals (*contra* Newman and Stine 660) or that the prophecy called for two animals. The Hebrew line "and upon a colt, the foal of a donkey" is Hebrew parallelism and means *even* upon a colt, thus identifying the donkey of the previous clause. The same is true for Matthew. One should read both Zechariah and Matthew, then, "on a donkey, even on a colt, etc."

The prophecy called for the king to ride a donkey's foal, a colt, and that is what Jesus did. This humble king will also enjoy a worldwide rule of peace (Zech. 9:10), which God will bring about in the eschaton, the end times.

Matthew did not mention Zechariah's "he is just and having salvation"—or as Bruner (2:355) translates, "triumphant and victorious is he." Writers agree Matthew did not include this phrase because he wanted his readers to see Jesus as a lowly Messiah, not as a victorious king bringing deliverance (Bruner 2:355; Hill 291). Jesus' intent was to make a *humble* entry. The symbolism in the part of Zechariah's prophecy that Matthew quoted conveys this idea. Israel's king would not enter Jerusalem on a warhorse as a conquering King. He would come in humility, riding a young donkey.

The two disciples did as instructed and brought the mother and her foal to Jesus (v. 6). They took their cloaks (their outer garments) and placed them on the animals. Though Matthew does not say, it is clear from the prophecy that Jesus then rode the colt (v. 7). That He sat "thereon" is, literally, "on them"—on the garments, that is.

A very great (Greek *pleistos,* elative of *polus*; BAGD 689, III) crowd of people was with Jesus, probably made up of travelers from all over Palestine and including residents of Bethany and Bethphage. There were also many travelers who were already in Jerusalem for the Passover feast. Some of these had heard of Lazarus' resurrection and went out to meet Jesus as He rode the colt their way (Jn. 12:9, 12-13, 18; Hendriksen 761). Others in the crowd that accompanied Jesus that morning knew Jesus and were excited to accompany Him into the city. Luke (19:37) calls them "his disciples."

Following the example of the two apostles, the crowd honored Jesus by placing their garments (v. 8) and branches from trees (v. 8) on the ground for the colt to walk over. The action is progressive (Greek imperfect): they *were placing* the branches on the ground as He rode along. See 2 Kings 9:13 for an O.T. example of this kind of honor.

As He rode down the Mount of Olives near the city (Lk. 19:37), all of the crowd, both those who went before Him and those who followed (v. 9), were calling out a portion of a Psalm (118:25-26). They cried out, "Hosanna." The crowds were not just shouting sounds (Newman and Stine 661). The crowds were specifically shouting praise to Jesus.

Hosanna transliterates the Hebrew and originally meant "Help," or "Save, I pray" (BAGD 899; Blomberg 65-66). Some interpreters suggest that by N.T. times the word had become an expression of intense joy or a shout of welcome rather than a prayer to God (ISBE II:761; Gundry 411; *Didache* 10:6). "Hosanna to the Son of David," then, was an exclamation of joy from a crowd thrilled about accompanying their king into the city. Bruner (2:356), however, prefers to understand "Hosanna" as a prayer and has the crowd praying, "God save the Son of David."

"Son of David" is a Messianic title (1:1; 9:27; 15:22; 22:41-45). This crowd believed Jesus was the promised Son of David, the king who would sit on David's throne. It is noteworthy that Matthew with his emphasis on Jesus as King did not include that portion of the crowd's confession. Luke 19:38 and John 12:13 each record that the crowd's praise included a specific reference to Jesus as king. This crowd was not offended by Jesus' lowly means of transportation. They understood Him to be the Messianic King of Israel (Jn. 12:13; Archer and Chirichigno 89). However, they were still thinking nationalistically and expected an imminent, visible kingdom (Mk. 11:10; Keener, *Matthew* 493). Not until after the cross and the resurrection would some understand the suffering aspects of the messianic king and then only after they were taught

(Lk. 24:4-7, 25-26, 45-46; Acts 3:18; Heb. 2:10).

The crowds also confessed they believed that God's blessings were on Jesus and acknowledged He was there "in the name of the Lord" (v. 9). They were quoting Psalm 118:26. This portion of their praise meant He was there on God's behalf, speaking God's word (Jer. 11:21; 14:14; ISBE III:482), and enjoying God's approval. The religious leaders had identified Jesus with Satan (12:24), but this crowd believed otherwise. See 23:39 where Jesus used this same O.T. quote in His condemnation of the city of Jerusalem.

Luke (19:37) says they also praised Him for all of the mighty works He had done. Since no miracles had been done on this occasion, they were speaking of miracles they had witnessed or heard about during Jesus' ministry. For these people the miracles had accomplished Jesus' purpose for doing them. They saw in them proof that the kingdom had arrived (12:28; see comments on 11:3-5).

Finally, the crowds also proclaimed, "Hosanna in the highest," meaning "highest places" or "highest heaven" (Wigram 763; Grimm's 647). See also Mark 11:10, Luke 2:14; 19:38. "Hosanna in the highest places," according to Gundry (411; Ps. 148:1-2), calls for praise among the angels, as Luke 2:14 depicts in the voices of angels themselves. However, "Hosanna in the highest" is probably simply praise to God (Newman and Stine 661). "In the highest" speaks of God without actually saying His name, something devout Jews were careful to practice. This means that the crowds were praising God for this day, i.e., for sending the Messiah (Carson, *Matthew* 439), rather than calling for praise from the angels. Either way, from the earthly road between Bethphage and Jerusalem to the highest heavens, this was a joyous occasion. The long-awaited Son of David was entering the city of Jerusalem.

Such volume, crowd size, and praise got the city's attention. This entire episode surely disrupted the day, for Jesus' entrance, though humble, did not go unnoticed. The whole city was stirred (v. 10). Jesus' entrance into the city on the colt as the crowds shouted caused great anxiety and commotion. Compare this with 2:3. It is therefore strange that Keener (*Matthew* 493) suggests the entry happened "relatively quickly" and that "the messianic commotion did not spread beyond the portion of the crowd already excited by Jesus' reputation."

The Gospel writers identified three groups in attendance that day: the crowd from Bethany (Lk. 19:28, 36), the crowd that went out of Jerusalem to meet Jesus (Jn. 12:12-13), and the rest of the city that was stirred at His arrival. This latter group, people still unfamiliar with Jesus, asked who this man was. The answer shows another dimension of the accompanying crowds' understanding. They identified Jesus as a prophet and they identified Him as the prophet from Nazareth in Galilee (2:23). One will notice that this crowd did not confess Him as the Prophet to come (Hagner 33B:596; Dt. 18:15; Jn. 1:25; 6:14; 7:40). He was the prophet from Nazareth.

Some Pharisees in the crowds disagreed with these disciples' assessment of Jesus and called for Jesus to rebuke them (Lk. 19:39-40). Jesus refused. The Pharisees denied that a prophet could come from Galilee (Jn. 7:52) but the crowd was not so blind. These Pharisees were wrong on several levels. (1) Jonah, the O.T. prophet, was from Gath-hepher, located three miles (5 km) north of Nazareth in Galilee. (2) Isaiah 9:1-2 promised that Galilee was God's choice for where His great Messianic light would first shine. In other words, the Prophet-Messiah was prophesied to come from Galilee. See comments on 4:15-16. (3) Nowhere in the O.T. did God limit Himself to any particular location from which He could select His prophets. (4) Jesus was the Prophet who was promised to come from Galilee.

The Twelve also witnessed and probably participated in this celebration. However, they did not understand the meaning of these events. It was not until after Jesus went back to heaven that they understood that His colt ride into Jerusalem was a fulfillment of Scripture (Jn. 12:16; Hendriksen 762).

B. Monday: Jesus Initiates a Confrontation (21:12-22)

Mark's comments (11:11) help the reader see that Palm Sunday was a big day for Jesus. His celebrated entry drew the attention of the city (Mt. 21:10). However, the whole city did not welcome Him with Hosannas. Many were curious but not worshipful. Once in the city, the celebration stopped, and after looking around inside the temple court Jesus and the Twelve returned to Bethany.

On Monday, the situation changed drastically. Mark mentioned that Jesus had looked around Sunday evening before He left for the day. Perhaps a plan was forming in His mind even then, for Matthew, Mark, and Luke each described Monday's scene as immediate and intense. Jesus took action as soon as He entered the Temple court.

1. The royal Messiah cleansed the temple (21:12-17)

12 And Jesus went into the temple of God, and cast out all them that sold and bought in the temple, and overthrew the tables of the moneychangers, and the seats of them that sold doves,
13 And said unto them, It is written, My house shall be called the house of prayer; but ye have made it a den of thieves.
14 And the blind and the lame came to him in the temple; and he healed them.
15 And when the chief priests and scribes saw the wonderful things that he did, and the children crying in the temple, and saying, Hosanna to the son of David; they were sore displeased,
16 And said unto him, Hearest thou what these say? And Jesus saith unto them, Yea; have ye never read, Out of the mouth of babes and sucklings thou hast perfected praise?
17 And he left them, and went out of the city into Bethany; and he lodged there.

Jesus entered the city from Bethany and just a short distance from the temple precincts. Passing through the first gate into the outer court Jesus looked around. This was the Court of the Gentiles, as far as Gentiles were permitted to go. Only Jewish women, Jewish men, temple workers (Levites), and priests could enter beyond the Court of the Gentiles.

Notice the action words: He cast (or drove) out and He overturned. He cast out those who bought and sold animals and other items necessary for sacrifices (Newman and Stine 665). He overturned the tables and seats of money-changers—apparently while the seats were occupied! Moneychangers were for people who had to exchange their homeland currency for the required temple currency. Mark 11:16 states that Jesus even stopped people from carrying items through the temple. Evidently, some were using the courtyard as a shortcut to another destination.

John 2:13 says cattle, sheep, and doves (Greek *peristera*, possibly pigeons) were bought and sold in the temple. In short, part of the temple had become a holding and marketing area for livestock. Matthew did not mention Jesus using a scourge or emptying out the money, as in John's record of His first temple cleansing. The first cleansing had no permanent effect on these temple habits (Walvoord 157).

The reader is struck by the actions that seem so unlike Jesus and opposite the humble image of the previous day. This is the same Jesus who taught "blessed are the poor in spirit, for theirs is the kingdom of heaven" (Mt. 5:3) and "blessed are the meek, for they will inherit the earth" (Mt. 5:5). He told His followers to "turn the other cheek" (Mt. 5:39) and rebuked the two "sons of thunder" who wanted to call down fire on the Samaritans (Lk. 9:54). In a manner reminiscent of certain O.T. prophets (Hos. 4:1-2; Am. 2:4), Jesus chastised His audience for violating God's Word. By actions and words, Jesus defended God's honor by purifying the temple. By the same actions, He showed His own high "respect for the sacredness of the Temple precincts" (Lane, *Mark* 406). His actions in part fulfilled Malachi 3:1 and, as Hill (293) observed, were a further messianic sign to those who understood. John the Baptist was the messenger (Mal. 3:1), the "Elijah" who was to come. See comments on 11:10, 14. Jesus, then, was the LORD who came suddenly to His temple.

Quoting two O.T. prophets, Jesus condemned the temple trade. Citing Isaiah 56:7 Jesus gave the main reason for His anger. God's temple was to be a house of prayer (v. 13). It had become instead something that interrupted and prevented worship. The house where prayers are offered should be free of distraction, commotion, and day-to-day business (Jn. 2:16).

Mark (11:17) records that Jesus quoted a longer portion of Isaiah 56:7 than mentioned by Matthew. The house of prayer was to be "for all nations." God promised through Isaiah that Gentiles who "joined themselves to the LORD, to minister to him, to love the name of the LORD, and to be his servants" (Is. 56:6) would joyfully worship in the temple and He would accept their sacrifices. Isaiah 56 is eschatological but it is clear from Jesus' actions that He expected some fulfillment of this already. As Blomberg (67) noted, the temple practices approved by the current leadership prevented God's stated desire for His temple.

The second reason Jesus cleansed the temple area appears to have been price gouging. That worshipers purchased sacrificial animals was not wrong. God had made this provision before Israel settled in the land of Canaan (Dt. 14:24-25). Looking ahead to the time when the Israelites would possess Canaan and a central location would be established for worship, God provided a means for those who lived great distances to bring their tithes to the temple. Crops and animals could be sold and the money used to purchase replacement offerings in Jerusalem. God had also assigned the priests with the task of insuring that all sacrifices met His standards (Lev. 22:17-25). One thousand years later Malachi (1:6-14) gave a scathing rebuke against the priests for dishonoring God by not insisting that the people bring acceptable animals for sacrifice.

It is easy to imagine how the need to provide animals preapproved for sacrifice became a business and how this business became an abuse. This sort of temple trade might have been going on for centuries. See Zechariah 14:21 where the Hebrew word translated "Canaanite" could instead be translated "merchant" or "trader" (as in the ESV; TWOT I:446).

Extra-biblical Jewish writings from that time period report that pigeons were sold at inflated prices (Evans, *Mark* 172-173). Other animals might also have been. Worshipers might have been forced to pay inflated prices for animals that had the priests' approval for sacrificial purposes. Keener (*Matthew* 497), however, says the historical substantiation that there were financial abuses is lacking. He thinks the problem was "paying money in the temple."

Though one cannot be certain about the extent of the abuses, surely, some wrongs were being done or Jesus' cleansing and rebuke would have been baseless. God had provided laws to make worship less of a hardship for those who traveled great distances, but some folks selfishly capitalized on the situation and made worship a hardship for those who had to purchase their animals. Jesus called such men thieves and quoted Jeremiah's condemnation of his contemporaries who turned the temple into a haunt for dishonest people (Jer.7:11).

The context of Jeremiah's words was of judgment and impending doom. Jews of Jeremiah's day thought God would never destroy the temple. They thought they could practice sin and still worship in the temple and have God's favor. God assured them they were wrong. He planned to destroy the temple (Jer. 7:14-15) even as He had destroyed Shiloh.

If this is the proper understanding of Jesus' use of Jeremiah, Jesus' violent actions and Scriptural quotations were not just to cleanse the temple of corruption but they were also a prophetic harbinger of the A.D. 70 destruction of Jerusalem and this temple. The temple was no refuge, no sanctuary, for practicing sinners. What had happened at Shiloh in Eli's day and to the first temple in 586 B.C. would happen to this first century temple as well.

Following the cleansing of the temple, Jesus performed His final, recorded healing miracles (v. 14), mentioned only by Matthew. Jewish authorities restricted the deaf, blind, and lame to certain areas of the temple (Carson, *Matthew* 442; Jeremias, 117-118). (For lame, see comments on 15:30-31.) People with various handicaps came into the Court of the Gentiles where Jesus was and He healed them, thus qualifying them for further access to the temple area. Jesus' philosophy of ministry was radically different from that of the Jewish leaders (9:13; 12:7; Hos. 6:6; Hagner 33B:601). His actions were merciful and continued supporting His claims that the kingdom had arrived (11:5-6).

Some of the chief priests and the scribes witnessed Jesus' healings (v. 15). They knew His miracles were legitimate. They also heard the children in the temple repeating what the adults had said about Jesus the day before: "Hosanna to the Son of David." One assumes these were children of the crowds of disciples that escorted Jesus from Bethphage to Jerusalem. Regardless, the children caught and (at least) mimicked the praise actions of the adults, a worthy goal of all godly parents.

Osborne (764) believes these children were doing more than mimicking what they had heard the previous day. He believes they were "used as disciples" to pass on inspired revelation (11:25-26). It is possible, indeed probable, that children believed in Jesus also and that God chose to use these young disciples on this day to further His purpose.

The priests and scribes reacted toward Jesus in anger and asked Him, "Are you hearing (Greek present tense) what these [children] are saying?" The children's praise was ongoing. Jesus responded by quoting Psalm 8:2, a Psalm that speaks of the universal majesty of the Lord. The Lord has so ordered creation that He receives praise from the highest heaven and from the weakest of humanity, babies and sucklings. These children would have been older than the Psalmist's babies and sucklings but they fall well within the parameters set by this Psalm for those who should give praise to the Lord of the earth. Walvoord (158) suggests these were twelve-year-old boys in the temple for their first time, but the text is silent about this.

Where Matthew has "perfected praise" (v. 16, matching the LXX), the Hebrew of Psalm 8:2 says, literally, "ordained strength" (KJV Ps. 8:2). This means that He has firmly established, founded, or ordained strength in the vocal utterances of the little ones. The Hebrew word for strength denotes a stronghold (BDB 738). Compare Jeremiah 16:19. This means that even the praises of little ones form a defense against God's enemies. How apt for Jesus to use this O.T. Scripture at this time when His enemies were gathering against Him. His defense was not sword and spear but children shouting His praises and Scripture that validated their doing so. (One may suspect that the chief priests and scribes remembered the last two lines of Psalms 8:2, even though Jesus did not quote them, and considered that He might have been inferring that the two lines applied to them as His accusers.)

Jesus (1) justified the children's praise of Him with this verse from Psalm 8 and (2) thus identified Himself as the LORD of that Psalm. By using this verse, He (3) at least inferred that the children were praising Him as part of the Lord's plan. Jesus was not going to forbid the children to call Him "Son of David," because this was exactly what He wanted them to do. Rather, He used the objection from the priests and scribes to further state His claim that He was more than just the human descendant of David. In other words, as offended as they were that Jesus would assume the title "Son of David," He was assuming even more than that. See comments on 22:41-45.

After this exchange, Jesus and the Twelve went to Bethany for the night. They probably stayed at the home of Simon (26:6) or perhaps the home of

Jesus' good friends, Lazarus, Mary, and Martha (Lk. 10:38; Jn. 12:1). Soon He would spend the nights just outside the city rather than go back to Bethany.

2. The fig tree cursed and withered (21:18-22)

18 Now in the morning as he returned into the city, he hungered.
19 And when he saw a fig tree in the way, he came to it, and found nothing thereon, but leaves only, and said unto it, Let no fruit grow on thee henceforward for ever. And presently the fig tree withered away.
20 And when the disciples saw *it*, they marvelled, saying, How soon is the fig tree withered away!
21 Jesus answered and said unto them, Verily I say unto you, If ye have faith, and doubt not, ye shall not only do this *which is done* to the fig tree, but also if ye shall say unto this mountain, Be thou removed, and be thou cast into the sea; it shall be done.
22 And all things, whatsoever ye shall ask in prayer, believing, ye shall receive.

Matthew, by the words "in the morning" and his placement of this incident, appears to mean that the entire fig tree incident happened on Tuesday morning after the cleansing of the temple on Monday. Mark 11:12, however, placed the *cursing* of the tree on the morning of the temple cleansing, and then the *lesson* drawn from its withering on the next morning. Perhaps Matthew's apparent practice of putting events side-by-side for thematic purposes (even though they happened on different days) applied to this matter also.

Monday morning, then, if the reader follows Mark's chronology, Jesus returned to Jerusalem from Bethany. The time was early (Greek *prōi*), apparently indicating the fourth watch of the night, from 3:00 to 6:00 a.m. (Grimm's 554). The fact that He saw a fig tree "in the distance" (Mk. 11:13) means it was daylight.

Jesus needed nourishment. He was hungry. Seeing a fig tree He went to it, hoping to find figs. But because it was not the season for figs (Mk. 11:13) there were none. Jesus might have hoped for either of two types of fruit at this time of the year: (1) He might have been looking for figs left hanging from the previous season (Gundry 417); or (2) He might have been looking for new, immature figs. According to ISBE (II:302), there are two crops of figs gathered each year.

> The first is ripe about June and grows from the midsummer shoots of the previous year, while the second, ripe about August, is produced from the new spring shoots. By December all figs in the mountainous areas have shed their leaves, and new leaf buds appear only in March (cf. Mt. 24:32), when the tiny figs appear simultaneously in the leaf axils. The figs grow to about the size of a small cherry and then the majority fall off (cf. the "winter fruit" of Rev. 6:13; AV "untimely figs"). ... In April and May the fig leaves develop and the fruit reaches maturity about June.

Perhaps this answers why Jesus approached this fig tree even though it was not the time of the year for ripe figs. Normally, small figs would have been on the tree because it had leaves. A tree with leaves and no fruit, however, would (according to the same source) "be barren for the entire season."

Because the tree was barren, Jesus commanded that the tree never produce fruit again (v. 19). Matthew said the tree withered instantly (Greek *parachrēma*, KJV presently = an archaic usage meaning immediately), a reference to its leaves, and by the next day according to Mark 11:20 it was dead to the roots.

Matthew offers no explanation for why Jesus condemned this tree and apparently the disciples did not ask. Surely Jesus was not angry at the tree but He was disappointed, a mark of His true incarnation. To be sure, He was hungry; but there was probably more to it than that.

Commentators divide over the significance of this miracle. Hagner (33B:604) says this miracle can only be understood as anticipation of national Israel's soon demise and the temple's soon destruction. Walvoord (159-160) thinks this cursing of the fig tree had nothing to do with Israel and was only about faith and miracles, nothing more.

It seems probable, however, that the fig tree incident fits in with the theme of the cleansing of the temple and the challenge to Jesus' authority (Carson, *Matthew* 444-445). Both were about hypocrisy. Jesus' condemnation of the tree for its barrenness, when it looked like it should have had at least some fruit, was a sign of judgment against Jerusalem's spiritual hypocrisy and barrenness (Lk. 13:6-9). If this is the right understanding, Jerusalem and all Israel were facing severe judgment for their hypocrisy (23:38; 24:2, 15-22) and spiritual barrenness (v. 43; 23:3; Hagner 33B:605).

The disciples were surprised at the quickness of the fig tree's demise (v. 20), and Peter (Mk. 11:21) pointed it out to Jesus. Grammatically, the last part of 21:20 can be understood as a statement of surprise (Grimm's 559) or as a question, as in some versions. Either way, this was a surprise even for men who had witnessed many miracles.

Jesus' response appeared to be, but was not necessarily, an answer to a question. What is more important was His teaching that the disciples could receive the same answers to their prayers. Faith that God will answer prayer—i.e., faith without doubt—will enable Jesus' followers to do what Jesus did and receive answers to prayers concerning works that are much more difficult. Moving mountains (v. 21) is hyperbole (1 Cor. 13:2) and speaks of doing very difficult things (17:20; Zech. 4:6-9) that might seem impossible.

Faith is especially effective in prayer (v. 22; Jas. 1:6). God is honored when His children ask, believing He can and will do as they ask. See also 7:7-11, 8:26, 17:20, and accompanying comments.

"This mountain," if Jesus was speaking of where He was standing, was the Mount of Olives. The sea might have been the Dead Sea (Hendriksen 775) or one might consider the Great Sea, the Mediterranean. If, however, Jesus was speaking in the abstract (as seems more probable) and using hyperbole, the reader does not need to limit Jesus' comments to any particular mountain or sea.

C. Tuesday: Debates and Questions (21:23—25:46)

The Jewish religious leaders directed four questions at Jesus to challenge His authority and ability as a Rabbi. In addition to answering their questions, sometimes with questions of His own, Jesus also asked one challenging question of them (22:42). As in the Sermon on the Mount, Jesus showed Himself to be the final authority in all matters of Scripture.

1. Temple court debates (21:23-22:46)

The religious leaders approached Jesus early Tuesday. They had clearly given thought to Jesus' expelling of the businesses from the temple court on Monday. They were offended by His actions and determined to challenge His authority.

a. A question of authority (21:23-27)

23 And when he was come into the temple, the chief priests and the elders of the people came unto him as he was teaching, and said, By what authority doest thou these things? and who gave thee this authority?
24 And Jesus answered and said unto them, I also will ask you one thing, which if ye tell me, I in like wise will tell you by what authority I do these things.
25 The baptism of John, whence was it? from heaven, or of men? And they reasoned with themselves, saying, If we shall say, From heaven; he will say unto us, Why did ye not then believe him?
26 But if we shall say, Of men; we fear the people; for all hold John as a prophet.
27 And they answered Jesus, and said, We cannot tell. And he said unto them, Neither tell I you by what authority I do these things.

When He arrived at the temple on Tuesday morning, the day after He cleansed the temple, Jesus apparently began teaching immediately. Luke 20:1 says He was preaching the gospel as well. The gospel at this time was not the death, burial, and resurrection of Jesus as Paul would later define it (1 Cor. 15:1-8) but rather the good news that the kingdom was dawning (Hagner 33B:609). It had arrived in the Person of Jesus (12:28).

Very soon, the chief priests and elders approached Him. For chief priests and elders see comments on 16:21. These would have a direct hand in Jesus' death. Their concern on this occasion was not His teaching but rather His authority. They, members of the Sanhedrin, were the Jewish authority and they challenged Jesus' authority. What right did He have making the sellers and moneychangers leave the temple (v. 12)? According to Evans (*Matthew* 396), the high priest and his chief priests alone had authority over the temple. They were hoping Jesus would incriminate Himself (Osborne 776).

Rather than immediately answer their question, Jesus promised to answer their question if they would answer one for Him concerning John's baptism: From where did John get the authority to baptize people and call them to repentance? Did John baptize and people repent in response to God's initiative or was John acting on his own (Barclay

2:300)? The inference was if John had authority and that authority was not from men, then it must have been from heaven (circumlocution for God). Likewise, if God gave John authority to baptize, could He not also have given Jesus authority necessary to fulfill His ministry? Also, John spoke of the arrival of the Messiah and the kingdom. If John were validated, then the one he spoke of would be too.

Surely, this was not the first time these men had considered this question. An official delegation from the Pharisees in Jerusalem had visited John the Baptist with just that question (Jn. 1:19, 25). It is possible that some of them were part of this crowd too (Mt. 21:45).

The chief priests and elders identified the possible answers and realized they were trapped either way they answered (vv. 25-26). Identifying John's authority as from God legitimized his ministry and meant they should have believed him. Identifying John's authority as from men, i.e., without divine backing, set them at odds with the general populace and they were afraid of the people. Therefore, they refused to answer. They wanted to win an argument not determine the truth about John or Jesus.

As stipulated, their refusal meant that Jesus also would not answer—and it further condemned them. They should have believed John; then they would have recognized and acknowledged the source of Jesus' authority as well.

Summary (21:1-27)

Sunday before the crucifixion, Jesus entered Jerusalem on a donkey's colt. He intentionally acted out Zechariah 9:9, which foretold the entrance of Israel's king into Jerusalem. In this way, He openly proclaimed that He was Israel's Messiah. Crowds reacted with enthusiasm and proclaimed Him the heir of David's throne and prophet. The praise continued into the next day, only this time it came from children.

Monday Jesus returned to the temple. As He walked from Bethany to Jerusalem He became hungry and approached a fig tree to see if it had any figs on it. It did not. Jesus responded to the tree's barrenness by cursing the tree. By Tuesday the tree was completely dead. His judgment on this tree demonstrated His disapproval of hypocritical barrenness and pointed to the impending judgment on Jerusalem for the same things.

After cursing the fig tree, Jesus entered the court of the Gentiles in the temple compound. There He interrupted the business of selling and buying animals and exchanging money. The temple, including the court of the Gentiles, was to be a place where prayer was offered. As it was, the atmosphere of animal noises and business dealings hindered prayer. Also, dishonest gain was being realized, which in effect turned the temple into a haunt for thieves. The cursing of the fig tree and Jesus' cleansing of the temple together showed that Jerusalem was ripe for judgment.

Tuesday Jesus returned to the temple. This was a day of challenging questions. The Jewish temple leadership and the Sanhedrin sent representatives to question Jesus in order to find justification to arrest Him. He responded to their first attempt with a question of His own: "What was the origin of John's authority?" For personal and political reasons they would not answer Jesus, so

He refused to answer their question about the source of His authority.

Application: Teaching and Preaching the Passage

Jesus' entry into Jerusalem on a donkey's colt was His first public declaration of His Messianic Kingship. Up to this point He had explicitly shared this information with only His closest followers. To communicate the importance of this historical event for the life and death of Jesus, one might develop a sermon or lesson on the triumphal entry of Jesus around the question the Jerusalem crowd asked: "Who is this?" There are three answers. (1) Jesus presented Himself as Messiah-King (vv. 1-6). (2) Jesus' disciples (Lk. 19:37) honored and praised Him as the heir of David's throne (vv. 7-9). (3) The crowds recognized Him as a prophet, God's messenger to them (vv. 10-11).

There were at least three reasons the triumphal entry was important: (1) It gave Jesus opportunity to declare His kingship publically; (2) It gave His followers opportunity to praise His Highness publically; (3) It gave nonbelievers a good look at Jesus and a reason to ask, "Who is this?"

The cleansing of the temple demonstrates principles for how one should act in places dedicated to God's worship. (1) Our places of worship should be free of all hindrances to worship (vv. 12-13); (2) Our places of worship should be open to all regardless of nationality, social stigmas, age, or objections (v. 14-16); (3) Our places of worship should be a place where praise to God is always encouraged, welcomed, and fitting (v. 16).

The cursing of the fig tree (v. 19) teaches two truths about hypocrisy: (1) Hypocrisy is non-productive, i.e., spiritually barren; (2) Hypocrisy is sure to bring God's judgment. The cursing of the fig tree also teaches two truths about personal faith: (1) God will empower His people according to the sincerity of their faith (v. 21); (2) Faith is the essential ingredient in prayer (v. 22).

b. Three parables to illustrate the unbelief and disobedience of the Jewish religious leadership (21:28—22:14)

This exchange continues the one recorded in verses 23-27 between the chief priests, elders, and Jesus. The previous one ended with neither party answering the other's question. However, Jesus did not allow His questioners to leave. He told three parables to make His point.

(1) A question of obedience: The parable of the two sons (21:28-32)

28 But what think ye? A *certain* man had two sons; and he came to the first, and said, Son, go work to day in my vineyard.
29 He answered and said, I will not: but afterward he repented, and went.
30 And he came to the second, and said likewise. And he answered and said, I *go*, sir: and went not.
31 Whether of them twain did the will of *his* father? They say unto him, The first. Jesus saith unto them, Verily I say unto you, That the publicans and the harlots go

into the kingdom of God before you.
32 For John came unto you in the way of righteousness, and ye believed him not: but the publicans and the harlots believed him: and ye, when ye had seen *it*, repented not afterward, that ye might believe him.

Matthew alone records this parable about obedience. Who was obedient, the one who promised to obey but never did as instructed, or the one who at first refused to submit to commands but later repented and did as he was told? Neither wanted to obey the father's will at first. Jesus' accusers answered this question correctly, identifying as obedient the one who repented and did what he was told to do. For repent, see comments on 3:2.

Jesus then applied the leaders' answer to their situation. The ones who thought they should enter God's kingdom, these religious leaders, would not because they did not repent and prepare for the kingdom's arrival as John preached. Their failure to act on John's message showed their lack of intent to follow the Father's will (Nolland 864), even though they professed otherwise. By answering as they did, these men condemned themselves as Jesus quickly declared. They corresponded to the second, disobedient son.

Those whom these leaders thought could never enter God's kingdom would enter before them, not because they were good—after all, they were tax collectors and prostitutes—but because they had believed John's message and repented. They obeyed God's instructions through John. Matthew must have rejoiced again as he heard these words (9:9).

To "go before you" expresses precedence, not time. Jesus was saying that those who repent and believe are given preference over those who do not. The unrepentant and unbelieving leaders would not be granted any entrance into God's kingdom at all. Religious professions and practices alone are not enough (5:20; Carson, *Matthew* 450). Jesus had indirectly declared the scribes and Pharisees outside the kingdom in His Sermon on the Mount (5:20). Now He plainly told the chief priests and elders that they, who viewed themselves as the best and most righteous, were out as well.

On the other hand, some of society's worst—dishonest tax collectors and female prostitutes—were entering the kingdom (v. 31; Lk. 3:12) by following John's preaching. For publicans (tax collectors) see comments on 5:46. Jesus here put belief, repentance, and obedience together. Initial faith in John's message moved those who heard John's preaching to repent and to act on (an expression of saving faith) his claim that the kingdom of God was near. This is Jesus' plan of salvation.

Jesus had previously asked His accusers if they believed John's baptism was from heaven (v. 25). Though they would not answer, Jesus now answered for them, in five parts. (1) John came "in the way of righteousness" (v. 32). The way of righteousness is the path of right living and right standing before God (Prov. 8:20; 12:28; 2 Pet. 2:21). It is the path of those who are in the kingdom of God. According to Jesus, John was right with God. He was doing God's work. He had heaven's authority. See Luke 3:2 where John received his prophetic call ("the word of God came to John"). (2) John had come to these men too ("to you") but they had refused to believe him. (3) John's ministry was proven by its results—changed lives. Tax collectors and prostitutes believed his message that the kingdom was near, repented of their sins, and were baptized in preparation for the coming king. (4) These religious leaders witnessed John's ministry and the changed lives it wrought, but even then (Greek *oude*, Metzger 32) they still refused to repent and believe. They appeared oblivious (13:13-15) to God's spiritual work in their midst. Their rejection resulted in their blindness. (5) These men preached but did not practice what they preached (23:3; Hendriksen). They were like the second son in the parable. If they had believed John, they would have believed Jesus. Because they rejected John, they were not ready to receive the king or enter the kingdom.

The power of choice is one of the presuppositions that made this parable work. Both sons made a real choice. The father did not choose for them. By His application, Jesus showed that individual choices determine entrance into the kingdom.

Greek manuscripts show various readings of this parable, and so the English versions show some differences. Metzger (55-56) organizes the readings into three main groups. In some (as in the KJV, ESV, and NIV) the order is the repentant son followed by the disobedient son. The first son did the will of the father. In some others, with the same order, the answer is that the last son did the will of the father—which would make the answer sarcastic—or nonsense! In yet other manuscripts (as in the NASB, REB, NEB, and Wuest), the order is reversed: the disobedient son is followed by the obedient son. (Carson, *Matthew* 449, favors this order. See Aland and Aland, 307-311 for technical discussion.) As Metzger explains, the order in the Authorized Version is probably original.

The point of the parable does not change regardless of the order: Jesus' accusers were living in disobedience to the will of the Father. For this they were excluded from the kingdom.

(2) A question of justice: The parable of the householder (21:33-46)

33 Hear another parable: There was a certain householder, which planted a vineyard, and hedged it round about, and digged a winepress in it, and built a tower, and let it out to husbandmen, and went into a far country:

34 And when the time of the fruit drew near, he sent his servants to the husbandmen, that they might receive the fruits of it.

35 And the husbandmen took his servants, and beat one, and killed another, and stoned another.

36 Again, he sent other servants more than the first: and they did unto them likewise.

37 But last of all he sent unto them his son, saying, They will reverence my son.

38 But when the husbandmen saw the son, they said among themselves, This is the heir; come, let us kill him, and let us seize on his inheritance.

39 And they caught him, and cast *him* out of the vineyard, and slew *him*.

40 When the lord therefore of the vineyard cometh, what will he do unto those husbandmen?
41 They say unto him, He will miserably destroy those wicked men, and will let out *his* vineyard unto other husbandmen, which shall render him the fruits in their seasons.
42 Jesus saith unto them, Did ye never read in the scriptures, The stone which the builders rejected, the same is become the head of the corner: this is the Lord's doing, and it is marvellous in our eyes?
43 Therefore say I unto you, The kingdom of God shall be taken from you, and given to a nation bringing forth the fruits thereof.
44 And whosoever shall fall on this stone shall be broken: but on whomsoever it shall fall, it will grind him to powder.
45 And when the chief priests and Pharisees had heard his parables, they perceived that he spake of them.
46 But when they sought to lay hands on him, they feared the multitude, because they took him for a prophet.

Matthew, Mark, and Luke record this parable. Presumably, Jesus taught this on Tuesday also. (For parable, see introductory comments to chapter 13.) This second parable also illustrates the unbelief and disobedience of the Jewish religious leaders.

Using a setting common for that day—and probably Isaiah 5:1-7 as a backdrop (Blomberg 71)—Jesus spoke of a landowner who planted a new vineyard and prepared it in every way for a good harvest. The landowner placed a protective fence, perhaps a thorny hedge or stone (ISBE II:671; Greek *phragmos*), about the vineyard and built a watchtower to provide shelter for the watchman (ISBE IV:881). He also built a wine press. Such presses had two pits, one for tramping grapes and one for catching the juice (ISBE IV:1072; Is. 16:10; Jer. 48:33). The owner then turned his vineyard over to tenant vinedressers and went away.

The word translated "Into a far country" (Greek *apodēneō*) simply means to leave one's home or country, but can imply a lapse of considerable time and great distance (Louw and Nida I:189). Nolland (871) thinks this landowner moved to town rather than left the country. Either is possible and does not change the impact of the parable. A move to a far country seems more in keeping with the boldly wicked attitude of the tenants. "Let out" (v. 33; Greek *ekdidōmi*) is to lease or rent (Louw and Nida I:578). Husbandmen were farmers or vinedressers (as in Jn. 15:1).

At harvest time, literally, "when the time for fruit came," the owner sent his servants to get the portion of the harvest that was to be his in the agreement. This might have been grapes (Num. 13:23; Neh. 13:15) or raisins (1 Sam. 25:18; 30:12; 2 Sam. 6:19; 16:1) but was probably mainly juice. Rather than send the owner his part, the tenant farmers beat, killed, and stoned his servants. Matthew summarized what Mark (12:2-5) and Luke (20:10-12) described as several trips with several servants. The point was that the tenant farmers acted wickedly toward the rightful owner instead of living by their agreement as tenant farmers.

Finally, the owner declared he would send his son, for the tenants would surely reverence (respect) his son. Mark (12:6) included that it was the owner's only son. Rather than honor the son by giving him the harvest, the tenants killed the son, thinking the vineyard would then be theirs (vv. 38-39). They sinned by killing the son and then mistakenly failed to consider how the owner might react to their evil actions (Nolland 874).

Jesus asked His accusers what they thought the landowner would do to the tenant vinedressers (v. 40). They believed he would do two things: (1) he would "miserably destroy" (Greek *kakōs apollumi*) those wicked men and (2) he would lease his vineyard out to new tenants who would give the owner what was rightfully his. According to Luke 20:9 and 16, Jesus' hearers were shocked at the thought of the tenants being replaced.

Before interpreting the parable, Jesus cited Psalm 118:22-23 to make another point. God sometimes chooses to use what man has chosen to reject and in spite of man's rejection, God does a marvelous work anyway. See Stephen's message in Acts 7, especially verses 35, 52.

According to Psalm 118, world powers had rejected Israel and tried to destroy her (Ps. 118:2, 10) but God had delivered her (Ps. 118:14), chosen her, and used her as the cornerstone (see below) of His plan (Carson, *Matthew* 453; ESV Study Bible 1092; VanGemeren 730-705). In the same way, the Jewish leadership was rejecting and planning to kill the Son, but that did not thwart the Father's plan. He would make His Son the cornerstone of His new building anyway, something that could only be characterized as marvelous. In the parable, the tenant farmers left the son dead. The cornerstone analogy required that the Son be brought back to life for use by His father (Nolland 878). Anyone who opposed God's choice stone will either be broken to pieces (Greek *sunthlaō*; Louw and Nida I:226) or crushed to powder (Greek *likmaō*; Louw and Nida I:227; v. 44).

At this point, Jesus interpreted the tenant farmer parable (v. 43). The vineyard stands for Israel, or more particularly for the kingdom of God in Israel's hands (vv. 41, 43; Hagner 33B:620). As with the landowner and the tenant farmers, God will remove the kingdom from under the watchcare of these Jewish leaders and give it to another nation that will produce fruit. Jesus did not identify this other nation. This writer believes this new nation is the new people of God (1 Pet. 2:9). See below for further comments on these matters.

By citing Psalm 118:22-23 Jesus implied that though these Jewish leaders rejected Him and would ultimately kill Him (vv. 38-39), God had chosen Him and assigned Him a most important role. These leaders, on the other hand, would be severely punished and relieved of their responsibilities. It is not certain the leaders understood Jesus' veiled references to Himself in these two parables, but they certainly understood His references to them (v. 45).

The importance of Psalm 118:22-23 to the early church is seen in the number of times it appears in the N.T. Mark 12:10-11 includes the complete quotation. Luke 20:17 records the first half. Peter alluded to it (Acts 4:11) and stated plainly that Jesus is the stone that was rejected by the Jewish leaders. Later (1 Pet. 2:7) he quoted Psalm 118:22 in connection with Isaiah 28:16, showing that Jesus is the fulfillment of both prophecies. His close positioning of these two quotes suggests that Peter understood the stone to be a foundation cornerstone (Greek *kephalē gōnia*; lit. head of the corner), not capstone—though not all interpreters agree (Gundry 429; Hagner 33B:622). Some writers think that the stone in Psalm 118:22 is a capstone and the stone in Isaiah 28:16 is a foundation stone (TWOT II:825, 911; BDB 910-911). Jesus' proverbial saying in verse 44 may support this. To fall on the stone suggests tripping over it as if it is at foot level, hence a cornerstone. To have it fall on someone suggests it is falling from a height, hence, a capstone.

This much is clear: Jesus is the stone rejected by men (1 Pet. 2:4, 8; Is. 8:14) but chosen by God and placed (Is. 28:16) in Zion as the cornerstone of a new edifice, a spiritual house. (A capstone would not be used to begin construction.) All who come to Him in faith (1 Pet. 2:4, 7; Rom. 9:33) are as living stones placed on the foundation of the apostles and prophets (Eph. 2:19-22), Jesus Himself being the chief cornerstone. All who come in faith are made part of the growing temple structure ("being built up," 1 Pet. 2:5).

As already indicated, God the Father is the farmer in the parable. The vineyard is Israel and the tenant farmers are the ungodly Jewish leadership of then present and previous generations. The fruit is proper, God-honoring behavior of the people (Evans, *Matthew* 399; Wilkins 699; Eph. 5:9, 11; Col. 1:10). The servants who were treated so terribly are the O.T. messengers of God and the son who was killed is Jesus. The first point of the parable is that the tenant farmers are accountable to God—always—and He is about to justly replace them. These wretches were about to be brought to a wretched end (NIV, v. 41). Second, God will bring replacement leadership to lead His people, leaders who will remain aware of their own accountability to God, the Landowner (Nolland 876).

In the parable of the cornerstone, Jesus is the stone the builders rejected. The original builders were the Jewish leadership and the Father made Jesus the most important stone in the new building of God. The main point of this parable is that these leaders needed to side with the Son. Their refusal meant their judgment.

Jesus applied both parables directly to His accusers. Their condemnation came from their own mouths (v. 41) as well as from His. Jewish leadership was not doing its job (9:36). They "serve[d] themselves rather than God" (Keener, *Background* 103)—just as they had been doing for centuries (Jer. 23:1-4; Ezek. 34:1-24)—and so God would replace them. In the parable of the tenant farmers was justification (v. 43, "therefore") for their judgment and the appointment of new leadership who would direct fruit to God. The new fruit-bearers are the new covenant people, the church (Wilkins 699), and the new leadership are true believers, both Jew and Gentile, who will lead others to produce the fruit that God expects (Evans, *Matthew* 403).

Jesus declared that the kingdom of God (v. 43; the vineyard in v. 41) would be taken from these men. He was not speaking to these men as representatives of all Israel (*contra* Hill 301 who says Israel had now forfeited its elect status). Rather, He was speaking of the present leadership who had rejected John and were now rejecting Him also—in the pattern of Jewish leadership over the years who had rejected God's messengers and thus turned people away from God. The tenants were being replaced, not the vineyard (Keener, *Matthew* 511). The leaders' rejection of Jesus, and subsequently His rejection of them, meant they would have no part in the kingdom of heaven.

The parable infers that the vineyard was being opened and expanded to include Gentiles, not that it was being closed to Jews (see 8:11-12; Rom. 11:1-2, 29). The Jewish people can still be part of the people of God, though they would not exclusively make up the new people (v. 43) who will bear kingdom fruit. When natural descendants of Abraham trust Jesus as personal Savior, they receive personal salvation (Rom. 10:1-4) even as do all others (Rom. 10:12-13). When natural Jews reject Jesus as personal Savior, they are rejected from the kingdom.

Jesus taught that resistance against Him is fruitless (v. 44). No one overcomes the stone. Some trip over it and are broken (Is. 8:14-15); others oppose it and are pulverized (Dan. 2:34-35, 45). No one who resists the stone escapes destruction. Verse 44, then, adds to the thought begun in verse 43: the kingdom will be transferred and those who failed to return to God with works of righteousness, i.e., proper fruit in its season, will be replaced (v. 41; Hagner 33B:623).

Jesus' hearers included Pharisees (v. 45). Perhaps the elders mentioned earlier were also Pharisees (v. 23), or perhaps Jesus' listening audience grew as the day progressed. Regardless, Jesus' enemies understood enough to know that Jesus had prophesied their demise and replacement. They would have arrested Him then and there, but the crowds were friendly toward Jesus and they were afraid of the crowds. The crowds believed that He was a prophet.

(3) A judgment based on response and privilege: The parable of the wedding feast (22:1-14)

This is the third parable Jesus gave to illustrate the unbelief and disobedience of His accusers. The first focused on their rejection of John the Baptist and his message (21:28-32). The second focused on their rejection of Jesus, the Son (21:33-46). This third parable focuses on their rejection of God's invitation to His Son's celebration.

1 And Jesus answered and spake unto them again by parables, and said,
2 The kingdom of heaven is like unto a certain king, which made a marriage for his son,
3 And sent forth his servants to call them that were bidden to the wedding: and they would not come.
4 Again, he sent forth other servants, saying, Tell them which are bidden, Behold, I have prepared my dinner: my oxen and *my* fatlings *are* killed, and all things *are* ready: come unto the marriage.
5 But they made light of it, and went their ways, one to his farm, another to his merchandise:
6 And the remnant took his servants, and entreated *them* spitefully, and slew *them*.
7 But when the king heard *thereof*, he was wroth: and he sent forth his armies, and destroyed those murderers, and burned up their city.

8 Then saith he to his servants, The wedding is ready, but they which were bidden were not worthy.
9 Go ye therefore into the highways, and as many as ye shall find, bid to the marriage.
10 So those servants went out into the highways, and gathered together all as many as they found, both bad and good: and the wedding was furnished with guests.
11 And when the king came in to see the guests, he saw there a man which had not on a wedding garment:
12 And he saith unto him, Friend, how camest thou in hither not having a wedding garment? And he was speechless.
13 Then said the king to the servants, Bind him hand and foot, and take him away, and cast *him* into outer darkness, there shall be weeping and gnashing of teeth.
14 For many are called, but few *are* chosen.

Jesus continued teaching, using parables as His vehicle of choice to convey kingdom truths. (For comments on the description and use of parables, see introductory comments to chapter 13. For why Jesus spoke in parables, see 13:10-17. For the words "the kingdom of heaven is like unto" see remarks on 13:24.) Why Matthew speaks of parables in the plural (v. 1) is unclear, unless he is perhaps speaking of verses 1-10 as one parable and verses 11-14 as another (Hagner 33B:629).

There are some similarities between this parable and one in Luke 14:15-24. Though they share a common theme there are significant differences between the two. Matthew and Luke record them as if they were different parables given on different occasions. Some source critics, however, (e.g., Hill, 301, though Nolland, 884, disagrees) think they share a common source.

The setting was a royal wedding. A king prepared a wedding feast for his son. He sent servants to tell those to whom he had earlier sent invitations that the time had come. According to Keener (*Background* 104), Jewish wedding feasts could last seven days and guests were expected to stay the entire time. In the parable, those who had received invitations earlier now did not want to come and ignored this second call (v. 3). The king sent other servants (v. 4), making a third contact. This time the servants emphasized the dinner was ready—and it was a meal fit for a king! The oxen and fattened animals had been killed and prepared. The guests needed to come immediately (Greek *deupo*; see 21:38; 25:34; 28:6).

Those invited responded different ways. Some ignored the third invitation also, going on about life's business as if they had not received an invitation. Others turned on the servants, even killing some. Compare these attitudes with those of the wicked tenants (21:35-36). Such a blanket refusal was an insult to the king (Keener, *Matthew* 520). The king reacted with anger and sent his army to destroy those who had murdered his servants. He even had his army burn their city.

The referents seem straightforward. The King is the Father. The Son is Jesus and the servants are the O.T. prophets who invited the nation of Israel to join the heavenly celebration. The Jews refused the Father's invitation, choosing instead to go about life's business. Some even killed their prophets. Rejecting God's invitation and killing His servants were insults. The Father will punish those who killed His prophets and will even burn their city. Those who killed the prophets were the Jewish leadership over the years and the burned city represented the upcoming destruction of Jerusalem in A.D. 70 and the punishment of the nation. Thus, this parable was a warning.

According to the parable, after punishing those who rejected his offer, the king declared the original invitees (Israel and her leadership) unworthy. They had shown themselves to be unworthy of the gracious invitation (Hendriksen 796), so the king sent his servants to invite anyone who would come (vv. 8-9). This represented the opening of the gospel invitation to include everyone, both Gentiles and Jews (Rom. 11:11-32; Bruner 2:389). "Go therefore," though a different verb mood (Greek present imperative), is the same beginning as in 28:19 (Bruner 2:388).

The servants assembled all they could, both good and bad people, and filled the feast room with guests. The bad people (v. 10) were those who typically would not have been invited to a royal feast: the lame, sick, poor, etc. (21:14; 11:4-5). These represented tax collectors and prostitutes (21:31), "sinners" thought by these religious leaders (9:11) to be unworthy of the kingdom of God.

The bad are not the same as the wicked in 13:49 in the parable of the net. The wicked there were the unrepentant. Here the bad are those judged unworthy of a place at the king's table from a human perspective (Hendriksen 796) but permitted access because they accepted the invitation and put on the wedding garment.

All of this happened in a single day (Gundry 434) according the parable: the invitation to an early meal, the refusals, the repeated invitations, the repeated refusals, the sending of the army to destroy those who spurned the invitation, and then the invitation to all who were on the roads. The apparently "unrealistic" portions of the parable (undertaking a military expedition while the food is getting cold, for example; Keener, *Matthew* 521) serve to accentuate the point.

After the room filled with guests, the king entered. He saw one man who had not clothed himself with a wedding garment. Exactly what the wedding garment was is unclear. Wealthy families sometimes provided wedding garments for their guests at weddings (Gower 69). If that were the case here, this man was being very disrespectful (Keener, *Background* 105) toward the king by not wearing the offered garment. Gundry (439; also Keener, *Matthew* 522) thinks more probably the man did not put on freshly washed clothes before coming and suggests Zechariah 3:4-5 and Revelation 3:4-5, 18; 19:8; 22:14 as examples of persons dressing in clean clothes, some on occasions such as this. However, others point out that the meal was ready and these guests were rushed in from the streets, which meant those invited did not have time to go to their homes, clean up, change clothes, and return to the banquet (Hendriksen 797). A wedding garment provided by the king may make the most sense.

Regardless, the man's dress was unacceptable. The king asked the underdressed guest how he got into the room without a wedding garment but the man was speechless (v. 12). The question concerned the man's right to be there

(Gundry 440). Clearly, the king held the man responsible for his failure to have on an acceptable garment. The man came thinking he would share in the feast but he soon learned otherwise (7:21-23). The king condemned him to binding and painful punishment. His servants, perhaps a different group from those who delivered the invitations, were commanded to prepare him for judgment and take him there.

For outer darkness, weeping, and gnashing of teeth, see comments on 8:12. Jesus was talking about eternal destinations. How one responds to the Father's invitation to honor the Son determines one's eternal destination. Here was a man who accepted the invitation but who did not want to accept the requirements that went with the invitation. He could have had a wedding garment but he chose not to, as the king's question and judgment revealed.

What the garments represented is unstated. To suggest they speak of Christ's imputed righteousness as Paul would later explain (Rom. 4:22-25) would mean that no one there that day could possibly have understood what Jesus meant. On the other hand, if the garments represent one's actions, good and bad, wearing proper wedding garments might have been another rebuke specifically aimed at the religious leaders. They claimed to be genuinely devoted to God's ways but Jesus knew their sinful ways (Mt. 23:23) and their sinful hearts (23:25-28). Their external righteousness was not enough for the kingdom (5:20). They needed to repent and obey kingdom entrance requirements (3:8; 21:32; Keener, *Matthew* 522). Verse 15 suggests that the Pharisees understood this to be another parable against them (21:45).

Verse 14 speaks of a division. "Many" refers to all, without limits ("bid as many as ye shall find" v. 9), as opposed to a limited number. Many are called, i.e., many receive the gospel invitation. The "few" are those who actually accept the invitation and wear wedding garments. Those who accept the invitation are the "chosen." Once again, the Jews heard Jesus say that the chosen people, Israel, are not all chosen to enjoy the blessings of the kingdom of heaven but that some Gentiles are.

Verse 14 answers why there will be weeping and gnashing of teeth (Gundry 441). All who reject the kingdom offer and wedding garment are destined for eternal punishment. Verse 14 includes all those who rejected repeated invitations and were destroyed by the king's army as well as the one with no wedding garment.

This parable is not about the wedding supper of the Lamb in Heaven (Wilkins 718; Rev. 19:5-8). No one will be asked to leave that table. This parable is about the earthly, kingdom ministry of Jesus. Like the parable of the sower (13:1-9, 18-23), this parable is about responses to the gospel. All receive an invitation but only those who accept the invitation and all of its requirements enter the kingdom (Jn. 1:12-13). This, then, is a second reason for this parable. The first was to illustrate the unbelief and disobedience of Jesus' accusers.

Summary (21:28—22:14)

On Monday of the Passion Week, Jesus cleansed the temple. The next day when He entered the temple complex, the religious leaders approached Him. They questioned His authority to cleanse the temple. Because they refused to answer His question about the source of John the Baptist's ministry, He refused to answer theirs about the source of His authority. Instead, He spoke three parables against them.

In the parable of the two sons, Jesus showed that obedience is doing, not just promising. Like the second son, Jesus' accusers promised to work in the Father's vineyard but they never did. In the parable of the tenants, Jesus again showed these leaders were not doing their God-assigned tasks and consequently would be replaced. They would reject and murder Jesus and, for this, God would punish them. However, in spite of Jesus' rejection and murder by these men, still God would do a marvelous work with Him. In the parable of the wedding feast, Jesus taught that these men and their nation would be punished for their rejection of God's invitation to be part of His kingdom. Even those who thought they should be permitted in will be excluded if they do not obey the entrance requirements.

These three parables illustrate the leaders' rejection of God's invitation through His prophets and Son. Their rejection resulted in their punishment and in the kingdom invitation being extended to non-Jews. This does not mean that entrance requirements were lessened. Full obedience is still required of everyone, Jew and Gentile. While Jesus' accusers did not fully understand these parables, they understood the parables well enough to know Jesus had spoken of their demise (21:45; 22:15). This understanding added to their determination to destroy Him and in effect act out their roles in the parables.

Application: Teaching and Preaching the Passage

The parable of the two sons is more than a rebuke of those accosting Jesus. It was that, but it was also Jesus' message of salvation, His explanation of what was required to enter His kingdom. All who would enter must (1) believe the message, (2) repent of sin, and (3) obey the Father's commands. Those who refuse either of these are lost and remain outside the kingdom.

As with the cursing of the barren fig tree, the parable of the wicked tenants concerns Israel's barrenness. This parable, however, went beyond the point made by the cursing of the fig tree. Not only would God judge Israel's barrenness but God specifically would also judge Israel's leaders as the ones most culpable for Israel's failure to produce God's desired harvest. The unique parts of this parable are the setting aside of Israel's failing leadership and the transfer of the kingdom of God to another people, the new people of God. See comments above. Using details and referents of the parable and comments included in the commentary above from other N.T. passages about God cutting off some branches of Israel and grafting in Gentiles (Rom. 11:17), a sermon or lesson might be developed. (1) The making of the new people of God (v. 43; reasons for judgment of the original people of God and God's purpose for choosing a new people). (2) The makeup of the new people of God (both Jewish and Gentile believers). (3) The marvel of the new people of God (v. 42; built on a rejected stone—include vv. 37-39; built on a resurrected stone; built by the Lord).

This parable also teaches the serious responsibility of spiritual leadership: (1) the vineyard is the Lord's; (2) leadership is in place by the Lord's determination; and (3) continuation in leadership is dependent on (a) fruit-bearing and returning a harvest to the Lord of the vineyard, (b) continued receptivity to God's messengers, and (c) respect for His Son.

The third parable can be used to teach God's grace in salvation. (1) God graciously offered salvation to the Jews multiple times (vv. 1-4). (2) The Jews as a nation dishonored God by rejecting His many gracious offers (vv. 5-7). (3) Following the Jew's rejections, God graciously offered salvation to all, Jew and Gentile alike (vv. 8-10). (4) God's gracious offering of salvation to all did not mean a lowering of entrance requirements (vv. 11-14).

This parable might also be presented as truths of God's grace to everyone as illustrated by His dealings with Israel. (1) God graciously offers salvation to sinners multiple times. (2) All who reject God's gracious offers of salvation show Him great dishonor. (3) Rejection of God's gracious offers of salvation does not mean God's program of grace will fail. (4) Entrance requirements into Christ's gracious kingdom are the same for all.

c. Four Questions (22:15-46)

The Jewish religious leaders directed four questions at Jesus to challenge His authority and ability as a Rabbi. In addition to answering their questions sometimes with questions of His own, Jesus also asked one challenging question of them (22:42; "Whose son is he?"). As in the Sermon on the Mount, Jesus showed Himself to be the final authority in all matters of Scripture.

The question about taxes is the first of four questions in this exchange. All three Synoptics include this question in their records (Mk. 12:13-17; Lk. 20:20-26). The first three questions were directed to Jesus and were designed to entrap Him. The last one He directed to the Pharisees. On the previous day, probably Monday, Jesus upset the religious leaders by ridding the temple area of those whom He viewed as interfering with prayer and worship. The day following the temple cleansing, the leaders challenged His authority to do such a thing (21:23). They asked Him who gave Him this authority. Jesus agreed to answer their question if they would answer His (21:24). They refused to answer His question and so He refused to answer their question. He then proceeded to give them the parable of the two sons (21:28-32) and the parable of the wicked tenants (21:33-44).

Following the parable of the wicked tenants, the leaders began seeking ways to arrest Him (21:46). These next verses record how the leaders "took counsel" or plotted to trick Him into saying something that they could use to lay a charge against Him (22:15; see 12:14 also). "Entangle" ((Greek *pagideuō*, v. 15) denotes trapping (Louw and Nida, I:330). Their actions were premeditated (Evans, *Matthew* 421) and directed toward a single goal: to get rid of Jesus (Lk. 20:19-20). They planned well. Their questions should have been enough to catch Jesus.

(1) Question one: Should God's people pay taxes to secular governments? (22:15-22)

15 Then went the Pharisees, and took counsel how they might entangle him in *his* talk.
16 And they sent out unto him their disciples with the Herodians, saying, Master, we know that thou art true, and teachest the way of God in truth, neither carest thou for any *man*: for thou regardest not the person of men.
17 Tell us therefore, What thinkest thou? Is it lawful to give tribute unto Caesar, or not?
18 But Jesus perceived their wickedness, and said, Why tempt ye me, *ye* hypocrites?
19 Shew me the tribute money. And they brought unto him a penny.
20 And he saith unto them, Whose *is* this image and superscription?
21 They say unto him, Caesar's. Then saith he unto them, Render therefore unto Caesar the things which are Caesar's; and unto God the things that are God's.
22 When they had heard *these words*, they marvelled, and left him, and went their way.

First, the Pharisees sent some of their own disciples, their understudies, along with some Herodians (Mk. 12:13) to trick Jesus. For Pharisees, see 3:7. One can assume these disciples would have been some of the Pharisees' advanced students.

The Herodians were one of the major sects in Palestine at this time. They were Jewish men of prominence who supported Herodian rule and the Roman rule on which Herodian rule rested (ISBE II:698). It is possible (but not certain) that they had close ties with the Sadducees. See the interchange between Sadducees in Matthew 16:6 and Herod in Mark 8:15 ("Herodians," ESV margin). The Pharisees were not supporters of Herod, so for these two groups to work together was unusual. They joined forces against Jesus, hoping to catch Him either way He answered their question.

This bi-partisan group approached Jesus in public (Lk. 20:26) and addressed Him as teacher (Greek *didaskalos*, equivalent to *Rabbi*; Wilkins 720). They began by extolling Jesus' reputation for clear and truthful teaching about how to live pleasing to God (Newman and Stine 704) and for His impartiality (v. 16), surely hypocritical flattery on their part (Picirilli, *Mark* 327; Lk. 20:20). Had they believed what they were saying they would have accepted His words (Hagner 33B:635).

They asked His opinion about paying taxes to Caesar. Is it right, i.e., is it in agreement with God's will, to pay taxes to Rome (Gundry 442; Bruner 2:398)? The tax they spoke of (Greek *kēnsos*) was the one denarius head tax collected from males ages fourteen to sixty-five and women ages twelve to sixty-five (Keener, *Matthew* 525; Barclay 2:317). Some scholars "estimate that a Jewish family paid 49 – 50 percent of its annual income on various taxes," so the people would have been tax-burdened (Wilkins 720).

This tax was offensive to Jews because a foreign ruler collected it and because the ruler, Tiberius Caesar, had his image and his father's deified name on one side of the coin (in Latin): "Tiberius Caesar, son of the deified

Augustus." On the other side was his mother's image as "an earthly incarnation of the goddess Pax (peace) and the legend *Pontifex Maximus* (high priest)" (Marshall 735-736).

The Herodians agreed with these taxes while the Pharisees did not. Jesus was caught either way—or so it seemed. If He answered yes, the Pharisees and the general public present who opposed foreign rule and oppressive taxation would be offended and Jesus' popularity would suffer (Hill 303). If Jesus answered no, the Torah-abiding Jews would be happy but the Herodians would be offended and an accusation could be made against Him to the governor (Evans, *Matthew* 420).

Jesus recognized their wickedness (Greek *ponēria*), saw through their ploy, and denounced them as hypocrites. (For hypocrites, see comments on 6:2.) Their hypocritical actions masked their murderous hearts. He rebuked them for trying to put Him to the test (Greek *peirazō* as in 4:1; not entrap, as in v. 15; see comments above on "entangle"). In this matter at least, His questioners were right. He was not afraid to answer them directly and truthfully.

Calling for the coin that was used to pay this tax (v. 19; Newman and Stine 705; Carson, 459, says using this coin was customary but not mandatory), the Roman denarius, Jesus used it as an object lesson. Caesar's likeness and the writing on the coin spoke to their question (v. 20). In short, Jesus answered, "Yes." "Render" (v. 21; Greek *apodidōmi*) properly means to "give back" (Bruner 2:399), implying that the hearers were to return what the government and God first gave them. The Herodians rightly believed that the Roman government should be supported with taxes, "the things that are Caesar's" (v. 21). The Pharisees were also right to believe that worship of the divine, "the things that are God's," should be directed to God alone, not Caesar (Hendriksen 803). Both human government and God's kingdom, each in its own right and realm, require respect and support. In truth, human government is founded by God (Rom. 13:1-7; 1 Pet. 2:13-17) and Jesus supported this understanding. Payment of taxes is part of the kingdom citizen's duty toward human government. All who "use Caesar's money must pay Caesar's taxes" (Marshall 733). Where there is a conflict between the two, God has priority (Acts 4:19; 5:29; Carson, *Matthew* 460). Jesus did not in any way imply that Caesar and God are equals.

Matthew remembered that Jesus' answer surprised both parties. Even their most carefully prepared trick questions (v. 15) were no challenge for Him. There were elements of truth in both positions. He had answered their question but had said nothing to offend the Torah-abiding Jews. Neither had He said anything His accusers could fairly use to incriminate Him before the governor (Marshall 733). He was not against government. His enemies did, however, later accuse Him before Pilate of prohibiting the payment of taxes to Caesar (Lk. 23:2), but Luke was careful to show that the accusation was not true (20:25). His questioners left without achieving their intent (Hagner 33B:636).

(2) Question two: Whose wife will she be in the resurrection? (22:23-33)

23 The same day came to him the Sadducees, which say that there is no resurrection, and asked him,
24 Saying, Master, Moses said, If a man die, having no children, his brother shall marry his wife, and raise up seed unto his brother.
25 Now there were with us seven brethren: and the first, when he had married a wife, deceased, and, having no issue, left his wife unto his brother:
26 Likewise the second also, and the third, unto the seventh.
27 And last of all the woman died also.
28 Therefore in the resurrection whose wife shall she be of the seven? for they all had her.
29 Jesus answered and said unto them, Ye do err, not knowing the scriptures, nor the power of God.
30 For in the resurrection they neither marry, nor are given in marriage, but are as the angels of God in heaven.
31 But as touching the resurrection of the dead, have ye not read that which was spoken unto you by God, saying,
32 I am the God of Abraham, and the God of Isaac, and the God of Jacob? God is not the God of the dead, but of the living.
33 And when the multitude heard *this*, they were astonished at his doctrine.

For the context of this exchange, see the introductory comments on subsection "c" above entitled "Four questions." This is the second question designed to trap Jesus. Still on Tuesday of the Passion Week, the Sadducees next approached Jesus with their trick question (also Mk. 12:18-27; Lk. 20:27-40). (For Sadducees, see comments on 3:7.)

According to Josephus (*Antiquities* 18.1.4; 13.10.6), the Sadducees observed only what the law commanded them. Some commentators (e.g., Blomberg 75) understand this to mean they relied only on the Books of Moses for their doctrine; but present scholarship is still debating this (ISBE IV:279). It is certain the Sadducees believed the soul dies with the body and thus they believed in no resurrection or rewards after death (Josephus, *Antiquities* 18.1.4; *Jewish Wars* 2.8.14).

The Sadducees, then, did not believe in an afterlife or a resurrection, although O.T. books other than the Pentateuch teach both. See Job 19:26, Isaiah 26:19, and Daniel 12:2. Jesus had spoken of both throughout His ministry (Mt. 8:11; Lk. 14:14; Jn. 5:29; 11:24-25) and had the reputation of one who could raise the dead (Jn. 11:45-48; 12:17; Mt. 9:26; 11:5; Lk. 7:11-17). The Sadducees thought they had the perfect question with which to play "stump the teacher." Their hypothetical question was exaggerated to make their point.

According to the Mosaic Law (v. 24), if a man died without children, his brother was required to marry the widow. Their first male child would carry on the name of the deceased brother (v. 24; Dt. 25:5-6) and the child would be his legal heir. In this way, a family name and inheritance would continue and the widow would have a secure place in society (Evans, *Matthew* 423; Josephus, *Antiquities* 4.8.23). This is called the law of levirate marriage (Latin *levir* = brother-in-law; ISBE III:263). See Genesis 38:6-11 for an example of this. Also, see comments on Matthew 1:3, 5.

The Sadducees imagined a scenario where seven brothers died, each without a son, and each having successively married the same woman. Last, the wife died, still childless. Understanding the doctrine of a resurrection to teach a bodily (physical) resurrection and a continuation of earthly life and relationships, they identified a problem, an inconsistency (Evans, *Matthew* 422) between the two doctrines. The seven-time wife could not be the wife of all seven in the resurrection. Whose wife would she be? (One may suggest this is a good question even for those who believe in the resurrection, for many people have had more than one spouse!)

They brought their question to Jesus to ridicule the doctrine and Him and to challenge Him to decide whose wife she would be (Blomberg 75). Jesus' answer was direct and corrective. First, He told them they were wrong not to believe in the resurrection. "You err," He said (v. 29).

Second, their error was because of ignorance. They were ignorant of two things: the teaching of the Scriptures and the power of God, i.e., His ability to raise the dead in the end times (Hagner 33B:641). The resurrection was no challenge to God's power. Their faulty doctrine was clear proof that they were unfamiliar with God's Word and God's ability. Jesus may have been telling them they should believe the entire O.T., not just the first five books.

Third, the Sadducees had a wrong understanding of resurrected life (v. 30). Life after the resurrection will not be a continuation of life as lived on this earth. Luke (20:34-36) gives the fullest account of Jesus' answer: namely, that resurrected people do not marry. There are no husband-wife relationships or births in heaven. The resurrected are raised to live like angels. Angels are sexless and eternal. They do not procreate. Resurrected people will not marry because "sons of the resurrection" cannot die. Jesus' doctrine on the resurrected life was new revelation. He was not explaining doctrine already revealed in the O.T.

As for the woman who was married to seven brothers, she will be no one's wife for no one in the resurrected life will be married. "She will be no one's wife" is the answer to the Sadducees' question. This does not mean the resurrected will be nameless people without identities in heaven or that all earthly memories will be erased. Peter, James, and John recognized Moses and Elijah on the Mount of Transfiguration (17:4). One should assume Moses and Elijah knew each other as well and how each had served the Lord while on earth. Jesus' words mean only that the resurrected will not be married.

Jesus did not promise that humans would become angels. He stated they would become *like* angels in this matter of singleness and eternality. "To marry" probably refers to the groom and "to be given in marriage" to the bride given by her father (v. 30; 24:38). Blomberg (75) suggests Jesus may have referred to angels as a dig, for the Sadducees did not believe in angels either (Acts 23:8). One wonders how the Sadducees could accept Genesis as Scripture but not believe in angels since angels are mentioned multiple times in that book (19:1; 28:12; 32:1).

Fourth, even Moses' writings assume life after death. Quoting Exodus 3:6 ("I am the God of Abraham, the God of Isaac, and the God of Jacob") Jesus argued that according to this Scripture even now these men are alive. God is "not God of the dead, but of the living." They have not ceased to exist. Even in death, they are alive. Using the present tense, "I am," not the past or future tense, God declared to Moses that He is still the God of the patriarchs. God and the patriarchs still have a living relationship and Jesus' reference to the patriarchs as being still alive and in a living relationship with God further teaches that while the bodies of these men are dead, their souls live on in a conscious state. Jesus' teaching also clearly implies God is not finished with these men and will raise them to fulfill His promises to them. Only in the world of the resurrected will these promises be realized (Heb. 11:13-16, 39-40).

Not every interpreter agrees with this explanation. Blomberg (79) thinks Jesus was quoting this passage only to refute the Sadducees, not to say it teaches a resurrection. However, it seems that Jesus' statement "He is not God of the dead, but of the living" was God's point to Moses in Exodus 3:6. If this is true, Jesus' statement was a real argument based on God's original intent and the syntax of Exodus 3:6.

Jesus also supported the doctrine of the inspiration of Scripture (cf. v. 43) when He said "what was said to you by God" (v. 31; Blomberg 78). Exodus 3:6 is God speaking. It is an accurately written record of God speaking. It is also God speaking directly to readers of later generations ("to you"; Bruner 2:407).

In summary, God is not the God of the dead (Bruner 2:408, translates "corpses") but of the living. If these men were no more, God would not be speaking of them as if they were still alive. The Sadducees were dead wrong about the future of the dead.

This passage is important in that it reveals information about the state of the righteous dead. Between death and the resurrection, what theologians call the intermediate state, the souls of people live on and they are in a conscious state. For the righteous, God is still their God, which implies that they are in a living relationship. For Moses (Ex. 3:6) the fact that God was still in a living relationship with the patriarchs also meant God was still going to honor His promise to the patriarchs that their seed would possess the land of Canaan, their Promised Land.

Other N.T. passages speak of the righteous dead also as being yet alive and conscious. See Matthew 17:3, where Moses and Elijah appeared in glorified form and talked with Jesus. See also Hebrews 12:22-23, which speaks of the *spirits* of the righteous as being alive, in the presence of God, in the company of angels, and in a perfect state. Jesus taught also that the unrighteous dead are conscious, not comatose (Lk. 16:23-24). Those in hell are conscious of their pain and suffering. Those in God's presence are conscious of their comforts.

Matthew recalls that the crowd was astounded at Jesus' words. The Pharisees' disciples had marveled at Jesus' answer (v. 22) but now the crowds were astounded (v. 33; Greek *ekplēssō*; to be so amazed as to be practically overwhelmed, Louw and Nida I:312). It is probably safe to say that no one there had ever thought of this passage in this light.

Luke 20:39 says some scribes heard Jesus' answer and commended Him. Luke does not say to which religious sect these scribes belonged. They might have been Sadducees since they were the ones who brought the question to Jesus (v. 23), but more likely they were Pharisees. See comments on 13:52 for scribes. Scribes were serious students of the Word, the biblical scholars of the day. These scribes recognized in Jesus, on this occasion, an honest and accurate understanding and exegesis of Scripture.

For the Christian the resurrection is a crucial doctrine (Rom. 1:4; 1 Cor. 15:12-19). There was a lot at stake in this question (Hagner 33B:640). Jesus condemned the Sadducees' doctrine as false.

(3) Question three: Which Bible command is the most important? (22:34-40)

34 But when the Pharisees had heard that he had put the Sadducees to silence, they were gathered together.
35 Then one of them, *which was* a lawyer, asked *him a question*, tempting him, and saying,
36 Master, which *is* the great commandment in the law?
37 Jesus said unto him, Thou shalt love the Lord thy God with all thy heart, and with all thy soul, and with all thy mind.
38 This is the first and great commandment.
39 And the second *is* like unto it, Thou shalt love thy neighbour as thyself.
40 On these two commandments hang all the law and the prophets.

The Pharisees had sent their disciples to Jesus earlier, along with some Herodians (vv. 15-22), with a tax question. The Sadducees next asked about the resurrection. Jesus answered both groups in such a way there was no further discussion. Clearly, His answers were final. This time the Pharisees themselves came. Mark 12:28-34 records this exchange also and includes information Matthew does not. For further comments on context, see remarks on subsection "C."

A lawyer, not a legal practitioner but one who was an expert in interpreting O.T. law (Greek *nomikos*; Louw and Nida I:427), asked a question. He asked which of the O.T. commandments was the most important. Jesus gave a two-part answer. The most important commandment of all is to love the Lord supremely and with every facet of one's being—quoting Deuteronomy 6:5. The second most important commandment is to love one's neighbor as oneself (Lev. 19:18). The word translated love (Greek *agapaō*) is the same in both commands. In contexts such as this it denotes "love and affection based on deep appreciation and high regard" (Louw and Nida I:294). Such love is an emotive and comprehending love that shows itself in decisive attitude and action. All the O.T. (the Law and the Prophets; see 5:17) is founded on these two commandments.

Love for God must be with all the heart, all the soul, and all the mind. "Heart" (Greek *kardia*) is figurative, "the most frequently used term in the Bible for man's immaterial personality functions" (TWOT I:466). In Scripture, it can refer to emotion, thought, or will—here apparently to the will. "Soul" (Greek *psuchē*) also has many meanings throughout Scripture but seems to refer here to "personal desire or inclination" (TWOT II:589). "Mind" (Greek *dianoia*) is "the faculty of understanding, feeling [and] desiring" (Grimm's 140). There is considerable overlap in meanings between the three words.

In Deuteronomy 6:5, "might" translates the Hebrew superlative which means "exceedingly" (TWOT I:487). According to this source the Hebrew word is mainly used as an adverb in the O.T., but here and in 2 Kings 23:25 it amounts to a substantive meaning "force" or "strength." In these two verses, the Hebrew word speaks of total commitment to Yahweh (TWOT II:589). Mark 12:30 renders it "mind and strength," Luke 10:27 "strength and mind," and Matthew (22:37) simply "mind." Mark's and Luke's wording gives a more exact equivalence of the Hebrew text in Greek (Blomberg 81).

Taken together, then, the three words (heart, soul, strength) were not intended to denote a trichotomous being. Rather, they "describe the engagement of a person's whole personality" (TDOT VII:41). Deuteronomy 6:5 calls for singular devotion to God. Many prophetic messages in the O.T. rebuked Israel for her divided love. She was commanded to have a single love, i.e., a love for the Lord God alone (Ex. 20:3), but she committed spiritual adultery multiple times with other gods (Is. 1:21; Hos. 1:2; 2:2).

The second command (v. 39) is the most important command in the Mosaic Law dealing with one's relationship with others. See comments on 5:43 and 19:19. See also Luke 10:25-37 (the good Samaritan) where Jesus also quoted this command and then illustrated who one's neighbor is and what He meant by loving one's neighbor. Jesus did not command that we love ourselves (Newman and Stine 717). To love oneself is assumed. Jesus commanded His followers to love others to the same extent they already love themselves. Later N.T. writers carried this command forward (Rom. 13:9-10; Gal. 5:13-14; Phil. 2:1-4; 1 Jn. 4:21) and James 2:8 called it "the royal law according to Scripture," i.e., the law of the King (ESV Study Bible 2393).

Multiple prophetic messages concerned Israel's mistreatment of her people. Many Israelites did not love their neighbors as they should have. See Isaiah 1:17, 58:3-7, Hosea 4:2, Amos 2:6-8 and 5:11. As illustrated in Jesus' parable of the Good Samaritan (Lk. 10:30-36), love for one's neighbor still needed to be taught in His day.

By quoting Deuteronomy 6:5 Jesus not only answered the lawyer's question, He also showed that "love is the heart of both the law and the gospel" (Blomberg 81). Without love for God and others, it is impossible to obey all the commands (Carson, *Matthew* 465). See comments on the Golden Rule also (7:12).

(4) Question four: Whose Son is He? (22:41-46)

41 While the Pharisees were gathered together, Jesus asked them,
42 Saying, What think ye of Christ? whose son is he? They say unto him, *The son* of David.
43 He saith unto them, How then doth David in spirit call him Lord, saying,
44 The LORD said unto my Lord, Sit thou on my right hand, till I make thine enemies thy footstool?
45 If David then call him Lord, how is he his son?

46 And no man was able to answer him a word, neither durst any *man* from that day forth ask him any more *questions*.

It was Jesus' turn. Three groups had challenged Him with their hard questions and He had answered them well. See remarks on verse 15 for context. According to Matthew, Jesus at this time asked the Pharisees for their opinion about the Christ's lineage. From whom would the Messiah descend? Mark 12:35-37 and Luke 20:41-44 both phrase the opening question differently. In their records, Jesus questioned the adequacy of the common description of Messiah as "Son of David" (Evans, *Matthew* 428). All three writers identify the question as, "Whose Son is the Christ?"

This is the most important question of the four, for an accurate identification of Jesus would make His answers authoritative (Bruner 2:421). As the Lord of David, He can speak authoritatively on government (vv. 15-22), the afterlife (vv. 23-33), and the law of God (vv. 34-40). The Pharisees answered Jesus (v. 42): the Messiah would descend from King David. See comments on 1:1 for O.T. references and explanation.

Jesus followed with a second question: "How can David call Him Lord?" "In spirit" means "by the Spirit" (Greek instrumental case for the agent) and speaks of the inspiration of Psalm 110. Under the direct influence of God the Holy Spirit, David penned these words. Compare 2 Peter 1:21. By ascribing this Psalm to David, Jesus testified to the accuracy of the superscription, the divine origin of the entire Psalm, and the status of King David as a prophet. See verse 31 also.

These Pharisees did not understand the Person of the Holy Spirit as post-Pentecost believers would (progressive revelation). However, they understood Scripture came from God and that David's prophetic utterances originated with God. They also understood this Psalm was Messianic. The Pharisees did not challenge Jesus on either of these points.

Jesus continued. In Psalm 110:1, David in the Spirit spoke of two persons who possessed higher honors than he. One was the LORD: Jehovah or, better, Yahweh. The other was David's Lord. By calling his descendant "my Lord," David ascribed to the coming Messiah greater honor than he himself possessed as the Messiah's kingly ancestor. Jesus asked how the son, the Messiah, could have greater honor than the father, King David. Jesus' question was not about the Messiah's human descent; all agreed that the Messiah would descend from David. Jesus' question was about the Messiah's position *over* David.

The Holy Spirit revealed in this Psalm that the human descendant of King David would have divine privilege. He would be invited to share God's throne until the day when God demonstrates final power over the heathen nations (Ps. 110:1-2, 5-6). This Psalm foretells the same exaltation of the Messiah as Daniel 7:13-14 (Wilkins 727). See 26:64 and comments.

The Jews believed the Messiah would be great, but few if any understood the kind of greatness this Psalm foretold and the greatness of which Jesus spoke. (However, see in the LXX Ps. 109:3 where the LORD seems to be speaking of a divine birth; Blomberg 83.) To rephrase Jesus' question, then, one might ask, "Is calling the Messiah 'son of

David' really adequate in light of His heavenly status?" The kingdom of the Son of David would not be an earthly kingdom like David's but a kingdom whose throne is "situated at God's right hand"(Lane, *Mark* 438).

None of the Pharisees answered Jesus (v. 46). His question called for them to believe something they had never before considered—a human who was also the unique Son of God (Hagner 33B:651). Jesus inferred with His question and quote that David's Lord was and is the Son of the LORD.

Those who had questioned Jesus also realized that they were no match for Jesus. His level of Scriptural understanding was beyond all of theirs combined. No one tried to entrap Him with trick questions again.

How can the Christ be both the son of David and David's Lord? The answer is in the incarnation. The Messiah is the God-man. He is both the son of King David (Mt. 1) and the Son of God (3:17; 17:5). The king-prophet saw the heavenly seating of the Messiah following His earthly ministry and ascension. Yahweh would invite the Messiah to share with Him the throne of heaven. Later Christian writers understood this Davidic prophecy to be fulfilled in Jesus at His ascension. See Acts 2:30-36; 1 Corinthians 15:25; Ephesians 1:20-22; Colossians 3:1; Hebrews 1:3, 13; 8:1; 10:12-13; 12:2; and 1 Peter 3:22. Jesus alluded to this at His trial also (Mt. 26:12).

This passage reveals considerable information about God. First, God is a Triune God. The Spirit gave the Psalm to King David and David wrote of the LORD and the Lord. See 1:18, 20, 22-23; 3:13-17; and 28:19 for other Matthean references to the Trinity.

Second, this passage teaches a strong and clear doctrine of Christ (cf. 11:27). He is God incarnate. He is the human descendant of King David but also the second Person of the Godhead. Following His earthly ministry, He has been ruling alongside the LORD in heaven. One day He will also finally and completely subdue and rule over all His enemies.

This idea of two Lords on the one throne in heaven challenged Jewish monotheistic understanding (Bruner 2:424; Mt. 26:63-66; Jn. 19:7). It challenges the non-Trinitarian, oneness doctrine as well. Jesus' teaching, however, requires that His followers accept the reality of the Triune God.

Jesus' question, then, though a conundrum, was no trick question. It was an invitation to all to consider His total person and to place personal trust in Him. Jesus was not finished with His accusers, for He turned to the crowds and to His disciples and warned them about the Pharisees and the scribes (23:1-12).

Summary (22:15-46)

Following three parables in which Jesus warned His accusers of their own impending judgment and demise, they schemed to ensnare Him. They began with a question that they thought would put Him on the horns of a dilemma. They asked if it was right according to the Mosaic Law to pay taxes to Caesar, the idolatrous Gentile ruler. If Jesus answered yes, He would lose popularity with the people. If He answered no, He could be in trouble with the government. He answered that human government and God both deserve what is rightfully theirs. His interrogators marveled at His answer and left Him.

Second, the Sadducees brought their question. They imagined a scenario in which in keeping with the O.T. levirate law, a woman married seven brothers, successively, but remained childless. They asked, "Whose wife will she be in the resurrection?" They designed their question to show the foolishness of the doctrine of a resurrection, for the Sadducees believed body and soul die together.

Jesus faulted the Sadducees with error and ignorance: they did not know Scripture, the power of God, or the truth about resurrection life. Long after the patriarchs died, God has declared that He is still the God of Abraham, Isaac, and Jacob, thus He is the God of living souls, not souls that have ceased to exist. Rather than look bad in the eyes of the people as the Sadducees intended, Jesus favorably astonished the people with His answer.

Third, a Pharisee lawyer approached Jesus with a question rabbis regularly debated: which commandment is the most important? Jesus answered that there are two primary commandments, primary in the sense they are fundamental to all the rest: love God with your entire being and love other people as you love yourself.

Jesus then asked the Pharisees a question. One assumes the lawyer and other legal scholars were present also. Using Psalm 110:1 Jesus asked a question intended to force His enemies to see past His humanity. Jesus asked whose son the Messiah would be. All knew that He would be the son of David. Jesus' next quote and comments implied, "Yes, but is that all? Is 'son of David' an ample Messianic title? Why would David in the Spirit call his descendant 'Lord' and why would this descendant be invited to share the throne of the Almighty?"

Application: Teaching and Preaching the Passage

Jesus' statement about taxes has become an aphorism and could be the title of a topical lesson or sermon. One might develop an outline with two major sections: (1) the things that are Caesar's and (2) the things that are God's. Some of the things that are Caesar's are listed in Romans 13:1-7, 1 Timothy 2:1-7, Titus 3:1, and 1 Peter 2:13-17. Some of the things that are God's include all of creation (Ps. 24:1; 50:12), all governments and powers (Dan. 4:32; Col. 1:16-17), the church (1 Cor. 3:9), our worship (Mt. 4:10; Jn. 4:23), and our material offerings (Mal. 3:8).

One might also develop the subject of the Christian and citizenship: (1) As a citizen, the Christian has obligations to human government, to "render to Caesar's what is Caesar's." This calls for the believer to submit to human government (Rom. 13:1-5), pay taxes (Rom. 13:6-7), show honor (Rom. 13:7), pray for government leaders (1 Tim. 2:1-7), obey the laws of the land (Tit. 3:1), and do all of this for the Lord's sake (1 Pet. 3:13-17). (2) Jesus did not explain what kingdom citizens are to render to God. However, as a citizen of God's kingdom (Phil. 3:20; Mt. 5:3; 25:1, 14), the Christian has obligations to honor (Mal. 1:6-14) and worship God (Jn. 4:23; Lk. 17:18), give Him tithes and offerings (Mal. 3:6-12; 1 Cor. 9:13-14), give Him service (Rom. 12:1-2), and fulfill one's obligations to human government as service to God. (3) Where there is conflict between one's loyalty to human government and God's kingdom, loyalty to God supersedes obligations to earthly government (Acts 5:29).

Exegetically, one might consider the trap set (vv. 15-16), the trap sprung (v. 17), and the trap avoided (vv. 18-22).

The discussion about the resurrection yields the following truths that can be developed into a lesson about the resurrection event and life. (1) Ignorance of God's Word and power is the cause of false doctrine about the resurrection (v. 29). (2) Resurrection life will not be a continuation of present, mortal life (v. 30, 23-27). (3) There will be a resurrection of all the dead (vv. 31-32). (4) The resurrection will be a resuscitation of the body, not an awakening of the soul (v. 32).

The greatest commandments are two and are foundational to all other commands. A sermon might explain the first command's importance: (1) its decisive action (love), (2) its object (the Lord thy God), and (3) its extent (with one's entire being); and then the second command's (1) importance, (2) decisive action (love), (3) object, and (4) extent (as oneself).

The final question of the four was Jesus' question. One might develop a sermon or lesson by answering "Whose Son is He?" (1) He is the son of David. (2) He is the Lord of David. (3) He is Co-Regent with the Lord Almighty.

2. Further warnings to the religious leadership (23:1-39)

Much of this chapter is unique to Matthew. Mark's record is considerably shorter (Mk. 12:37b-40). According to Luke 11:37-52, some of these same denunciations were spoken a few months before Jesus' crucifixion at the private home of a Pharisee who had invited Him for a meal. Luke included only a brief portion of this material in his Passion Week narrative (20:45-47).

Writers disagree about whether this material is another discourse. Some say it is (Hendriksen 820), but most say it is not. Most writers understand chapters 24 and 25 to contain the fifth and final major discourse in the Gospel (e.g., Wilkins 744). Regardless, chapters 23-25 are linked by common subject matters, namely the kingdom of heaven, Jerusalem's judgment, and the Lord's return (23:37-38; 24:1-3), suggesting that even if Matthew did not intend that chapters 23-25 be a single unit, they have a lot in common.

a. A warning about the scribes and Pharisees (23:1-12)

1 Then spake Jesus to the multitude, and to his disciples,

2 Saying The scribes and the Pharisees sit in Moses' seat:

3 All therefore whatsoever they bid you observe, *that* observe and do; but do not ye after their works: for they say, and do not.

4 For they bind heavy burdens and grievous to be borne, and lay *them* on men's shoulders; but they *themselves* will not move them with one of their fingers.

5 But all their works they do for to be seen of men: they make broad their phylacteries, and enlarge the borders of their garments,

6 And love the uppermost rooms at feasts, and the chief seats in the synagogues,

7 And greetings in the markets, and to be called of men, Rabbi, Rabbi.
8 But be not ye called Rabbi: for one is your Master, *even* Christ; and all ye are brethren.
9 And call no *man* your father upon the earth: for one is your Father, which is in heaven.
10 Neither be ye called masters: for one is your Master, *even* Christ.
11 But he that is greatest among you shall be your servant.
12 And whosoever shall exalt himself shall be abased; and he that shall humble himself shall be exalted.

This day's confrontations began in 21:23 when the chief priests and elders challenged Jesus about His authority to cleanse the temple. He responded with three parables that illustrated the failings of the religious teachers and leaders. The leadership countered with three questions designed to provide them with opportunity to accuse Him. Jesus ended the debate with a question of His own. It so surprised His accusers that they did not ask Him any more questions (22:46).

Matthew did not specifically mention in chapter 23 that the Pharisees and scribes were still present. However, neither did he mention they left after Jesus' question in 22:41-46. One may conclude that though Jesus turned His focus to the crowds and His disciples, the Pharisees and scribes were still within hearing range.

The disciples were more than just the Twelve. There were many of His followers in Jerusalem for the Passover (Lk. 19:37). Some had come up with Him from Galilee (Mt. 27:55-56).

According to Jesus, the scribes and Pharisees "sat in Moses' seat." This means at the least that they were the authoritative teachers of the law, the legal successors of Moses (Carson, *Matthew* 472). However, some writers believe that recent archaeological finds support the idea that the synagogue teacher sat in a literal chair when teaching the law and that Jesus was speaking of this chair (Wilkins 745).

For scribes, see comments on 13:52. For Pharisees, see comments on 3:7. Luke 11:37-54 shows that the scribes and the Pharisees were two distinct groups even though there was some overlap between them (Keener, *Background* 107). John 19:38-39 demonstrates that all Pharisees were not wicked and Matthew 8:19 and 13:52 that all scribes were not opposed to Jesus.

The scribes and Pharisees filled an important role in Israel, so important that Jesus endorsed their teaching role. Nonetheless, He denounced their lifestyles (v. 3). These men were hypocrites. They knew the law and they taught it, but they did not obey their own teachings (Rom. 2:21) even though they wanted others to believe they did. In other words, Jesus did not "attack ... the ideal set up by the Pharisees [but] the fact that they [did] not reach it" themselves (TDNT IX:43). See 5:20 and comments. Jesus had not forgotten the oral tradition of the Pharisees (15:3) and He had not changed His mind about traditions that contradicted God's Word. Rather, He supported honest, accurate teaching of Scripture.

Some Greek manuscripts do not have the first "observe" (v. 3). Its presence clarifies but its inclusion or absence does not affect the meaning of the verse.

God's laws are to be obeyed, not just discussed.

Jesus mentioned three sins of these men. First, the religious leaders went beyond the law, adding to its requirements more rules and regulations (v. 4). This was a clear violation of Deuteronomy 4:2 and 12:32. In addition, these new laws were like a heavy load, grievous and hard to carry. These leaders, however, would not help the lay people bear them, not even a little bit (v. 4, "with a finger"). Nolland (924) thinks that Jesus, using the image of a backpack, was apparently scolding these men for not even helping situate the load on their backs. These teachers provided no help to people who struggled with obeying the difficult commands. Jesus had high demands also, but He helped His followers carry the load (11:29). All who handle the Word of God should help people obey, not add to the difficulty of their loads.

Second, these religious leaders lived to be seen (v. 5). Jesus denounced this in His earlier Sermon (6:1-18) and gave two illustrations here. They broadened their phylacteries and lengthened their tassels. For tassels, see comments on 9:20 (hem) and 14:36. Numbers 15:37-38 and Deuteronomy 22:12 are behind this practice.

This is the only reference to phylacteries in the N.T. These were small boxes worn on the left hand, the left arm just above the elbow, and on the center of the forehead (ISBE III:864-865; Keener, *Background* 107; Evans, *Matthew* 432). The box on the forehead was divided into four compartments. Each contained one of the following portions of Scripture: Exodus 13:1-10, 11-16; Deuteronomy 6:4-9; and 11:13-21. Phylacteries were an attempt to apply literally commands that were originally meant metaphorically ("as" frontlets; Dt. 6:8, 11:18 and Exodus 13:16; TWOT I:348). According to some scholars, these rectangular boxes could be lengthened (ISBE III:864-865). Other scholars say the leather straps that were used to tie the boxes to the forehead and arm were widened (Evans, *Matthew* 432; Hendriksen 823). Regardless, Jesus condemned the wearing of oversized, religious symbols for showiness.

Third, still denouncing their desire for visibility, Jesus rebuked the scribes and Pharisees for their desires and efforts to be honored by others (vv. 6-7). He gave four examples. They wanted to have the honored guest's seat at feasts and the most important seats in the synagogues. They liked men to recognize them in public places and relished titles that set them above others. (Regarding vv. 4, 5, 7, Newman and Stine 725, 727 point out that "men"—Greek *anthropos*—means people in general, not just males. They are technically right and this is often how the word should be understood and applied today. However, given the prevalent attitude of Rabbis of that day toward women and their strong aversion to speaking with women in public places—see ISBE IV:1094, Jesus probably intended "men.")

Jesus mentioned three titles that He did not want His disciples to covet or use: rabbi, father, and teacher. The Jewish religious leaders liked to be called "Rabbi" which meant "my master" or "my teacher." Jesus instructed the crowds and His disciples not to seek this title. All followers of Christ are equals (v. 8). Only one is "Teacher" and He is the Messiah, Jesus.

Followers of Christ should also not want to be called "father" (v. 9). Jesus was not speaking of the normal title of the male parent but of this as a title of honor. All followers of Christ are siblings. There is only one Father, "the heavenly [one]." He alone births children into His family (Jn. 1:12-13; 1 Pet. 1:3, 23). He alone is the source of spiritual life.

Finally, Jesus alone is our personal teacher (v. 10): literally, "For one, the Christ, is your instructor" (Greek *kathēgētēs*). This word probably means tutor in the sense of one who gives private instruction (Moulton and Milligan 312; Hagner 33B:661; Nolland 928). Jesus is God's communicator and interpreter (Heb. 1:1-2). Jesus did not mean the church would not have teachers, because she would and does have them (Rom. 12:7; 1 Cor. 12:28; Eph. 4:11). Jesus meant that none of His disciples would have absolute authority over others in the family of God.

Greatness in the kingdom does not come by title or position of authority. Greatness comes by service (v. 11). Being a servant (Greek *diakonos*) is Jesus' prescribed path to greatness in His kingdom (20:26). Such service is deliberate. As Wilkins (750) writes, the ideal servants of Christ "must arrange their lives with the ambition to give themselves for the benefit of others." See also 18:1-4 and 20:20-28 and comments.

Jesus closes this section with a truism (v. 12) about His kingdom to emphasize what He had just stated. It is not honorific titles that make one great in the kingdom of heaven, it is service. This is one of the many differences between Christ's kingdom and secular society (Mt. 18:4; Lk. 14:11; Jas. 4:6, 10). Greatness in Christ's kingdom belongs to those who give themselves in selfless service. The future passives in this verse (will be humbled, will be exalted) speak of the judgment (Bruner 2:441; Osborne 839) and the rewards and punishments meted out at that time.

With these words, Jesus denounced pride and aggression in the church as sin. Vying for positions of power and influence is wrong. Such positions need to be filled but not with those hungry for power and not with prideful people. Rather, the church should seek people with good reputations who are filled with the Holy Spirit and wisdom (Acts 6:3).

Jesus' words caution that honorary titles and names must be absent in the church. Christ's church is not the place to insist or encourage titles that set some people above others. "Brother" and "sister" speak of family relationship and equality. Pastor, deacon, and Sunday School teacher speak of services and roles more than positions of authority. However, see Hebrews 13:7, 17, 1 Peter 5:2, and Acts 20:28.

The church must also exercise spiritual wisdom in her use of professional titles among her ranks because social strata are also not to be carried into the church (Jas. 2:1-13). Professional titles alone do not qualify anyone for service or position in the Christian community. Professional pride, academic jealousies, pride on one's alma mater, and pursing degrees (earned or unearned!) are some ways this sin of pride can creep into the kingdom community and destroy the unity of the Spirit (Eph. 4:3).

All of this is not to say that professional people cannot or should not be used in church government and ministry. Skilled people are essential to effective organization (Acts 7:22; Dan. 1:4-5), and people should not be judged negatively because they have enhanced personal skills and abilities or professional titles. However, Spirit-filled, skilled people are most essential to the church (Acts 20:28). May their kind increase.

b. A warning to the scribes and Pharisees (23:13-36)

13 But woe unto you, scribes and Pharisees, hypocrites! for ye shut up the kingdom of heaven against men: for ye neither go in *yourselves*, neither suffer ye them that are entering to go in.

14 Woe unto you, scribes and Pharisees, hypocrites! for ye devour widows' houses, and for a pretence make long prayer: therefore ye shall receive the greater damnation.

15 Woe unto you, scribes and Pharisees, hypocrites! for ye compass sea and land to make one proselyte, and when he is made, ye make him twofold more the child of hell than yourselves.

16 Woe unto you, *ye* blind guides, which say, Whosoever shall swear by the temple, it is nothing; but whosoever shall swear by the gold of the temple, he is a debtor!

17 *Ye* fools and blind: for whether is greater, the gold, or the temple that sanctifieth the gold?

18 And, Whosoever shall swear by the altar, it is nothing; but whosoever sweareth by the gift that is upon it, he is guilty.

19 *Ye* fools and blind: for whether *is* greater, the gift, or the altar that sanctifieth the gift?

20 Whoso therefore shall swear by the altar, sweareth by it, and by all things thereon.

21 And whoso shall swear by the temple, sweareth by it, and by him that dwelleth therein.

22 And he that shall swear by heaven, sweareth by the throne of God, and by him that sitteth thereon.

23 Woe unto you, scribes and Pharisees, hypocrites! for ye pay tithe of mint and anise and cummin, and have omitted the weightier *matters* of the law, judgment, mercy, and faith: these ought ye to have done, and not to leave the other undone.

24 Ye blind guides, which strain at a gnat, and swallow a camel.

25 Woe unto you, scribes and Pharisees, hypocrites! for ye make clean the outside of the cup and of the platter, but within they are full of extortion and excess.

26 *Thou* blind Pharisee, cleanse first that *which is* within the cup and platter, that the outside of them may be clean also.

27 Woe unto you, scribes and Pharisees, hypocrites! for ye are like unto whited sepulchres, which indeed appear beautiful outward, but are within full of dead *men's* bones, and of all uncleanness.

28 Even so ye also outwardly appear righteous unto men, but within ye are full of hypocrisy and iniquity.

29 Woe unto you, scribes and Pharisees, hypocrites! because ye build the tombs of the prophets, and garnish the sepulchres of the righteous,

30 And say, If we had been in the days of our fathers, we would not have been partakers with them in the blood of the prophets.
31 Wherefore ye be witnesses unto yourselves, that ye are the children of them which killed the prophets.
32 Fill ye up then the measure of your fathers.
33 *Ye* serpents, *ye* generation of vipers, how can ye escape the damnation of hell?
34 Wherefore, behold, I send unto you prophets, and wise men, and scribes: and *some* of them ye shall kill and crucify; and *some* of them shall ye scourge in your synagogues, and persecute *them* from city to city:
35 That upon you may come all the righteous blood shed upon the earth, from the blood of righteous Abel unto the blood of Zacharias son of Barachias, whom ye slew between the temple and the altar.
36 Verily I say unto you, All these things shall come upon this generation.

In the previous verses, Jesus spoke about the Pharisees and scribes. In these next verses, He directed His comments to them (Nolland 932), comments that were public and stinging. Before a crowd of people and His disciples, Jesus named sins and showed these leaders to be religious frauds. In the previous verses, He spoke of the scribes and Pharisees as good illustrations of how not to be (v. 3). They were proud and this pride motivated them to seek high positions and honorary titles. They wanted to be above others. In this section, He showed more of their sinful hearts and corrupt lifestyles.

Jesus began eight (seven if one does not count v. 14) statements with "woe to you." "Woe" (Greek *ouai*) as a substantive means disaster or horror (Louw and Nida I:243). Used as an interjection, as Jesus' used it here, it was a warning that "intense hardship or distress" was coming their way (Lk. 6:24). Their easy lives would be disrupted with judgment. See comments on 11:21. Woes serve as "the opposite of the beatitude" (Hagner 33B:668).

Jesus called these scribes and Pharisees hypocrites. See comments on 6:2 for hypocrite. They were pretending to be one thing while in reality they were something else.

First, rather than entering the kingdom and encouraging others to join them, they were keeping people from entering (v. 13). In essence, they were blocking the path into God's kingdom by their lifestyle, teachings, and opposition to Jesus (Wilkins 751). According to Luke 11:52, they had "taken away the key of knowledge," suggesting that their wrong interpretations of Scripture kept people from understanding and accepting Jesus' kingdom message. Marshall (507) takes Luke's phrase to mean that knowledge is both the key and the result to which it leads (interpreting the Greek genitive as both appositional and objective): namely, the knowledge of God and of salvation. These scribes so distorted the Word that instead of bringing people to God, they locked people out (Newman and Stine 732). See comments on 16:19.

For kingdom of heaven, see remarks on 3:2 and the introductory remarks on chapter 13. The hypocrisy of the scribes and Pharisees was their claim to be anticipating God's kingdom, while in reality they opposed it now that it had arrived. This verse along with 12:28 teaches that the kingdom had indeed arrived (Carson, *Matthew* 477).

Jesus taught human will and responsibility here (*contra* Hendriksen 827-828). According to Jesus there were people who could have and would have entered into the kingdom had these false teachers not blocked the door. In fact, these false teachers themselves could have entered. Their faults were their refusal to enter and their active blocking of the door so others could not enter (Osborne 848). No wonder Jesus pronounced this woe and later sentenced these men to hell (v. 33)!

Second—there are two sins behind this woe—these men used their positions to take unfair advantage of widows, taking the widow's wealth for themselves (v. 14). God's care for widows and His condemnation of those who treat widows unfairly are common Bible teachings (Ex. 22:22-24; Dt. 10:18; 14:29; Jer. 7:6; Zech. 7:10; 1 Tim. 5:3, 16; Jas. 1:27). The hypocrisy was the leaders' claim to represent God while using their positions to take advantage of the defenseless.

These men prayed long, public prayers as if they were sincerely interested in spending long periods of time talking to God. See also 6:5. Jesus denounced them as hypocrites. They were not talking to God but rather were trying to impress people. They were hiding behind length of prayers as if that were proof of godliness. In 6:5, Jesus stated that if being seen by others was the motivation behind long prayers, then being recognized by men for such prayers was also their reward. Here in 23:14, however, He condemned those who prayed with such motivation and assured them that greater condemnation would come upon them. This meant that they would experience a heavier penalty or sentence because of their sin. (Here, damnation—Greek *krima* = condemnation or judgment; TDNT III:942.) With these words of warning, Jesus taught degrees of punishment. These men's sins were especially offensive to God.

Verse 14 is not in the Greek manuscripts of Matthew that the textual scholars rely on most, and so some translations do not include it or place it in brackets. However, Mark 12:40 and Luke 20:47 both record this woe, confirming that it was part of Jesus' teaching that day.

Third, Jesus rebuked these leaders for gathering people for hell (v. 15). They aggressively proselytized Gentiles to Judaism (Evans, *Matthew* 434), which Jesus did not condemn; but after indoctrinating the new converts these teachers made their new converts twice as certain (hyperbole; Hagner 33B:669) for hell as the scribes and Pharisees themselves. Their hypocrisy was they claimed to be bringing people to God, but in reality—by teaching them man-made rules—they were placing insurmountable hurdles between the proselyte and God.

Jesus plainly told these men that in their present spiritual condition they were going to hell. Even though Jesus knew everyone's spiritual condition and whether or not individual persons would be saved before they left this world, still such a statement about a particular person's eternal destination was rare on the lips of Jesus. Jesus was warning these men. They needed to repent, not reject His message.

Fourth, Jesus pointed out their misevaluations (vv. 16-17). The Pharisees taught that one's level of obligation to an oath was determined by what they swore by in their oath (ISBE I:906). If they swore by the temple, the obligation was not binding. But if they swore by the gold of the temple, the obligation was legally binding (Osborne 849). Jesus showed they wrongly considered sanctified gold more valuable than the temple that sanctified it. If gold has its greatest worth when sanctified by the temple, then the temple has greater worth than even sanctified gold. For their misevaluation, He called these scribes and Pharisees "fools and blind." They had no real spiritual understanding or perception. See comments on "blind guides" below (v. 24).

This same skewed valuation was seen when these men taught that oaths were binding when one swore by the gift on the altar but when one swore not by the altar itself (v. 18). Again Jesus pointed out their spiritual blindness (v. 19). Like gold used in temple service, so the gift upon the altar is only valuable because it is sanctified by something greater—in this case, the altar (Ex. 29:37). This meant also that the altar and the gift were inseparable. A person could not swear by one without the other (v. 20). (The words "fools and" are not in some Greek manuscripts.)

Swearing by the temple included not just the gold in the temple but also God who dwells in it (v. 21). This statement is noteworthy. Jesus thus stated that the Lord's presence was in the temple at this time, apparently in the O.T. Shekinah sense. See verse 38. The Lord had withdrawn from the temple before its destruction by Nebuchadnezzar (Ezek. 10), but He had returned at least in some sense at an undisclosed time. Perhaps the temple's reconstruction and dedication (Ezra 6:1-18) marked His return. See also Haggai 2:9. In the same way, according to Jesus, one could not swear by heaven without including God, for heaven is His throne (v. 22; Is. 66:1).

The hypocrisies here were their claims to be trustworthy and their use of honorable witnesses to support their claims. This graduated system of binding oaths was nothing more than a cover for lies, manmade loopholes to make promises non-binding. See 5:33-37 and comments.

Fifth, Jesus warned these men that distress was headed their way. Though they were meticulous about certain minor aspects of the law such as tithing, even to the point of measuring out their spices, yet they lived in violation of the more important matters of the law. These more important matters have to do with treating people fairly and mercifully as well as living faithfully. Living faithfully means having a trustworthy character (v. 23; Grimm's 514) founded upon a faith relationship with God. Obedience to the minute matters of the law was commendable, but only if the most important aspects of the law were honored by obedience. All points of the law were important, and breaking just one made the lawbreaker a sinner (Jas. 2:10). However, some laws were more important than others and so carried a weightier judgment. See 22:39 and James 2:8, 9. These men claimed to keep the whole law, even the smallest points. Jesus saw behind their masks and revealed they were in violation of very important principles of the law. Micah 6:8 may have been behind Jesus' specific mention of justice, mercy, and a faithful lifestyle, the latter being comparable to "walk humbly with your God" (Blomberg 85).

Jesus commended tithing, giving the tenth, even to the point of tithing spices. He said, however, these men should also have obeyed the weightier matters of the law, i.e., those dealing with their interaction with others. He never suggested tithing was optional, temporary (Lev. 27:30-33), or could be substituted for right behavior.

Some Christians believe tithing was strictly pre-cross. However, 1 Corinthians 9:13-14, drawing from Numbers 18 and Deuteronomy 18, state that like O.T. temple workers, N.T. ministers of the gospel are to receive support from those to whom and for whom they minister. The only support system the temple workers knew was in tithes and offerings.

One may also consider Hebrews 7:8 where the writer argues that Melchizedek is a type of Christ. Just as Melchizedek received tithes, so the one who lives today, the immortal one, receives tithes today. If Jesus is receiving tithes today, Christians are still giving them.

Jesus gave another aphorism in verse 24, using humour and hyperbole to illustrate further the problem of majoring on minors and minoring on majors. First, He called them blind guides. They were false interpreters and teachers of the law (Bruner 2:449). They were a poor choice of guides for any who wanted to enter God's kingdom. All who followed them were doomed to fall into a ditch (15:14). These legalistic leaders were extremely careful about some points of the law but not so careful about others. Jesus compared them to individuals who meticulously strained their drinks to remove every gnat while swallowing a camel, the largest land animal in Palestine (Keener, *Matthew* 552; 19:24). In other words, they took great pains (strained) to avoid the smallest possible means of becoming unclean (a dead gnat in their drink) yet practiced without any apparent awareness large and obvious ways to become unclean (by eating a camel, an unclean animal, Lev. 11:4; Gundry 464; Newman and Stine 739). Their attention to the smallest detail was commendable, but they had missed the main points of the law (Keener, *Background* 109).

Sixth, distress was coming to these men because they were all about externals, i.e., ceremonial cleansings rather than heart holiness (v. 25; Walvoord 173). Like a cup and dish washed only on the outside, they appeared clean. However, inside they were full of the corruption that comes from robbery and dissipation. The contrast is between being clean and being guilty of sins of greed.

As often in the N. T., the third "of" in verse 25 (Greek *ek*) appears to mean "from" (Newman and Stine 739), speaking of the uncleanness and filth inside the vessel that results from greed and lack of self-control. Literally translated with the ellipsis, the last portion of the verse reads, "but on the inside they are full [of uncleanness] from robbery and dissipation."

"Robbery" speaks of their greed, and "dissipation" speaks of their lack of self-control. This latter word (Greek *akrasia;* Grimm's 23; Louw and Nida I:752) can imply a lack of sexual restraint (1 Cor. 7:5), but it does not have to. These scribes and Pharisees were hiding wicked hearts behind ceremonial washings. This was hypocrisy.

The presence of wickedness in such outwardly good people demonstrates the powerlessness of the human spirit and body over its own depravity. Even rigid, religious observances do not sanctify or change the makeup of the inner person. A change of habits does not cancel or overpower depravity. These men needed what all mankind needs—regeneration. They needed to be born again (Jn. 1:13; 3:3-8; 2 Cor. 5:17). Sanctification is God's remedy for sinful hearts. See comments on 15:11, 19-20.

A fifth and final time in this exchange Jesus described these men as "blind" (v. 26), using direct address—"You blind Pharisee!"—and including them all. They really were clueless to God's way of salvation. Salvation begins within, and once salvation is applied internally, the outside will automatically change (2 Cor. 5:17). This is the reason Jesus said they should first cleanse the inside of the cup and plate, so the outside also might be clean (v. 26).

A seventh time Jesus foretold distress for these men. This time He compared them to whitewashed tombs (v. 27). These tombs were hewn caves in which the bodies of the dead were placed. Some people decorated the tombs of their loved ones by whitewashing them (Gundry 466, Nolland 940-941). Also, at Passover each year the Jews whitewashed the tombs to keep people from accidently touching them and becoming unclean for the Passover week (Carson, *Matthew* 482; Num. 19:16). Compare Luke 11:44. Which whitewashing Jesus had in mind is unclear. In both instances, the tombs looked better (appeared beautiful) but their exterior beautification did not purify the inside. Still inside were bones and every impurity. Jesus was alluding to the process of decay and the ceremonial uncleanness that accompanied death and burial.

Just as tombs cannot be beautified to the point they no longer house the remains of the dead, so also outward obedience to the law will never change the heart (v. 28). These scribes and Pharisees looked righteous to others but were in reality full of deceit and wickedness. As in verses 25 and 26, Jesus again taught that external actions are powerless to change the heart.

The eighth and final woe condemned these men for continuing the habits of their sinful and rebellious forefathers (vv. 29-36). By admission, they built and decorated the burial places of murdered prophets and other righteous men. They did this to "distance themselves" from their murderous ancestors (Evans, *Matthew* 436). Jesus pointed out that their actions testified instead that by their own admission they were "sons of" those who murdered the prophets. According to Jesus, they were not only fleshly descendants but also "character" descendants. See comments on "children of" in 5:45 and 13:38; also 1 John 3:10 and John 8:44. Jesus ironically instructed them to go ahead and act like their fathers (v. 32; Keener, *Background* 110). "Fill up the measure of your fathers" can mean complete what the fathers have begun (Hagner 33B:672; see Acts 7:51-52), to act according to the pattern or standard lived by their ancestors, or it can mean to add to their generational sins to the point that God determines it is time for judgment. (See 1 Thessalonians 2:16 for this latter idea.) There is a shared element of all three in Jesus' statement but the judgment theme in this discourse make the last option the probable emphasis of Jesus. According to Jesus, there is a point where God must act against sin (Osborne 854, 855). Their rejection and murder of Jesus as well as the persecutions and murders of His followers (vv. 34-35) would fill the cup of sin for the Jewish nation to the point where God would act against them in judgment. The hypocrisy of the leadership in this instance was their claim to be unlike their ancestors who killed God's prophets, while at the same time they were plotting to kill Jesus, God's prophetic messenger to them.

Jesus called them snakes and the offspring of serpents (v. 33). They were snakes in their own right and their parents had been serpents as well, thus showing that they had both the heritage and character of snakes. Jesus' use of the question form "intensified the guilt" of these men and "emphasized the inevitability of their judgment" (Gundry 469).

John the Baptist had used the same snake imagery (3:7) when speaking to the Pharisees and Sadducees. Snakes are crafty and can be poisonous. These religious leaders were subtly killing the nation and God held them accountable. Jesus promised they would be judged in Gehenna (see comments on 5:22), that eternal place of punishment.

Because of the failure of these leaders (v. 34), Jesus promised to send—the "I" is emphatic—more prophets, wise men and scribes (10:16-42; 28:18-20). His promise to send them was a hint of His deity. The coming prophets, wise men, and scribes would be messengers sent to replace the scribes and Pharisees of Jesus' day. The religious leaders to whom Jesus addressed His remarks would not receive the next generation of messengers at all. Rather, they would have some of them crucified and flog others in their synagogues. Jesus spoke of the early years of the church. For synagogue flogging, see comments on 10:17. For crucifixion as a form of death, see comments on 27:35. For some fulfillments of this prophecy, see 1 Thessalonians 2:15.

Prophets were part of the church's gifted servants (1 Cor. 12:28-29; Eph. 4:11). They foretold events (Acts 21:10, 11) and proclaimed God's message. Both men and women could have this gift (Acts 2:17-18; 21:9). Apparently, God stopped giving new revelation to His prophets after the N.T. canon was completed (1 Cor. 13:8). Wise men are part of the church's intellectually gifted who "are regarded as capable of understanding the philosophical aspects of knowledge and experience" (Louw and Nida I:384; 1 Cor. 1:26; 6:5; Jas. 3:13). For scribes, see comments on 13:52.

This persecution would be extensive, aggressive (from city to city), and murderous—and the final act before judgment. These persecutions would justify and result in God's judgment (v. 35). Severe judgment would fall on this generation as opposed to a later generation (v. 36) and on leaders and people alike (Nolland 948). This judgment would be on behalf of all innocent deaths from Abel (Gen. 4:8; Heb. 11:4), the first righteous or innocent man (Greek *dikaios*, faultless, guiltless; Grimm's 148) murdered for his faith, to Zechariah, son of Barachiah (Zech. 1:1).

There is no biblical record of this Zechariah's martyrdom. Many commentators suggest that Zechariah, son of Jehoiada (2 Chr. 24:20), was who Jesus meant. This Zechariah was stoned in the temple court and was the last martyr listed in the Hebrew Scriptures as they were ordered at that time (Hagner 33B:677). One respected manuscript of Matthew does not have "son of Barachiah" in Matthew's Gospel adding a little weight to this possiblity. However, according to Blomberg (85), "later rabbinic traditions believed that the prophet Zechariah, son of Berekiah, who is depicted in the O.T. book that bears his name, was also killed in the temple."

Regardless, both Jesus and His audience knew of whom He spoke. His point was that His generation would be judged for all of the persecutions and martyrdoms since the first murder (v. 36). In other words, not only would God judge the religious leadership, He would also judge that entire generation of Jews.

c. A warning to Jerusalem (23:37-39)

37 O Jerusalem, Jerusalem, *thou* that killest the prophets, and stonest them which are sent unto thee, how often would I have gathered thy children together, even as a hen gathereth her chickens under *her* wings, and ye would not!
38 Behold, your house is left unto you desolate.
39 For I say unto you, Ye shall not see me henceforth, till ye shall say, Blessed *is* he that cometh in the name of the Lord.

In the previous section, Jesus had warned the religious leaders of imminent judgment on them. He gave this warning on Tuesday of the crucifixion week. He was in the temple courtyard teaching openly. He had warned that judgment would fall on this generation (v. 36) because of its rejection and murders of God's messengers. Now Jesus declared that the whole city, not just the scribes and Pharisees, was guilty of murdering the innocent. These words to Jerusalem are also in Luke 13:34-35. Mark does not include them in his record.

In these verses, Jesus focused specifically on the city of Jerusalem and lamented that the city He loved (Bruner 2:458) had often refused His efforts to draw her close to Himself for protection and care. He was referring to the many appeals through O.T. prophets (e.g., Is. 22:12; Jer. 4:3-4; Jl. 1:1-17) and to His own appeals. In fact, the city, i.e., her inhabitants (Lk. 19:41-44), had killed the messengers Jesus had sent (Mt. 5:12). Jerusalem was a prophet killer.

Jesus claimed responsibility for the O.T. messengers of the Lord sent to prophesy. With these words, He also claimed a pre-incarnate existence as God. He would have gathered Jerusalem to Himself.

Jesus switched from the singular reference to the city (*thou*, thy, her) to the plural (ye). From the city to individuals, Jesus turned the discussion from the abstract—the city—to the concrete reality—the people (Carson, *Matthew* 486; Osborne 862). Jerusalem was a responsible rejecter and killer of prophets. Jesus drew her to Himself but she refused to come. Responsibility and free will are present. Jerusalem's rejection brought condemnation and judgment. Not only would the city be judged because she rejected and killed God's messengers, she would also be judged because she rejected and killed the Lord.

He spoke of the city's impending physical and spiritual desolation (v. 38). Her citizens thought that with the temple in her city and her copies of the law she was spiritually rich (Jn. 5:39). She was not, however. The only one who could give her life she was rejecting (Jn. 1:11).

Jerusalem's rejection of Jesus meant judgment. The temple (24:15) and the city proper ("your house") would fall (Lk. 21:20-24). Instead of life and prosperity there would be physical desolation and ruin (v. 38). The destruction of the city in A.D. 70 fulfilled this prophetic warning (Osborne 862). Jesus gave this warning during Passover week when Jerusalem was literally overflowing with people. It would have been hard to imagine that Jesus' words would be fulfilled, especially so soon.

Jesus declared also that He was about to leave and this city would not see Him again until they recognized Him as from the Lord (v. 39). For "henceforth," compare 26:29 and 26:64. Each use of this phrase (in Greek) "mark[s] a major transition point" (Nolland 952). Jesus' death would change everything. His withdrawal following His resurrection meant the city would be left spiritually desolate as well.

Quoting from Psalm 118:26, Jesus spoke the words directed toward Himself only three days prior. As He entered the city on a colt, the crowds included these words in their praise: "Blessed is he that cometh in the name of the Lord" (v. 39). See comments on 21:9.

Both in Psalm 118 and in Jesus' mouth, these words refer to a person of great importance on whom the blessings of the Lord clearly rest. The next time Jerusalem would look on Him, it would be with belief that He was who He claimed to be. This confession would be proof of the city's repentance and acceptance of her Messiah (Evans, *Matthew* 440). These were words of judgment (you will not see me again until then) and hope (until you say this). The crowds had welcomed Jesus with Psalm 118:26 on Palm Sunday. According to Jesus, this beloved city will one day welcome Him again with these same words (Bruner 2:461; Rom. 11:1, 17-32). Her desolation was not permanent.

Jesus spoke of a future coming, a return (10:23; 16:27; 24:30). However, He did not explain the context of that coming to this audience. It does seem, though, that for Matthew, these comments led into the questions of the disciples in 24:3 (the sign of your coming).

Summary (23:1-39)

In chapter twenty-two Jesus interacted with the religious leaders and their representatives as they tried to trick Him into making a verbal misstep. They were unsuccessful. In chapter twenty-three Jesus turned His attention to the crowds and to His disciples and warned them specifically about the scribes and Pharisees. He warned that though one can and should obey their teachings, their lifestyles were not to be followed. According to Jesus, these religious teachers filled an important role but they were not good role models.

He condemned them for three sins. First, they added to the law. Second, they did everything to be seen. Third, they wanted to be treated with special honor everywhere they went.

Jesus spoke about the scribes and Pharisees but His words were for His followers. They are not to practice kingdom living as the scribes and Pharisees practiced their religion. Instead, kingdom citizens are to serve humbly.

In verses 13-36 Jesus switched from talking *about* scribes and Pharisees to speaking directly *to* them. Judgment was coming to them because of their hypocritical habits. Jesus gave eight examples of their hypocrisy and warned them they would experience the just punishment of God.

Jesus warned that these men were not alone in their sin and impending judgment. The city of Jerusalem would feel the judgment of God as well, so much so she would be left desolate. Here desolation in part was the long-term absence of Jesus. However, Jesus ended this warning with a word of hope: the city's people would one day recognize Jesus for who He is and turn to Him.

Application: Teaching and Preaching the Passage

Jesus' warnings in verses 2-12 contain timeless instructions for all who train others in the Word of Christ. All Bible teachers must (1) teach the Word of God authoritatively (vv. 2-3a); (2) practice what they preach (v. 3b); (3) not make living for God difficult but rather help people live in obedience to God's Word (v. 4); (4) not make oneself the focus (vv. 5-6); (5) not consider oneself better than one's fellow kingdom citizens (v. 7-10); and (6) seek greatness in servanthood (vv. 11-12).

Jesus condemned the scribes and Pharisees in verses 13-36 for their hypocrisy in leadership. Embedded in these condemnations are positive instructions as well as warnings to preachers and teachers. (1) Those who handle the Word of God must make sure they are teaching accurately the way into the kingdom (v. 13). (2) Those in positions of spiritual leadership must not take advantage of the less fortunate and the defenseless (v. 14). (3) Those who pray publicly must pray sincerely, not with pretense (v. 14). (4) Those who make disciples must make sure they are making disciples of Truth (v. 15). (5) Those who handle the Word must model and teach absolute honesty in all circumstances (vv. 16-22). Manmade, legal loopholes do not remove or lessen one's obligation to a promise or debt. (6) Those who handle the Word must major on the majors and minor on the minors (vv. 23-24). (7) Those who handle the Word must teach sanctification as the only cure for the evil heart, not attempts at internal change by external conformity to the law (vv. 25-28). (8) Those who handle the Word must separate themselves from the sins of their fathers (vv. 29-31).

Verses 37-39 are Jesus' sorrowful and hopeful words to the city of Jerusalem. He loved her (v. 37); she rejected Him (v. 37). He will judge her (v. 38); she will turn to Him (v. 39).

3. The Olivet Discourse, 24:1—25:46

The Olivet Discourse is Jesus' fifth and final major teaching section in Matthew's Gospel. (His final discourse before the cross was the Upper Room Discourse, but only John (13-16) records that.) This section ends with 26:1, "When Jesus had finished all these sayings," though for outlining purposes I have ended the section with 25:46. See comments on 26:1. Some, like Gundry (474), believe chapter 23 is also part of this discourse but the fact that the denunciation of the religious leaders and the eschatological discourse so clearly took place in separate locations and to different audiences favors their separation in Matthew's plan as well.

In these chapters Jesus foretold events from the destruction of the temple and the city of Jerusalem to His return and judgment. Parallel passages are in Mark 13:1-37 and in various places in Luke (and will be referenced at the appropriate places below). A comparison of Matthew, Mark, and Luke demonstrates that all three organized Jesus' teachings differently. For an example, see Matthew 24:45-51 and Luke 12:42-48 along with their historical and literary contexts. This is not to say that Jesus did not speak everything in chapters 24 and 25 on this occasion as Matthew recorded, but rather that being an itinerate preacher Jesus probably taught some—surely not all—of this material on other occasions as well.

Opinions vary on the interpretations of many of Jesus' statements in these two chapters. As Blomberg (87) summarizes, "The main debate involves the question of how many details of Jesus' prediction concern first-century events, how many deal with still future events, and how many treat both." Some interpreters believe these verses describe events that are all future (the futurist view; Walvoord 182). In fact, Walvoord says that nothing in this chapter was for the first century. He thinks the Olivet Discourse is a summary of the time period described in Revelation 6-19, the second half of the great tribulation. Hagner (33B:685) provides names of interpreters on the opposite extreme who understand *everything* (up to v. 35) as having taken place in the first century (the preterist view). Still other interpreters understand this passage to contain prophecies about first century events, e.g., the destruction of Jerusalem, as well as the second coming of Christ. Turner (9) in his summary article calls this the "traditional preterist-futurist" view and notes that there are several variations among interpreters about exact details. This third understanding is that of this writer.

This much is certain: the return of Christ and its accompanying judgment are at the ultimate point of this discourse. Among all the lessons these chapters teach, Barclay (2:367) rightly highlights two. First, Jesus wins. There is no doubt that the one who rides the clouds is victor. Second, this world is going somewhere. Life on earth is not an endless, meaningless continuum.

These chapters describe events that will transpire in the end times, events that come under the study of eschatology. This doctrine is informed by teachings from lengthy passages and whole books in both testaments. The Olivet Discourse intertwines with many prophetic texts throughout the Bible, making it impossible to treat it as a standalone text; yet the space here does not permit lengthy interaction with other Scriptures. Some end time events mentioned in other Scripture texts, e.g., the resurrection of the saints (1 Th. 4:13-18), are assumed but not specifically taught in these chapters; readers will have to fit them in according to their own personal eschatology. On the other hand, one must be careful not to read into the text what is not there or add events the passage does not plainly say will happen—a secret rapture, for example (cf. vv. 23-28)—just because one's eschatological system seems to call for it. Consider Revelation 22:18-19 in this light.

a. The prophecy concerning the destruction of the temple (24:1-2)

1 And Jesus went out, and departed from the temple: and his disciples came to *him* for to shew him the buildings of the temple.
2 And Jesus said unto them, See ye not all these things? verily I say unto you, There shall not be left here one stone upon another, that shall not be thrown down.

This was Tuesday of the Passion Week. It had been a long day. Jesus had been in the temple area since morning. The religious leaders were upset because on Monday Jesus had physically forced those selling sacrifices to leave the temple court and had overturned the tables of the moneychangers. On this day, the leadership challenged Jesus' authority to clear the temple area, and He responded with parables that spoke of God's judgment on them and the nation. The leaders made several attempts to entangle Him in His teachings but were unsuccessful. Jesus finished the day teaching the crowds and His disciples as He did every other day that week (Lk. 21:37-38).

As He left the temple for the last time (Bruner 2:470) Jesus' disciples joined Him, and one of them (Mk. 13:1) remarked about its amazing beauty and architecture. Herod the Great began its construction in 20-19 B.C. and it evidently was still under construction in Jesus' day (Jn. 2:20; ISBE IV:770). Others joined in the discussion (Mt. 24:1). Jesus never commented on the temple's beauty. Perhaps the disciples did not fully comprehend the implications of Jesus' declaration in 23:38. The city and temple would be desolate as God brought judgment against the "religious establishment" (Keener, *Matthew* 560). The temple would be destroyed to such an extent that not one stone would be left on another. Compare Luke 19:44. With certainty (Greek *amēn*, verily, truly) Jesus promised this destruction. History proves the accuracy of His words. Titus, the Roman General, had the entire city, including the temple and most of the city walls, razed to the ground (Josephus, *Wars of the Jews* 7.1.1; Osborne 868).

Destruction of the temple had huge implications for first century Jews. It is no wonder the disciples wanted to ask Jesus about this. It would be difficult to imagine the Jewish people without their temple—again. It is also no surprise that when early disciples like Stephen preached this part of Jesus' prophecy (Acts 6:14) they met with serious opposition.

b. General signs that indicate God's plan for this age is unfolding (24:3-8)

3 And as he sat upon the mount of Olives, the disciples came unto him privately, saying, Tell us, when shall these things be? and what *shall be* the sign of thy coming, and of the end of the world?
4 And Jesus answered and said unto them, Take heed that no man deceive you.
5 For many shall come in my name, saying, I am Christ; and shall deceive many.
6 And ye shall hear of wars and rumours of wars: see that ye be not troubled: for all *these things*

must come to pass, but the end is not yet.
7 For nation shall rise against nation, and kingdom against kingdom: and there shall be famines, and pestilences, and earthquakes, in divers places.
8 All these *are* the beginning of sorrows.

As Jesus sat alone on the Mount of Olives facing the city, perhaps resting from the intense week and the long day of teaching and debate, His disciples came to Him. He spent the last few nights of His life before the cross on this mount (Lk. 21:37). Whether He spent this particular night in Bethany (Mt. 21:17) or on the Mount of Olives is unclear. His disciples knew where He would be (Jn. 18:2), for He "often met there with His disciples." Mark 13:3 says Peter, James, John, and Andrew came to Him privately and asked Him these questions.

They were concerned about three subjects, apparently thinking that all three were closely related in time. Jesus addressed this misunderstanding by showing there would be a delay in His coming. The temple would be destroyed in "this generation" (v. 34), but there would be a significant delay before His return and the end (Carson, *Matthew* 495, 497). Thus He addressed all three aspects of the questions.

The first two questions apparently arose from His earlier comments. The question "When shall these things be?" was in response to Jesus' prophecy about the destruction of the temple complex (v. 2) and perhaps the lament over Jerusalem's coming desolation (23:38). O.T. prophets had asked similar questions (Dan. 12:6; 1 Pet. 1:11). The question "What shall be the sign of your coming?" was perhaps partly in response to His reference to His return in 23:39. The disciples had some knowledge of His coming in glory (16:27), but their knowledge was limited.

"Coming" (Greek *parousia*) means coming, arrival, advent (Grimm's 490; so vv. 3, 27, 37, 39). Fifteen of the twenty-four times this word appears in the N.T. it refers to Jesus' return. One time (2 Pet. 1:16) it refers to His first coming, His incarnation, once to the arrival of the Anti-Christ (2 Th. 2:9), and once to the day of the Lord (2 Pet. 3:12). The remaining six times it refers to "common human arrivals" (ISBE III:664).

Only Matthew included the question about signs of the end of the world or age (Greek *aiōn*). This part of the question does not have an immediate antecedent but may be in response to 22:28 and 22:30-32. "End" (Greek *sunteleia*) is the consummation of the age. Matthew always uses it with this meaning (13:39-40, 49; 28:20).

Jesus addressed the last item first, signs announcing the end. He cautioned the disciples there would be many deceivers who would come claiming to be Him (v. 5). These false christs would lead many away from the truth. Jesus warned His followers not to be fooled, to "take heed" or "beware" lest someone mislead them.

Second, He told them human suffering would be constant. The world will be in continual strife (vv. 6-7) and famines and earthquakes will be common (v. 7). Some Greek manuscripts of Matthew include pestilence (Greek *loimoi*, a widespread, contagious disease; Louw and Nida I:271) in the list of troubles, while other (those that textual scholars rely on most) do not. Mark does not include pestilence in his record, but Luke (21:11) does, adding support to the notion that Jesus included pestilence in His teaching. Further, there will be many international wars and more wars rumored to come. Such human suffering gives rise to thoughts that the end must be near (Hagner 33B:691). However, Jesus' disciples are not to be troubled by these reports, for wars are part of the master plan (v. 6) and do not indicate the nearness of the end. These are just the beginning of the pains this world will experience (v. 8). Jesus called them beginning birth-pains (Greek *ōdin*), i.e., "preliminary troubles to the development of a catastrophe" (AGL 282).

Third, Jesus implied by this reference to birth-pains that until impostors, strife, and natural calamities get much worse the end is not near. In other words, if wars, famines, and earthquakes are only the *beginning*, the tribulation that follows will be much more intense and difficult. Wilkins (774) says that the birth-pains metaphor suggests irreversibility once the process has begun and the "repetitive nature of the waves of pain until the end." Bruner (2:482) thinks the metaphor also suggests joy is coming. "It is going to get worse before it gets better ... but it will get better." However, Jesus' tone seems to be somber, not one that attempts to arouse joyful anticipation.

Jesus, then, did not give any specific signs of the end in these verses. Rather, He gave signs of normal life on a sin-cursed planet. He inferred that this world's troubles would increase greatly as the end approached but He said nothing any more specific than that.

c. Signs that indicate when the end is nearing (24:9-14)

9 Then shall they deliver you up to be afflicted, and shall kill you: and ye shall be hated of all nations for my name's sake.
10 And then shall many be offended, and shall betray one another, and shall hate one another.
11 And many false prophets shall rise, and shall deceive many.
12 And because iniquity shall abound, the love of many shall wax cold.
13 But he that shall endure unto the end, the same shall be saved.
14 And this gospel of the kingdom shall be preached in all the world for a witness unto all nations; and then shall the end come.

In the previous verses, Jesus told His disciples that false christs, wars, and natural troubles would be commonplace (vv. 5-7). The world will be experiencing suffering throughout this age (Wilkins 774). In verses 9-14, however, Jesus spoke of areas of life where troubles would increase as the end nears. He warned that worldwide persecution will arise against Jesus' followers, bringing suffering beyond the devastation of war (Gundry 479) and the otherwise usual suffering of this age. The disciples in this discussion represent the church throughout the church age, not just the first century. Persecution began almost immediately for the church (Acts 4:1-3; 5:17-18, 40; etc.) but has grown in intensity throughout the centuries. Jesus promised these persecutions would end in death for some (10:28; 21:35; 22:6; 23:34, 37), being motivated by an ongoing (Greek periphrastic participle emphasizing progressive action) and universal hatred of Jesus (v. 9; 5:11; 10:22; Jn. 15:18-21; 2 Tim. 3:12). Such widespread hatred shows Jesus was speaking of a significant passage of time. This intense persecution would cause some disciples to "be offended": that is, to desert (Greek *skandalizo*; Grimm's 576; Mt. 13:21; 26:31, 33) Christ and betray their former fellow-believers to the persecuting authorities. Mutual hatred will replace shared Christian love (v. 10), which love is one mark of a true Christ-follower (Jn. 13:34, 35).

In addition to false christs (v. 5), there will be false prophets (v. 11; Acts 20:29-30; 2 Pet. 2:1). See 7:15-23. These individuals will pretend to be Christians, but inwardly they will be sheep killers. Their actions will betray their unsaved and depraved hearts as they lead believers into sin and away from Christ (2 Tim. 3:6-7). This is the third stimulus that Jesus warned would influence believers to turn from Christ. Persecution (v. 10) was the second; false christs the first (v. 5).

"Iniquity" (v. 12) is lawlessness (Greek *anomia*) in the culture, a fourth stimulus that will increase and influence many believers to move away from Christ. Jesus was speaking of more than individual sin or even sin inside the Christian community. Societal sin will increase dramatically. The increase will be such that many believers (vv. 10-12) will lose their love (Rev. 2:4). Their love will grow cold as they give in to the pressures of society to amalgamate. Matthew did not identify the object of this love. It could be either the Lord (2 Tim. 3:4) or one's fellow believers. The context argues for the latter (v. 10), though both are probably intended (22:37-40) since they are inseparable (1 Jn. 3:14-15; 4:16). Regardless, the result will be a large-scale desertion from Christ, something later Scripture writers foretold as well (2 Th. 2:3; 1 Tim. 4:1; Picirilli, *2 Thessalonians* 121). In other words, the Christian community will lose many as they place hope in false christs, are won over by the doctrines of false teachers, refuse to remain faithful under persecution, and/or are drawn by society away from Christ and into an antinomian lifestyle.

However, there will be those who will not desert Christ, believe the false prophets, fail in persecution, or give in to the sinful culture. Jesus was emphatic about this (v. 13): literally, "The one who endures to the end—this one will be saved." Jesus went from the many to the one (Bruner 2:489). Salvation is an individual matter and belongs to those who finish well. Believers who endure, i.e., remain true and faithful followers of Jesus to the end, will experience final salvation. See comments on 10:22. The end can be either death, the end of persecution, or the Lord's return (Hagner 33A:278). Jesus was speaking of His return and its accompanying judgment (25:46), so this is the primary referent here. Believers who commit apostasy will be lost.

Jesus promised that all through this age this gospel of the kingdom will be being preached (v. 14; Greek future, viewed as progressive) throughout the whole world. To preach (see on 3:1) in the post resurrection, kingdom sense is to publicly announce the death and resurrection of Jesus and its implications for lost mankind's salvation. By definition, to "preach" (Greek *kērussō*) includes "urging acceptance and compliance" (Louw and Nida I:417). These messengers will be preaching for decisions. Such worldwide preaching requires a strong and growing church during this time of difficulty (Bruner 2:492). Even though many believers will be killed and many others commit apostasy, still a strong, evangelistic church will survive and grow even in troublesome times. In fact, worldwide proclamation of the gospel is a must for the church (Mk. 13:10; 2 Pet. 3:8-9, 15). All nations are to hear throughout this age the same message of Jesus' kingdom (Mt. 9:35). Only one gospel, His, will prepare this world for the end, and He intends that the whole world hear it (Mt. 28:19; Lk. 24:47; Rev. 14:6). After an extended time of preaching the gospel throughout the entire world, God will bring this world to an end.

Early missionaries made it their goal to evangelize the whole world (Rom. 15:19-21, which also demonstrates their goal had not yet been realized; Turner 8), but church history reveals several centuries when missionary zeal was not part of the church. However, the nineteenth and twentieth centuries witnessed a resurgence of Protestant missionary fervor (Cairns 437-440). With the aid of print, radio, television, the internet, and satellites, gospel witnesses are reaching more of this world in near and remote places than ever before.

The faithful will know, then, when societal sin greatly increases, and large numbers of believers apostatize, that the end is getting nearer. However, even then, the faithful will continue evangelizing the whole world. They will remain faithful until the Lord returns for them.

d. Signs that indicate the nearness of the destruction of Jerusalem and of the temple (24:15-22)

15 When ye therefore shall see the abomination of desolation, spoken of by Daniel the prophet, stand in the holy place, (whoso readeth, let him understand:)
16 Then let them which be in Judaea flee into the mountains:
17 Let him which is on the housetop not come down to take any thing out of his house:
18 Neither let him which is in the field return back to take his clothes.
19 And woe unto them that are with child, and to them that give suck in those days!
20 But pray ye that your flight be not in the winter, neither on the sabbath day:
21 For then shall be great tribulation, such as was not since the beginning of the world to this time, no, nor ever shall be.
22 And except those days should be shortened, there should no flesh be saved: but for the elect's sake those days shall be shortened.

Jesus had been addressing the question of His four disciples, "What will be the sign ... of the end of the age?" "When ... therefore" (v. 15) marks a "major temporal shift" (Wilkins 777) in Jesus' discussion. At this point He turned His discussion from worldwide evangelism to the judgment of contemporary Jerusalem, as well as to the implications ("therefore"; Nolland 968-969) these events have for similar events of the end times. He had foretold Jerusalem's desolation and destruction earlier (Mt. 22:7; 23:38; 24:2). One of the questions the four asked was, "When shall these things be?" Verse 15 begins Jesus' explanation of His statement that one temple stone will not be left on another, and his explanation of signs marking its nearness in time. "When you see" speaks of physical sight of recognizable events, events Jesus put forward as signs.

Walvoord (185) denies these verses are about the destruction of Jerusalem. He says (182) that Jesus' words describe the great tribulation that immediately precedes the second coming, and that Jesus, in Matthew and Mark, did not address the destruction of Jerusalem. He thinks only Luke does that. However, as Carson observes (492), it is hard to imagine that any first century Christian would read this prophecy without thinking of the destruction of the temple and Jerusalem.

According to Jesus, Jerusalem's desolation will happen as Daniel prophesied. One sign of Jerusalem's approaching desolation will be the presence of the abomination foretold by Daniel. Daniel used the terms "abomination" and "desolation" together three times (Dan. 9:27, 11:31, and 12:11), and "desolation" by itself one time (Dan. 8:13). See also "desolations" in Daniel 9:26. Like Matthew, Mark did not include any explanation of the "abomination of desolation." However, Mark 13:14—and Matthew following his lead—addressed the readers at this point, encouraging them to give special attention to these words and apply them to their particular situation (Turner 12). This is somewhat akin to Jesus' words, "He who has ears, let him hear" (13:9). Surely, Daniel and Jesus' prophecies must be considered together if either is to be understood fully (Evans, *Matthew* 450). Perhaps the political climate was such that Mark and Matthew believed, when they wrote (if prior to Jerusalem's destruction), that Rome would soon move against Jerusalem. In that case, they might have been adding their own (inspired) warning for their current readers' sakes.

Jesus' use of Daniel in this manner shows that He accepted the book of Daniel as Scripture. He spoke of it as authoritative and accurate. He acknowledged the historicity of Daniel as a person and as the author of the book carrying his name. Daniel was a true prophet whose prophecies would be fulfilled.

Carson (*Matthew* 500) understands the words "let the reader understand" to have originated with Jesus rather than Mark or Matthew. Understood in this manner, Jesus was speaking to the reader of Daniel and emphasizing the importance of Daniel's words to Jesus' discussion. However, Mark, who probably wrote before Matthew and was one of Matthew's sources, did not specifically mention Daniel and, as Fee and Stuart observe (137), it seems unlikely that Jesus would address a potential reader of Daniel without mentioning Daniel by name (Mk. 13:14). If Fee and Stuart are right, Matthew may have added the words "spoken of by Daniel the prophet standing in the holy place" as an explanation of the abomination of desolation. However, the specific mention of Daniel was probably by Jesus as explained above.

The abomination is the "despicable thing" (Greek *bdelugma*), a word used well over one hundred times in the LXX. Opinions vary concerning exactly what Daniel's prophecy and Jesus meant. The NIV translates "the abomination that causes desolation" and makes the abomination responsible for the desolation that follows. Zerwick (78) understands the desolation of the temple to be the abomination, the despicable thing (taking desolation as a Greek appositional genitive). Keener (*Background* 112-113), understands the abomination and desolation as two events. He believes the abomination was the slaughter of the priests in the temple in A.D. 66 by Jewish Zealots (Josephus, *Wars of the Jews* 4.5.2) "for which God later brought about the desolation of the temple" in A.D. 70. Keener explains that human bloodshed in the temple desecrated it and this event would have been a sign to Christians that they needed to leave Jerusalem as Jesus forewarned (v. 16). Further, Christian prophets warned Christians to leave Jerusalem at this time. However, Nolland (970-971) argues that "one looks in vain in Josephus's account of the Jerusalem war for a distinct event that would stand out clearly as deserving the label 'the desolating sacrilege.'"

Of the several possibilities, Nolland believes the most probable was late in the war after the city and temple were already in flames when the Romans carried their standards into the temple court and offered sacrifices to them (Josephus, *Wars of the Jews*, 6.6.1). The problem is that for this prophecy to be a warning that provided time to escape, it had to precede the destruction (Carson 500). In other words, the abomination could not have been something the Romans set up in the temple. By the time they stood in the temple, it was too late for anyone to escape.

Daniel's prophecy seems first to be about the Syrian ruler Antiochus IV Epiphanes, who desecrated the temple in 167 B.C. (Hays, Duvall, and Pate 9) by offering swine on the temple altar and evidently placing something (an altar or image?) representative of the Olympian god Zeus in the temple (1 Macc. 1:47; 2 Macc. 6:2, 18, 21; 7:1). The writer of 1 Maccabees states in 1:54: "Now on the fifteenth day of Chislev, in the one hundred and forty-fifth year, they erected a desolating sacrilege upon the altar of burnt offering" (RSV). Two years later, Antiochus sent a chief collector of tribute who killed many people, destroyed city walls and burned houses, and accomplished the prophesied desolation (1 Macc. 1:29-40). He then rebuilt and fortified the city and made it his citadel. Lawless Gentiles governed the city. See especially Daniel 11:29-35 for Daniel's prophecy concerning these events.

In this Olivet Discourse, Jesus referred to the abomination of desolation as a future event. This means that either Daniel's prophecy was not about Antiochus IV Epiphanes or that Daniel's prophecy was intended to have multiple fulfillments. See further below.

Luke also wrote of the desolation to which Jesus referred (Lk. 21:20): "And when ye shall see Jerusalem compassed with armies, then know that the desolation thereof is near." Either Luke omitted any reference to the abomination or he told his readers what Jesus meant by "the abomination." If Luke interpreted Jesus' saying, which seems likely, the Roman army was the abomination that brought desolation on the city and the temple. Gentiles overthrew Jerusalem. See Luke 19:43-44 also. Matthew wrote, "When you see the abomination." Luke wrote, "When you see ... armies." The Roman army would completely destroy Jerusalem and the temple. Jesus warned His followers to leave as quickly as possible when they saw the Roman armies if they wanted to avoid severe suffering and death.

The fact that Jesus applied Daniel's prophecy to the coming destruction of Jerusalem in A.D. 70 suggests that Daniel 9:26 must also be factored into this prophetic equation (Nolland 969) and that the Daniel 9:27 prophecy would have multiple fulfillments, at least two: the destruction by Antiochus IV Epiphanes and the A.D. 70 destruction. Bruner (2:497) disagrees but he appears to be in the minority. He sees only the A.D. 70 destruction in Daniel and Jesus' words. However, some scholars think there is also a third fulfillment, yet to come. They believe Israel will rebuild the temple and reinstitute the sacrificial system during the first part of the seven-year tribulation and then the temple will be desecrated by the Antichrist (Walvoord 186-187). See Revelation 11:1-2; 2 Thessalonians 2:4. Walvoord believes that Daniel's prophecy has no application to the destruction of the temple in A.D. 70, only to the Syrian ruler Antiochus' desecration and to the future desecration of the temple during the Great Tribulation by another individual who will repeat Antiochus' actions. Walvoord (182) also believes Jesus did not say anything about the destruction of Jerusalem in Matthew.

However, Jerusalem's destruction is the point of this prophecy. That event anticipated the final and great tribulation (see below), but this anticipation was not Jesus' primary concern at this point. Jesus was warning (v. 15) Judean inhabitants of the awfulness, suddenness, and completeness of Jerusalem's looming desolation. His reference to Judea points specifically to the A.D. 70 destruction. When the time comes, those in Jerusalem and those in all Judea should run to the mountains (v. 16). According to Eusebius (*Eccl. Hist.* III.V.3), many Christians believed Jesus' words applied to the Roman army's invasion and fled north to Pella after the first Jewish revolt in A.D. 67 (ISBE III: 738). Though some writers challenge Eusebius' accuracy on this point, Hagner (33B:701) says this has been successfully defended.

Summarizing Beitzel (186-187) and Evans and Porter (274-276), this is what happened. The Roman general Vespavian did not attack Jerusalem at first. He entered Palestine from Syria in A.D. 67 and took control of Galilee and several western cities including Joppa and Azotus. This gave him control of the supply routes from Egypt into southern Palestine and the major supply routes north through Galilee. In 68 Vespavian took control of Perea and then Idumea, followed by most of Judea. He stopped in June 68 after Nero committed suicide because a military command terminated on the death of the emperor who gave it. He waited a year but then continued his campaign in June of 69. He strengthened his control of Judea but stopped again when the Roman forces in the east proclaimed him Emperor. In the spring of A.D. 70, he went to Rome to assume the throne and made his son Titus general. Titus moved his army against Jerusalem from three sides. He set siege against Jerusalem during Passover week, April A.D. 70. In July, his army broke through the northern wall. August 10th they burned the temple. In September, they burned and leveled the city.

Jesus described an aggressive army and the need for an emergency escape. Anyone on the roof of his house who saw approaching armies should leave immediately and not try to gather any provisions (Wilkins 779) from inside (v. 17). Gundry (483) thinks this is a leisurely man in contrast to laborers, of whom Jesus next speaks. Those working in a field should not even try to get their outer garments they had removed for work and laid down. Jesus showed special concern for expectant mothers and mothers of nursing children because they would have an especially difficult time fleeing (v. 19).

He instructed His disciples to pray that they would not have to make their escape in the winter or on a Sabbath (v. 20). Winter is mainly a rainy season in Palestine, with some frost and snow in higher elevations (ISBE IV:375). According to Beitzel (52), there is snow in Jerusalem two years out of three. January is Israel's coldest month with an average temperature of 47 degrees Fahrenheit (8 Celsius).

The difficulties of escaping and hiding in mountains in the cold, rainy weather would add more suffering to what would already be an extreme hardship. Rigid Sabbath practices might increase the difficulty in preparing for an extended stay in the mountains, even for Christians who knew they were no longer under Sabbath restrictions. They would be unable to buy supplies (Gundry 483) and otherwise gather necessary items, thus increasing the hardship.

Jesus commanded His disciples to be making (Greek present tense) this a matter of prayer. By this, Jesus showed that God honors prayer and changes events in response to the prayers of His people. In fact, Jesus stated that God had already willed the reduction of the number of days of this tribulation in order to spare His people's total destruction (v. 22). The elect are the faithful, not blood descendants of Abraham. By this, Jesus also showed that some of His own followers would be present for this tribulation and would experience suffering along with others. He warned them ahead of time so their sufferings would be lessened according to their prayers, preparations, and attentiveness to His warnings. Jerusalem would be judged and any righteous people in her would suffer as well.

Luke 17:22-37 placed some of these same warnings in the context of Jesus' return (Nolland 973). This suggests Jesus intended that readers of all generations benefit from His warnings and directives concerning the A.D. 70 destruction of Jerusalem. It also suggests that Jesus merged the events of Jerusalem's destruction with the end times' tribulation and the return of Christ. In other words, the same urgency and preparation required of any who would escape Jerusalem's demise is required of all who would be delivered from earth's judgment when Jesus returns.

"For then shall be great tribulation" (v. 21) is "*in* those days shall be affliction" in Mark 13:19. Literally, Mark reads, "those days shall be affliction" without any indication of time. By adding "then," Matthew more clearly connects the tribulation in verse 21 with the arrival of the abomination of desolation in verse 15.

Jesus forewarned there would be "tribulation"—trouble or suffering—beyond what this world had ever witnessed or would ever witness again (v. 21). Compare with Daniel 12:1. One wonders if Jesus was using hyperbole but this warning appears as literal as the previous warnings. Jesus foretold suffering so intense that it would never be repeated. Carson (501) observes that to describe the Great Tribulation in this manner would be inane if it is to be immediately followed by the Millennium or the new heaven and the new earth. See comments below on verse 29. Jesus' point seems to be to give reason for escaping the invading army as quickly as possible. Josephus (*Wars of the Jews*, 5.10.2, 3) details some of the horrors of this war. So intense would the suffering be "in those days" (compare v. 19) that unless the Lord (Mk. 13:20, meaning God the Father) lessened the number of days of this judgment no one would survive (v. 22). Jesus promised God would shorten this judgment so His people, the elect, who would also be present in this judgment, would not be completely destroyed in it. This promise reminds God's people that He is in control of every aspect of this judgment (Wilkins 780).

This destruction of Jerusalem was judgment against the Israelite nation. See 23:32 and comments. Luke calls Jerusalem's destruction "days (no "the" in Greek) of vengeance, that all things which are written may be fulfilled" (Lk. 21:22).

In summary, though Jesus began speaking primarily of Jerusalem's A.D. 70 destruction and desolation, He merged in thought Jerusalem's localized judgment with a later time of judgment that will come upon the entire world. Some interpreters like Walvoord (189) apply these verses totally to the Great Tribulation with no application to the destruction of Jerusalem; others like Bruner (2:497, 502) apply these verses totally to the A.D. 70 destruction of Jerusalem. See comments below on verse 29. Also, see Luke 21:23-24 where "this people" will experience the sword and captivity among the nations "and Jerusalem will be trodden down by the Gentiles, until the times of the Gentiles are fulfilled." Luke's comments suggest God's judgment against Jerusalem went beyond her A.D. 70 destruction (until the times of the Gentiles are fulfilled). That judgment foreshadowed the greater time of judgment that would come upon the whole earth. This later judgment will be greater in that it will be against the entire earth and not just against Jerusalem, but it apparently will not equal or surpass the intensity of suffering the victims of the A.D. 70 war experienced. The final tribulation will last three and one half years (forty-two months, Rev. 13:5). Jerusalem's siege lasted only four months but Roman soldiers systematically attacked parts of Palestine from the spring of A.D. 67 to 74 when the last Jewish stronghold, Masada, fell (Beitzel 187).

e. More information on the coming and work of false christs and false prophets in the days leading up to Jesus' return (24:23-28)

23 Then if any man shall say unto you, Lo, here *is* Christ, or there; believe *it* not.
24 For there shall arise false Christs, and false prophets, and shall shew great signs and wonders; insomuch that, if *it were* possible, they shall deceive the very elect.
25 Behold, I have told you before.
26 Wherefore if they shall say unto you, Behold, he is in the desert; go not forth: behold, *he is* in the secret chambers; believe *it* not.

27 For as the lightning cometh out of the east, and shineth even unto the west; so shall also the coming of the Son of man be.
28 For wheresoever the carcase is, there will the eagles be gathered together.

Jesus had already foretold the coming of many false christs (v. 5). Here He expanded on this subject with another warning. They must not believe any claims He has returned (v. 23) or He is working in secret somewhere—i.e., away from public scrutiny and verification by those familiar with His previous teachings (v. 26; Gundry 486). In the context of severe trouble (v. 21), people will be looking for hope. There will be many false christs and false prophets (see above on v. 11) at that time ("then," v. 23) of tribulation and they will perform "great signs and wonders" in their efforts to lead people astray. There are no records of signs and wonders in the context of the A.D. 70 destruction of Jerusalem.

This is the third time Jesus warned about being led astray. See verses 4 and 11. These false christs and prophets will perform miraculous signs and have as their goal to deceive, if possible, even true believers, the elect (v. 24). (Note: Signs and wonders do not always indicate that a prophet is from God. See Deuteronomy 13:1-2.) However, Jesus' disciples know better than to believe the claims of these imposters because Jesus has told them beforehand (v. 25). They should also know better than to believe false claims of a secret return with secretive meetings because Jesus has said He will not return in secret (v. 26). His coming will be as lightning that shines from horizon to horizon (v. 27; Lk. 17:24). His coming will be obvious, not secretive, and grand as well as powerful.

These verses are about the appearances of false christs and prophets near the end of the church age. Here also is Jesus' first direct reference to His return in answer to the disciples' question in verse 3, "What will be the sign of your coming?" He is coming back to this earth (Greek *parousia*, cf. v. 3) and His coming will be as visible and powerful as lightning. For His coming, see comments on verse 30.

Jesus ended this section with a proverbial saying (Zerwick 79; Job 39:30), the meaning of which is a mystery to the modern reader. Jesus observed that vultures visibly gather where there are corpses. Some suggested interpretations are these: in this context the vultures can be either (1) the people who are deceived and gather to feed on the spiritually dead false christs and prophets, (2) Jesus' disciples who will gather to Jesus when He comes (Nolland 981), (3) judgment of the unsaved, the dead, when Jesus and His angels descend upon them (suggested as a possibility by Hagner 33B:707, though not his preference), (4) real birds that gather to feed on the judged, those slain in battle (Keener, *Matthew* 583; Rev. 19:17) or (5) the visibility of Christ at His return: i.e., Christ's return will be as visible and unmistakable as circling vultures over a carcass (Newman and Stine 768). The latter seems the most likely. Jesus' return will be unmistakable. There will be ample evidence that He has returned to judge this world. Jesus' promised visibility at His return is opposed to the secrecy of the false christs (Grundry 487).

The parallel passage in Luke 17:37 has a different application. There the proverb emphasizes the universality of the separations for judgment that will happen at Jesus' return (Lk. 17:34-35; Marshall 669). Wherever there are people there will be separations for judgment.

f. Signs that will immediately precede Jesus' coming (24:29-31)

29 Immediately after the tribulation of those days shall the sun be darkened, and the moon shall not give her light, and the stars shall fall from heaven, and the powers of the heavens shall be shaken:
30 And then shall appear the sign of the Son of man in heaven: and then shall all the tribes of the earth mourn, and they shall see the Son of man coming in the clouds of heaven with power and great glory.
31 And he shall send his angels with a great sound of a trumpet, and they shall gather together his elect from the four winds, from one end of heaven to the other.

Following His discussion of the tribulation and His very visible coming, Jesus turned to the four disciples' second question (v. 3): "What will be the sign of your coming?" "Sign" is the emphasized word. Jesus had spoken of His coming in 23:39 and 16:27. With all that had happened this week, beginning with the Triumphal Entry and His most recent comments about His return, they were anxious with anticipation, expecting a glorious manifestation of the kingdom soon. See 20:22 and comments.

Though not translated in several English versions, verse 29 includes an adversative "but" (Greek *de*; Osborne 892). In contrast to the seemingly never-ending events of the tribulation in "those days" (vv. 21-22), the end is now in sight. "But immediately after" the judgment of the earth, "the tribulation of those days," there will be signs (Lk. 21:25) in the sky. "Immediately after" links the destruction of Jerusalem and the suffering that was part of that event (Mt. 24:15-20) with the final tribulation (Lk. 21:20-28), that time of earth-wide suffering, that Jesus' coming finishes (Kenner, *Matthew* 583).

Blomberg (88) thinks Jesus taught the "great tribulation" began with the destruction of Jerusalem and continues until His visible return at the end of the age. He says this makes verse 21 make sense. If verse 21 applied only to the final tribulation described in Revelation then it obviously would never be repeated. However, if Jesus spoke of the tribulation that accompanied Jerusalem's destruction as being the worst ever to be experienced and that tribulation would continue throughout the church age, then His words have "great significance and poignancy." I prefer to think that Jesus simply linked Jerusalem's troubles with the great tribulation, but Blomberg's opinion may have merit in light of constant persecution against the church throughout its history. See comments above on verse 21.

"Immediately after the tribulation of those days" suggests that the tribulation will end and there will be a lull in end-times suffering. Perhaps this will be the time when people will be saying, "Peace and safety" (1 Th. 5:3), because they think the worst is past. Regardless, this quiet time will be short-lived, for just after this tribulation God will darken the heavenly lights. The sun, moon, and stars will no longer be visible and the powers of heaven, i.e., the forces of nature both in the heavens and on earth, will be altered to such an extent people will be filled with fear (Lk. 21:25-26). In Luke, Jesus described these heavenly signs as having such an effect on people they will be perplexed "because of the roaring of the sea and the waves." One thinks of the gravitational influence of the moon upon the waves. Luke further records people's hearts will be "failing them for fear, and for looking after those things which are coming on the earth." Some writers think the heavenly powers that will be shaken are "the spiritual forces of wickedness in heavenly places" (Gundry 487). However, it is difficult to understand how people on earth would be aware of such a spiritual upheaval in a realm they are unable to sense (2 Kg. 6:17).

Isaiah (13:10; 24:23), Ezekiel (32:7), and Joel (2:10, 31) each foretold that the celestial lights would be signs of God's judgments. Isaiah uttered his prophecy in the context of God's judgment against Babylon. Ezekiel warned that God would block the celestial lights with clouds when He judged Egypt (Ezek. 32:7-8), and Joel (2:2, 10) warned the same if Israel did not repent. It is possible the Lord was also speaking of thick clouds in Matthew 24:29 when He spoke of the darkening of the sun and moon. However, the fact the stars will fall, evidently suggesting an awesome meteor shower, and their falling will be visible from earth suggests that thick clouds may not be the best explanation for no longer seeing the sun and moon. Perhaps there will be an eclipse that will darken both luminaries. It is certain that all the heavenly lights will not be extinguished at the time Jesus was speaking of because, according to Isaiah (24:23), following the judgment of the whole earth, the Lord will reign in Jerusalem with such glory the sun and moon will appear dim. The same kind of contrast will be true at Jesus' return. His brilliant glory will be set against an unusually dark sky, which will accentuate his brilliance.

These signs did not happen in the first century A.D. The noonday darkness that took place during Jesus' crucifixion (Mt. 27:45) was a sign, but it was not the sign Jesus was speaking of here because the sign He foretold would take place after "the tribulation of those days" (Mt. 24:29). In addition, on the day of Pentecost (Acts 2:19-21) Peter quoted Joel 2:30-32 as if Joel's words were still for the future, not for the past or Peter's present circumstances. At the time the Apostle John recorded the Revelation (mid 90's?), he saw in his prophetic vision an apparent future celestial upheaval (Rev. 6:12-17). This may be the same event of which Jesus spoke.

In addition to the celestial upheaval, Joel also promised that all who call upon the Lord will be saved from the judgment of that day. Peter preached this portion of Joel's message in Acts 2:21 to convey there is time to repent before these signs and judgments arrive. In Acts 2:40, he encouraged the people to "save" themselves. The celestial signs were still future. It was time for people to call on the Lord in order to be saved before the day of the Lord's judgment arrived.

When God darkens the heavenly lights, Jesus will return in radiant glory (v. 30, quoted in the *Didache,* 16:8). Everyone will see Him coming on the clouds (Rev. 14:14-16) with power and great glory as prophesied in Daniel

7:13-14. There are different ideas about what "the sign of the Son of Man" (vv. 3, 30; Osborne 893) may be. The sign might be His coming itself (v. 30; Evans, *Matthew* 456; Greek appositional genitive) that marks the end of the age (16:27; Wilkins 83). It might be a standard and the trumpet sound (Newman and Stine 770; Carson 505) that announces His arrival. Or His splendid glory might be the sign that He is coming. The text seems to emphasize the glory of His return. See Daniel 7:14 and Matthew 26:64 with accompanying comments. Walvoord (189, 192) thinks the great tribulation is the sign that Jesus' coming is near.

Jesus will return with great glory and power. "Power" in this discourse is a reference to the Father according to 26:64. Jesus will not return as the humble, turn-the-other-cheek Nazarene. He will return with the Father at His side, as Almighty God.

At His return, Jesus will pass through each hemisphere, in view of all earth's inhabitants as He circles the globe. Everyone will see Jesus sharing the Father's throne. Accompanied by all His angels and with full heavenly glory, this will be a magnificent sight. The enormous size of the company and the brightness of their glory will insure no one misses this event that stretches from horizon to horizon (v. 27).

Wilkins (783) understands "tribes" to refer to the twelve tribes of Israel (as in 19:28) and the "earth" to be the "land" of Israel. Though this use of "tribes" is common in both testaments, it seems too restrictive to limit it to Jews, in this passage, in light of 16:27, 24:14, and 25:32 (Hagner 33B:714). See also Revelation 1:7, 5:9, 11:9, 13:7, and 14:6. The same can be said for "land." It can refer to the land of Israel but it regularly does not. The people of the whole earth will feel immediate, overwhelming mourning or regret (Greek *koptõ*; Grimm's 355: to beat one's self in grief) over their failure to prepare for His return. The Jews will feel additional regret at His coming for their role in piercing Him (Zech. 12:10; Jn. 19:37; Rev. 1:7).

Jesus will return with all of His angels (16:27; 25:31) and will dispatch them (24:31) with a great trumpet sound (v. 31; 1 Cor. 15:52; 1 Th. 4:16). They will gather His people (His elect; 2 Th. 2:1) from one end of the sky to the other. As Hill (323) notes, there is no specific mention of a resurrection as in Paul's later writings. However, such a resurrection is clearly assumed. Later texts convey this gathering will have multiple stages. (1) There will be the resurrection of the dead saints in their glorified bodies and the immediate rejoining of their souls with their bodies. (2) Angels will separate the living saints from the living sinners. (3) There will be the transformation of the living saints into their glorified bodies. (4) There will be the ascension of all saints and they will be escorted by angels to meet the Lord in the air.

"From one end of heaven to the other" is hyperbole and means not one of God's children will be left behind. His angels will enforce His judgment, separate the righteous from the unrighteous, and cast the sinners into eternal punishment. See 13:36-43, 47-50, and comments. See also 2 Thessalonians 1:5-10, Jude 14-15, and Revelation 14:14-20. Jesus will resume His discussion about His coming in 25:31.

g. The certainty of Jesus' words stressed (24:32-35)

Four disciples had asked specific questions about future events (Mt. 24:2-3; Mk. 13:3). Jesus gave general answers in verses 4-14 teaching that the end would not be soon. Only after considerable time has passed, during which the whole world will be evangelized, will the end come. Beginning in verse 15, He gave a sign that would signal the imminent destruction of Jerusalem. This sign was the Roman army assembling against her. More events (the rise of false christs and prophets) would characterize the extended delay of His return. He will return and when He does, He will come visibly and powerfully, not in secret. In these next verses, 32-36, Jesus emphasized the absolute certainty of His words.

32 Now learn a parable of the fig tree; When his branch is yet tender, and putteth forth leaves, ye know that summer *is* nigh:
33 So likewise ye, when ye shall see all these things, know that it is near, *even* at the doors.
34 Verily I say unto you, This generation shall not pass, till all these things be fulfilled.
35 Heaven and earth shall pass away, but my words shall not pass away.

Whenever Jesus taught, He wanted His disciples to learn, but now it seems He took His desire for them to learn to a higher level. The Greek word translated "learn" (Greek *manthanō*) can mean to "learn from experience, often with the implication of reflection" (Louw and Nida I:327). Jesus wanted the disciples to think about this parable of the fig tree. New leaf growth on the fig tree announced the soon arrival of summer. See comments on 21:19 for fig tree. In the same way the fig tree heralded approaching summer, the signs (vv. 15-29) would announce approaching events. "It" (v. 33) should probably be understood as "He," the "Son of man" in verse 30 being the probable antecedent. He is at the door (compare Jas. 5:9), i.e., He, the Judge, is near. But, if summer (v. 32) is the antecedent, then "it" is the proper translation (Wilkins 786) and refers either to the destruction of the temple or the end of the world or both (Bruner 2:517). Luke 21:31, however, explains this fig tree parable in this way: "When you see these things taking place, you know that the kingdom of God is near." The kingdom had already arrived in one sense (12:28). What is yet to happen is the full, visible manifestation of that kingdom. Thus, the fig tree points primarily to the return of Christ and the full manifestation of the kingdom at the end of the age. However, according to Matthew the fig tree parable also refers to the first-century destruction of Jerusalem.

"Ye" (v. 33) now includes all of Jesus' followers and is not limited to the four asking questions (see comments on v. 3) or to Jesus' contemporaries. See more below on "this generation." "All these things" in verses 33 and 34 refers to the end time troubles and signs mentioned in verses 21-28 (of which the first-century troubles were types) and the celestial signs of verse 29. Believers living at the time of these signs will recognize the nearness of Jesus' return. In the words of Luke 21:28: "When these things begin to come to pass, then look up, and lift up your heads; for your redemption draweth nigh."

"This generation" can refer to those alive in Jesus' day or to those alive in the end time. If Jesus meant the fig tree parable to refer to the A.D. 70 destruction of Jerusalem, "this generation" refers to Jesus' contemporaries (Newman and Stine 773-774), as in 23:36; and "all these things" refers to the signs pointing to the city's destruction. If the fig tree parable refers to the end time, "this generation" is not Jesus' contemporaries but the final generation, and "all these things" refers to the signs pointing to Jesus' return and the end.

It seems certain Jesus meant that the destruction of Jerusalem would happen during the lifetimes of His contemporaries. This is the most natural interpretation of "this" generation (11:16; 12:45; 23:36; Keener, *Matthew* 578). That very generation saw Jerusalem left desolate (v. 15). However, the fig tree parable seems also to speak of end time signs. This seems clearest in Luke's record. Immediately following the fig tree parable, Luke 21:31-32 adds: "So also, when you see these things taking place, you know that the kingdom of God is near. Truly, I say to you, this generation will not pass away until all has taken place" (ISBE III:667). This suggests that just as the tribulation that took place during the destruction of Jerusalem foreshadowed the final great tribulation, so the A.D. 30-70 generation also foreshadowed the final generation. The generation of believers alive in the late 60's saw the signs of the approaching desolation of the temple (see verse 15 and comments above). The final generation will likewise see the signs that "summer is near" (Wilkins 787): that is, that the end of the world and the consummation of the kingdom are close. If this understanding is correct, the last generation will see more intense tribulation (vv. 21-22), increased attempts at deception (vv. 23-26), and heavenly signs (v. 29). Once these end times events begin to unfold, things will move quickly toward the end of the age when relief will come to the persecuted and judgment will fall on the unrepentant. The final generation will witness the return of Christ (Lk. 21:28).

Some writers take a third approach. They believe Jesus meant the end of the age would come during the lifetime of His contemporaries but that He was wrong. Bruner (2:519-520) says plainly, "Jesus made a mistake." He believes that Jesus' true humanity requires "the possibility of Jesus' mental fallibility about the exact time of the end of the world." Nolland (989) is more discreet: "As the prophets before him had regularly done, the gospel of Jesus presents as part of a single development things that belong together in principle but turn out to be separated chronologically in a manner that he did not anticipate." Jesus' words in verse 35 (and in verse 25) are meaningless if these men are right. Verses 6, 8, and 14 show that Jesus did not expect His own return and the eschatological end of all things to take place before His own generation died.

Jesus assured His disciples that His words are true and eternal. They will never (Greek double negative for emphasis) pass away. They will never cease to exist (Greek *parerchomai*) or fail. What He told His disciples would certainly be what would come to pass. His words will outlast heaven and earth (Ps. 102:25-26; Is. 51:6; 2 Pet. 3:10; Rev. 20:11; 21:1).

h. The need for constant readiness for Jesus' return emphasized (24:36-44)

Throughout His lifetime on earth, Jesus revealed His complete humanity in different ways. In these verses, He spoke of His limited knowledge concerning the timing of His return. His disciples had asked "when" (v. 3). He assured them that their generation would see the desolation of the temple; but in answer to any questions about when the end would come, He said, to paraphrase, "I do not know." This was one bit of information He could not give to His disciples because He Himself did not know. However, He knew some things about life at the end time so He shared this information with His disciples and instructed them to be ready for His coming at all times.

36 But of that day and hour knoweth no *man*, no, not the angels of heaven, but my Father only.
37 But as the days of Noe *were*, so shall also the coming of the Son of man be.
38 For as in the days that were before the flood they were eating and drinking, marrying and giving in marriage, until the day that Noe entered into the ark,
39 And knew not until the flood came, and took them all away; so shall also the coming of the Son of man be.
40 Then shall two be in the field; the one shall be taken, and the other left.
41 Two *women shall be* grinding at the mill; the one shall be taken, and the other left.
42 Watch therefore: for ye know not what hour your Lord doth come.
43 But know this, that if the goodman of the house had known in what watch the thief would come, he would have watched, and would not have suffered his house to be broken up.
44 Therefore be ye also ready: for in such an hour as ye think not the Son of man cometh.

Some knowledge about the end time events the Father did not will to reveal to Jesus. The exact date of Jesus' return was one such matter. Concerning this Mark 13:32 states plainly only the Father and not even the Son knew that date. (Most of the textual scholars believe, because of its inclusion in important Greek manuscripts, that that same exception belongs in Matthew also.)

Jesus' lack of knowledge raises rather thorny theological concerns. How can Jesus be God and unaware? The answer lies in the mystery of the incarnation and the two natures of Christ. (See comments on 1:20; 8:26; and introductory remarks to chapter four.) One might suggest with Grudem (560) that Jesus had two intelligences, one divine, the other human. Though His human consciousness could access His divine intelligence at will, yet much of the time He did not exercise that privilege. This allowed Him to experience full humanity. From infancy Jesus grew in His human mind and understanding as any other human (Lk. 2:40, 52), developing as any other child, and He never grew to omniscience in His human mind. He was, nonetheless, omniscient in His divine nature (Jn. 16:30) all the while this human development was taking place. None of this changed when Jesus became an adult and began ministry. He still did not know everything in His human mind. His human mind was limited. His divine intelligence was not. The exact time of His return, then, was one example of something Jesus did not know in His human mind but in His divine mind did (Grudem 562).

Others suggest Jesus had limited knowledge because He "gave up the independent exercise of His divine attributes" (Erickson 771). This means He used certain attributes (omniscience, omnipotence) only when His and His Father's wills agreed that He should. Jesus would ask the Father and together they would agree whether to use divine power or knowledge. Thus, Jesus did not know everything while He was on this earth because He gave up independent exercise of His omniscience; some would say He gave up coordinate exercise of His omniscience for subordinate exercise (Forlines 177-178). Jesus thus possessed only knowledge that the Father agreed was right for Him to have during His humanity.

Jesus' mention of angels suggests they have a higher level and capacity of awareness than humans (Wilkins 800). "Not even the angels [know]," Jesus stated. Their mention also assumes their closeness to God and their familiarity with many details of God's overall plan (Hendriksen 869), though see their extensive knowledge qualified in 1 Peter 1:12. Matthew included several descriptive statements about angels in his record. See 13:39 and comments.

To emphasize the need for readiness in light of this ignorance (Nolland 992), Matthew records that Jesus gave two illustrations. Luke includes a third. First, Jesus spoke of Noah's generation as a reminder of an earlier visitation of God's judgment. He spoke of Noah and the flood as historical facts and as one who had firsthand knowledge. According to Jesus, there are parallels between God's workings in the flood and His working in the coming judgment (2 Pet. 3:5-7; Hendriksen 847), between the responses of Noah to God's warnings and those of His generation, and between the responses of the people of God and their unsaved generation at the time of the judgment at Jesus' return.

(1) Noah prepared (an ark) while the people ignored God's warnings through Noah (2 Pet. 2:5). Rather than prepare along with Noah, people continued normal living. Eating, drinking, marrying, and giving in marriage stress ongoing action in past time (Greek periphrastic present participles). "Eating and drinking," suggests satisfying one's needs for personal survival. "Marrying and giving in marriage" suggest normal marriage habits in keeping with God's approved creative design for racial propagation (Gen. 1:27-28; 2:18-24; Mt. 22:30). "Marrying" possibly refers to the man who marries and "giving in marriage" possibly refers to the parents giving their daughter in marriage. Jesus' point was that people will be living the normal habits of life when the final judgment comes.

(2) Normal life continued for most people even as Noah built the ark right up to the day he entered the ark. His generation was oblivious to—they did not know or understand—his entrance into the ark and what that meant for them. Judgment was close and they did not recognize it, whereas Noah and his family were prepared. This characteristic grounds Jesus' warning (vv. 42, 44) that His disciples must be awake and

ready (Gundry 493). Jesus' point was that in the end people will be oblivious to the nearness of God's judgment.

(3) The Judge who delivered Noah and his family destroyed everyone else. The flood came and took them away, signifying the suddenness, severity, and finality of the judgment of God. The flood interrupted and ended their earthly lives. They were gone. God literally washed them off the face of the earth.

(4) The flood was worldwide. No one escaped its reach. The coming judgment will also be worldwide (all, v. 39; Evans, *Matthew* 459). Scripture says nothing about the antediluvians' wickedness (Gen. 6:5) paralleling that of the people alive at the end time, though one may expect from verse 12 that the moral climates are similar. As in Noah's day, mankind's wickedness will provide justice for the end-times' judgment.

In the same way (v. 39; Greek *houtōs;* in the way described; Grimm's 468), the generation alive when Jesus returns (Greek *parousia*) will experience God's judgment. Some will be prepared. Some will be unprepared. The unprepared will be pursuing normal life activities (vv. 40-41), oblivious to their own imminent danger. At His return, Jesus will take away His own and leave the rest for judgment. This is how it will be: two men will be working together in the field. Jesus will take one and leave the other. Two women will be working side-by-side milling grain. Jesus will take one and leave the other. See comments on 18:6. On Son of Man, see comments on 26:64.

Jesus' point was not that people in close proximity are separated but close associates will be separated unexpectedly while they are going about the normal business of life (Gundry 494) simply because only some are ready for Jesus' return. The separation will be so unexpected and fast that advance preparation is essential. The separation is part of God's judgment against the ungodly, and Jesus emphasized that all who are not watching will be caught totally by surprise.

The ones "taken" may be those taken in judgment (Keener, *Background* 115; Walvoord 193) or those taken away to heaven. Verse 31 suggests the latter. Verse 39 suggests the former. That Jesus is coming for His own makes the latter understanding more attractive. Jesus' application is straight forward: always be watching (v. 42; Greek *grēgoreō* present imperative; to be awake, watchful, vigilant, also v. 43; 25:13; 26:38, 40-41; Louw and Nida I:260). Always be ready for the return of "your Lord" because no human knows when He will come again. Mankind's ignorance of the exact time of his judgment is part of God's master plan. (Some Greek manuscripts have "day" in verse 42 while others have "hour." The meaning is essentially the same.)

Jesus gave a second illustration, this one from His own time period, to make His point about the unexpected timing of His return. This illustration utilized a familiar happening, the surprise breaking and entering of a thief (also Lk. 12:39-40). "Broken up" (v. 43, Greek *deorussō*) speaks of a thief digging through the dirt wall of a house in order to gain access. See comments on 6:19. If the master ("goodman") of the house had known when the thief was coming, he would have prepared and prevented the undesired entry. He did not know and consequently suffered loss. Apparently, the thief dug through the house while the homeowner slept inside.

The homeowner made a serious mistake by not having all of the "watches" covered (Nolland 995). Although Jesus did not tell His followers when He would return, He told them He would come again. Because they have been told, they not only must but they always can be ready and watchful—the point of verse 44.

Luke recorded a third illustration of folks not ready when judgment fell, Sodom (Gen. 19). Sodom's citizens too were ignorant of the nearness of their judgment. There was a general unpreparedness (Lk. 17:28-29) that characterized their day. They ate, drank, bought, sold, planted, and built, but on the morning Lot left, God suddenly destroyed them with fire.

Jesus warned His followers, not the crowds (Gundry 495; v. 44). Literally, He said, "You (plural, emphatic position) must also be (Greek pres. imperative) ready" (Greek, *hetoimos*; cf. 25:10 where "the ready" went in), i.e., you must have all of the watches covered. Jesus spoke not only to individuals but also to the church about her need to be a ready people, in a constant state of readiness for His return (Bruner 2:530). Readiness means to be living always as a follower of Jesus (Hagner 33B:721), aware of the signs and awake. Jesus will arrive with the unexpectedness of a thief (1 Th. 5:2; 2 Pet. 3:10; Rev. 3:3). Inherent in this warning is the idea of surprise, finality (no second chance; Hendriksen 871), and possible loss. For Noah's generation, the burglarized home, and Sodom, advance preparation would have prevented surprise and loss and provided salvation.

Summary (24:1-44)

This discourse began with Jesus predicting the destruction of the temple in Jerusalem. His disciples asked Him when this destruction would happen and what sign would precede His coming and the end of the age. Answering the last question first, Jesus stated there will be an extended time period when false christs and false prophets will preach their false doctrines and deceive many. There will be wars, rumors of wars, and natural catastrophes. During this same period there will be intense persecution against Jesus' followers, and many who knew Christ will turn from Him. As this period progresses, societal sin will increase and influence some believers to the point that many who once possessed a fervent love for the Lord and their fellow believers will allow that love to grow cold. These characteristics of the age are not signs of the end's nearness. Concurrent with these events, preachers of the true gospel will carry the kingdom message to every nation. This is the church age.

Jesus next addressed the disciples' first question. Their generation would see the Lord punish Jerusalem by destroying the city and the temple. He would use Gentiles to carry out this judgment and give them control of the city until their time, the times of the Gentiles, is complete (Lk. 21:24). The destruction of Jerusalem and the temple anticipated the final tribulation. After the times of the Gentiles are complete, according to Luke, the Lord will bring intense judgment on the whole earth and everyone will suffer. The suffering of this final tribulation will mirror that experienced in Jerusalem in the years A.D. 66-70 but it will be on a worldwide scale. The Lord will limit the length of that judgment in order not to destroy His elect also.

Immediately after this latter tribulation, there will be signs in the heavens. God will darken the celestial lights and alter heavenly forces. At that time and against that backdrop of darkened heavens, Jesus will return in bright glory to gather His people. This was Jesus' answer to the disciples' second question: He will return after the heavenly signs that follow the final tribulation.

Jesus gave a parable of a fig tree. Even as the fig tree begins to leaf out in spring and so is a sign that one season is about to end and another to begin, so "all these things" Jesus spoke of in verses 21-28 will indicate Jesus' return is close. However, this was as specific as He would get. In His humanity, Jesus did not know the exact date of His return, so He commanded His followers to be ready always for His return. They had to be alert always lest they be caught unawares as Noah's generation was when the flood came and swept away in judgment all but eight. They had to be alert lest they be surprised and suffer loss as an unprepared homeowner does when his home is burglarized.

Application: Teaching and Preaching the Passage

Teaching and preaching Matthew 24 will be challenging but satisfying and edifying. It is part of the "whole counsel of God," the Word that God wants His people to hear (Acts 20:27; 2 Th. 2:1-5; 2 Tim. 3:16-4:2). The preacher will be tempted to ignore completely this chapter, or to proof text and refer only to selected portions of the chapter, or to make Jesus' words conform to one's already decided eschatology. The teacher or preacher must resist such an "easy" way, as well as the temptation to read into the text his or her own preconceptions (eisegesis) instead of doing honest and full exegesis so that the words of Jesus will speak for themselves. One's fullest eschatological understanding comes from this and other large portions of Scripture in both Testaments. Consequently, one must resist the temptation to make Jesus conform to one's understanding of other texts, say what He did not say, or arrange His prophecies so they depict an end-time chronology that He did not. Since Scriptures do not contradict, any seeming contradiction is really a failure on our parts to comprehend fully what we are reading. We should share what is clear and be honest about areas where we are still searching for clarity. Healthy study wrestles with difficulties, including apparently irreconcilable differences, until mature understanding dawns.

One might develop a series of sermons or lessons around Jesus' answers to the three subjects raised in verse 3. (1) When will we know the end is near (vv. 3-14)? (2) How did the disciples' generation know Jerusalem was about to be destroyed (vv. 15-28)? (3) When will we know Jesus' second coming is near (vv. 29-31; 36-44)?

A sermon could be entitled "Summer might be nearer than you think" using verses 32-34 as the text. The title comes from verse 32 and assumes "all these things" (v. 33) have double fulfillments. See comments above. If the fig tree parable was for two generations, one might explain first how this parable applied to Jesus' contemporaries and the destruction of Jerusalem: (1) Jerusalem will be destroyed within one generation (v. 34); (2) as the budding fig tree heralded the coming summer, so the approaching armies of Rome signaled Jerusalem's approaching demise (v. 15); (3) Jesus' advanced warning was an opportunity to escape the destruction (experience individual "salvation," vv. 16-19); (4) God promised to help those who ask (v. 20); (5) suffering was the worst ever (v. 21); and (6) God was in control of the entire event (v. 22). Second, one might explain how this parable applies to the generation alive at Jesus' return: like those who lived in Jerusalem at the time of her desolation, the final generation (1) will also have a sign (the abomination that causes desolation, v. 15); (2) should heed Jesus' warning to be prepared to leave immediately (vv. 16-18); (3) should pray for easiest circumstances (v. 20); (4) should expect troublesome times (v. 21-22a); (5) should trust in God's oversight and control during this time of severe troubles (vv. 22b); and (6) must stay true to Christ while waiting for His return (vv. 23-28).

One might develop a lesson or sermon on clear facts in Matthew 24: (1) normalcy in this world includes many troubles (wars, rumors of wars, famines, and earthquakes, vv. 6-7); (2) Christians will experience some troubles only because they are following Christ (v. 9); (3) this world will end (vv. 6, 14, 35); (4) the gospel will go worldwide even during troublesome times (v. 14); (5) Jesus is coming again, visibly (v. 27), powerfully (v. 30), and gloriously (v. 30); (6) Jesus' words are more certain and eternal than the universe and this planet (v. 35); (7) no human knows exactly when Jesus is coming again (vv. 36-44); and, (8) followers of Jesus will be judged for their service when He comes again (vv. 45-51; see comments on these verses in the next section).

Jesus gave five essentials for His people who wish to survive tribulation. First, for those who wanted to survive the Roman destruction of Jerusalem, Jesus instructed them to (1) know what the Scripture says (v. 15); (2) be ready to leave (v. 16); (3) do not become attached to things (vv. 17-18); (4) pray for deliverance from troubles (vv. 20-22); and, (5) keep faith in the Jesus they know (vv. 23-28). Second, these same guidelines plus one more are for Christ's followers to live by today also: (1) know your Bible; (2) be ready to leave; (3) do not be attached to things; (4) pray for deliverance from troubles; (5) keep your faith in the Jesus of the Bible; and, (6) never doubt Jesus' words. Just as His prophecies about Jerusalem's destruction happened, so will His prophecies about the final destruction of this world.

Bruner (2:494-495) finds in verse 14 "a panorama of God's plan of salvation": the what, how, where, why, and when. I would add "to whom."

Verses 27-31 lend themselves to a sermon on the characteristics of the return of Christ. Jesus' return will be visible (vv. 27-28), after tribulation (v. 29), after a series of heavenly signs (v. 29), an occasion of sincere regret for some (v. 30), powerful (v. 30), glorious (v. 30), noisy (v. 31), with His angels (v. 31), and purposeful: to gather His people to Himself (v. 31).

One might speak on what Noah's generation can teach every generation (vv. 37-39). (1) What you do not know can hurt you. (2) What you do not believe matters can matter (sin). (3) What you do not expect can happen (God's judgment: the fact, the means, the timing).

There are at least five truths Jesus wants His people to learn from the universal flood: (1) normal life can blind people to real danger (vv. 38-39); (2) ignorance does not stop judgment ("they were unaware," v. 39); (3) divine judgment is final ("swept them all away," v. 39); (4) divine opportunity can end quickly (vv. 40-41); and, (5) preparation is the key to survival (vv. 38, 43-44).

One might give a miniature message on Jesus' end-times teachings: (1) what Jesus knew He told (v. 25); (2) what Jesus did not know He admitted (v. 36); and, (3) what Jesus wants His people to do until He returns He emphasized (vv. 43-44).

There are lessons for everyday living in Matthew 24. (1) Life is more valuable than things (vv. 15-18) (Keener, *Matthew* 580); (2) God's Word and warnings should always be heard and heeded (vv. 16-18); (3) we can pray for deliverance from troubles (v. 20); (4) we must always measure every teacher's claims against Jesus' incarnational teachings (v. 23-25); and, (5) we must expect a visible return (vv. 26-27).

i. Three parables to illustrate the need for constant readiness for Jesus' return (24:45—25:30)

In 24:30, Jesus spoke of His return. He did not say exactly when that would be (24:36). Only the Father knew exactly when the Son would come. Jesus concluded from this that His followers must always be ready; to illustrate this point, He gave three parables: the parable of the faithful and wise servant, the parable of the ten virgins, and the parable of the talents. All three parables are eschatological. To make one or more of them apply to the Jewish nation or the scribes and Pharisees (Barclay 2:374, 377) is to deny them their eschatological context (Hill 328). For parables, see the introductory remarks to chapter 13.

(1) The parable of the faithful and wise servant (24:45-51)

Even though Jesus' followers cannot know the exact time of His return for them, still they must live prepared. The flood caught Noah's generation by surprise and Jesus' return will surprise the last generation in the same way. However, Jesus wants His followers to be expectant and ready. They are to live out this expectant readiness in faithful service to the Lord throughout His lengthy delay. See Luke 12:41-46.

Included throughout this discourse are Jesus' strong teachings on the final judgment at the end of the age. He will be the judge. Everyone who has ever lived will stand before Him. Based on Jesus' determination at that judgment, each person will be directed to one of two eternal destinies. With three parables about judgment and the portrayal of the final judgment as a shepherd dividing sheep from goats (Bruner 2:533), Jesus ended the Olivet Discourse, His final teaching session before the cross.

45 Who then is a faithful and wise servant, whom his lord hath made ruler over his household, to give them meat in due season?
46 Blessed *is* that servant, whom his lord when he cometh shall find so doing.
47 Verily I say unto you, That he shall make him ruler over all his goods.

48 But and if that evil servant shall say in his heart, My lord delayeth his coming;
49 And shall begin to smite *his* fellowservants, and to eat and drink with the drunken;
50 The lord of that servant shall come in a day when he looketh not for *him*, and in an hour that he is not aware of,
51 And shall cut him asunder, and appoint *him* his portion with the hypocrites: there shall be weeping and gnashing of teeth.

Jesus spoke these words to His followers (v. 44). Faithfulness as Jesus defined it means continually working at one's assignment until the Lord returns, even if the return is delayed (Evans, *Matthew* 459). Gundry (495) thinks Jesus was speaking to church leaders (and Peter's question in Luke 12:41 might suggest this), but Jesus' words should not be limited to the leadership. Jesus promised He would reward all faithful servants well by assigning to them positions of greater honor (vv. 46-47).

In this parable, the household, including the servants, belonged to the master. The master placed his servant "over" a certain area of responsibility. In this instance, the servant was to feed the household when it was time to eat. "In due season" suggests timeliness, i.e., at the right time (Lk. 12:42; 20:10). Faithfulness required ongoing work on the assignment in the master's absence. Being busy at the master's assignment when he returned assured (v. 47, "verily," Greek *amēn*) the servant of his master's approval and reward. The master promised to elevate the faithful servant to the position of a household steward, the person over all of his master's possessions.

If, however, that same servant expects delay (Greek *chronizō*, an extended absence; BAGD 88; Nolland 999) and considers that an opportunity to slack off his assigned duties and abuse his privileges by mistreating his fellow servants, having parties, and associating with the drunken (v. 49), the Lord promised the master would come unexpectedly and he would judge that servant harshly. The master would come unexpectedly in the sense that he would come sooner than the servant expected. Jesus described such servants as wicked, not at all like the faithful servants in verses 45-46. It is clear that the evil servant's activities are opposite those of the master and the servant's drunken associates were not part of the master's household. (The words "his coming" after "delayeth" (v. 48) are not in all manuscripts but are clearly understood.)

It is possible to understand the wicked servant to be a second servant (Carson 510). If one does not consider Luke, a second servant is the most natural reading of Matthew. The essential meaning of the parable remains the same either way.

The wicked servant's punishment will be in two stages. The master will "cut him asunder": that is, in two parts (Greek *dichotomeō*; compare Jer. 34:18; Lk. 12:46). (See Luke 19:27 for similar ferocity but a different word.) This means the master will inflict a punishment of extreme severity "that appropriately launches him into" an eternal punitive afterlife (Gundry 497). The Lord will assign the evil servant to the same place of punishment as the hypocrites, a reference to the difference between this servant's feigned loyalty to his master and his real practice. The place of punishment is one of extreme pain and suffering. For "weeping and gnashing of teeth," see comments on 8:12.

The master rewarded service that continued until he returned. Jesus called such service faithful and wise. The master punished the servant who stopped serving because his master was away. The Lord called such servants wicked and such service unfaithful and unwise.

The household, then, belongs to the Lord. Jesus is the master. He assigns ministry responsibilities to His servants. He expects effective time management. He rewards long-term faithfulness and He punishes hypocrisy and laziness. Each of His servants must keep serving Him the whole time He is away and be serving Him when He returns (Tit. 2:11-14; Lk. 21:34-36). Jesus spoke this parable not to the ungodly but to His disciples about their responsibility to faithful service. He expected them to stay busy doing the task He assigned them until He comes for them (Lk. 12:47-48; Nolland 1000). He also expected them to teach this obligation to all disciples (28:20).

(2) The parable of the ten virgins (25:1-13)

1 Then shall the kingdom of heaven be likened unto ten virgins, which took their lamps, and went forth to meet the bridegroom.
2 And five of them were wise, and five *were* foolish.
3 They that *were* foolish took their lamps, and took no oil with them:
4 But the wise took oil in their vessels with their lamps.
5 While the bridegroom tarried, they all slumbered and slept.
6 And at midnight there was a cry made, Behold, the bridegroom cometh; go ye out to meet him.
7 Then all those virgins arose, and trimmed their lamps.
8 And the foolish said unto the wise, Give us of your oil; for our lamps are gone out.
9 But the wise answered, saying, *Not so*; lest there be not enough for us and you: but go ye rather to them that sell, and buy for yourselves.
10 And while they went to buy, the bridegroom came; and they that were ready went in with him to the marriage: and the door was shut.
11 Afterward came also the other virgins, saying, Lord, Lord, open to us.
12 But he answered and said, Verily I say unto you, I know you not.
13 Watch therefore, for ye know neither the day nor the hour wherein the Son of man cometh.

This second of three parables uses customs common to the first century Jewish wedding to illustrate the need for readiness for the Lord's return. Only Matthew records this parable. Jesus' regular references to weddings suggest He was familiar with them. He might even have attended the weddings of His siblings (1 Cor. 9:5; Mt. 13:55-56). Indeed, His first miracle was at a wedding (Jn. 2:1-11).

Throughout His ministry, Jesus used the form of the Jewish wedding to make and illustrate various teaching points. In Matthew 22:1-13, He gave the parable of the wedding feast to illustrate the

Pharisees' hypocrisy and to illustrate that though everyone receives a gospel invitation, only those who accept the invitation and its requirements enter the kingdom. In Luke 14:7-11, Jesus used proud habits of some at wedding feasts to teach humility. In Luke 12:36, Jesus used a story of a master returning late at night from a wedding feast to teach that He too wanted His servants ready to greet Him at any hour of the day or night. This same idea of readiness is the theme of the parable of the wise and foolish virgins.

For "the kingdom of heaven shall be likened to" see comments on 13:24. The kingdom of heaven will be like what happens to the virgins in this story (Hagner 33B:728). The future tense refers to that time when the kingdom will be consummated, when it will enter its final stage, whereas the present tense in Matthew 13:24, 44-45, 47 speaks of the early days of the kingdom during Jesus' ministry.

Virgins (Greek *parthenos*; Mt. 1:23; Lk. 1:26-27) were young, unmarried women invited to accompany the wedding party throughout the streets as the groom went to get his bride. On the day of the wedding, at the end of the day, the groom would leave his home and go to the bride's home in order to take her where they would live. The procession would include guests who carried lamps to light the way. Together the wedding party would walk in festive fashion to either the groom's and his parent's home (Newman and Stine 878) or the home of the bride and groom (Gower 66) for a week long wedding celebration.

Jesus described two opposite groups of these women. Five He called wise because they took extra oil for their lamps in case there was a long waiting period. Their wisdom showed in their preparation for a possible lengthy delay of the bridegroom. The other five He called foolish because they took lamps with oil in them but no extra oil. They did not prepare for a delay. They expected the groom to come soon. The "lamp" (Greek *lampas*) can mean lamp or torch (Louw and Nida I:66), and scholarship is divided over which Jesus meant. Though a torch might be expected for walking through the streets (see Jn. 18:3) and lighting the way for festive dancing, the action of trimming their lamps (v. 7) argues for a small vessel with a wick (Evans, *Matthew* 463) rather than oil-soaked rags wrapped around a stick or sticks (Gundry 498; Keener, *Background* 116). Either will fit the story.

The bridegroom was later than anticipated by the foolish virgins. This is the turning point of the plot (Carson, *Matthew* 512). The idea of a soon coming groom is the opposite of the evil servant's idea of a delayed master in 24:48 (Bruner 2:544). All ten virgins expected the groom to arrive after dark but five believed he would come much earlier than he did. Because the groom extended his delay, the ten virgins slept and their lights began to go out. In the middle of the night (v. 6), the crier announced the arrival of the bridegroom and his party. All ten awoke but only five had enough oil to refill their lamps so they could join the procession. The five who had not brought extra discovered their oil was almost depleted and their lamps "gone" (or "going") out. The unwise wanted the wise to give them some of their oil, but the wise refused, saying they did not have enough for both—meaning none of them would have enough oil to finish the procession if they shared (Keener, *Matthew* 598). They recommended that the foolish virgins go buy oil for themselves.

While the foolish were buying oil, the wedding party came by and "the ready" (v. 10, literally; cf. 24:44, "ready") virgins joined in the groom's procession and continued on to the home where the celebration would take place (Hagner 33B:729). The door was shut and the festivities begun. When the foolish virgins arrived and tried to enter for the wedding feast, they were refused entrance. The groom denied knowing them (v. 12; 7:23; 10:33; Lk. 13:25, 27) meaning not that he did not know who they were but that he was treating them as strangers as punishment for their failure and their insult (Keener, *Matthew* 598-599). The foolish virgins had missed the groom's arrival and the wedding procession, which was the reason for the oil. Consequently, they were denied access to the wedding feast.

Gundry (499) understands the oil to represent good works. He bases this understanding on Jesus' use of the wise and foolish in 7:24, 26 and light being good works in 5:16. However, it is not good works Jesus emphasized in this parable but the state of being prepared, which includes good works. Jesus emphasized the need to be prepared for the long-term because one does not know how long the bridegroom will delay his coming. Having the foresight and will to bring an oil reserve is a mark of wisdom for one who faces a night of undetermined length. Going into the night without enough oil to keep the light burning all night long, if necessary, is foolish. For the followers of Jesus, being wise begins with being desirous and ready for the Groom's possible soon coming; but it also includes having the foresight and will to be ready to meet the Groom regardless how long His delay may be. Being foolish is thinking that short-term preparation is sufficient or that once prepared means one is automatically forever prepared. Being ready to meet Jesus at His coming is about preparing for both the immediate and the long-term. (In v. 13, the words "wherein the Son of Man cometh" are not in the Greek manuscripts the textual scholars rely on most. However, it is clear from the context—see 24:42—that this is what Jesus meant.)

Jesus told the parable in the context of His return. He directed it to His followers but it applies to everyone. The main lesson is to be ready when He comes. Jesus made this point with these supporting truths: (1) Individual, advanced preparation is essential to readiness. (2) Readiness includes preparing for a lengthy delay and staying prepared until He comes. Those who do not prepare for the long delay will be caught unprepared as in a trap (Lk. 21:34) when Jesus finally arrives. (3) It will be too late to prepare once He arrives. (4) No one joins the wedding party unless he or she is ready at the time the groom arrives. (5) One can be "too late": either be ready when Jesus comes or be forever outside. (6) "Check your 'equipment' now because [no one] knows how much longer it will be before [he has] to be sure that [he is] ready" (Nolland 1010).

Both this parable and the previous one teach long-term faithfulness. The wicked servant stopped serving his master and so was unprepared when the master returned (24:50-51). The foolish virgins failed to make adequate preparations for a long-term delay and consequently were not prepared to join the wedding procession and celebration when the groom came. People who are not following the Lord faithfully when He comes will find themselves unprepared for His arrival and denied entrance into the kingdom celebrations.

(3) The parable of the talents (25:14-30)

14 For *the kingdom of heaven is* as a man travelling into a far country, *who* called his own servants, and delivered unto them his goods.
15 And unto one he gave five talents, to another two, and to another one; to every man according to his several ability; and straightway took his journey.
16 Then he that had received the five talents went and traded with the same, and made *them* other five talents.
17 And likewise he that *had received* two, he also gained other two.
18 But he that had received one went and digged in the earth, and hid his lord's money.
19 After a long time the lord of those servants cometh, and reckoneth with them.
20 And so he that had received five talents came and brought other five talents, saying, Lord, thou deliveredst unto me five talents: behold, I have gained beside them five talents more.
21 His lord said unto him, Well done, *thou* good and faithful servant: thou hast been faithful over a few things, I will make thee ruler over many things: enter thou into the joy of thy lord.
22 He also that had received two talents came and said, Lord, thou deliveredst unto me two talents: behold, I have gained two other talents beside them.
23 His lord said unto him, Well done, good and faithful servant; thou hast been faithful over a few things, I will make thee ruler over many things: enter thou into the joy of thy lord.
24 Then he which had received the one talent came and said, Lord, I knew thee that thou art an hard man, reaping where thou hast not sown, and gathering where thou hast not strawed:
25 And I was afraid, and went and hid thy talent in the earth: lo, *there* thou hast *that* is thine.
26 His lord answered and said unto him, *Thou* wicked and slothful servant, thou knewest that I reap where I sowed not, and gather where I have not strawed:
27 Thou oughtest therefore to have put my money to the exchangers, and *then* at my coming I should have received mine own with usury.
28 Take therefore the talent from him, and give *it* unto him which hath ten talents.
29 For unto every one that hath shall be given, and he shall have abundance: but from him that hath not shall be taken away even that which he hath.
30 And cast ye the unprofitable servant into outer darkness: there shall be weeping and gnashing of teeth.

Jesus' third parable is similar to Luke 19:11-27, the parable of the minas (or pounds), yet they are distinct parables. Jesus gave the parable of the minas between Jericho and Jerusalem, perhaps on Friday of the previous week. Jesus spoke the parable of the talents on Tuesday evening of the Passion Week as part of the Olivet Discourse.

"For" (Greek *gar*, explicative) indicates that this parable further explains the previous two parables (Bruner 2:552). More particularly this parable further explains the core truth that the Lord's coming will be after a long delay, the exact timing of which is unknown, and that faithful service in the interim is required. This parable also teaches that Jesus' disciples have responsibilities in the interim and will give an accounting to Him in the end (Hagner 33B:734; Osborne 923).

Jesus told of a man who entrusted his property to his servants. His property was money (v. 27; Greek *argurion*; silver or silver money). He divided his money between three servants according to what he determined to be their abilities. One talent was worth about six hundred day's wages (Keener, *Background* 95), so one servant received an amount approximately equivalent to two years' wages (one talent), one received an amount approximately equivalent to four years' wages (two talents), and the last received an amount approximately equivalent to ten years' wages (five talents).

Whether "straightway" means the master left on his journey immediately, or the servant began trading his master's money immediately is not certain. Translators and interpreters differ. The overall thrust of the parable seems to favor the latter, meaning the servant wasted no time getting started.

The servants entrusted with five or two talents went, traded and gained (v. 16). The inference is that from the time they received the talents, and the whole time the master was away, these two servants faithfully put his money to work. Both doubled it. "Work" (Greek *ergazomai*) means "to be involved in business, ... to do business, to trade" (Louw and Nida I:580). In contrast to the first two, the servant who had received only one talent hid his master's money rather than used it gainfully. Hiding wealth in the ground was common. See comments on 13:44. The third servant made no effort to increase his master's wealth. The only work he did was digging a hole so he would not have to do anymore work.

After a long time (v. 19), the master returned and called his servants in for an evaluation. He began to settle accounts. Compare 18:24. The servants who had received five talents and two talents reported their gains for the master. Both stated they had done the work to produce the gain (Nolland 1016). The master commended these servants for their faithfulness and promised them both positions of greater responsibility and honor (25:21, 23). He invited them to share in his joy—an ongoing state and not just a short-term celebration.

The servant who had received one talent reported next. He began by trying to justify his actions (Hagner 33B:735). He knew the master to be a hard man who gained from the labors of others. Hard (Greek *sklēros*) in this context can denote harsh and cruel or hard and demanding (Louw and Nida I:757). The latter might have been the servant's intended meaning, but the former might have been in his heart as well (Bruner 2:559). The servant claimed he had been afraid of his master and hid the talent, implying that he had taken good care of it. He brought the talent to give back to his master. Perhaps he believed the master would accept this and be pleased there was no loss: "Behold! You have what is yours!"

The master responded with immediate condemnation. He judged the servant to be evil and lazy, not fearful. The servant knew the master wanted gain on his money. This made the servant knowledgeable and responsible. He could as a minimum have given the talent to moneychangers or bankers (Greek *trapezitēs*; Louw and Nida I:582), where it would at least have earned interest. The servant did not want to make money for his master. He showed no initiative. He believed it wrong for the master to expect him to work for the master's gain. The servant's insolence and indolence were costly. First, he lost favor with his master. The master's favor was evident in his original entrustment of the talent. He had every right to expect labor from his servant. Further, the master did not expect more than he should have from his servant. The master had assigned responsibilities according to ability. Second, the master ordered the talent be taken from the servant, which implies the servant lost any further opportunity to work for the master. The master commanded that the one talent be given to the servant with ten talents and then stated the principle involved: those who show gain will receive more and those who show no gain will lose even what they initially received. Third, the master judged this servant to be useless and condemned him to punishment in ongoing horror and intense chastisement. His final state was opposite that of the productive servants. For outer darkness, weeping, and gnashing (grinding) of teeth as descriptors of hell, see comments on 8:12.

As in the previous two parables, Jesus addressed His followers in this parable. The final points of this parable are in verses 29 and 30. Evans (*Matthew* 464) observes, "The principle of spiritual receptivity (as in Mark 4:24-25) is here applied to the principle of productivity, or lack thereof." The Lord will reward handsomely those who faithfully work and show gain using what the Lord has provided them. The Lord will punish in hell-fire servants who refuse to work for His gain. The servant with the ten talents is the example to follow (Gundry 509). One must avoid falling into the trap of the lazy servant. What the third servant did not have was gain. He had a talent; he just did not have any produce from it. Because he was unfruitful, he lost what he had been given, the talent, and he lost his place as servant.

Interpreters have understood the "talent" to represent money (which it clearly is in this parable), aptitude, spiritual gifts, and divine appointments and opportunities. Bruner's application is helpful (2:554): a talent stands for "whatever the Lord gives now and will ask about later."

j. A scene from the final judgment (25:31-46)

Jesus returned to His teaching about His coming and included a lengthy description of the final judgment. In 24:30-31 Jesus assured His disciples that He would return. In 24:36-44, Jesus told His followers always to be ready for His coming because He could not give them the date of His return. He then told three parables to illustrate the need to be ready at all times for His coming. Now in 25:31, He resumes His discussion discontinued after 24:31. In order to connect the two sections together, Jesus used the terms Son of Man, glory, and angels.

31 When the Son of man shall come in his glory, and all the holy angels with him, then shall he sit upon the throne of his glory:
32 And before him shall be gathered all nations: and he shall separate them one from another, as a shepherd divideth *his* sheep from the goats:
33 And he shall set the sheep on his right hand, but the goats on the left.
34 Then shall the King say unto them on his right hand, Come, ye blessed of my Father, inherit the kingdom prepared for you from the foundation of the world:
35 For I was an hungred, and ye gave me meat: I was thirsty, and ye gave me drink: I was a stranger, and ye took me in:
36 Naked, and ye clothed me: I was sick, and ye visited me: I was in prison, and ye came unto me.
37 Then shall the righteous answer him, saying, Lord, when saw we thee an hungred, and fed *thee*? or thirsty, and gave *thee* drink?
38 When saw we thee a stranger, and took *thee* in? or naked, and clothed *thee*?
39 Or when saw we thee sick, or in prison, and came unto thee?
40 And the King shall answer and say unto them, Verily I say unto you, Inasmuch as ye have done *it* unto one of the least of these my brethren, ye have done *it* unto me.
41 Then shall he say also unto them on the left hand, Depart from me, ye cursed, into everlasting fire, prepared for the devil and his angels:
42 For I was an hungred, and ye gave me no meat: I was thirsty, and ye gave me no drink:
43 I was a stranger, and ye took me not in: naked, and ye clothed me not: sick, and in prison, and ye visited me not.
44 Then shall they also answer him, saying, Lord, when saw we thee an hungred, or athirst, or a stranger, or naked, or sick, or in prison, and did not minister unto thee?
45 Then shall he answer them, saying, Verily I say unto you, Inasmuch as ye did *it* not to one of the least of these, ye did *it* not to me.
46 And these shall go away into everlasting punishment: but the righteous into life eternal.

This is Jesus' final story in His earthly ministry (Bruner 2:563). It is not a parable but rather a depiction of that final evaluation of all people (Hagner 33B:740). Matthew alone recorded it. Jesus' return is the pinnacle event in chapter 24. His judgment is the pinnacle event in chapter 25. In addition to the events Jesus (earlier in this discourse) disclosed would happen when He returns, at this point He revealed the final and great judgment will also take place in conjunction with His return. At His glorious return, He will bring all of His angels with Him and sit on His glorious throne to judge the nations (16:27; 19:28). Jesus emphasized the glory that will be His on that day by speaking of it twice in one sentence (v. 31).

In 24:31, Jesus said He will command His angels to gather the elect. The unsaved were not mentioned. Now, however, it appears the angels will gather everyone, all nations, believers and unbelievers, before Jesus' throne. For Jesus' throne, see comments on 26:64. There will be a division of the people. For other times Jesus spoke of the final separation see 7:19-23; 8:11-12; 10:32-33; 12:36-37; 13:30; 13:40-43; 22:12-13; 24:40-41, 45-51. Instead of separating wheat from chaff (3:12), wheat from tares (13:30), or good fish from bad (13:47-50), the image is that of a shepherd dividing his sheep from goats. The end is the same. Chaff, tares, bad fish, and goats will all be cast into eternal punishment. Wheat, good fish, and sheep will be gathered to the Lord to share in His glory.

The Son of Man is now "King" (v. 34). The kingdom inaugurated in His earthly ministry will then be consummated (Dan. 7:13-14). He speaks to the sheep first and addresses them as the blessed ones, the ones favored by the Father. He invites them to receive their heavenly inheritance, the heavenly kingdom prepared for them since creation (something not mentioned in Genesis 1). The reason they will share in this inheritance is their service to Jesus during their lives on earth. They ministered to Jesus in their service to other disciples: food to the hungry, drink to the thirsty, hospitality to the traveler, clothing to the naked, and ministry visits to the sick and imprisoned. The righteous did not realize they did these actions to King Jesus—who sees a king so needy?—but Jesus assured them that they had. He said whenever they helped even the least important of Jesus' brothers, i.e., His followers (12:49-50), they were helping Him. Consider also Matthew 6:1-4 and the "true fast" described in Isaiah 58:6-7.

Though one would not want to limit the application of Jesus' words to one group of Christians, His comments in verses 36-40 seem especially fitting to persecuted Christians and itinerate missionaries of the type described in chapter 10 (Gundry 513). Disciples who travel without money, preaching the kingdom, need food and lodging (10:9-14). Those who are persecuted and imprisoned need ministry and visits (10:17-19). Those who are thirsty need a drink (10:41-42). Jesus will reward His people who provide for these needs.

Multiple interpretations arise from these verses. Hill (331) thinks Jesus is referring to all in need, not only Christians, when He speaks of "my brothers." However, in 12:49-50 Jesus limited the term "brother" to those who do the will of His Father. Jesus never called the unsaved His brothers. Walvoord (201-202) thinks Jesus' brothers are Israel (neither sheep nor goats) and the great tribulation is the context of their need. At that time, Gentile believers (the sheep) will help individual Jews survive severe anti-Semitism thus demonstrating they are Christians and recognize the Jews as the chosen people. These saved Gentiles who help the persecuted Jews are invited to share in the kingdom. One problem with this interpretation is Jesus nowhere teaches there are three groups of people: the saved, the lost, and Israel.

Some Calvinists see in these verses hope for those who have never heard the gospel. They believe that "some people at the Judgment will not have served Christ *consciously*. Yet these *un*conscious servers will be given the kingdom" (Bruner 2:572; emphasis his), even to their own astonishment (Sell 90), because they showed love to Christ in their service to others. This is the gospel inverted. Salvation does not follow works directed to Jesus through others, whether intentional or not. Christ-honoring works follow salvation (Eph. 2:8-10). The Bible's teaching about those who have never heard is that they are lost until they hear and believe the gospel. Only those who call on the Lord are saved. Only those who believe in the Lord can call on Him. Only those who have heard about the Lord can believe in Him. Only those who have a witness can hear. Gospel witnesses are God's only means for unsaved people to find the only salvation that saves in the final judgment (Rom. 10:9-17).

Faith is Jesus' message of salvation throughout Matthew's Gospel. Faith was the proper response to John the Baptist (21:32). Jesus commended the centurion (Mt. 8:10) from Capernaum for his faith and showed that He wanted everyone in Israel to have such faith in Him. He required faith from the blind men before He would heal them (9:28-29). He commended the Gentile woman from the area of Tyre and Sidon (15:28) for her great and persistent faith. His kingdom consists of those who believe in Him (18:1, 6) and includes Gentiles who place their hope in Him (12:21; Greek *elpizō*; put one's hope in someone; BAGD 252). In short, giving of oneself and one's resources to meet the needs of people in general or even of Christ's followers does not gain an entrance for anyone into heaven. Rather it indicates the relation of the giver to the kingdom and to Jesus (Carson, *Matthew* 520). Such giving is important or this account of the judgment would not include the same list four times (Nolland 1031). However, faith in Jesus as Savior is the sole condition of salvation.

The wicked, on the other hand, are the cursed ones (v. 41). "Cursed" (Greek *kataroauai*) means these individuals will suffer great affliction by the power of Jesus' declaration (Louw and Nida I:442). They will hear the frightful words, "Depart from me." Jesus will reject them. They will have no inheritance in glory. They will hear their doom. They will be condemned to an eternal existence in a fire that never goes out. They will share in the punishment prepared for Satan and his fallen angels. The reason ("for," v. 42) for their awful fate is they did not minister to Jesus while on this earth. They lived opposite the righteous. They gave no food to the hungry, no drink to the thirsty, no hospitality to the traveler, no clothes to the naked, and made no ministry visits to the sick and imprisoned. As was true with the righteous, the wicked had no idea where they had encountered a needy Jesus. He assured them that every time they said "no" to even the least of His disciples, they had said "no" to Him. In short, these wicked individuals had contributed to the suffering of the righteous and of their Lord.

Many will be surprised that their works will be reviewed at the judgment, especially works such as these. God's people should not be surprised, for Scripture regularly teaches this truth (Rom. 2:6-11; 14:10-12; 2 Cor. 5:10; Rev. 20:11-15). Works reveal whether or not one is a new creation in Christ (Eph. 2:10).

This judgment, condemnation, and separation are final. The wicked will "go away" to a place not prepared for them while the righteous will go to an inheritance prepared for them (Gundry 515), "into eternal life" (v. 46). Though opposites experientially, both punishment and kingdom life are equal in duration. Any who might suggest that heaven is forever but hell is not must take into account verse 46.

One's personal eschatology will, of course, influence each interpreter in his or her understanding of the relationships and order of final events, including when this judgment will take place. There is no outline of end-time events acceptable to everyone. For example, premillennialists disagree on whether this judgment precedes or follows the millennium. Wilkins (813) summarizes the problem. (1) If one is a premillennialist (such as Walvoord 200) and places this at the Second Coming of Christ, then an explanation is necessary for why Jesus spoke of entering "eternal" life at the beginning of the millennium; (2) if one is a premillennialist and identifies this judgment as the Great White Throne Judgment that follows the 1,000 year millennium (Rev. 20:11-13), then an explanation is necessary for why Jesus spoke of an immediate judgment that would take place at His coming but that would in reality not happen for 1,000 years.

Nonetheless, one must not allow questions of timing to keep one from teaching, preaching, or otherwise bearing witness to the coming Judgment Day. The judgment depicted here is one of the most sobering truths in all of Scripture. On this day, souls will be separated—forever. All will go into eternity, some into glory and others into punishment, never to be together again.

Summary (24:45—25:46)

The disciples wanted details about Jesus' coming. They wondered how they would know when it was close. Jesus gave some general signs but nothing time specific. He told them their ignorance of the specific date of His coming was good reason to be ready for His return at all times. He gave three parables to illustrate the kind of readiness He had in mind and then described one scene of the final judgment to show why always being ready to meet Him is essential. Everyone will stand before Him in judgment and—based on their relationship to Him as manifested in their works while on this earth—will be directed to one of two eternal destinies.

Application: Teaching and Preaching the Passage

In all three parables, readiness for Jesus' return and judgment is the focus. In each parable, there is a positive and a negative that explains what the Lord means by being ready for His return (Nolland 1020). For the wicked servant, the master came too early. For the unwise virgins, the groom came when they were unprepared. For the unprofitable servant, the master came with unyielding expectations. In the first parable, the faithful servant was promoted to a permanent position of high management. In the second parable, the wise virgins were permitted to share in the festivities. In the third parable, the faithful and hardworking servants were rewarded with positions of greater honor and responsibilities. In each parable, the judgment was fair, firm, and final.

These three parables challenge some contemporary wrong thinking about God. For example, God as a gracious God has been variously misunderstood in the church. For some, grace is a license to sin. They think that because God's grace covers all sin, believers can sin without conscience or consequence. Romans 6:1-14 says such thinking is fallacious. So does the parable of the wicked servant (24:45-51). For others, preparation for the Lord's return is a single act of the will, a decision of the mind that does not have to translate into a lifestyle. Some think that once prepared, always prepared, regardless of one's apparent readiness for the Lord's return. The parable of the foolish virgins shows how erroneous such thinking is. For others, grace is a license to do nothing. They think because believers are saved by grace through faith, not of works, believers are not required to work for God. They ignore texts that teach that believers are saved for good works (Eph. 2:10). Some professing Christians appear to believe that the Master has no right to expect them to work for His benefit, that any such expectation is unfair and an infringement on their freedom in Christ. The parable of the talents addresses such thinking and teaches that laziness in kingdom matters is evil (24:48; 25:26). It also teaches that God is no "grasping tyrant" but ... "He is Lord of all and will ultimately make good that claim" (Nolland 1018).

The teacher or preacher can present this passage in an overview fashion following Wilkins' (816-822) outline: We are to be prepared (24:43-44). Here is how: (1) be responsible (the two kinds of servants, 24:45-51); (2) be ready (the virgins, 25:1-13); (3) be productive (the talents, 25:14-30); (4) be accountable (the judgment of the sheep and goats, 25:31-46).

The parable of the wise and wicked servants might be developed as two servants, two services, and two rewards. The wise and foolish bridesmaids might be considered under the characteristics and rewards of each. The wise prepared, participated, and were permitted entrance. The foolish did not prepare, were unable to participate, and were refused admission. There are several truths in the parable of the ten virgins that are characteristic of the Lord's return. Some are as follows: (1) the Lord's coming is certain; (2) the Lord's coming should be anticipated by all of His people; (3) a significant delay in the Lord's coming is part of God's plan; (4) the Lord's coming will be visible; (5) preparation for the Lord's coming is possible and recommended; (6) only those who are prepared at the time of His coming will be permitted to go with Him; (7) preparation can be done only on an individual basis; and (8) entrance into the marriage supper at His coming is limited to those who are prepared.

The parable of the talents explains the state of readiness for the Lord's return in the sense of ongoing faithfulness and productivity. This parable might be considered by listing the characteristics of each person in the parable. The characteristics of the hardworking servant are these: (1) he has abilities to produce for his master (v. 15); (2) he wastes no time getting started in his work for his master (v. 16); (3) he works the whole time his master is away (v. 16); (4) he works to produce gain for his master (vv. 16-17); (5) he knows he is responsible for his work product (v. 20); (6) he receives commendation for producing gain with his master's goods (v. 21); (7) he receives a generous reward from his master (v.21); and (8) he receives increasing opportunities for further service (vv. 28-29).

The characteristics of a lazy servant are these: (1) he has the ability to produce for his master (v. 15); (2) he hides his master's talent rather than work it (v. 18); (3) he blames others instead of accepting responsibility himself (v. 24); (4) he believes the master wrongfully expects to profit from his labor and the labors of others (v. 24), unlike the hard-working servant who never questions the master's expectations to receive profit from his labors; (5) he has no gain to bring to his master (v. 25); (6) he foolishly expects commendation for simply preserving the master's goods (v. 25); (7) he is evil and lazy (v. 26); (8) he receives condemnation (v. 26); (9) he forfeits all opportunities for further service (v. 28); and (10) he receives severe punishment for his laziness (v. 30).

The characteristics of the master are these: (1) he owns the servants and the talents; (2) he knows each servant's abilities; (3) he assigns responsibilities according to abilities; (4) he leaves for a long time which gives his servants opportunity to demonstrate faithfulness and ability; (5) he returns to check the faithfulness and productivity of his servants; (6) he holds each servant accountable; and (7) he judges each servant fairly and finally.

The final judgment needs to be taught and preached. As Bruner (2:534) observed, "Only where there is real judgment can there be real grace." One might develop the sermon or lesson in the following manner: (1) there will be a final and great judgment (v. 31); (2) there will be a final and great assembly of everyone (v. 32); (3) there will be a final and great division of all humanity into two groups (v. 32); (4) there will be one great difference that divides the two groups: how each served Christ in ministry to others (vv. 35-40; 42-45); and (5) there will be the final and great eternal rewards (vv. 34, 41, 46).

D. Thursday Through Saturday: The Royal Messiah's Death and Burial (26:1—27:66)

The words "when Jesus had finished all these sayings" (v. 1) mark the end of the Olivet Discourse. Matthew used a similar construction at the end of each of the five major discourses (7:28; 11:1; 13:53; 19:1). With these words, Matthew also concluded all of Jesus' sayings and began his record of the final events of Jesus' earthly life. In two days Jesus would be betrayed; in three, dead. The crucifixion would take place on the same day (by Jewish reckoning, Nisan 15) the Passover meal was eaten (the day after the Passover animal was killed; see accompanying timeline). The crucifixion, then, would be the day after the Passover lamb was killed, which was only two days away from this prophecy.

The reader soon realizes that Jesus' death, burial, and resurrection are the end goals of Matthew's Gospel, the reason the virgin-born baby came to this world. He came to die as a sacrifice to pay for the sins of the world (26:28; 1:21) and then to rise again to be exalted and seated at the Father's right hand.

1. Events leading up to the Royal Messiah's Crucifixion (26:1—27:31)

Sunday, Monday, and Tuesday were eventful days in the week of Jesus' death. Neither Gospel specifically records any events from Wednesday. After the Olivet Discourse, which took place Tuesday evening, Matthew and the other writers pick up the story with the preparation and observance of the Passover meal, which apparently was on Thursday.

a. Jesus' fourth prophecy of His death (26:1-5)

1 And it came to pass, when Jesus had finished all these sayings, he said unto his disciples,
2 Ye know that after two days is *the feast of* the passover, and the Son of man is betrayed to be crucified.
3 Then assembled together the chief priests, and the scribes, and the elders of the people, unto the palace of the high priest, who was called Caiaphas,
4 And consulted that they might take Jesus by subtilty, and kill *him.*
5 But they said, Not on the feast *day,* lest there be an uproar among the people.

The Feast of Passover was instituted by God the night He delivered Israel from Egypt (Ex. 12:1-28, 43-49; Lev. 23:4-8; Num. 9:9-14; Dt. 16:1-8). This annual feast commemorated the death of Egypt's firstborn and the sparing of all who were inside houses marked with the blood of a lamb. The Lord had promised as He passed through Egypt to kill the firstborn of man and beast,

FROM PASSOVER TO THE RESURRECTION
(NOTE: Times are approximate)

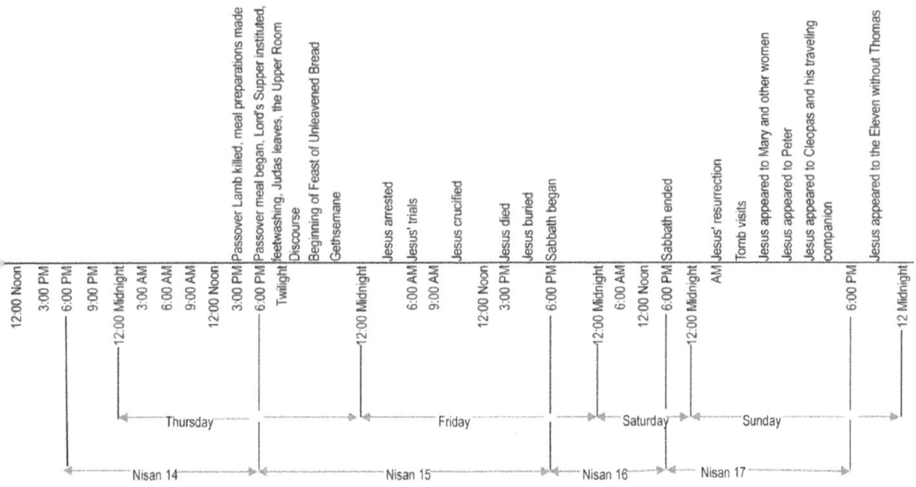

when He saw the blood on the doorposts and lintels, He would pass over those houses and the death angel would not kill their firstborn. Over fourteen hundred years later, the Jews still observed this commemorative feast. On this evening, though, it took on additional meaning. See verses 26-29.

"After two days" identifies the day of this prophecy as probably Tuesday evening since Jesus and the Twelve began eating the Passover lamb on Thursday "at even": that is, just after sunset (Carson, *Matthew* 523). The lamb was killed on the afternoon of the fourteenth day of Abib, the first month in the Jewish calendar (Num. 28:16-17; Lev. 23:5; called Nisan after the Babylonian captivity, ISBE III:543; Mk. 14:12), and preparations made for the meal. At sunset, which marked the beginning of the fifteenth day of Abib, the meal began. This was the rite observed in private homes (Ex. 12:3) when each family ate their own lamb.

Scholars debate whether Jesus actually ate the Passover meal. Matthew, Mark, and Luke clearly state Jesus ate the Passover with His disciples (Mk. 14:12). John 18:28 sounds like Jesus might have been crucified on Passover, which would mean the meal He and His disciples ate would not have been the Passover (Evans and Porter 376), or He ate it one day early because He knew He would be dead the next day (Keener, *Matthew* 623). See P. Harrison (87-96) and Carson (*John* 455-458) for discussions of issues and possible solutions concerning identifying the Passover meal Jesus and His disciples ate.

One solution understands John's Passover reference (Jn. 18:28) to be a second Passover rite observed the afternoon following the Passover meal, the afternoon of the fifteenth (Archer, *Difficulties* 376). According to Archer, this was the national observation when the people gathered for a holy assembly and killed another Passover lamb (Ex. 12:16-17; Lev. 23:4-8; 2 Chr. 30:15-19; 35:11-16)—as opposed to the family or small group observation the previous evening.

The Jewish day was reckoned from sundown to sundown; so if Archer is right, Jesus was crucified on the first day of Unleavened Bread at the time the temple Passover lambs were sacrificed (Archer, *Difficulties* 376). In other words, Jesus would have eaten the Passover meal on Thursday evening as everyone else did and was crucified on Friday at the time the Passover lambs were being slain in the temple for the nation.

Another approach that seems more satisfactory is to understand John's reference to the Passover to include the continuing Feast of Unleavened Bread begun the previous evening. Luke 22:1 indicates that the two feasts, the Passover and the Feast of Unleavened Bread, were at this time spoken of as one. Matthew's description below (v. 17) shows he spoke of the two feasts as one also. The historical record shows how the two feasts came to be regarded as one. The original Passover lamb was killed in the afternoon of the 14th and its blood placed on the doorposts and lintel of each house (Ex. 12:1-28), symbolizing that death had already visited that home. At twilight the meal began. Twilight (Ex. 12:6) is literally "between the two evenings" (TWOT II:694). The Passover meal that began in the twilight of the 14th and 15th concluded a few hours later in the evening/night hours of the 15th, the first day of the

Feast of Unleavened Bread. Later, still in the first evening/night of the 15th, just after midnight, Israel was directed to leave Egypt in a hurry. Because Israel did not have time to prepare food for the journey they took with them unleavened bread. The Feast of Unleavened Bread reminded them of their hasty exodus from Egypt on the 15th. So while these two feasts were distinct, they shared this one evening, which explains how they could be spoken of as one.

Second Chronicles 35:1-19 records an occasion where efforts were made to follow strictly Scriptural guidelines for the observance of these feasts. Apparently, the chronicler meant that Passover went from the 14th through the Feast of Unleavened Bread (Keil and Delitzsch III:501). Only lamb or goat was eaten on the evening of the 14th but from the 15th on roasted lamb and goat as well as boiled oxen were eaten. This, then, is historical precedent for the two feasts to be treated as one.

The O.T. records plus Luke and Matthew's references argue that John's Passover reference is probably referring to the Feast of Unleavened Bread that followed the Passover Meal. This means all four Gospels agree that Jesus ate the Passover meal the night before He was crucified. For a similar argument, see Carson (*Matthew* 531) and his explanation based on Numbers 28:18-19. Archer's proposal mentioned above is possible but understanding that John referred to the two feasts by the same name seems the more probable explanation.

Jesus told His disciples He was only two days away from His betrayal and crucifixion (v. 2). He had spoken before of His death (16:21; 17:22-23; 20:18-19), but this was the first time He gave them a specific day on which He would be crucified (Hendriksen 895). Jesus foretold He would be handed over (Greek *paradidōmi;* betray, hand over; Louw and Nida I:485; Mt. 5:25; Mk. 9:31; Acts 3:13) to be crucified. Bruner (2:594) points out that the verb translated "betray" or "hand over" is used fourteen times in chapters 26 and 27 (26:2, 15, 16, 21, 23, 24, 25, 45, 46; 27:2, 3, 4, 18, 26). Judas handed Jesus over to the Jewish leaders, the Jewish leaders handed Jesus over to Pilate, and Pilate handed Jesus over to the soldiers to be crucified.

At the same time Jesus was foretelling His coming betrayal and death, the religious leaders were meeting at the home of the high priest, Caiaphas (v. 3). "Palace" (v. 3, Greek *aulē*) can refer to a courtyard or to a dwelling with an interior courtyard (Louw and Nida I:82, 90; v. 69; Lk. 11:21). For chief priests and elders see 16:21.

Caiaphas was high priest from ca. A.D. 18-36 (ISBE I:570). He presided over one portion of Jesus' trial, which ended with Jesus being condemned (vv. 58-68). This meeting in Caiaphas' house was a separate meeting from that mentioned by John (11:45-54), since the latter was precipitated by Lazarus' resurrection and resulted in Jesus being more careful to avoid an early arrest. Matthew's point is that Caiaphas hosted this meeting of powerful men whose design was to get rid of Jesus permanently.

Some older Greek manuscripts of Matthew do not include the scribes in verse 3. But Mark 14:1 and Luke 22:2 definitely indicate the scribes were present.

The reason for this meeting was to "consult" together or plan (Greek *sumbouleuō*; 12:14 noun form) Jesus' arrest and death. His triumphal entry, cleansing of the temple, parables against the Jewish leaders, and stern rebukes (chapters 21-23) left them sore (Hendriksen 896). They wanted to arrest Him by stealth (Evans, *Matthew* 468; v. 4) so neither the general population nor Jesus would know—so they thought—what they were doing until it was too late. The Jewish leaders agreed they would not arrest or kill Jesus on (or during) the feast because they feared the people, many of whom believed in Jesus (v. 5). However, Judas' proposal (vv. 14-16) presented them with an acceptable alternative (Barclay 2:383).

b. Jesus' early anointing in preparation for His burial (26:6-13)

6 Now when Jesus was in Bethany, in the house of Simon the leper,
7 There came unto him a woman having an alabaster box of very precious ointment, and poured it on his head, as he sat *at meat*.
8 But when his disciples saw it, they had indignation, saying, To what purpose is this waste?
9 For this ointment might have been sold for much, and given to the poor.
10 When Jesus understood it, he said unto them, Why trouble ye the woman? for she hath wrought a good work upon me.
11 For ye have the poor always with you; but me ye have not always.
12 For in that she hath poured this ointment on my body, she did *it* for my burial.
13 Verily I say unto you, Wheresoever this gospel shall be preached in the whole world, *there* shall also this, that this woman hath done, be told for a memorial of her.

Matthew inserted this pericope into his narrative with no time indicators. John 12:1 said it took place six days before the Passover, which was probably the Saturday evening before the crucifixion, the evening before Jesus' triumphal entry. Matthew and Mark (14:3-11) apparently placed it here because it provided a link between the evil plans of Jesus' enemies and Judas' betrayal (Wilkins 828). It also explains how the Jewish leaders were able to arrest Jesus without the knowledge of the general population. What better way than to have a traitor inside Jesus' own circle of disciples? This event is not the same one Luke recorded in Luke 7:36-38.

The village of Bethany was located less than two miles (3 kilometers) east of Jerusalem (Jn. 11:18). Jesus at least spent Saturday night (Jn. 12:1, 12), Sunday night, and Monday night of the Passion Week in Bethany (Mt. 21:17). Probably from Tuesday on that week He stayed in the Garden of Gethsemane, up to the night of His betrayal (Lk. 21:37). Bethany was the home of Simon the leper (v. 6) as well as the hometown of Lazarus and his sisters, Mary and Martha. There Jesus raised Lazarus from the dead (Jn. 11). The Gospels do not mention the healing of Simon but he had to have been healed or no one could have been around him. For information about how lepers had to live separate from society, see comments on 8:1-4.

Simon, Lazarus, Mary, and Martha made a dinner for Jesus (Jn. 12:2). Simon opened his home for this meal. According to John, Lazarus reclined with Jesus, Martha served the meal, and Mary anointed Jesus. Matthew did not identify her, which suggests that what she did was more important than who (Nolland 1056). Matthew just told what she did and how the disciples reacted to it.

As Jesus ate, Mary entered the room with a small alabaster jar of extremely expensive perfume and poured it on Jesus' head (v. 7) and His feet (Jn. 12:3). She then wiped His feet with her hair. It seems probable that she emptied the contents of the container onto Jesus. Such alabaster jars normally had a long neck which was broken to open the container (Louw and Nida I:69; Mk. 14:3). Some writers suggest that anointings at feasts were common (Evans, *Matthew* 469; Keener, *Matthew* 618; Ps. 23:5; Lk. 7:46).

Mary was able to pour the perfume on Jesus' feet because He was reclining on a low couch. "As he sat *at meat*" (v. 7, Greek *anakeimai*) can refer simply to the act of eating or it can refer to the reclining position one is in while eating (Louw and Nida I:218, 251). Reclining seems probable in this instance especially when one considers John's comments (12:3) about her wiping His feet with her hair. See also Luke 7:37-38 where the sinful woman also anointed Jesus' feet and wiped them with her hair. Luke specifically says she "stood at his feet behind him."

Jesus was the main guest of honor (Jn. 12:2) but Lazarus was being honored as well, doubtless because of His recent resurrection (Jn. 11:44). It is apparent this was a planned celebration. This family loved Jesus. Martha served and Mary anointed Jesus, thus designating His honored place at this meal. This anointing was also her gesture of "genuine religious love, gratitude and devotion" (Hendriksen 899). It may also have been a testimony of her faith. If she accepted Him as the Messiah, the Anointed One, then why not anoint Him (Evans, *Matthew* 469)?

John 12:5 says Judas declared the value of the perfume to be three hundred denarii. A denarius was the normal day's wage for a soldier or day laborer (ISBE I:923; 20:2; see comments on 18:28 and 20:9). Three hundred workdays meant this ointment was worth almost a year's wages.

The other disciples agreed with Judas (Hendriksen 899) and with great anger labeled Mary's action a waste (v. 8). They believed the perfume would have been better used if sold and the money given to needy people. They judged Mary's gift to be worth too much just to pour on Jesus and they verbally criticized Mary for her lavish gift.

Jesus knew what they were saying (v. 10). In contrast to their condemnation, He judged her actions "a good work," a good work done to Him. The Twelve scolded Mary for extravagant giving (Mk. 14:5) but Jesus scolded them. He accepted her offering. It was expensive. It was from the heart. It was something for which there was only a small window of opportunity to give and she was wise to do what she could while she could (v. 11). It had greater meaning than even she knew (v. 12).

The disciples' desire to give to the poor (v. 9) was honorable (except for that of Judas, Jn. 12:6) and reflected their grasp of Jesus' teaching about wealth and how best to use it (6:2-4;

6:19-20; 19:21). However, there would always be opportunity to give to the poor because there would always be such needs (v. 11; Dt. 15:11). Giving to honor Jesus in this manner was an opportunity that would soon be gone. Jesus' earthly stay was about to end.

Though Mary did not intend it this way (Hendriksen 901, says she might have), Jesus said her anointing was in reality preparatory for His burial (v. 12). These were surely strange words to her ears. Jewish custom included anointing the body of the deceased prior to burial as Nicodemus and Joseph did before they buried Jesus (Jn. 19:39-40). Mary, however, by showing how highly she valued Him, anointed Him before His death. This made her anointing worshipful, caring, and prophetic.

Were Mary and her siblings wealthy? Did she give from her wealth or did she give sacrificially? Was this gift only from Mary or did her family contribute as well? Was this the family's life savings? Scripture does not answer these questions. Jesus said, "She hath done what she could" (Mk. 14:8), meaning Mary did according to her understanding and ability (Picirilli, *Mark* 375). The perfume was at least Mary's gift to Jesus, and He who knows all hearts accepted it. No one, not even the Twelve, had the right to come between this worshiper and her Lord.

Jesus' words were prophetic. He spoke of His departure (v. 11). He also spoke of the gospel, what would be the good news of His death and its accomplishments (v. 13), and He promised that her action on this day would be retold throughout the whole world along with the gospel. Though such honor was never her intent, Jesus' blessing on her showed His satisfaction for her gift. One can never out-give the Lord. As promised, her story lives on in the records of Matthew, Mark (14:3-9), and John (12:1-8).

c. Judas made plans to betray Jesus (26:14-16)

14 Then one of the twelve, called Judas Iscariot, went unto the chief priests,
15 And said *unto them*, What will ye give me, and I will deliver him unto you? And they covenanted with him for thirty pieces of silver.
16 And from that time he sought opportunity to betray him.

Apparently, all of the Twelve were placated but Judas. Judas opened himself up to Satan (Lk. 22:3-4) and went to the chief priests where he offered to hand Jesus over to them. Scripture does not tell why Judas handed Jesus over, except that he was motivated by Satan (Hagner 33B:761). Anger over Jesus' handling of Mary's extravagant gift might have been a contributing factor (Mt. 26:8; Jn. 12:4-5). "What will you give me?" (v. 15) hints at another reason (Gundry 523): perhaps greed played a role (Jn. 12:6). Perhaps he thought he was saving his own life by distancing himself from Jesus (Evans, *Matthew* 471).

Such hypocrisy of character inside the Twelve is hard to imagine, but the records are clear. Judas "sought ... to betray him." No doubt, even the chief priests were surprised, but glad, that one of the Twelve would turn traitor (Lk. 22:5).

This meeting between Judas and the chief priests took place sometime after the meeting described in verses 3-5 (Lk.

22:1-6). The Jewish leaders now had what they wanted—a way to get to Jesus when He was away from the crowds. Waiting until after the Feast was no longer as critical.

Thirty pieces of silver, the real value of which is unknown (Hagner 33B:761), was the selling price, a ridiculously low price prophetically founded in Zechariah 11:12-13 (Barker 677). Barclay (2:387) says a piece of silver (Greek *argurion*) was equivalent to four days' wages but gives no support for this statement. This would mean Judas betrayed Jesus for less than five months' wages, a pitifully small amount that pales in comparison to Mary's sacrificial gift of a year's worth of income.

The chief priests agreed to pay (Greek *histēmi;* to pay, establish; Louw and Nida I:575, 682; Mk. 14:11; Lk. 22:5) Judas and finalized their arrangements. Perhaps they paid him up front, but Mark and Luke suggest they did not. From this point on, Judas watched for a time when there would be no crowds around (Lk. 22:6) so he could hand Jesus over to them.

The N.T. writers do not reveal what Judas thought would happen to Jesus. He might not have expected Jesus to be killed (27:3-5). His actions fulfilled prophesy (Ps. 41:9) and according to Jesus were reprehensible. Judas was guilty of a horrendous sin, a sin so great that no mortal can imagine the torments of hell that are his (Mt. 26:24; Mk. 14:21; Lk. 22:22). Even though Jesus knew perfectly Judas' scheme, yet five days after Judas decided to betray Jesus, he was still numbered with the Twelve. Jesus even washed his feet (Jn. 13:1-30). Oh, the vileness of the sinner! Oh, the grace of the Savior!

The disciple Judas had been designated an apostle (10:2, 4; Acts 1:17) and given power to perform miracles (10:5-8). He would have been foundational in the building of Christ's church (Eph. 2:20) and a ruler in the final kingdom age (19:28; Wilkins 830). For some untold reason Judas lost confidence in Jesus and forfeited a glorious salvation (Acts 1:25). His devotion turned to hatred; rather than just walk away, his hatred became so passionate that he turned traitor (Bruner 2:608). Judas' calculated treachery (v. 16) was no surprise to Jesus (Jn. 6:64) and his sin has become synonymous with his name—Judas, the betrayer. Keener (*Matthew* 641) rightfully understands Judas' apostasy to serve as a warning that "one's current commitment is no guarantee of one's perseverance."

d. Jesus observed His final Passover and instituted the Lord's Supper (26:17-30)

17 Now the first *day* of the *feast of* unleavened bread the disciples came to Jesus, saying unto him, Where wilt thou that we prepare for thee to eat the passover?
18 And he said, Go into the city to such a man, and say unto him, The Master saith, My time is at hand; I will keep the passover at thy house with my disciples.
19 And the disciples did as Jesus had appointed them; and they made ready the passover.
20 Now when the even was come, he sat down with the twelve.
21 And as they did eat, he said, Verily I say unto you, that one of you shall betray me.

22 And they were exceeding sorrowful, and began every one of them to say unto him, Lord, is it I?
23 And he answered and said, He that dippeth *his* hand with me in the dish, the same shall betray me.
24 The Son of man goeth as it is written of him: but woe unto that man by whom the Son of man is betrayed! it had been good for that man if he had not been born.
25 Then Judas, which betrayed him, answered and said, Master, is it I? He said unto him, Thou hast said.
26 And as they were eating, Jesus took bread, and blessed *it*, and brake *it*, and gave *it* to the disciples, and said, Take, eat; this is my body.
27 And he took the cup, and gave thanks, and gave *it* to them, saying, Drink ye all of it;
28 For this is my blood of the new testament, which is shed for many for the remission of sins.
29 But I say unto you, I will not drink henceforth of this fruit of the vine, until that day when I drink it new with you in my Father's kingdom.
30 And when they had sung an hymn, they went out into the mount of Olives.

Jews were forbidden to eat leavened bread on Passover, the fourteenth of Nisan (Ex. 12:18; Abib) and throughout the following week when the Feast of Unleavened Bread was observed (Lev. 23:6). The Feast of Unleavened Bread was one of the three pilgrimage festivals required of Jewish men (Ex. 23:14-17), thus Jesus and His disciples were in Jerusalem in obedience to the law. For more discussion concerning the Passover, see comments on verse 2 above. "The first day of the feast of unleavened bread" reflects the contemporary way of referring to Passover and the Feast of Unleavened Bread as a single feast, even though strictly speaking they were two separate feasts.

Preparations needed to be made ahead of time. The lamb had to be purchased, dressed, and roasted. A room suitable for a group this size had to be procured as well. Either Jesus had already made arrangements with a homeowner or He once again demonstrated perfect foreknowledge and control (v. 18; Mk. 14:13-16). Peter and John made the necessary preparations (v. 19; Lk. 22:8).

"Master" (v. 18) is literally the Teacher (Greek *didaskalos*). "My time is at hand" was Jesus' way of speaking of His death (Jn. 2:4; 7:6, 30; 8:20; 12:23, 27; 13:1; 17:1). "At your house" is literally "with you." Gundry (525) suggests this means others besides the Twelve shared in this Passover meal with Jesus.

Scholars divide over whether Jesus actually ate the Passover or ate His "last supper" the day before Passover. See the discussion on verse 2. For details of what was included in a normal Passover ritual meal, the reader is referred to a Bible encyclopedia.

When evening came, i.e., at twilight (v. 20), Jesus and the Twelve (Luke 22:14, "the apostles") gathered in the upper room to observe this fourteen-hundred-year-old rite. They sat down, or more probably, reclined (see discussion above, v. 7). According to Keener (*Matthew* 625), men would recline with their heads nearest to the table. When women ate in the same room, they would sit. During the meal and following the feet washing event (Jn. 13:1-20) Jesus shocked the Twelve with an announcement that one of the Twelve would betray Him (v. 21). "Verily" (Greek *amēn*) means "truly."

Eleven of the Twelve responded with deep grief and sadness (v. 22). One by one all twelve asked Him, "I am not the one, [am I]?" None doubted Jesus' words; each wondered if Jesus meant him. None suspected Judas. He kept his plans and movements hidden from the others (Barclay 2:389).

Jesus answered them indirectly. It would be one who shared His dipping dish, one who was eating with Him at that moment (v. 23; Hagner 33B:767). Only John records that Jesus gave Judas the bread (Jn. 13:26), which means Judas had to be near Jesus as well. Jesus' point was that the betrayer would be a person who enjoyed close familiarity with Him (Keener, *Background* 120). He was, in fact, a friend (Ps. 41:9; Jn. 13:18) and at this meal he was one of the closest to Jesus at the table.

Jesus would die as prophesied (v. 24) but that did not lessen the sin of the betrayer. Judas was responsible for his actions. Jesus did not mince words about the dire future of this traitor. His punishment would be so great that he would have been better off never to have been born (v. 24). What a tragedy! From the inner circle to outer darkness, Judas fell from eternal favor to eternal fire.

Jesus knew His impending death was settled from eternity past (1 Pet. 1:19-20; Isaiah 52:13—53:12), but Judas did not have to participate in it. Judas' betrayal was his decision and action even though he was influenced directly by Satan (Lk. 22:3). Neither God nor Satan forced Judas to betray Jesus. Though we do not know what Judas' main motivation was, there is no doubt about Satan's. The kingdom of darkness had been invaded by the Light and Satan wanted Him out (Jn. 1:5; Mt. 12:28-29).

Apparently, Judas was the last to speak. He asked, "Is it I, Rabbi?" (v. 25). Unlike the others, he did not call Jesus "Lord." The hypocrisy of Judas surfaces in his question. Jesus answered with an indirect affirmative (Zerwick 86): (literally) "You said [so]." According to John 13:27-30, at this point Jesus told Judas to "do quickly" what he planned to do. It is hard to imagine Judas would follow through with his plans once he was made aware that Jesus knew about them. Such was the power of his disillusionment toward Jesus and of Satan's presence in him. Rather than heed the Savior's warning (v. 24), Judas yielded to Satan and turned his back on the Savior.

According to Luke 22:21-23, Jesus warned of Judas' betrayal after the institution of the Lord's Supper, whereas Matthew and Mark place Jesus' warning before the Lord's Supper. This makes it difficult to determine whether Judas partook of the Communion cup and bread. It seems that he probably did (Bruner, 2:630). Compare Matthew 26:20-25 and John 13:21-30 with Luke 22:14-23.

During the Passover meal, Jesus took the unleavened bread and blessed it, broke it, possibly into two pieces, and passed the bread to His disciples who then broke off pieces for themselves. He told them to eat and called the bread His "body" (v. 26). What had been "the bread of affliction" (Dt. 16:3), i.e., bread that reminded Israel of her hard slavery in Egypt, now represented His body

(Nolland 1074). It will remind His followers of His affliction, His own torn body. Jesus did not suggest that this bread would become His body in some "real" sense, as Catholic doctrine teaches (transubstantiation). The parallel passage in Luke 22:19 clarifies Jesus' intentions: "Do this in remembrance of me." The Apostle Paul later reported that Jesus told him the same thing (1 Cor. 11:23-24). In other words, the unleavened bread in the Lord's Supper is a memory aid that represents Jesus' body, not a re-sacrificing of Jesus (Heb. 9:28). The unleavened bread reminded Israel that she left Egypt hurriedly and in hardship. This same bread would now remind Jesus' followers that He had suffered greatly for them.

After passing the bread, Jesus then took a cup of grape juice (v. 27), gave thanks for it, and passed it around for all of His disciples to drink. Scripture is silent about whether He drank from the cup also; one would think He did (v. 29, again, ESV). In the words "Drink ye all of it," "all" modifies "ye": all the disciples were to drink and each was to drink some (Newman and Stine 829). See Mark 14:23: "They all drank of it."

Just as the bread represented Jesus' body, the juice represented Jesus' blood (v. 28). His blood is the blood of the new (Lk. 22:20) covenant (Jer. 31:31-34; 1 Cor. 11:25; 2 Cor. 3:6, 14; Heb. 8:6-13; 10:16-18, 29; 12:24). The old covenant was the Sinai Covenant (Ex. 19:5). It too was initiated and sealed with blood (Ex. 24:5-6, 8).

A covenant is an agreement between two parties that binds them together (ISBE I:790-793). Covenants were made between people and between God and mankind. God made a covenant with Israel at Mt. Sinai that He would be their God and they would be His people, provided they would abide by the stipulations of the covenant. The most basic stipulations were the Ten Commandments recorded in Exodus 20. Strictly speaking, though, the Book of the Covenant (from Ex. 24:7) in its narrowest sense included Exodus 20:22—23:33 but more broadly speaking included 19:1—23:33 (Kaiser, *Exodus* 449).

The first covenant was confirmed by the application of blood on the altar and on the people. In this manner, the blood spoke of the two sides of the agreement (covenant). The blood on the altar (Ex. 24:6) represented the atonement and spoke of God's "forgiveness and acceptance of the offering"; the blood on the people spoke of the "blood oath that binds them in obedience" (Kaiser, *Exodus* 449). In other words, the people agreed to do everything the Lord commanded in the covenant (Ex. 24:7), and the blood on them witnessed they had promised to obey the covenant stipulations. "The blood, shared between the altar and the people, [bound] God and the people together, with the people aligned with the holiness of God, and with solemn commitment on both sides" (Nolland 1079).

The old and new covenants have similarities. (1) In both covenants, shed blood, i.e., lifeblood poured out, meant death of the sacrifice (Newman and Stine 830) as the basis for a covenant relationship. Moses stated (Ex. 24:8) after he sprinkled the blood on the people: "Behold the blood of the covenant, which the LORD hath made with you concerning all these words." In other words, "the blood by which the covenant was ratified and sealed was *the basis for the union between Yahweh and the people*" in the O.T. (Kaiser,

Exodus 449; emphasis mine). In the same way, Jesus' shed blood, which He offered on the cross for mankind's atonement (Heb. 9:12-14) and symbolized by the "fruit of the vine" at the Lord's Table, *is the basis of the union between the Lord and His people under the new covenant* (Forlines 191-194). In both covenants, blood was the basis for a union between sinful mankind and God. (2) In both covenants, faith was the condition for having the benefits of the blood atonement applied and the union effected (Rom. 3:28; 4:13-14; Gal. 2:15-16; 3:1-18, esp. v. 7; Picirilli, *Romans* 79).

Verse 28, then, is at the heart of Matthew's Gospel account (1:21; 20:18). Jesus, by His own blood, ratified the new covenant (Is. 42:6). In these verses, the reader gains understanding of the cross event. Chapter 27 records Jesus' crucifixion as historical fact but offers no doctrinal explanation for why it happened or what it accomplished. Jesus' teaching about the Lord's Supper is Matthew's only explanation of the purpose and accomplishments of the cross. The cross event is the basis of the new covenant, the basis for a union between holy God and sinful mankind.

Some Greek manuscripts (and some contemporary translations) do not have "new" in verse 28. However, Luke 22:20 and 1 Corinthians 11:25 both have the word, so it is certain that He said it (whether Matthew included it in his summary or not.)

Jesus spoke of His blood being shed, i.e., "poured out" (Greek *ekcheō*). Whereas the O.T. sacrifices were animal sacrifices, His was a human sacrifice (Nolland 1081). He was comparing His sacrifice to the O.T. sin offerings when the blood of animals was poured out at the base of the altar of burnt offering (Lev. 4:7, 18, 25, 30, 34; Evans, *Matthew* 478). These were atonement offerings, offerings that by identification (of the sinner with the sacrifice), by substitution (of the sacrifice for the sinner), and by representation (of the sinner by the sacrifice to God) paid for sin and restored broken fellowship between the guilty and God. According to Carson (*Matthew* 533), the same pouring out happened when Passover lambs were slain. The priests "took the blood and passed it along lines until it was poured out at the foot of the altar." Jesus, then, was speaking of blood sacrifices in general when He spoke of His blood being shed. He was referring to both sin offerings and the Passover lamb offerings when He said His own blood would be "poured out." By shedding His blood, Jesus brought the new covenant into force (Heb. 9:14-17).

In both covenants, forgiveness (Greek *aphesis*, remission, the cancelation of an obligation) is possible only through the shedding of blood (Heb. 9:22). This is why Jesus needed to shed His blood (Mt. 26:28; see also 1:21). Mankind is in debt to God. Mankind owes God perfect righteousness (Mt. 5:20) and payment for sin (Rom. 6:23). He can provide neither. Mankind is bankrupt. Jesus came to die—the meaning of shed His blood—in mankind's place and pay mankind's sin debt. Through faith in the sacrificial work of Jesus Christ as the only and all-sufficient means of salvation, the condition for inclusion in the benefits of the new covenant (Rom. 5:1, 2; Eph. 2:8-9), sinful man is united with Christ (Rom. 6:5). Through this union with Christ, the believer identifies with Jesus' death on the cross. Because of this identification, Jesus' death is counted as payment for the believer's sin debt and the believer is forgiven by God, justified (declared not guilty) before God, and reconciled (Rom. 5:10) to God. Also, because the believer is joined to Christ he is given (imputed) Christ's righteousness as his own, the righteousness God requires (2 Cor. 5:21). The believer is thus made a member of the new covenant people and a child of God.

The new covenant, then, is about forgiveness (Jer. 31:34). The cup used in the Lord's Supper represents the blood Jesus shed to pay the sinner's sin debt so that he or she can be forgiven (v. 28). See 1 Corinthians 10:16, 18, 21 and 1 Corinthians 11:17-34 for further meaning and implications of the Lord's Supper. See also Picirilli's comments on these passages (*1 Corinthians* 145-147, 164-173).

The entire Passover was the Lord's ("the Lord's Passover," Ex. 12:11). It is also proper to designate this new covenant meal as "the Lord's Supper" (1 Cor. 11:20). Both meals are to be characterized by special respect and care. Both originated with God.

Verse 29 speaks of the kingdom as if it is still future. Some aspects of the kingdom are future, while others are present. See comments on 3:2 and 12:28. The reference here appears to be the kingdom banquet, the marriage supper of the Lamb (8:11; 25:10; Rev. 19:6-9) that will take place in heaven. At that marriage supper, Jesus will lead in celebrating the success of the new covenant by providing and participating in the marriage supper. He will also at that time—for the first time since the night of His betrayal—drink grape juice, the symbol of His sacrifice. Until that time, Jesus will not again ingest the memorial. It seems possible—perhaps probable—that the kingdom meal Jesus spoke of will be a Passover meal (Lk. 22:16).

Following the institution of the Lord's Supper, Judas left to make preparations. If the authorities planned to arrest Jesus on this night, they were possibly waiting on word from Judas before making final arrangements (Hendriksen 922). Guards and soldiers needed to be gathered. The Sanhedrin needed to be notified, as did Caiaphas and Annas. Since this was Passover night one could expect that these men would be up, dressed, and able to leave their homes immediately (Ex. 12:11).

After the Passover meal was completed, Jesus and the Eleven (Jn. 13:30) remained in the room for Jesus' final teaching, the Upper Room Discourse (Jn. 13:31—16:33). He may have taught some of this discourse as they walked to the Mount of Olives. Matthew's order suggests this (26:30-36; Jn. 13:36-38). However, the interaction between Jesus and His disciples also suggests a close, private setting. The same can be said for His high priestly prayer (Jn. 17).

Following the meal and the discourse, they sang a hymn, probably a Psalm. Scholars suggest their final song might have been Psalm 114-118 (Carson, *Matthew 539*). Singing these Psalms was customary for the Passover rite. At any rate, it is worth noting that Jesus sang and led His disciples to do the same.

It was nighttime (Jn. 13:30) both naturally and spiritually. The sun had set and Satan was at work through Judas. The Eleven would sleep outside that night (v. 40) on the Mount of Olives. This was something they did at times

(Lk. 22:39), which was one reason Judas knew where to find Jesus (Jn. 18:2). The darkness, however, was temporary (Mt. 28:1; Jn. 1:5).

e. Jesus foretold the disciples' flight (26:31-35)

31 Then saith Jesus unto them, All ye shall be offended because of me this night: for it is written, I will smite the shepherd, and the sheep of the flock shall be scattered abroad.
32 But after I am risen again, I will go before you into Galilee.
33 Peter answered and said unto him, Though all *men* shall be offended because of thee, *yet* will I never be offended.
34 Jesus said unto him, Verily I say unto thee, That this night, before the cock crow, thou shalt deny me thrice.
35 Peter said unto him, Though I should die with thee, yet will I not deny thee. Likewise also said all the disciples.

According to Matthew's order of events, as Jesus and His disciples walked toward the Mount of Olives, Jesus revealed another shocking upcoming event: the Eleven—including Matthew!—would leave Him this night. He knew His future and theirs. Quoting a Messianic prophecy from Zechariah 13:7 (Blomberg 91, 92), Jesus spoke of His own death again (16:21; 17:22-23; 20:18-19; 26:2) and of His disciples' failure to support Him in His trial (v. 31).

Zechariah 11-13 is notoriously difficult to interpret and the reader is referred to commentaries on that passage. While the Messianic Shepherd is readily discerned in these three chapters, the disciples' place is not. It may be that the prophet Zechariah was speaking of the nation Israel scattering after the Messiah's death (as part of God's judgment against disobedient Israel; Barker 687) and that Jesus applied this passage in principle form to His disciples, i.e., sheep without a shepherd scatter. This would mean that what the disciples would do at His arrest, the nation would do after His death. Or, Jesus might simply have meant that both He and His followers would experience great affliction, out of which would come refinement and ultimately salvation (Zech. 13:7-9; TDNT VII:349).

The prophet also saw that God held the sword that would strike the Good Shepherd (Zech. 13:7). That this was the Holy Spirit's intent is clear from Jesus' use of the first person to refer to God: "I will smite the shepherd" (v. 31). In Matthew 16:21 and 20:17-19, the Jewish and Gentile leaders will kill Jesus but in 26:31, Jesus stated that the one who spoke in Zechariah 13:7, Israel's God, would kill the Shepherd. With these words, Jesus identified His death with the judgment of God (Nolland 1089). See Isaiah 53:4: "smitten of God."

The disciples were not ready to accept the reality or necessity of His death. Jesus' arrest and subsequent death would "offend" them (Greek *skandalizō*, cause to stumble). They would fall away and lose their faith in Him (TDNT VII:349). Because of the events of that night, they would leave Jesus alone and go in different directions. The picture is one of chaos and uncertainty.

Jesus' death, however, was not the end and neither was their failure (v. 32). The Father would raise Him from the dead (v. 32; Rom. 10:9; 1 Cor. 6:14; 15:15; 2 Cor. 4:14; Gal. 1:1; Eph. 1:20; Col. 2:12; 1 Th. 1:10; 1 Pet. 1:21) and after His resurrection He would meet them in Galilee (Mt. 28:7, 10, 16). The mention of a future meeting assured them their failure would not be final (Hendriksen 913). "The smitten shepherd and the scattered sheep will be reunited" (Hagner 33B:777). They would leave Jerusalem, but they would not be leaving Jesus in the grave. He and they would regroup in Galilee.

Peter adamantly rejected the idea that Jesus' words included him (v. 33). So confident was he of his own stability and loyalty that he assured Jesus he would be true to Jesus even if he had to stand alone. He would accompany Jesus to prison or even to death if necessary (Lk. 22:33). Peter's attitude toward Jesus' death was different from what he voiced in 16:22 where he rebuked Jesus. As Luke 22:31-32 reveals, there was more to this conversation than Matthew recorded.

Jesus assured Peter that he would also fail and gave him a sign (v. 34). Before the morning rooster crowed on this night, Peter would deny Jesus three times. "Deny" (Greek *aparneomai*) is "to say that one does not know about or is in any way related to a person or event" (Louw and Nida I:420; Mt. 10:33; Lk. 8:45). "Deny" is the opposite of confess (Evans, *Matthew* 480). Again Peter stubbornly rejected the Lord's prophecy (v. 35), and this time his profession was so strong that the other ten disciples joined in with him. Jesus was wrong about all of them—or so they wanted to believe. The previous week James and John had also voiced their commitment to Jesus even in suffering (20:22) and He had assured them they would suffer with Him; but this night would be different. None of the Twelve would stay with Him.

Opinions vary about the rooster crowing, especially in light of Mark's two crowings (Mk. 14:30). However, God's control is evident throughout this entire event. The God who made a donkey talk (Num. 22:28), a fish transport a prophet (Jon. 1:17; 2:10), and another fish bring tax money up from the Sea of Galilee (Mt. 17:27) also controlled when and how often the roosters in Jerusalem crowed this night. On this, Matthew and Mark agree.

f. Jesus prayed in the Garden of Gethsemane (26:36-46)

36 Then cometh Jesus with them unto a place called Gethsemane, and saith unto the disciples, Sit ye here, while I go and pray yonder.
37 And he took with him Peter and the two sons of Zebedee, and began to be sorrowful and very heavy.
38 Then saith he unto them, My soul is exceeding sorrowful, even unto death: tarry ye here, and watch with me.
39 And he went a little farther, and fell on his face, and prayed, saying, O my Father, if it be possible, let this cup pass from me: nevertheless not as I will, but as thou *wilt*.
40 And he cometh unto the disciples, and findeth them asleep, and saith unto Peter, What, could ye not watch with me one hour?

41 Watch and pray, that ye enter not into temptation: the spirit indeed *is* willing, but the flesh *is* weak.
42 He went away again the second time, and prayed, saying, O my Father, if this cup may not pass away from me, except I drink it, thy will be done.
43 And he came and found them asleep again: for their eyes were heavy.
44 And he left them, and went away again, and prayed the third time, saying the same words.
45 Then cometh he to his disciples, and saith unto them, Sleep on now, and take *your* rest: behold, the hour is at hand, and the Son of man is betrayed into the hands of sinners.
46 Rise, let us be going: behold, he is at hand that doth betray me.

The upper room events and teachings behind Him, Jesus led His disciples into the Garden of Gethsemane on the Mount of Olives. The word Gethsemane means "oil press" and from John's record (Jn. 18:1) one may conclude it was a walled garden (ISBE II:457). This was probably an olive tree garden located on the Mount of Olives, east of the city.

The weight of His death upon His mind, Jesus withdrew from eight of His apostles and any other disciples who accompanied them (Mk. 14:51-52). He took with Him the inner circle, three of His first four disciples (4:18-22), the same three privileged to witness His restoring of Jairus' daughter to life (Lk. 8:51) and His own transfiguration (17:1). This time, rather than more of His deity, they saw more of His humanity. With great emotion (literally, he was sad and greatly distressed) He led them a distance from the others and then directed them to remain awake and watchful with Him. Verse 41 states He meant for them to do more than stay awake. He wanted them to pray with Him. He also wanted privacy as He prayed and they were to shield Him from intrusion (Evans, *Matthew* 483).

He was very sad (Greek *perilupos*), so much so He felt as if His sorrow could kill Him: "unto death" suggests the intensity of His distress (Nolland 1098). Jesus might have been quoting and applying to Himself Psalm 42:5-6 and 11 (Archer and Chirichigno 69). Leaving Peter, James, and John, Jesus moved "about a stone's throw" away (Lk. 22:41) and began to pray.

Face to the ground, Jesus begged for a way out. "If it is possible" (v. 39; Greek first class condition) assumes the possibility for the sake of the prayer, but there was no other way to save lost mankind. Doctrine is strong here. Jesus prayed earnestly that He not be required to experience the cross. With loud cries and tears, He begged to be spared this death (Heb. 5:7, 8). Jesus' prayer and the fact that the Father did not provide another way show that the cross was God's only plan of atonement. It also shows that even Jesus did not get everything He asked for (Osborne 947). Sometimes it is God's will that the greater good come through temporary pain.

"This cup" spoke of His upcoming suffering (Jn. 18:11; cf. "the hour," Mk. 14:35). It is also reminiscent of the Lord's words, "and he took the cup ... saying, 'This is my blood of the new testament" (vv. 26-27). See below on verse 44 for what this cup included that He wanted to avoid.

Jesus returned to find His disciples sleeping. They (v. 40) were unable to stay awake for Jesus for even one hour. Had Jesus prayed for an hour? Jesus directed His rebuke specifically to Peter (v. 40; esp. Mk. 14:37) at first, but the plural "you" in the original shows that His comments applied to James and John as well. The apostles were not as strong (comp. v. 35) as they claimed to be (Lk. 22:33-34).

This time Jesus told them to stay awake and pray (Greek imperatives) so they could avoid temptation (v. 41; Greek *peirasmos;* for comments about temptation and tests, see 4:1; 6:13). They were about to face the most difficult test they had ever faced and they needed spiritual strength more than they needed sleep. He still wanted them to pray with Him, but they needed to pray for themselves as well.

Jesus knew their hearts, their human spirits. They wanted to be strong for Him (v. 35) but they were weak physically (v. 41; Carson, *Matthew* 545). The flesh here is their physical bodies not the Pauline depraved human nature (which would be strong, not weak; Nolland 1102; *contra* Bruner 2:658-659). The spirit is their human will (Hill 342). Jesus' words were not "to excuse human weakness" (Wilkins 842) but to show how they and all of Christ's followers could find strength to obey God's will. They were tired physically and emotionally (v. 43; Lk. 22:45). They understood enough to know these next hours would be difficult for Jesus and them. They gave up and slept. Jesus said they could find strength in prayer. Prayer is the believer's source of strength in temptation and tests.

Leaving them awake, Jesus returned to His prayer spot. Again He prayed, this time not asking for a way out ("if this cup may not pass away from me") but rather submitting to this cup—if it was the only way to satisfy the Father's will (v. 42). It was God's will that this cup, God's judgment against sin, be poured out but it had to be done in a way that satisfied His holiness and paid mankind's debt for sin. See the discussion above on the new covenant (v. 28).

He returned to His disciples to find them sleeping again (v. 43). He woke them and might have rebuked them this time also because Mark (14:40) says they did not know what to answer Him. He left them a third time to pray (v. 44). One assumes He again commanded them to pray with Him. He prayed the same prayer. He agonized. They went back to sleep.

The struggle was intense, but Jesus once again proved Himself to be the perfectly obedient Son (4:4; Heb. 5:7-9). There was no other plan to deliver lost mankind from sin's penalty. He willingly submitted to the desire of His Father.

Wilkins (841) states this was Satan's "last-ditch effort to convince Jesus that the cross was unnecessary." However, Scripture never states Satan was in the Garden with Jesus or that this was a satanically motivated temptation. To conclude this was such a temptation, one must believe that Jesus was praying as Satan wanted Him to and was at least to some degree resisting the Father's will. Jesus never followed Satan or resisted His Father's will. The only role of Satan the Gospel writers describe in this entire experience is to get Jesus to the cross (e.g., through Judas and the Jewish leaders) and to add to Jesus' physical suffering (Jn. 14:30). Scripture offers no evidence that Satan was trying to keep Jesus from the cross at this time.

These prayers originated with Jesus. Just like the time He prayed all night before He chose the Twelve (Lk. 6:12), Jesus again needed the Father's direction and strength ("the flesh is weak" applied to Him too; v. 41). Hebrews 5:7-9 states that Jesus learned obedience, and this obedience included death (Phil. 2:8). The struggle appears to have been on two levels. His humanity struggled with the knowledge of the intense suffering and death He knew would be His at the hands of sinners and His knowledge it was the Father's will that He experience this suffering and death. He also struggled in His divine nature knowing He would experience the full wrath of His Holy Father against the cumulative sins of mankind and this too was His Father's will. Jesus was the propitiatory sacrifice, the atoning sacrifice. This experience was His "cup" to drink.

So intense was this inner struggle that His sweat fell as drops of blood to the ground (Lk. 22:44). The struggle was within Himself, not between Himself and His Heavenly Father. Sinners would kill Him with a Roman cross. The Father would treat Him as if He were a sinner (Is. 53:5, 8-12; 2 Cor. 5:21) even though He had never known sin. He was willing to die at the hands of sinners and He was willing to obey His Father unto death, but He asked three times that He not be asked to go through this if there was another way. Though Jesus' own desire seems different from His Father's at this time (Keener, *Matthew* 639), Jesus was solidly committed to obeying the Father's will (Forlines 179). His prayer was for assurance and strength. The angel's visit (Lk. 22:43), at least in part, addressed that need as angels did at the end of His forty-day temptation (Mk. 1:13).

Further details of this struggle are hidden in the mystery of the incarnation. Mark 14:35-36 records that Jesus prayed—in addition to "if it were possible"—that "all things are possible unto thee," suggesting at least two things. (1) He was searching for another way to satisfy the Father's requirements for saving the world, and (2) He might not have known that there was no other way, suggesting this may have been another divinely-imposed limitation in His knowledge (see Mt. 24:36; Carson, *Matthew* 544). For further study, consult theology books concerning the two natures of Christ and the impeccability or peccability of Christ.

Having ended His third prayer session, Jesus returned to find His disciples asleep again (v. 45). They could have prayed with Him in His trial. They could have encouraged their Master. His next words could be translated as either a statement (Sleep on, rest, KJV, ESV) or a question (Are you still sleeping and resting? NIV, RSV). Carson (*Matthew* 545) says it was a statement of irony. Either way, Jesus addressed their failure. Three times, He told them to watch with Him and pray. There is no indication they prayed even once.

There might have been a time interval between verses 45 and 46 (Walvoord 219). If so, then having permitted the disciples a few more minutes of sleep, Jesus woke them again and told them to get on their feet. The dreadful hour (v. 45), the one He had been speaking of for so long, had arrived. It would begin with the arrival of the "sinners" and His betrayal by Judas.

Jesus spoke of those coming to get Him as "sinners." Though He came to die, He condemned those who took part in His death. He was innocent of any wrongdoing. They were guilty of wrongdoing. They might have had the title of religious leaders or were representing the religious leaders, but to Jesus they were sinners. This included Judas, His former, trusted disciple.

g. Jesus' betrayal and arrest (26:47-56)

47 And while he yet spake, lo, Judas, one of the twelve, came, and with him a great multitude with swords and staves, from the chief priests and elders of the people.
48 Now he that betrayed him gave them a sign, saying, Whomsoever I shall kiss, that same is he: hold him fast.
49 And forthwith he came to Jesus, and said, Hail, master; and kissed him.
50 And Jesus said unto him, Friend, wherefore art thou come? Then came they, and laid hands on Jesus and took him.
51 And, behold, one of them which were with Jesus stretched out *his* hand, and drew his sword, and struck a servant of the high priest's, and smote off his ear.
52 Then said Jesus unto him, Put up again thy sword into his place: for all they that take the sword shall perish with the sword.
53 Thinkest thou that I cannot now pray to my Father, and he shall presently give me more than twelve legions of angels?
54 But how then shall the scriptures be fulfilled, that thus it must be?
55 In that same hour said Jesus to the multitudes, Are ye come out as against a thief with swords and staves for to take me? I sat daily with you teaching in the temple, and ye laid no hold on me.
56 But all this was done, that the scriptures of the prophets might be fulfilled. Then all the disciples forsook him, and fled.

Jesus knew who approached Him in the darkness and why (v. 46). Matthew identified him as "Judas, one of the twelve." The betrayer was one of their own. Jesus had spent the previous few nights, perhaps since Tuesday, in this same area (Mt. 21:17; 24:3; Mk. 11:12, 19; Lk. 21:37; 22:39; Jn. 18:2) so Judas knew exactly where to find Him.

Judas came with a large crowd armed with swords (Greek *machaira*; a short sword; Louw and Nida I:58; vv. 51-52) and "staves": that is, clubs. They came with the authority of the chief priests and elders. John 18:3 says they had lanterns and torches also. Jesus might have been watching them come across the Kidron Valley and into the Garden (Wilkins 843) while His disciples slept. These were probably Roman soldiers and Jewish temple guards (Jn. 18:3; Wilkins 858; *contra* Keener, *Matthew* 640). Though Matthew does not say, it seems certain this arrest was carried out under the cloak of darkness in order to hide it from the public eye (26:3-5).

The size of the arresting party was probably determined by the number of men Jesus had with Him. Twelve men (eleven disciples plus Jesus) could put up considerable resistance, especially if some were armed (Lk. 22:38). Judas knew some of the disciples carried swords. The arresting officers needed to show a clear display of force in order to discourage resistance as they moved in to arrest Jesus. They also needed to be able to make the arrest should resistance arise.

With premeditated calculation (v. 48), Judas greeted Jesus with "Hail, Master" or "Greetings, Rabbi," normally a greeting of respect, and stepped up to kiss Jesus. This was the prearranged sign between Judas and the arresting officers. Judas' positive identification of Jesus assured that the right person would be arrested even in the darkness.

Judas, however, did not merely give the kiss of normal greeting. He kissed Jesus with a great show of affection (Greek *kataphileō*; Grimm's 338) making the identification unmistakable. This is the word Luke used to describe the sinner woman's kissing of Jesus' feet (7:38, 45) in comparison to the kiss (Greek *philēma*) the Pharisee did not give. The affectionate kiss is what the father gave the returning prodigal (Lk. 15:20) and the Ephesian elders gave Paul when he told them they would never see him again (Acts 20:37). Judas was a hypocrite. His kiss showed how low he had sunk (Bruner 2:669).

Jesus showed no anger. Rather, He called Judas "friend" (v. 50). Matthew alone of the Gospel writers used this word (11:16; 20:13; 22:12). Here (as the Greek vocative of address), it means "My good friend" (Grimm's 254). Jesus then asked Judas, "Why are you here?" (The Greek can also be understood as a statement: "Friend, do what you came to do.") If Jesus asked a question, it was not for information but for rhetorical effect (Newman and Stine 846). John 18:2-8 shows that Matthew abbreviated his account.

With Judas' kiss, the arresting officers had a positive identification of Jesus and they laid hands on Him, i.e., arrested Him and restrained Him (Jn. 18:12). According to Luke (22:49), the disciples asked Jesus if He wanted them to fight, but Peter did not wait for an answer. He acted in keeping with his promise (Mt. 26:33-35). He would be loyal to death. Drawing his sword (Jn. 18:10-11), Peter sought to defend Jesus. In his fervor, he took off a man's right (Lk. 22:50; Jn. 18:10) ear (v. 51), probably aiming to take off his head instead. Evans (*Matthew* 488) thinks Peter was intercepting a man who was headed for Jesus to deliver a blow. John 18:10 says the man's name was Malchus and he was the high priest's servant.

God does not rely on the sword or human might to advance His kingdom (Wilkins 858). Rather than urging resistance and before the crowd could understand and react to what Peter had just done, Jesus healed the man with the severed ear (Lk. 22:51)—His final miracle before the cross. He told Peter to sheathe his sword and warned him that such actions would bring swift death, a reference either to death in battle or to death by execution (v. 52; Blomberg 93; Gen. 9:6). He reminded Peter of His relationship to God the Father. Jesus did not need human weapons. A simple request to the Father would bring thousands of angels (v. 53). Writers differ in their understanding of the exact number of soldiers in a legion. Grimm's (373) suggests that a legion (Greek *legeōn*) at this time would number 6,820 men, Wilkins (860) says a legion had 6,000 men and Heggie (35) says 4,800. Either way, when one multiplies these numbers by twelve it is easy to understand that Jesus did not need Peter's help or that of the other disciples for that matter (Lk. 22:36-38, 49). Perhaps this was Jesus' point, using "legion" to refer to a large and powerful number of spiritual forces rather than a specific number as such (ISBE III:101). Jesus was neither helpless nor defenseless. Surely, His mission was not dependent on human strength. Help was only a prayer away.

A second reason Peter's sword was wrong was because Jesus' arrest without any resistance was part of the plan of God (vv. 54, 56; Is. 53:7; Jn. 18:11). Jesus offered Himself willingly. This seems to have been His point in verse 55 as well. He was no threat, yet His enemies treated Him as one. They arrested Him as if He were a violent criminal, a threat to society. Events moved quickly as the Jewish leaders unknowingly (Lk. 23:34; Jn. 11:51, 52; Acts 3:17, 18; 1 Cor. 2:8) fulfilled prophecy by taking steps to put to death their own Messiah (Ps. 22; Is. 52:13-53:12; Zech. 12:10; 13:7). Even the disciples fulfilled prophecy when they all ran (v. 56; vv. 31-35; Zech. 13:7). After all, Peter's resistance meant he and perhaps the other disciples could now be legally arrested as well (Wilkins 860).

"In that same hour" (v. 55) means "then" or "at that time" (8:13; Newman and Stine 849; Hagner 33B:790; BAGD 896). Jesus asked why they were treating Him as a violent criminal since He taught openly in the temple every day. Then He answered His own question: they were acting as they were in order to fulfill Scripture, the writings (Scriptures) of the prophets (v. 56): "He was numbered with the transgressors" (Is. 53:12; Bruner 2:675).

h. Jesus' first trial before the Sanhedrin (26:57-68)

57 And they that had laid hold on Jesus led *him* away to Caiaphas the high priest, where the scribes and the elders were assembled.

58 But Peter followed him afar off unto the high priest's palace, and went in, and sat with the servants, to see the end.

59 Now the chief priests, and elders, and all the council, sought false witness against Jesus, to put him to death;

60 But found none: yea, though many false witnesses came, *yet* found they none. At the last came two false witnesses,

61 And said, This *fellow* said, I am able to destroy the temple of God, and to build it in three days.

62 And the high priest arose, and said unto him, Answerest thou nothing? *what is it which* these witness against thee?

63 But Jesus held his peace, And the high priest answered and said unto him, I adjure thee by the living God, that thou tell us whether thou be the Christ, the Son of God.

64 Jesus saith unto him, Thou hast said: nevertheless I say unto you, Hereafter shall ye see the Son of man sitting on the right hand of power, and coming in the clouds of heaven.

65 Then the high priest rent his clothes, saying, He hath spoken blasphemy; what further need have we of witnesses? behold, now ye have heard his blasphemy.

66 What think ye? They answered and said, He is guilty of death.

67 Then did they spit in his face, and buffeted him; and others smote *him* with the palms of their hands,
68 Saying, Prophesy unto us, thou Christ, Who is he that smote thee?

The arresting officers took Jesus to the home of Caiaphas, the high priest. Once again, Matthew abbreviates his record. John 18:13 says they took Jesus to Annas before taking Him to Caiaphas. For Matthew the point is men had already gathered to try Jesus (v. 57).

Peter did not run far. He followed Jesus from a distance (v. 58) to Caiaphas' house where he entered the courtyard and sat with the "servants" (Greek *hupēretēs*; servant, attendant, officer; Louw and Nida I:460)—perhaps these were guards (Newman and Stine 852)—beside a fire (Jn. 18:18). Peter wanted to know the outcome of this trial but he also wanted to remain unidentified. So while his presence in the courtyard took some courage (Wilkins 862), Peter was not willing to be identified with Jesus. Matthew mentioned nothing about John being with Peter.

The Sanhedrin gathered for this meeting (v. 59). The Sanhedrin was the highest Jewish court in Jerusalem who "had both religious and political powers and comprised the elite (both priestly and lay) of society" (ISBE IV:331-334). There were seventy members plus the High Priest who was the head; but all members might not have been present for this meeting (Lk. 23:51). Their hatred toward Jesus was such that they had called a special session of the Council several weeks earlier (Jn. 11:47-54) just to decide how to deal with Him. They were afraid of losing their positions of power individually and as a nation. Now they met to carry out their earlier decision.

The meeting in Caiaphas' house was called to hear allegations against Jesus. It was for a single purpose (v. 59): the leaders wanted Jesus dead. They looked for people who would lie about Jesus so they could kill Him—or, more specifically, so they could ask the Romans to kill Him (Evans, *Matthew* 491). Evans says this was not an official meeting of the Council and that all members were not present. Other writers say it was an official meeting but illegal because it did not follow established judicial rules. Keener (*Matthew* 647) gives five reasons this hearing was illegal. (1) Capital trials were to be conducted during daylight. (2) Trials were not to occur on the eve of a Sabbath or festival day. (3) Pharisaic rules required that a day pass before issuing a verdict of condemnation. (4) The Sanhedrin was not supposed to meet at the High Priest's palace. (5) Jewish law prohibited the use of false witnesses in trials.

Other writers suggest other improprieties in Jesus' trial. However, Carson (*Matthew* 550) is probably right that "expediency partially motivated" the religious leaders because they wanted to be rid of Jesus before the Sabbath. To do so they had less than twenty-four hours and so had to move quickly. In order to expedite matters they perhaps decided to set aside some of their normal rules.

Many testified against Jesus but their testimonies did not agree (v. 60; Mk. 14:56). According to the Mosaic Law, there had to be at least two witnesses in agreement before anyone could be put to death (Num. 35:30; Dt. 17:6; 19:15). It is noteworthy that Judas was not called to testify (Barclay 2:392). One supposes he could have contributed information to help the Sanhedrin, but there is no evidence that he was at the trial, although Matthew 27:3 could possibly imply his presence.

Finally, two men testified that Jesus claimed to have the ability to destroy the temple and rebuild it in three days (v. 61). John 2:19 recorded words similar to these as Jesus' words but explained to the readers that Jesus was speaking of His body, not the physical temple complex in Jerusalem (2:20-22). The high priest took this as a claim of supernatural power and he was right, for so it was whether Jesus spoke of the temple Herod built or of His body. The resurrection of either in three days would require supernatural power. Rather than deny or admit the inference, Jesus remained silent (v. 63; Is. 53:7).

Caiaphas then "adjured" (Greek *exorkizō*, command under oath) Jesus by the living God to tell them if He was "the Christ, the Son of God" (v. 63). These words were not original to Caiaphas. He was using words Jesus had used to refer to Himself. They were also O.T. words (Ps. 2:2, 7; Evans, *Matthew* 492). For "Christ," see on 12:18 and 16:18.

Mark (14:61) says Caiphas said "Son of the Blessed" rather than Matthew's "Son of God." "The Blessed" was a common Jewish substitute for God's personal name Yahweh (TWOT I:13) and was probably what Caiphas said. Matthew made sure his readers understood that "the Blessed" is God.

What Caiaphas meant by his question is uncertain. Wilkins (864) thinks Caiaphas used "Messiah" and "Son of God" as equivalent titles but not in our Trinitarian sense (16:16; 2 Sam. 7:14; Ps. 2:7; 89:26-27). However, Caiaphas might have remembered earlier claims Jesus made about Himself that He was the Son of God and equal to the Father (Jn. 10:24, 30, 36).

In response to the command from the High Priest, Jesus answered and agreed. The reader should understand Jesus' indirect answer, "You have said," (v. 64) to mean "I am" (Mk. 14:62). It was an evasive affirmative (Carson, *Matthew* 555). This is clear from verse 25 (Hendriksen 932). Without waiting for more questions, Jesus told His accusers more about Himself.

This was a pivotal time as He had told His disciples earlier that night (v. 29). From that time on ("henceforth"), the time of the Lord's Supper, He would not drink grape juice until the kingdom was fully realized. Speaking now to the high priest (v. 64) and to all those judging Him, Jesus stated clearly that from that time on ("hereafter")—i.e., after the cross and His resurrection, ascension, and exaltation—He would take His seat beside God Almighty, the "right hand of Power," and they would see Him there. Jesus claimed He would soon share the throne-chariot of God (Blomberg 93; Dan. 7:9; Ezek. 1:4-28). This was blasphemy unless it was true. See Evans (*Mark* 453-455) for a discussion of blasphemy. These men would also see Him coming on the clouds of heaven (Acts 1:9-11; 1 Th. 4:17; Rev. 1:7; 14:14-16).

Though the kingdom had arrived earlier (12:28), Jesus' exaltation as king of His heavenly kingdom is based on His work on the cross (Ps. 110:1; Keener, *Matthew* 650). What appeared to be weakness was strength (1 Cor. 1:18). What seemed the end was the beginning. It was there that atonement was made for the transgressors and His kingdom established (Is. 53:13—54:12). It was there that the stone began to grow into a mountain (Dan. 2:35, 44).

With this claim, Jesus identified Himself as the apocalyptic subject of Daniel 7:13-14 and the Davidic Messiah of Psalm 110:1. Two actions are in view: first, the prophet Daniel saw one like a son of man—a human, in other words—approach God and receive an eternal kingdom. Second, as ruler of this eternal kingdom, this Son of Man would return to earth "on the clouds of heaven" and be recognized as Lord by all. This is His Second Coming. See comments on 24:30. In effect, Jesus told the High Priest and the Sanhedrin that though they were sitting in judgment over Him now, one day they would be kneeling before Him. The victim will be victorious. These men will see this man on God's throne.

This "Son of Man" was human yet divine. He was being judged yet He is the Judge of all the earth. His cryptic use of the title "Son of Man" throughout His ministry now comes into full view. His confession included His identity as also the Son of God, the second Person of the Trinity incarnate. He claimed divine rights and privileges. The high priest had unwittingly provided Jesus with a public platform from which to declare in plain terms His true identity (Keener, *Matthew* 649).

The high priest's reaction was immediate. He understood Jesus to claim that He possessed a divine relationship to the Almighty and He was both human and divine (Wilkins 865). The high priest considered such humanizing of the Divine to be blasphemous and tore his outer garment, an expression of shock and grief (Gen. 37:29, 34; 44:13; 1 Sam. 4:12; Ezra 9:3, 5; Job 1:20). He then called on the Sanhedrin to acknowledge what they had just heard (v. 65) and give their decision (v. 66). They ruled that Jesus must die. There was no need for further witnesses. The Council members had heard for themselves Jesus' words to the high priest. Jesus' claim to be God was ultimately what put Him on the cross (Jn. 10:33; 19:7). His claim to be king was what the Jews used to get Pilate to condemn Him (Lk. 23:2-3; Jn. 19:12-16).

No one in that room misunderstood Jesus' claims about Himself (Bruner 2:687). They understood what He said; they just did not believe Him (Acts 3:17; 1 Cor. 2:8). Throughout His ministry, He had carefully revealed His true identity progressively and selectively. On this occasion, however, He answered in plain terms. For the first time unbelievers received Jesus' full self-revelation, in fact, His fullest self-revelation to date—and they used it to condemn Him.

Matthew does not say who, but some (of the council members? So Gundry 457; Wilkins 866; Walvoord 223) in the room began to dishonor Jesus by spitting in His face as well as beating and slapping Him (v. 67). Mark 14:65 said they covered Jesus' face and then slapped Him as they were challenging Him to tell them who hit Him (Mt. 26:68). They were making light of His claim to be a prophet and the Messiah. Too late, they would realize He knew who threw every punch and who disgraced Him with every spit (Hagner 33B:802).

They turned Him over to the guards who "received him with blows" (Mk. 14:65). One can imagine the pain these guards inflicted on this gentle man. The process of disgracing Him had begun. However, Jesus lived what He taught

(5:39; 26:52-53) and left a clear example for His disciples to follow (1 Pet. 2:21-23).

i. Peter's denials of Jesus (26:69-75)

69 Now Peter sat without in the palace: and a damsel came unto him, saying, Thou also wast with Jesus of Galilee.
70 But he denied before *them* all, saying, I know not what thou sayest.
71 And when he was gone out into the porch, another *maid* saw him, and said unto them that were there, This *fellow* was also with Jesus of Nazareth.
72 And again he denied with an oath, I do not know the man.
73 And after a while came unto *him* they that stood by, and said to Peter, Surely thou also art *one* of them; for thy speech bewrayeth thee.
74 Then began he to curse and to swear, *saying,* I know not the man. And immediately the cock crew.
75 And Peter remembered the word of Jesus, which said unto him, Before the cock crow, thou shalt deny me thrice. And he went out, and wept bitterly.

Matthew turned his focus once again to Peter. While Jesus was in the priest's quarters (Lk. 22:54), Peter and John (Jn. 18:15-16) were outside in the courtyard (v. 3; Greek *aulē*, courtyard, any dwelling having an interior courtyard; dwelling, palace, mansion; Louw and Nida I:82, 90). Peter's denials took place over an extended period that night (Lk. 22:59).

As Peter warmed himself by the fire (Mk. 14:67) the slave girl (Greek *paidiskē*; Lk. 1:48; Gal. 4:31) who kept the gate (Jn. 18:17) recognized him and approached him. She stated that he was one of Jesus' disciples (v. 69). Peter had courageously entered the courtyard and sat among Jesus' enemies (Keener, *Background* 123), but when confronted about his relationship to Jesus his courage failed. He denied it—before everyone (v. 70). Peter did not realize he was on trial also. His loyalty to Jesus was being tested.

One has only to remember 10:33 to understand the seriousness of Peter's actions. Gundry (548-549) states, "Peter is forfeiting his salvation," which, he says is why Peter's name is not included in chapter 28 and which further proves that Peter is not the rock upon which Jesus was going to build His church (16:18). While it is clear Peter did not forfeit his salvation, this was surely a step in that direction. Had he failed to repent (v. 75), he would have had the same eternal end as Judas.

Matthew did not include any details concerning how this woman knew Peter was with Jesus. Perhaps she had seen them earlier that week when Jesus and His disciples were in the city or perhaps she had seen Peter in the garden when Jesus was arrested. Regardless, she was right.

Peter, realizing that he too might be in danger, moved away from the light of the fire and toward an exit: "porch" (Greek *pulōn*) can mean gate, entrance, vestibule (Louw and Nida I:87). But, subsequently another woman recognized him as having been with Jesus (v. 71). Mark 14:69 ("began to say") suggests that the allegation was repeated to several of the bystanders. Peter denied even knowing "the man" and swore an oath to that effect.

After a while (v. 73; about an hour according to Lk. 22:59) some others approached Peter and made a similar allegation. This time they accused him of being one of Jesus' disciples. They were convinced the first two women were right because of Peter's Galilean speech. "Bewray" (v. 73) is an outdated form of betray. Again, he denied any knowledge of Jesus, this time calling a divine curse down on himself if he were lying. For more on swearing and using oaths, see on 5:33-37. This man who had been one of Jesus' closest confidants for over two and one half years, had seen Him raise the dead (9:25; Mk. 5:37, 41), saw Him glorified (17:1-4), walked on water with Him (14:29), and had tried to defend Him (26:51), now denied ever knowing Him. Then two things happened that Peter did not expect: (1) Jesus turned and looked at him (Lk. 22:61), and (2) the rooster crowed. What was in Jesus' look? Was it love? Hurt? Sorrow? Disappointment? Compassion?

Jesus used these two things to bring Peter back to truth and reality. Just a few hours earlier He had told Peter that he would deny Him. Peter had adamantly denied even the remotest possibility of this. Peter's actions and the rooster's voice proved that Jesus knew Peter's heart better than he knew himself. Peter had claimed he would die for Jesus but when confronted with a real cross, Peter backed down. The danger had reached a point beyond Peter's level of dedication.

Peter was stricken with shame and "wept bitterly," i.e., with great mental anguish (v. 75). Confronted with his failure, Peter had difficulty accepting that he had done what he had. He left the courtyard and—one may surmise from the silence of Scripture—never saw Jesus alive again until after His resurrection.

Two were on trial that night, Jesus and Peter. The innocent was condemned to die and the guilty remained free—except from his conscience. It would be a long three days before Peter saw and heard his gracious and forgiving Savior again (Lk. 24:34). Peter should have prayed with Jesus in the Garden (Gundry 548).

One wonders where John was in all of this. Did he hear Peter's denials? The writers of the Gospels do not say, but John's record of Peter's denial (18:15-18, 25-27) suggests an eyewitness account.

Summary (26:1-75)

This portion of Matthew's Gospel conveys some of the final events in the life of Jesus. He began with chronologically parallel events. As Jesus was announcing to the Twelve He would be dead in two days, His enemies gathered to bring about His demise (vv. 1-5).

Matthew then went back in time to the previous Sabbath evening when Jesus' friends in Bethany had a dinner in His honor. It was here that Mary anointed Him with the expensive perfume and Judas got so angry that he decided to hand Jesus over to the authorities. Sometime the following week, after the meeting described in verses 3-5 but before the Passover, Judas met with the chief priests and they made their plan.

Thursday afternoon Peter and John made the preparations for the Passover meal and Thursday evening Jesus and the Twelve observed this ancient memorial dinner. During the extended meal, Jesus announced that one of the Twelve would betray Him. The betrayer would hand Him over to Jewish authorities. Jesus identified him as a close friend with whom He was presently sharing table fellowship. It was also at this same time that Jesus instituted the new covenant memorial service, the Lord's Supper. Jesus instituted this memorial to help His followers regularly remember His death for them.

At some point in the evening, perhaps even after they left the room for the night, Jesus gave another startling announcement: all of the Twelve would deny Him that night. Peter refused to accept this prophecy but Jesus assured him that even he would deny the Lord. Peter would deny the Lord three times and then a rooster would crow.

Jesus and His disciples left the Passover room and walked to the Mount of Olives and the Garden of Gethsemane. Here Jesus prayed that the Father would provide another way, something other than the cross. After a lengthy time in prayer, Jesus accepted that the cross was the Father's will for Him and unquestioningly submitted to that.

Following this intense prayer time, Judas came with the arresting crowd from the Sanhedrin. They arrested Jesus and the Apostles ran. The officers took Jesus to the home of the high priest where the Sanhedrin tried Him. The Sanhedrin ruled that He was guilty of blasphemy because He claimed rights to the throne of God. They began immediately abusing Him.

At the same time Jesus was on trial, Peter was being tested. Satan was in the courtyard (Lk. 22:31). A few hours earlier Peter had rejected Jesus' prophecy and warning that he would deny Him. However, when put the test, Peter did just that—three times. Peter had been one of Jesus' closest associates but he denied even knowing Him. Peter failed the test.

Application: Teaching and Preaching the Passage

This chapter shows the heights and the depths of humanity. The perfect human, Jesus, excelled in every way. Imperfect humans failed to pray, betrayed Jesus, denied Him, and voted to crucify Him. Mary of Bethany and her siblings demonstrated their love sacrificially. Judas and the religious authorities sacrificed Him. Ministry outlines might be developed from these records as follows:

Mary's gift (vv. 6-13) was lavishly sacrificial, largely distasteful, and lovingly accepted. The Lord's Supper can be used to teach the following features of the new covenant: (1) the provisions of the new covenant are sacrifice and forgiveness (v. 28); (2) the symbols of the new covenant are unleavened bread and the fruit of the vine (vv. 26-28); and (3) the promises of the new covenant are Jesus' temporary abstinence and table fellowship with Christ in the Father's kingdom (v. 29).

A lesson on the Lord's Supper might be prepared around the following: (1) the context (the Passover meal, v. 26); (2) the content (unleavened bread, fruit of the vine, vv. 26-28); and, (3) the continuation (for Jesus, v. 29; for His followers, Lk. 22:19; 1 Cor. 11:26).

A sermon or lesson might be developed on the following aspects of Judas' betrayal of Jesus: (1) Judas betrayed Jesus for personal gain (vv. 8, 14-16);

(2) Judas betrayed Jesus in spite of loving confrontation (vv. 23-25); (3) Judas betrayed Jesus under a cloak of friendship (v. 48-50); and (4) Judas betrayed Jesus to his own ruin (27:1-5; see comments on next chapter).

Jesus taught several lessons about temptation in verses 36-46. (1) Exhaustion can make one more vulnerable to temptation (v. 43: "their eyes were heavy"). (2) The best time to pray is before temptation (vv. 41, 75). (3) Prayer enables one to withstand temptation (v. 41). (4) The desire to do right by itself will not enable one to win over all temptation (v. 41). (5) Those fall who do not through prayer seriously prepare for temptation (v. 56, 69-75).

The Garden events might be presented under the headings of (1) the struggling Lord (vv. 37-39, 42, 44), (2) the sleeping disciples (vv. 40-41, 43, 45), and (3) the submissive Savior (vv. 39, 42, 44).

The trial of Jesus before the Sanhedrin might be taught using the following: (1) His confrontation (vv. 57-63); (2) His confession (v. 64); and (3) His condemnation (vv. 65-68).

Jesus (1) is worthy of worship (vv. 11, 12); (2) was self-giving (vv. 26-28); (3) was obedient to the Father (vv. 39-44); and (4) is our soon-coming King (v. 64).

Wilkins (846) speaks of divine inevitability in these verses. A sermon or lesson might be organized around "Divine Destinies": (1) Judas and his betrayal; (2) the disciples and their defection; and (3) Jesus' suffering and death. See comments above for specific prophetic passages.

j. Jesus' second trial before the Sanhedrin and other leaders (27:1-2)

1 When the morning was come, all the chief priests and elders of the people took counsel against Jesus to put him to death:
2 And when they had bound him, they led *him* away, and delivered him to Pontius Pilate the governor.

By this time, Jesus had appeared before Caiaphas and members of the Sanhedrin (26:57-68). They had decided that He deserved to die and held Him in custody until daylight. All the chief priests then assembled on this Friday morning to meet with those who had first tried Jesus and together they finalized their plan to kill Jesus (Lk. 22:66). Matthew (27:62), Mark (15:42), and Luke (23:54) each indicate that Jesus was crucified on Friday. For discussion on the day of Jesus' crucifixion, see comments on 26:2, 17.

The Jewish officials bound Jesus again (v. 2; Jn. 18:12) and took Him to Pilate, the Roman governor. Pilate was governor (procurator) from about A.D. 26 to 37 (ISBE III:869). (Some Greek manuscripts, and so some translations, do not include the name "Pontius" before "Pilate.") "Delivered" (Greek *paradidōmi*) means, "to hand over" and is the same word translated betray. Judas handed Jesus over to the Jewish authorities (v. 3). The Jewish authorities handed Jesus over to Pilate (v. 2). Pilate handed Jesus over to his soldiers to crucify Jesus (v. 26). Handing Jesus over to Pilate began the fulfillment of 20:19.

The Jews needed Pilate's permission to kill Jesus (Jn. 18:31). According to Longenecker (302), they had authority to decide all non-capital cases. They were permitted to decide only one capital offence, that of a Gentile accused of trespassing beyond the posted walls of the temple area (Acts 21:28-29).

k. Judas' suicide (27:3-10)

3 Then Judas, which had betrayed him, when he saw that he was condemned, repented himself, and brought again the thirty pieces of silver to the chief priests and elders,
4 Saying, I have sinned in that I have betrayed the innocent blood. And they said, What *is that* to us? see thou *to that.*
5 And he cast down the pieces of silver in the temple, and departed, and went and hanged himself.
6 And the chief priests took the silver pieces, and said, It is not lawful for to put them into the treasury, because it is the price of blood.
7 And they took counsel, and bought with them the potter's field, to bury strangers in.
8 Wherefore that field was called, The field of blood, unto this day.
9 Then was fulfilled that which was spoken by Jeremy the prophet, saying, And they took the thirty pieces of silver, the price of him that was valued, whom they of the children of Israel did value;
10 And gave them for the potter's field, as the Lord appointed me.

Judas was close to the trial proceedings. Neither Gospel writer states he was present for the trial, but he must have been (cf. comments on 26:60) for he knew the verdict before it became public knowledge. That he "repented" means he regretted (Greek *metamelomai,* to feel regret as the result of what one had done; Louw and Nida I:318) his action of handing Jesus over to the leaders. He returned the money (v. 3; 26:15). This is not the usual word for repentance (Greek *metanoeō*), which adds credibility to the position that Judas stopped short of real repentance. On the thirty pieces of silver, see comments on 26:15.

Judas confessed Jesus' innocence, which showed his own evil. He admitted he had betrayed an innocent man (v. 4). The leaders were not about to change their minds just because Judas changed his. In short, they said the betrayal of the innocent was his problem, inferring that the problem was his alone; but they were wrong. Shedding innocent blood was their problem too (Nolland 1151), for shedding innocent blood was strongly condemned in Scripture (Gundry 554; Dt. 27:25; Prov. 6:17, Is. 59:7; Jer. 22:3, 17; Joel 3:19). They could not absolve themselves of wrongdoing by denial any more than Pilate could by simply washing his hands (v. 24).

Judas was so upset (Bruner 2:707 suggests he was furious) he threw the silver pieces "in" the temple, either *in* the temple area or through a door or over a wall *into* the temple (Hagner 33B:812). "In" may suggest Judas was in the temple where he should not have been. "Into" may suggest Judas was in the temple area and "implies strong emotion and physical exertion" (Metzger 66; Carson, *Matthew* 566).

Leaving the money, Judas promptly committed suicide by hanging himself (v. 5). Peter further described Judas' death (Acts 1:18-19) as being gruesome and stated that everyone in Jerusalem became aware of his death and the horrific details. Some interpreters assume the structure (a tree limb growing out over a precipice?) from which Judas hung himself gave way and he fell as described by Peter (Wilkins 879; Hendriksen 945). Judas' remorse stopped short of repentance and stands in contrast to that of Peter (26:75; Keener, *Background* 124). Nolland (1153), however, believes Judas truly repented and received restoration, a position hard to reconcile with Jesus' comments concerning Judas while in the upper room (Mt. 26:24), in His high priestly prayer (Jn. 17:12), and Peter's statement in Acts 1:25. Jesus had foreseen the falling away of the Twelve (26:31, 56), the denials of Peter (26:34, 69-75), the betrayal by Judas, and Judas' awful end (26:24, 47-49).

The chief priests concluded because the silver had been used to buy the death of a man (Jesus), it could not be placed into the temple treasury (v. 6). They thus confessed they had paid money for Jesus' death and this was therefore tainted money (Keener, *Matthew* 661). The hypocrisy of the Jewish leadership is clear (v. 6). They would not break the law with improper use of blood money but they were more than willing to break the law to put Jesus to death (Keener, *Background* 125). The fact they spoke of its going into the treasury suggests that they might have used temple money to pay Judas. The chief priests decided to use the returned money to purchase a field previously used by potters, which explains how Judas purchased a field as recorded in Acts 1:18. This field became a burial ground for strangers (v. 7). It became known as "The Field of Blood" (v. 8) or "The Bloody Field" (Evans, *Matthew* 501) because of Judas' treasonous act of betraying Jesus to death and because of his own gruesomely bloody death (Acts 1:18-19). The Bloody Field, then, spoke of the deaths of two men. Scripture does not suggest Judas was buried in this field (Gundry 556), although he might have been (Carson, *Matthew* 562). It was still known by that name at the time Matthew penned his account some thirty years or more later.

Scripture says nothing of Judas' family. However, one may understand that their suffering over Judas' failure and suicide must have been intensive and long-term. This would have been especially true if they were also followers of Jesus and heard about it back in Galilee.

Matthew again turned to the O.T. where he found some prophetic experiences that paralleled that of Judas and Jesus (vv. 9-10). Jeremiah visited a potter (Jer. 18:3), prophesied of a future burial site in the valley of Topheth, and purchased a potter's flask (Jer. 19:1-13). Zechariah prophesied that he would be sold for thirty pieces of silver (Zech. 11:11-13). The exegetical problems are that Matthew credits Jeremiah with the prophecy that is only in Zechariah and Zechariah does not mention purchasing property with the thirty pieces of silver. The solution appears to be that Matthew quoted Zechariah but merged subject matter from both Jeremiah and Zechariah (Keener, *Background* 125; Evans, *Matthew* 501), a common way of handling multiple Scripture texts in Matthew's day (Blomberg 95). Though Matthew referred to two prophets, he only mentioned the most prominent of the two (Hendriksen 948). Mark does the same thing in his Gospel (Archer and Chirichingo 163). See Mark 1:2-3 where Mark credits Isaiah with both prophecies.

Matthew referenced Zechariah in order to parallel the corrupt leadership of Zechariah's day with the corrupt leadership of Jesus' day. In both instances, the good Shepherd was rejected by His own and sold for a pitifully cheap price; then the thirty pieces of silver were thrown back into the temple. While Jeremiah and Zechariah were neither one foretelling a future Messianic event, there were points of contact in their experiences that Matthew understood as paralleling the circumstances involving Judas, Jesus, and Jewish leadership.

l. Jesus' trial before Pilate (27:11-26)

11 And Jesus stood before the governor: and the governor asked him, saying, Art thou the King of the Jews? And Jesus said unto him, Thou sayest.
12 And when he was accused of the chief priests and elders, he answered nothing.
13 Then said Pilate unto him, Hearest thou not how many things they witness against thee?
14 And he answered him to never a word; insomuch that the governor marvelled greatly.
15 Now at *that* feast the governor was wont to release unto the people a prisoner, whom they would.
16 And they had then a notable prisoner, called Barabbas.
17 Therefore when they were gathered together, Pilate said unto them, Whom will ye that I release unto you? Barabbas, or Jesus which is called Christ?
18 For he knew that for envy they had delivered him.
19 When he was set down on the judgment seat, his wife sent unto him, saying, Have thou nothing to do with that just man: for I have suffered many things this day in a dream because of him.
20 But the chief priests and elders persuaded the multitude that they should ask Barabbas, and destroy Jesus.
21 The governor answered and said unto them, Whether of the twain will ye that I release unto you? They said, Barabbas.
22 Pilate saith unto them, What shall I do then with Jesus which is called Christ? *They* all say unto him, Let him be crucified.
23 And the governor said, Why, what evil hath he done? But they cried out the more, saying, Let him be crucified.
24 When Pilate saw that he could prevail nothing, but *that* rather a tumult was made, he took water, and washed *his* hands before the multitude, saying, I am innocent of the blood of this just person: see ye *to it*.
25 Then answered all the people, and said, His blood *be* on us, and on our children.
26 Then released he Barabbas unto them: and when he had scourged Jesus, he delivered *him* to be crucified.

Following the parenthetical recounting of Judas' death, Matthew turned his discussion back to Jesus' trial before the Gentiles (v. 2). Pilate's question reveals the allegations the Jews brought to him against Jesus (Lk. 23:2, 5). At first, they did not mention blasphemy. See 26:64-66 and comments; also John 19:7.

Pilate would have had no interest in such matters. However, the political charge of claiming to be the King of the Jews was a more serious matter for Pilate. If Jesus were trying to lead a rebellion against Rome, Pilate needed to know. This was one of three charges they made against Jesus (Lk. 23:2; Barclay 2:417).

Jesus only indirectly answered the governor (v. 11). See John 18:36-38 for a fuller version of this exchange. After this, He neither denied nor affirmed the allegations. While His accusers were charging Him before Pilate, Jesus stood silent. Pilate tried to get Him to answer (v. 13), but Jesus refused. His silence was so unusual that Pilate was astonished (Greek *thaumazō*, marveled; 8:10). One can almost hear Pilate's elevated volume as he said to Jesus, "Can you not hear what they are saying about you?" (Bruner 2:715). Jesus did not at all appear to Pilate to be the kind of person He was accused of being (Hendriksen 951). He was unwilling to "fight for His life," something Pilate found very unusual (Nolland 1164).

Matthew stated that it was customary ("wont") for Pilate to release a prisoner at each Jewish feast (v. 15). Matthew, Mark 15:6-15, Luke 23:18-19, John 18:39-40 and Acts 3:14 all mentioned this release. Evans (502) gives other historical references that speak of political leaders releasing prisoners on various occasions such as this.

Pilate picked a prisoner who was the extreme opposite of Jesus. His name was Barabbas (v. 16), which means "son of (his) father." Some older Greek and Syriac manuscripts have "Jesus" Barabbas or "Jesus bar Abba" and some scholarship supports this reading (Metzger 68). This would mean that "Jesus" the murderer was set free while Jesus the Messiah was condemned (Hill 350). It also helps one understand why Pilate identified Jesus as "Jesus, which is called Christ" (vv. 17, 22) and not just "Jesus."

Barabbas was a well-known robber, murderer, and insurrectionist (Mk. 15:7; Lk. 23:19; Jn. 18:40; Acts 3:14). "Notable" (v. 16, Greek *episēmos*) means "well known" and can infer positive or negative characteristics (Louw and Nida I:338). Here it may suggest he was popular with the people (Bruner 2:717).

Pilate saw that Jesus was not guilty of anything worthy of death (v. 24). Jesus' accusers were motivated by envy (v. 18), but Pilate would not have known why. He recognized that theirs was not a desire for righteous judgment. Barabbas, however, deserved to die. He was guilty of violent crimes. A crowd gathered to see which prisoner would be released (v. 17; Mk. 15:8) on this holy day and were themselves unexpectedly faced with a choice. Pilate hoped the people would choose Jesus over Barabbas (Acts 3:13), but that was not to happen.

As Pilate sat on the judgment seat (Greek *bēma,* v. 19) his wife sent word to him. She advised him not to have anything do with Jesus, meaning that she cautioned Pilate against punishing Jesus. She called Jesus a righteous man and said she had suffered that day in a dream because of Him. God used Pilate's wife to warn him regarding the sin he was about to commit in sending Jesus to His death. Dreams were one way God communicated His messages at this time (Osborne 1018; 1:20; 2:12-13, 19, 22).

The chief priests and elders, probably the same members of the Sanhedrin who had tried Him earlier that morning, urged the people to choose Barabbas over Jesus (vv. 20-21). Apparently, there were no dissenters in the crowd; they all called for Jesus' crucifixion. Pilate appears to have been surprised and asked for something Jesus had done wrong (v. 23: "Why ... ?"). In an unusual move he allowed the crowd to determine Jesus' fate when he asked, "What shall I do then with Jesus" (v. 22; Nolland 1174-1175).

The crowd listened to their religious leaders again and called for Jesus' death by crucifixion: "Let Him be crucified!" (vv. 22-23). Pilate offered some resistance to the crowd's wishes (v. 23) because he believed Jesus was innocent of the charges (Lk. 23:4, 13-15). He wanted to release Jesus (Jn. 19:12; Acts 3:13), but the crowd would settle for nothing less than Jesus' blood.

Pilate could see that a "tumult" or uprising or riot was beginning. In order to keep peace he acquiesced and tried to pass off the responsibility for shedding innocent blood. He publicly washed his hands to demonstrate that he wanted no part in Jesus' death (v. 24). Clearly, he believed Jesus should not be killed, but it is also clear he did not have the courage his position as governor and judge needed. He was responsible to protect the innocent. Instead, he gave official approval of Jesus' death and then denied responsibility. Pilate's statement, "See to it yourselves" reminds the reader of the chief priests and elders' words to Judas (v. 4; Carson, *Matthew* 571). (The word "just" (v. 24) does not appear in some manuscripts and translations.)

In the end, as Barclay (2:423) observed, Pilate went against his sense of justice, his own conscience, and the advice of his wife. He sided with evil Herod (Lk. 23:12) and fulfilled prophecy (Ps. 2; Acts 4:25-28) by acting against the Lord and His Christ. Pilate condemned Jesus to die but never pronounced Him guilty of any wrongdoing.

The people understood Pilate's wish and act of washing his hands and accepted full responsibility for Jesus' death. They even offered future generations of Jews to share in any judgment that might be given if they were wrong to crucify Jesus (v. 25). In their minds, they were sending Jesus to the cross and were right in doing so (Acts 3:17). Pilate was only making it official.

This crowd of Jews had no right to commit future generations of Jews to special judgment because of their actions. It is clear from the Scriptures that God does not hold the Jewish people *as a whole* responsible for Jesus' death. The thousands of Jews saved in the weeks and months following this event, as well as specific teaching to the contrary, support this statement (Acts 2:41; 4:4; 5:14; Rom. 11:1-32)

Pilate accepted the Jewish crowd's statements and released Barabbas. It seems certain that Jesus died on a cross intended for Barabbas. Neither writer says Barabbas would have been crucified then, but given the crucifixion of the two robbers (v. 38) it seems safe to assume this.

Pilate had Jesus scourged or whipped (Greek *phragelloō*; v. 26), perhaps a second whipping. The first would have preceded His final condemnation by Pilate (Jn. 19:1) as an attempt on Pilate's part to avoid Jesus' crucifixion. The latter whipping would have been the more serious of the two. Such scourgings prior to crucifixion consisted of the victim's being tied to a post (Wilkins 878; Acts 22:25) and then beaten with "leather straps or knotted cords often weighted with metal or bone" (ISBE IV:359). These beatings could shorten the victim's time on the cross and could be so severe that victims would die just from the beating. One can hardly imagine the increased pain of the second beating over the fresh wounds of the first.

Isaiah prophesied that the Lord's Servant would be beaten (Is. 50:6; 53:4-5; Blomberg 97) and that His beatings would so mar Him that He would not be recognizable (Is. 52:14). Jesus' beatings prior to His crucifixion marred Him in this way. Jesus had told His disciples He would be beaten and killed by the Gentiles (20:19). Isaiah explained why this was important: His stripes were the means of our healing (Is. 53:5; 1 Pet. 2:24; Hendriksen 958). This means the suffering of Jesus both prior to and upon the cross were in our place (vicarious atonement and propitiation) and for our benefit (justification, sanctification, and reconciliation).

m. Jesus' abuse and mockery at the hands of the Roman soldiers (27:27-31)

27 Then the soldiers of the governor took Jesus into the common hall, and gathered unto him the whole band *of soldiers*.
28 And they stripped him, and put on him a scarlet robe.
29 And when they had platted a crown of thorns, they put *it* upon his head, and a reed in his right hand: and they bowed the knee before him, and mocked him, saying, Hail, King of the Jews!
30 And they spit upon him, and took the reed, and smote him on the head.
31 And after that they had mocked him, they took the robe off from him, and put his own raiment on him, and led him away to crucify *him*.

Following the beatings (v. 26), Pilate's soldiers took Jesus to the "common hall," the praetorium (Mk. 15:16). This was the official residence in Jerusalem for the Roman governor (ISBE III:929). Scholars divide over whether this was the palace of Herod the Great or the Fortress Antonia, a Hasmonean era fortress adjoining the temple (Nolland 1171). Here a cohort of Roman soldiers gathered. The "band" (Greek *speira*) can refer to a full cohort (six hundred soldiers) or to a portion of a cohort (Louw and Nida I:550; BAGD 761), as few as from one hundred and twenty to two hundred men. (Hagner 33B:830 suggests that Matthew might have intended "cohort" as hyperbole rather than a literal number of soldiers.)

The soldiers removed Jesus' robe and replaced it with a scarlet robe, the color of royalty. This may have been a reaction to the "gorgeous robe" (Lk. 23:11) Herod and his men put on Him before sending Him back to Pilate. Pilate's soldiers ridiculed Jesus and His claim to be a king. They treated Him as if He were powerless and a common criminal. They also platted (Greek *plekō*, twist together, weave) a crown of thorns and put it on His head. They placed a reed in His hand as if it were a royal scepter and then bowed before Him as one would a king. The reed (Greek *kalamos*) was the heavy, rigid stalk of a reed plant (Louw and Nida I:35).

They disgraced Him with spit (Is. 50:6) and took the reed and repeatedly (v. 30; Greek imperfect tense) hit Him on the head with it. Finished with the mockery, they put His own clothes back on Him and took Him away to crucify Him. If the entire cohort went along, Jesus had a substantial number of soldiers escorting Him to Golgotha (Nolland 1185).

Hendriksen (959) noted that thorns were part of the curse mentioned in Genesis 3:18. Hence, Jesus was also bearing the "curse that lies upon nature, in order to deliver nature and us from it." It is possible that Jesus wore the thorns all the way to the cross (Jn. 19:5) even though He was redressed in His own clothes before He left the praetorium (Mt. 27:31).

The mockery and torture were clearly not only physical. The abuse was intended to break the victim's mental and emotional stability as well. No wonder He prayed, "If it be possible, let this cup pass from me" (26:39).

2. The royal Messiah's crucifixion (27:32-44)

32 And as they came out, they found a man of Cyrene, Simon by name: him they compelled to bear his cross.
33 And when they were come unto a place called Golgotha, that is to say, a place of a skull,
34 They gave him vinegar to drink mingled with gall: and when he had tasted *thereof*, he would not drink.
35 And they crucified him, and parted his garments, casting lots: that it might be fulfilled which was spoken by the prophet, They parted my garments among them, and upon my vesture did they cast lots.
36 And sitting down they watched him there;
37 And set up over his head his accusation written, THIS IS JESUS THE KING OF THE JEWS.
38 Then were there two thieves crucified with him, one on the right hand, and another on the left.
39 And they that passed by reviled him, wagging their heads,
40 And saying, Thou that destroyest the temple, and buildest *it* in three days, save thyself. If thou be the Son of God, come down from the cross.
41 Likewise also the chief priests mocking *him*, with the scribes and elders, said,
42 He saved others; himself he cannot save. If he be the King of Israel, let him now come down from the cross, and we will believe him.
43 He trusted in God; let him deliver him now, if he will have him: for he said, I am the Son of God.
44 The thieves also, which were crucified with him, cast the same in his teeth.

As the Roman soldiers walked Jesus to Golgotha, they initially made Him carry His own cross (Jn. 19:17). Whether His was the whole cross or just the cross beam, neither writer says. Hendriksen (962) believes the whole cross was intended. Bruner (2:731), along with many other modern writers, says it was the cross beam only. Regardless, Jesus was too weak from the beatings to carry His cross the entire way, so the soldiers conscripted a passerby, Simon from the northern African city of Cyrene, to carry Jesus' cross. Cyrene was located in modern Libya, the ruins of which remain today. Simon was just walking into the city (Lk. 23:26) when he was forced to carry Jesus' cross. Soldiers had the authority to conscript civilians to help them in this manner (see comments on 5:41).

The soldiers walked Jesus and Simon outside the city (Heb. 13:12) to a place called Golgotha (v. 33). Golgotha is the Aramaic word for "skull." If the name describes the appearance of the hill then what is today known as Gordon's Calvary may be the place where Jesus was crucified. The "Church of the Holy Sepulchre" built by the Roman Emperor Constantine marks the traditional spot and is believed by many scholars to be the more probable spot (Wilkins 897-898; Hagner 33B:834; Carson, *Matthew* 574).

Once they arrived at the place of His crucifixion, they (the soldiers?) offered Jesus a drink of wine and gall mixed (v. 34). Wine might have eased the pain (Prov. 31:6). Gall in O.T. usage was a bitter herb that made the wine taste bad (Ps. 69:21). Mark 15:23 said the wine included myrrh. One writer thinks this "aromatic, resinous gum" was intended to enhance the flavor (Nolland 1190). However, most scholarship thinks the opposite was the case (Carson, *Matthew* 575; ISBE II:393; Louw and Nida I:103).

With this in mind, the mixture may have been intended to add to His misery (Gundry 569). His body was dehydrated from the intense prayer times of the previous night (Lk. 22:44) and the severe, bloody beatings shortly before. He needed hydration but the gall caused Him to reject the wine. Evans (*Matthew* 511) suggests Jesus refused to drink because He was unwilling to participate in their mockery. Keener (*Matthew* 678) suggests two other reasons: Jesus' vow in 26:29 and His need to experience humanity's pain in full. One thing seems certain: there was a connection between Jesus' experience and that of the composer of Psalm 69:20-21.

"And they crucified him" (v. 35): these are words to ponder. Without embellishment, Matthew stated in simple terms that Jesus had been fastened to a cross to die. Thomas said Jesus was nailed to the cross through His hands (Jn. 20:25), the scars of which were visible and could be felt in Jesus' resurrected body. Jesus had said that He would be killed (16:21; 17:22-23; 20:19; 26:2). Twice He had foretold that He would die by crucifixion (20:19; 26:2).

Crucifixion was a cruel form of death. The crucified person was stripped naked (Nolland 1193) and suspended from a cross beam (Keener, *Background* 126). Some were tied with ropes. Others, like Jesus (Jn. 20:25), were nailed. The crucified would have to pull himself up to breathe. When he lacked strength to pick himself up, he would die from asphyxiation. The victim could last for days before death. The soldiers now had only to wait until He died (v. 36), to guard Him in order to keep anyone from taking Him down from the cross.

The words "that it might be fulfilled which was spoken by the prophet, They parted my garments among them, and upon my vesture did they cast lots" (v. 35) are not in the oldest manuscripts. They are present in John's Gospel (19:24) without question, which shows that a specific prophesy was given and fulfilled (Walvoord 233). In fulfillment of prophecy (Ps. 22:18), then, the four soldiers who remained at the cross (Jn. 19:23) gambled for Jesus' clothes (v. 35). They gambled for the long, shirt-like undergarment worn next to the skin because they did not want to divide it. It was seamless. One wonders why anyone would want this garment for it was surely a bloody mess (v. 31). The outer garments they divided into four parts, each soldier getting a part. If He still had the outer robes Herod and his men put on Him (Lk. 23:11) then the soldiers would have been glad to get these.

Scholars agree the Romans normally crucified their victims nude to add to their humiliation. However, one cannot be certain that Jesus was not given a loincloth in consideration of Jewish sensitivities. Regardless, teaching and preaching this passage requires care lest the speaker add additional humiliation to the image of the Savior on the cross.

The soldiers placed His indictment over His head, which suggests the cross shape was used in which the upright beam extends above the crosspiece (✝ not an **X** or **T**; ISBE I:826). The trilingual sign (Jn. 19:20) read, "This is Jesus, King of the Jews" (v. 37). This was what the Sanhedrin accused Him of claiming (27:11) and this was the official reason Pilate put Jesus on the cross. Indeed, He was this (1:1; 2:2) but it grated the Jewish leaders to read this as factual (Jn. 19:21) even though they used this to have Him crucified. Bruner calls this sign, "The Gospel according to Pilate" (2:735). For Matthew, it summarized the theme of his Gospel (Carson, *Matthew* 568).

The soldiers crucified two robbers alongside Jesus (v. 38). Robbery could be a violent crime and Rome had no tolerance for those who practiced it. Keener (*Background* 127) suggests these men were colleagues of Barabbas. Though three men were crucified that day, one received the most attention.

Three groups mocked Jesus. Passersby mocked Him (v. 41, likewise), "reviled" or blasphemed Him (v. 39, Greek *blasphēmeō*), and shook their heads (v. 39; Ps. 22:7) as they recounted His claims about Himself. They mocked His claim to have miraculous power (destroy and rebuild the temple in three days) and taunted Him, pointing out the apparent absurdity of God's Son hanging on a cross. See these two claims discussed above (26:61-64).

Their words "If you are the Son of God" (v. 40) hurled at Jesus as He hung on the cross had a history. This was not the first time Jesus heard them. They had come from the evil one during Jesus' great temptation (4:3, 5). At least one interpreter believes Satan was still trying to get Jesus to "evade the Father's will and avoid further suffering" (Carson, *Matthew* 576).

The religious leaders participated in the mockery (vv. 41-43) and jokingly promised each other they would believe in Jesus if He would come down from the cross (Wilkins 901). "If" is not in many older Greek manuscripts, making them read, "He is the King of the Israel" rather than "If He is the King of Israel." Both wordings mean they mocked His claim to the throne.

They also mocked Jesus' claim to trust God and concluded that if such a relationship did exist, God would deliver Jesus from the cross (v. 43). The fact that Jesus remained on the cross proved to them He was not God's Son and God wanted nothing to do with Him—but looks were deceiving (Bruner 2:741).

Isaiah 53:4-5, says: "We did esteem him stricken, smitten of God, and afflicted. But he was wounded for our transgressions"). One needs only to contrast "he" and "him" with "our," "us," and "we" in this Isaiah prophecy to understand some of what happened on that cross. Whether unwittingly or not, these men expressed Psalm 22:8 (v. 43). See below on verse 46. While Jesus suffered their punishment from the Father to save them and became their wrath bearer, their propitiatory sacrifice (Rom. 3:25; 1 Jn. 2:2; 4:10), they mocked. Psalm 22 was fulfilled throughout this crucifixion.

The thieves hanging there with Him also participated in the verbal abuse of Jesus (v. 44). Everyone, it seemed for a time, turned against Him. However, one thief later repented (Lk. 23:42-43) and received eternal life even as he was dying on the cross.

3. The royal Messiah's death and the supernatural events that followed (27:45-56)

45 Now from the sixth hour there was darkness over all the land unto the ninth hour.
46 And about the ninth hour Jesus cried with a loud voice, saying, Eli, Eli, lama sabachthani? that is to say, My God, my God, why hast thou forsaken me?
47 Some of them that stood there, when they heard *that*, said, This *man* calleth for Elias.
48 And straightway one of them ran, and took a spunge, and filled *it* with vinegar, and put *it* on a reed, and gave him to drink.
49 The rest said, Let be, let us see whether Elias will come to save him.
50 Jesus, when he had cried again with a loud voice, yielded up the ghost.
51 And, behold, the veil of the temple was rent in twain from the top to the bottom; and the earth did quake, and the rocks rent;
52 And the graves were opened; and many bodies of the saints which slept arose,
53 And came out of the graves after his resurrection, and went into the holy city, and appeared unto many.
54 Now when the centurion, and they that were with him, watching Jesus, saw the earthquake, and those things that were done, they feared greatly, saying, Truly this was the Son of God.
55 And many women were there beholding afar off, which followed Jesus from Galilee, ministering unto him:
56 Among which was Mary Magdalene, and Mary the mother of James and Joses, and the mother of Zebedee's children.

Jesus' crucifixion had dramatic and powerful effects on Jerusalem and the area about it. The Synoptics say that from noon to 3:00 p.m. darkness was upon the land. Scripture does not say if the darkness went beyond the borders of Judea, just that it was "over all the land." Neither writer says how the darkness was brought about but Scripture teaches that God controls the light of day (Gen. 1:3-5; Ex. 10:21-23; Joel 2:31; Acts 2:20). Noonday darkness was one of the supernatural signs that accompanied Jesus' death.

Nor does Scripture say why the darkness was present, how intense it was, or what it meant. The darkness probably represented God's judgment (Hendriksen 970; Nolland 1205). Perhaps it was during these hours that Jesus bore the most intense portion of God's wrath against man's sin, and God intended that the darkness show His holy displeasure and judgment as manifested in the propitiatory and atoning sacrifice.

About 3:00 p.m., just before He died, Jesus quoted in a loud voice the prayer of Psalm 22:1. "*Eli, Eli, lama sabachthani*?" is a transliteration of the Hebrew (Keener, *Background* 128; Hill 354) which means, "My God, My God, why have You forsaken Me?" Mark's "*Eloi, Eloi*, etc." transliterates the Aramaic equivalent. (According to Metzger 70, various Bible translations have slightly different spellings of the words, reflecting similar, slight differences in Greek manuscripts. The meaning of each is the same.)

Was Jesus actually abandoned and calling on God from His sense of abandonment? Or was He primarily saying this for the benefit of His human audience? Some interpreters understand Jesus' question to mean that the Father did in some sense forsake His Son as He hung on the cross as the atonement for the sin of the world (Hendriksen 971; Hagner 33B:844). Others understand Jesus to have been implying, "Read the twenty-second Psalm. It tells you what this crucifixion is about. I may look forsaken (Mt. 27:43) but I am not" (Ps. 22:24). This makes Jesus' quote and question mainly rhetorical.

The twenty-second Psalm recounts the Psalmist's struggles as his enemies surrounded him for the kill, at the same time prophetically looking into the future at the crucifixion of Christ. There are several parallels between the Psalmist's experience and that of Jesus on the cross. Both felt forsaken (v. 1). Neither had their prayers for personal deliverance answered immediately (v. 2). Both were despised and ridiculed (vv. 6-8). Both appeared to be abandoned by God (v. 8). Both suffered extreme physical torture (vv. 14-15). Both had their hands and feet pierced—by "dogs" (a band of evil men, NIV) in the Psalmist's distress and by nails in Jesus' (v. 16). Both had their clothes divided and gambled for as spoils from one who would need them no more (v. 18; VanGemeren 206-207). However, both were ultimately delivered (vv. 22-24).

Those who understand Jesus' use of Psalm 22 as applying literally to His own experience—i.e., that the Father forsook His Son while He bore the sin of lost mankind—view Psalm 22 as prophetic and Jesus' death on the cross as fulfillment. Some also see the Father and Son as separating in some way for this time. Carson (*Matthew* 579) allows for some type of real separation; Wilkins (902-903) does not. Blomberg (100) says those who cannot accept a real absence of the Father "probably reflect an unwitting Docetism—the heresy that Christ was not fully human." A real separation and absence of the Father are difficult concepts to accept and, this writer believes, unnecessary.

It seems more probable that Jesus was not forsaken (Ps. 22:24) even though it *appeared* to those on the ground that He was and even though He Himself felt forsaken (Evans, *Matthew* 514). He had suffered forty days in the wilderness at the beginning of His ministry and endured extreme loneliness in the Garden the previous night in prayer. In like manner, on the cross at the time of His greatest suffering Jesus again felt isolation, only this time the sense of isolation was the most intense of His entire human experience—because He bore the wrath of God for the sins of the entire world.

The interpreter will want to consider the implications of the position he determines to be Scripture's intent. Can the Father and Son really separate in their beings (Jn. 10:30)? Would such a real separation agree with Psalm 22:24?

Some bystanders heard Jesus say, "Eli," and thought He called for Elijah (v. 47). Popular Judaism at this time believed that Elijah was a heavenly helper in time of need (TDNT II:930-935). These bystanders misunderstood on both counts. One of them offered Jesus vinegar or sour wine, perhaps to ease His discomfort. (Extending to Jesus a sponge on the end of a reed suggests that He was elevated above the people.) Others stopped the person from giving Jesus the drink. Perhaps they wanted Jesus to continue praying, wanting to see if His prayers would be answered (v. 49). This would prove His innocence. It is also possible they did not want to ease Jesus' suffering.

Just before He died, Jesus shouted three statements, a surprise for one so near death. The first was Psalm 22:1. The order of the last two statements is unknown. Possibly the next statement was "It is finished" (John 19:30) followed closely by "Father, into your hands I commit my spirit" (Lk. 23:46). Either of these last two could have been Jesus' last loud cry and the one that Matthew referred to in verse 50; or the last cry could have been without words (Hagner 33B:843).

Matthew said Jesus "yielded up" (v. 50) His spirit, which can simply mean He died. Other N.T. passages use the same imagery and express the same idea in different words (Mk. 15:37, 39; Lk. 23:46; Jn. 19:30; Acts 12:23). However, it may be that Jesus' shout and self-control are in view here to show that Jesus did not *just* die; rather, He died as "an act of the will" (Gundry 575). He decided when He would die. Jesus thus died violently (11:12) and voluntarily. Even though He died voluntarily, yet humanity had just committed its greatest sin by crucifying its God and Savior (Acts 2:23-36; 4:10-12; 5:30). For the salvific meaning of Jesus' death on the cross, see 26:28 and comments.

Jesus' spirit went immediately to Paradise (Lk. 23:43), the place of the departed spirits of the righteous. He did not go to hell to experience further suffering. His suffering was complete. It was finished (Jn. 19:30).

Immediately at His death, several events took place that can only be explained as supernatural. The temple veil was torn (v. 51). There were two such curtains (ISBE I:838; IV:774). If this was the curtain visible from outside, it was the first curtain that separated the holy place from the outer porch (Evans, *Matthew* 515). If this was the inner veil (Keener, *Background* 128; Hill 355), then it was the veil that separated the holy place from the Holy of Holies, the Most Holy Place.

The miracle included tearing the curtain from top to bottom. The time of the evening sacrifice was at 3:00 p.m. (Keener, *Matthew* 686; ISBE IV:273-274). This means that priests would have been in the temple at this time.

They would have witnessed the rending of the curtain.

Matthew offers no theological explanation for this, only that it happened. One writer thinks the tearing of the veil meant God was leaving the temple (Keener, *Matthew*, 686). Other writers rightly understand this tearing meant that the way to God is now open (Wilkins 905; Hendriksen 974; Hagner 33B:849; Heb. 10:19-20). The way for reconciliation between God and man was at this time complete (Col. 1:20). The tearing of the veil also marked the end of the O.T. sacrificial system, which happened in practice when the temple was destroyed in A.D. 70 (Hagner 33B:853).

There was also an earthquake, so violent that rocks split and tombs opened. These tombs were probably sepulchers like Joseph's (v. 60) or cave graves like those the Gadarean demoniacs inhabited (8:28). Following Jesus' resurrection, raised saints—no sinners were in this resurrection—came out of the tombs and went into Jerusalem where they visited many people (v. 53). These events were some of the Father's responses to His Son's death.

The Greek text of verses 52-53 may be understood to mean that the saints were resurrected on Friday and stayed in the tombs until after Jesus' resurrection. This seems strange, but Gundry (576) argues that it is the most natural reading. However, the Greek text, (which originally had little if any punctuation) may also be understood to mean that the graves were opened at the time of the earthquake, but the saints were raised on Sunday (Wilkins 906; Carson, *Matthew* 581-582). Punctuated this way, the text reads, "And the earth was shaken and the rocks were split and the tombs were opened. Many bodies of the saints who had fallen asleep were raised and came out of the tombs after His resurrection and went into the holy city and appeared to many." This seems probable and is the basis of the interpretation expressed in the previous paragraph.

There are questions about this miracle that Matthew did not answer. Did these raised saints (like Lazarus) die again? Or did they have a resurrection body like that of Jesus? If the latter, how long were they in Jerusalem and did they eventually ascend to heaven, perhaps when Jesus ascended? Were these saints the recently departed loved ones of those living in Jerusalem at the time? Or were they people who had perhaps been dead for centuries? Wilkins (906) and Osborne (1045) think these saints were O.T. heroes of the faith, raised to bear witness of Jesus' resurrection. (See this matter more fully explored in Hagner 33B:850-852.)

Regardless of our unanswered questions, these resurrections were and are strong arguments for Jesus' authenticity. They supported the testimony of Jesus' own resurrection and post-resurrection appearances (Nolland 1217). They also prove that the cross is as efficacious to save those who trusted in God's salvation in the O.T. as it does for those after the cross (Bruner 2:763). Third, these resurrections point to an even greater resurrection, that of all God's people.

Then there was light. Around the time Jesus died, light returned. Scripture does not give a strict chronology of all the events surrounding Jesus' crucifixion, but Jesus apparently died in the dark. At the time of His death, God tore the veil, sent an earthquake, split rocks, opened some graves, and unveiled the sun again. The point of Matthew's testimony to these miraculous events is that Jesus is God's Son whom He claimed to be.

The soldiers standing guard recognized the unusual nature of these events and concluded that they were associated with Jesus' death (v. 54). The whole scene frightened them—they had just killed Jesus (Nolland 1220)—and they concluded He was the (or "a": there is no "the" in the Greek) Son of God. They had heard the taunts of verse 43 (Hendriksen 977) and joined in the mockery (Lk. 23:36), but they came to realize their error and were sobered. In keeping with one of Matthew's themes, he showed again that Gentiles can believe in Jesus (Mt. 28:19; Jn. 12:32).

The drawing power of the elevated Savior had begun (Jn. 12:32-33). This does not mean these men exercised saving faith at this time since they had no understanding of God's plan of salvation. However, they spoke more than they knew. They recognized Jesus to be "of God," something the Jewish leaders and most onlookers did not.

The centurion and his fellow soldiers accepted the testimony of a long list of objectively verifiable witnesses that day. The midday darkness, the major earthquake, the split rocks, the torn temple curtain (if one assumes that it was the outside curtain and that they could see it from Golgotha), and the opened tombs all testified this death had clear supernatural implications. The centurion and his men were so convinced that they were very afraid. They thought God was responding to Jesus' death in an angry way. He was not. Rather, He was marking Jesus' death in a powerful way.

According to Luke (23:47), the centurion saw the signs as proof of Jesus' innocence. Along with Pilate (Lk. 23:4, 14; Jn. 19:4), Herod (Lk. 23:14-15) and the repentant thief on one of the other crosses (Lk. 23:41), the centurion stated that Jesus was innocent (Evans, *Matthew* 517). Jesus was crucified as an imposter (Jn. 19:7; Mt. 27:43), but the centurion concluded that He was not. Jesus was the Son of God.

The miraculous signs also impacted the crowds (Lk. 23:48). These were folks who had gathered just to watch a crucifixion. Seeing the events that accompanied Jesus' death, they returned home in mourning, beating their breasts (Bock 377).

Up to this point, Matthew mentioned mainly those who did not really know Jesus. At this point, he turned his attention to those who were Jesus' friends and followers (disciples). He mentioned none of the remaining eleven apostles. He mentioned only women. These women had accompanied Jesus from Galilee to Jerusalem, "ministering" to Him (v. 55). This means they prepared meals for Jesus and the Twelve as they traveled between towns. Some of these women had been Jesus' support workers, traveling with and ministering to Jesus and the Twelve for months (Lk. 8:2).

Matthew identified only three among the several women present: Mary from Magdala, Mary the mother of James and Joseph (Joses), and the mother of James and John. For the names of other women at the cross, see John 19:25-26. It seems probable that Mary, the mother of James and Joseph, is Jesus' mother (13:55), though several writers disagree (Osborne 1048). Why Matthew identified her this way is unclear. The mother of Zebedee's children, James and John, may have been Salome. See comments on 20:20. Though the writers say nothing about Mary's pain in the context of her miracle son's crucifixion, surely the prophetic words of Simeon were fulfilled: "A sword shall pierce through thy own soul also" (Lk. 2:35).

4. The royal Messiah's burial (27:57-61)

57 When the even was come, there came a rich man of Arimathaea, named Joseph, who also himself was Jesus' disciple:
58 He went to Pilate, and begged the body of Jesus. Then Pilate commanded the body to be delivered.
59 And when Joseph had taken the body, he wrapped it in a clean linen cloth,
60 And laid it in his own new tomb, which he had hewn out in the rock: and he rolled a great stone to the door of the sepulchre, and departed.
61 And there was Mary Magdalene, and the other Mary, sitting over against the sepulchre.

Jesus probably died about 3:00 p.m. He was the first of the three crucified that day to die. His body remained on the cross until early evening. The soldiers made sure He was dead by thrusting a spear in His side (Jn. 19:34).

According to the Mosaic Law (Dt. 21:22-23) all three bodies had to be removed from the crosses and buried. This had to be done quickly because evening and the Sabbath were upon them (v. 57; Lk. 23:54). Joseph, a wealthy and respected member of the Sanhedrin (Mk. 15:43; Lk. 23:50-51) who was from the Samarian city of Arimathaea (the O.T. City of Ramah; ISBE I:290), came upon the crucifixion (v. 57; Nolland 1228). Apparently recognizing that Jesus was dead and needed to be removed from the cross, He went to Pilate and asked for permission to bury Jesus. This took courage (Mk. 15:43). Pilate made sure of Jesus' death (Mk. 15:44-45) and gave Joseph the permission he sought.

Joseph was a believer in Jesus. He had become a disciple though he had not previously made his faith public for fear of reprisal (Jn. 12:42; 19:38-39). "Disciple," though translated as a noun here, is a verb in the original language; one could translate, literally, "who also himself was (or had been) discipled to (or for) Jesus." (See BDF 82, par. 148.3). Compare with 13:52 where scribes "were trained" for the kingdom of heaven.

Joseph had not consented to Jesus' death (Lk. 23:51). Luke's record that Joseph did not consent and Matthew's account that Joseph "came" may suggest he had just arrived in Jerusalem and had not been in the area at the time of Jesus' trial and sentencing. At any rate, assessing the situation, Joseph decided to act and get Jesus' body off the cross and into his own sepulcher if Pilate permitted.

John recorded that Nicodemus assisted Joseph with the burial and provided a large amount of aromatic spices for Jesus' body. Joseph provided a new, fine linen shroud and his own newly hewn rock tomb (v. 60; Mk. 15:46) in which no one had ever been buried (Lk. 23:53). They laid Jesus' body in the tomb and closed the opening with a large stone, thus fulfilling another of Isaiah's prophecies (Is. 53:9: "with the rich") and providing substantiation to the gospel message (1 Cor. 15:4).

Joseph and Nicodemus both became ceremonially unclean because they touched a dead body (Num. 19:11; Osborne 1049). Their uncleanness would last one week, the entirety of the Feast of Unleavened Bread.

Joseph and Nicodemus gave Jesus' body special care and so honored their Savior with a respectful burial. This stands in stark contrast to the way Jesus had been treated in the previous hours: beaten, insulted, nailed to a cross, and pierced with a spear. Then, as quickly and as quietly as Joseph entered the picture, he departed (Bruner 2:773). His work was done, but he is forever remembered for this one act of loving discipleship.

Once again, Matthew wrote of two women disciples who were close to Jesus. They had followed Joseph to the sepulcher and watched as he and Nicodemus entombed the Lord. Mary Magdalene and the other Mary (vv. 56, 61) had stayed with Jesus from Galilee to the tomb. They were among the last to see Jesus alive and among the last to see Him before He was buried. Following Jesus' burial, they left to prepare spices and ointments for His body (Lk. 23:56), planning to return to anoint Jesus after the Sabbath. Their love and loyalty would be rewarded (28:1).

5. The royal Messiah's tomb secured (27:62-66)

62 Now the next day, that followed the day of the preparation, the chief priests and Pharisees came together unto Pilate,
63 Saying, Sir, we remember that that deceiver said, while he was yet alive, After three days I will rise again.
64 Command therefore that the sepulchre be made sure until the third day, lest his disciples come by night, and steal him away, and say unto the people, He is risen from the dead: so the last error shall be worse than the first.
65 Pilate said unto them, Ye have a watch: go your way, make *it* as sure as ye can.
66 So they went, and made the sepulchre sure, sealing the stone, and setting a watch.

On the day after His death and burial—that is, on Saturday, the Sabbath—the same groups responsible for His crucifixion went to Pilate. They remembered Jesus' promise that He would rise again. They were concerned that His disciples might steal His body and claim, based on an empty tomb, He had risen. ("By night," in v. 64, is not in some manuscripts.)

The Jewish leaders believed the claim of a resurrected Jesus could potentially cause them more problems than He had caused them before His death. The "first error" was Jesus' claim to be their Messiah and the fact that many people believed in Him before His crucifixion. The "second error" would be a fake resurrection (France 405) which could result in increased numbers of people believing in Him as a resurrected Messiah. The leaders were right: claims of a resurrected Jesus would cause them great trouble (Acts 5:14, 17, 27-33).

Their statements reveal they knew and understood Jesus' resurrection promises (*contra* Hagner 33B:862). They knew what He meant when He spoke of the sign of Jonah (12:40). They understood the implications of a resurrection. A resurrection would validate Jesus' claims (Rom. 1:4). They considered Him a deceiver (v. 63; Greek *planos*; imposter), but they knew that many people could potentially believe in a professed, resurrected Jesus.

Pilate gave them a guard (probably Roman soldiers; Keener, *Background* 129; Mt. 28:14; though Carson, *Matthew* 586, says they were temple police) and permission to secure the tomb. They secured the tomb two ways: (1) they sealed the tomb so that if the stone was moved they would know, and (2) they put the Roman guard in place to guard the tomb against intruders. The seal (Greek *sphragizō*; BAGD 796) could have been either a soft clay tablet (Dan. 6:17; Archer, *Daniel* 81) or wax on which a ring seal was impressed. The intent was to secure the tomb against unlawful entry; but the result was further corroboration of the resurrection (TDNT VII:948).

One can assume that the Jewish leaders were careful to locate and identify the proper tomb. Jesus' body had been unguarded all Friday night (Hagner 33B:863). At least one writer thinks that either the guards or the Jewish leaders who accompanied them to the grave checked to make sure Jesus' body was in the tomb before they sealed it (Nolland 1239). Although neither Gospel suggests the Jewish leaders made sure Jesus' body was in the tomb, this seems probable given that they had not been physically present when Jesus' body was laid to rest. Rome and religion joined forces to take Him down and keep Him down (Bruner 2:776)—but Sunday was just a few hours away.

Summary
(27:1-66)

Following Jesus' trial before Caiaphas, Jesus was held over until morning light. The Sanhedrin gathered to plan how they could convince Pilate to put Jesus to death. When Judas realized that Jesus was condemned to die, he tried to undo his part. He wanted to return the betrayal money and change his story. He confessed to betraying innocent blood, but the Jewish leaders refused to accept his recantation. He threw the money in (or into) the temple and found a spot to hang himself. The chief priests and elders used the money to purchase a place to bury strangers and named it "The Field of Blood."

While Judas was on a course of self-destruction, Jesus was taken to Pilate, the Roman governor. The Jews accused Jesus of treason. Pilate questioned Jesus but found no fault. Hoping to set Jesus free, Pilate offered the people a choice, Jesus or Barabbas, a murderer and insurrectionist. Urged on by the Jewish leadership, the people chose Barabbas and demanded that Pilate crucify Jesus.

Pilate had Jesus scourged, possibly twice, and sent Him to be crucified. The soldiers first took Jesus to their quarters where they mocked Him and showed Him great disrespect. Then they placed the upper beam of His cross on His shoulders and made Him carry it. When He could carry it no further by himself, they conscripted Simon to help Him.

At Calvary, they crucified Jesus along with two thieves. Mockers were common. Even those crucified with Him turned against Him. From noon until just after His death, darkness covered the land. Around 3:00 p.m., Jesus cried out to His Father, expressing His sense of aloneness and abandonment. He cried out again and then died. It was finished. Sin's debt was paid.

Supernatural events took place in quick succession following Jesus' death: the temple curtain was torn in two pieces from top to bottom, an earthquake occurred, tombs were opened, and daylight reappeared. So powerful were the signs, that the Roman soldiers guarding Jesus decided that Jesus' claims to be God's Son were in fact true. Even the crowds who earlier had mocked Him so vehemently were beating their breasts, seeming finally to recognize to some extent the weightiness of what had just happened.

After Jesus died, Joseph of Arimathea requested and received permission from Pilate to entomb His body. Aided by Nicodemus (Jn. 19:39), Joseph prepared Jesus' body for burial and placed Him in his own new tomb. Certain women who had been at the cross watched as they placed Him in the sepulcher.

The next day, Saturday, certain chief priests and Pharisees approached Pilate with a request to place a guard on Jesus' tomb. They wanted to prevent anyone from stealing Jesus' body and claiming He came back to life. He gave them permission, and with some soldiers, they secured the tomb.

Application: Teaching and Preaching the Passage

This is one of the most important chapters in all of Scripture. Therefore, it requires serious and regular attention. Many people still prefer signs and discourses laced with the wisdom of the age and addressing felt needs, but we must continue to preach Christ crucified (1 Cor. 1:21-23).

The apostasy of Judas can be presented as his conviction, confession, and consternation. See also the application section at the end of the discussion on chapter 26.

Because Matthew did not discuss the meaning of the cross, the preacher or teacher will need to include several Scripture passages in any discussion of the cross and its meaning. One way to approach this might be to discuss Jesus' death on the cross under three broad headings. (1) The facts of His crucifixion (His condemnation, His abuse, His crucifixion, His death, and the supernatural events that immediately followed); (2) the meaning of the crucifixion (from Is. 53: payment for our sins, vv. 4-5; God's provision for all lost people, v. 6; an offering for sin, v. 10; God's way to make sinners righteous, v. 11 and 2 Cor. 5:21; as when and where Christ opened the way into the presence of God, Heb. 10:19-20, 22); and (3) the message of the crucifixion (as our message, 1 Cor. 2:1, 2; as essential, 1 Cor. 15:3; as having the power to change lives, 1 Cor. 1:17-18; as God's only provision for our salvation, 1 Cor. 1:21; as God's perfect display of power, 1 Cor. 1:22-24; as God's perfect display of wisdom, 1 Cor. 1:24).

One might present the crucifixion event ("and they crucified him") as (1) what "they" (crowds, soldiers, Jewish leaders) did, (2) what He did (suffered, prayed, died), and (3) what the Father did (supernatural events). Jesus died (1) violently, (2) and voluntarily, but (3) He rose victoriously (28:6; Rev. 1:18).

A gospel lesson might be developed around the following supernatural events. (1) The torn curtain spoke of the end of the old sacrificial system and the beginning of a new and open way to the Father. (2) The earthquake demonstrated God's power over nature and His presence at the crucifixion of His Son. And (3) the resurrection of the holy people testified of God's power over the grave, the efficaciousness of the cross to save people of every generation, the certainty of life after death, and the future resurrection of God's people.

The truths implied in the taunts might serve as a suitable outline: (1) Jesus was and is the king of the Jews; (2) God did desire His Son; (3) He could have saved Himself; (4) He was and is the Son of God; and (5) He did raise the "temple" again after three days. Using Psalm 22, one might present a lesson or sermon on the sufferings of the Savior, or on intense sufferings and the faithfulness of the Father as revealed in Psalm 22 and Matthew 27 and 28.

Using the records of all four Gospels, one might consider "The Seven Last Sayings of Jesus on the Cross" or "The Cries from the Cross."

The burial and resurrection of Jesus might be presented by bringing out that His body was shrouded (27:57-61), secured (27:62-66), and set free (28:1-10).

VII. THE RESURRECTION NARRATIVE: THE ROYAL MESSIAH RAISED FROM THE DEAD (28:1-15)

Matthew concluded his record of Jesus' life and ministry with events from two days of Jesus' post-resurrection appearances. Matthew first summarized the testimonies of the earliest eyewitnesses on resurrection day (vv. 1-15), and then he summarized a single meeting Jesus had with the Eleven and some other disciples on a mountain in Galilee (vv. 16-20). Matthew's inclusion of these events at the end of his Gospel record shows that following the resurrection Jesus intended that His disciples purposefully tell and retell His story until the end of the age. See comments on 28:16-20.

A. The First Appearance of the Resurrected Jesus (28:1-10)

1 In the end of the sabbath, as it began to dawn toward the first *day* of the week, came Mary Magdalene and the other Mary to see the sepulchre.

2 And, behold, there was a great earthquake: for the angel of the Lord descended from heaven, and came and rolled back the stone from the door, and sat upon it.

3 His countenance was like lightning, and his raiment white as snow:

4 And for fear of him the keepers did shake, and became as dead *men*.

5 And the angel answered and said unto the women, Fear not ye: for I know that ye seek Jesus, which was crucified.

6 He is not here: for he is risen, as he said. Come, see the place where the Lord lay.

7 And go quickly, and tell his disciples that he is risen from the dead; and, behold, he goeth before you into Galilee; there shall ye see him: lo, I have told you.

8 And they departed quickly from the sepulchre with fear and great joy; and did run to bring his disciples word.

9 And as they went to tell his disciples, behold, Jesus met them, saying, All hail. And they came and held him by the feet, and worshipped him.
10 Then said Jesus unto them, Be not afraid: go tell my brethren that they go into Galilee, and there shall they see me.

The Sabbath was from sundown Friday to sundown Saturday. Having witnessed Jesus' crucifixion and burial, certain women began immediately making preparations to anoint Him as soon as possible (Lk. 23:56). Saturday evening after sundown, Mary Magdalene, Mary the mother of James and Joseph (probably Jesus' mother and brothers, Mt. 13:55; 27:56; Mk. 6:3; 15:40), and Salome bought more spices to anoint Jesus (Mk. 16:1; Gundry 585). Early the next morning (Lk. 24:1, Jn. 20:1; Nolland 1245-1246), these same women, Joanna, and possibly other women as well (Lk. 24:10) returned to the sepulcher, spices in hand, where they had earlier witnessed His entombment (27:60-61). They knew Joseph had rolled the stone against the entrance of the tomb (Mk. 15:46; 16:3), but they were evidently unaware that the tomb had been sealed and a guard put in place (27:66). Either of these would have prevented them from anointing Jesus' body (Gundry 586). Matthew did not mention spices. He said they came "to see the sepulcher," suggesting that perhaps they came to mourn (Hagner 33B:869).

Matthew's record could mean that the women's arrival happened in conjunction with the earthquake and the angel's movement of the stone that covered the entrance to the tomb. However, Matthew more probably is summarizing the morning's events and the women did not appear on the scene until verse 5. (See the chronology in Mk. 16:1-5, Lk. 24:1-4, and Jn. 20:1-13.) All four Gospels mention the angelic presence. (The words of v. 2, "from the door," are in later Greek manuscripts only but are certainly accurate. See 27:60.)

Matthew said an angel, in glorified form (v. 3), came down from heaven and sat on the stone. His appearance was as bright as lightning and as white as snow. Mark 16:5 described him as dressed in white. Luke 24:4 said there were two angels and they wore shining or dazzling apparel. Though dark outside (Jn. 20:1), God's angel provided light. Glorious angels celebrated Jesus' birth (Lk. 2:9-14), and they celebrated His resurrection.

The angel did three things; he rolled back the stone so people could see the empty tomb (Wilkins 937); he gave the first vocal witness to the resurrection of Jesus; he then gave instructions to the women for the Eleven. That women were the first humans to witness and testify of Jesus' resurrection is significant because women were not considered credible witnesses in that culture (Keener, *Matthew* 698-699).

The angel was visible to everyone at the tomb (v. 4). The guards, unbelievers though they were, saw the descending, glorious angel as he rolled back the stone and sat on it, and they shook and then either fainted (Keener, *Matthew* 702) or became paralyzed with fear and fell to the ground (Newman and Stine, 905). Men who were used to causing fear in others were themselves overcome with fear. The dead lived; the living became as dead (Hagner 33B:869). The angel had no direct message for them (Hill 359), but they could have believed their own eyes and ears.

The women were also afraid when they saw the angel. The angel spoke to calm their fears (v. 5; Greek negative and present imperative = "stop being afraid") and address their desire to anoint the body of Jesus. Mark 16:1 and Luke 24:1 state they had come to anoint Jesus' body with the burial spices they had begun preparing just after His burial (Lk. 23:56).

However, there was no need for burial spices this day for three reasons: (1) Mary of Bethany had anointed Jesus for burial before He died (26:12); (2) Joseph and Nicodemus had anointed Him just after He died (Jn. 19:39-40); and (3) the real reason: there was no dead and decaying body (Acts 2:31). The angel knew what the women needed to know: Jesus had been raised (v. 6; Greek passive stressing the Father's role; Acts 2:24, 32) on the third day just as He said (16:21; 17:23; 20:19; 27:63). The proof offered by the angel was the empty tomb. "Come!" he said to the women.

The women had seen Jesus buried and the stone rolled into place. Now the angel directed the women to come and see the empty tomb for themselves. When they entered the tomb (Mk. 16:5), they could see by the light of the angel's glory that Jesus was gone. The empty tomb spoke of Jesus' bodily resurrection (Keener, *Matthew* 713). The women must have seen the neatly folded grave clothes that Peter and John saw when they came later (Lk. 24:12; Jn. 20:6-7). The angel did not command blind faith. He invited sensory investigation (Bruner 2:790).

The words "he is risen" are pivotal. Without the resurrection, nothing Jesus said or did matters. Without Jesus' resurrection, we are still in our sins and hopeless (1 Cor. 15:14-19; Picirilli, *1, 2 Corinthians*, 219-220). Jesus' resurrection became the foundation of the church's message (Hagner 33B:870; Acts 2:24, 32; 3:15; 4:10; 10:40; 13:30, 37; 17:31-32; 26:23; Rom. 10:9; 1 Cor. 15:1-4).

In keeping with Hebrew thought, a part of a day was reckoned as a whole day (Wilkins 936). Jesus was crucified on Friday afternoon, day one. He was in the grave all of Saturday, day two. He arose from the dead Sunday morning, on the third day just as He had promised. He was raised on the first day of the week, not the holy day of Judaism (Bruner 2:779-780). This, in turn, became the basis of a weekly worship and celebration meeting of His followers (Acts 20:7; 1 Cor. 16:2; Picirilli, *1, 2 Corinthians,* 239).

"The Lord" (v. 6) is clearly the Person who had been raised even though several Greek manuscripts simply have "the place where he lay." David prophesied of this resurrection (Ps. 16:8-11) and the early church preached David's prophecy as proof that Jesus is the Messiah, the one foreseen by David (Acts 2:22-36; Longenecker, 280).

The angel further instructed the women to tell the disciples of His resurrection (v. 7). They were also to remind the disciples that Jesus would meet them in Galilee as He had told them three days earlier, the night of His betrayal (Mt. 26:32).

The women did not delay. They left the tomb quickly with the guards still motionless on the ground and ran to tell the disciples. They were fearful, still unsure of what all of this meant, and yet excited (v. 8). They had "great joy."

They did not have time to process the implications of Jesus' resurrection, but this was a new, an exciting and joyous day. The Lord had risen! Jesus' resurrection was the firstfruits of a bodily resurrection (Wilkins 939). A greater harvest of the dead would follow (Mt. 27:53; 1 Cor. 15:20-23).

The women left the tomb to go where the disciples were so they could pass along the message of the angel. (Some manuscripts do not have "And as they went to tell his disciples," but this simply repeats what has already been said in v. 8.) At some point between the tomb and the disciples—Matthew did not give a specific location though John said that they were still in the vicinity of the tomb (Jn. 20:14-18)—Jesus appeared to them (v. 9).

First, Jesus gave them a common, friendly salutation: "All hail!" or "Greetings!" (Greek *chairō,* lit. rejoice!; Louw and Nida 1:393), which was similar to our "Hello!" This was the first word He spoke after His resurrection (Bruner 2:796). These women were the first to see the stone rolled back, the first to learn of Jesus' resurrection, the first to see the empty tomb, the first to see and hear the risen Lord, the first to worship the risen Lord, and the first to tell the completed gospel story that Jesus died, was buried, and rose again. They fell before Him—He is God—and grasped His feet—He is human, a testimony to His bodily resurrection (Lk. 24:39; Wilkins 940; Bruner 2:796). The God-man lives. They worshiped Him and He accepted their worship, an acknowledgement of His deity for only God is to be worshiped (4:9-10).

The women at this point had three proofs of Jesus' resurrection: the angelic announcement, the empty tomb, and the personal meeting with Jesus (Nolland 1233). The first two were proof enough to convince them to tell the disciples what they had heard and seen, but the third was indisputable. They heard, saw, and touched the resurrected Jesus.

Jesus instructed the women to tell His "brothers" to meet Him in Galilee (v. 10), which would not only put them back in their home area but provide greater privacy for meetings. Evidently, Jesus spent most of His post-resurrection time in Galilee (Mt. 28:16; Jn. 21). Also, there they would see Him. Jesus promised sensory verification (Bruner 2:793-794) even as the angel had (v. 7). These "brothers" were primarily the Eleven but Jesus probably intended that the women spread the good news to more than the Eleven. He wanted other believers in Jerusalem told too, which the women did (Lk. 24:23). The resurrection was not a secret to be kept but a story to be told. He wanted all those He called His brothers told (12:49-50; 25:40; Carson, *Matthew* 589; Wilkins 941). By calling them His brothers, Jesus spoke of their close relationship to Him. This meeting in Galilee was for all who wanted to see the risen Savior. See comments on 28:17.

As mentioned earlier (see 4:15), there is reason to believe Jesus appeared to both Jewish and Gentile disciples, for Galilee was the land "of the Gentiles" (Walvoord 241). It is probable that Jesus went to Galilee in order to prepare His disciples for His final set of instructions that included making disciples of all the world, not just the Jews (Carson, *Matthew* 590). They would no longer focus only on Israel (10:5; 28:19).

Scripture records that Jesus appeared to the following persons after His resurrection: (1) Mary Magdalene and the other women in the Garden (Mt. 28:9; Jn. 20:16); (2) Simon Peter (Lk. 24:34); (3) Cleopas and his friend as they traveled to Emmaus (Lk. 24:15, 31); (4) the apostles without Thomas, Cleopas, and his friend after they returned from Emmaus, plus others in Jerusalem all together in one room (Lk. 24:33, 36; Jn. 20:19); (5) the Eleven including Thomas in Jerusalem (Jn. 20:26); (6) those who had accompanied Jesus when He traveled from Galilee to Jerusalem on His way to the cross (Acts 13:31), both men and women, including His mother (Mt. 27:55-56; Mk. 15:41; Lk. 23:55; Jn. 19:25); (7) the seven disciples in Galilee who went fishing (Jn. 21:1); (8) the more than five hundred "brothers" in Galilee (1 Cor. 15:6); (9) James (the Lord's brother? 1 Cor. 15:7); (10) all of the apostles (1 Cor. 15:7: may mean more than just the Eleven); (11) Joseph and Matthias and other men with them (Acts 1:21-23); and after Jesus' ascension, (12) Paul (Acts 9:3, 17; 23:11; 1 Cor. 15:8); and (13) the Apostle John (Rev. 1:12-18). Scripture is clear. Many people saw the resurrected Lord.

B. The Testimonies of the Guards (28:11-15)

11 Now when they were going, behold, some of the watch came into the city, and shewed unto the chief priests all the things that were done.
12 And when they were assembled with the elders, and had taken counsel, they gave large money unto the soldiers,
13 Saying, Say ye, His disciples came by night, and stole him *away* while we slept.
14 And if this come to the governor's ears, we will persuade him, and secure you.
15 So they took the money, and did as they were taught: and this saying is commonly reported among the Jews until this day.

Following their meeting with Jesus, the women did as He instructed and went to tell the disciples (v. 10). At the same time, some of the guards went into the city (the tomb was outside the city walls; Hagner 33B:876) to the chief priests and reported the events they had witnessed. Both the women and the guards who reported told the truth. Perhaps the other guards remained at the tomb until they were officially relieved of duty (Wilkins 944). Those reporting would have included in their account the earthquake, the angels and their glory, their own fear and powerlessness, the rolled back stone, the empty tomb, and perhaps even the angel's instructions to the women if they were conscious at that time. Matthew does not say whether they heard the angel tell the women Jesus was no longer there or that they looked into the tomb themselves after the angel left. What is clear is that the guards who were entrusted with keeping Jesus' body in the tomb were in fact among the first witnesses of the empty tomb. They told the chief priests, and apparently the entire Sanhedrin, what they had witnessed even as the women told the disciples.

Being mainly Sadducees (Acts 5:17), the men denied both the existence of angels and the possibility of resurrection from the dead (Mt. 22:23; Acts 23:8; see comments on 3:7). The chief priests were at a loss for what to do. They had what they feared, an empty tomb (27:64; Hagner 33B:875). They were not interested in truth (Hill 360) even though the guards' report was credible and unbiased. The chief priests should have believed them. They knew Jesus' promise to rise again (12:39-40; 16:4; 27:63), and here was proof He had. Their unbelief was inexcusable (Gundry 592).

Instead, they assembled the elders (v. 12) in order to craft a lie to stop the spread of the gospel. While the women ran to tell the good news, the elders dispatched messengers to stop it (Bruner 2:799). As Keener observed (*Background* 130), they never denied the empty tomb; they just tried to explain it. Their worst fear was about to materialize (27:64) and they had to stop the spread of such a story whether true or not. The priests never argued with the soldiers or tried to discredit them. Instead, they paid the soldiers a large sum of money (from the temple treasury? Cf. comments on 27:6) to lie. The largeness of the payoff points to the dishonesty of the leadership, the seriousness with which they approached this situation, the fear of the soldiers for their lives, and the certainty of these soldiers about what they had just witnessed.

The lie cast the soldiers in a bad light so the priests promised to protect them. Sleeping while on guard duty was a serious offense and Pilate might have them killed (Acts 12:19). Fear for their own lives might also have encouraged these guards to do as they were told (Keener, *Background* 130). Paying the guards to spread the lie distanced the lie from the priests while assuring the story was endorsed by the authorities, in this instance, the guards.

The ridiculousness of the lie is clear for several reasons. First, all of the guards would not have gone to sleep while on duty (Wilkins 945). Second, the probability is slim that men would have been able to move such a large stone and carry the body of Jesus out past the guards without making enough noise to wake the guards. According to Evans (*Matthew* 521), "wheel-shaped stones are typically four to five feet in diameter and a foot or so thick, weighing hundreds of pounds." Third, trained soldiers would not position themselves to allow free and unhindered access to the tomb. Fourth, how could they know what happened if they had been asleep (Hendriksen 996)? Sleeping people make poor witnesses (Bruner 2:801). Fifth, if the body had been stolen, the Jewish leaders would have complained since this was their reason for placing the guards in the first place (Hagner 33B:877).

Those who question that anyone would deny such signs must remember that these leaders were operating in ignorance (1 Cor. 2:8) as well as rebellion. Their refusal to acknowledge Jesus as Messiah resulted in God's judgment of a closed mind (13:12-15). Their refusal to believe the guards shows that their earlier promise to believe if Jesus would come down from the cross was a lie as well (Carson, *Matthew* 591).

According to Matthew, the soldiers took the money and spread the lie (v. 15). From day one, resurrection Sunday, the gospel has been opposed (Bruner 2:800). Those who heard the guards repeated their story and at the time of Matthew's writing the story was still being told as truth. The presence of this charge against the disciples (that they stole Jesus' body) was probably why

Matthew included the account of the guards in his narrative (Keener, *Matthew* 713). How long this lie was believed is uncertain but some still believed it in the second century A.D. (Justin Martyr, *Dialogue with Trypho* 108).

Summary (28:1-15)

Matthew summarized the resurrection day events around witnesses and testimonies. The women told the Eleven and other disciples that they had seen Jesus alive and He would meet them in Galilee. The guards told that a glorious angel had descended from heaven, rolled back the stone, and that now the body of Jesus was gone. A bribe was enough to get them to change their story and tell that Jesus' disciples stole His body while they all slept.

The reader is not left to wonder long about whom to believe. In the final portion of his record, Matthew reported that the women were not the only ones to see Jesus alive. He saw Him too (vv.16-17).

Application: Teaching and Preaching the Passage

When used with the final verses in the chapter, a lesson or message might be developed around the idea of the resurrection testimonies: God sometimes uses the unlikely (vv. 1-10; in this case, women disciples); God sometimes uses unbelievers (vv. 11-15; Roman guards); and God today uses all who know the living Lord (vv. 16-20).

One might develop a study on the resurrection day: its miracles, messages, and message.

One might prepare a lesson or sermon on why we believe in the resurrection. (1) There were supernatural signs that accompanied it (earthquake, angels, moved stone, empty tomb). (2) There were sightings of the angel (by guards and by the women) and sightings of the risen Savior: (by several women). (3) There were sensory proofs (they saw, heard, and touched).

VIII. THE GREAT COMMISSION: MATTHEW'S CONCLUSION TO HIS GOSPEL (28:16-20)

16 Then the eleven disciples went away into Galilee, into a mountain where Jesus had appointed them.
17 And when they saw him, they worshipped him: but some doubted.
18 And Jesus came and spake unto them, saying, All power is given unto me in heaven and in earth.
19 Go ye therefore, and teach all nations, baptizing them in the name of the Father, and of the Son, and of the Holy Ghost:
20 Teaching them to observe all things whatsoever I have commanded you: and, lo, I am with you alway, *even* unto the end of the world. Amen.

Between the upper room and Gethsemane (26:32), Jesus had told the disciples that after His resurrection He would go before them to Galilee. On resurrection day both the angel (v. 7) and Jesus (v. 10) told the women to tell the disciples to meet Him in Galilee. The guards told that Jesus' disciples stole His body (v. 15), but Matthew contrasts that tale with his account of Jesus' appearance to the others and himself in Galilee (Gundry 593). Even the place in Galilee was pinpointed, but Matthew did not include that information. In obedience to this prearranged plan (v. 16), the Eleven left Jerusalem and went to Galilee of the Gentiles (4:15). A few days earlier, the Eleven were the Twelve but one was lost (27:3-5; Jn. 17:12).

The Gospels did not give the time for this appointment, but Jesus' two appearances in Jerusalem (Jn. 20:19, 26) tell readers that the disciples did not go before the second week after His resurrection. The meeting by the Sea was Jesus' third appearance (Jn. 21:1, 14), and the meeting on a Galilean mountainside (Mt. 28:16) took place sometime after that and before His return to Jerusalem (Lk. 24:50) for the Acts 1:8 commission and His ascension (Lk. 24:51; Acts 1:9). The seaside meeting described in John 21 and this mountainside meeting suggest that the Eleven and Jesus spent several days in Galilee (Acts 1:3). Matthew's account also assures us that Peter and the others (Jn. 21:2) were in Galilee in obedience to this command of Jesus (Carson, *John* 669).

The Eleven worshiped Him: that is, they knelt before Him (v. 17; Greek *proskuneō*; Louw and Nida I:540). Matthew had begun his account of Jesus with the Magi worshiping Jesus (*proskuneō*, 2:2, 8, 11) and now his final depiction was of people kneeling in worship before Jesus as well. What better way to bring his Gospel to a close?

Matthew adds, "But some doubted" (v. 17), not identifying them. Commentators make several suggestions. Some think these are some of the Eleven (Gundry (594; Hill 361). Hagner (33B:885) agrees but says their doubt is not unbelief in Jesus as much as uncertainty of the future in light of the recent events. The strength of Hagner's position is the way Jesus' words in verses 18-19 address such doubt. Other writers (Carson, *Matthew* 593) see a hint of a larger crowd present and suggest that some other than the Eleven doubted. By this time, most of the Eleven had seen Jesus at least three times. Peter had seen Jesus at least four times and Thomas at least once. Others besides the Eleven had seen Jesus as well. If there were others beside the Eleven present on this occasion, this might have been for some their first look at the resurrected Lord. It might have been the occasion when over five hundred "brothers" saw Him (1 Cor. 15:6). As with the Eleven, perhaps for these first-time witnesses the scars were the proof that this really was Jesus and this was His same body (Jn. 20:20, 25; Lk. 24:40). Regardless whom these doubters were, Jesus took great care to strengthen their faith because they would be His mouthpieces. They would tell His story.

First, Jesus established His "power": that is, His right or authority (v. 18; Greek *exousia*). He had every right to give the instructions He was about to give. Matthew recorded earlier mentions of Jesus' authority. Jesus had taught them as one having authority (7:29). He had authority to forgive sins (9:6, 8). He gave His disciples authority against unclean spirits (10:1). He claimed authority over the temple (21:23-24). Now, following His resurrection He declared possession of all authority in heaven and on earth. He is Supreme Commander of the universe. He is Ruler. He has the right to govern. He has authority over all—even over those who do not want His story told (vv. 11-15).

With the words "All power/authority is given unto me in heaven and in earth," Jesus again alluded to Daniel 7:13-14 (26:64; Archer, *Daniel* 91; Blomberg 100). This time, there were no challengers (Jn. 19:10-11). That it "is (or has been) given to me" indicates the activity of God the Father (understanding this as a "divine passive"; Hagner 33B:886; Eph. 1:22-23) who was directing all authority through the Son (Carson, *Matthew* 595). Jesus' words in Matthew are for the present and future, pointing both to the present aspect of the kingdom and that future time when the kingdom will be fully realized. For kingdom, see the discussion on 3:2 and under "Special Doctrines" in the Introduction.

Based on His authority alone (Greek inferential *oun*, "therefore"), the resurrected Jesus commanded His followers to do certain, specific things. He told them to go, teach (make disciples), baptize, and teach. Make disciples (v. 19), is the main verb in this sentence in the original and the only imperative. The other three actions—go, baptize, and teach—are participles that function as adverbial modifiers of this main verb and are part of the command.

Jesus commanded His followers to make disciples (Greek *mathēteuō;* imperative) for Him (not themselves, 23:8-10). Proclamation alone is not enough. Jesus wants His followers to proclaim purposefully. He wanted them to proclaim in order to make disciples. The grammar (Greek ingressive aorist) may suggest both the beginning of an action and a sense of urgency, i.e., begin now.

The command is plural: all of Jesus' disciples are addressed in this command. All disciples from that point on are obligated to obey this command. This was not just for the apostles.

A disciple is a follower, a learner. This suggests people will be won over time (Bruner 2:815-816; Hagner 33B:887). This does not mean that there will not be a point of conversion. Rather it means there will be a process leading up to conversion as well as a process that follows conversion. See 13:52 and Acts 14:21 where persons were discipled, i.e., trained to follow Christ. At conversion, a person becomes a disciple of Jesus. Also at conversion, the disciple of Jesus becomes responsible to learn how to grow into a mature disciple of Christ, which includes learning to make disciples of others.

Jesus desired that all His disciples work to convince others to follow Him too, to make Him their Master and Lord (Wilkins 952). As will become clear in the fourth part of the command, "teaching them to observe...," a disciple is more than an intellectual adherent. Disciples are people who live after their conversion according to Jesus' prescribed teaching and lifestyle.

The target group is the whole world: literally, "all the nations." What better place for Jesus to give such a command than in "Galilee of the nations"? See discussion on 4:12-17. Jesus is the Savior of every ethnic group in every geographical place in the world. This has been a theme in Matthew's Gospel (2:1-12; 8:11-12; 12:21; 15:21-28; 21:43; 22:8-10; Hendriksen 999; compare with 10:5). Here the theme blossoms.

The Eleven did not leave immediately for parts unknown (Acts 1:4). They had to wait until the Holy Spirit anointed and enabled them (Acts 1:8). However, their first evangelistic effort had a massive impact on the Gentile world (Acts 2:9-11) and introduced the gospel to people from many areas that would later be evangelized by traveling missionaries.

There is an invitation in Jesus' words. The greatest commission includes the greatest invitation: anyone and everyone in all the world can become a disciple of Jesus. All can enter a disciple-Lord relationship with the resurrected Jesus. No nation and no ethnic group is outside the bounds of this invitation.

"Go" in the original (a Greek participle) modifies "make disciples." The grammatical relationship is such (a participle of attendant circumstances) that it has the same imperative force as the main verb it modifies. This means that Jesus commanded His disciples to go. He did not assume they would go on their own (*contra* Evans, *Matthew* 531; see comments on 9:38) nor did He mean they were only to go wherever they already were and not go somewhere special to do missionary work (a position explained but not espoused by Carson, *Matthew* 595). To translate or understand "go" as "while [or "as"] you are going," (as a Greek temporal participle) is to miss Jesus' intent. (Other examples of this construction are (1) in 11:4, where Jesus told John's disciples, "Go and tell John, etc." and (2) in 21:2, "loose [them] and lead [them] to Me" in 21:2.)

The third action in this final list of commands is baptize. Grammatically, "baptizing them" (v. 19) and "teaching them" (v. 20) could be understood adverbially as the means, i.e., the way, to make disciples (Keener, *Background* 130; Newman and Stine 913). It is true that the means Jesus prescribed for making disciples was by going, baptizing, and teaching—all three. However, faith in Jesus (18:6), not baptism or learning, brings one into a discipleship relationship with Jesus. Baptism is a testimony that grace has been received ("the answer" or "the pledge" (NIV) in 1 Pet. 3:20-21). It is not a means of grace (*contra* Bruner 2:821; 1 Cor. 1:14). Once a person becomes a disciple of Christ, the first act of obedience for that individual is to follow Jesus in baptism. According to N.T. practice, only believers were baptized (Acts 2:41; 18:8), which is one reason gospel baptism is only for those who are mentally mature enough to place personal faith in Jesus as Savior. In other words, baptism is not for children too immature to place saving trust in Christ.

Therefore, "baptizing them"—like "going" and "teaching them"—has the same imperatival force as "make disciples" (Hagner 33B:882, 886; however, see Carson, *Matthew* 597). The record of the early church shows she understood baptism to be part of the Great Commission command (TDNT 1:539; see below for references). "Them" covers all disciples. Present believers are commanded to baptize all new believers. All believers are to submit to baptism. Christian groups such as the Salvation Army that do not baptize converts are in violation of these plain words of Jesus.

"Baptize" is a transliteration of the Greek verb (*baptizō*). In its most basic sense, it means to dip, to immerse. John the Baptist, Jesus, the Twelve during Jesus' earthly ministry, and the early church all practiced immersion as their mode of baptism. (See this commentary on 3:6 for further discussion on this mode of baptism.) Other forms were introduced into church practice decades later but they were not part of the original practice. Extended teaching times between profession of faith and baptism were also a later introduction.

The book of Acts shows that the early church took Jesus' instructions concerning baptism literally. There were no salvation decisions that were not followed by baptism. Following Pentecost, baptism was the initiatory rite that identified a new believer with the existing Christian fellowship (Acts 2:41; 8:12, 38; 9:18; 10:48; 16:15, 33; 18:8). This is why some Baptist groups say baptism is the door into the church and make baptism the way to join local church membership. In Paul's case, three days passed between his conversion and baptism but this apparently was an anomaly. Baptism was generally done immediately at one's profession.

Jesus commanded that baptism be done, literally, "*into* the name" (note the singular "name"). Biblically, the person being baptized demonstrates identification with the one in whose name he or she is being baptized (Rom. 6:3, 5; 1 Cor. 10:2; Picirilli, *1 Corinthians* 137). See an example of this in Acts 19:1-5. In Christian believers' baptism, Jesus' disciples identify with the Triune God. This is the fullest revelation of the divine, greater than the revelation of the O.T. In the N.T., devotion to God encompasses all three Persons of the Godhead. The doctrine of the Trinity is distinctive to kingdom theology and mandates a commitment to Jesus and the Holy Spirit as well as to the Father. This N.T. doctrine challenged the Jewish understanding of O.T. monotheism (Jn. 5:17-18; 19:7; Wilkins 955).

This listing of the members of the Godhead also reflects Jesus' own baptism. The Father spoke, the Son was in the water, and the Holy Spirit descended in the form of a dove (3:16-17). It is important to note that in 28:19 each member is mentioned equally. Neither Person is presented as being superior to or less than either of the other members. This is a clear pronouncement of Jesus' deity (Wilkins 955).

This Trinitarian baptismal formula is unique to Matthew. There are no specific examples of its use recorded in the book of Acts. See Acts 10:48. For this reason, some groups baptize in Jesus' name only and several commentators believe that this Trinitarian statement does not represent the exact wording of Jesus (Hagner 33B:887; Carson, *Matthew* 598). However, all known Greek manuscripts include these words and there is no objective reason to believe they did not come from the lips of Jesus. A Trinitarian emphasis was clearly Matthew's intent and the Trinity is the revealed God on whom all persons being baptized are to focus. Salvation is the work of the Trinity (1 Pet. 1:2).

The fourth action Jesus commanded of His followers was teaching (v. 20), also imperatival in force as already indicated above. All disciples are to be baptized and taught. "Teaching" means to provide instruction (Louw and Nida I:413). New converts, immediately upon their profession, are to begin receiving further instruction (Acts 2:41-42) and it is understood that this teaching will be over an extended period of time (Bruner 2:824). They in turn are to instruct others who also decide to follow Jesus (2 Tim. 2:2; Tit. 2:1, 3-4). Making disciples, then, is more than convincing sinners to make a decision to follow Christ. Making disciples is convincing sinners to accept the gospel, be baptized in the name of the Father, Son, and Holy Spirit, and submit to long-term Bible instruction while living in obedience to Jesus' teachings.

Jesus did not leave the lesson content vague. Mature disciples are to teach newer disciples two things: first, obedience; second, what Jesus had taught them. Discipleship is obedience (12:49-50; Jn. 14:15, 21; 15:10; 1 Jn. 2:3-4; Rom. 8:29: "conformed to the image of His Son"). Obedience is discipleship. Thus, Jesus deals with antinomianism (Gundry 597).

Mature disciples are to teach new converts what to obey. Specifically, new converts are to learn all of Jesus' teachings in order to obey them. The first covenant had the words of the Law. The new covenant has the words of Jesus. It is Christocentric (Hagner 33B:889; Col. 3:16). Matthew's inclusion of the large teaching sections illustrates this emphasis (chapters 5-7; 10:5-42; 13:1-52; 18:1-35; chapters 24-25). The great commission is satisfied only when disciples go, make new disciples, baptize all new disciples, and teach all new disciples to do as they have done, i.e., go, make, baptize, and teach more new disciples to do as they have done.

These instructions must have been a surprise to the disciples. Their expectations were probably neither worldwide (Acts 1:6; Wilkins 954) nor long-term. Compare the question in Acts 1:6 with "unto the end of the age." However, these mountainside instructions were the long-term marching orders of the church. All disciples must make other disciples and teach disciple-making—or we have failed (Carson, *Matthew* 599).

This commission may well give a hint of Matthew's purpose for penning his Gospel. He brought together large blocks of Jesus' teaching to share with later generations of believers. This written record was one way Matthew obeyed and satisfied his obligation to make disciples and teach Jesus' commands. (This writer hopes this commentary will do the same!)

Jesus began His Great Commission with an assertion of absolute authority (v. 18). He closed with an assurance of constant presence (v. 20). He was not sending His disciples out on this worldwide mission alone. He assured them of His presence (Greek present, "I *am* with you," not "I *will* be"; Bruner 2:828) always (Greek, literally "all the days") until the end of the world—i.e., the age (Greek *aiōn*). This was an important statement in light of His resurrection and His approaching return to the Father. It was also an important statement for each succeeding generation of disciples from the early church to the end of this age. Compare with 18:20.

With these words, Matthew brought his record to a close. The King has come (1:1). He is God with us, Immanuel (1:23; Blomberg 100). He is God in the midst of the assembly (18:20). He is God who is always with His people as they carry His kingdom news to the ends of the earth (28:20) in this the end of the ages (1 Cor. 10:11).

Summary
(28:16-20)

These verses conclude this Gospel. Matthew moved from the resurrection day appearances of Jesus (1-10) and tales of the guards (11-15) to a day in Galilee. In obedience to Jesus' instructions, the Eleven met Jesus at a predetermined place in Galilee. There they learned what their post-resurrection ministry would be. Because all divine authority is now being mediated through

Him, He will empower them to reach the whole world with His gospel. They will tell everyone, all nations, about Jesus with the goal to make them disciples of Christ. They will continue baptizing as before, only now they will baptize in the name of the Triune God. In conjunction with their going, making new disciples, and baptizing, Jesus' disciples will also teach everything He taught them. Going, making disciples, baptizing, and teaching are the responsibilities of the church until the end of the age.

Application: Teaching and Preaching the Passage

This chapter might be developed into a single lesson or sermon. For example, there are three ways this chapter teaches that God wants the world to hear Jesus' story: (1) the angel commanded the women, "Go and tell" (v. 7); (2) Jesus commanded the women, "Go and tell" (v. 10); and (3) Jesus commanded all of His disciples, "Go and make disciples" (v. 19).

One might present lessons or sermons on the resurrected Lord: (1) His praise (v. 9); (2) His promises: "I have ... all authority" and "I am with you always" (vv. 18, 20); and (3) His prescriptions: go, make disciples, baptize, and teach (vv. 19-20). The resurrected Lord's followers (1) worship the risen Savior (v. 9), (2) give witness of the risen Savior (vv. 10-20a; Lk. 24:48), and (3) walk with the Savior (v. 20b). The resurrection generates considerable discussion: (1) between believers (vv. 8-10); (2) between unbelievers (28:11-15); and (3) between believers and unbelievers (vv. 16-20).

Adapting Wilkins (958), one might consider the commission's great promise—I am with you always (v. 20)—through every stage of this commission (v. 19). (1) I am with individuals who carry the gospel throughout the world, both near and far; (2) I am with individuals who become My lifelong disciples; (3) I am with individuals who demonstrate their union with Me in baptism; (4) I am with individuals who live their lives according to My teachings; (5) I am with individuals who teach others so they can live like Me too; and (6) I am with the church as she travels through this age.

A sermon might focus on the all-encompassing aspects of the great commission: (1) all authority; (2) all nations; (3) all of Jesus' teachings; and (4) all the days. Likewise, Jesus gave the greatest commission: (1) the greatest charge (go); (2) the greatest invitation (become a disciple of Jesus); (3) the greatest drama (baptism, a reenactment); (4) the greatest lesson (Jesus' words); (5) the greatest communion (I am with you); (6) the greatest promise (I am with you always, to the end of the age).

One might speak on the great deception: (1) the great effort (27:62-66); (2) the great event (28:1-10); (3) the great elusion (vv. 11-15); and (4) the great evangelization (vv. 16-20).

MATTHEW

BIBLIOGRAPHY: WORKS CITED IN THIS COMMENTARY

Books (cited by author's last name or abbreviation)

Aland, Kurt and Barbra Aland, *The Text of the New Testament: An Introduction to the Critical Editions and to the Theory and Practice of Modern Textual Criticism.* Translated by Erroll F. Rhodes (Eerdmans, 1987).

Allen, Ronald, *Numbers* in *The Expositor's Bible Commentary*, vol. 2 Genesis—Numbers (Zondervan, 1990).

AGL: *The Analytical Greek Lexicon Consisting of an Alphabetical Arrangement of Every Occurring Inflexion of Every Word Contained in the Greek New Testament Scriptures with a Grammatical Analysis of Each Word, and Lexicographical Illustration of the Meanings* (Zondervan, 1970).

Archer, Gleason, *Daniel* in *The Expositor's Bible Commentary*, vol. 7 Daniel—Malachi (Zondervan, 1985).

Archer, Gleason, *Encyclopedia of Bible Difficulties* (Regency, 1982).

Archer, Gleason L. and Gregory Chirichigno, *Old Testament Quotations in the New Testament* (Moody, 1983).

BAGD: Arndt, William F. and Gingrich, F. Wilbur, *A Greek-English Lexicon of the New Testament and Other Early Christian Literature: A Translation and Adaptation of the Fourth Revised and Augmented Edition of Walter Bauer's Griechisch-Deutsches Wörterbuch zu den Schriften des Neuen Testaments und der übrigen urchristlichen Literatur;* Second Edition Revised and Augmented by F. Wilbur Gingrich and Frederick W. Danker from Walter Bauer's Fifth Edition, 1958 (University of Chicago, 1979).

Barclay, William, *The Gospel of Matthew:* Volume 1 Revised Edition (*The New Daily Study Bible Series*, Westminster John Knox Press, 2001).

Barclay, William, *The Gospel of Matthew:* Volume 2 Revised Edition (*The New Daily Study Bible Series*, Westminster John Knox Press, 2001).

Barker, Kenneth, *Zechariah* in *The Expositor's Bible Commentary*, vol. 7 Daniel—Malachi (Zondervan, 1985).

BDB: Brown, Francis. *The New Brown—Driver—Briggs—Gesenius Hebrew and English Lexicon with an Appendix Containing the Biblical Aramaic* (Hendrickson, 1979).

BDF: Blass, F., A. Debrunner, and Robert W. Funk, *A Greek Grammar of the New Testament and Other Early Christian Literature: A Translation and Revision of the ninth-tenth German Edition Incorporating Supplementary Notes of A. Debrunner* by Robert W. Funk (University of Chicago, 1961).

Beasley-Murray, G. R., *Baptism in the New Testament* (Eerdmans, 1962).

Beitzel, Barry J., *The Moody Atlas of Bible Lands* (Moody, 1985).

Blomberg, Craig L., *"Matthew"* (*Commentary on the New Testament Use of the Old Testament*, eds. Beale and Carson, Baker, 2007, 1-109).

Bock, Darrell O., *Luke* (IVPNTCS, InterVarsity Press, 1994).

Bruner, Frederick Dale, *Matthew: A Commentary, Volume 1: The Christbook: Matthew 1-12*, Revised and Expanded Edition (Eerdmans, 2004).

Bruner, Frederick Dale, *Matthew: A Commentary, Volume 2: The Churchbook: Matthew 13-28*, Revised and Expanded Edition (Eerdmans, 2004).

Cairns, Earle, *Christianity through the Centuries* (Zondervan, 1967).

Calvin, John, *Institutes of the Christian Religion in Two Volumes.* Translated by Ford Lewis Battles and Philip Schaff (Westminister, 1960).

Carson, D. A., *Exegetical Fallacies* (Baker, 1984).

Carson, D. A., *The Gospel According to John* (Eerdmans, 1991).

Carson, D. A., *Matthew* in *The Expositor's Bible Commentary, vol. 8 Matthew—Luke* (Zondervan, 1984).

Carson, D. A., *The Sermon on the Mount: An Evangelical Exposition of Matthew 5-7* (Baker, 1978).

Ciampa, Roy E. and Biran S. Rosner, "1 Corinthians" (*Commentary on the New Testament Use of the Old Testament*, eds. Beale and Carson, Baker, 2007, 695-752).

Delitzsch, F., *Isaiah* in *Commentary on the Old Testament in Ten Volumes* (Eerdmans, n.d.).

Dowley, Tim, ed., *Eerdman's Handbook to the History of Christianity* (Eerdmans, 1977).

Eccl. Hist: Eusebius: The Ecclesiastical History (in the *Loeb Classical Library*) vol. 1 with an English Translation by Kirsopp Lake; vol. II with an English Translation by J. E. L. Oulton (Harvard University Press, printed 1980).

Elwell, Walter A. and Robert W. Yarbrough, *Encountering the New Testament: A Historical and Theological Survey* (Baker Academic, 2005).

Erickson, Milliard J., *Christian Theology* (Baker, 1985).

ESV Study Bible: English Standard Version (Crossway Bibles, 2008).

Evans, Craig A., *The Bible Knowledge Background Commentary: Matthew—Luke* (Victor, 2003).

Evans, Craig A., *Mark 8:27—16:20*. Word Biblical Commentary, vol. 34B (Nelson, 2001).

Evans, Craig A., and *Stanley E. Porter, Dictionary of NT Background* (InterVarsity Press, 2000).

Fee, Gordon D. and Douglas Stuart, *How to Read the Bible for All It's Worth* (3rd Edition, Zondervan: 2003).

Feinberg, Charles L. "Jeremiah" in *The Expositor's Bible Commentary*, vol. 6, Frank E. Gaebelein, gen. ed. (Zondervan, 1986).

Forlines, Leroy, *The Quest for Truth: Answering Life's Inescapable Questions* (Randall House, 2001).

France, R. T., *The Gospel According to Matthew: An Introduction and Commentary* (Eerdmans, 1985).

Gesenius' Hebrew Grammar as Edited and Enlarged by E. Kautzsch, revised in accordance with *the Twenty-eighth German Edition (1909)* by A. E. Cowley (Clarendon, Oxford, n.d.).

Giese, Ronald L. and D. Brent Sandy, *Cracking the Old Testament Codes: A Guide to Interpreting the Literary Genres of the Old Testament* (Broadman, 1995).

Grimm's: Greek-English Lexicon of The New Testament being Grimm's Wilke's Clavis Novi Testamenti translated, revised and enlarged by *Joseph Henry Thayer* (Zondervan, 1977).

Gower, Ralph, *The New Manners and Customs of Bible Times* (Moody, 1987).

Grogan, G. W., *Isaiah* in vol. 6 (*Isaiah—Ezekiel*), *The Expositor's Bible Commentary*, (Zondervan, 1986).

Grudem, Wayne., *Systematic Theology: An Introduction to Biblical Doctrine* (Zondervan, 1994).

Gundry, Robert H., *Matthew: A Commentary on His Handbook for a Mixed Church under Persecution*, 2nd Edition (Eerdmans, 1994).

Guthrie, Donald, *Jesus the Messiah* (Zondervan, 1972).

Hagner, Donald A., *Matthew 1-13. Word Biblical Commentary,* vol. 33A (Nelson, 1993).

Hagner, Donald A., *Matthew 14-28. Word Biblical Commentary*, vol. 33B (Nelson, 1995).

Harrison, Everett, *Introduction to the New Testament* (Eerdmans, 1971).

Hays, J. Daniel, J. Scott Duvall, and C. Marvin Pate, *Dictionary of Biblical Prophecy and End Times* (Zondervan, 2007).

Hendriksen, William, *New Testament Commentary: Exposition of the Gospel According to Matthew* (Baker, 1973).

Hill, David, *The Gospel of Matthew* in *The New Century Bible Commentary* (Eerdmans, 1972).

ISBE: *The International Standard Bible Encyclopedia.* Bromiley, Geoffrey W., ed., (4 volumes, Eerdmans, 1982).

Jeremias, Joachim, *Jerusalem in the Time of Jesus* (Fortress, 1969).

Kaiser, Walter C., *Exodus* in *Expositor's Bible Commentary,* vol. 2 Genesis—Numbers (Zondervan 1990).

Kaiser, Walter C., *The Uses of the Old Testament in the New Testament* (Moody, 1985).

Kalland, Earl S., *Deuteronomy* in *The Expositor's Bible Commentary*, vol. 3 (Zondervan, 1992).

Keener, Craig S., *The Background Commentary: New Testament* (InterVarsity, 1993).

Keener, Craig S., *Commentary on the Gospel of Matthew* (Eerdmans, 1999).

Keil, Carl Frederick, *Twelve Minor Prophets* in *Commentary on the Old Testament in Ten Volumes* (Eerdmans, n.d.).

Keil, C. F. and F. Delitzsch, *Commentary on the Old Testament in Ten Volumes*, Vol. III: *I & II Kings, I & II Chronicles, Ezra, Nehemiah, Esther* (Eerdmans, reprinted 1982).

Lane, William L., *The Gospel According to Mark: The English Text with Introduction, Exposition and Notes* (Eerdmans, 1974).

Lane, William L., *Hebrews 1-8* in *Word Biblical Commentary*, vol. 47A (Word, 1991).

Lenski, R. C. H., *The Interpretation of St. Matthew's Gospel* (Augsburg, 1961).

Liddell, Henry George, and Robert Scott, *A Greek-English Lexicon*, 9th Edition (Clarendon Press, 1985).

Liefeld, Walter L., *Luke* in *The Expositor's Bible Commentary, vol. 8: Matthew - Luke* (Zondervan, 1984).

Longenecker, Richard, *Acts* in *The Expositor's Bible Commentary, vol. 9 John - Acts* (Zondervan, 1984).

Louw and Nida: *Greek-English Lexicon of the New Testament Based on Semantic Domains,* ed. Johannes P. Louw and Eugene A. Nida (two volumes, United Bible Societies, 1988).

Maier, Paul, *Josephus, The Essential Works: A Condensation of Jewish Antiquities and The Jewish War* (Kregel, 1994).

Marshall, I. Howard, *The Gospel of Luke: A Commentary on the Greek Text* (TNIGTC: Eerdmans, 1978).

McComiskey, Thomas E., *Micah* in *The Expositor's Bible Commentary*, vol. 7: Daniel—Malachi (Zondervan, 1985).

McDonald, Lee Martin and Stanley E. Porter, *Early Christianity and Its Sacred Literature* (Hendrickson, 2000).

Metzger, Bruce. M., *A Textual Commentary on the Greek New Testament: A Companion Volume to the United Bible Societies' Greek New Testament,* Third Edition (United Bible Societies, 1971).

Moulton, James Hope and George Milligan, *The Vocabulary of the Green Testament Illustrated from the Papyri and Other Non-Literary Sources* (Eerdmans, 1930).

MacArthur, John, *Matthew 8-15* in *The MacArthur New Testament Commentary* (Moody, 1987).

Newman, Barclay M. and Philip C. Stine, *A Translator's Handbook on the Gospel of Matthew* (United Bible Societies, 1988).

Nolland, John, *The Gospel of Matthew: A Commentary on the Greek Text* (Eerdmans, 2005).

Ong, Walter J., *Orality and Literacy: The Technologizing of the Word* (Routledge, 1982).

Osborne, Grant R., *Matthew* in *Zondervan Exegetical Commentary on the New Testament* (Zondervan, 2010).

Picirilli, Robert E., *Ephesians and Philippians* in *The Randall House Bible Commentary, Galatians through Colossians* (Randall House, 1988).

Picirilli, Robert E., *1, 2 Corinthians* in *The Randall House Bible Commentary* (Randall House, 2003).

Picirilli, Robert E., *2 Thessalonians* in *The Randall House Commentary, 1 Thessalonians—Philemon* (Randall House, 1990).

Picirilli, Robert E., *Mark* in *The Randall House Bible Commentary* (Randall House, 2003).

Picirilli, Robert E., *Paul the Apostle* (Moody, 1986).

Picirilli, Robert E., *The Book of Romans* (Randall House, 1975).
Ryken, Leland, *How to Read the Bible as Literature and Get More out of It* (Grand Rapids, 1984).
Rykan, Leland, *Words of Life: A Literary Introduction to the New Testament* (Baker, 1987).
Sauer, Ron, *Various Aspects of New Testament Greek Grammar* (n.p., n.d.).
Sell, Alan P. F., *The Spirit Our Life: Doctrine and Devotion* (Ragged Edge Press, 2000).
TDNT: *Theological Dictionary of the New Testament,* ed. Gerhard Kittle (10 volumes, tr. Geoffrey W. Bromiley: Eerdmans, 1971).
TDOT: *Theological Dictionary of the Old Testament,* ed. G. Johannes Botterweck, Helmer Ringgeren, and Heinz-Josef Fabry (8 volumes, tr. Douglas W. Stott; Eerdmans, 1983).
Tenny, Merrill C., *New Testament Survey,* Revised by Walter M. Dunnett (Eerdmans, 1985).
Thiessen, Henry Clarence, *Introductory Lectures in Systematic Theology* (Eerdmans, 1949).
TWOT: *Theological Wordbook of the Old Testament*, ed. R. Laird Harris (2 volumes, Moody, 1980).
VanGemeren, Willem A., *Psalms* in The *Expositor's Bible Commentary, vol. 5 Psalms—Song of Songs* (Zondervan, 1991).
Walvoord, John F., *Matthew: Thy Kingdom Come: A Commentary on the First Gospel* (Kregel, 1974).
Wessel, Walter W., *Mark* in *The Expositor's Bible Commentary*, vol. 8 Matthew—Luke (Zondervan, 1984).
Wigram, George V., *The New Englishman's Hebrew Concordance Coded to Strong's Concordance Numbering System* (Hendrickson, 1984).
Wilkins, Michael J., *Matthew* in *The NIV Application Commentary: From Biblical Text ... to Contemporary Life* (Zondervan, 2004).
Williams, Ronald J., *Hebrew Syntax: An Outline* (2nd ed. University of Toronto Press, 1976).
Wood, Leon. *A Survey of Israel's History* (Zondervan, 1986).
Wuest, Kenneth S. *The New Testament: An Expanded Translation*. (Eerdmans, 1961).
Young, Edward J., *The Book of Isaiah: An English Text, with Introduction, Exposition, and Notes,* vol. 1: Chapters 1-18 (Eerdmans, 1965).
Young, Edward J., *The Book of Isaiah: An English Text, with Introduction, Exposition, and Notes*, vol. 3 Chapters 40-66 (Eerdmans, 1965).
Youngblood, Richard F., *1 Samuel* in *The Expositor's Bible Commentary, vol. 3 Deuteronomy—2 Samuel* (Zondervan, 1992).
Zerwick, Max, and Mary Grosvenor, *A Grammatical Analysis of the Greek New Testament*, 3rd Revised Edition (Editrice Pontificio Istituto Biblico, 1988).

MATTHEW

Articles: cited by author's last name

Campbell, Ken M., "What Was Jesus' Occupation?" (*Journal of the Evangelical Theological Society* 48.3 [September 2005] 501-519).

Harrison, Paul V., "Chronology and the Gospels: Issues in the Life of Jesus." (*Integrity: A Journal of Christian Thought* 5 [Summer 2010] 75-97).

Heggie, Jon, "Rome's War Machine" (*National Geographic: Exploring History* [Fall 2011] 30-43).

Turner, David L., "The Structure and Sequence of Matthew 24:1-41: Interaction with Evangelical Treatments." (*Grace Theological Journal* 10.1 [1989] 3-27).

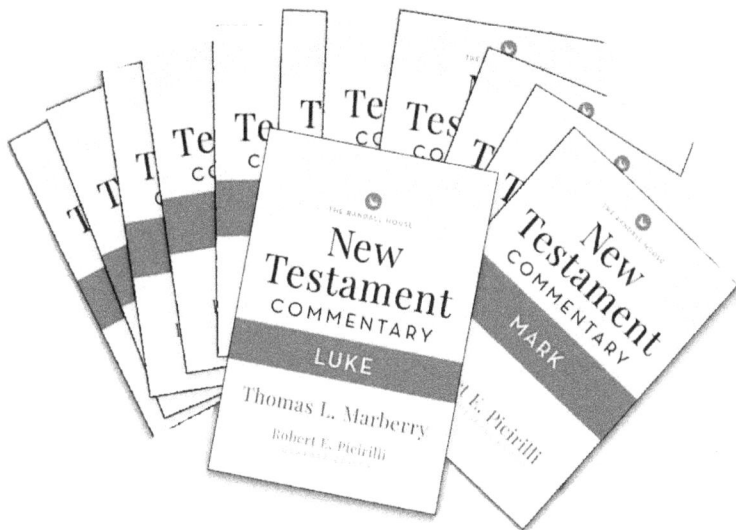

www.ingramcontent.com/pod-product-compliance
Lightning Source LLC
Chambersburg PA
CBHW020408100426
42812CB00001B/247
* 9 7 8 0 8 9 2 6 5 7 3 7 7 *